Identity

INTELLECTUAL HISTORY
OF THE MODERN AGE

Series Editors
Angus Burgin
Peter E. Gordon
Joel Isaac
Karuna Mantena
Samuel Moyn
Jennifer Ratner-Rosenhagen
Camille Robcis
Sophia Rosenfeld

IDENTITY

The Necessity of a Modern Idea

Gerald Izenberg

PENN

UNIVERSITY OF PENNSYLVANIA PRESS

PHILADELPHIA

Published by
University of Pennsylvania Press
Philadelphia, Pennsylvania 19104-4112
www.upenn.edu/pennpress

Printed in the United States of America on acid-free paper
1 3 5 7 9 10 8 6 4 2

Library of Congress Cataloging-in-Publication Data
ISBN 978-0-8122-4808-1

For Toby and Miri
To Whom I Owe a Dedication

and

For Ziva
To Whom I Owe Everything

Contents

Introduction. The New "Discourse" of Identity   1

Chapter 1. Identity Becomes an Issue: European Literature
Between the World Wars   25

Chapter 2. The Ontological Critique of Identity: Heidegger and Sartre   62

Chapter 3. Identity Becomes a Word: Erik Erikson and Psychological
Identity   105

Chapter 4. Social Identity and the Birth of Identity Politics, 1945–1970   144

Chapter 5. Collective Identities and Their Agendas, 1970–2000   187

Chapter 6. The Practical Politics of National and Multicultural Identity:
Germany, France, Canada, and the United States, 1970–2010   234

Chapter 7. The Problem of Collective Identity in Liberal Democracy   264

Chapter 8. The Contradictions of Postmodern Identity   301

Chapter 9. Identity Transforms the Social Sciences   355

Chapter 10. The Kinds of Kinds: Explaining Collective Identity   398

Chapter 11. Identity as an Ethical Issue   427

Conclusion. The Necessity of Identity   445

Notes   459

Bibliography 499

Index 517

Acknowledgments 541

Introduction. The New
"Discourse" of Identity

Identity is so "in" that the question about the identity of a
culture has in many places created a culture of identity.
—Wolfgang Bergem, *Identitätsformationen in Deutschland*

In the contemporary Western imagination nothing about the self seems more self-evident than the idea that we have, or seek, an identity. People need to define themselves, we believe, to know and to be able to tell others "who" or "what" they are. Identity has so permeated academic and popular discourse that it can appear to have always been a fixture of both. We speak readily in the family, the media, and the marketplace of "gender identity," "identity crisis," "identity politics." Only the availability of large electronic databases enables scholars to survey the otherwise unmanageable numbers of books and articles in the humanities and social sciences with the word "identity" in their titles, let alone their content.[1] When I suggested to students in courses on the history of identity that it was a new idea, they invariably responded skeptically, "Didn't people always have identities?"

Though the answer to their question is in one sense yes, we know from recent research that the use of the word identity with the meaning my students took for granted *is* historically new.[2] As a problem in the logic of "sameness," identity goes back to ancient philosophy, its best-known formulation Plutarch's conundrum about the ship of Theseus: is a ship whose every part has been replaced with a new one the same ship? What it means to talk of the identity, or sameness, of two numerically distinct things was a standard topic in medieval and early modern philosophy. John Locke first raised the issue of *personal* identity—the self's continuity or sameness in relation to the ever-changing stream of our sense impressions—in the seventeenth century. But the notion of identity as *substantive self-definition*, self-definition as *something*, which purportedly determines what I believe and do, came into common usage only with the work of Erik Erikson in the

1950s. It was then that he coined the term "ego identity" to describe a psychic structure fundamental to psychological equilibrium in the mature adult,
and the more famous "identity crisis" to denote the disturbances that disrupt the self while it is being established in the adolescent. And though
American sociology had also begun to use the word in the 1950s to refer to
an individual's definition in terms of social roles, it was only in the 1960s
that political activists, social theorists, and historians extended Erikson's
psychological concept to wider group identities—gender, sexual orientation,
ethnicity, and nation. Since then, the expansion of the term has not only
encompassed ever more instances of collective identity and multiplied its
definitions but has generated claims for the concept's existence, if not the
word's presence, *avant la lettre*.[3] Not surprisingly, it has also produced a
strong backlash: is identity a valid concept at all?

Like "class" or "unconscious," identity is one of those words that have made
the transition from technical concept in social science to everyday language. It
undoubtedly helped that in virtually all such cases the words already existed
in the vernacular with related meanings. But the newness of usage in the case
of identity is easy enough to document.

Disciplinary encyclopedias and manuals tell the story for the academic
disciplines and the professions. The first *Encyclopedia of the Social Sciences*,
published in 1936, had no entry for identity; it appeared for the first time in
the 1968 edition. Identity is not to be found in the original *Dictionary of the
History of Ideas* in 1973, nor in the magisterial German reference work of basic
historical concepts, *Geschichtliche Grundbegriffe* in 1982;[4] the *New Dictionary
of the History of Ideas* published in 2005, on the other hand, has multiple
entries and subentries for identity, including "Identity of Persons," "Personal
and Social Identity," and "Multiple Identity" (the latter referring not to psychopathology but to hyphenated or plural identities).[5] The authoritative reference work of psychiatric illnesses, the *Diagnostic and Statistical Manual of
Mental Disorders* (*DSM*), first published by the American Psychiatric Association in 1952, contained no diagnostic category for problems of identity. "Gender Identity Disorder" was only introduced in *DSM III* of 1980, and *DSM IV*
added "Personality Identity Disorder" to its diagnoses in 1994, replacing the
much-contested "Multiple Personality Disorder."[6] The ultimate imprimatur
from the academy—and the publishing industry—came with the publication
of the *Encyclopedia of Identity* in 2010.[7]

The shift in the meaning of identity in everyday discourse was equally
abrupt. Identity had long been an everyday word in English, French, and German, though *identité* and *Identität* seem to have had somewhat more technical

implications than the English word from early on. The first edition of the classic German *Brockhaus Concise Dictionary* (*Conversations-Lexikon oder kurzgefasstes Handwörterbuch*) in 1809–1811, intended as a reference work for the would-be educated speaker, defined *Identität* with implicit reference to its meaning in logic as "Oneness. Identical statements, statements with the same meaning, though differently expressed." The more ambitious and for a long time authoritative French dictionary of Emil Littré, published between 1863 and 1872, defined *identité* as "the quality which makes one thing the same as another," but differentiated jurisprudential, medical, grammatical, and philosophical uses of the word. Examples of the first two were discovering the identity of a suspect or a corpse, and determining whether someone is really who he claims to be. Significantly, the word's listed philosophical meanings included Locke's concept of self-identity—the consciousness that one has of oneself as the same person through time—and Hegel's concept of absolute identity, the unity of particular and universal, or subject and object. Apparently educated Frenchmen were expected to be familiar with both.

Webster's American dictionary of 1828 defined "identity" as "Sameness, as distinguished from similitude and diversity. We speak of [the identity] of things, . . . of persons, or of personal identity." Examination of American newspapers and periodicals from the nineteenth and early twentieth centuries shows that the word identity was an everyday word in all these meanings, and more. Its most common use was to identify persons by objective markers that located them along a set of public axes established for bureaucratic purposes in the modern state: name, sex, age, address, occupation, parentage for minors, and physical appearance. Such markers were employed, among many other purposes, to identify crime victims and adjudicate inheritance claims by those purporting to be the persons named in a will. They determined what was understood before Erikson as a person's identity.[8] The phrase "personal identity" might refer, depending on context, either to the set of objective indicators necessary to establish identity for civic purposes, or to the subjective sense of personal continuity through the memory of one's past, in the sense that Locke had given the concept.[9] That educated Americans in the nineteenth century might, like Europeans, be expected to be familiar with Locke is apparent from an article in the *Philadelphia Recorder* of April 9, 1825, titled "Identity and Diversity," which it summarized in the following terms: "Personal Identity—Mr. Locke considers this to be constituted by consciousness." "Personal identity" also had the important religious connotation of continued existence of the soul or self after death. It was a regular subject of articles in the many religiously oriented periodicals published in the United States through the nineteenth century, and newspapers not infrequently reported talks with that theme.[10]

Less frequently, though not uncommonly, identity referred to group rather than individual continuity, as in articles about the identity of a political party; the reference was always to specific policies with which the party was identified. There was even the rare use of the phrase "national identity"—only three appearances in the *New York Times* in forty years—as an almost throwaway term with the sense of national uniqueness but without any indication of what constituted it.

Starting in the mid-1950s, however, and with increasing frequency after 1960, identity appeared with a new meaning which soon almost completely usurped the old, though the latter of course persists. Often the reference was to the idea of a "quest for identity," a search for self-definition conceived as a psychological state that had to be subjectively achieved. Thus a *New York Times* reviewer described a recently published autobiography as recording "A Desperate Need for Identity" (October 23, 1955); another *Times* reporter described Eastern European refugees in German camps as "People in Search of Identity" (September 20, 1956). Writing in the *Chicago Daily Tribune*, a reporter asked "Can the Jewish People Retain Its Identity?" noting that "When an age enters on a time of radical transition, loss of identity ensues. Societies and civilizations which had once enjoyed a clear sense of purpose and self-understanding seem to forget what they are" (July 17, 1960). A *Tribune* article a few years later with the headline "Women Told How to See True Identity" reported a commencement address by the chairman of the Atomic Energy Commission in which he said that one of the problems of today's educated woman is "finding her true identity among all the external forces telling her to do this or to be that, or to fit into a prefabricated pattern" (June 6, 1963).

Within four decades the uses of identity in its new meaning had proliferated wildly, penetrating not only politics and academic disciplines but also culture high and low. The celebrated Czech novelist Milan Kundera published a novel *Identity* (French original *L'Identité*), which became a bestseller in the United States and *New York Times* notable book in 1998.[11] Hollywood produced the movie potboiler *Identity*, described by a prominent film critic as somewhere between horror film and classical whodunit;[12] the only thing new about it was the title, which capitalized on the contemporary cachet of the word. The popular mystery novelist Brad Meltzer came out with an amusing, widely read graphic series titled *Identity Crisis* concerned with the identity problems of superheroes.[13] Lecrae Moore, a Christian rapper, featured the song "Identity" on his 2008 album *Rebel*, the first Christian hip-hop album to reach No. 1 on the *Billboard* Gospel chart ("I'm not the car I drive, no. . . . I'm not the job I work. . . . My identity is found in Christ"). Unsurprisingly, the expansiveness of the term produced more confusion than clarity.

Currently definitions and distinctions abound, none agreed on by everyone. As one author of a book on German identity put it, "Whoever tries to get a grip on the enormous difficulties of merely identifying the . . . phenomenon of identity, never mind defining it, soon finds himself reminded of Ludwig Wittgenstein [writing to Bertrand Russell] . . . 'Identity is the very devil.' "[14] To other researchers, less sympathetic, the apparent multiplicity of meanings has served as an argument to abandon the term altogether as empty, even pernicious.[15] In his lexicon of "plastic words," which he defined as "connotative stereotypes," words that mean everything and therefore nothing but sound scientific, the German literary scholar Uwe Pörker headed his list of examples with "identity."[16]

Devil or not, the problem of defining identity has to be addressed, precisely because of the promiscuity of its use and the skepticism it has aroused. Identity has become so central a term in so many contexts that the questions of what it means and whether it has validity matter a great deal—to scholars and professionals, certainly, who rely on it as an explanatory concept, but also to anyone who cares about meaningful talk rather than fashionable buzzwords. In turn, the problem of definition requires a more complex approach, historical as well as analytic. The "meaning" of identity is, in important part, how it has been used. Only after a historical and critical investigation can we hazard some conclusions about the commonalities and distinctions among those uses, some explanation for their varieties, and a judgment about their validity.

At the same time we can, and must, make some preliminary distinctions concerning identity in order to set the parameters of a meaningful investigation. To claim that identity is new is to say, for one thing, that it is not the same as "self." Self was a matter for reflection in the West as far back as classical philosophy and early Christianity. But it is also to say that contemporary identity is something different from the concept of "personal identity" that John Locke introduced in the seventeenth century, and that was revived as a topic of lively debate in the Anglo-American analytic philosophical tradition in the twentieth century, most notably through the work of Derek Parfit.[17]

In his comprehensive history of the modern Western idea of the self, Jerrold Seigel wrote that the terms self and identity are "closely related."[18] By "self" we ordinarily mean the particular being any person is, that which draws the parts of our existence together, persists through changes, and gives us a sense of agency about fashioning ourselves. This everyday sense of self is implicitly underwritten, Seigel argued, by a more systematic philosophical way of conceptualizing it. The concept of the self took shape as the intersection of three dimensions of personhood: the bodily self, with its urges and desires; the relational self, arising from social and cultural interaction, which gives us the shared language and values that shape and constrain us; and the reflective self, which can observe both our bodies and our social relations and so become an active agent of self-realization. The reflective self establishes order among our various desires and beliefs and gives direction to our actions.[19] There is bound to be tension and conflict among different aspects of the self, and humans often strive for at least a measure of stable unity and integrity. Presumably it is that "measure of stable unity" that constitutes the self's identity. But while the ordering of our desires for manageability is undoubtedly one important result of having an identity, that idea sidesteps the core meaning of identity as subjective self-definition. And even as a possible explanation of why we strive for identity, it doesn't tell us why ordering our desires takes the form of defining the self as *something*.

The claim that self and identity are the same thing is strongly implied in the title of Raymond Martin and John Barresi's book *The Rise and Fall of Soul and Self: An Intellectual History of Personal Identity*.[20] As the authors pointed out, jokes about whether the self remains identical over time can be found as far back as fifth-century Greek comedy. One ancient play features a debtor who denies his obligation to repay a loan on the grounds that, since people are always changing, he is no longer the same person who borrowed the money. When the creditor then hits the borrower over the head, he in turn denies responsibility, claiming he is no longer the person that struck the blow.[21] Assessing the postclassical contributions of Western monotheistic faiths to the idea of the self, the authors concluded that religion "bequeathed to the philosophy of self and personal identity its most enduring preoccupations: personhood, subjectivity, and identity over time,"[22] the latter referring above all to the question of the immortality of the soul. It is clear that the authors understood personal identity as our consciousness of self-continuity, in the terms originally defined by John Locke. The religious question was whether it persisted after death.

Locke had taken up the topic of the self in the second edition of his *Essay Concerning Human Understanding* (1694), in a chapter devoted to the broader question of what constitutes the identity of things over time. The empiricist epistemology he had put forward in the first edition seemed to raise serious problems for the possibility of a continuous self. If there was nothing in the mind that did not come from the senses, the self threatened to disintegrate into a mere procession of transient sensory experiences. His rescue effort rested on the facts of self-consciousness and memory: "since consciousness always accompanies thinking and it is that which makes every one to be what he calls self," Locke claimed, "and thereby distinguishes himself from all other thinking things, in this alone consists personal identity."[23] Self is nothing but the subjective "I-consciousness" that accompanies all our mental contents. Furthermore, the self exists "as far as this consciousness can be extended backward to any past action or thought. . . . [F]or it being the same consciousness that makes a man be himself to himself, personal identity depends only on that."[24] It is enough to be able to say, "I remember that I did that" for my present self to be the same as my past self.

Locke's empiricism was intended to refute the idea that some metaphysical substance underlies the perceived qualities of things. His definition of the self took the same approach; the self is not a substance but a modality of consciousness. He took up the problem of personal identity, however, for primarily ethical and religious reasons. Empiricist philosophy appeared to pose a particularly serious problem for law, morality, and faith. If my self was not a continuous substance, I could, with apparent justice, disavow in the present responsibility for what as some other self I had done in the past—as the Greek comedian had long ago noted—and anticipate denying it again in the future for present deeds, ultimately perhaps before the seat of divine judgment. The discontinuous self rendered promising, legal responsibility, morality, and sin nugatory. For these reasons Locke insisted on the legal bearing of identity: "In this personal identity is founded all the right and justice of reward and punishment"; the term person "is a *forensic* term, appropriating actions and their needs, and so belongs only to intelligent agents, capable of a law, and happiness and misery."[25] Continuity through memory could secure—and was sufficient to secure—the sameness of self that was necessary for the legitimacy of judgment of all one's deeds over time, whether by conscience, the state, or God.

But is continuity of memory enough to secure another kind of sameness, one whose absence certain subjective experiences of discontinuity show can be deeply troubling? Take, for example, the experience recorded in this diary entry by the British writer Katherine Mansfield: " 'To thine own self be true' . . . which self? Which of my many . . . hundreds of selves? . . . [T]here are moments when I feel I am nothing but the small clerk of some hotel without a proprietor, who has all his work cut out to enter the names and hand the keys to the wilful guests."[26]

In Mansfield's wonderful metaphor, the only permanent resident of "Hotel Self" is a beleaguered, faceless underling whose job is to register the temporary but demanding guests and allow them entry—an empty consciousness whose sole continuity is in accommodating different selves that come and go. Like hotel guests, Mansfield's separate selves have their own identities but have nothing to do with one another, nor, ultimately, with her. And while the hotel has a clerk, it has no proprietor—no one to give the residence its own distinct identity. Under these circumstances, the demand for self-integrity can have no meaning, because there is no one self to be true to. Mansfield's torment was precisely that of self-continuity *without* self-identity.

It is just *this* sense of missing identity, the continuous self, empty of content, that is nothing but a gatekeeper for transient occupants, which decisively marks the modern issue of personal identity off from that of John Locke. In the concise distinction made by the philosopher Amélie Rorty, Locke's problem was that of individual *re-identification* as distinct from the different problem of individual *identification*. Re-identification concerns the question of how one identifies oneself as the same human being, in different contexts, under different descriptions or at different times. Individual identification by contrast is concerned with the sorts of characteristics that identify a person as "essentially" the *person* she is, with the implication that if those characteristics were changed, she would be a significantly different person, to herself and to others—though she could still be differentiated and re-identified by others and by herself as the same human being.[27]

Rorty's distinction, however, is not quite so clear-cut. In some famous cases of individuals who suddenly appeared in a community claiming to be someone who had disappeared many years before, attempts to establish their identity included not only physical signs and confirming memories but also continuity of personal characteristics as attested by former intimates.[28] The philosopher Paul Ricoeur attempted a more precise differentiation. There are, he claimed, two kinds of personal identity: identity as *sameness*, which he designated by the Latin word *idem* (the same), and identity as *selfhood*, designated by the Latin *ipse* (the person—or thing—itself). Though both entail some sort of personal continuity or permanence, they do so in quite different ways. "Selfhood," Ricoeur asserted, "is not sameness."[29]

The distinction between idem- or sameness-identity and ipse- or selfhood-identity, Ricoeur elaborated, is the difference between the kind of permanence entailed in the idea of "character," and the kind of permanence entailed in the idea of "keeping one's word."[30] "Character" designates the set of lasting dispositions, acquired identifications, habits, and patterns by which a person can be recognized as the same over time. In terms of the question "Who or what am I?" it is the answer to the "what": character designates individual instances of general categories—thriftiness, masculinity, Italian-ness—and implies the inertia of determinism: I am (and must be) courageous because I am a man. The permanence involved in keeping one's word is of a quite different order; it is permanence through self-constancy, the act of committing oneself to fulfilling one's promises. It is sustained not by the inertia of character but by the will of a subject, the "who" that asks the identity question. The "who" and "what" of the identity question are not just two ways of asking the same question; they entail quite different views of the self.

Ricoeur's project of the self was ultimately, like Locke's, an ethical one. He wanted to ground ethics in the permanent nature of the self. But he couldn't proceed like Locke, setting aside the issue of the self's "content sameness," or idem-identity. By the late twentieth century identity in this sense had become central to the self-understanding of the person. So Ricoeur put forward a narrative theory of the self that, he argued, accommodated both kinds of identity, the inertia of character and the continuity of commitment. Narrative identity allows for both stability and change; a character in a story, and in life, is to some extent fixed, pushed along by its inner dynamic, yet is also able to alter itself in the face of new circumstances.

Sameness-identity is indispensable to narrative identity: without it, we would not be "characters," and we therefore could not have stories. But for Ricoeur sameness of character was too precarious to secure ethical constancy. It is vulnerable to change, and at the extreme can break down completely, as it did, he claimed, in Robert Musil's seminal novel *The Man Without Qualities* (*Eigenschaften*, or "characteristics," in the original German). Ricoeur called the novel a "fiction of the loss of identity." Its protagonist, having abandoned work, social commitment, and sense of purpose, becomes strictly unidentifiable to others and to himself. He no longer has a character, and therefore can no longer be a character; as a result, Ricoeur claimed, the novel loses narrative form and becomes essentially a nonfiction essay. The protagonist makes nothing happen and nothing happens to him; he can only observe and analyze others. Yet unsettling cases of loss of identity like that of Musil's protagonist can also be interpreted, Ricoeur argued, as revealing the ultimately ethical nature of selfhood. When the support of sameness-identity is removed, we see that we still retain our capacity for self-constancy, for staying true to our word.[31] Self persists even when identity is lost.

We need not go into Ricoeur's further derivation of ethical imperatives from ipse-identity.[32] What matters here is his insistence that identity as character-sameness is both vital to the way we live our lives yet separable from selfhood. In fact making the distinction between self and identity in the second half of the twentieth century did not even require Ricoeur's elaborate analysis. In a rather less rigorously founded way, academic psychology after the 1970s also held that there is an empirically useful distinction to be made between the two concepts, as the title of an influential contemporary reference work, *Handbook of Self and Identity*, indicated. "Self" in academic psychology is equivalent to the total person or the experiencing subject; "identity" is a person's "self-concept," how someone consciously defines himself, a subordinate but necessary dimension of selfhood as a whole.[33]

*   *   *

If, however, identity as stable self-definition is a necessary dimension of the lived self, why has it only recently been talked about? Charles Taylor raised this question in his pioneering *Sources of the Self*. It was an unavoidable issue for him since he claimed that identity is the "ontologically necessary" foundation of selfhood. Humans, Taylor argued, can only act within a set of commitments and identifications. These provide the "frame" or "horizon" within which alone we can determine from case to case what we endorse or oppose. Such frameworks make up our identity because they enable us to know who we are: "To know who you are is to be oriented in moral space, a space in which questions arise about what is good or bad, what is worth doing and what not, what has meaning and importance for you and what is trivial and secondary."[34] Furthermore, only seeing myself as a particular "who" enables me to place myself as an interlocutor among others with their own standpoints, without which we could not communicate with them. For these reasons the space that our frameworks seek to identify, our identity, is "ontologically basic."[35]

But as Taylor himself pointed out, in the past we didn't talk about moral orientation in terms of the question, who are we? In fact talk about identity in the modern sense would have been unintelligible to our forebears. More than unintelligible: had he been able to understand it at all, Martin Luther would have found Erik Erikson's psychological account of his crisis of faith reprehensible. What has changed since Luther's time is that we no longer believe that questions of moral orientation can be answered in objective universal terms. Modern loss of belief is the outcome of our post-Romantic validation of individual differences along with the importance we give to self-expression.[36] After the Enlightenment turn to secular rationalist individualism, the Romantics aspired to recover contact with transcendent moral and spiritual truths not through dogma but through the exercise of the unique creative imagination. Modernism in art and thought, of which we today are the legatees, is a late version of this Romantic aspiration. But unlike art produced in eras marked by the unquestioning acceptance of "publicly established order of references"—traditional religious symbols of transcendence, which even the Romantics shared—modernists had to invent their own symbols for it. Whatever they meant by spirituality, universality, or oneness could only be refracted through their unique individual sensibilities, couched in symbols of purely private inspiration. Though others might be able to decipher and enter into the meaning of modernist art, its creations could never be the publicly shared references of a deeply ingrained tradition,[37] and they certainly could not inspire the belief in their objective truth that traditional religion enjoyed. We still aspire to objective norms but today we can express and support them only through personal feelings. This is "the modern identity"—and the modern dilemma.

Nuanced as it is, Taylor's explanation is one version of a long familiar story: modernization as the rise of secular individualism. In his telling, the longing for transcendence remains even as the past intellectual frameworks that provided it no longer persuade. However understandable, and in many ways beneficial, the modern validation of autonomy and subjectivity, the inner demands we feel to honor the worth of human beings and treat them justly cannot be adequately sustained with merely subjective feelings. "High standards," Taylor observed, "need strong sources."[38] "Modern" identity needs to recognize the true nature of identity, which reveals itself in the contradiction between its relativist beliefs and its deepest inner urgings for objectively believable standards that can ground and justify our inescapable universal imperatives.

Another long-term explanation of the emergence of identity, if in broad agreement with Taylor's story about modernization, rejected his religious nostalgia. For the sociologist Anthony Giddens, the problem of "self-identity" was the inevitable psychological byproduct of the sociological conditions of "high modernity." By this he meant the historian's conventional set of economic and political institutions that characterize the Western (and increasingly the entire) world—industrialization, capitalism, and the nation-state—but most of all the state of mind produced by them, which contrasts sharply with that of traditional society. Modern social life is endlessly dynamic, a "runaway world" not only in the pace of its changes but in their scope and profundity.[39] People are uprooted from a sense of time and space determined by their concrete location and subjected to the abstractions of global parameters. Similarly, social institutions are "disembedded" from their original local contexts, their structure and processes governed only by monetary considerations and the demands of technical expertise. The result is that social life is freed from the hold of preestablished precepts and practices, and subjected to the imperative of "reflexivity," the need to constantly monitor and revise one's actions and situations in the light of new information and knowledge.[40]

Inevitably, Giddens argued, "the reflexivity of modernity extends into the core of the self. . . . [I]n the context of a post-traditional order, the self becomes a *reflexive project.*"[41] This is to say more than that the self has to constantly reinvent itself to meet new conditions. Giddens started with the premise, similar to Taylor's, that "to be a human being is to know, virtually all of the time, in terms of some description or another, both what one is doing and why one is doing it."[42] This demands the kind of "ontological secur- ity" that is furnished by answers to the fundamental existential questions which human life necessarily addresses. In the Western past, tradition supplied those answers. Under the conditions of modernity, we have to furnish our own sense of continuity by constantly reinterpreting ourselves in relation to our past and creating a coherent self-narrative: autobiography, "in the broad sense of an interpretive self-history produced by the individual . . . is at the core of self-identity in modern social life."[43]

How Giddens thought to reconcile the modern demand for continual reflexive self-adjustment with the existential need for ontological certainty is not clear. Leaving aside their internal difficulties, however, the obvious prob- lem with philosophical explanations of the rise of identity like Taylor's and sociological explanations like that of Giddens is their lack of historical speci- ficity. The conditions both of them describe, the breakdown of faith and the rise of the modern economy and state, predate by many years the emergence of the discourse of identity they are supposed to account for. "Modernity," however defined, is simply too broad-gauged a notion to account for the rela- tively sudden emergence and rapid rise of identity.

Lack of historical precision is not a problem for the explanation offered by the historian Lutz Niethammer. He was ostensibly concerned only with the idea of collective identity, but this was misleading, since he argued that Erik Erikson's concept of individual identity was derivative of his own earlier con- cern with collective identity, and on that idea other writers predated Erikson. Niethammer's book made two significant revisionist claims: the idea of collec- tive identity preceded individual identity, and it was a concern of major Euro- pean thinkers in the interwar years who were responding to deep-lying social and political crises created by World War I.

He began with a brief interpretation—ironically quite plausible—of the "legend" of the conventional account. According to the story, Erikson's "psy- chosocial identity" was a wholly new construct of the mid-twentieth century, created in reaction to the increasingly discontinuous processes of individual socialization resulting from the rapid social changes of modernity. Emerging from the individualist and democratic traditions of the United States, it was intended to enable people to gain more control over their lives by using its formulations about individual psychological development to guide their expectations and actions through the turmoil. In this way it was a contribution to strengthening individual autonomy against increasing pressures for conformity amid the social upheavals that, in destroying traditional society, had helped bring about the totalitarian catastrophes of the twentieth century. In the German reception of Erikson, the story continued, emphasis shifted from the anxieties of the individual to the discontinuities in Germany's collective life, above all the problem of coming to terms with the meaning of the Third Reich and with the division of Germany after 1945. From a German perspective it was German theorizing in the 1970s and 1980s that introduced the idea of collective identity.[44] American and British scholars disagreed, claiming that the turn from individual to political or collective identity had already taken place in the United States in the 1960s. But both German and Anglo-American accounts agreed that there are no examples of explicit concern with collective identity before then.

This version of the history of identity, Niethammer asserted, is completely wrong. His revisionism rested on the appearance of the word "identity" in the political theories of Carl Schmitt and Georg Lukacs, C. G. Jung's concept of the collective unconscious, Maurice Halbwachs' sociological theory of collective memory, Aldous Huxley's picture of mindless homogeneity in a future dystopia, and Freud's famous acknowledgement of Jewish identity in a talk to his B'nai B'rith club. All these instances date from between 1916 and 1931, with particular concentration in the years 1923–1926.[45] Niethammer acknowledged that he researched the word identity only in its collective—political, social, and cultural—contexts, since he was perfectly willing to buy the conventional account of Erikson as discoverer of individual identity, but his conclusions radically demoted its significance. Collective identity took priority, both chronologically and in its impact on politics and the subsequent history of ideas.

It is impossible here to do justice to the detail and finesse of Niethammer's analyses of ideas and their biographical origins. On the broader historical question, though, he did not make his case. Three of his exemplars, Schmitt, Lukacs, and Huxley, used the word "identity" in its accepted logical and Hegelian contexts. The other three, Freud, Jung, and Halbwachs, are indeed very relevant to the origins of modern identity, but not in the way Niethammer thought. His own analyses show that the idea of collective identity appeared in their work explicitly in relation to individual identity. They point, in other words, to a quite different historical genesis of modern identity.

Erik Erikson had himself noted Freud's declaration of his "inner identity" as a Jew as the (singular) psychoanalytic precursor of his own concept.[46] Niethammer rightly claimed that Freud defined himself in terms of what we later learned to call "ethnic identity," but he also acknowledged that it was as an expression of Freud's sense of himself.[47] The example highlights both the individual psychological dimension of collective identity, and the confusion that can result from drawing an overly sharp distinction between the two. What Niethammer did importantly emphasize was how much a mystery his Jewish identity was to Freud himself, citing Freud's foreword to the Hebrew edition of *Totem and Taboo* published for the Zionist community in Palestine:

> No reader of this book will find it easy to put himself in the emotional position of its author, who does not understand the holy tongue, is alienated from the religion of his fathers—as from all others—and is not able to share in nationalist ideals, and yet has never denied belonging to his people, feels that he is in his essential nature a Jew, and does not wish it otherwise. If you were to ask him: What is Jewish about you, when you have given up all these common characteristics with your people? he would answer, a great deal still, probably the most important thing of all. But he would not be able to express this essential thing in clear words. . . . [B]ut some day, no doubt, it will become accessible to the scientific mind.[48]

Niethammer took the lack of content in Freud's Jewish identity and his inability to articulate its meaning to be essential features of collective identity as such. Collective identity, he argued, is not constituted by a set of objective characteristics that others might rely on to identify someone but only by the subjective emotions of those who feel bound by it.[49] This is wrong on the face of it; people can and do cite reasons for their adherence to ethnic groups and religions, which come equipped with both identifying public criteria and beliefs that serve as their legitimation.[50] More importantly, and ironically, Niethammer's analysis was self-refuting; in labeling Freud's avowal of Jewishness as "ethnic identity," and explaining it as the feeling of identification with a group that partly defines to oneself and others who one is, he was offering the very "scientific" account of it that Freud hoped for. If Niethammer did not credit his own explanation it was for ethical and moral reasons: he thought the deep, ineffable loyalties behind ethnic identity dangerously irrational and destructive.

Freud's inarticulateness about his Jewish identity was not a necessary feature of the idea of collective identity; it represented rather his particular historical-theoretical problem with it, and hence with identity as such. As his analysis of group psychology showed,[51] the idea of "group identity" did not fit comfortably into the individualist and rationalist psychological theory he had spent his lifetime creating. He had discovered the concept of identification, on which the modern concept of identity would depend, but had explained identification with one's parents in the biological terms of survival and gratification. Psychologically these categories translated into desires for autonomy and self-interest.[52] Group belonging was thus nothing more than mass infantile regression to love of and submission to the father. Freud's puzzlement at the assertion of his Jewish identity, in the context of his theories about how the psyche works, expressed his sense of the illegitimacy of "identity" from a nineteenth-century liberal individualist point of view.

The critique of identity implicit in Freud was explicit in the early depth psychology of his follower and rival C. G. Jung. Jung, as Niethammer acknowledged, was the only one of his figures to use the actual term "collective identity." It appeared but once, in an unpublished draft, and was eliminated from the published version of the piece, replaced by the phrase "identification with the collective psyche."[53] The revision was significant: from Jung's point of view, identification with the collective psyche was pathological because it represented an individual's refusal of individuation. Such a refusal could manifest itself in one of two ways, since "collective psyche" had two different meanings in Jungian psychology. It referred both to the conventional norms of society, from which the psychically immature individual had not yet differentiated himself, and to the universal figures of the collective unconscious, the archetypes that dwelled in the unconscious of every human being. To the extent that the nonindividuated person became aware of the archetypes' existence, as in dreaming, he might treat them as dangerous psychic intrusions and defend against them by regressively trying to restore his "persona," his conventional public self. Or he might attempt to wholly identify one's self with one or another of the archetypes, in the megalomaniacal effort to become one with the universal figure of Hero or Prophet. In either case—at least in Jung's early psychology, before he fatefully added a racial collective unconscious to the universal collective unconscious—"collective identity" appeared as the essence of loss of self.

The third figure whose interwar work bore on identity was Maurice Halbwachs, a French sociologist who would be taken up in the 1970s and 1980s by poststructuralists and memory theorists as a precursor. In his analysis of what he was the first to name "collective memory," Halbwachs described the historical "memories" shared by members of a society as fictions, constructed over time out of mythified bits and pieces of real events and bequeathed to future generations. Their crucial function is to provide society with a sense of continuity and stability. As Niethammer acknowledged, Halbwachs did not talk of collective identity but of "collective tradition." He used the phrase "the feeling of identity" with regard only to the individual members of a society: "We preserve," Halbwachs wrote, "a number of memories from each of the epochs of our lives which we reproduce repeatedly, and through these the feeling of our identity is sustained as if in a continuous interconnection."[54] If collective memory was a social enterprise, "identity" was an individual, subjective concern. Halbwachs's insistence on the social context of personal identity was aimed in part at Bergson's and Freud's purely psychological conceptions of memory. Against them he argued that identity was the internalization of "social memory," which, necessarily oblivious to the changes it underwent in order to fulfill its function of social continuity, also gave individuals their sense of *personal* substantive sameness (Ricoeur's "idem-identity") over time. Niethammer argued that Halbwachs's enterprise had a specifically political context. Exposing the fictional character of "collective memories" served to undermine the myths underpinning the dangerous right-wing nationalisms of the interwar period Halbwachs feared. But demystifying the collective memories of nationalism also had destructive implications for personal identity. If the individual's feeling of identity was founded on the constructed and fictional nature of collective memory, it was itself nothing but illusion.

I have dwelt on these three examples because they do reveal something important about the history of identity, though the opposite of what Niethammer claimed. To the extent that the thinkers he discussed did talk of something like collective identity, they understood it explicitly in relation to an individual's sense of himself, or personal identity, and they found both problematic. Furthermore, the three represent merely the tip of an iceberg. Identity was at best a peripheral concern in their work. During the interwar period, however, many creative writers were centrally preoccupied with it. The entry from Katherine Mansfield's diary dates from 1920; it describes with emotional precision and metaphorical flair the dilemma of wanting and being unable to answer the question "Who am I?" *The Man Without Qualities*, characterized by Paul Ricoeur with exactitude as a novel about the loss of identity, dates from the late 1920s. They are only two of many literary explorations of personal identity in the twenties and early thirties. Nietham-mer was right about the importance of the interwar period for the history of identity, but not about its significance: it was during those years that the sense of individual identity became a self-conscious, and highly problematic, issue for the first time.

* * *

Shortly after the end of World War I, the French poet Paul Valéry wrote that among the many things the Great War had damaged was the mind. The European mind had come to doubt itself profoundly because it had turned its vaunted science, learning, and morality into instruments and justifica-tions of destruction.[55] Not the least of what avant-garde European writers came to doubt was the beneficence and viability of the identities connected with those corrupted ideals: the moral bourgeois, the cultivated person, the patriotic nationalist. So deep did disillusion with previously honorific identi-ties go that it implicated the possibility of defining the self by *any* set of fixed categories. Virginia Woolf's Clarissa Dalloway put it most starkly, "She would not say of any one in the world now that they were this or that. . . . She would not say of herself, 'I am this,' 'I am that.'"[56] It was out of such skeptical reticence that the modern concern with identity was born, though not yet named.

Some who attacked the possibility of identity saw no alternative and ended in theoretical confusion or despair (countered in some cases by a leap into Fascism or anti-Fascist politics). Others, while dismantling the idea of stable identity, simultaneously explored new conceptions of selfhood that might avoid identity's false fixities and determinism. These two reactions established the framework within which identity would be taken up in the following decades. Between the mid-twenties and early forties Martin Hei-degger and Jean-Paul Sartre developed the philosophical arguments against the idea of "essential" identity that were the implicit basis of the contempo-rary literary critique and the foundation of later attacks. But Heidegger went beyond the purely negative to try to work out a philosophically viable con-ception of collective identity in order to deal both with the ontological prob-lem of the anxiety of "being" and the fragmentation of Weimar Germany as he interpreted it.

After World War II, partly as a response to the disruptive psychological effects of this second twentieth-century catastrophe, the pendulum swung toward positive individual identity. The psychoanalyst Erik Erikson broached his theory of psychosocial identity, naming the idea explicitly for the first time, in the clinical conviction that a stable identity was essential to psychic health. But he too found it necessary to steer his concept between the need for inner stability and the realities of ongoing adult psychological development, historical contingency and social change, and the dangers of identity that World War II only heightened. The interwar critique had left a permanent legacy.

Erikson's concepts of "ego identity" and "identity crisis" came at a propitious historical moment. They reflected and crystallized the situation and mood of segments of educated middle-class youth in the United States during the 1950s, disenchanted with the narrow security and success goals of the Depression parent generation, and quickly established themselves in popular and scholarly discourse. Within a decade and a half, however, Erikson's concern with individual identity was overtaken by social and political upheaval. Public and intellectual focus shifted from the individual to issues of collective identity and identity politics. A similar shift to the political had taken place almost two decades earlier within existentialism; awakened by the war and the Holocaust to the realities of ongoing identity oppression in colonialism, racism, and sexism, Sartre and Simone de Beauvoir applied the ontological concept of the "Other" to political domination. But the Eriksonian language of identity demonstrated its uniquely transformative power: to conceive of social and political conflicts explicitly in terms of identity was to alter them substantively. The language of identity made it possible to conceptualize the hurt of groups denigrated by and excluded from power because of physical or cultural differences. Augmented by the existential analysis of the role of "otherness" in the creation of devalued selves, identity could take political expression in the form of demands of subordinate identities for recognition in psychological, moral, and material terms.

The politics of identity spread widely and across ideological boundaries, from disadvantaged blacks, women, and gays to conservative representatives of established elites who felt their national or religious identity threatened, ultimately making its most far-reaching claims in demands for global multiculturalism. But the politicization of identity also rebounded on it. From disparate, sometimes otherwise opposing perspectives, collective identity came to seem like a bad idea. Liberal democrats argued that identity politics undercut universal rights and licensed chauvinism. Radicals thought it obscured economic inequality and the need for economic reform. Lesbians and women of color felt excluded by the identity politics of middle-class white feminists. The original existential attack on identity was renewed in the 1970s and 1980s with new philosophical arguments by poststructuralism and postmodernism, which claimed that the inevitable but illegitimate partiality of all identities erased from view individuals and whole groups who did not meet their definitions. By the 1990s such attacks had discredited identity for many in university humanities departments, especially scholars of race and gender, who nevertheless found themselves arguing for the rights of groups they could no longer define. Other academic activists, pointing to the contradiction, tried to frame a version of identity that could withstand the philosophical criticism of "essentialism."

At the same time, in the less politically charged arena of the social sciences, the concept of identity was embraced because it was seen as solving a problem that had long bedeviled them. Identity could bridge the seeming contradiction between causal explanation by objective social structures and explanation by the subjective motives of individual action. Anthropology, economics, history, linguistics, sociology, and psychology were enriched and sometimes transformed by incorporating identity as a major explanatory factor. The effort to adjudicate the argument between proponents and opponents of the idea of collective identity led theorists to explore its validity and scope by analyzing the foundations of group identity claims: how they arise, how they are couched, how they relate to one another, how they justify themselves. And, since both individual and collective identities make demands on the self and on behalf of the self, a number of philosophers took the position that identity was an ethical as well as a psychological or a sociological concept, with unique ethical claims that could be differentiated and subjected to validation.

*   *   *

In its effort to document this set of developments, this book can be seen as an attempt at a history of the "discourse of identity," to use a contemporary academic term of art. I mean the phrase, however, more loosely than strictly. I have tried to tease out and make explicit the network of observations, assumptions, and values that were folded into the idea of identity at its birth and those it generated as it was extended into new areas. For the most part, and especially after Erikson, the word itself was my guide; I followed wherever it led me. But I also include in the discourse of identity the issues, in whatever terms they were couched, that led to the introduction of the word in the first place. The thing existed as a problem before the word was called on to name it; it is as evident in Katherine Mansfield's brief cri de coeur as it is in Robert

Musil's lengthy novel. Conversely, Heidegger and Sartre, in whose work identity *was* a central term, did not mean it in the psychological sense Erikson would give it but in its sense in German Idealist philosophy. Nevertheless, their critique of the Idealist tradition was their way of raising the question whether it is possible to answer the vernacular question "What am I?" in a philosophically legitimate way. Before Erikson the absence or presence of the word identity itself is neither a sufficient nor a wholly reliable guide to the presence of the discourse.

As history, this book makes no claim to completeness; it is *a* history of identity, not *the* history. While I discovered identity in places I did not anticipate, I have undoubtedly omitted others, some that I am even aware of. I did not have space, for example, to discuss the literature on masculine identity, in particular the provocative work of French philosopher Elizabeth Badinter, nor the highly abstract "systems theory" of German sociologist Niklas Luhmann, in which identity functions as the very criterion of a social system. I did not examine the debate on the question of whether the European Union represents a new kind of transnational identity, nor could I go into popular culture except for the barest of references. The literature of identity is vast and constantly growing; its disparate materials, from philosophy to history to social theory, parliamentary proceedings, political polemics, whodunits, and graphic novels are dizzying in their range. Complete coverage is a chimera and any attempt would not only have made an already long book longer but would be doomed to failure from the outset. What I hope to have done is to map the outlines of the new landscape identity has created like the outflow of a volcanic eruption, with as many of its main features as I could discern.

At the same time, if the vicissitudes of identity's rise and spread were greatly influenced by the unpredictable currents of history, the internal logic of the idea, however fuzzy, ensured that the same set of issues would arise again and again as identity was adapted to new uses and thinkers tried to define it in new situations. Through the multiplicity of applications and definitions it is possible to discern four consistent areas of theoretical concern. I call them the *ontological, psychological, social,* and *historical* dimensions of identity. The meaning and scope of these concerns can be defined by the questions that were recurrently raised within each of them. *Ontological:* Is identity a necessary concept in defining the human being, or is it to the contrary philosophically indefensible? Even if we think of identity as a construct rather than as a preexisting "essential self"—that is, something we create rather than something we discover—to what degree is it determined by our "facticity," our unchosen birth in a concrete time, place, and body, and to what degree by our capacity for reflection and choice? *Psychological*: Do our emotional and physical well-being, as well as our ability to act effectively in the world, depend on having a subjective, positive *sense* of identity, whatever its philosophical standing? What would be the components of such a sense of identity? Where does it come from developmentally? What is the connection between identification as a psychological process and identity as stable self-definition? *Social*: What is the relationship between individual identity and the collectives we are inevitably part of? What kinds of collective identities are there and how do we define them? Are collective identities naturally antagonistic to one another, mutually hostile aggregations of Us and Them, or is antagonism a sociohistorical artifact? *Historical*: How does the felt sense of identity as sameness through time relate to the objectively perceived reality of historical changes in identities? Is identity nothing but the product of history or does identity make history? If identity is a universal category of human existence, why did it emerge as an idea only recently?

These are, it is almost needless to say, extremely difficult questions—almost, because I will try to offer answers to them. And in doing so I also want to make the claim that despite well-reasoned opinions to the contrary the answers constitute a strong argument for the validity, indeed indispensability, of identity, though carefully defined and qualified.

Even if not metaphysically necessary (as religious and other believers certainly hold some identities to be), identity is contingently necessary for us—necessary, that is, given how we humans are factually constituted. Psychologically we do not seem to be able to feel at home in our bodies, act effectively in the world or interact emotionally and intimately with others without a stable sense of who or what we are. Our identities necessarily include, though they are not exhausted by, our self-definition in relationship to our sexual bodies; our relationship to the world of subsistence and work; membership in one or more groups who speak the same language and share a common sense of place and time as well as formal observances marking basic life passages; a set of ultimate beliefs about human destiny and basic norms of right and justice (which may or may not derive from those groups); and finally perhaps, at least in some times and places, the sense of something that makes one a unique self.

The sense of identity may, however, and quite often does, derive from an implicit commitment to the belief in the permanence and all-encompassing nature of our identities, as expressed in the words "I *am* this or that," where the copula verb appears to freeze human existence into the inertness and determinism of thinghood. Our feelings and actions show in fact that we are strongly tempted to absolutize and reify our identities, out of a desire for the metaphysical security—the feelings of necessity, legitimacy, and belonging—that such a sense of the "being" of identity can convey.

This is especially evident in relation to the collective dimension of identity. To become human is to become socialized into the prevailing norms of our time and place, more precisely, to "identify" with them. We could not otherwise orient ourselves in the world, know what is good and bad, know what to choose and how to behave. We could not begin to interact with others with any degree of consistency and predictability without the rules and regularities prescribed by the collective identities we are born into or later choose to belong to. We take these identities to be not just what we do but what we are. Collective identities are internalized as a major, if not, as in many cases they are, the determining dimension of individual identities. Some kinds of groupings, moreover, seem much more important than others in defining ourselves, so basic, unavoidable, or "primordial" that we manifest our desire for ontological security by absolutizing their particular form as ordained, metaphysical necessities—whether our sex, our ethnicity or nationality, or our cosmic beliefs about destiny and the human condition.

It is this propensity to absolutize collective identities above all that has made many hostile to the very concept. Collective identities, with their invidious distinctions of friend and foe, superior and inferior, breed conflict, exclusion, and annihilation. Furthermore they do so based on false beliefs about the permanently ordained natures or essences of human groupings. Collective identities, critics argue, are nothing but dressed-up historical constructs that come and go, most often in the service of power that seeks to dominate others.

This argument, however, throws out the valid with the illegitimate. Particular collective identities are indeed mutable human creations; the aspects of human life around which they coalesce are permanent structural features of human existence. Nor does the historical and constructed nature of collective identities undermine in principle the legitimacy of their emotional appeal and their binding force. Finite creatures of time and place that we are, we have both the psychological need and the philosophical right to embrace our particularity, our concrete identities, without having to claim some kind of transcendental justification for them.

That is precisely what the historical emergence of the category of identity has taught; it is in fact at the heart of the meaning of the concept itself. If most Westerners were not self-conscious about their identities before the word, it was not only because they took them for granted. It was because they endowed their basic identity categories with the permanence and justification, the "being" that they aspired to as finite beings. The shock of the First World War exposed and undermined this propensity, and in doing so appeared at first to destroy identity itself. What it ultimately did instead was to make us redefine identity to include the human contribution, social and individual, to its creation, without forcing us to abandon the sense that it has a solid basis both in what we permanently are as a species and in what we have created as historical and temporal beings.

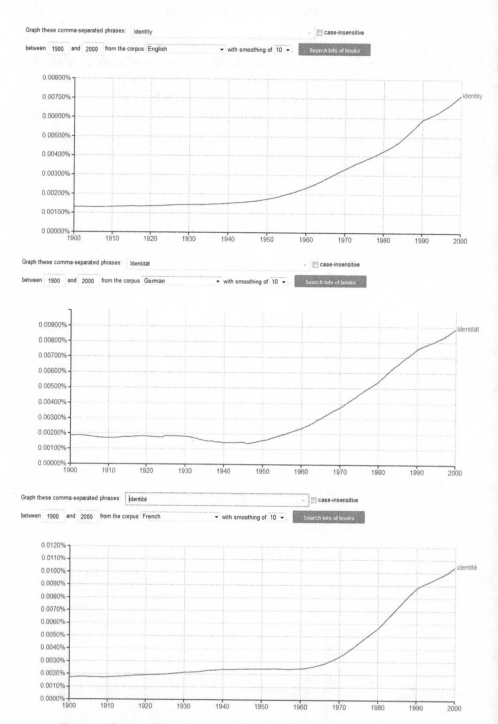

Figure 1. The rise of identity: Google N-Gram for identity in English, German, and French, 1900–2000. Source: Google Books Ngram Viewer.

Chapter 1

Identity Becomes an Issue: European Literature Between the World Wars

> I am never anything but what I think of myself—and this varies
> so incessantly, that often, if I were not there to make them
> acquainted, my morning's self would not recognize my
> evening's. Nothing could be more different from me than
> myself.
>
> —André Gide, *The Counterfeiters*, 1925

> There is no ideal to which we can sacrifice ourselves, for all we
> know is lies. . . . The earthly shadow which falls behind marble
> gods is enough to keep us from them. How firmly man is
> bound to himself! Fatherland, justice, grandeur, truth—which
> of his statues does not carry such a trace of human hands as
> would evoke in us the same ironic sadness as old and once-
> loved faces?
>
> —André Malraux, *The Temptation of the West*, 1926

As Virginia Woolf's Orlando drives out of London toward her country estate—at precisely 11:00 a.m. on October 11, 1928, we are told—her view from the speeding car is a kaleidoscopic succession of fragmentary images: half-words of shop signs, red flashes of meat in butchers' windows, women passed so quickly "they almost had their heels sliced off." Immediately the description becomes a spectacular metaphor—in both literal and vernacular senses—for an ultimate truth about the self:

> Nothing could be seen whole or read from start to finish. What was
> seen begun—like two friends starting to meet each other across the

street—was never seen ended. After twenty minutes the body and mind were like scraps of torn paper tumbling down from a sack and, indeed, the process of motoring fast out of London so much resembles the chopping up small of identity which precedes unconsciousness and perhaps death itself that it is an open question in what sense Orlando can be said to have existed at the present moment.[1]

This passage represents the first serious use of the word "identity" that I have found in its now-prevalent sense of the self as a continuous *something*. Woolf's metaphor entails a complex understanding of its meaning and historical moment. The automobile vignette brings together in brilliant compression three distinct realms: a psychological experience of self-fragmentation; the ontological condition of the self's insubstantiality that underlies it—hinted at in Woolf's evocation of the sense of ephemerality provoked by the thought of death; and finally a concrete situation, the motorcar as a personal technology of speed widely available only after the Great War, which provides the historical occasion for the breakthrough of fragmentation and nothingness into daytime consciousness.[2]

If the language of identity was rare in the 1920s, a deep sense of the self's lack of substantial being was not. Few may have used the word, but the experience Woolf describes is at the core of much European fiction and drama during the decade. Woolf herself had probed identity even more deeply three years earlier in *Mrs. Dalloway*. She and writers like André Gide, Marcel Proust, Luigi Pirandello, Hermann Hesse, Robert Musil, and Hermann Broch stand as the discoverers of the modern idea of identity as *self-definition* in their works of the interwar years. And the paradox that will haunt the concept from then on is that they discovered identity in the negation of its possibility as it had been taken for granted until then: the ability to define what the self "was" as a stable, permanent something—sexual, racial, national, social, or religious. For some writers—Pirandello, for example—the discovery led to a kind of nihilism; identity was impossible but selfhood without identity was unlivable. For others like Proust, Musil, and Woolf, identity had to be fundamentally reconceived if it were to be rescued at all. For all of them, however, the old idea of identity, along with so many other things, had been done to death by the Great War.

The Inadequacy of Memory

He was still seeing [his] baby shoes. Or not seeing them: he merely saw them as if he were seeing them. . . . And he thought:

"This having-nothing-to-do-with-me-anymore somehow
expresses the fact that all our lives, we're somehow only half
integrated with ourselves."
—Robert Musil, *The Man Without Qualities*[3]

It was Marcel Proust who most directly tested Locke's equation of memory and personal identity and found it wanting. *Time Regained*, the last volume of *In Search of Lost Time*—significantly the only one set in the postwar years—offered an interpretation of memory that was meant to finally explain the epiphany Marcel had experienced years before, when the taste of a *madeleine* soaked in tea had released overwhelming memories of childhood happiness.[4] In the despairing reflections that preceded a second and final epiphany, which would reveal to Marcel the saving power of art derived from memory rightly understood, Proust confronted the defects of Locke's idea. He acknowledged the continuity of memory in Locke's forensic terms, but suggested its relative insignificance for the deepest concerns of the self. "The memory of the most multiple person," Marcel asserts, in defending the moral reliability of even the flightiest soul (he is thinking of Gilberte), "establishes *a sort of identity* in him and makes him reluctant to go back on promises which he remembers, even if he has not countersigned them."[5] A *sort* of identity—but not, as Marcel says again and again in the novel, the kind whose absence tears at us most painfully. Proust easily conceded the possibility of ethical constancy within identity inconstancy because he did not see ethics as the crux of the problem.

At the Guermantes' party, which takes up much of *Time Regained*, Marcel analyzes the experience of meeting friends and acquaintances he had not seen since before the war and recalling what he knew about them:

> As I followed the stream of memory back towards its source, I arrived eventually at images of a single person separated from one another by an interval of time so long, preserved within me by "I's" that were so distinct and themselves . . . fraught with meanings that were so different, that ordinarily when I surveyed . . . the whole past course of my relations with that particular person I omitted these earlier images and had even ceased to think that the person to whom they referred was the same as the one whom I had later got to know, so that I needed a fortuitous lightning flash of attention before I could re-attach this latter-day acquaintance, like a word to its etymology, to the original significance which he or she had possessed for me.[6]

Because the self changes so radically, memory is substantively discontinuous—one can encounter recognizable memories of someone that nonetheless don't at all seem like one another or like the person one knows in the present. Despite his recourse to the Bergsonian and Jamesian metaphor of the stream of consciousness, Marcel's analysis of his encounter suggests that memory is not a continuous stream which can only artificially be disarticulated into separate elements. It is more like discrete bundles floating in a stream, bundles so apparently different from one another that it takes an act of focused attention to connect them. And even that kind of attention is not under one's conscious control, depending rather on "a fortuitous lightning flash." Such disconnectedness is shockingly true even of love, the most consuming of human attachments. At one point Proust had described it as "like an evil spell in a fairy tale against which one is powerless"; when in love, one can't let go of the beloved no matter how hard one tries. But that is true only until the enchantment has passed.[7] Then love may disappear so completely that one cannot recognize either the once beloved in the other person or the self that once loved her. In his most shattering evocation of ephemerality, Proust asserted the impermanence even of loss: "For in this world of ours where everything withers, everything perishes, there is a thing that decays, that crumbles into dust even more completely, leaving behind still fewer traces of itself than beauty: namely grief."[8] Memory is discontinuous not because one cannot remember that one once loved and lost, but because the memory no longer carries existential weight. It no longer constitutes who one is now.

Identity Before the War

The anguish of Marcel's discontinuous stream of memory is its insubstantiality. But for a more historical sense of what that might have meant to writers in the 1920s, it should be understood not against Locke's account of identity but against identity as they had understood it before the war. Two vignettes from other novels of the decade can give an initial sense of the world their authors felt they had lost, for good and ill.

The first is from Robert Musil's *The Man Without Qualities*. Written during the late 1920s, it is set in Vienna in 1913, the last, blissfully unselfaware year of Austro-Hungarian innocence before the catastrophe that destroyed the empire. An early chapter titled "Even a Man Without Qualities Has a Father with Qualities" introduces readers to the protagonist Ulrich's father, his antitype. Father is a middle-class Viennese law professor who by dint of assiduous service in his student years as a tutor in the houses of the high aristocracy had risen to become their legal adviser. Though now retired, professionally respected, and independently wealthy, he remains fawningly subservient to "the owners of horses, fields and traditions." For their part, while happy to have used his services, the nobility "never regarded him as anything but the personified spirit of the rising middle class."[9] Yet despite the aristocracy's indelible if genial condescension, Ulrich's father is completely at one with himself, never doubting the legitimacy of the existing social and political order or the justice of his subordinate place in it. From the vantage point of an unquestioned sense of who he is he criticizes Ulrich for flouting his proper station by buying a large house that however run-down could still be considered an aristocratic chateau. With such pointed details Musil sketches the picture of the quintessential European upper bourgeois, the same picture that will reappear in later historical accounts of the "persistence of the Old Regime" and the "feudalization of the middle class" in late nineteenth-century Central Europe.[10] But above all the image depicts the quintessential man of identity: Ulrich's father "sincerely venerated the state of affairs that had served him so well, *not because it was to his advantage, but because he was in harmony and coexistent with it.*"[11] What matters to him, *pace* Marx or Weber, is not the material interest or social status that his class position and belief system serve but the self-definition they offer him. He is a solid, undivided self because he has a definite place in the Austro-Hungarian imperial and social structure, sanctioned by history and God; more exactly, he *is* that place. It is against the ontological density of his father's social and political identity that the irreverent Ulrich, with no attachments, no vocation, and a mordant sense of the rickety hollowness of Austria-Hungary, is "The Man Without Qualities."

The second vignette, from Hermann Hesse's *Steppenwolf* (1927), involves an equally alienated protagonist, in the postwar years, who however measures the self-awareness that dawns on him against a very different previous reality. Before the war, in partial rebellion against his bourgeois upbringing, Harry Haller had come to think of himself as divided into two distinct and antagonistic selves, man and wolf. The "man" is decent, humane, cultured, and orderly, the embodiment of all the nineteenth-century bourgeois virtues. The wolf is wild, potentially destructive, a creature of impulse, passion, and anger longing to tear up the fabric of orderly society out of hatred for its decency and lawfulness. So frightening is the wolf to Haller that after one of its particularly egregious eruptions he contemplates suicide. He can neither shake the bourgeois in himself nor fully accept him, and sees no other way out of this inner conflict than death.

The "Treatise on the Steppenwolf" thrust on Haller one night by a mysterious stranger transforms him. It first articulates the man-wolf polarity in more precise terms than Haller had ever been able to do, then seeks to disabuse him of it. It ascribes the dualistic way of thinking primarily to artists, alluding to the "two souls" warring within Goethe's Faust that had become an integral part of the nineteenth century cultivated German's self-image. Faust's two souls, originally evoking the Romantic conflict between the wish to embrace earthly finitude and the desire to transcend it, had by the late nineteenth century come to mean something less exalted and more dangerous. The division between rational human and instinctual animal that bedevils Haller was the common trope of a European-wide rebellion against bourgeois rationalism. The nonrational might indeed include "higher" infinite spiritual yearning but more commonly it was "low" sexual and aggressive drives, morally unacceptable, culturally problematic, and hence consciously unavailable to the normative middle-class personality. Artist versus bourgeois, immoralist versus moralist, unconscious versus conscious, charisma versus bureaucratic rationality, instinct against intellect, Apollo and Dionysus, Dr. Jekyll and Mr. Hyde—in different but parallel figures the art and thought of prewar Europe painted a dualistic portrait of humanity in order to subvert the false unity and harmony of its "Victorian" self-image. Whether enthusiastically embraced, vehemently rejected, or, as in most cases, regarded with deep ambivalence, the irrational was omnipresent in prewar avant-garde culture as the suppressed other of the bourgeois self.

To the author of the Steppenwolf treatise, however, this prewar dualism is false. It is, he claims, only a paradoxical instance of the inborn human need to create an illusory unity within the self. Though dualism begins to recognize multiplicity, it is still too bounded a formulation of the self, even if someone who arrives at it can be thought "almost a genius," a rare exception to the usual self-deception, so pressing is the human need for the illusion of unity. Even so, the trope of "two souls" is an unacceptably reduced account of the self. Every "I" is in reality "a manifold world, a constellated heaven, a chaos of forms, of states and stages, of inheritances and potentialities." Not all that bites is wolf, nor is "man" exhausted by the bourgeois. The artist who divides man into two fails to see that "this whole world, this Eden and its manifestations of beauty and terror, of greatness and meanness, of strength and tenderness is crushed and imprisoned by the wolf legend just as the real man in him is crushed and imprisoned by that sham existence, the bourgeois."[12]

In correcting Haller, Hesse was correcting himself. His own early novels had been constructed around the very dualism the Steppenwolf treatise excoriates. There is no better evidence for the radical novelty of the analysis of the self in Steppenwolf and The Man Without Qualities than the artistic trajectories of their authors. Both Hesse and Musil had written novels before the war with dualistic premises that had brought them considerable acclaim.

Hesse had actually used the wolf image to describe one side of the "split within myself" in his most popular prewar novel, Peter Camenzind (1903), but there the animal was more benign than the snarling beast of *Steppenwolf.* Camenzind is a self-described "poet, wanderer, drunkard, lone wolf," a soulful melancholic from a tiny farming village in the Alps who experiences early in life the infinite grandeur of nature in the mountains. His talent for writing wrenches him out of his rural idyll and sends him to the city, to higher education and the world of commercial publishing. He yearns to translate his "dispassionate" love for nature into great literature to convey the message of the oneness of all life to humanity, but is stymied by both personal shortcomings and the corruptions of modernity. Too consumed by narcissism to be able to give himself up to nature, the ambitious artist is the exemplar of modern man who has abandoned it. To save himself, Camenzind returns to his little village to look after his dying father, and nourishing himself on the memory of the people he first loved, leaves his magnum opus unfinished in a drawer. *Peter Camenzind* was the epitome of a widely popular genre, an expression of the late upsurge of nostalgic nature-Romanticism in early twentieth-century Germany in the face of a rapidly urbanizing and industrializing society. Its core was conflict within a self divided between country and city, nature and capitalist industrialism, the modern striving egoistic self and the timeless unity of the All.

The divided self in Musil's early work is darker and less vaporous than Hesse's neo-Romantic sentimentalist, more like Hesse's wolf of the steppes. Where *Peter Camenzind* gestured vaguely to the higher regions, Musil's *Young Törless* probed the lower, with a mix of lurid external detail and fearful inner exploration. The ambitious scion of an upper middle class Austrian bureaucrat, Törless is sent to a prestigious military boarding school to prepare for an illustrious career in state service. In his unsavory friends, however, and within the psyche that draws him to them, he discovers shocking currents of sexuality, gender confusion, and sadism for which the respectable conventional life of his parents had not prepared him:

> He felt as though torn between two worlds: one was the solid everyday world of respectable citizens, in which all that went on was well regulated and rational, and which he knew from home, and the other was a world of adventure, full of darkness, mystery, blood, and undreamt-of surprises. It seemed as though one excluded the other. . . .
>
> [Yet] from the bright daytime world, which was all that he had known until now, there was a door leading into another world, where all was muffled, seething, passionate, naked, and loaded with destruction. . . . [B]etween those people who moved in an orderly way between

the office and the family . . . and the others, the outcasts, the blood-stained, the debauched and filthy . . . there was some bridge—and not only that, but . . . the frontiers of their lives secretly marched together and the line could be crossed at any moment.[13] (translation slightly modified)

This is one of the most succinct literary evocations of the ubiquitous prewar dualism that would be most famously epitomized by Freud's conscious and unconscious selves.

Dualism was jarring enough to its discoverers. Before he reached the climax of Törless's descent into the world of "darkness, mystery and blood," Musil tried to save him by abruptly breaking away from narrative to explain how as an adult, Törless will be able to integrate these "adolescent experiences" without regrets through a process of self-development whereby he comes to understand their usefulness in reaching a higher level of maturity. Törless will discover that externally correct behavior would preserve him from "spiritual coarseness" while allowing him a sense of irony toward the pretensions of law and morality to absolute truth. He will be able to gloss over the problems that agnosticism about moral truth presents because truth is not important; the only real interest that "aesthetically inclined intellectuals" feel, Musil editorializes, "is concentrated on the growth of their own soul" through the absorption of new experiences.[14] This was a restatement of the German tradition of *Bildung* with a modernist twist that subordinated ethics, originally central to the idea of self-cultivation, to aesthetics. By the early twentieth century the concept of the ethical personality was no longer a realistic version of the human ideal even to the dedicated nineteenth-century humanist. Yet by falling back on the notion of *Bildung* at all, Musil offered the clearest demonstration of that desire to unify the self that Hesse would deconstruct in *Steppenwolf* and Musil himself would savage in *The Man Without Qualities*. The irony and nostalgia of the prewar exposé of bourgeois identity, from the perspective of the 1920s, is that it did not give up the ideal of identity; not only did it preserve identity in a well-defined dualism that would have been a comfort to the fragmented self of the 1920s, but it also still aspired to overcome that dualism in a higher unity.

The examples of *Peter Camenzind* and *Young Törless* belie the notion that to speak of prewar dualism is to suggest a simple conflict of opposites. The other side of "the bourgeois" was a richly diverse set of counterselves, whose only unity lay in the fact that each represented the contradiction of some presumably essential bourgeois characteristic. The "anti-bourgeois" had many faces, dark and light. It could be the sexual, the "perverse," the occult, the transcendent, the primitive, the charismatic, the demonic—anything that was the obverse of reason, science, empiricism, material self-interest, duty, or moral restraint. Some of its versions glanced in the direction of chaos and the unbounded—Bergson's "élan vital," Freud's "primary processes" unconstrained by logic or reality, Kandinsky's "spiritual" quest for the infinite in abstract painting. But before the war none drew the most radical inferences from their attacks on rationality and form. Bergson argued for the moral direction of the life force; Freud's purpose was to shine the light of consciousness on the irrational in order to control it; Kandinsky's abstraction was intended as a more inclusive version of harmony that would take into account the realities of dissonance. One way or another, the reconciliation of opposites under the banner of unity was the prewar order of the day.

Perhaps the most revealing reinterpretation of the prewar self in the retrospect of the 1920s is to be found in Hermann Broch's trilogy *The Sleepwalkers* (1931–1932). Each of the first two volumes, *1888: Pasenow, or Romanticism* and *1903. Esch, or Anarchy*,[15] centers on a character meant to represent an entire prewar cultural-political epoch in Germany. The trilogy parallels Musil's project in *The Man Without Qualities* but from the vantage point of an elaborately developed philosophy of history that is only fully articulated in part three, *1918: Huguenau, or Realism*. I will take it up when I discuss how it came out of Broch's reaction to World War I; here I want to suggest the way the first volume of the novel transformed the conventional prewar dualistic interpretation of the iconic Prussian Junker.

Broch's picture of the aristocrat Joachim von Pasenow was refracted through his thesis that prewar identity was a late stage in the total collapse of identity in Europe. From a dualist perspective, Joachim von Pasenow would have been the quintessential divided self, caught between the rigid forms and expectations of the life of a Junker scion and the lure of a lower-class Slavic girl who embodies sexual and sensuous possibilities otherwise unavailable to him. But in Broch's postwar construction of Pasenow's inner conflict, the rigid carapace of his military uniform was meant not just to ward off forbidden sexual desire but to protect against the total disintegration of the self. The "cult of the uniform," as Broch called the veneration of the army in the Prussianized German Empire, was the characteristic Romanticism of its time; it elevated the secular institutions of army and state to embodiments of the absolute. The true function of "superterrestrial and supertemporal" ideas like Romanticism, Broch claimed, is to ordain and to manifest order in the world, thus to arrest the inherent chaos and formless flux of life. Exclusion is the other side of absolute identity, since the ideal is necessarily the opposite of the finite and degraded. The contents of the ideal may change; rigid separation between the ideal and what it excludes does not. As Broch sardonically put it, it is "on intolerance and lack of understanding [that] the security of life is based."[16] We need the rigidities of unchanging personal structure to feel secure in the world, but structure and form mean falseness to oneself and injustice to others. This is the authentic voice of the postwar disillusion with identity.

Life Without Identity

> She would not say of any one in the world now that they were this or were that. . . . [S]he would not say of herself, I am this, I am that.
>
> —Virginia Woolf, *Mrs. Dalloway*

The language of identity—"I *am* this, I *am* that"—is one crux of Woolf's novel; the word "now" is the other. Once, Clarissa Dalloway would have taken for granted that everyone *was* something fixed and definite; now she can't. The pivot on which time has turned from "then" into "now" is the Great War. This is true for all the writers I discuss here. But before examining why the war and its consequences relegated the prewar self, whether monolithic like Ulrich's father or divided like Haller's Steppenwolf, to an unrecoverable past, I want to explore the landscape of life without identity that they descried.

One apt guide to that terrain is the apparently recovered madman "Henry IV," the eponymous "hero" of Luigi Pirandello's play. Pirandello learned a good deal about the self's lack of stability from the paranoid delusions of his psychotic wife, but it was in his postwar masterpieces, *Six Characters in Search of an Author* and *Henry IV*, written in a hectic six-week period in 1921, long after the onset of his wife's illness, that he generalized the special case of madness into a theory of identity. "Henry IV" is an Italian aristocrat who while playing the role of the medieval German emperor in a pageant was knocked unconscious and woke up believing he was his dress-up character. For many years he has been supported in his delusion by servants and friends; when with him, they put on appropriate costumes and play the roles of figures from the great historical drama of Henry IV's conflict with Pope Gregory VII. Except that Henry has not been mad for much of this time; long before the action of the play he awoke from his delusion.

The explanation he offers for continuing the masquerade after he has ceased believing it is an analysis of the disorienting temporality of the self and of the consolations offered by history. Though we are all fixed in good faith in a certain concept of ourselves, Henry says, we are always faced with the possibility of acting out of character. It is just because of the chaos that lurks beneath the costume that we cling so tightly to it. But an estranging glance from someone we love, someone whose recognition we crave but who does not see us as we see ourselves—as happened to Henry just before the pageant—is enough to shake our very existence. So Henry, disappointed in love, took refuge in history, where the script has already been written and no improvisation is required. Though the historical Henry IV had been defeated and humiliated by Gregory at Canossa, the role provided "Henry" with the kind of certainty life denies. "Sad as is my lot," he tells his servants on revealing his deception, "hideous as some of the events, bitter the struggles and troublous the time—still all history! All history that cannot change, understand? All fixed forever! And you could have admired at your ease how every effect followed obediently its cause with perfect logic, however every event took place precisely and coherently in each minute particular! The pleasure, the pleasure of history, in fact, which is so great, was yours."[17] Of course, Henry knew on awakening that he was playacting; his revived consciousness must corrode the containing framework of his historical identity. But, he claims later, when he reveals the truth of his deception to the visitors who have come to cure him, he is saner than they because he at least plays his role with the lucid consciousness that it is a role, while they continue to live their madness, the illusory fixity of their roles, agitatedly, without knowing it or seeing it.[18]

Theater provides the same benefits of identity as history—though only to the characters within a play, not to the actors—which is to say that identity is possible only after death or in art, not in life. Pirandello stated the devastating truth explicitly in a climactic exchange in *Six Characters in Search of an Author* between the Father, one of the characters in an unfinished play who have come to the theater to have their play completed, and the "real life" character of the theater manager. When the Father asks the manager "Who are you?" the manager answers testily that it takes some nerve for a character to ask a real person who he is. A character, the Father returns calmly, may always ask a man who he is because a character is always "somebody" while a man in a deep sense is nobody:

Our reality doesn't change: it can't change! It can't be other than what it is, because it is already fixed forever. It's terrible. Ours is an immutable reality which should make you shudder when you approach us if you are really conscious of the fact that your reality is a mere transitory and fleeting illusion, taking this form today and that tomorrow, according to the conditions, according to your will, your sentiments, which in turn are controlled by an intellect that shows them to you today in one manner and tomorrow . . . who knows how?"[19]

In one final twist, however, the dramatic denouement of the play nihilistically destroys even the certainty of fictional characters, when the Boy, silent throughout the play, drowns his younger sister and then shoots himself, plunging the stage, and presumably the audience, into chaos. Characters are, after all, at the mercy of their author, as open-ended and unpredictable, therefore, as life itself.

The two plays proclaim many essential features of the self without identity that are rehearsed throughout the literature of the 1920s. Identity is immutable; the self is forever changing. Identity is a unity; the self is a heap of fragments, a metaphor made flesh by the musician-magus Pablo in *Steppenwolf's* Magic Theater when he takes materialized pieces of Harry Haller's life and shows how they can be arranged and rearranged in an infinite number of configurations like the pieces in a game of chess. And the radical mutability of the self underlies the ever-present possibility of uncanny self-estrangement. "Nothing could be more different from myself than me," says Edward in Gide's *The Counterfeiters*.[20] The horror of self-estrangement may be partly moral—Edward, unlike Proust's Marcel, does worry about the disintegration of his sense of responsibility that seems to go along with the "decentralization" of his self—but more fundamentally it is the horror of nothingness, the "nobody" a man may become to himself when he realizes that nothing he believed essential to who he is, is so in fact. The judge who in a sudden seizure of self-awareness realizes he could be the criminal standing before him tries to suppress the moment not for moral reasons but because it opens under him the abyss of formlessness.

Even Pablo in *Steppenwolf* concedes that a human being cannot live in a fragmented state, that psychiatry, which labels self-fragmentation schizophrenia, is right in pointing out that the multiplicity of selves within the self can only be dealt with in the framework of a coherent structure, an orderly grouping. But it is wrong in holding that only one binding and lifelong order is possible for the "multiplicity of subordinate selves."[21] The ordered self is a constructed self that can be endlessly made and remade like the infinite possible configurations of game pieces on a board, each of which will yield a different game. In a quite different spirit, but with similar self-awareness, Clarissa Dalloway sits before her mirror preparing for the party that is the end, in both senses, of the novel:

> She pursed her lips when she looked in the glass. It was to give her face point. That was her self—pointed; dart-like; definite. That was her self

when some effort, some call on her to be her self, drew the parts together, she alone knew how different, how incompatible and composed so for the world only into one centre, one diamond, one woman who sat in her drawing-room. . . . [For others she] had tried to be the same always, never showing a sign of all the other sides of her.[22]

Here Woolf is talking about a social motivation for wanting to present oneself as unified, and Clarissa Dalloway has only one social self in her repertoire. But her party-giving sociability is "metaphysically" inspired, motivated by the same desire to overcome the ultimate disconnectedness in the macrocosm of humanity that underlies the microcosmic act of pulling the different parts of herself together.

There are no universal guidelines for how to do that, however, no blueprints for constructing identity. Henry IV was drawn to historical role-playing because of the seductiveness of the notion, which is also the nemesis of historians, that what happened in that past had to happen—else why did it? The past is ineluctably there, like a thing; it must be the necessary effect of preceding causes, which it's the historian's job to discover. To act one's role then is simply to obey the law of cause and effect, no decision involved: "You could have admired," as Henry put it about his behavior as Emperor, "how every effect followed obediently its cause with perfect logic." Musil's "Man Without Qualities," however, has discovered another, opposite, law of history and identity, the principle of insufficient cause: "in our real, I mean our personal lives, and in our public-historical lives, everything that happens happens for no good or sufficient reason."[23] Young people plead inner necessity to justify their acts, but there is no such thing; when they reach middle age they don't really know how they got to be what they are, how they came by their pastimes, their outlook, their wife, their character, or their profession: "nowhere is a sufficient reason to be found why everything should have turned out the way it did; it could just as well have turned out differently."[24] Contingency rules life—"'I'm only fortuitous,' Necessity leered"; so Ulrich reflects—not simply in the empirical sense that life is impinged on by accidents, but in the metaphysical sense that everything could be other than it is—the universe as well as one's personal choices.

*　*　*

The novel of the 1920s that took as its central task to challenge the contingency of identity is Kafka's *The Castle* (1924); its pointed failure served only to confirm it. *The Castle* takes two existential steps beyond *The Trial*. What was at

stake in *The Trial* was the law, and while everything about its earthly instantia-
tion in the existing legal system and in the church was discredited by corruption or human fallibility, Kafka seemed in no doubt that Law in the
transcendent sense existed within its inner sanctum, though unreachable by
man. The proximate and ultimate proof of its existence is not its revelation
but its effects—Joseph K's very real sense of guilt and his ceaseless quest for
justice. In *The Castle* the stakes are higher: the possibility of a transcendental
foundation for human identity. And while the castle that presumably hired K.
as a land surveyor also exists (and is also impenetrable), there are serious
questions as to whether it really did hire him, whether it is inhabited by anyone with authority to do so, or whether indeed it is inhabited at all. The only
evidence for any of these is K's desire that it be so.

The metaphor of land surveyor is almost too obvious. K. wants to know
"the lay of the land," to define final and legitimate boundaries, and he wants
sanction for his task and its results from a higher authority. His first exchange
with the castle, by telephone, is unpropitious. He hesitates to say who he
"really" is because he's too easily intimidated on the phone, and announces
himself instead as his old assistant. The voice on the other end initially rejects
that self-definition, but when K. responds "Who am I, then?" the voice
answers definitively that K. is indeed the old assistant. K., unfortunately, is
only whoever he says he is.

That is not what he wants, but he can get no other unambiguous satisfaction. There is a letter, ostensibly from the castle, apparently confirming his
appointment, though without saying as what; it is signed by an anonymous
bureaucrat and is delivered by a mere messenger. The letter is full of contradictions, and it is clear to K. that it has been left up to him to decide what to
make of them, "whether he wanted to be a village worker with a distinctive
but merely apparent connection to the Castle, or an apparent village worker
who in reality allowed the messages brought by Barnabas to define the terms
of his position."[25] Should he, that is, take on a real, socially defined identity
within the existing division of labor, with a claim to, but no real evidence for,
higher legitimation, or should he insist that he is really of a higher world, that
his social identity is not his real self, but then accept his legitimation from a
bureaucrat whose only evidence that he actually represents that higher world
is his own assertion?

K. never chooses between the options. He will accept neither mere social
role status, except provisionally, nor instructions from above from a mere
intermediary. Instead he continues his endless battle for recognition of his
identity directly from the castle. "What I want from the Castle is . . . my
rights," he insists;[26] "My greatest and indeed my only wish is to settle my

affairs with the authorities."[27] But this proves difficult. He can obtain no direct access to them. The chairman of the village council, who has the executive power of appointment, judges the purported letter from the castle authorities to be a private rather than an official communication and refuses to appoint K. In fact, he informs him, K. has never really come into contact with the authorities; all his supposed contacts have been merely apparent. In any case the wording of the letter implies that K. may not have been appointed at all, that perhaps he has been trying to foist himself on the castle, and that therefore "the burden of proving that you've been taken on rests with you."[28]

He is not relieved of the burden throughout the novel, which ends inconclusively, or rather, since it was not completed or published by Kafka, appropriately does not end at all. K. never meets with Klamm, the castle official in charge of his case. The only promise of official connection with him and therefore of recognition by the castle is in the deposition that Momus, Klamm's village secretary, demands of K. But it will be filed in the village registry and Klamm will never read it—Kafka's droll hint at the only certain, the bureaucratic, construction of identity. K. refuses to be interrogated. He remains suspended between castle and village. But that has dire implications for his sense of who he is. "You're not from the Castle, you're not from the village," his landlady had told him early on, "you are nothing. Unfortunately, though, you are something, a stranger, one who is superfluous and gets in the way everywhere."[29] Intentionally or not, the English translation uses terms that have become familiar to readers of the English translations of Camus and Sartre. Without transcendental recognition, one's identity is not metaphysically necessary, and one who continues to seek it is a stranger in a double sense, at home neither within himself nor with others.

What complicates the status of nothingness, however—because in life, unlike in a vacuum, the void is complex—is that even a man without qualities has qualities nonetheless, or rather, as Musil puts it in another of his playful-serious chapter titles, "A Man Without Qualities Consists of Qualities Without a Man." Even as K. quests for transcendental recognition he has acquired a home, a position, real work, and a fiancée in the village. The problem of not having a sanctioned identity is worse than being empty; it is being empty and busy at the same time. "One is," Ulrich acknowledges, "undoubtedly conditioned by one's qualities and is made up of them, even if one is not identical with them."[30] As much as one may feel that one is metaphysically nothing, contingently one is inescapably something, indeed many things. If one can't have metaphysical necessity, one can't escape contingent necessity. Living inexorably plunges us into situations in which we make choices or are drawn to things to which we get emotionally attached. However we came to be constituted as we are, we are de facto bodies and social beings. Ulrich himself counts his contingent identities in what is probably the most detailed list of identity parameters to be found not only in the fiction of the 1920s but in psychology or social theory today, after decades of theoretical identity-consciousness: "the inhabitant of a country has at least nine characters: a professional, a national, a civic, a class, a geographic, a sexual, a conscious, an unconscious, and possibly even a private character to boot."[31] (At least nine, says Musil: he strangely omitted religion, though he had written extensively about it.) But however many identities one might add, they don't add up to a whole. For, as Musil goes on to say,

> He unites them in himself, but they dissolve in him, so that he is really nothing more than a small basin hollowed out by these many stream-lets that trickle into it and drain out again. . . . Which is why every inhabitant of the earth also has a tenth character that is nothing else than the passive fantasy of spaces yet unfilled. This permits a person all but one thing: to take seriously what his at least nine other characters do and what happens to them; in other words, it prevents precisely what should be his true fulfillment."[32]

That tenth "identity" is the space between consciousness and all the others. It is what prevents us from ever fully identifying with any of our "characters," the corrosive self- awareness that we may be this and that but we are not wholly this and that and therefore not ultimately this or that. The horror is that we can feel all the impulsions of desire and belonging while at the same time standing back detachedly observing our own frenzy and knowing that it is, in the ultimate sense, unwarranted. The reverse however is also true. When Henry IV sees his former lover's daughter, who resembles her mother, dressed as she was on the fateful day of the pageant, his vaunted lucidity flees him completely. Caught up once again in the passion that gave his life meaning then, he falls back into the very madness of self-deception he has just exposed to those who would cure him. But just as he has never escaped the dream of identity-by-love that had always lurked within his lucidity, he will never again, even in passion, be able to escape the lucid awareness that the dream is just a dream.

That space between consciousness and identity is our freedom, but as Ulrich says, it is a purely "negative freedom,"[33] which can be liberating but is never fulfilling: "this inner freedom," he reflects bitterly, "consists of being able to think whatever one likes; it means knowing, in every human situation, why one doesn't need to be bound by, but never knowing what one wants to be bound by!"[34] A decade later Sartre will describe this negative freedom as the sentence to which we are condemned, catching up the sense of Ulrich's despair at his inability to be motivated deterministically enough to overcome the ironic detachment of nonidentity. The ultimate tragedy of nonidentity is the impossibility of wholeheartedness.

The Great War and the Unmaking of Identity

> This late age of the world's experience had bred in them all,
> men and women, a well of tears.
>
> —Virginia Woolf, *Mrs. Dalloway*[35]

Musil's analysis is certainly meant as an exposé of the universal human condition, but unlike Sartre later he did not make it in a historical vacuum. On the contrary, he thought that the tenth identity, that "empty invisible space" within the self, had only become apparent for the first time under very particular historical conditions. "Insofar as this can become visible to all eyes," Ulrich claims, "it had happened in Kakania," his playfully obscene nickname for the Austro-Hungarian Empire, derived from the denomination officially attached to all its entities, *kaiserlich-königlich*, or imperial-royal, abbreviated as "k&k" and pronounced in German "ka (und) ka"—the ordinary children's term for excrement.[36] It was the absurd contradictions in the structure of the empire, and the inconsistent self-definitions it fostered in and demanded from its subjects, that ultimately revealed to them the insufficiency of the grounds of their identities:

> the Austro-Hungarian state . . . did not consist of an Austrian part and a Hungarian part that, as one might expect, complemented each other, but of a whole and a part; that is, of a Hungarian and an Austro-Hungarian sense of statehood, with no country of its own. The Austrian existed only in Hungary, and there as an object of dislike; at home he called himself a national of the kingdoms and lands of the Austro-Hungarian Monarchy as represented in the Imperial Council, meaning that he was an Austrian plus a Hungarian minus that Hungarian; and he did this not with enthusiasm but only for the sake of a concept that was repugnant to him, because he could not bear the Hungarians as little as they could bear him.[37]

Who's on first? Given the manifest sham of Austro-Hungarian "identity," it was little wonder that the introspective "Austro-Hungarian" could not believe in the reality of what he was officially told he was.

Austria-Hungary was not, however, a lone case. Writers elsewhere in Europe had become similarly aware of the friability of identity. Furthermore, while Musil was questioning what Austria-Hungary stood for before the war, it was only after its disappearance that he was able to see fully into the contradictions that had destroyed it and expose its unreality, more exactly, as the title of the main section announces, its pseudoreality. In every work I examine here, the turning point for the idea of identity is World War I, whether the events of 1914–1918 or their later consequences for the individual countries of their authors and for the common culture of Europe.

∗   ∗   ∗

A debate about World War I as a cultural turning point to our own time has been ongoing since the publication of Paul Fussell's *The Great War and Modern Memory*, which famously made the claim that irony as the dominant form of modern sensibility originated in the social and literary response to the events of the war.[38] Fussell's materials were largely English. Modris Eksteins made a similarly large claim for European culture as a whole in *Rites of Spring: The Great War and the Birth of the Modern Age*,[39] though the "birth" he had in mind was that of Fascism, offspring of the marriage of artistic modernism and war with its glorification of action for action's sake and aesthetics of violence. Opposing such views, some biographers of modernist writers minimized the war's significance. They noted that writers had documented a widespread and deepening sense of crisis in European culture before the war, and claimed that its outcome did little more than vindicate their subjects' earlier sense of European decline.[40] The idea that the Great War was a seismic cultural event was challenged on the postwar side by Jay Winter, who argued in *Sites of Memory, Sites of Mourning: The Great War in European Cultural History* that Europeans mourned after the war with traditional prewar tropes and symbols.[41]

The literary works I look at here strongly support the idea of radical change with regard to identity. Though Broch, Musil, and others did share deep forebodings about the fate of European culture before 1914—along with, in the case of Musil, optimistic hopes for cultural renewal—the war's traumatic psychological and intellectual impact did more than realize the cultural decline they had anticipated before it. Just as some in the years before 1914 predicted the inevitability of war but not the kind of war that came, writers and intellectuals who predicted cultural disaster in the prewar years did not foresee the depth of change war would bring about, least of all in their own ideas.

*   *   *

The war figures not just as background in *Mrs. Dalloway* but as its other main protagonist, directly embodied in the shell-shocked veteran Warren Septimus Smith and more obliquely in the discrediting of the symbols of "king and country" as refracted through the narrator's ironic consciousness.[42] It is because Woolf did not believe in the sacred character of those symbols that Clarissa Dalloway can no longer believe in the reality of fixed identities. The disillusion of war has extended itself to the ideals and sociopolitical structure that legitimized it. As Nietzsche had written about the coming of nihilism with the death of the Christian God, the untenability of one interpretation of the world on which a tremendous amount of energy had been lavished awakens the suspicion that all interpretations of the world are false. For Clarissa Dalloway nothing could replace the icons of meaning and authority that had constituted English identity over hundreds of years.

Clarissa herself is not quite aware that she no longer believes in the symbols; she is still impressed enough with an official-looking closed car that possibly carries the Queen, "the majesty of England . . . the enduring symbol of the state" to put on "a look of extreme dignity" when it passes her in the street.[43] But the look is put on, not spontaneous. She has come to despise the ideologies and passions that can take one over so completely that they extinguish the capacity to be open and generous, to respond to and connect with "life" in its infinite, unclassifiable variety. Clarissa's ideological aversions are intensely personal; they are for those enthusiasms that threaten to make totalitarian demands on her or to seduce her daughter away from her. But they are nonetheless universal targets: "Love and religion! . . . How detestable, how detestable they are! . . . The cruelest things in the world, she thought, seeing them clumsy, hot, domineering, hypocritical, eavesdropping, jealous, infinitely cruel and unscrupulous."[44] For the author, however, well ahead of her protagonist, the hatred of abstract ideals implicated all those which constituted English identity in the late Victorian England in which she grew up, and which lingered into the postwar period.

Woolf was merciless at the expense of a wide range of basic English identity types: the fatuous aristocrat Lady Bruton who, needing a cause in middle age to replace the self-adulation of her long-lost youth, has fixed on solving England's economic problems by getting young people to emigrate; the odiously smug psychiatrist Sir William Bradshaw, for whom the therapeutic ideology of "proportion" is nothing but class-based disgust at the "irrationality" of the psychically ill, and a device to isolate the disturbers of good society out of sight in country asylums while getting rich and famous in the bargain. But what takes these character sketches beyond Wildean satire to bitter revulsion is their guilty implication in the ideology of Englishness that destroyed Warren Septimus Smith morally, psychologically, and physically.

Observing a group of young boys in uniform, Clarissa's long-ago suitor Peter Walsh admires the expressions on their faces that seem to read "duty, gratitude, fidelity, love of England." He had just passed the statue of a young duke and remarked to himself that the future of civilization lay in the hands of young men like that, "of young men such as he was, thirty years ago; with their love of abstract principles" and books and reading sent to them while serving their country abroad.[45] It was precisely that love of abstraction that had made Clarissa reject him. And it was those same abstract principles, mediated through the eager improver of the lower classes Miss Isabel Pole, which had transformed Septimus Smith from vaguely ambitious lower middle class youth to passionate lover of England's cultural heritage. In this regard, Septimus and Miss Pole are representative characters. As Paul Fussell pointed out, the Great War occurred at a moment when the appeal of popular education was at its peak because it was imagined that the study of great literature would actively assist those of modest origins to rise in the class system, and there were few common soldiers who had not been assured that the greatest of modern literatures was the English.[46] When the war broke out, Septimus was one of the first to volunteer, to "save an England which consisted almost entirely of Shakespeare's plays and Miss Isabel Pole." He became the ideal British soldier, manly, dutiful, stoic. So perfect of type he was that when the only friend he had ever made in his life, his commanding officer Evans, was killed, Septimus prided himself on feeling "very little and very reasonably. The War had taught him. It was sublime. He had gone through the whole show, friendship, European War, death, had won promotion, was still under thirty and was bound to survive."[47]

The war was indeed a sublime teacher, but Septimus had mistaken its lesson. The desperate effort to sustain his refusal to mourn has been broken through by irrepressible emotion and by the war's revelation of the lie of Englishness. The nation and its culture were lies as he had been taught them. Shakespeare was not about great language; like all great writers, he revealed the loathsome truth about humanity that Septimus had discovered for himself, and most devastatingly about himself, in the war, but had worked to deny in the name of his identity as a British soldier. The truth was "that human beings have neither kindness, nor faith, nor charity beyond what serves to increase the pleasure of the moment. They hunt in packs. . . . They desert the fallen. They are plastered over with grimaces."[48] He was guilty like everyone else, guilty above all of not caring when Evans was killed because his identity was about caring for higher things. The death of one man, even one he loved, could not be allowed to matter if it unmanned him for doing his duty. For this, for all his other crimes of using people, like his innocently loving wife, he has come to feel he deserves no less a judgment than death.

Clarissa the socialite party-giver must, surprisingly, fight off a similar temptation when she hears of Septimus's suicide that evening at her party. Her attraction to death seems quite different from his, but is in fact closely related. Septimus killed himself to avoid being locked away by Bradshaw's hypocritical ideals, which denied the reality of his experience and his suffering, as he himself had initially tried to do for the sake of those same ideals. Knowing nothing of Septimus, Clarissa nonetheless scents, projecting her own self-knowledge, that his death was an act of defiance in the name of an obscure truth: "Death was an attempt to communicate; people feeling the impossibility of reaching the centre which, mystically, evaded them; closeness drew apart; rapture faded, one was alone. There was an embrace in death."[49] Clarissa doesn't kill herself—though in the introduction to a later edition of the novel Woolf wrote that she had originally intended to have her do so after the party.[50] Instead, Woolf found a counter to death for Clarissa in the party itself, in the communicative sociability, the connectedness, which is for her the deeper reality of its superficial frivolity. But the truth that makes death tempting to her in the first place, the realization that because of the absence of a common center one is ultimately alone, is the result of the collapse of that center in the war. If the center "mystically" evades people, it is because its previous incarnation, the myth of "England," no longer exists. Since it was *the* center, its collapse makes it impossible to believe in any center, any common identity which could unite people in the "imagined community" of those who are not in physical proximity. The party, the ephemeral but physically real coming together of isolated selves, is for Clarissa the substitute for national identity.

*   *   *

For Hermann Broch too, the center had ceased to exist by the 1920s, though he had a different conception of it. In the longer temporal perspective of *The Sleepwalkers* the center had been crumbling since the Middle Ages. But the war gave it the coup de grace, indeed made the long trajectory of destruction fully visible for the first time. He laid the process out in a ten-part essay titled "The Disintegration of Values," whose sections were interspersed throughout the third volume of the novel, *1918: Huguenau, or Realism*. It provides the retrospective key to the novel's characters as much as to Broch's thought.

The essay, however, does not begin directly with Broch's philosophy of history but with a raw cry of pain, an enraged funeral lament:

> Is this distorted life of ours still real? is this cancerous reality still alive? the melodramatic gesture of our mass movement toward death ends in a shrug of the shoulders,—men die and do not know why; without a hold on reality they fall into nothingness; yet they are surrounded and slain by a reality that is their own, since they comprehend its causality.

The cause of humanity's "distorted life," the cause of the war, is the triumph of irrational "life" completely divorced from and no longer constrained by reason:

> this age seems to have a capacity for surpassing even the acme of illogicality, of anti-logicality: it is as if the monstrous reality of the war had blotted out the reality of the world. Fantasy has become logical reality, but reality evolves the most a-logical phantasmagoria. An age that is softer and more cowardly than any preceding age suffocates in waves of blood and poison gas; nations of bank clerks and profiteers hurl themselves upon barbed wire; a well-organized humanitarianism avails to hinder nothing, but calls itself the Red Cross and prepares artificial limbs for the victims.[51]

The passage continues the litany of contradictions in which every aspect of prewar European civilization has been turned upside down by the war, the good turned into bad, the bad transformed into virtues, though only to better serve the purposes of destruction.

The depiction of prewar European civilization here is quite different from what it is in the long process of disintegration that Broch went on to describe in the later installments of the essay. In the ensuing analysis the prewar world is already in an advanced stage of spiritual and moral decay. But in the opening the prewar world is depicted as benign, integrated, and progressive, its culture at so high a level that it makes the transformation into the opposite in the war all the more inexplicable:

> This age harboured somewhere a disinterested striving for truth, a disinterested will toward art, and had after all a very definite social feeling; how could the men who created these values and shared in them "comprehend" the ideology of war, unresistingly accept and approve it? How could a man take a gun in his hand, how could he march into

the trenches, either to die in them or to come out again and take up his work as usual, without going insane? How is such adaptability possible?[52]

The purpose of the rest of the treatise is to answer these questions by putting recent history into longer and more philosophical perspective. Broch described a European medieval civilization governed by an image of infinity that fused the material and spiritual realms in the figure of the Trinity and permeated every sphere of life, unifying them all in purpose and in an aura of sensuous spirituality. Over the centuries, however, the idea of the infinite became ever more abstract and remote, until by the end of the nineteenth century it was nothing but a mathematical expression and social life nothing but the reign of soulless specialization, each activity and sphere of life isolated from the others with its separate goal and rationale. The contradiction between this analysis of gradual disintegration over centuries and the sudden, total catastrophe described in the essay's opening passage resulted from the fact that the parts of the essay come from different periods in Broch's life, and clearly show the war as dramatic turning point in his view of the world.

A businessman by family origin and occupation, Broch had long been interested in literature but had begun to write cultural criticism only in his late twenties, five years before the outbreak of the war. His first essays exemplified the widespread sense of cultural pessimism intensifying in those last pre-war years and shared its common diagnosis. The arts, he claimed, literature and painting in particular, were atrophying from an overly rationalist, scientific penchant for mere realistic description. Art had lost touch with its true vocation, beauty, because it had abandoned its roots in "life," in the instinctual. "Art was the sexuality of culture," he wrote provocatively. "Now it is dying from psychic impotence."[53] The aesthetic sensibility is the heightened will to life, and is thus directly connected to sex. That is why dance is the most basic art form; it is the most original and primitive artistic expression of the erotic. In another conventional trope of the contemporary ethical-aesthetic reaction against commercial civilization Broch even made the claim, hugely ironic in the light of what would come later, that the most intense form of the dance was battle.[54]

It was only in his essays of 1917–1919 that Broch turned from a narrower concern with the decline of high culture to the problem of the destruction of the values that underlay Western civilization as a whole. The dramatic opening words of the first section of "The Disintegration of Values" in *The Sleepwalkers* are in fact taken from an unpublished essay of 1917 called "The Ethical Reality of Our Time," the first of four collected under the general title "Towards an

Understanding of Our Era." All four essays are concerned with what the second calls "The Construction of Historical Reality," and they trace the historical rise of positivism, the scientific veneration of facts that characterizes modernity. They are highly academic exercises in the history of the philosophy of history, however, without the immediacy, fervor, or existential despair of the treatise in *The Sleepwalkers*. They were begun before the war and were meant to put Broch's prewar analysis of the decay of art into broader context.[55] But they were carried over more or less intact into the novel, by which time the solution they had implied seemed to Broch himself grotesque.

The freeing of instinctual vitality that before the war was his hope for cultural regeneration now represented pure nihilism, the destruction of values and the possibility of form, which in personal life meant identity. It is through one of his minor characters in the third novel that Broch makes the connection between war and the loss of identity explicit. Gödicke, a bricklayer in the Territorial Guard, had been buried under the rubble of a trench destroyed during a bombardment. Barely alive when unearthed, he survives against all expectations but remains terribly injured and in such pain that he lies on rubber air cushions to make it bearable. Worse, however, than the injury to his body is the damage to his "soul." The simplest action like lifting a spoon to his mouth is made difficult by the fact that he is not clear in his mind who it is that is being fed. The problem is not that he doesn't remember his past; on the contrary, he remembers quite clearly all the previous phases of his life, all the different selves he has been:

> The difficulties with which the man Gödicke had to contend, then, were certainly not caused by the fact that he felt this whole series of persons living within him, but rather sprang from the sudden interruption of the series at a certain point, from the fact that there was no connection between the earlier biography and himself, though he himself should obviously have been the last link in the chain, and that being cast adrift in this way from something which he could hardly any longer describe as his life, he had lost his own identity [*Existenz*].[56]

The English translator was quite correct to translate Broch's *Existenz* as "identity"; it is the continuity of his person, not of his physical existence or his memory, that Gödicke can no longer experience. In part it is of course his physical disability that makes it impossible for him to be the man he was, the man who slept and still wants to sleep with the carpenter's bride; he is so helplessly angry at the body which has betrayed him that he can manage only by splitting himself psychically and trying to starve the self he can no longer be. But his near death has also detached him reflectively from who he was, made him aware of all the different, irreconcilable selves he can be, and of the impossibility of subsuming them all into one unified personality who could be named "Gödicke." The war is that "sudden interruption" which has cut him off from his previous biography, not just by the physical changes in him but through them by his traumatic awakening into consciousness of the true, identity-less nature of the self.

The same awakening infects even the central figure of the novel, the "realist" Huguenau, who conned and exploited his way through the war without patriotic scruple. Once the wartime anarchy that made it possible for him to operate with impunity has passed, he returns to conventional respectable bourgeois life as a prosperous businessman and active citizen. He is no longer simply the amoral opportunist but a believer in the profit system, a capitalist by conviction and representative figure of the present age. Yet he finds himself at times unaccountably questioning the value and meaning of money. His incipient self-awareness begins to separate him from his less aware fellow citizens who live their lives with unquestioning immediacy. Every social gathering begins to disintegrate for him into a mere collection of isolated beings with no center, no meaning. Though Huguenau is not given to reflection, his feelings of separateness in a group supposedly united by a common identity point to an unavoidable conclusion. Had he in fact thought further, said Broch,

> he would certainly have discovered that the unity of any event and the integrity of the world are guaranteed merely by enigmatic, although visible, symbols, which are necessary because without them the visible world would fall asunder into unnameable, bodiless, dry layers of cold and transparent ash—and so Huguenau would have perceived the curse of the casual, the fortuitous, that spreads itself over things and their relations to each other, making it impossible to think of any arrangement that would not be equally arbitrary and fortuitous.[57]

The symbol of modernity is money, the supposedly objective value that unites society. To recognize it as a symbol, which Huguenau incipiently does, is to recognize that it is not objectively real but man-made. The curse of the "arbitrary and fortuitous" that hovers over the unity of society also hovers over the supposed unity of the self; Huguenau feels so alone in the company of his peers because he does not ultimately share the value that gives them purpose. The war, which had destroyed all values, had destroyed even the possibility of believing in the value of self-interest. Identity has dissipated, if not quite into nothing, then into the insubstantiality of bodiless layers of transparent ash—dead particles so small they do not hang together and so slight one can see through them.

* * *

Huguenau's postwar fate exemplifies how the war lived on in the European psyche through its aftereffects even where life seemed to have resumed its normal course. The war's destructive effects were even clearer in the literature dealing with those identities which couldn't return to their prewar normal, the patriot and the cultivated man in defeated Germany, those and others shaped by the Austro-Hungarian Empire in a now-shrunken Austria. In *Steppenwolf*, Hermann Hesse responded to the emergence of virulently revanchist chauvinism among the German educated elite with a bitter attack on nationalism and *Bildung*. In *Man Without Qualities* Musil anatomized the pseudoreality of the empire and its honorific identities, exposed as such when it did not survive its military defeat.

Harry Haller's breaking point comes at a dinner at the home of a young professor of Eastern mythology whom he had met in previous visits to the town. As Hesse describes him, the professor is a paragon of *Bildung*: "He believes in the studies whose servant he is; he believes in the value of mere knowledge and its acquisition, because he believes in progress and evolution."[58] But he is also a nationalist and jingoist; he hates Jews and Communists, and rails against traitors who like the one he has unwittingly invited to dinner have openly mocked the Kaiser and blamed Germany equally for the outbreak of the war. Appropriately, however, Haller finally snaps not over a disagreement about politics, which he realizes they can't discuss without unpleasantness, but on noticing a portrait of Goethe, the Christ-figure of *Bildung*, in his host's drawing room. The portrait, he says contemptuously, is that of a conceited sentimentalist who radiates a false sense of superiority. Though he himself had criticized Goethe's "venerable pomposity," he finds this portrayal too extreme in sentimentalizing what Goethe truly represented—knowledge of the dark side as well as the sunny ideal. The offended professor angrily protests. Unable to restrain his anger at the professor's morally repulsive use of culture to justify bigotry and violence, Haller bursts out that he himself is in fact the "traitor" whom the professor had earlier condemned, and that it would be better for their country and the world if people who were capable of thought stood for reason and the love of peace instead of heading with a blind obsession toward another war. With that, he rushes from that house, aware that his outburst is a "leave-taking from the respectable, moral and learned world," a complete break with his past identity as a bourgeois. Now all wolf, having abandoned that part of himself that connected him to the only social world he knew, he is prepared to kill himself. It is at that moment that he meets Hermine, the mysterious young woman who will show him how to live the truth of existence he had previously just read about in the "Treatise on the Steppenwolf," and thus assist at his rebirth not just as a new self but a new kind of self—a self without fixed identity.

Hesse himself had actually taken a somewhat equivocal position during the war. Living in Switzerland when it broke out, he had volunteered for army service with the German embassy, and didn't serve only because he failed his physical exam. He went on to aid the war effort by setting up a mail-order library service for German war prisoners in France. But unlike most of his German literary colleagues, he was not a war enthusiast. In private correspondence he had declared himself a nationalist, and expressed the common sentiment of the educated bourgeoisie that the very survival of culture demanded a German victory. His first published piece, however, which became notorious in Germany, a feuilleton titled "O Friends, Not These Tones" after Schiller's "Ode to Joy," rebuked writers on both sides for the stridency of their partisanship, and invoked a human European culture constituted by the work of Shakespeare, French poetry, and German music. As he put it in a letter, which declared in the contemporary idiom of the German intelligentsia that the war had an ethical value, "nationalism has always also signified a certain education for the ideal of humanity."[59] It was this taken-for-granted equation of German cultural ideal with universal humanity that led to puzzlement, then bitterness, when his wartime pieces were greeted with rage in the German press; he had assumed that the German intelligentsia shared his understanding of the cosmopolitan nature of *Kultur*. As he came to realize that this was not the case, he turned not only against the war but against the equation of culture with nationality, a turn that helped precipitate a severe emotional and intellectual crisis of identity. By the end of the war it had led to the revolution in his writing first announced in the autobiographical coming-of-age novel *Demian* and epitomized by *Steppenwolf*.

Neither war nor postwar make their appearance in Musil's *Man Without Qualities*, which is set the year before the war's outbreak, yet it is a novel of 1914, or more exactly 1918, when the Austro-Hungarian Empire dissolved into successor states. As Stefan Jonsson points out, it was only when the material and institutional support of the imperial apparatus had vanished that the values and traditions that had anchored the Austrian subject's idea of himself in the imperial order were revealed in all their contingency.[60]

In his essay "Political Confession of a Young Man. A Fragment," published in 1913, Musil admitted that he had been little interested in politics till then.[61]

Even in the flurry of essays he published around that time, only the brief "Politics in Austria" addressed the failings of the political entity that were to be at the heart of his later exploration of the illusion of personal identity. That compact essay certainly anticipates the causal connection between nation and identity in *Man Without Qualities*, but before the war there is still a note of hope. Somewhere in this state there must be hidden a mystery, an idea, he wrote. But it is impossible to ascertain what it is. It is not the idea of the state, not the dynastic idea, not that of a cultural symbiosis of different peoples— though, he added, Austria could have been a world experiment in that regard. The whole thing appears to be just aimless movement because of the lack of a driving idea, like a spinning bicycle wheel that doesn't move forward. "Such deplorable political conditions always have their grounds in deplorable cultural conditions. Politics in Austria have no human [i.e., universal] goal, just an Austrian one. One can't become a self [*Ich*] through them."[62] Self as essential identity was at this point something both real and positive for Musil. The self aspires to be universal and depends for identity on being animated by a universal idea through identification with it. Austrian politics, however, was all passion *without* ideas: the conflicts between nationalities and classes within the empire had neither moral nor other grandeur, only particularist aims and ambitions. But, as the parenthesis suggests, Musil believed before the war that Austria could have been a universal idea because of its multicultural identity. It was only the collapse of the Austrian empire that enabled him to see that the "identityless self" of prewar Austria was not merely a remediable political defect but the human condition as such.

Musil demonstrated this with an ingenious reversal. In the novel the absence of an Austrian "idea" becomes the symbol of an ultimate human emptiness that cannot be filled. Musil brought that absence to satirically hilarious life in the novel's antiplot, the fruitless effort to find a central theme for a mooted seventieth jubilee year of Emperor Franz Josef in 1918. The jubilee project is the novel's central "action," and its very name proclaims its nullity. It is called the Parallel Campaign [*Aktion*] because even the idea of a jubilee celebration is not a spontaneous Austrian initiative but is generated in imitation of and rivalry with the thirtieth jubilee of the German Kaiser Wilhelm planned for the same year. From the beginning the Parallel Campaign is an empty phrase in search of content. Ulrich, who has taken a sabbatical from life, becomes, at his father's anxious instigation, the secretary of the campaign's planning committee through his family connection as cousin of its organizer, the Viennese cultural doyenne he ironically names "Diotima." It is from his mocking perspective that we see the campaign's absurdities.

For a year and more than a thousand pages, the committee cannot arrive at a central theme for the celebration. There are various proposals, each reflecting the particular political or cultural perspective of its promoter, each representing the essence of the most prestigious prewar Austrian, indeed Central European, identities, and each mercilessly exposed as contradictory, ridiculous, or vaporously insubstantial. The hollowness of these imperial identities taken together explains in retrospect why the empire could not survive, but it more significantly speaks to the bankruptcy of those identities in the postwar period. They were mere pseudoreality then, and with the end of the political structure that sustained them, they are no longer viable even as illusions.

The driving political force behind the campaign is Count Leinsdorf, embodiment of the Old Austrian aristocracy. He has come up with four slogans for the jubilee: "Emperor of Peace, European Milestone, True Austria, Property and Culture," but they signify nothing. In part this is because he himself, a tissue of contradictions, stands for nothing. He hates the modern age because it is a "whirlpool of materialist democracy," and wishes to return to the past era of faith, hierarchical authority, and noblesse oblige, but he runs his estates like an opportunistic capitalist who "could not imagine how industry . . . or a stock-exchange deal in wheat or sugar could be conducted on religious principles; nor was there any conceivable way to run a modern large-scale landed estate rationally without the stock exchange and industry."[63] Because he knows, however, that establishing the connection between the eternal verities and business that the campaign requires is more complicated than evoking the "lovely simplicity" of tradition, and because he believes that such a connection can only be found today "in the profundities of middle class culture," he has entrusted the campaign to the middle-class socialite and culture worshipper "Diotima."

If Musil treated Diotima with more ambivalence than he did Leinsdorf, it is because within her absurdities there lurks an idealism he once shared, the aim of reconciling the world's contradictions through culture; Ulrich can allow himself to be attracted to her physical beauty with a degree of authenticity. But Musil also exposes Diotima's idea of culture as vapid, clichéd, and egocentric. Culture is concerned not with the body and material things but with the "soul," which in her case, Musil writes, "was probably nothing more than a small amount of capital in love she possessed at the time of her marriage," that is, her sexual desire and sexual attractiveness. Unfortunately, her husband, the indomitably prosaic middle-class bureaucrat Tuzzi, "was not the right business opportunity to invest" her passion in.[64] In quest of a more adequate object, she has turned to literature, the repository of the Good, the

True, and the Beautiful—which turn out to be nothing but expressions of her own reductive understanding of spirit as "a force analogous to the power of love."[65] If this definition is narcissistic, sentimental, and self-deluded, it at least explains why Diotima believes woman is the carrier of culture, a common prewar trope among artists themselves.[66] Since men in the modern world developed only their rational intellects, "only the unfragmented woman still possessed the fated power to embrace the intellect with those vital forces that, in her opinion, it obviously sorely needed for its salvation."[67] It is only natural then that a woman be the appointed organizer of the committee to plan the Parallel Campaign.

Except that, having no real ideas of her own, she turns to someone else to provide a theme for the Year of Austria. Her choice of the Prussian industrialist Paul Arnheim is not only the most ironic of Musil's novelistic moves; Arnheim is the most important of Musil's targets. If the aristocrat Leinsdorf is the man of the past, and the pretentious Diotima the avatar of a cultural ideal she discredits by representing it, Arnheim is the man of the present and the hope of the future. An intellectual businessman who has made fortunes and published philosophical works, he embodies the unity of "capital and culture," industrial modernity with spirit, *Geist*. Some of Ulrich's spleen toward him is obvious jealousy of a man capable of acting successfully in the modern world, but Arnheim is nonetheless unmistakably a charlatan, the more despicable for espousing an ideal that, superficially attractive, is self-contradictory. The supposed union between "the soul and the price of coal" represented by Arnheim's intellectual and commercial ventures is a "con game" that serves to keep separate "what Arnheim did with his eyes wide open and what he said and wrote in his cloud of intuition."[68] The con's broader social purpose is to cloak the takeover of political and social power by money with the veneer of traditional values that had once legitimized the aristocracy's preeminence. In truth, the "soulful" German middle classes "look down upon art and literature, which they once regarded as the ultimate fulfillment, as upon an earlier stage of development."[69] Arnheim himself, more sophisticated and far-seeing, recognizes that the power of business has to be elevated by the ideology of soul to pacify the contemporary social rebellion against money, science, and calculation. But "keeping the world in order was perhaps his truest and fiercest passion, a craving for power far surpassing everything even a man in his position could afford."[70]

The aristocrat, the female doyenne of passion and art, the cultivated capitalist—all these preeminent identities of the prewar world had completely lost any semblance of persuasiveness after it, victims of the social and political reality that had been preparing a cataclysm before their unseeing eyes. The perfervid nationalism that succeeded them had never had credit with Musil, who before the war had been a believer, however disappointed, in the cosmopolitan "Austrian idea." The outpouring of rabid patriotism when the war broke out both shocked him and educated him to humanity's ineradicable need for chauvinist passion. In a trenchant postwar essay, "The Nation as Ideal and Reality," Musil insisted that the modern nation could not be a genuine expression of the ethical universal and hence not a valid foundation for identity; modern nationalism was either a cover for racism, the contemporary form of the traditional authoritarian state, or the deceptive idealization of purely material interests.[71] But none of the other supposedly universalist ideologies of the age could make good their claim to totality either. "Our time," says Ulrich, gently needling General Stumm von Bordwehr, the comically unimaginative representative of the military mind, who is hopelessly infatuated with Diotima and her quest for the great Austrian idea,

> rejoices in a number of great ideas, and by a special kindness of fate each idea is paired with its opposite, so that individualism and collectivism, nationalism and internationalism, socialism and capitalism, imperialism and pacifism, rationalism and superstition, are all equally at home in them, together with the unused remnants of countless opposites of an equal or lesser contemporary value.

With amused irony, Musil gives the last word on this self-cancelling set of totalizing opposites to General Bordwehr's simple minded but insightful practicality: "When you spend a lot of time with ideas you end up itching all over, and you can scratch till you bleed, without getting any relief."[72]

The problem goes beyond the deficiency of any particular modern ideology; it is inherent in the very quest for value. Values, not in the sense of how we should treat others but what we should live for, are a matter of feeling, of enthusiasm, the "state of mind in which all . . . feelings and thoughts have the same spirit." But, Ulrich continues, "there is nothing to sustain such an enthusiasm" because the desired galvanizing goal is a matter of feeling, not of objective knowledge. Man "believes in ideas not because they are sometimes true but because he needs to believe." The forms of rationality that can solve scientific and mathematical questions are therefore of no help. For "although, all in all, the number of choices based on feeling is infinitely greater than those based on clear logic, and every event that moves mankind arises from the imagination, only the purely rational problems have achieved an objective order, while nothing deserving the name of a joint effort, or even hinting at any insight into the desperate need for it, has been done for the world of feeling and imagination."[73] With this acknowledgment of the irrelevance of objectivity and the primacy of imagination, any possibility for what had up to then been understood as identity is gone.

Reinventing Identity

> For him, morality was neither conformism nor philosophic
> wisdom, but living the infinite fullness of possibilities.
> —Robert Musil, *The Man Without Qualities*[74]

The demolition of "old" identity was only a first step for some of these authors, a necessary ground-clearing for proposed alternatives. The three clear exceptions are Pirandello, Broch, and Kafka, whose works end in apparent nihilism, though in life the first two took political paths out of the chaos they depicted in their literary work: Fascism in the case of Pirandello, anti-Fascism in the case of Broch.[75] Arguably the alternatives to fixed self-definition are in fact the real "point" of *Steppenwolf, Time Regained, Mrs. Dalloway*, and *The Man Without Qualities*, and it would require more extensive discussion of these alternatives than is possible here for anything approaching a full understanding of the novels. Nonetheless noting their revisionary projects can amplify our sense of what the authors were rejecting through the contrast with what they believed to be "other than identity."

I have already touched on the alternative Woolf was suggesting with Clarissa Dalloway's party. Woolf's genius with her character was to make a plausible metaphysician out of an apparently superficial socialite. Clarissa's ruminations on death and immortality are no less profound for being unsophisticatedly expressed: "she must inevitably cease completely . . . but . . . somehow in the streets of London, on the ebb and flow of things, here, there, she survived. . . . part . . . of the trees at home; of the house there . . . part of people she had never met."[76] The timing of these ruminations on timelessness is precise: they are followed immediately by her reflection on the sad horror of the recent war. Clarissa's concern is not with life after death but how to live in the present in the face of the transience of the individual and the desuetude of collective ideals that the war has brought home to her, in the face of the "supreme mystery" of the insuperable separateness of people. Wholeness of being can no longer be found within individual identity anchored in abstract collectives like the nation. In response to, as compensation for, this loss, Clarissa has the quasi-pantheist intimation that she is not a limited something in time and space but "everywhere; not 'here, here, here,'" on the bus where she was sitting as the thought came to her, but part of everyone and everything she noticed from it. "She was all that. So that to know her, or anyone, one must seek out the people who completed them."[77] Creating the wholeness that completes her is the deep purpose of her parties. They are, as Clarissa tries stumblingly to articulate for herself, "life," attempts "to combine, to create" by bringing together otherwise separate existences in a simulacrum of totality.[78] For Woolf the project was explicitly, challengingly linked to Clarissa's "frivolous" femininity. In a diary entry in 1916, Woolf angrily referred to "this preposterous masculine fiction"[79] of war projected through the grandiloquent idioms of the press. The virtues the war discredited were masculine: the soldier's courage, stoicism, and sense of duty to king and country were but mandates to kill feeling as well as bodies in the name of purportedly universal ideals. But idealism itself was masculine; it was fealty to abstractions, the self-proclaimed sphere of men, instead of to the pulsing reality found only in life's particulars. (Doris Kilman, who hides her *ressentiment* in religious fanaticism, shows that women can be men, too.) Woolf constructed a feminine counter-image to the patriotic fictions that elevated war. Though Clarissa knows skepticism and existential despair, she, unlike Septimus, will not sacrifice immediate feelings of connectedness to abstract concepts. Her anti-intellectualism is not know-nothingism; it is a refusal of false solutions. Parties, in their evanescence, may implicitly proclaim the ultimate unattainability of permanent collective identity but their messy, lively heterogeneity, their sheer "thereness," concretely images our sought-for feeling of completeness. Peter Walsh, who has never stopped loving Clarissa despite his disdain for her frivolity, senses why without being able to relate his insight to her parties: she had "that extraordinary gift, that woman's gift, of making a world of her own wherever she happened to be."[80]

A similar belief in woman's gift animates the final lesson Hesse must impart to the Steppenwolf to complete his reeducation, though it has a quite different outcome. Pablo's lecture to Harry on the infinite number of configurations into which life's fragments can be arranged is not sufficient to transform him, despite its striking visual aids. Its existential meaning must be driven home by brutal enactment, just because the seductive power of the eternal feminine is stronger than theory. Harry's guide throughout his sentimental education has been the mysterious Hermione, the young woman who has opened him up to worlds of sensuality and experience he never knew or had shunned. Yet she herself has remained teasingly aloof, seeming only to intimate that she will give herself to him as the climax of, the reward for, his reeducation. Enlightened about the many possibilities of his life as he has become, able not just to think them but live them, he is nonetheless completely invested in the woman who has midwifed his rebirth. "I belonged to her not just as this one piece in my game of chess," he reflects as he goes to meet her at the end of his adventure in the Magic Theater, "I belonged to her wholly."[81] When he finds her sexually sated in the arms of Pablo, he is overwhelmed by jealous rage and stabs her to death.

This event too, however, is part of the Magic Theater. Hermione is the lesson he has not yet learned. Belonging to anyone or anything wholly is precisely what Hermione, Pablo, and the Magic Theater mean to *unteach*. No one thing, person, or even artistic creation can be the infinite, so that one could become whole oneself by belonging to it, losing oneself in it. While aspiring to the infinite is indeed the essence of human desire, one must learn at the same time not to take anything within the world seriously as its adequation. What he must learn with regard to Hermione is what he must also learn about music, which for him is the purest expression of sublimity, a cliché of *Bildung* in the Wagnerian era, though Haller's musical god is the classical Mozart. He learns it by shedding his initial horror at hearing the divine music of Mozart strangulated by the tinny reproductions of radio. Primitive radio's extreme distortions only make exaggeratedly manifest a general truth. The perfection of the greatest music is an unreachable ideal; *all* reproductions of it are at most aspirations toward it, never its attainment. "When you listen to the radio you are a witness of the everlasting war between idea and appearance, between time and eternity, between the human and divine," Pablo tells him at his "trial" for killing Hermione (who, this being a Magic Theater, is of course not really dead—or alive either): "exactly as [the radio] strips this music of its sensuous beauty, spoils and scratches . . . it and yet cannot altogether destroy its spirit, just so does life, so-called reality, deal with the sublime picture-play of the world."[82] Nothing in the world can live up to the Idea. One's only recourse is to laugh—at oneself for making the inevitable mistake, at the mistake itself. This is Romantic irony a hundred years later though much chastened, lacking the buoyant optimism of the original Romantic celebration of creative destruction.[83] For Hesse, humor is necessarily gallows humor, laughter in the face of the death of transcendental hope. There will always be Mozart, and he will never be played perfectly. For that matter, Haller has learned that Mozart's music itself is not "perfect"; it too only aspires to a totality it can never reach. Pablo the modern jazz saxophonist is as "good" as Mozart; in fact he *is* Mozart, in the metamorphic play of the Magic Theater. When Mozart offers to resurrect Hermione so that Harry might marry her, Harry, in his newfound wisdom, refuses, knowing that a marriage burdened with the expectation of wholeness is doomed to unhappiness. He will try instead to live the sentence Mozart ultimately pronounces on him: "You are to learn to listen to the cursed radio music of life and to reverence the spirit behind it and to laugh at its distortions."[84] Whether this is a viable prescription for life, or is possible only in art, is a question Hesse left open; the novel ends in the Magic Theater.

Though, perhaps tellingly, Musil never finished his novel—there are more unpublished than published pages—he did canvass a solution for the man without qualities *within* life, in the very sphere that served as Hesse's ultimate object lesson in self-deception, love. While the second volume of *The Man Without Qualities* reprises all the themes of the first, and ends in the doom of the Parallel Campaign, its center is an entirely new plot, the relationship between Ulrich and his sister Agathe, who doesn't even appear in the first volume. Volume two is meant as the positive to volume one's negative, but though it may surely be characterized as depicting a love relationship, its nature defies easy characterization—not least Musil's own. His struggle is apparent in every encounter between brother and sister; their scenes are generally more talky and less precise, more portentous and allusive than the interactions between other characters. The term "mystical" sometimes used to describe their love is, however, a cop-out, even if Ulrich sometimes uses it himself. The attraction between Ulrich and Agathe is clearly strongly erotic, though it is never consummated. Sexual union would destroy the relationship by reducing it to a delimited act in space and time, erasing the permanent tense force field between two opposite poles that never touch. Consummation would also destroy it by reducing its nonmateriality to physical gratification or worse, self-centered possession. Musil's incestuous pair is a late version of the Romantic trope of incest, which figured the brother-sister relationship as the ideal love because the lovers were both the same and opposite, able by coming together to create wholeness.[85] As Ulrich puts it, "It's the ancient longing for a doppelgänger of the opposite sex, for a lover who will be the same as yourself yet someone else, a magical figure that is oneself and remains magical, with the advantage over something we merely imagine of having the breath of autonomy and independence."[86] Nonconsummation plays the same role for Ulrich's imagination of the infinite as it does for Hesse's; it protects desire from disappointment and disillusion. But what is unique to Ulrich's understanding of the permanent force field between himself and Agathe is not the negativity that keeps desire alive by permanent frustration. It is the positive ability of distance to keep in play what Ulrich understands as true morality. Morality is not merely "a sort of police regulations for keeping life in order"; it is the faculty of "imagination," which makes possible "living the infinite fullness of possibilities."[87] Fixating on the inherently transient "will of the time, or . . . spirit of the era" by identifying with one's nation or culture was "a moral weakness," for it meant developing one's potential one-sidedly, "never taking the measure of one's own will, never achieving a complete form, and in disjointed passions doing now this, now that."[88] Incestuous desire is an obstacle to the stultifying conformism of fixed identity because, Ulrich points out, psychologists couple it with antisocial disposition and a rebellious attitude toward life, possibly even "a not sufficiently rooted gender identification."[89] But breaking down categories maintained by rules and taboos is precisely what allows infinite openness to possibility as such. The force field of incestuous love creates infinite possibility by rejecting the closure of fixed sex roles as well as by avoiding the closure of consummation.

For Proust, however, avoiding sexual consummation would only put off the inevitable. Totality could not be arrived at by forever staving off one of its most compelling temptations and thus keeping alive what he knew to be its false promise. On the contrary, love had to be experienced in order to learn that it was only a stage on the way to solving the problem of identity, not its solution. Proust's project of recuperating time through art surrenders unique personal identity in return for capturing the eternal substance of human selfhood. The epiphany by which Marcel arrives at the solution comes in a progressive series of realizations. They begin with the famous aperçu that "the true paradises are the paradises we have lost."[90] For while "paradisal experiences" have something extratemporal about them, experience, because necessarily in time, is always corrupted by it—by the imperfection of the beloved or the limitations of the lover that are inevitably revealed in time's passing. The memory of those experiences, in virtue of being the present memory of a past event, can recreate in us the sense of a "minute freed from the order of time."[91] But contrary to a common misunderstanding of Proust's "memory recaptured," it is not simply the recollection of those moments of eternity through involuntary memory that recreates paradise. What one must understood about such memories in order to benefit from them beyond the moment of recollection is what makes them return involuntarily with such overwhelming force. What Marcel suddenly realizes is that involuntarily returning memories are involuntary because they contain eternal truths which, though embedded in transitory sensory experiences, can be extracted from them. Such memories are nothing less than signs of laws of human nature.[92] Their uncontrolled recurrence, independent of the will to remember, is the evidence of their authenticity as "renewable, durable . . . mouthpieces of a psychological law."[93] Such laws can be deduced by "comparing a quality common to two sensations . . . extracting their common essence and . . . reuniting them to each other, liberated from the contingencies of time."[94] It is not the love for this or the other person, each of whom is imperfect and impermanent, but *loving* that is the permanent structure of selfhood: "if our love is not only the love of a Gilberte (and this fact is what we find so painful), the reason is not that it is also love of an Albertine but that it is a portion of our mind more durable than the selves which successively die within us."[95] It is both the power and the task of art to "exactly reconstitute life, around the truths to which we have attained inside ourselves."[96] If the individual person does not have a permanent identity in loving, humanity does. But it is only through the experiences of the unique person that it can be discovered. That is why only art (rather than, for example, philosophy) can accomplish the task. The beloved dies, the lover no longer loves, but a beloved must have lived, and a lover have loved completely, for loving to be revealed as definitional of the human.

*　*　*

Whether any of the alternatives to fixed personal identity that these writers proposed are viable as ways of life is literarily, if not existentially, unimportant. What is common to the interwar solutions is that they were proposed in works of the imagination as self-conscious fictions, as thought-experiments. They demand of their protagonists a state of mind able to tolerate and live with metaphysical contradiction, so that they constantly strive for a wholeness they are aware they can never attain, remaining fully involved while observing their own passion with ironic detachment. Pirandello, the most radically consistent of them, called into question the possibility of sustaining such a state of mind even in a fiction—neither "Henry IV" nor the Six Characters are able to—but it isn't clear what their fictions committed other authors to believing about identity outside of art. Proust seems to have genuinely believed that the artist, at least, could demonstrate through his fictions that there is such a thing as a basic human, if not individual, identity; the "solution" of Hesse's Magic Theater, on the other hand, remained forever in the realm of the unreal and he went on to other explorations.

What is clear is that all these authors, usually implicitly but sometimes explicitly, challenged all the hidden beliefs inherent in what it meant to contemporaries to have an identity. What they depicted in novel and drama, Martin Heidegger in the same decade and Jean-Paul Sartre a decade later analyzed and systematized theoretically, articulating the hidden beliefs implicit in identity and putting them to explicit philosophical examination. It is against the background of the fictions discussed here that the full import of Heidegger's and Sartre's work for the dismantling of the possibility of identity becomes clear.

Chapter 2

The Ontological Critique of Identity:
Heidegger and Sartre

It all depends on what the meaning of the word "is" is.
—U.S. president William J. Clinton

Some of the writers discussed in the last chapter were well-read in European philosophy; all were philosophically attuned, and their fictions were at times as much dramatizations of ideas as of characters (for which they were occasionally criticized). Their rejection of fixed identity was an implicit critique of the ontology that underlay the idea, its assumptions about the basic nature of self, consciousness, and time. It remained for philosophers to articulate and probe those assumptions in the contemporary idioms of their discipline. This was precisely the task that Martin Heidegger and Jean-Paul Sartre set themselves. Both worked with the same methodological approach, Edmund Husserl's descriptive phenomenology, and both went beyond it with the same intent, using phenomenological insights to undermine the ontological premises on which fixed identity rested. Both also attacked the philosophical errors of identity by analyzing its historically specific form in post-World War I European bourgeois society. But they came at identity from different ideological perspectives and with opposed agendas; not surprisingly, they ended with radically different conclusions.

Martin Heidegger: Inauthentic and Authentic Identity

Martin Heidegger's *Being and Time*, published in 1927, was the first and remains in many ways the most powerful philosophical critique of fixed, substantive identity. His book presented itself with daunting abstractness as an inquiry into "the meaning of Being,"[1] a work of "fundamental ontology."

Such an inquiry, Heidegger argued, was necessary to establish the foundations for any empirical investigation in science, particularly in the human sciences; we must have a correct idea of the nature of the entities we study before we can ask appropriate research questions about them. Ostensibly, then, he was not concerned with a "merely" empirical psychological idea of identity, as the interwar creative writers clearly were. But for Heidegger the meaning of "Being" could only be arrived at by investigating the nature of the human beings who posed the question, since meaning exists only for human consciousness. Nor could there be any distinction for him between analyzing the fundamental, or timeless, categories of human existence and placing humans in their concrete social and historical context, because "sociality" and "historicality" were two of those basic categories. The general categories of human existence ("existentialia") always appeared in people's lives clothed in the particular forms of their time and place.

Heidegger presented his ontological venture as a much-needed intervention in the history of Western metaphysics, which had become "forgetful of Being." But its social and historical context, which crucially determined the way he posed and resolved the question, were the same circumstances that had disrupted and revolutionized the creative writers' previous understanding of personal identity—the Great War and its consequences. Heidegger's historical problem was above all with the consequences of the war for the contemporary German's sense of himself as person and as German. The creative writers had responded to the discrediting of received identities by subjecting the possibility of fixed identity to destructive criticism, but with few exceptions—Pirandello's dramatic nihilism being the most notable—they had also attempted literary prescriptions for life without it. Pirandello, having found none, made an ungrounded leap to Fascism. As an already committed conservative German nationalist, however, Heidegger faced a different problem. He wanted to rescue a philosophically viable version of identity out of what he regarded as the disastrous wrongheadedness of current conceptions. Consequently he set himself the philosophical task of destroying what he condemned as the reigning "inauthentic" understanding of individual identity in order to construct a valid notion of collective identity, one that would also make true individuality possible for the first time.[2] His critical argument, however, as I will contend, overshot the mark. His demolition of personal identity was powerful enough to bring down his concept of collective identity as well. If Heidegger failed to see this it was because, despite his own warning, he largely identified what was problematic about identity with one particular historical version of it while believing he had overcome the problem in his own version. Aporias like this would repeat themselves again and again in the subsequent history of identity. What would soon come to look like a theoretical compulsion to repeat the same impasse suggests the conundrum that identity presented even to many of its most astute critics: identity was simultaneously philosophically impossible yet humanly necessary. Heidegger was the first, and most dramatic, casualty of the dilemma.

Identity as Inauthentic Self

"We are ourselves the entities to be analyzed," Heidegger announced. To understand what Being is we must first understand who and what *we* are, such that "Being" can be an issue for us. But why put *this* particular concept to the question in the first place? Heidegger's critical starting point was the claim that we inevitably do take a certain meaning of Being for granted in how we define ourselves, and usually, most especially in his own time, it is a false meaning and the sign of a serious historical crisis.

"Dasein," Heidegger's neologism for the individual human being, in fact asks about its Being by asking who it is. Most of the time, Heidegger claimed, in a central passage that defines what we now mean by identity,

> The question . . . "who" [am I] answers itself in terms of the "I" itself, the "subject," the "Self." *The "who" is what maintains itself as something identical throughout changes in Experiences and ways of behavior, and which relates itself to this changing multiplicity in so doing.* Ontologically we understand it as something which is in each case already constantly present-at-hand. . . . *Substantiality is the ontological clue* for determining which entity is to provide the answer to the question of the "who." (italics added)[3]

"Presence-at-hand" was Heidegger's term for the mode of being of entities without subjectivity, that is, things. Things do not ask about or relate to their existence; they just are. Yet in thinking of myself as a self, I am thinking of myself precisely as a thing, though one with subjectivity; an unchanging essence underlies and persists through any and all empirical changes that I may undergo over time. Such an understanding of the self, Heidegger argued, had historically invaded even the most sophisticated philosophical attempts to avoid it. Kant had rejected the idea of the empirical self as a substance, and correctly characterized the "I" as nothing but the subjective consciousness that accompanies all our thoughts and acts. Nevertheless he also spoke of the "I" as the "subject" of logical behavior, a persisting self that binds our experiences into a unity. Kant's "subject" in the end is a thing-like entity that remains always the same: "To define the "I" ontologically as "*subject*" means to regard it as something always present-at-hand. The Being of the "I" is understood as the Reality of the *res cogitans*" (367). The fundamental modern ontological error in characterizing what is distinctively human was in Descartes' very attempt to make the distinction between mind (*res cogitans*) and matter (*res extensa*). By using the same word "*res*"—thing or matter—for both, he assimilated subjectivity to thinghood. So powerful is the hold of this reified distortion of the nature of human existence that it had proved impossible—up till now—to avoid replicating in philosophy the way we think of the self in everyday life. Our error is that we both feel naively and believe sophisticatedly that we have identities in the sense of persisting things.

Since, however, presence-at-hand is a mode of being that only "belongs to entities that are not that of Dasein," the usual way we answer the identity question "Who am I?" must be wrong. "It could be," Heidegger suggested, with stylized coyness, "that the 'who' of everyday Dasein just is not the 'I' myself" (150), that the "self" I proclaim that I am in answer to the question "Who am I?" is not in fact the real I. "Perhaps," he went on, "when Dasein addresses itself in the way which is closest to itself, it always says 'I am this entity,' and in the long run says this loudest when it is 'not' this entity. Dasein is in each case mine . . . but what if this should be the very reason why, proximally and for the most part, Dasein is *not* itself?" (151). Not only, then, is Dasein in error to say "I am this or that," I *am* this person, subject, or self, but the way Dasein stubbornly insists on it suggests that its error is motivated, not a simple mistake. The insistent assertion of the self's identity is a protest, and Dasein protests rather too much. Against what?

The essential characteristic of Dasein, the peculiarly human way of being, Heidegger called *Jemeinigkeit*, "mine-ness," the experience/knowledge of my experience *as* mine (67). To call it essential was to say that we are unable *not* to relate to ourselves this way. It is the nature of human subjectivity to be reflexive, to look at and know itself. Our capacity to "own" our experience is not elective; it is our inevitability. What made this apparently obvious, if not tautological, point worth making and subjecting to deeper analysis is that we can on some level refuse to recognize *Jemeinigkeit* while at the same time seeming to acknowledge it. It is in this sense that Dasein can fail to be itself. To claim an identity, to say, "I am this entity," is to fail in precisely this way. Such failure raised three questions, the questions *Being and Time* was above all intended to answer. If "mine-ness" defines the self's relation to its experience, how can we possibly deny it? Why should we want to do so in the first place? And finally, what can we do about it? How can we become truly ourselves?

Dasein as "Having to Be"

One further specification of the nature of Dasein offered a first answer to the question of how we can deny the subjectivity of our own experience. *Jemeinig-keit* also entails that Dasein is characterized by its "*Zu-sein*," by the fact that it "has to be." "Having to be" is the opposite of inertly "just being." Our characteristics, attributes, habits, and dispositions are "not 'properties' present-at-hand of some entity which . . . is itself present-at-hand . . . as if it were a table, house or tree. . . . they are in each case *possible* ways for it to be" (67, italics added). Heidegger's notion of "possibility" means that, unlike things, we have some sort of control over who we are—though exactly what kind of control turns out to be the crucial, and problematic, issue. Initially he put it this way: "Dasein has always made some sort of decision as to the way in which it is in each case mine. . . . In each case Dasein *is* its possibility, and it 'has' this possibility but not just as a property, as something present-at-hand would. . . . And because Dasein is in each case essentially its own possibilities, it can . . . 'choose' itself and win itself; it can also lose itself and never win itself, or only 'seem' to do so" (68). The difference between the alternatives of choosing itself and losing itself is the difference between the "authentic" and "inauthentic" modes of Dasein's being.

The wording of this passage, specifically the talk of "decision," made it superficially plausible to think that what Heidegger intended by Dasein's choosing, in contrast with the inertia of things present-at-hand, was absolute freedom of choice: possibilities, unlike the objective attributes of things, are take-it-or-leave-it propositions. Dasein can freely choose to realize certain of its possibilities while not choosing others. This is how Sartre would later inter-pret the matter, but it is not how Heidegger understood Dasein's fundamental situation. The first important clue lay in his assertion that Dasein *is* in each case its own possibilities at the same time that it can choose or not choose them. Everything depends, so to speak, on what the meaning of the word "is" is. The ambiguous, not-so innocent copula was the pivot on which both Heidegger's deconstruction and consequent reconstruction of identity turned. Its full meaning lies only in his unfolding of the ultimate essence of Dasein, its (our) temporality.

Before explicating temporality, however, Heidegger offered a preliminary description of the way in which Dasein usually was inauthentic, the way it normally denied *Jemeinigkeit*. Inauthenticity was grounded in his analysis of Dasein's dynamic interaction with the world, encapsulated in the root notion "being-in-the-world." Our world, that is, the world of our experience, is not a world of entities with preexistent, objective meanings, which we have pas-sively to discover. Rather, the meaning of entities is disclosed to us only as we actively live our possibilities, and in relation to them. What the self gets out of the world, the aspects of reality that are revealed to it, are functions of the purposes with which it addresses the world. This conception was aimed in the first instance against an empiricist subject-object version of self-world relations, in which the outside registers itself on our senses as if humans were purely passive screens. But it was no less aimed at idealism, according to which the mind knows the world by organizing sense data by fixed internal schemata. Both wrongly made "knowing" our primary relationship to the world. At the same time though, Heidegger was also critical of the then-prevalent vitalist "philosophy of life," which privileged biological or "irrational" needs and desires over cognition as our address to the world. The problem with all of these philosophies was their causal determinism, whether from outside or inside the body. It ignored the sense in which we own, we are, our desires and actions, our possibilities. The concept of being-in-the-world said nothing about the content of our "possibilities"; the word was meant to articulate their dynamic, the peculiar way in which our ways of being are actions and choices for which we are responsible, and how the meaningfulness of the world is their result.[4]

Denying True Selfhood Through Self-Alienation in "the They"

The important critical payoff for interpreting Dasein as being-in-the-world was the idea that "at first and for the most part" Dasein remains oblivious to its role as the agency by which meaning comes into the world. Dasein is generally "out there" in the world, working with things as they have already been conceptualized, so that they seem to be what they are independently of us. In his central example, Heidegger talked of the way in which entities in the world are deemed by us to be "ready-to-hand"—*zuhanden*—useful things with objective purposes. A hammer is a "thing for hammering." "Readiness-to-hand," he wrote, "is the way in which entities as they are 'in themselves' are defined" (101). In truth, however, things are not what they seem to be "in themselves." They have meanings only in relation to "a possibility of Dasein's being." Tracing the meaning and purposes of things (tree as wood, wood for hammering, hammering for building a shelter) back to their ultimate origin inevitably leads to "Dasein's Being as the sole authentic 'for-the-sake-of-which'" (117).

Or it *could* lead us back to the origin, to ourselves—except that regarding things inauthentically as having ready-made meanings has its counterpart in an everyday inauthentic way of understanding ourselves as well. Just as we fail to see Dasein's active role in opening up meaning in general, we fail to acknowledge our own individual role in sustaining the existing meanings of things through our participation in the ways of being that disclose them. Thus we do not acknowledge our personal commitment to those existing ways of being, that is, we do not acknowledge them as *mine*. It is not that we can't or don't say "I do this for such and such a purpose" or "I believe thus and such," but that the way we say it so does not reflect a truly individuated sense of *Jemeinigkeit*.

What the "I" refers to instead is to a self that is not differentiated from other selves except as a spatial locator. "By Others we do not mean everybody else but me. . . . They are rather those from whom for the most part one does *not* distinguish oneself—those among whom one is too" (154). I exist as a physically separate Dasein but not as a truly individuated one, because I understand what I do and what I believe as just my particular realization of what "everyone" does and believes. I don't first know myself through introspection and then come to believe that others are subjects like me by projecting consciousness onto them. Rather I know who I am *through* them, as being one of them. Being-in-the-world is from the very beginning a being with others [*Mitsein*], and "Knowing oneself is grounded in Being-with" (161). But being-with-others can also be either authentic or inauthentic, and for the most part it starts off inauthentically. Though others are encountered as "Daseine," human existences, they are also first encountered as "what they are," as reified, thing-like entities. Above all, "they *are* what they do" (163). In a world where things are defined as use-values, people are also defined in terms of their social functions. And as just one of everybody, Dasein too defines its being, its identity, the same way: "'One is' what one does" (283). The advent of American sociological role theory some years later looks in ironic retrospect as if it had been invented to support Heidegger's argument. Social science seemed to codify the inauthentic everyday mentality: we *are* (nothing but) our social roles.[5]

A paradox of inauthentic Being-with is that precisely because of the fundamental sense in which we are all the same, "there is a constant care as to the way one differs from them" (163), whether in order to achieve equality with or superiority to them. But this initially surprising competitiveness can be easily understood in relation to the essence of inauthentic being-with-one-another, because in that mode "Dasein . . . stands in *subjection* to Others. It itself *is* not; its Being has been taken away by the Others. Dasein's everyday possibilities of Being are for the Others to dispose of as they please. . . . One belongs to the Others oneself and enhances their power" (164). Because we know who we are only through others, because we let them define us, we resent their primacy over us. We either hanker enviously to catch up with them or to be better at being them than they are themselves.

Who are these "others"? Everyone and no one. "The 'who' is not this one, not that one, not oneself, not some people, and not the sum of them all. The 'who' is the neuter, the "they" [*das Man*]" (164). In German, the English idiom "they say . . ." is rendered in the singular as "*man sagt*," one says, but in both languages the idiom is meant to attribute the saying in question to everyone in general and no one in particular. Heidegger used this idiom to characterize the conscious identity of the everyday self, a self-definition that is also a whole way of life. It reads better in the German singular with its punning overtones of " *der Mann*," man, the male. In its everyday existence, Dasein *is das Man*, "one," "anyone," "everyman," man in general. One is *das Man*, for example, when one gets one's knowledge and opinions from newspapers and holds them because they are what "everyone" knows and opines. "We take pleasure and enjoy ourselves as *they* take pleasure; we read, see and judge about literature and art as *they* see and judge; likewise we shrink back from the 'great mass' as *they* shrink back; we find 'shocking' what *they* find shock-ing" (146). (Here Heidegger's point might be better conveyed in English by the translation "We enjoy the things 'one enjoys.'") It is not even necessary to refer explicitly to "them" at all. *Man sagt* can be translated by the passive "it is said." I may say, using the passive, "I just do what is done," with the "by everyone" implied. Heidegger meant here to ventriloquize the exact state of mind in which one is able to say "I" yet at the same time deny *Jemeinigkeit*.

In such a state of mind one is above all denying personal responsibility for or commitment to what one believes and does. In effect we offer explanations of what we do that are simultaneously excuses and evasions, though without our conscious awareness; called to account, we are saying that we do what we do because "that's what people do." The "they-self" "can be answerable for everything most easily," Heidegger wrote, "because it is not someone who needs to vouch for anything. It 'was' always the 'they' who did it, and yet it can be said that it has been 'no one'. . . . Thus the particular Dasein in its everydayness is *disburdened* by the "they." Not only that; disburdening it of its Being, "the "they" accommodates Dasein if Dasein has any tendency to take things easily and make them easy" (165). The English "disburdened" is intended to capture the force of the German *entlasten*, which has the active sense of "taking away or taking off" but the self who "takes away the burden" of responsibility is the same self from whom it is taken. The language plainly suggests both a factual description and a moral critique, despite Heidegger's disclaimer that he was not doing moral philosophy. Dasein *is* responsible but refuses responsibility, and the way Dasein "disburdens" itself of the responsi-bility demanded by *Jemeinigkeit* is through its identity as "everyman." As Hei-degger concluded, with the neat paradox of inauthentic identity, "Everyone is the other, and no one is himself" (165). "Normal" self-identity is in the deepest sense self-alienation.

In retrospect it has been glaringly obvious to historians that many of the universal features Heidegger assigned to *das Man* bear the stamp of a particular historical moment and milieu. *Das Man* is characterized by "distantiality" (from one's own experience), "averageness" and "leveling down," all of which constitute *das Man*'s "publicness," its self-referral to the standards and norms that are publicly available, broadcast through modern means of information and mass communication. It is through "publicness" that Dasein discovers what "they" are saying and therefore who it is. What is thus "common knowledge" is the subject of "idle talk," which Heidegger defined as the kind of communication between people that gives one "the possibility of understanding everything without previously making the thing one's own" (213), parroting the conventional wisdom without the backing of personal immersion in the subject at hand. Similarly "curiosity," fanned by the constant availability of novelty, is not interested in things in order to truly know them, but "seeks novelty only in order to leap from it anew to another novelty . . . restlessness and the excitement of . . . changing encounters" (216), or, to use a once-popular, post-Heidegger idiom, to be "where it's at." Finally, since "common knowledge" is just that, accessible to everyone and the source of most of what people know, we have no idea whether what they communicate is genuinely understood or not, whether what they pass along is true or just what everyone is saying. Thus all social communication is infected with "ambiguity"; we may think we are learning something new, but we already know what to think about it (217).

These abstract categories of inauthentic being-with were all barely disguised concrete descriptions, and indictments, of uprooted modern urban society with its anomie and anonymity, from the standpoint of a disdainful critic from a small provincial town rooted in a traditional agrarian economy and culture.[6] But the description also hints at a greater social specificity than the abstract idea of modernity alone suggests and that the concept of "mass society" actually gets wrong. When Heidegger said of *das Man* that "we shrink back from the 'great mass' as they shrink back" he was referring to the bourgeoisie and its disdain for "the masses"—workers, lower middle classes, above all the rural population—as expressed by its intellectual representatives. His allusion to *das Man*'s competitiveness, and his frequent references to its constant "busyness," point in the same direction. Heidegger's contemptuous depiction of *das Man* was an attack from the conservative right against the modern urban bourgeoisie who were the historical agents of capitalist modernity, economic, social, and political.

Nevertheless Heidegger is to be taken at his word that he meant the category of "everydayness," the inauthentic way of being-in-the-world and with others, as a universal category applicable to other societies and cultures than his own. Arguing against confusing everydayness with some anthropologically primitive mode of life—which presumably could and would be outgrown with progress—Heidegger asserted that "primitive Dasein . . . has a specific everydayness of its own" (76). "Tribal man" was inauthentic in his own unique way. If anything, Heidegger claimed, everydayness could be seen even more clearly in primitive cultures than in modern ones because they were less complicated and hidden, less overlaid with the pseudodifferentiation and misleadingly individualist self-interpretations of modernity. The essence of everydayness was its "primordial absorption" in things, in what he called Dasein's everyday "thrownness" and "fallenness," which occluded its true relationship to them and to itself and which were the usual states of Dasein in every society. Inauthentic identity is a structural feature of many different kinds of society; more exactly, it can be and generally is a feature of every society. To the extent that people understand their actions as deriving from, and justified by, an external, collective authority, they are inauthentic.

The key word to describe the inauthentic state of everyday Dasein is "submission." Dasein is always already in the world; it has "fallen" into things with supposedly objective meanings before it ever reflects on and takes hold of itself as the ultimate source of their meanings. It discloses the meanings of things in the world through its prereflective "moods" and "attunements" but is unaware of how those meanings are dependent on its own states of mind. On the one hand, for example, "Only something which is in the state-of-mind of fearing (or fearlessness) can discover that what is environmentally ready-to-hand as threatening" (176). On the other hand, in these states of mind "Dasein constantly surrenders itself to the 'world' and lets the 'world' "matter" to it in such a way that somehow Dasein evades its very self" (178). It surrenders and evades, in this particular instance, by taking things as objectively "fearful in themselves," rather than in relation to who and what Dasein is, that is, to Dasein's "possibilities." In the "fallen" state, Dasein takes its possibilities "From the world . . . and it does so in accordance with the way things have been interpreted by the "they." This interpretation has already restricted the possible options of choice to what lies within the range of the familiar, the attainable, the respectable—to that which is fitting and proper" (239). Modern and primitive societies—and presumably all those in between—have their own characteristic versions of "the they," of the external authority that dictates to the individual Dasein what is fitting and proper, what things "mean." In primitive society it is the gods, or nature, rather than the public. What all have in common, however, is their failure to understand that the origins of meaning are in Dasein itself.

The Paradox of Authentic Possibility as Determinism

The example of fearing was not incidental; it points to one crucial element of what Heidegger meant by possibility, but also to what he didn't mean. What possibility *didn't* mean was above all an activity or social role or way of life that Dasein could either choose or not choose to realize at will. "Possibility . . . does not signify a free-floating potentiality-for-Being in the sense of the 'liberty of indifference'" (183). Dasein's being-in-the-world is not a matter of "comporting oneself towards a plan that has been thought out, and in accordance with which Dasein arranges its Being" (185). But this was to say more than that Dasein is always doing and being in the world before it reflects on its purposes and intentions. Taken in isolation, as the proposition that reflective thought is always necessarily parasitical on existence, it might suggest that once we reflect on what we are doing, which of our possibilities we are acting on or "projecting," we might decide to stop, withdraw from that possibility, and do something else. But fear as a "possibility" is neither a choice nor a plan. Given who we are, we are not free to fear or not to fear. The only thing we are free to do in relation to our fear is own it or deny it, not in the psychoanalytic sense of repressing it into the unconscious, but by saying something like "Well, of course I'm afraid; isn't everybody in this situation? Isn't it natural to be afraid?" This is the language of *das Man*, language that denies *Jemeinigkeit* by removing the sting of terror, of being alone with the naked reality of one's own fear.

From the very beginning there was a built-in, indefeasible determinism in Heidegger's notion of possibility. Our possibilities are who we permanently, unavoidably *are*, though we can be them either in the mode of acknowledging them as "mine" in a deep experiential sense or defending oneself by passing them off as objective. "Dasein is such," Heidegger wrote, "that in every case it has understood (or alternatively, not understood) that *it is to be thus or such*" (184; italics added). In the first half of his exposition it wasn't at all clear where the "thus and such" came from, what determined them. The example of fear might suggest biology, though nothing could have been further from Heidegger's meaning or concern. The crucial source of possibility became clearer—a relative term in Heidegger—only later in the context of his attempt at the philosophical refurbishing of national identity, when he introduced the idea of Dasein's essential "historicality."

Anxiety: The Motive for Identity

Given his ultimate purpose, however, Heidegger first had to take up the question of why Dasein falls into inauthenticity in the first place, since that was the obstacle to overcome to create a new, "authentic" identity. It is not just because it is "natural" to be occupied with things in the world as we go about our business and therefore not reflect on the source of the meanings we take for granted. Rather Dasein's falling, its absorption in the world, is a deliberate flight from just such reflection. Why Dasein flees is immanent in the very comfort that falling provides. "The supposition of the "they" that one is leading a full and genuine 'life' brings Dasein a *tranquillity* for which everything is 'in the best of order'"[7]. . . . Falling . . . is at the same time *tranquillizing*" (222). Dasein's being-in-the-world as the origin of meaning is the source of an anxiety that unsettles it and demands quieting. But this anxiety is not an empirically caused psychological state that could be alleviated by concrete achievement, material acquisition, or psychotherapy. Its existence is in fact perfectly compatible with "complete assurance and self-sufficiency in one's everyday concern" (234), in other words, with what psychotherapy would generally consider mental health. And that is precisely the point of falling: it gives us the feeling of being at home in the world because in the state of inauthenticity everything is objectively as it is and "should be." This is true even if I feel that I personally am not as I should be, that I haven't lived up to my values, because I am at least confident that I know what they are. And because being-in-the-world means there is no such objective order, because meaning exists only in relation to Dasein's own possibilities, the tranquilizing effect of falsely believing in such an order tells us that what we are fleeing is the fundamental sense of *not* being at home in the world. "When in falling we fell into the "at-home" of publicness we flee in the face of the "not at home"; we flee in the face of the uncanniness which lies in Dasein—in Dasein as thrown Being-in-the-world. . . . This uncanniness pursues Dasein constantly, and is a threat to its everyday lostness in the "they," though not explicitly. . . . *From an existential-ontological point of view, the "not-at-home" must be conceived as the more primordial phenomenon*" (234).

What Heidegger offered here—though he would have abhorred the wording—was nothing less than a motivational theory of identity, derived by backward deduction from the phenomenological texture of the feeling of identity. The theory's central claim is that human beings desire to be cosmically "at home." To be at home is to be where one "belongs," where "belonging" implies an absolute, metaphysical right, one not conferred by revocable human agency, or dependent on achievement. Robert Frost brilliantly expressed the sense of it in the homely exchange between the two interlocutors of his poem "The Death of the Hired Man," so different from Heidegger's abstractions yet the same in meaning: "'Home is the place where, when you have to go there / they have to take you in.' / 'I should have called it / Something you somehow haven't to deserve.'" "They" can't refuse to take you in, because you belong there as a matter of right independently of human will. Nor do you have to earn the right to be home; it is yours in virtue of your birth, hence of who you are. To exist, Heidegger claimed, is to want to feel that the world is home in this way. But as being-in-the-world, Dasein is precisely *not* at home. Nothing is ordained for Dasein; meaningfulness is not simply there, conferred from the outside, not guaranteed as a matter of objective or metaphysical truth. Dasein's world is only what Dasein's realizing its own possibilities makes it. That is what Heidegger meant in saying that "what Dasein is anxious about is Being-in-the-world itself " (232). Being-in-the-world feels uncanny—in German, *unheimlich*, with its semantic reference to home—*Heim*—and being homeless, *heimatlos*.

The inauthenticity of everydayness, by contrast, is the state of mind in which everything—above all Dasein itself—is as it is, metaphysically necessary. Difference and alternatives are not thinkable; to realize the human, subjective origins of meaning would be to admit Dasein as its own source, and therefore the impossibility of being at home in the absolute, objective sense in which Dasein desires it. *Das Man* is the impersonal, objective, and universal authority that gives that assurance. Yet at the same time, on some level, Dasein knows its error, which is announced to it by the "uncanny" that lurks in all experience. It is not hard to recognize, as many commentators have, the religious origins of this interpretation of ultimate human desire, the aspiration to the security of transcendent truth and justified belonging, which Heidegger understood, and as we will see, still retained in secular form after abandoning orthodox Catholic belief and a flirtation with Protestantism.[8] His debt to Kierkegaard's concept of anxiety is the latter's most obvious legacy.

It is the secular transformation of religion that also gave *Being and Time* its structure as a pilgrim's progress, with the first part an analysis of the "fallenness" of Dasein followed by a second which offered the prescription for salvation and rebirth, the path from inauthentic to authentic being. Heidegger even used the Latin term for the religious aspiration to grace, *perfectio*, to characterize Dasein's true end, which however he defined in purely secular terms as Dasein's "transformation into that which he can be in Being-free for his ownmost [*eigenst*] possibilities (projection)" (243; "Ownmost" overlooks the lexical connection in German between *eigenst* and *eigentlich* "authentic"). Dasein's "ownmost," or "most authentic" possibility was the possibility of

finally becoming authentic in relationship to itself and hence all its possibilities. At the end of the first division of *Being and Time*, Heidegger had prepared
the ground to answer the questions which had motivated the work to begin
with: how can Dasein go about leaving inauthentic identity behind—a redundancy, because fixed identity is inauthenticity—and what will it be when it
does? What, in other words, replaces the identity of *das Man*?

Becoming Authentic

That something *can* replace it represents, in the light of Heidegger's analysis
of identity up to this point, an apparently astounding turn of argument. As he
acknowledged at the beginning of the second division, "Any entity whose
Essence is made up of existence, is essentially opposed to the possibility of our
getting it in our grasp as an entity which is a whole" (276). Identity is a
definition of the self as a whole. If Dasein, as being-in-the-world, is nothing
but the ongoing enactment/realization of its possibilities, it is in principle
indefinable, not only before its death but even afterward. After death, the
summed total of Dasein's enacted possibilities during its lifetime is a mere
aggregate that does not constitute a unified whole. (Even if one's life activities
seem to have a consistent theme, it is not out of the logical necessity of a
closed self-definition, but because Dasein had continuously enacted certain
possibilities.) In a word, being-in-the-world would seem to be the very opposite of identity. But at this point Heidegger announced that this preliminary
conclusion is wrong because it does not go deeply enough into the fundamental nature of Dasein. A "primordial" interpretation can indeed disclose
Dasein's "possibilities of authenticity *and totality*. . . . Dasein has an authentic
potentiality-for-Being-a-whole" (276, 277; italics added). This was a remarkable statement. Totality or wholeness is definitional of identity; it is what identity promises. If one can be somehow "totalized," wrapped up in a definition,
one can be wholly, definitively *something*.

The solution to the apparent squaring of the circle represented by the
reconciliation of authenticity and totality lay in Heidegger's conception of
temporality. All the creative writers who had questioned the possibility of
substantive personal identity between the wars saw time as the crucial and
problematic category of identity. Their common insight, expressed most
straightforwardly by Pirandello, was that the possibility of self-identity rests
on the effort to freeze time's unstoppable flow. For humans, the passage of
time does not simply mean that things change but that even when they don't,
change is a lurking possibility. Living in time means not only traversing the
predestined temporal arc from birth to death but also knowing the ineradicable discontinuity of temporal moments—unless we hold them all together by

our choices. This is not a truth we welcome. We are all, says Pirandello's Henry IV ironically, fixed "in good faith" in a concept of ourselves, meaning that we sincerely lie, denying the terrifying truth that from one moment to the next we can step out of what we thought was our character. To acknowledge this would be to confront vertiginous indeterminacy. Heidegger turned this argument upside down and transformed the idea of temporality itself into a species of determinism.

To begin with, Heidegger argued, we *do* in fact concern ourselves about ourselves as a whole, and not just about our various possibilities. We can discover this in the way we relate to the "possibility" of our death, which is the certainty that our not-being is not only inevitable but possible at any time. Ultimately, this is what anxiety is anxious about; the fact of death tells us that we are not "necessary": "Death is the possibility of the absolute impossibility of Dasein" (302). Death is the ultimate proof we are not at home in the world; we are finite, ephemeral beings whom the cosmos can obviously do without, since it will go on without us. If I am not necessary, and that is what I want to be, I am nothing. That is why we "fall" into the world of things as they "objectively" are according to *das Man*: it enables us to deny death by passing it off as something that of course eventually happens to everybody, and thus avoid the *Jemeinigkeit* of *my* death, the shattering realization that at any moment *I* may cease to be.

Despite my effort at denial, however, my "nothingness" does announce itself to me experientially, according to Heidegger, in the phenomena of conscience and guilt. The ontological meaning of conscience is not that it consists of absolute rules that may declare me guilty of some violation, but that I am able to negate them by violating them. What my guilt reveals to me is the power of the "not" in relation to what is ostensibly absolutely binding: if I can violate the absolute, I am free in relation to it: "we define the formally existential idea of the 'Guilty' as "Being-the-basis for a Being which has been defined by a 'not'"—this is to say, as "Being-the-basis of a nothingness" (329).[9] When I accept at last the call of conscience, which reveals my power to negate, and the personal reality of my death, which reveals my ownership of and responsibility for my own life, I can make the "anticipatory resolve" to leap into authenticity, individualizing myself out of the generality of *das Man*.

But—and this is crucial—negation is the only real power that Dasein has. Dasein is not and cannot be the foundation of itself, choosing itself ex nihilo. It is not the uncaused cause of its being-in-the-world. Thrown by its birth into a preexisting situation, "Dasein constantly lags behind its possibilities. It is never existent *before* its basis but only *from* it and *as this basis*. Thus 'being a basis' means *never* to have power over one's ownmost being from the ground up. This '*not*' belongs to the existential meaning of 'thrownness' "(330). This was a proclamation of the determinism that circumscribes Dasein's freedom: Dasein doesn't create its own possibilities, and can only choose what it has been thrown into.

It might appear at first that even with that limitation Dasein has more than one option: "Freedom . . . is only in the choice of one possibility—that is, in tolerating one's not having chosen the others and one's not being able to choose them" (331). But while "not being able to choose others" might be interpreted simply as a version of the law of the excluded middle (you can't choose two opposites simultaneously) or as a consequence of human finitude (you can't have it all, even sequentially), they are clearly not what he meant: authentic Dasein, liberated from *Das Man*, has only one choice, period.

Dasein's possibilities are defined by its "facticity." "Thrown into its "there" every Dasein has been factically submitted to a definite 'world'—its world. . . . [After Dasein frees itself from the inauthenticity of *das Man*] the 'world' which is ready-to-hand does not become another one 'in its content,' nor does the circle of Others get exchanged." This is reminiscent of a Zen koan about enlightenment: before enlightenment, mountains are mountains and rivers are rivers; on the path to enlightenment, mountains are no longer mountains and rivers no longer rivers; after enlightenment, mountains are mountains and rivers are rivers. What changes for Dasein with authenticity is not the content of its world or the circle of others with whom one is together in the world, but one's understanding of who one truly has been all along.

But if nothing changes with authenticity, what can Dasein's "choice" and freedom mean? It would appear to be the familiar trope of much nineteenth-century German thought that freedom is the acceptance of necessity.[10] And why in any case should Dasein make the leap of anticipatory resolve into freedom, when that entails embracing its nothingness? Why give up the comfort of the certainty about the world that Dasein's identity as *das Man* provides? Heidegger's answer was that that is the only way to achieve real, as opposed to false and in any case precarious, identity. At this point the attack on identity in the first part of *Being and Time* is seen in a whole new light: as an attack only on the kind of identity that is illusory and false.

Das Man, after all, offers only the illusion of stability. To be *das Man* is to be prey to the arbitrary shifts, fads, and fashions of the conventional wisdom. *Das Man* has no control over its own self-definition. In surrendering to public-ness, I have actually given up the possibility of being constant and self-consistent. By contrast "the . . . authentic potentiality-for-Being [one's self] . . . opens our eyes for the constancy of the Self, in the sense of its having achieved a position. The constancy of the Self, in the double sense of steadiness and steadfastness, is the authentic counter-possibility to the non-Self-constancy that is characteristic of irresolute falling" (369).[11] *Das Man* turns out not to be identity at all, as I desire it—a steady, constant self that knows what and where it is. Self-constancy only becomes possible through "anticipatory resoluteness," the resolute "leaping ahead," as the German literally puts it, into the anguished abyss of true individuation, that is, of choice and taking responsibility. Being able to choose means that one is able to commit to something permanently.

Choice, Heidegger was arguing, was a necessary aspect of true *self-definition*. Neglect of the self's freedom was precisely the flaw in previous theories of the self's identity as a permanent essence or substance underlying the vicissitudes of life. But Dasein also wants permanence, definition; doesn't freedom of choice negate it? How can commitment be objectively defining, binding, if it is freely chosen? This would appear to be the insoluble dilemma of the desire for identity. Heidegger did not think so. Choosing in his view is not an agonizing problem for the self; it is not a problem at all. When Dasein realizes its authenticity it is no longer preoccupied with its own ego, because its choice is only an internal shift in attitude to what it already is. "*As something that keeps silent*, authentic *Being*-one's-Self is just the sort of thing that does not keep on saying "*I*"; but in its reticence it '*is*' that thrown entity as which it can authentically be" (370). When it chooses to be itself, it accepts that which it already is in an act of commitment, not, like before, in unthinking thrownness into the world.

Dasein's Temporality as the Source of Authentic Identity

But what, finally, *is* it as that "thrown entity" which it already is but now for the first time can choose to be? Taking over one's thrownness, Heidegger asserted, means "being Dasein authentically *as it already was*," that is taking up its past not simply as an inert given, but as an active project for the future. "Only as far as it is futural can Dasein *be* authentically as having been" (373). Heidegger was unreservedly asserting here a version of essentialism, while at the same time attempting to rescue identity from complete determinism. Dasein unalterably *is* what the past has made it. This was meant as a very strong claim, one quite different from what Sartre would make. It entails that the past has made the self something quite definite, something fixed that, when properly understood, commits it to a *particular* future. That Dasein "is" permanently what it was, that it is *something* (rather than everything, as *das Man*, being one of "everybody," thinks that it is) is the badge of human finitude (378). But for Dasein to be itself authentically, it must take up the something that it "is" freely and actively. It must make what it "is" into a project for the future, not let itself be in the mode of the past inertly, as if it has no control whatsoever over it.

Heidegger's essentialism was grounded in this idea of temporality. Being-in-the-world is being in a situation that was created by the past and has become Dasein's present. But the present is not presence-at-hand, an inert past that washes over one as if one were floating along passively in a moving stream. Because one does not choose the circumstances of one's birth it can seem that way. Dasein does not choose its thrownness, or as Marx had put it more transparently long before, man does not make history in circumstances of his own choosing. Nonetheless he does make history. In Heidegger's somewhat different terms, Dasein makes the past present, turning what it has been given from past into its present by enacting its various possibilities. And in acting in the present we are necessarily also future oriented, since any action intends a result that is not yet. "Self-projection upon the 'for-the-sake-of-oneself' is grounded in the future and is an essential characteristic of *existentiality. The primary meaning of existentiality is the future*" (376). Dasein is in its fundamental structure (if not in its everyday self-awareness) a future-oriented actualization in the present of its possibilities as handed down by the past.

So far, this interpretation of temporality could be consistent with the notion that each moment of time in Dasein's life is self-sufficient, that Dasein is "the sum of the momentary actualities of Experiences which come along successively and disappear" (426). Only as opposed to inauthentic temporality, in which discrete experiences passively "come along" moment to moment as if by themselves, in authentic temporality these moments would be chosen enactments. This, however, was exactly the temporality that Pirandello's Henry IV feared: disconnected points of time at any of which the self could choose to do and be something different. Such an understanding of temporality entails a radical version of decisionism or voluntarism.[12] But this was not Heidegger's understanding of time. Dasein does not fill up a divisible stretch of life with only momentary actualities, living life as if time were like the discrete moments of Newtonian dynamics, t1, t2, and so on. Rather, Dasein "stretches *itself* along in such a way that its own Being is constituted in advance as a stretching along" (426). In a (Heideggerian) word, Dasein has a care for its own "connectedness" (427), its sameness from moment to moment. In other (non-, even anti-Heideggerian) words, Dasein creates its identity across the span of its life by actively taking up its factical thrownness as possibility, rather than just passively identifying with it in the way *Das Man* has defined it, and actively sustaining it in the present by projecting it as a goal for the future.

Historicality: *Identity as the Free Choice of (National) Destiny*

But exactly what are these possibilities of our thrownness? "We must ask," Heidegger wrote, "whence, *in general*, Dasein can draw those possibilities upon which it factically projects itself" (434). In one sense, Dasein doesn't have to look far. They already "circulate" in the "average" public way of interpreting Dasein today, he answered; indeed they are well known to everybody, but they have been made "unrecognizable" *as* possibilities by "ambiguity." That is why when they are seized resolutely, it will necessarily be, as he put it succinctly, "for, against and yet again for them" (435) as they have been interpreted up until now. That is to say, their true "deep" content will be affirmed, but that content will have to be stripped of the false ways it has been interpreted by *das Man*, so they can then be projected into the future in a genuine manner.

What is this deep content? When Dasein "comes back" to itself in authentic resolve, back to what it truly is, it discloses its authentic possibilities to itself "in terms of the *heritage* . . . which that resoluteness . . . *takes over*" (435). Dasein *is* the heritage of its past, which up to now it has been only passively, not as something it can do anything about but as a mere fact about itself, like the brownness of a table. Furthermore, it understands this heritage in the context of the present, as it has been interpreted by contemporary public opinion. In resoluteness, Dasein for the first time consciously hands down to itself, that is, makes into a conscious, future-oriented goal, that which it has up to now merely passively inherited. Choosing freely what it has inherited, Heidegger fatefully wrote, "brings Dasein into the simplicity of its *fate*" (435). Here was the explicit confirmation of the determinism that had been implicit all along in Heidegger's interpretation of temporality and the facticity of the past. We have no choice but to live our heritage; that is who we *are*.

He had yet to specify what the fundamental elements of one's "heritage" were. When he finally did, he came as close as he ever would in *Being in Time* to concreteness, leaving just enough ambiguity for misinterpretation if he is read without sufficient attention to historical context. Since Dasein is "always already" a being with others, the authentic "historizing" of one's existence is necessarily a "co-historizing" with those others "which is determinative for it as *destiny*. This is how we designate the historizing of the community, of a people [*der Gemeinschaft, des Volkes*]" (436). If *fate* points backward, to the determinism of the past in constituting the individual's communal identity, *destiny* points forward to the way that identity is to be actualized by the community in the future. The English translation at this point is a significant mistranslation. Heidegger's original says "of the community, of *the* people," not "a" people. One need not read this as a barely veiled reference to the right-wing notion, ultimately made infamous by Hitler and the Nazis, of the racialized *Volksgemeinschaft*[13] to see that for Heidegger the most basic element of one's fated inheritance was one's "peoplehood," and further, that he understood peoplehood as a *Gemeinschaft*, a fraught word with polemical implications in German thought at least since the publication of Ferdinand Tönnies's *Gemeinschaft und Gesellschaft* (*Community and Society*) in 1887.

The idea of the *Volk* had long had overtones of kinship by blood and rootedness in the land.[14] A *Gemeinschaft* is a community united by noninstrumental, affective bonds. Its sense of unity and solidarity comes from the feeling of belonging to one organism, something more than the sum of its individual parts, to which the individual is subordinate and for which he is always ready to sacrifice himself. With the exception of friendship, Tönnies's concept of *Gemeinschaft* was authoritarian and hierarchical. A *Gesellschaft*, by contrast, is a society in which social relationships are a means to serve the interests of the separate individuals that constitute it. It is based on contract and held together by laws whose rational purpose was to protect individual interests against contract violation. Tönnies's distinction was originally intended to theorize the difference between modern capitalist commercial and industrial society and the traditional society of hierarchy and devotion that it was overtaking in late nineteenth-century Germany.

For Heidegger, Germany—and ostensibly any "authentic" collective—was in its essence a *Gemeinschaft*. "Destiny," he wrote, "is not something that puts itself together out of individual fates [as in an individualistic *Gesellschaft*], any more than Being-with-one-another can be conceived as the occurring together of several Subjects. Our fates have already been guided in advance, in our Being with one another in the same world and in our resoluteness for definite possibilities. Only in communicating and in struggling does the power of destiny become free. *Dasein's fateful destiny in and with its 'generation' goes to make up the full authentic historizing of Dasein*" (436; italics added). Fate, destiny, community, people, struggling, generation—put in historical context these terms indicate just what Heidegger meant when he said that in taking over its fate, Dasein acted "for, against, and yet again for" the received way it interpreted itself in everydayness, as exemplified by the German case.

Germany after the war was a defeated nation; what it was in the present—territorially, internationally, and even in its domestic political system—had been decided by others and passively acquiesced to by Germany's present leaders. To be German in the inauthentic way was to submit to that version of German identity as just the way things were, the way things had happened historically. But the Germany of the Weimar Republic was not "authentic" in

Heidegger's sense, that is, it was not in control of its own destiny. To be authentically German was to take up one's national identity but reject its current form and move toward a national self-determination and assertiveness that would make it once again master of its fate. One's *fatedness* was to be German in the current situation Germany found itself. One's *destiny* as a German, however, should and could be decided and realized by Germans alone. It was wholly consistent with this notion of identity in *Being and Time* that six years later, in an address to the students of the University of Freiburg as the newly installed Rector under the new Nazi regime, Heidegger spoke of the "*Deutsches Dasein*" that had been revolutionized by National Socialism.[15] Whether or not one can already read his later Nazism into *Being and Time* is irrelevant to the more general meaning of his theory of identity. The idea of a collective identity acting on its own behalf that could and should at the same time be embraced as one's own personal identity was the climax of his philosophical treatise.

All these elements of identity were contained in a concept that fused total historical determinism with the freedom to act and innovate: the idea of "repeatability." Repeatability was the temporal-historical dimension of Dasein's (limited) control over its possibilities. "*Repeating*," as Heidegger defined it, "*is handing down explicitly*—that is to say, going back to the possibilities of the Dasein that were already there. The authentic repetition of a possibility that has been—the possibility that Dasein may choose its hero—is grounded existentially in anticipatory resoluteness; for it is in resoluteness that one first chooses the choice which makes one free to struggle for loyally following in the footsteps of that which can be repeated" (437).

The notion of "choosing one's hero" has suggested to some commentators that Dasein could in fact choose any figure or model from the past to inspire the future, but this is clearly not the case, given that the writ of the hero is circumscribed by the primacy of the organic national community; only nationalist heroes qualified. In repeating the past, one should not accept the version of national community prevailing in the present, in the form recent events had determined it, or even as it had existed in the past. On the contrary, "the repetition makes a *reciprocative rejoinder* to the possibility of existence. But when such a rejoinder is made to this possibility in a new resolution, it is made in a *moment of vision; and as such* it is at the same time a *disavowal* of that which in the "today," is working itself out as the 'past'"(438). "Authentic" handing down of tradition demands not passive acceptance of what is, but a creative response that retrieves tradition's "true" meaning and promotes it in the present circumstances. It demands that Dasein disavow the false way that the present defines national identity and hence the nation's future destiny.

Heidegger called the present self-understanding of the community "the 'actual' that is left over, the world-historical that has been, the leavings and the information about them that is present-at-hand. Lost in the making present of the "today," it understands the 'past' in terms of the 'Present'" (443). The "actual" is the "merely" empirical, not the essentially "real." In the concrete terms of Germany's historical situation, present-day Germans presume that Germany "is" what world-historical events—the war and its aftermath—have made it, the Weimar *Gesellschaft* Republic. They regard German history in the retrospect of the present as progress toward this present. But that is inauthentic thinking, because in it the world-historical is "experienced and interpreted" as something that simply "comes along, has presence and disappears." That is, history is what happens *to* Dasein, not what Dasein makes happen. It is a thing-like force that pushes us where it will.

Interpreting history this way, Dasein has been "dispersed" in the many kinds of things which daily "come to pass," which just happen. It is driven about by its "affairs." So if it wants to come to itself, "it must first pull itself together from the dispersion and the disconnectedness of the very things that have 'come to pass'" (442). It is precisely because Dasein is "dispersed" in *das Man*, with no unified core of its own, that the problem of how it establishes a sense of its connectedness—its oneness or identity—comes up in the first place. Heidegger's point was that unity and connectedness are subjectively an issue for Dasein; Dasein *wants* identity, as its cleaving to the false certainty of *das Man* shows; it wants connectedness and certainty, but has been looking for them in all the wrong places.

The *right* place to look is the idea of Germany as the organic "people's community," a renewable ideal whose realization depends on the active committed will of its members. It is already there, in people's sense of themselves as German, but the true nature of German-ness is obscured by its current incarnation. In the "moment of vision," Dasein responds to and takes over the eternal idea of Germany creatively, not imitatively, not by trying to restore the unrecoverable forms of the past—for example, the Wilhelmine Empire. That past version of German-ness is gone forever. The present situation demands a reassertion of the "possibility" of national community oriented to the future, taking into account the falseness of the present—that against which the idea of Germany must be reasserted, and which consequently shapes its future as different from the present. In a paragraph whose importance Heidegger signaled by italicizing the whole and bold-facing the key temporal terms he wrote that "*Only an entity which, in its Being, is essentially* **futural** *. . . can, by handing down to itself the possibility that it has inherited, take over its own thrownness and be* **in the moment of vision** *for 'its time'*" (437; boldface in original). "For its time"—to have an authentic future, Dasein must adapt the eternal idea of Germany to the present situation, which is after all what it factically *is*, into which it has been thrown and which it cannot escape.

And when it does so Dasein will at last constitute itself as a connected whole. "The Self's resoluteness against inconstancy of distraction, is in itself a *steadiness which has been stretched along*—the steadiness with which Dasein as fate 'incorporates' into its existence birth and death and their 'between' and holds them as thus incorporated" (442). This is the very definition of modern identity. Identity is the self's unity through time, and that can be achieved only through active commitment to and the sustaining of a continuous idea that gives every moment of life, retrospectively and prospectively, the same meaning. The totality of one's life comes under one's control in the realization of identity: one need not wait until death to sum up one's life because one has its meaning already in view before death, and one redeems the inauthentic present and its falsely interpreted past by understanding its relation to that same meaning. But that ideal is not different in content from what Dasein already is in its thrownness. "Resoluteness," he wrote, "constitutes the loyalty of existence to its own Self. . . . [T]his loyalty is at the same time a possible way of revering the sole authority which a free existing can have—of revering the repeatable possibilities of existence" (443). Heidegger recognized the contradiction of identity but insisted that it was only a paradox, not a contradiction. That Dasein is fated in its thrownness is no limitation on its freedom. That Dasein is free is not inconsistent with its being forever something over which it had no choice—being born into membership in a historical community.

The idea of revering repeatable possibilities, however, suggests that to Heidegger, the repeatable facticity of the past was not a "mere" facticity, as it would be for Sartre—that is, a contingent, accidental truth one might continue to sustain by acting on it or not. Rather, one's facticity was to be revered because it carried the aura of the metaphysically necessary, indeed, as the word "revered" suggested, of the holy. Though not metaphysically necessary in content, in the sense that every community's past was different—there is no universal history—the past of one's community was inescapably there for each human being, completely defining who she or he was. At the same time it guaranteed human freedom within that necessity, since instead of living it passively one could consciously take up one's past and promote it. The ultimately misleading but subtle ingenuity of Heidegger's argument consisted in this: though he insisted that one's past was only contingently necessary, thus apparently avoiding the determinist metaphysics of essentialist or thing-like identity, he characterized it as having one-dimensional content and one-directional thrust. In the concrete example of Germany, not only was one inescapably German, there was only one genuine kind of German-ness, only one way of being German. By interpreting "heritage" in this deterministic way, he in effect converted contingent into metaphysical necessity, or rather, he had his cake and ate it too. One's communal heritage is an accident of history yet it is one's unalterable destiny.

Precisely because the conceptual shaping of Heidegger's argument seemed to fit with Germany's historical situation so closely, it must constantly be kept in mind that it was meant as a fundamental analysis of the human, not just the German, condition. It would not otherwise have had the influence on the philosophical world that it did, or inspire the claim that Heidegger's philosophy is separable from his politics. The most immediate and plausible evidence for such a claim is its impact on Jean-Paul Sartre, as far from Heidegger's politics as can be imagined. Yet fashioning a general argument with a specific case in mind cannot avoid skewing the general categories. One might, for example, accept Heidegger's notion of heritage as the unavoidable facticity into which one is born and with which one must reckon, while objecting that it does not entail Heidegger's concept of destiny as a necessary, one-dimensional future orientation. One's heritage—national or religious—may be subject to a number of different interpretations, or arguments, as to its true meaning and as to how it is best adapted to change and to the future. The philosopher Alasdair MacIntyre would later take exactly such a position on the relationship between tradition and identity.[16]

Turning heritage into destiny fulfilled a two-fold desire on Heidegger's part: to theorize a valid concept of collective identity in general and to defend a conservative nationalist definition of German identity in particular. But the very way he did it was ultimately self-defeating. While there was no necessary contradiction between *Jemeinigkeit* and collective identity as such—one could consciously commit to the nationality into which one was born—there was also no *ontological* reason to argue that this was the only authentic response to it, let alone that Heidegger's conservative version of *Gemeinschaft* was the only authentic version of peoplehood. As some defenders of Heidegger themselves pointed out, the "facticity" of German nationality was not one-dimensional; it contained a number of historical possibilities, among them Weimar's democratic republicanism. There was no ontological reason to reject it as authentically German, as incompatible with "German-ness" in principle. More radically, there was no ontological reason to believe that the fact of German birth had to be "revered" as the sole repeatable possibility legitimately dictating one's future destiny. It was equally possible to disidentify with one's birth nationalism on behalf of another or (though more problematically than would-be cosmopolitans argued, as we will see) with all nationalisms. Heidegger's legislative sleight of hand on behalf of the communal destiny of birth could only be true for someone who in the end desired of identity the security of determinism that he himself had argued was inauthentic. His notion of collective identity transformed peoplehood into an inert thing whose characteristics, by Heidegger's own analysis of thinghood, had not been decided or chosen by Dasein. It was *vorhanden*, present at hand. The definition of German-ness could only be there for Dasein as given to it by some external authority, such as "tradition" or "the hero"; such authority thus became determinative for the individual's identity, precisely as *das Man* was for modern Dasein, as his tribal gods were for the "primitive" tribesman. To conceive national identity as "destiny" was no less an alienation of self in otherness than the modern's submission to *das Man* or the primitive's to the tribe.

Nothing better proved that such alienation was entailed by Heidegger's concept of peoplehood than his investing of Adolf Hitler six years later with the authority to determine the destiny of the German people. The blunt concreteness of his exhortation was shocking only in comparison with the remote abstractions of *Being and Time*, but it was wholly consistent with their import. "Doctrine and 'ideas' shall no longer govern your existence," he told students; "The *Führer* himself, and only he, is the current and future reality of Germany, and his word is your law."[17]

My point is *not* that Heidegger was already a Nazi in spirit when he wrote *Being and Time*. Nor is it even that *Being and Time* worked out the conceptual foundation that underlay his later formal commitment to Nazism (though I believe this to be true). The important issue for the history of modern identity is that the same book brilliantly, and fatally, undermined the possibility of a metaphysically substantive foundation for individual identity—the notion of the self's identity as thing-like, stable essence—only to reinstate it, presumably without the dubious metaphysics, in the context of a fixed substantive collective identity. This attempt, however, depended as I've argued on philosophic sleight of hand. That it took the historical form of affirming National Socialism compounded conceptual error with historical horror, and helped make the idea of collective identity for some forever suspect.

Jean-Paul Sartre: Self as the Negation of Identity

The essential difference between Jean-Paul Sartre's and Martin Heidegger's ontologies of the self is implied in the titles of their master treatises. *Being and Time* suggests that being is a positive concept to be explicated in terms of the temporal nature of human existence. Sartre's title, *Being and Nothingness*, sets one against the other. It suggests the negation—in fact the annihilation—of being, and with it the possibility of a philosophically acceptable concept of identity as permanence. That was precisely what Sartre intended. With ruthless consistency he carried through Heidegger's destruction of identity into every area of life where human beings tried to achieve it—from initial attempts at internal self-definition to the most intimate forms of human "being-with," love and sex, to which Heidegger's project was utterly indifferent, and finally to the kind of collective identity that was central to it. It has been claimed that Sartre's work was derivative of Heidegger, and this is certainly true of Sartre's fundamental argument that identity is an illusion and that existential anxiety is its motive. But Sartre's notorious conclusion that "man is a useless passion" because he seeks identity in vain was wholly antithetical to the redemptive spirit of Heidegger's rescue operation and was in fact Sartre's refutation of it.

To the difference in their conclusions there corresponds a difference in the historical contexts of their projects. Like Heidegger, Sartre was writing, albeit a decade later, in the shadow of the post-World War I disillusion with prevailing identities. In the case of both, furthermore, there was a deeply personal edge to their disillusion. There is an almost perverse similarity between Heidegger's disdain for urban middle-class modernity and Sartre's contempt for the French bourgeoisie.[18] On one level this was an expression of the not uncommon convergence of reactionary right and revolutionary left during the interwar years in rejecting bourgeois liberalism for its economic, political, and spiritual failures. But Sartre's hatred of the bourgeoisie was initially apolitical, or more accurately, not aligned theoretically or practically with left-wing politics, even if vaguely leftist in its social sympathies.[19] Sociologically, he was a representative of the middle-class high intelligentsia, that segment of the national leadership elite educated at the École Normale Supérieure that represented the contemporary version of the Enlightenment "republic of letters." Its members, though brought up in the French republican tradition, and in some cases adopting socialist and even communist politics, saw themselves above all as independent critics of society from the privileged vantage point of universal Reason. The theoretical ground of Sartre's attack on the fatuousness of liberal middle-class identity, unlike Heidegger's on *das Man*, left him with no fallback identity, which in any case he initially neither needed nor wanted. French nationalism in the virulently reactionary and anti-Semitic version represented by Action Française that he encountered in the 1920s and 1930s was just another aspect of the middle class's entitled arrogance and violent repressiveness.[20] Liberal humanism, which Sartre lampooned in the figure of the Self-Taught Man in *Nausea*, was a hypocritical sham. Even proletarian solidarity, however morally and politically understandable, was an ontologically dubious concept. Personally and politically, Sartre wrote *Being and Nothingness* from a social and psychological vantage point from which he could, as he ruefully put it years later in his autobiography *The Words*, cheerfully expose man's impossibility.[21]

For Heidegger, Dasein's apprehension of its "nothingness," its power to say no to apparently binding obligations and so realize its freedom, was only a moment on its way to authentic being. For Sartre, on the other hand, man's nothingness was everything in relation to his aspirations to "being," to wholeness, absoluteness, and timelessness. Heidegger did not introduce the idea of nothingness until well into his analysis of Dasein; Sartre's book began by introducing it as man's defining feature: "Man is the being through whom nothingness comes into the world."[22] Furthermore, Sartre deliberately defined man's "nothingness" from the outset in relation to the very "something" in which Heidegger found the ultimate source of Dasein's true identity, the past. Just as Heidegger had argued that our freedom reveals itself in our ability to contravene what we initially take to be absolutely binding morally, Sartre claimed that it reveals itself in our negating of the past as constraining us, determining who we forever *are*: "Freedom is the human being putting his past out of play by secreting his own nothingness." "Putting out of play" is not a deliberate, conscious act; it is the nature of consciousness to be separate from its past in its ability to reflect on it and thus distance itself from it. Even when consciousness isn't actively doing so it "continually experiences itself as the nihilation of its past being" (28).

There is, or can be, according to Sartre, crucial experiential evidence that we are in touch with our nothingness even if we don't know it consciously. We can know it in anguish, the emotion that tells us that we are absolutely free in the sense that nothing prevents us from doing anything at all. Most shockingly, nothing prevents us from doing even what we don't want to do; our psychological motives are not enough to determine our actions. The experience of vertigo proves this. Vertigo is not the fear of falling from a precipice but the fear of throwing myself over it. The fact is I *can* jump; furthermore, I know that I can, and even though I don't want to die, I might jump anyway. Perhaps, the psychologically inclined might add, I feel the urge to jump because I desire to challenge my fear, or my human limitations, or I also do want to die. But producing motives to jump would be beside Sartre's point. If I have conflicting motives, I must choose between them, and nothing can decide for me which one to act on. If I invoke yet a third motive as a criterion by which to choose between two opposing ones, it is my choice of it alone that validates the criterion. What I fear, then, in existential anguish, is myself, or rather, I fear for myself: "I am in anguish precisely because any conduct on my part is only *possible*. . . . My possibilities [are] filled with anguish because it depended on me alone to sustain them in their existence" (31, 35). More definitively, "It is certain that we can not overcome anguish for we are anguish" (43). But if so, why is the actual experience of anguish so rare? In the first instance, he answered, because of our thrownness, or, as he also put it, our always and necessarily being "in situation": we are involved in the world before we reflect on it, acting on its norms as the natural way things are before we are able to think of them as *my* possibilities. But beyond that there is the ultimate inner barrier to reflection: we don't *want* to think of ways of being as mere possibilities. We want the certainty of absolute necessity.

To argue that we know our freedom in and as anguish is to say that freedom terrifies and repels us because it negates our deepest need. Heidegger had talked about our anguish as a response to the realization that we are not "at home" in the world. Sartre first depicted it literarily in *Nausea* as a violent visceral and emotional response to a parallel anti-epiphany: we don't matter. We are not ultimately *necessary*. "The essential thing" that nauseates Roquentin "is contingency. I meant that one cannot define existence as necessity. To exist is simply *to be there*."[23] In *Being and Nothingness*, Sartre described anguish in more technical philosophical terms as the sense of being "separated from our essence." Essence is "everything in the human being which we can indicate by the words—that *is*" (35). The copula points both to the idea of the self-contained totality of a thing, and its nontemporality, its timeless "is-ness." That is the wholeness and timelessness we wish for. To be able to be that would make us feel necessary. But the only "essence" man is in touch with is the past, Sartre said, quoting Hegel's epigram partly for its rhetorical neatness: *Wesen ist, was gewesen ist*, essence is (only) what was. The past alone is permanent because it can't change. But even the past is only contingent—things could have happened otherwise—and in any case we can't simply be an inert extension of what was because we have to choose and act in the present. If we want the past to define us we have to choose to be continuous with it—and we do choose even if we simply don't choose to break from it. So much for Heideggerian "fated destiny."

One other way Sartre talked about the sense of "being" reveals more directly how symbiotic his theory of motivation, like Heidegger's, was with traditional Christian religion, in his case even more clearly Protestant. Just as there is nothing to appeal to in order to adjudicate among my conflicting motives, there is nothing, and no one, to appeal to in the sphere of ethics. "Absolutely nothing," Sartre said, "*justifies* me in adopting this or that particular value, this or that particular scale of values. As a being by whom values exist, I am *unjustifiable*. My freedom is anguished at being the foundation of values while itself without foundation" (38; italics added). We humans want to be "justified" in the sense of being "in the right," not legally or socially but absolutely. In the background, hardly hidden, lurks the Lutheran formula of "justification by faith." Sartre knew the idiom at first hand. He had grown up from infancy in the home of his liberal Protestant grandfather, Charles Schweitzer, who had trained for the ministry and "retained the Divine," as Sartre put it, even after abandoning it. Jean-Paul himself was a believer until the age of twelve.[24] Religion was not just an idiom for Sartre; the religious impulse was the wellspring of his understanding of the need identity fills. But he interpreted that impulse inversely from the believer. Religion was not the positive quest *for* Truth. It was, like every form of determinism that projected the meanings, norms, and desires motivating human action onto outside entities, an escape *from* truth. "Everything," Sartre wrote, "takes place . . . as if our essential and immediate behavior with respect to anguish is flight" (40).

It is how Sartre conceptualized the way we flee the anguish of our freedom/nothingness that makes *Being and Nothingness* a landmark in the history of identity. "The supreme value," he wrote, "toward which consciousness at every instant reaches beyond itself," he declared, "is *the absolute being of the self with* its *characteristics of identity, of purity, of permanence,* etc., and as its own foundation" (93; translation slightly modified; italics added). The idea of the "absolute being" of the self is to be taken at its face value. It is the heart of what Sartre called the fundamental human project, that which we all strive for. And identity is its key feature, entailing all the others he lists. To be an absolute self is to have an identity characterized by necessity, wholeness, goodness, and permanence.

Sartre derived his concept of "identity" from the Hegelian concept of consciousness as—ideally and ultimately—being one with, or identical with, itself. The motor of Hegel's philosophical system was the idea that human consciousness does not historically start out as identical but strives to become so. It comes into full self-possession and self-awareness only through a lengthy historical process that began with its self-alienation. Human consciousness originally perceived its full potentiality, its attributes, powers, and possibilities as existing in things outside itself. Above all the two essential dimensions of human possibility, freedom and "totality," man's capacity for universality, were seen by men to reside in external institutions and metaphysical powers: in the despotic, divinely ordained ruler, in capricious multiple gods, in natural law, in the transcendent creator God of Western monotheism as the source of absolute Law. Human consciousness was divided from itself because it did not realize that these beliefs and institutions were nothing but the projections and embodiments of its own ideals and aspirations. Through the long historical process of man's institutional and intellectual development, consciousness came gradually to recognize itself in otherness, to realize that what it had deemed external and coercive, like political sovereignty and the demands of ethical universality, were its own projections, residing in its own powers to realize, embody, and enact. The Protestant idea of salvation by faith in Christ as the union of the human and the divine unmediated by earthly authority was the ultimate symbolic realization of humanity's aspiration to unite its particular and universal, or finite and infinite natures within itself. Full human self-recognition, however, had only come to its climax and conclusion in the concrete achievement of the modern liberal state, which with its individualist economy and society and its legal institutionalization of equality of rights, realized concretely both individual human freedom and human universality, or ethical wholeness. This was the realization of the absolute idea.

Sartre's contribution to modern identity was to translate Hegel's analysis of the historical dialectic of universal human consciousness into an ontological dialectic of the individual personal consciousness. It was the individual who wanted to unite his particularity with wholeness, thus becoming one with himself, a universal yet also a unique and particular self. In his translation, Sartre turned Hegelian identity theory into a theory of individual identity. Except that, unlike for Hegel, the aim of the individual consciousness goal to become one with itself, to be both particular and universal, could in principle never be consummated.

To demonstrate its chronic failures in all their ironic and depressing specifics, Sartre adopted key terms from Hegel's philosophical vocabulary and in effect turned them against their originator. There are two basic kinds of entities in the world, which Hegel had called "for-itself" and "in-itself." These corresponded more or less to Heidegger's Dasein, human existence, and the *vorhanden*, entities without consciousness. For Sartre, consciousness and the for-itself were interchangeable because consciousness is reflexive, able to turn from attending to the world to look at its own content, at its mode of engagement with the world. Experience exists *for* consciousness. And the "for-itself-ness" of consciousness is in play even before reflection. One is always, even if only incipiently, self-aware. To know something is at the same time to know that one knows it.

The in-itself is the mode of being of things, inert, self-contained, and in that sense whole and unchanging. A table might be damaged, but then it is a damaged table, not changed in its essential being as table. In ontological terms, its being is just what it is (74); "a rose is a rose is a rose." The in-itself, however, is not just the kind of being of the material world other than the self. There are dimensions of the self that also have this sort of thing-like there-ness. This inertness is selfhood's facticity. Our past is one aspect of it; so are the bodies we are born with, the social structures we are born into, and not least, the presence of other people. None of these dimensions of our existence are of our choice or making, even if we may be able—within limits—to manipulate their circumstances.

How this relates to the experience of personal identity Sartre, with his gift for the particular example, illustrated in what became his most cited vignette, the "sincere" waiter. Sartre invoked the waiter as a paradigmatic example of bad faith, but the other side of that coin is that he is the quintessence of identity, described in the easily grasped terms of individual intention and belief. The waiter is "sincere" in that he genuinely believes himself to be a waiter. "Being" a waiter in his sense, in which one's every action feels internally determined by fixed and unchanging norms—"here I stand, I can no other"—is an instance of "the principle of identity" (58); self-consciousness takes itself to be the same as its object. The waiter in a word defines himself not just in terms of but *as* his social role; he is completely one with his "waiterhood."

To think of himself this way is, however, from the ontological point of view to falsify himself. He cannot "be what he is." In his very assertion "I am a waiter," his consciousness detaches the asserting/reflecting "I" from the waiter and regards it; he is no longer identical with it. In fact he never was. Nothing ever prevented him from ceasing at any time to wait on others (at whatever cost—Sartre was not concerned, as Maurice Merleau-Ponty was, with the practical ability to realize one's intention).[25] "In this sense," Sartre argued, "it is necessary that we *make ourselves* what we are" (59). At every instant the waiter sustains his identity by continuing to act like one. Sartre wasn't being metaphorical when he wrote that the man is "playing" at being a waiter, even if to drive the point home he ignored the weight of existential anguish in saying that the waiter was "amusing himself." Certainly the waiter as Sartre describes him is a caricature. His actions are stilted, formulaic, almost fanatical in their exactness; he bends forward too eagerly, his interest in his customer seems oversolicitous. But his point is that the waiter's "playacting" is not for fun, not for the theater of it nor even for bigger tips. In always acting as a waiter is supposed to act, the man is "playing with his condition in order to *realize* it." In other words, he does not want to act *as* a waiter, he wants *to be* one, the way a rock is a rock; his exaggerated behavior is above all an attempt to convince himself, and only secondarily his customers, that that is what he "is."

Ventriloquizing the waiter's demystified consciousness Sartre wrote, "What I attempt to realize is a being-in-itself of the café waiter, as if it were not just in my power to confer their value and their urgency upon my duties and the rights of my position, as if it were not my free choice to get up each morning at five o'clock or to remain in bed, even though it meant getting fired. As if from the very fact that I sustain this role in existence I did not transcend it on every side, as if I did not constitute myself as one beyond my condition" (60). This is the fatality of identity: I am always more than my identity. I sustain it, it doesn't determine me. Nor is this fatality limited to identity as social role. "I am never," he wrote, "any one of my attitudes, any one of my actions." As the rest of the book will demonstrate, this holds true for identities much more complex and subtle, more socially significant than the waiter with his mannered behavior.

First however, Sartre explained that there is in fact more to seeking identity than trying to escape nothingness by becoming one with one's facticity. Though desiring to escape its freedom, the self contradictorily doesn't want to deny its nature as a free consciousness. It doesn't want to be controlled and diminished by another consciousness. Hence it wants also to be the source of its objectified identity. In the waiter's case, he wants his existence to be both fully defined by his role and yet to have freely chosen it. Put in terms closer to their original religious inspiration, he wants to be both the creator of his identity and its creature. This duality would make the self completely self-contained—or would if consciousness could think of itself as absolute, not just *a* creator but *the* Creator. If it seems implausible that we can think so grandiosely of ourselves, Sartre wholly agreed. The power of our own consciousness to define us doesn't feel great enough. Our encounter with "the Other," who de-centers our world by making us feel like objects in his world, shows that quickly enough. It is the Other who seems to have the absolute power we lack. But in reality the Other is not different from us. He couldn't have the power to define us if it were not a projection of the power *we* have—or rather wish we had—to justify ourselves.

Our identity problem is that we know that our consciousness is not absolute, not self-contained, and hence not able to furnish the desired justification for who we are. We wouldn't need to be identical with something if we felt justified simply in existing, if we didn't feel our existence to be de trop, superfluous. Consciousness experiences itself as not being enough, as missing something, as a "lack" (86); this lack is evidenced in its very desire to become the in-itself, some solid, definite thing. As Sartre summarized things, "It is the self which *would be what it is* which allows the for-itself to be apprehended [by itself] as *not being what it is*; the relation denied in the definition of the for-itself . . . is a relation (given as perpetually absent) between the for-itself and itself *in the mode of identity*" (89; italics added). The "proof" of our subjective sense of lack of being is in our very desire to be Some*thing*, solid, permanent, necessary, of objective value. Of course by the same token, the knowledge that we *want* to be that Something reveals the futility of the project of identity, since we can never *just be* that Something.

Heidegger's concept of temporality was central to Sartre's description of the waiter's trying to realize his waiterhood through his exaggerated actions. His identity as waiter is underdetermined because he must always be making himself in the present what he was a moment ago, projecting his would-be identity into a future which will never be realized once and for all. Temporality enabled Sartre to formulate the contradictions of identity as the mind-bending paradoxes of the copula verb in which he reveled. In relation to its past, present, and future, the for-itself *is not what* is and *is what it is not* (137; italics added). With regard to the past, the self "is what it is not and is not what it is" because while we *are* inescapably our past—"we can not take a new decision except in terms of it" (496)—we are also *not it*, since we nullify its determinism by having to choose it at every moment if we are to sustain it. In fact, our choices in the present can even change what the past means. If I change my religion, I will reinterpret my past identity as myself-in-error, or myself-in-a-phase-that-led-up-to-myself-now. With regard to my present new religion, however, I am also simultaneously "it and not it." I practice my new religion diligently every day, and in that sense I *am* an X, but only in the mode of *not being one*, since I only sustain my religion by future acts of observance—which I am free not to perform.

Identity would be, were it realized, the denial of our temporality, our "having to be." It fulfills man's "desire of being-in-itself," the desire to have "the impermeability and infinite density of the in-itself," to be a self the way a stone is a stone, while yet also being, as a choosing consciousness, the foundation of that being-in-itself, that which confers identity on the self (566). Our ambition to be the cause of ourselves is the way medieval theology described God's self-sufficiency, in contrast to the dependence of everything else on God's creation: God, and only God, is *causa sui*. This is what Sartre meant by his provocative claim that man's fundamental desire is to be God. If it seems extreme, however, it is only because the phenomenology of experience implied by the words didn't get the feeling texture of many concrete identities right. For many, probably most identity seekers in Sartre's sense, it was enough to be the "child of God," whose worth and timelessness is guaranteed by His—so long as we could also conceive Him as justifying us, or get him to do so. This is in fact precisely what Sartre would set out to demonstrate with his introduction of the idea of the Other.

"If at first you don't succeed, try, try, try again," the proverb exhorts; "Ever tried. Ever failed. No matter. Try again. Fail again. Fail better," runs

Samuel Beckett's existential inversion. Together both describe the dramatic structure of *Being and Nothingness*. The for-itself does try again and again to achieve identity. Each succeeding effort works at a higher level of complexity, avoiding the contradictions of the previous one, only to contradict itself in more complex and subtle ways. It is only in this sense that the for-itself "fails better." The more complete version of Beckett's aphorism ends with ultimate failure. So does Sartre; *Being and Nothingness* purported to exhaust all the possible ways of trying, and failing, to achieve identity.

The first in ontological simplicity, though not in the chronology of human development, depends on the for-itself alone. Consciousness tries to constitute identity through an act of internal self-definition. That is what the waiter is doing by throwing himself so completely into his role. It is as if identity were an unspoken declaration to oneself—this is what I am—though it employs elements of facticity, here social role, that originate outside the individual consciousness. Sartre called this kind of attempt at identity "impure reflection," because it falsifies what happens in being conscious-of-oneself, where the for-itself creates a gap between itself as reflecting and itself as reflected-on. Because consciousness is always prereflectively aware of the gap, it is in being dishonest with itself, acting in "bad faith," when it claims to believe there is seamless identity between them, that the person acts as it does only "because he is a waiter" and can do no other.

Superficially it might seem difficult to imagine the desire to be God realizing itself in the low status occupation of waiter. But, Sartre argued, to accept one's inferiority does not necessarily mean to be content with it. One might assume it in an internal rebellion against the facticity of one's lowly status, with the aspiration to reach a place one believes is higher or better. In a yet unhappier relation to the facticity of low status, one might prefer to be the last in status rather than be lost in the mass, or even to choose "discouragement and shame as the best means of attaining *being*" (472). The choice of humiliation can only be fully explained through Sartre's analysis of sadism and masochism in relations with the Other. I bring it in here to point out that the example of the waiter doesn't necessarily contradict the qualities of absoluteness the in-itself must have to make it worthy of self-identification. But there are more cogent reasons not to dismiss it.

There are two qualities that the in-itself appears to have when consciousness deems it worthy of identification. One emerges in Sartre's critique of Freud's idea of the unconscious. The unconscious is ostensibly the "real me," the part of me that determines my actions but which is at the same time "not me," acting on me as an external causal force. Its supposedly object-like existence outside consciousness is precisely its attraction for identity. Through psychoanalysis I can finally know who I really am: my id, my complexes. This is the model for all identifications through which one constructs identity. Since I know myself to be metaphysically unnecessary, the in-itself that I wish to be one with must also be other than me, pure objectivity, not tainted by my freedom (155). Second, the in-itself must appear to have fullness of being, an idea my consciousness grasps in its very knowledge of the finitude of things but knows itself unhappily not to be (177). With these in mind we can begin to understand why a waiter might in fact be quite content with his role, as the philosopher Kwame Anthony Appiah would argue later about the butler Mr. Stevenson in Kazuo Ishiguro's novel *The Remains of the Day*. Stevenson genuinely seeks nothing more than to be the best butler he can be. Individual social roles are not isolated things; they are elements of a large-scale social construct that has been endowed—that we have endowed—with objective legitimacy. "Among the thousands of ways which the for-itself has of trying to wrench itself away from its original contingency there is one which consists in trying to make itself recognized by the Other as an existence by right. We insist on our individual rights only within the compass of a vast project which would tend to confer existence on us in terms of the function which we fulfill. This is the reason why man tries so often to identify himself with his function and seeks to see in himself only the 'Presiding Judge of the Court of Appeal,' the 'Chief Treasurer and Paymaster,' etc. Each of these functions has its existence justified by its end. To be identified with one of them is to take one's own existence as saved from contingency" (485). Individual roles have behind them the imprimatur of Society with a capital "S."

The full explication of the possibility of social role as necessary identity involves—demands—the presence of "the Other." This is not simply because roles are socially constituted, nor because we are born into a ready-made division of labor we must eventually occupy. These are merely empirical sociological and developmental facts. They don't explain the apparent metaphysical legitimacy that social structure acquires through the belief that it exists as a matter of right. The "recognition" of rights—which is in truth only their conferral—does not come just from empirical others. It comes from "the Other" with a capital O.

The Other is the consciousness of another person as absolute consciousness, as having the power to found and justify my identity that I myself don't have. The Other feels ontologically necessary for identity because the attempt of one's own consciousness to become one with some in-itself is doomed to failure. Consciousness can't constitute itself as a totality. We can't take a view of or grasp ourselves as a whole because we are also the observers; any effort to observe the observer obviously leads to an infinite regress. The self-constituted identity can never have the fullness of being our contingency desires; further-more, we know this. The only apparent way out of the impasse would be via a consciousness that I can somehow believe *is* able to constitute me as a whole, a consciousness outside me that can know the whole me, me as I really am. That is the consciousness, and the role, of the Other.

The concept of the Other was Sartre's most important contribution to the idea of identity, though as we will see later, it was in Simone de Beauvoir's version that it later became central to the politics of identity. For Sartre the Other was not originally a political concept, though power and conflict were always at its heart. It was an ontological category, the Other as absolute being.

Sartre addressed the problem of the Other with three questions in mind: why was another consciousness better positioned than my own to confer on me the identity I could not confer on myself? What evidence do we have that we were in fact relying on such a consciousness to achieve identity? What were the most important ways we used the Other to do so?

The answer to the first involves the role of the body in the constitution of identity. Initially Sartre alluded to it in another famous example of bad faith, the girl in the café flirtatiously allowing her companion to cover her hand while disavowing her act by pretending to be nothing but a disembodied con-sciousness engaging in intellectual conversation. The body however is just that element of facticity that allows us to believe that another could perceive us, get a purchase on us as a whole, because our bodies are circumscribed things in the world.[26] If Maurice Merleau-Ponty was the first philosopher to make the body central to our knowing the world,[27] Sartre was the first to make it central to identity.

We cannot do this ourselves because our bodies are not at first objects for us but a dimension of the for-itself. Consciousness is always embodied consciousness, that through which we grasp the world and orient ourselves in it. Concepts like near and far, fast and slow, big and small are produced through our embodied being-in-the-world. "Being for-itself," as Sartre put it, "must be wholly body and it must be wholly consciousness" (305). It is because the for-itself is body as well as consciousness that our experience of nothingness is not just anxiety but physical nausea or vertigo. As a result, however, the same problem that nullifies the possibility of our consciousness grasping itself as a whole nullifies the possibility of our grasping the body-self as a whole. When we turn to reflect on our body, it is through only our embodied consciousness that we can do so.

But the body *might* be known as a whole if we could take the point of view on it of another. My body is, after all, an object in the world. My body exists then as an object for others, for whom it is not a subjectively experienced, ungraspable for-itself. That is not to say that the body for others is like any other kind of object. On the one hand, the body for the other is animated; it is "life." At the same time, as a contingent material object, the body for another is inert "flesh," in Sartre's deliberately repellent term. It is through my awareness that my body is an object for others that it can also be an object for me, seen through the eyes of the other. But that awareness is of special importance to me. It is much more than the mere noting of a fact.

"O wad some Power / The giftie gie us / To see oursels as / ithers see us!" wrote Robert Burns. That, Sartre claimed, is indeed our most fervent wish, but in a spirit quite the opposite of Burns's. "It wad frae mony a / blunder free us," Burns continued, "an foolish notion: / What airs in dress an / gait wad lea'e us, / An e'en devotion." Seeing ourselves as others see us served a moral purpose for Burns: it would deflate us, humble our grandiosity. But in Sartre's view we want to know how the other sees us for a quite different purpose. Because our consciousness is enclosed in a determinate body, an object which others can see from the outside, we can plausibly imagine that they can do for us what we can't do for ourselves—get a purchase on us as a whole person. If I can then internalize the meaning of my body—my self—as it is for others, I can at last grasp myself as a whole, as what my being truly *is*. This desire reveals itself in my response to "the look" of the other.

Rather than expose the error of self-regard, as Burns thought, the look of the other produces it. Solipsism argues that we can't prove the existence of other consciousnesses because we can't experience another's subjectivity. However much that entity over there looks, talks, and acts like me, I can't *know* whether it has subjective experiences like my own. Nonetheless I don't react to him as if he were just the probabilistic hypothesis of a self; I react with the utter certainty that he is one. More than that, I act as if his consciousness is more authoritative than my own, one that can see the Truth of who I am. I experience the other not just as a contingent consciousness but as absolute consciousness, not merely as "an" other but as "the Other." This experience can't be knowledge; it can only be that I *want* the Other to be such an absolute consciousness. It is what psychoanalysis calls a fantasy wish fulfillment. While at certain points Sartre seemed to be arguing that our immediate experience of the Other refutes solipsism, his analysis in fact depends on the truth of its argument.

Dazzling as it is as phenomenological description, Sartre's analysis of "the look" can mislead if it is taken to reveal the necessary structure of all encounters with another. As description, it is self-enclosed; it only "proves" what it shows.[28] But Sartre was right to believe that it revealed a great deal about actual human relationships, more at any rate than critics of his sweeping onto-logical claims have seemed comfortable with. The quest for identity as self-certainty and security reaches far, and it is through others that we commonly try to achieve it.

In the look I become self-conscious about being looked at by another—whether he is actually looking at me or not. I am no longer the center of a world of experience, looking at things, but have become an object in his world. This is not a neutral experience; it is fraught with anxiety and the potential for shame because it matters to me how he looks at me. But I have made it matter, I have made him into an, or rather *the*, Other because of what he as the Other can do for me: "I, who in so far as I am my possibles, am what I am not and am not what I am—behold now I am somebody!" (263)—in other words, I have an identity. I have become this "somebody" only because I let the Other's freedom be greater than my own, in fact, absolute; not I but he or she is God. "I experience the Other's infinite freedom. It is for and by means of a freedom and only for and by means of it that my possibilities can be limited and fixed" (270). Only if I project the Other as absolute being can he limit my freedom and confer an identity on me as something definable: I am as he sees me to be. In his biography of Baudelaire a few years later Sartre also interpreted such projection developmentally as the way children first perceive their parents: not just as the nurturers and protectors their physical frailty requires, not as Freudian love-objects, but as Gods who lay down the absolute law of How Things Are that children's existential frailty demands.

What, however, if the look is negative? What if the Other looks at me belittlingly, with disdain or contempt? Self-identity as "the absolute being of the self" necessarily includes the idea of its objective value. The human desire "to be" is the desire for solidity, permanence, *and* goodness. Projecting the absolute freedom of the Other to define me is as dangerous as it is promising. This is the central dilemma of trying to use Otherness as the source of identity. Sartre's analysis of our concrete relations with others reveals them all as varia-tions of the only two strategies we have to cope with it.

His descriptions of love and sex, masochism and sadism are familiar.[29] Here I want to emphasize the different consequences the two strategies have for identity. They may be labeled for convenience passive and active strategies, though the terms are misleading; each strategy is both, though only one domi-nates consciousness. Sartre called the passive strategy "the first attitude toward others" because it begins with my sense of being (my wish to be) an object for the Other; it keeps my facticity in the foreground of consciousness and sup-presses awareness of my freedom. The active strategy, "the second attitude," is motivated by the failure of the first. It foregrounds my freedom and suppresses my facticity.

Love is the quintessential passive identity strategy. Loving means "recognizing," that is, projecting, the Other's absolute freedom and value; being loved by such a One thus justifies my existence. This is identity in the passive voice, the identity of the *Beloved*: "I identify myself totally with my being-looked-at" (365). At the same time, since the Other's absolute freedom can by definition at any time devalue or abandon me, I need to control it, though without acknowledging to myself that I can or even want to; to be able to manipulate the Other would contradict the absoluteness of his freedom. Concealing from myself my effort to actively seduce the Other, I try to make myself the *indispensable object* of his desire. But passive identity undermines itself by the very effort, let alone by such power as I might have to actually affect the Other's supposed self-sufficiency and impermeability. To want to be indispensable to the Other means to want to limit him by making me *his* supreme value. Sartre's formulation typically made the inherent contradiction as blatant as possible: "He wants to be loved by a freedom but demands that this freedom as freedom should no longer be free" (367). To put it in its original religious terms, God *must* love me unreservedly, but his love must be *freely* granted.

If awareness of the contradiction breaks through, I may try to sink deeper into passivity through masochism. The masochist seeks complete surrender to the Other, to be nothing but his object, courting abjection and pain to reduce his conscious self to a mere tool for the Other. But masochism too inevitably fails; insofar as the masochist must make himself into the object he wishes to be (which in contemporary versions of SM the masochist can undo simply by uttering a "safe-word") he is asserting his own free subjectivity.

Having failed at passivity, we may renounce it and move instead to be active in relation to the Other. This may superficially seem also like the renunciation of identity itself. By consciously enacting our freedom vis-à-vis others, we seem to be giving up the quest to be defined as something, to be limited and definite. But so long as *an* other is *the* Other to us, identity is still the goal of relationship. Being the sexual aggressor, the Lover, is the quintessentially active identity strategy. By coming on to the Other sexually I want to arouse her physical desire, ultimately stripping away her conscious being and reducing her to quivering flesh, pure materiality. But in that very effort I testify both to my acknowledgement of the Other's idealized personhood, her absolute freedom, as well as to my own inert fleshiness. Why would I want to reduce the Other to flesh if I did not in fact perceive her as a free consciousness who can reject me? It is just that absolute personhood that I want to rob her of in making her physically desire me. And tellingly, the way I do that is by myself becoming nothing but my physical desire for her. "Desire is not only the desire of the Other's body; it is . . . the . . . lived project of being swallowed up in the body. . . . The desire which desires is consciousness making *itself* body" (389). In the throes of desire, one's aspiration is to be the incarnate body. And the desire for sexual possession of the Other is "reciprocal incarnation": "I make myself flesh in order to impel the Other to realize for-*herself* and for-me her own flesh" (391). Ironically, then, sexual climax is the failure of desire—not for the contingent reason that after it desire subsides but because pleasure "motivates the appearance of a reflective consciousness of pleasure" (397). Consciousness pulls away from its attempted absorption in the body and becomes detached reflection, or nothingness, once again.

The postcoital sadness of inevitable detachment may also motivate a more violent attempt to reduce the Other to flesh, sadism. The sadist no longer wishes to be flesh himself but pure consciousness, a "free appropriating power" that uses the Other as his instrument and makes her feel her fleshiness as pain and humiliation. Sadism is nonetheless a blind alley rather than the road to identity for the same reasons all identity projects fail: here because the sadist, in enjoying the possession of the Other is trying to deny his own body yet must use it as the instrument for giving pain. Furthermore when the Other seems revealed to me in her pure facticity as flesh, desire for her rises up in me once more, and the vicious circle begins another cycle, the eternal recurrence of the same futility.

It is both jarring and unremarkable that the active and passive modes of identity-making are clearly "gendered," as we say today, male and female. It is of course jarring to the modern egalitarian sensibility. But it is also philosophically jarring because "consciousness" and the Other were intended as ontological, not empirical, categories that define ultimate human reality; embodiment is our common facticity, and thus all the variants of interpersonal relationships as Sartre described them are necessarily both active and passive. It is unremarkable on the other hand both because Sartre's identification of activity with masculinity and passivity with femininity was stereotypical for his time, and more importantly because his bias did not affect the essential point of his ontological analysis. It did not matter for the question of identity as an ontological category if one sex were consciously or initially more active than the other. Were women to be "active" in Sartre's sense, love and sex would be no less futile as ways of achieving identity. Critics who focus on Sartre's masculinist bias are both right and miss the point. It was not about sexual, or gender, identity, despite the importance of the factical body in his ontology, which led to his even coarser masculinist identification of femaleness with holes and slime (609, 613). It was about identity as "being"; (male) dread of these features of the (female) body is ultimately dread of nothingness, which men (and women who experience shame about the vagina) wrongly identify with one possible representation of them.[30]

Something similar might be said about critics who focus on Sartre's claim that human relationships are inherently conflictual. Here Sartre was even more directly responsible for a provocation that diverted attention from his main concern. Human relationships are necessarily conflictual to the extent that each tries to use another to achieve identity, because in that attempt each imagines the Other as simultaneously all-powerful ally and all-powerful enemy, and therefore tries to subdue the Other's power to his own purpose. But the view of another as the Other is, the way Sartre interpreted it in *Being and Nothingness*, a wholly internal fantasy resulting from the quest for identity; conflict is an inevitable consequence of that fantasy. Others may, and often do, happily play the parts in the real world into which we cast them in fantasy because of their own identity needs, but what that means is that conflict in the world, *insofar as it is a conflict of identity fantasies*, is the result of a folie à deux. Which is of course not to say that its often-disastrous consequences are only fantasy.

It is precisely the fact that the Other is a construction of the individual quest for identity that led to Sartre's interpretation of the impossibility of collective identity. The very brevity of Sartre's treatment of the subject by comparison with his treatment of the couple-in-relationship was a rebuke to Heidegger. Sartre had no problem with the notion of being-with as an ineluctable factical reality of being-in-the-world. The crucial difference was that Sartre's ontology of identity left no possibility of an "authentic" being with others. Quite to the contrary, any form of collective identity could only be another illusory quest.

The possibility of a collective identity, a "we-subject," entails the idea of a plurality of free subjectivities which recognize one another as such. But this would contradict the "primal" experience of my being-as-object for the Other and of the Other's being-as-object for me (413). Since we do in fact say "we," what can we mean by using the collective subject pronoun? Its meaning can only be rooted, Sartre argued, in our experience of yet another consciousness, a "Third" who looks at me and another as objects for it. "We" exist as a collective identity first as objects for others, before we can exist together as subjects. Group identity is not initially a "we-subject" but an "us-object," an object in virtue of some common feature the Third picks out in order to identify us with one another. This Third consciousness is the Other in relation to the group of us. We buy into its objectification of us for the same reason the individual buys into the desire to be loved by the Other. The Third consciousness seems more powerful than ours, absolute in relation to us, able to see "us" for who we really are.

At that point the dynamic of self-Other that operates between the members of a dyad in love and sex can unfold between the Third and the group of people objectified by him. The "us" can turn on him and try to make him into "our" object; it is in doing so that we constitute ourselves as "we," a group of subjectivities acting in concert. But the ontological status of the "we" is no different from that of the "I" which is using the Other to constitute my identity. We have become a collective identity only in our combined efforts to control the consciousness of the Third who has already defined us. "We" as a collective do not constitute an ontologically basic category because in the very act of rebelling against it the individuals composing it have each accepted their object status for the Third, defining themselves as he has defined them. "The experience of the We-subject," Sartre asserted, "is a pure psychological, subjective event *in a single consciousness*" (425; italics added). This psychological event must be in bad faith, since in constituting myself as one of the "we," I am actually letting the objectified "us" define me first. In Heideggerian terms, this is just another way of being "*das Man.*"

It should be clear that Sartre was not talking about the "factical" social situations of groups he offered as examples of "us-object" and "we-subject" but about their *identities*, about how they are defined, first in the eyes of the Others and consequently in their own. Individuals work in factories; they do not have a common identity a priori. It is only in the eyes of factory owners that they are not differentiated individuals but "workers" with a fixed—and, of course, inferior—set of characteristics. "Workers," however, may transform themselves internally from "them/us" to "we, the proletariat," a group that can assert themselves positively and make demands on the bosses. Yet they remain, in their identities, in thrall to the capitalists so long as they understand themselves as "workers," even if workers militant. As we will see shortly, however, this very example raised fundamental issues about identity that Sartre could not solve within his ontological framework. If all consciousnesses are ontologically equal, why and how does one group get to define another in the first place, while the other lets itself be defined? This became a central question for Sartre when he turned to politics after World War II.

* * *

There is no underestimating the fundamental importance of Heidegger's and Sartre's early work for the history of identity. If identity is taken to mean the answer to the question "Who or what am I," both philosophers showed that the apparently simple copula verb contains an irreducible ambiguity. It is betrayed by the two words "who" and "what," which the question slides over as if they were equivalent. The phenomenological approaches of *Being and Time* and *Being and Nothingness* offered fine-grained descriptions of the *inner experience* of the "am-ness" in "who or what I am." They showed that it could refer to two very different possible ways of experiencing time and the weight of circumstance. One was as a purely empirical description of one's present situation, with no necessary implications for the future or change. "I am a doctor" could be consistent with the possibility that one knew that one had chosen to pursue the practice of medicine and might also choose to abandon it. But this was not the ordinary state of mind of someone who asserted identity according to Heidegger and Sartre. It was rather an assertion of the felt inertia of thingness, with the determinist implication that one had been destined to be and would always be that something. A more nuanced version might concede the freedom that allowed a person to actively embrace one's destiny or fail to see it or even reject it. In all such cases, however, destiny in this sense was the result of a world ordained. Martin Luther's apocryphal words "Here I stand, I can no other," are the quintessential expression of this state of mind and reveal its origin in the appeal, conscious or unconscious, to transcendent necessity. After Heidegger and Sartre, identity could never legitimately be grounded in an ontology of metaphysical necessity, inert thingness. Heidegger ingeniously tried to rescue the certainty of identity by anchoring it in historical necessity. One does not, after all, have a choice about the circumstances of one's birth. There is such a thing as contingent, even if not metaphysical necessity. But as Sartre argued, contingent necessity only circumscribes choice. Even if Heidegger were right about being fully defined by the one-directional destiny of one's people, there would always be the choice of taking it up or refusing to take it up as "mine." But Heidegger was of course also wrong about the absolute determinism of national destiny, even if, despite his own disastrously failed political choice, he could never admit it.

Chapter 3

Identity Becomes a Word:
Erik Erikson and Psychological Identity

"We begin to conceptualize matters of identity," Erik Erikson wrote when he introduced the word in its psychological sense to a broad public, "at the very time in history when they become a problem."[1] Thus he staked his claim to originality while acknowledging that only large-scale historical change made it possible.

Erikson believed from the outset that "identity" was a radically new psychological idea. Though—as he knew—Erich Fromm had used the word in a psychological sense before him, though the existential philosophers had been concerned with much the same issue, if from a different point of view, he was largely right. Identity was never a central category for Fromm. Both Heidegger and Sartre were at pains to deny that in explicating the ontological character of Dasein and consciousness they were doing (merely) empirical psychology. It was precisely psychology, however—the stages of human development, the subjective feeling states and inner conflicts of individuals in concrete situations—that Erikson was concerned with. Most salient of all, for the existentialists, identity was a temptation to be overcome; for Erikson, it was something positive to be achieved.

This last is fundamental to the difference between the existential and the psychological concepts of identity. For the philosophers, the critical gauge of identity was fidelity, or lack of it, to ontological truth (though as we saw fidelity carried with it a strong if unacknowledged implication of ethical demand); from that point of view identity was a lie. For Erikson the therapist, the goal was not philosophical truth but psychological health. He first formulated his notion of identity in clinical work with World War II veterans suffering from what was then called battle fatigue. As he came to understand it, their ultimate emotional problem was that under the stresses of war, because of what they had done or seen, they had lost their previous sense of who they were, and were left adrift in unmasterable anxiety.[2] The concept of existential anxiety did not depend on the evidence of felt experience; to the contrary, it could best be deduced from the most successful efforts to escape it. The anxiety of identity loss was by contrast all too palpable. As an empirically derived need, identity seemed immediately testable by the vicissitudes of everyday experience.

A few years later, generalizing to normal human development, Erikson asserted, with dramatic urgency, that "in the social jungle of human existence, there is no feeling of being alive without a sense of ego identity."[3] The savage metaphor referred not only to the recent bloody conflict but even more to the longer historical moment, the social upheavals of modernity and its ongoing conflicts out of which the war itself had come. His sense that psychic chaos emerged from social chaos would deeply mark the content as well as the occasion of his new concept. Though pointedly psychological, Erikson's concept was not, he would always insist, *just* psychological.

The mostly implied, sometimes explicit contrast he intended was with psychoanalysis, the movement in which he had been professionally reared. In contemporary orthodox psychoanalytic theory, all neurotic conflict was purely "intrapsychic," between unconscious desires within the self. Further, such desires, according to Freud's metapsychology—his basic explanatory theory—were the mental representatives of the biological drives. This paradigm made desire and conflict both universal and largely impermeable to social influences. Even Freud's introduction of the superego as the internalized parent images (which also incorporated societal norms) did not fundamentally change his understanding of psychic causality, since both the child's need to resolve the Oedipus complex and the failures that resulted in repression and neurosis were rooted in biological necessity and constitutional factors. For Erikson, however, identity was as much social as psychological from the beginning. The first time the word appeared in his published work was in the phrase "group identity," which he defined as "a group's basic ways of organizing experience" for its children in terms of its economic system and above all as the "inventory of social prototypes" it makes available for the child's identification.[4] Individual identity is always, he asserted, a *"variant of a group identity"*;[5] as for identity pathology, "there is no individual anxiety which does not reflect a latent concern common to the immediate and extended group."[6] His belief in the integral relationship between group and individual identity was not incidental to his introduction of the word identity itself. One of his explicit purposes in adapting what had been till then a casual term in ordinary language for technical psychological use was to create a new discourse to mediate between the psychological and the sociohistorical, and thus to change the exclusively intrapsychic focus of contemporary psychoanalytic theory. For contemporary organized psychoanalysis this was not a timely intervention, and Erikson would be throughout his life a problematic, even marginal figure within it.

First Definitions

Though Erikson was a notoriously unsystematic writer, with something like an aversion to theoretical precision, his first published definition of personal identity—the first of many—was both succinct and dense with implication. "The conscious feeling of having a personal identity," he wrote, "is based on two simultaneous observations: the immediate perception of one's *selfsameness and continuity in time*; and the simultaneous perception of the fact that *others recognize one's sameness and continuity*."[7] Having an identity is on this definition first and foremost a subjective matter for the individual, an affectively toned perception *of* the self *by* the self. This does not preclude the role of others; on the contrary, subjective belief in its recognition by others is a constituent of self-identity. Erikson's definition was a phenomenology, not a causal theory, though for him the two were mutually entailed: no feeling of recognition without de facto recognition. Early on he thought of it as a conscious feeling, not necessarily couched in the language of identity—people had identities before they called them that—but of what it connotes: selfsameness and continuity. Later he extended this feeling to include unconscious strivings for continuity of personal character when the sense of selfsameness came under threat.[8] And he always thought of the identity crisis in adolescence, the process of creating selfsameness, as going on at a mostly unconscious level.

It is his idea of selfsameness that crucially marked Erikson's concept of personal identity off from Locke's. Identity is not just continuity of memory through whatever changes the self may undergo, but a feeling of the sameness of one's *substantive content* through time. The experience/belief in such an unchanging personal essence was just what Heidegger and Sartre were trying to demystify with their critiques of the thing-like "being" of presence-at-hand and bad faith. Both of these states achieved a sense of permanence by denying temporality and choice in the language of (timeless) "being," and Erikson frequently used similar linguistic terms—copula verbs whose illocutionary force was to affirm steady self-states and deny the flux of temporality—to describe the feeling of identity. A child's sense of identity, he wrote about one of his most vivid clinical vignettes, is the feeling of *"being* one's self, of *being all right*, and of being on the way to becoming what other people, at their kindest, take one *to be*."[9]

This second definition, however, seriously complicated the idea of self-sameness. Identity doesn't just want to be permanent and solid; it wants to be *good*, to be "all right." Our identities, Erikson pointed out later, *can* be negatively toned, because having a negative identity is emotionally preferable to having none at all; as Nietzsche had put a parallel insight about the terrors of nihilism, man would rather have nothingness as his purpose than not have a purpose. But humans are inherently valuing creatures, and first we want to be of value in ourselves. This is the source of another problem: we cannot initially be so *for* ourselves, since we begin as infants and children at the mercy of an unknown world far more powerful than ourselves. Having a positive identity depends, therefore, on positive recognition by more powerful others, even if, ideally, external recognition is eventually internalized to become inner self-valuation. And finally, because we keep developing even after adolescence—one of Erikson's major breaks with classical psychoanalysis—identity is dynamic. In his famous life cycle scheme, identity development continues until death. This was his ultimate paradox: identity is simultaneously being *and* becoming, status *and* process. The developmental perspective created logical problems for the concept (and existential problems for the living) by introducing the subjective awareness of time and change into an experience that was supposed to provide a sense of permanence and stability. Erikson would address this tension many times, never with explicit mention of the contradiction it seemed to entail but always deeply attentive to its concrete psychological, historical, and even political ramifications. It was—and remains—the foremost problem in any formulation of identity.

Origins

Biography

History and politics presided over the genesis of Erikson's concept of identity, both as personal biography and world event. In his early writings he explicitly made world history part of his explanation for the emergence of identity as a psychological theme. Only relatively late in life, however, did he acknowledge that his own personal history had attuned him in childhood to the problem he would name identity by making him feel "marginal in regard to family, nation, religion and profession," living life on the boundary between conflicting designations in each of these spheres.[10] In private correspondence he was even more straightforward. "Without a deep identity conflict," he once wrote a friend, "I would not have done the work I did."[11] It took a deeply researched investigative biography, however, to reveal just how profound, troubling, and unresolved were the inner conflicts he came to call "identity diffusion."

He was born the illegitimate son of a Danish Jewish mother and a father who would remain forever unknown to him, but who he came to believe—or hope—was a Danish Gentile, aristocrat, and artist. His mother and German Jewish stepfather, a doctor who married her when Erik was three, lied to him about his origins, telling him first that his stepfather was his biological father, then that it was his mother's Danish Jewish first husband. He came to doubt each story in turn, but had only rumors and wishes to oppose to them. Tall, blond, and blue-eyed, he was mocked as a "goy" in synagogue, and a Jew at school. During the First World War he was attacked by his German classmates for being Danish and became in reaction an ardent German patriot. Through adolescence he was increasingly alienated from his adoptive father's Judaism and drawn to Protestantism, though he never formally rejected the first nor embraced the second. Of the educated middle class, a Gymnasium graduate on a professional track, he nevertheless did not attend university, defying his stepfather's wish that he study medicine, and attempted instead the bohemian life of a wandering artist. Ultimately he was drawn to the socially marginal profession of psychoanalysis, which combined healing and art, putative father and real stepfather, but in which he would become an outsider twice over by breaking with the psychoanalytic orthodoxy of his teachers. Fearing the worst when the Nazis came to power in Germany, he left Vienna for Copenhagen and tried to reacquire the Danish citizenship he had lost by German adoption; when Denmark refused him, dubious about refugee psychoanalysts, he had no recourse other than exile once again. His parents would leave two years later for Palestine; completely removed from Zionism, he was able to immigrate to the United States in virtue of his wife's American citizenship. He was thirty-one years old, a cultured Central European in a raw New World whose language he did not speak. Though his inner familial, religious, and national conflicts were not fully revealed until after his death, their force might have been divined in his change of name when he became an American citizen in 1939, from his stepfather's all too German Jewish Homburger to the self-chosen Scandinavian-Gentile Erikson. The new name indicated the social choice of his non-Jewish identity, while simultaneously asserting his self-identification as his own father, one who had fashioned his own identity. But his enormous distress and embarrassment at public accusations late in his life that he, the preacher of identity integrity, had deliberately concealed his Jewish origins suggested that internally the matter was far from settled.[12]

Ideology

If, however, Erikson insisted that individual identity was a variant or expression of group identity, it was not from a desire to conceal personal conflicts; it was because he felt and understood them to be historically representative. His conflicting identifications were personal versions of the tensions within and the radical differences between the various collectives and changing historical eras to which he belonged. It was his sense of historical representativeness that allowed him to generalize a personal sense of identity diffusion into a universal category. At the same time the specifics of his historical situation shaped many of the general formulations of the identity concept. This vector of influence he was much less aware of; while he insisted that history provided the occasion for the discovery of identity, identity would always be for him a universally valid category. When he was criticized for this by feminists and others during the upheavals of the 1960s, he was not able to make distinctions between what might be essential to identity as a universal category and what might be the features of its historically specific formulation in his work.

One of the most significant historical factors in the genesis of Erikson's concept of identity has to do with what he was *not*, in the spectrum of contemporary European ideologies: he was not a Marxist. This meant first and foremost that "class" was never for him a central, let alone the definitive category for interpreting the social world. What was true in Erikson's case would prove true once again when psychological identity was analytically extended from individual to group identity from the late sixties on: the category of identity would implicitly function as an alternative to that of class. Significantly it was Jean-Paul Sartre, existentialist newly turned Marxist in the mid-1940s, who first made the point about the theoretical incommensurability of identity and social class at the very time Erikson was introducing the idea of psychological identity. Sartre argued that the Marxist categories could not adequately encompass the immediate psychological and historical situation of colonial Africans. Black intellectuals, he wrote, coined the term "negritude" and celebrated its virtues not because they felt economically exploited but because they had been made to feel that their human essence was inferior to that of whites.[13] Although there was no reason why identity could not logically encompass class as one of its subcategories—Erikson himself casually included it—the reverse was not true. A theoretical framework that viewed "real" group membership in terms of economically based social classes (as opposed to the ideological false consciousness in which it might be described by its members) could not logically generate an explanatory category of identity superordinate to class or even coordinate with it. Not surprisingly, many later twentieth-century critics of economic and social inequality would find the increasing predominance of identity thinking a serious obstacle to the kind of social consciousness and analysis they believed necessary to support structural economic and social reform.[14]

The exception that tests and confirms the conceptual dissonance between Marxism and identity is the case of Erich Fromm. There is little doubt that

Erikson first came upon the word identity in Fromm's popular and influential effort to explain the susceptibility of the German middle class to Nazism, *Escape from Freedom*, published in 1941. Like Erikson, Fromm was a psychoanalyst and Jewish refugee from Germany who had broken with psychoanalytic orthodoxy to argue for the social and historical determinants of psychic structure. Unlike Erikson, he had been steeped in Jewish religious spiritualism, from which he derived his view of man's existential aloneness, and then Marxism, which he drew on for his argument that existential aloneness was exacerbated by the social atomization, insecurities, and inequalities of capitalism.[15]

Erikson discussed Fromm's book at a meeting of the San Francisco Psychoanalytic Society in early 1943, before he used the word identity in his own writing.[16] Fromm had used it in *Escape from Freedom* with the same meaning Erikson would later give it. Describing how the defense of masochism, in which the individual wholly submits to a leader like Hitler, protects him from the anxiety of freedom, Fromm wrote, "He is also saved from the doubt of what the meaning of his life is or who 'he' is. These questions are answered by the relationship to power to which he has attached himself. The meaning of his life and the identity of his self are determined by the greater whole into which the self has submerged."[17] Farther on, in connection with the insecurities of the individual forced to compete in capitalist society, Fromm wrote, "The loss of self has increased the necessity to conform, for it results in a profound doubt of one's own identity. If I am nothing but what I believe I am supposed to be—who am I? . . . The identity of the individual has been a major problem of modern philosophy since Descartes. Today we take for granted that we are we. Yet the doubt about ourselves still exists, or has even grown." Tellingly, Fromm cited the work of Pirandello as representative: "In his plays Pirandello has given expression to this feeling of modern man. He starts with the question: Who am I? What proof have I for my own identity other than the continuation of my physical self? His answer is not like Descartes'—the affirmation of the individual self—but its denial: I have no identity."[18]

It was at least in part from such literary sources—he also cited Kafka's *The Castle* as articulating modern man's vain search for a higher authority to show him his place in the world—that Fromm got the idea of the desire "to be" something to which he attached the name identity. But the quest for identity was far from the most important element of his theory of motivation. Much more central were the ambiguous psychological effects of individuation, which as he interpreted the process gave the decisive role in psychological development to economic and social structure. Individuation separated the self from the security of its original "primary ties" and left it "free" but morally alone and insignificant in the face of the immensity of reality. The individuated self's greatest needs were for connectedness with others and for transcendence, a sense of purpose and meaning greater than the self. The organization of the socioeconomic structure could either furnish meaning and social solidarity in a way that simultaneously fostered freedom—as communitarian socialism promised—or make the individual feel even more alone and anxious, desirous of escaping his freedom, as the hostile competitiveness of capitalism in fact did.

Though uninterested in socialism, the young Erikson was hardly innocent of social ideology. Whatever the destabilizing antinomies of his familial, religious, and national origins, he was, before emigrating from Europe, the avatar of a late nineteenth-century German middle-class ethos since made familiar by a half century of historical scholarship: professedly apolitical but culturally and politically conservative, contemptuous of mass democracy, and hostile to modern industrialism from an agrarian, "organicist," and patrician point of view.[19] This set of values represented the latter-day adaptation of *Bildung*, the ideal of the unique but cultivated and integrated "whole personality" normative in Germany from the time of Goethe and Humboldt, to the political and economic realities of the post-1871 German Empire. The *gebildete Mensch* championed nature, art, and "spirit" against the grasping self-interest, materialism, and power politics of the industrializing empire, whether capitalist or socialist. In the years before World War I this countercultural antimodernism was epitomized socially in the *Wandervögel*, bands of adolescents who, temporarily at least, abandoned city and career for hiking in the countryside and communing with nature, and culturally in the anticommercial, antiurban late Romantic novels of writers like Hermann Hesse. Born in 1902, Erikson was steeped in this culture even if he came of age under the radically different postwar political system of Weimar Germany. In any case the advent of the democratic republic often only sharpened prewar conservative cultural attitudes, especially among the educated young. Though he did not join organized groups, Erikson was in his early twenties something of a lone *Wandervogel* while also embarked on a personal version of the apprentice artisan's traditional *Wanderschaft*, moving restlessly about Germany and Italy as he essayed the career of artist. In the journal he kept at the time he remarked contemptuously, and wholly conventionally, on the modern "craze for democracy" and its "futureless values." He lamented both its social "leveling"—the triumph of equality—that "creates [individual] loneliness" and the rise of the proletariat that "creates [social] division." Against divisive electoral and party politics he invoked the idea of the great leader whose personality "creates unity" because he embodies the homogeneous communal will, the basis of the only kind of social harmony in which an integrated, creative soul could develop and flourish. The scattered snippets of poetry in the notebook are the typical effusions of such a soul, yearning to combine classical humanist and Romantic values: eternal beauty beyond the physical, spiritual over "factual" truth, and the "balanced form" that could accommodate, without succumbing to, the temptations of the demonic.[20]

Whether or how his youthful political ideas changed in the late twenties and early thirties as he matured into a profession and Nazism began its ascent—we have no evidence on this point—emigration to American completely eradicated any trace of his earlier antidemocratic sentiment. Erikson gratefully and wholeheartedly embraced the politics of the country in which he found refuge. The idea of *Bildung* was always individualist in essence, if opposed to a narrowly defined material self-interest; perhaps immigration enabled Erikson to reconnect with the liberal political strain inherent in Wilhelm von Humboldt's original idea of individuality, which was submerged in its later metamorphosis.[21] But if he adapted easily to political democracy, other elements of his early cultural formation shaded his attitude to American society and American identity with ambivalence, and ultimately colored his concept of identity. As we will see, they also greatly contributed to identity's appeal to a generation of disaffected young Americans in the 1950s.

Erikson left no doubt that his own experience of immigration greatly contributed to his long-existing sense of marginality. At the same time, as a "nation of immigrants" America offered a template for the direct confrontation between cultures that he believed had brought the problem of personal identity to the fore, since it posed to newcomers the conscious problem of choice of self. America represented to Erikson the model scene of deliberate identity-fashioning as well as the specific challenge of its own distinctive identity. Like any immigrant Erikson brought with him the lens through which he observed his new world. In the United States he encountered a strain of social thought that gave his initial holistic orientation a more local expression. While it was the happenstance of the cultural moment and the accident of personal connections that brought Erikson in close touch with the "culture and personality" movement in anthropology, he was immediately drawn to it because there was a natural affinity between its approach to personality development and his original predilections.

"Culture," the central category of the anthropology of Margaret Mead, Ruth Benedict, H. Scudder Mekeel, and Alfred Kroeber, spoke to Erikson's original ideal of an organic society in two ways. It embraced equally all aspects of social life—economics, certainly, but just as important tribal self-definition and its ceremonial performance, family life, sexuality, education, religious belief and ritual, and the sphere of perhaps most immediate interest to a child psychoanalyst, modes of child rearing. It further represented these activities as harmoniously integrated, functioning together to realize a distinctive and unified way of life. In such a society the child was raised by techniques whose aims were calibrated to the specific role he or she would play as an adult, and thus suffered no sense of what Erikson later called identity diffusion.

It was the original triumph and contemporary tragedy of this ideal that Erikson saw in the evolution of the Native American societies to which his anthropological connections gave him access, the Oglala Sioux of the Dakota plains and the Yurok of the Pacific coast. Both figured in important chapters in *Childhood and Society*, the book that introduced identity to a general audience and made him famous, but their theoretical significance there has been little appreciated. In the original forms of Sioux and Yurok life, before the coming of the whites, Erikson saw actual historical instances of the ideal of seamless connection between individual identity and communal identity rooted in and attuned to nature. In their present existence, especially that of the Sioux, he saw the destructive impact of American industrialism and individualism on the traditional tribal way of life and on the psyches of individual Indians who could no longer live the identity they nevertheless still clung to symbolically.

Speculating about the connection between apparently contradictory Sioux customs surrounding breast-feeding and the tribe's need to foster the opposed values of generosity and a "hunter's ferocity" in its children, Erikson offered a revealing generalization about the integral relationship among social values, child-rearing modes, and individual identity:

> Such values persist because the cultural ethos continues to consider them "natural" and does not admit of alternatives. They persist because they have become an essential part of an individual's sense of identity, which he must preserve as a core of sanity and efficiency. But values do not persist unless they work, economically, psychologically, and spiritually . . . and to this end they must continue to be anchored, generation after generation, in early child training; while child training, to remain consistent, must be embedded in a system of continued economic and cultural synthesis.[22]

In this loaded passage Erikson unproblematically asserted as psychologically necessary what the existentialists before him had expressly rejected as the philosophically false "essentialism" of identity. For values to persist and function as a source of personal identity they must be "naturalized," believed to be universally and objectively valid because grounded in an unchanging, eternal nature. Further, and as evidence of their naturalness, they must be seen to "work," that is, to be logically consistent with one another and with actual social practice, whose success is the proof of their truth. Given these necessary conditions, society through its child-rearing practices is able to provide its members with the permanence and solidity inherent in its values. Such solidity is the very condition of personal "sanity," the ability to orient oneself to reality and to act in the world effectively and with confidence. In return, individuals preserve social values by enacting them as the imperatives of their personal identities.

Unfortunately, this ideal integration no longer existed for present-day Sioux. Erikson's objective yet anguished description of the lack of fit between traditional Sioux values and the reality of Sioux life on the reservation was a lament, not just for them but also for the lost world of traditional European society and its purported integration of individual and collective. The obverse of his idealization of the Native American past was his criticism of the American present. At some points it reads uncannily like the roughly contemporary Marxist critique of Theodor Adorno and Max Horkheimer in *Dialectic of Enlightenment*, but the terms of Erikson's explanations associate it with a recognizably right-wing indictment of modernity. The threat to a positive American identity was not industrial capitalism, but industrial technology, machines rather than classes—"complicated, incomprehensible, and impersonally dictatorial in their power to standardize . . . pursuits and tastes. These machines do their powerful best to convert [the growing adolescent] into a consumer idiot, a fun egotist, and an efficiency slave—and this by offering him what he seems to demand."[23] The parallels with the Frankfurt School's deft paradox of production slavery and consumerist self-indulgence is another reminder that many Marxist and conservative bourgeois critics of modernity had a shared background in the "mandarin" elitist tradition of *Bildung*, however much they differed in their causal diagnoses and preferred utopias. Erikson was finally open about what he saw as the historical European alternative to American identity when he characterized the identities overtaken by American "mechanization" as "agrarian and patrician," noting that mechanization threatened those identities in their lands of origin in Europe as well.[24] The reference to "patrician" identity was not just neutral description. His characterization of America's political culture combined a dash of Alexis de Tocqueville's nineteenth-century liberal aristocratism with a whiff of Hannah Arendt's more contemporary disdain for the democracy of the masses. Adopting terms from both, he defined America's "native" political polarity as the perennial conflict between "aristocracy" and "mobocracy."[25]

In the countercultural explosion of the 1960s Erikson would indeed be accused of conservatism—to his dismay and incomprehension, since he was sympathetic to many of its causes. Much of the criticism had to do with his apparently traditional Freudian view of sexual difference. But even apart from the gender issue, his critics were on to something, though interpreting his "conservatism" in purely American terms, they could not understand its European origins and meaning. At the same time, however, his allusion to Tocqueville also indicates the limits of Erikson's nostalgia for closed organic societies. So too does the way he described the threat represented by another major American villain, the "boss," in context more likely the corporate than the political boss, though the ambiguity of "machine" and "boss" could cover both. "'Bosses' and 'machines,'" Erikson wrote, "are a danger to the American identity, and thus to the mental health of the nation. For they present . . . to the generations with tentative identities, the idea of an autocracy of irresponsibility."[26] The threats Erikson perceived in American economic and social life were to creative individuality and to the personal autonomy he argued was the necessary condition of political freedom. If he was a cultural conservative, valuing the creative elite, he was also a committed political liberal and democrat. But the ultimate goals of Humboldt's humanist ideal of unique individuality and cultural creativity would be at the core of Erikson's notion of positive identity.

History

The unconflicted nature of Erikson's political, as opposed to his ambivalent social acculturation, and the way it too became a part of his definition of healthy identity, reflects another historical reality. He introduced the concept of identity during the "anti-totalitarian moment" in American political and intellectual history, the period beginning shortly before the end of the war when political theorists and polemicists, many of them European émigrés, were developing the theory of totalitarianism to mobilize intellectually against Soviet Communism by subsuming it under a common rubric with Nazism. It is no coincidence that the two versions of national identity that Erikson discussed along with American identity in the last section of *Childhood and Society* were the German and the Russian. His vehicles were national myths ("legends") of inner division and putative healing which, he asserted, explained why many young people rallied to totalitarian ideologies in broken societies. These chapters literally and figuratively bookend the earlier ones on Sioux and Yurok cultures, and serve to sharply demarcate the limits of Erikson's ideal of social homogeneity and identity integration. Whatever his youthful antidemocratic sentiments, Erikson as Jew and humanist psychoanalyst found the ethnonationalist and racist versions of Weimar radical conservatism wholly abhorrent expressions of them. Immigration sealed the difference.

It forever allied Erikson's elitist ideal of *Bildung* with liberal democratic political individualism, if not with the American ethos of economic individualism.

The antitotalitarian moment, however, also contributed a second element to Erikson's understanding of identity needs, one that was in permanent and precarious tension with individuality. He himself had experienced the attractions of belief as a young man, but the overwhelming appeal of a viciously destructive totalitarianism to German youth brought dramatically home to him the adolescent's deep need to fashion an encompassing "ideology." Erikson used the contemporaneously charged term rather loosely, citing but diluting Karl Mannheim's definition of it in *Ideology and Utopia* to include any set of ideas, whether rigorous philosophy, less systematic Weltanschauung, or vaguely defined "way of life," that purported to provide answers to the ultimate questions of human existence and directives to live it. The horrors wrought by totalitarian ideologies, however, made it necessary for him to try to distinguish "healthy" from "unhealthy" ideologies. Healthy ideologies were flexible and inclusive, cementing group cohesion while also permitting personal change and development and recognition of the rights of other identities. Unhealthy ideologies were characterized by "totalism" and exclusiveness and defined by absolute beliefs that left no room for difference or contingency. But the conceptual line between the two was hazy if not invisible in view of Erikson's general formulation of ideology. "All ideologies," he said, "ask for, as the prize for the promised possession of a future, uncompromising commitment to some absolute hierarchy of values and some rigid principle of conduct."[27] Such a formulation would seem, if anything, to favor the exclusionary and fanatic over the latitudinarian and tolerant belief system. In the end, not surprisingly, Erikson drew the line psychoanalytically. "It is in the totalism and exclusiveness of some ideologies that the superego is apt to regain its territory from identity," he wrote, meaning that under totalistic ideologies the individual loses his autonomy, regresses, and falls under the control of the superego's "paternalistic-primitive simplicity" and its external projections, the "superpolice chiefs on earth,"[28]—the Hitlers and Stalins. Whatever else identity meant, it entailed for Erikson psychological autonomy as understood by contemporary psychoanalytic theory (in this regard the psychological expression of liberalism)—control by the rational ego rather than by the uncompromisingly dogmatic "thou shalt" of the superego.

Psychoanalysis

This is evident in the name he first gave the new concept, "ego identity." The most obvious influence on Erikson's concept of identity was his work as a clinical psychoanalyst of his time. Inevitably, identity was framed from the standpoint of psychopathology, as that was understood in the theory he had absorbed under the tutelage of his analyst Anna Freud and others in the founder's immediate circle. That identity originated in this context gave rise to perhaps its greatest paradox and sharpest irony: the theory within which it germinated was conceptually inimical to it and finally unable to accommodate it.

When Erikson began learning and undergoing analysis in Vienna in the late 1920s, Freudian theory was in the process of shifting from its early focus on the contents of the repressed unconscious to an emphasis on the psychic agency of repression, or more broadly defense, and its methods. The change had begun with the publication in 1923 of *The Ego and the Id*, which introduced the tripartite division of the psyche into id, ego, and superego. While Freud's new "structural psychology" famously depicted a weak and beleaguered ego, the survival-oriented adaptive agency of the self continually functioning under heavy pressure from id, superego, and external reality, analysts led by Anna Freud soon began elaborating the inbuilt "mechanisms" available to the ego to defend against the dangers threatening from blindly demanding instinct and uncompromisingly punitive conscience. By the 1930s a more positive, optimistic picture began to appear of an ego equipped by evolution with faculties and strengths that enabled it to adapt, like all biological organisms, more or less automatically to its "average expectable environment"[29] unless thwarted by external circumstances. Erikson received his training in the early days of the new "ego psychology," and matured as an analyst as it was becoming the standard model.

The ego was the "structure" of the psyche that included such mental functions as perception, memory, and judgment. Its overall function was to gratify bodily urges while also protecting the self from pain and harm. This it could do only by coordinating the instinctual demands of the id in accordance with both the demands of conscience and the requirements of external, including social, reality. The ego thus had not only to assess those requirements and regulate internal demands in accordance with them; it had also to integrate conflicting internal demands with one another so as to minimize conflict. The ego was both the outwardly oriented agency of the psyche and the synthesizing or unifying function within the psyche. It was the only place, but also the apparently appropriate one, within the structural theory of psychoanalysis for a synthesizing concept such as identity, whose aim after all was also the unity of the self.

In fact there were two insurmountable conceptual problems with the idea of "ego identity." The forces that moved the psychic apparatus in psychoanalytic theory were the biological drives of evolutionary theory, survival and procreation of the species. Freud had called them the ego and libidinal instincts prior to the structural model of *The Ego and the Id*; afterward, though reformulated as Eros and the death instinct, biological drives were still understood as the main elements of the "dynamic" or conflict model of metapsychology. As such they were logically not categories of subjective intention but of external causation. But even when translated into empirical psychological desires (as they generally were in clinical description) they did not include or refer to anything like a subjective need for self-definition. Put simply, Erikson had introduced a radically new theory of human motivation into psychoanalysis, one not necessarily incompatible with drive theory but not reducible to it, and not capable of formulation in its terms.

The second problem with the idea of "ego identity" was that Erikson's identity was not merely a substructure of one agency of the self; it *was* the self. While as a *concept* it might be understood as a creation of the (Freudian) rational ego, identity was meant to embrace the self as a whole, including sexuality, perceptual and rational faculties, and morality, that is, id, ego, and superego. Freudian metapsychology had no superordinate structure uniting id, ego, and superego other than that of the organism, a biological category; it had no psychological self other than the "psychic apparatus" of the organism, which consisted of psychological representatives of the biological drives and their objects. Id, ego, and superego might be understood as reifications of modes of acting of a subjective self, but the self as such was not, and as things stood could not be, theorized within the structural model in psychoanalysis. Heinz Kohut would struggle with the same conceptual problem when he came to see narcissistic issues as the heart of psychopathology: where and what was the "self " of self-esteem? Kohut, however, ultimately broke formally with Freudian metapsychology in naming his version of psychoanalysis *self-psychology*. In his time and place, Erikson could not, or at any rate did not, do so; the furthest he went was to eventually drop the term ego identity and call it identity *tout court*.

Much less problematic for Erikson's idea of identity in his psychoanalytic heritage was the developmental orientation—the "genetic" level—of psychoanalytic theory. Identity formation was a process, just like sexual development, though with more stages, since it continued past adolescence. Erikson famously constructed an eight-stage schema for identity formation that spanned the whole of the life cycle from birth to death.[30] At the same time he tried to accommodate his schema to classical psychoanalysis theory by coordinating the early stages of the life cycle as closely as he could with Freud's stages of psychosexual development, oral, anal, phallic, latency, and adolescence. Thus the first stage of Erikson's life cycle, "basic trust versus mistrust" corresponded to Freud's oral stage, since the child learns she or he can or cannot trust in the support of the world through the consistency or inconsistency of the nurturing mother. Similarly the stage he called autonomy versus shame and doubt, in which the child experiments with the "social modalities" of holding on and letting go, corresponded to Freud's anal stage. But these superficial resemblances could hardly conceal the very different motivational foundation on which Erikson's "psychosocial" stages of identity development rested.

The issue of trust versus mistrust, for example, is not primarily related to the gratification or frustration of the infant's oral sensuality or need for food, though this is the arena where it plays out, but to laying the foundation for a sense of identity. It is through the maternal relationship that the infant first gains (or fails to gain) the foundation of that sense of being "all right, of being oneself" which is the essence of identity. It is crucial that this go well because, Erikson argued, even under the most favorable circumstances this stage "introduces into psychic life (and becomes prototypical for) a sense of inner division and universal nostalgia for a paradise forfeited. It is against this powerful combination of a sense of having been deprived, and of having been abandoned—that basic trust must maintain itself throughout life."[31] Similarly, the essential dynamic of Erikson's version of the "anal stage" concerned not issues of control over "anal gratification" but the child's ability to learn, and exert self-control at the behest of others without loss of self-esteem through their shaming. There is a limit to the child's (and the adult's) ability to maintain a positive sense of self "in the face of demands to consider himself, his body, and his wishes as evil and dirty."[32] The Freudian "phallic stage" was for Erikson the phase in which the child learns to initiate action, sexual or otherwise, with or without being constantly threatened by a sense of crippling guilt. The "oedipal stage" is less about sexual rivalry than it is about whether the moral sense established through it is so oppressive that it restricts the horizon of the permissible to a very narrow range. Each succeeding phase is one in which, as the child's faculties unfold, the prerequisites of autonomy, self-esteem, and productive labor that are themselves prerequisites for successful identity formation are either fostered or thwarted. They culminate in, though they do not end with, the identity crisis in adolescence and young adulthood, in which the crucial issue is choosing among the roles society makes available in order to settle on a career. Failure in this phase causes identity diffusion, the inability to settle on an occupational identity.[33]

A decade later, under the obvious if unacknowledged influence of existentialist thinking, Erikson claimed that human self-consciousness begins with the experience of "uprootedness," the sense of abrupt alienation from oneself first experienced in early infancy when the familiar face of the mother turns cold or angry, or is replaced by a strange and unfamiliar one. Suddenly the baby no longer knows either the other or himself, since his sense of being the (good) self he "is" depends on the affirming recognition of a constant, consistent, and benign other. This occasion of alienation from self is only the first of many to come, some inevitable stages of human development, some the result of historical vicissitude. The toddler, for example, gains an increasing sense of autonomy and mastery through the ability to move about on his own, but he also simultaneously becomes subject to disapproval and shaming, which make him aware that who he "is" is at the mercy of others, that he is the "exposed self by which man becomes an outsider to himself."[34] And even when the standards by which he is judged are internalized and fixed, he can become an outsider to himself by his own acts of critical self-judgment. Understood from the vantage point of such self-alienation, the quest for identity is the desire to be finally rooted, to be at home, in a double sense: to be in one place and to be one undivided self. However, Erikson warned, the biological metaphor of roots is partly also misleading, susceptible to a reactionary romanticism. Agrarian man, with his supposed attachment to nature, was no more securely rooted, in an absolute sense, than modern technological man, as his fearful need to placate hidden and arbitrary divinities testifies; he too was always in danger of exile and punishment. Ultimate rootlessness and self-alienation are the human condition. The immigrant, who experiences uprootedness most concretely and dramatically, is only the person whose life-circumstances impose this universal truth on him most nakedly. Erikson had now accepted Heidegger and Sartre's position on the impossibility of metaphysical identity.

By the same token, however, the immigrant experience, as well as certain forms of psychopathology, shows that the sense of rootlessness has its degrees, its *psychologically* tolerable and intolerable versions. Within the limits of possibility set by the human condition, the Eriksonian quest for identity *is* a quest for a sense of solid rootedness. Absolutist ideologies seek to abolish anxiety altogether by erroneously denying the limitations of human finitude, but within those limits, with include inescapable ontological anxiety, psychological uprootedness can generate unnecessary "surplus anxiety," which has its sociopsychological causes and hence also its possible cures.[35] Psychological self-alienation is emotionally sustainable only if it can be experienced as a stage of creative destruction in the forging of a final identity (though, Erikson pointed out, consciously chosen uprootedness can, under certain circumstances, itself be a viable identity). We can say that for Erikson, identity was the solution to the anxiety of psychological self-alienation, of not feeling one with oneself, that exceeded the inescapable minimum alienation and anxiety of the human condition.

At the same time, psychoanalytic developmental theory did provide a concept crucial to Erikson's (and as the future would prove, to any) theory of
identity: the idea of identification. Identification, too often employed in psychological description and explanation as if it were a self-evident notion, is in
fact one of the most mysterious of psychological concepts. For Freud, identification was primarily a fantasy way of retaining lost objects of desire.[36] One
"internalized" such objects by incorporating some of their characteristic traits,
behaving like them, ultimately, in some sense, "becoming" them. But in what
sense does one "become" someone else? Identification with someone certainly
involves something more than and other than desire for that person; as an act
it suggests assuming or taking on sameness with somebody else, thus becoming identical with or to that person. "Assuming sameness" or "becoming identical with," however, are imprecise linguistic stabs at defining an unconscious,
infralinguistic, literally fantastic process, whose outward results may be visible
but whose inner workings are inaccessible. In the tame language of the philosophical theory of action they are at best approximated by implied propositions of "as if" beliefs: I behave as if I believe I am my mother or father. The
psychoanalytic language of early identifications, however, conjures up much
more graphic physical imagery. Psychoanalysis speaks of infants "introjecting"
and "projecting" persons, or parts of persons, in unconscious fantasies of can-
nibalistic incorporation and physical expulsion. Whatever the realities of these
mental processes, however, what emerges at the end are verbalizable, and
indeed often stated, as propositions of identity: I *am* my father's son (that is,
I feel and act as if I were he), I *am* a woman, I *am* an American.

Identification throughout early development is automatic and unconscious, or at any rate unselfconscious; without noticing, the child adopts a
series of parental behaviors, values, and roles. Identity, by contrast begins in
Erikson's formulation where identification ends: "[Identity] arises," he wrote,
"from the selective repudiation and mutual assimilation of childhood identifications,"[37] that is, as a self-conscious process of self-making. Throughout
childhood, identifications provided "tentative crystallizations" which make
the individual "feel and believe . . . as if he approximately knew who he was—
only to find that such self-certainty ever again falls prey to the discontinuities
of psychosocial development."[38] Each provisional identity synthesis of childhood is undermined by the new possibilities and demands of succeeding
stages, which must be integrated into the old. But in adolescence, on the verge
of entering into the world of adult choices and responsibilities, the young
person is challenged to decide, out of the welter of past, often conflicting,
identifications, which to accept and which reject in order to become who he
will finally be. These include everything encompassed by contemporary

psychoanalytic ego psychology and more—preferred sexual modalities, erotic object choices, the balance of aggression, characteristic defenses, including character defenses—but above all, three crucial adaptations to the social world: *choice of work commitments, group affiliations,* and *philosophy of life.* These for Erikson were the essential constituents of identity.

The independent role of a conscious life-philosophy in identity was especially important to Erikson. His early case study descriptions demonstrate acute sensitivity to the unconscious conflicts of his young patients—by all accounts he was a gifted clinician—but his emphasis on the conscious element of identity creation seemed to mainstream analysts an abandonment of the very core of psychoanalysis. The charge was both true and untrue. Erikson never abandoned the idea or denied the importance of unconscious conflict: quite the contrary. He took for granted, for example, that Martin Luther, the subject of his most famous work on identity crisis, would not have been able to consciously connect his theological and institutional rebellion against the pope with his struggle against his father's authority, or even to be fully aware of it. But it is also true that (contrary to the way the work has sometimes been construed) Erikson did not *explain* Luther's religious rebellion as nothing but the displaced manifestation of an unconscious oedipal conflict over sexual and aggressive prerogatives.

Rather, he saw Luther's paternal conflict as one between autonomy and authority, which he took to be irreducibly fundamental categories of both personal identity and social arrangements. Tension between them is inevitably experienced first in the family, but it is interpreted within the reigning ideological structure that governs all thinking about such basic issues—at that time and place Catholic theology. Necessarily then, Luther's conflict over authority was expressed and enacted on two levels simultaneously, the secular-familial and the sacred. But it was within the sacred that the terms of both were articulated.

Furthermore, Luther's thrust toward independence was not simply instinctual oedipal rivalry; it was conditioned by the economic and social changes that were breaking down traditional hierarchies and ideas of obedience. These events had enabled Luther's own father to rise beyond the station to which he would have been confined in feudal times and model for his son new possibilities of social autonomy and independence. Ideology, however, lagged behind social and psychological reality. Christian conscience did not permit conscious acknowledgment of independence from either heavenly or earthly father. To want autonomy, let alone to actively rebel, was to be a sinner. It was only the contemporary delegitimizing of papal authority, exposed by its corruption as a seriously flawed representative of both paternal and divine authority, that made Luther's open rebellion against the Church imaginable for him. Never-theless the dilemma of *sacred* authority had to be solved before this break with institutional authority was possible. How could God, as Love, accept the sinner whom God as Law must condemn to damnation? The dilemma demanded the theological formulation of a new relationship between man's freedom and submission.

Luther's famous solution was salvation by faith alone. Man was an abject sinner who could only be saved by the faith in God's love as manifest in Christ's sacrifice, not by his own efforts. But at the same time this was a truth that man could discover by himself, without the mediation of priestly author-ity, by his independent reading and understanding of Scriptures. It was in such historical-theological terms, and only in such terms, that Luther's identity cri-sis could be solved.

Nonetheless it was the way the theology resolved a psychological crisis, and not the theology itself, that interested Erikson. As a result he cast Luther's theology in terms that put both the man and the theology in an odd, anachro-nistic light. "Martin's theological reforms," he wrote, "imply a psychological fact, namely, that the ego gains strength *in practice*, and *in affectu*, to the degree to which it can accept at the same time the total power of the drives and the total power of conscience—provided that it can nourish what Luther called *opera manum dei*, that particular combination of work and love which alone verifies our identity and confirms it."[39] It is no doubt possible to recognize Luther's theological tour de force of combining the absolute right of each individual to interpret Scripture with the absolute authority of Scripture in Erikson's claim about the foundation of true ego strength, but this was hardly what Luther had in mind. At the same time, however, despite the psychoana-lytic language of "drives" neither was it Freudian. From the point of view of identity, Erikson transformed Luther's theological revolution into a formula for psychic health, which allowed for the rights of individual autonomy within the framework of an authoritative objective identity.

The Mature Formulation of Identity

The difficulties Erikson had integrating identity into a psychoanalytic frame-work are nowhere more evident than in his essay "The Problem of Ego Iden-tity," first published in *Journal of the American Psychoanalytic Association* in 1956. It was reprinted three years later in a collection of his papers titled *Identity and the Life Cycle*, which appeared as the first volume of *Psychological Issues*, a series of monographs dedicated to providing source materials for a "general psychoanalytic theory of behavior." However congenial such a venture was to Erikson's enterprise, both publication venues, committed to "orthodox" psychoanalytic theory, exacerbated the difficulties of clarifying the originality of identity. The essay remains, however, the most detailed and explicit statement of what Erikson meant by it.

The need to integrate his idea within an uncongenial theory was not the only source of difficulty; there was also Erikson's characteristic casualness about conceptual rigor. He repeated his earliest formulation of identity as "a persistent sameness within oneself (selfsameness) and a persistent sharing of some kind of essential character with others," but now added a set of "connotations" in which the meaning of the term could "speak for itself": as "a conscious *sense of individual identity*"; "an unconscious striving for a *continuity of personal character*"; "a criterion for the silent doings of *ego synthesis*"; and "a maintenance of an inner *solidarity* with a group's ideals and identity."[40] In fact, except for the idea of "ego synthesis," his main concession to psychoanalytic ego psychology, these were all consistent with one another and with his original core definition, and even ego synthesis could be interpreted as the ego's activity to resolve conflicts between identifications rather than with instincts. The so-called "unconscious striving for continuity" was not necessarily unconscious in the psychoanalytic "dynamic" sense of repressed or otherwise defended against but rather preconscious or unselfconscious. It implied that identity is an inbuilt psychic need goaded by anxiety and motivating specific action, when needed, to harmonize future commitments with past and present ones. In simpler words, we desire that who we will become will be consistent with who we are and were—a desire that, as the Luther biography intimated, shapes the way we interpret even radical breaks with our past: "now we are saved who once were lost."

Of the possible elements of identity that an individual had to both choose for himself and find social support for during the "identity crisis" (the masculine pronoun is in accord with Erikson's own usage, and with the gender bias of the time), the one he emphasized most in the essay, almost to the exclusion of others except ideology, was work. Despite his early attention to nationalism and immigration, he took national and ethnic affiliation for granted when he discussed the individual, and for a psychoanalyst had surprisingly little to say about sexual or what later came to be called gender identity. Of Freud's famous double answer to the question of the purpose of life, love and work, Erikson focused primarily on the second, though the achievement of intimacy was one of the stages in the life cycle. "Man," he wrote, to take his place in society, "must acquire a 'conflict-free' habitual use of a dominant *faculty*, to be elaborated in an *occupation*; a limitless resource, a feedback, as it were, from the *companionship* it provides, and from its *tradition*; and finally, an intelligible *theory* of the processes of life."[41] The enumerated requirements—dominant faculty, occupation, companionship, tradition—embedded work in broader personal, social, and metaphysical contexts: existential mastery and creativity, social utility, emotional solidarity, and not least, time—specifically, the human desire to defeat the potential radical discontinuities of temporality. All of these Erikson took as basic identity needs that could be conjoined in the satisfactions of work suitably chosen. Perhaps no element in his concept betrayed more clearly its origins in the nineteenth-century European professional upper bourgeois ethos.

But the preeminent context of identity for Erikson the therapist was psychic health. That is what all the other desiderata like work and ideology were valued for. Discussing the question of whether the sense of identity is conscious, he argued that "identity consciousness," by which he meant overt, worried concern with identity questions, is an index of psychopathology, transient if developmental, more painful and serious if prolonged. A *sense* of identity, by contrast, is "experienced pre-consciously as a sense of psychosocial well-being." The elements of this state of well-being are "a feeling of being at home in one's body, a sense of 'knowing where one is going,' and an inner assuredness of anticipated recognition from those who count."[42] At the core of these, furthermore, is "a dominant sense of the goodness of individual existence" and of the basic, at least potential goodness of others, whom one can therefore also come to love and trust.[43] Even if all these assurances are never attained once and for all but are constantly lost and regained, they represented for Erikson both the ultimate aim of subjective psychological striving and his normative definition of psychic health.

Erikson's categorization of identity pathology further clarified the scope of the concept. The two basic pathologies he named were "identity diffusion" and "negative identity." The very possibility of identity diffusion implicitly acknowledged that even a "normally" developing young person has multiple identities. In the pathological case, however, they are not integrated with one another in a self-synthesis that feels unified, consistent, and whole. Torn between conflicting or incompatible identifications, loyalties, and commitments, the adolescent cannot create an assured sense of who he is and may attempt various external maneuvers to substitute for it. The most common is using others in distorted versions of friendship and love to mirror back a unified, idealized image of oneself, a move doomed to failure because the subject's inner reality doesn't permit him to believe in it. In the case of negative identity, an adolescent perversely takes on what he—and his important others—regard as a "bad" identity. Behind what appears a blatantly self-defeating appropriation is the feeling that the circumstances of his upbringing have generated in him the belief that he is unworthy of, excluded from, the identities his environment considers good. Rather than be at the mercy of others' definition of him, he will actively choose and celebrate a negative self-definition that makes him not just noticeable but notorious. Negative identity has its own paradoxical place in the social structure and one who bears it gets a perverse species of social recognition. But in the end, though our desire is for positive identity, the need for identity is powerful enough that it will take negativity over nothingness.

The Cultural Diffusion of Identity: America, Germany, France

Covering a speech by Mrs. William Graham Cole, "lecturer, teacher, mother, and wife of the president of Lake Forest college" to the local YWCA member-ship luncheon on September 30, 1963, a reporter for the *Chicago Tribune* quoted her as saying women do not usually encounter the "so-called identity crisis" until some of their domestic obligations have let up.[44] The piece nicely illuminates the process of diffusion of Erikson's ideas in the United States. It is one of the earliest appearances of the term in an American daily newspa-per.[45] The qualifier "so-called" suggests that while the speaker probably expected her audience to have heard the term, she thought they would regard it as still new and somewhat strange, perhaps not quite legitimate. The speaker is reported as having taken the theme of her talk, an exhortation to women to stop looking for their meaning in others and answer the question "Who am I" for themselves, from her speeches to college women. Finally, it is not irony, or at least not only irony, but history to note that reporting a speech calling for women to define their own identity, the female reporter, though putting the speaker's occupation first in the listing of her social identities, introduced her by her husband's name and ended with his obviously more prestigious position. The story was published in the same year as Betty Friedan's *The Feminine Mystique*—a book that also made much of Erikson's concept of identity.

The earliest newspaper mention of "identity crisis" I found is in a story in the *New York Times* of May 28, 1961, discussing the emotional difficulties faced by university students after their first year of college. Having been thrown into a new environment that challenged their previous beliefs and sense of self, returning students "are abruptly faced with the job of questioning everything: 'Who am I?' 'What am I?' 'What do I honestly believe in?' What do I really want and want to be?'" The writer was reporting on a "special session on the identity crisis" held by the mental health section of the American College Health Association. Its consoling message was that, while students' turmoil was upsetting to their parents and themselves, most specialists regard all but the "exaggerated extremes" of this crisis as "within the range of the normal" and that "some specialists say that the identity crisis is an intrinsic and necessary part of growing up."[46] Taken together, the *Times* and the *Chicago Tribune* story suggest a line of progression. Public discussion of the identity crisis was at first a matter for mental health professionals concerned with adolescents and influenced by the developmental sequence Erikson had described but who also wanted to convey a reassuring message about their children to a lay public of worried parents. Within a very short time, however, the identity crisis had overflowed its original boundaries to become relevant to women facing it, or being exhorted to face it, in middle age.

In just a few more years, identity crises were to be found everywhere. The painter Andy Warhol, his companion and model Edie Sedgwick and "her playmates and image makers" were described in 1965 as sitting around "sipping white wine punch and revealing themselves to be suffering from identity crisis and grappling earnestly with the problem of perceiving reality."[47] A year later the Pittsburgh Plate Glass Company was "having an identity crisis" because, though the company also produced glass fiber, coatings, resins, and chemicals, its name "projected an image of a company that made only plate glass."[48] On a more serious matter the *Los Angeles Times* headlined a story critical of the Black Power movement's tactics "Identity Crisis: Primitive Paranoia vs. Democratic Maturity,"[49] evidence of the politicization of identity then already underway. The term was still very much available for individuals, however: the flamboyant, much gossiped about Martha Mitchell, wife of Richard Nixon's attorney general, denied having difficulty adjusting to all the publicity about her in a story titled "Identity Crisis for Martha Mitchell,"[50] but in following years the *Los Angeles Times* also reported the identity crises of the clergy,[51] Yugoslavia,[52] and the game of squash.[53] The *Baltimore Sun* explained to its readers that the actor Sean Connery's visit to a private psychiatric clinic in Norway was the result of a "temporary identity crisis" created by his apparent overidentification with his screen persona James Bond.[54] The frivolous mixed with the more scholarly as in the *Sun*'s report of an academic lecture in which an art historian attributed an identity crisis to the painter Van Dyck who felt overshadowed by Rubens, while individual crises alternated with those of organizations and groups in the *Sun*'s pages as in its announcement that the Baltimore Medical Society was "in the midst of an identity crisis,"[55] and that despair over integration was stimulating an identity crisis among blacks that was leading to black separatism.[56] Even the *Wall Street Journal* got into the Zeitgeist, reporting about "something of an 'identity crisis'" caused in corporate culture by the merger of two disparate companies.[57] All told there were some 13 mentions of identity crisis in the *Sun* between 1960 and 1970, 46 in the same span in the *Los Angeles Times*, 35 in the *Chicago Tribune* in 1963–1969, and 91 in the *New York Times*. Between 1961 and 2008, the term appeared in the *New York Times* in more than 1,900 stories.

These citations coincide with the years in which Erik Erikson became a public intellectual and cultural celebrity. In the fall of 1960, he took up a tenured academic position at Harvard, an unheard-of achievement for someone who had never even attended university. While *Childhood and Society* had sold a respectable number of copies in the 1950s, sales more than tripled when the Norton publishing company brought out a revised paperback edition in 1963. The book became required reading in a large number of college courses in sociology, social work, and psychology, and was not infrequently assigned in history, philosophy, theology, and anthropology classes as well. As an index of his public stature during the decade, Erikson was twice invited to the White House, once to a small reception in 1965 with President Johnson and prominent African American leaders, and again in 1969, this time to address a White House dinner for President Nixon's staff to explain student protests against the Vietnam War.

In fact, however, the ground for the recognition Erikson received in the 1960s had been more than prepared in the previous decade. This was true not only in the sense that the publications of the 1950s had already established his reputation among social scientists but that his writings were very much part of the intellectual and social spirit of the decade, influenced by it and influencing it in turn. In an essay at the end of the 1970s surveying twentieth-century trends in the academic study of "personality" in the United States, a leading American intellectual historian wrote that after the Ages of Freud and Adler in the 1920s and 1930s and the contemporaneously styled Age of Anxiety in the 1940s, "From the end of the 1940s to almost the end of the 1950s the cultural problem [of the self] was fundamentally redefined as that of personal identity. Who could object to seeing this as the Age of Erik Erikson?"[58]

Many university courses in psychology and sociology were already assigning *Childhood and Society* by the mid-1950s. In her 1955 review of current literature on social issues, Margaret Mead, certainly an interested voice as Erikson's long-time mentor and friend, claimed that "a new concept is clamoring for acceptance—the concept of identity," which was about to become "one of the most burning problems of the age." She predicted, correctly, that Erikson would soon become a central public figure and nominated *Childhood and*

Society as the most important book of the past quarter century.[59] As if in corroboration, two widely read books appeared just a few years later whose titles and analyses paid extended tribute to Erikson's innovation, Alan Wheelis's quirkily insightful *The Quest for Identity* and Helen Merrell Lynd's *On Shame and the Search for Identity*. Perhaps even more telling about Erikson's direct impact were the many letters he received during the decade from faculty members reporting that their students had found deep personal meaning in his volume.[60] "Identity" in its new meaning made the newspapers some years before "identity crisis," if not as frequently. A 1955 *New York Times* book review of French-Jewish Algerian expatriate Albert Memmi's wrenching autobiographical novel *The Pillar of Salt* was titled "A Desperate Need for Identity";[61] a report the following year on German expellees from Eastern Europe after World War II described them as "People in Search of Identity."[62]

Attempting to explain why identity "so quickly became an indispensable term in American social commentary," the historian Philip Gleason suggested that the growing prestige of the social sciences in the United States since the 1930s and the vogue of national-character studies during the 1940s were contributing factors. But by far the most important consideration was that the word identity seemed "ideally adapted to talking about the relationship of the individual to society as that perennial problem presented itself to Americans at midcentury" because it promised to "elucidate a new kind of conceptual linkage" between them. It was the discovery of "mass society" and the "central problem of personal isolation" within it, as analyzed by David Riesman in *The Lonely Crowd*, published in the same year as *Childhood and Society*, that caused people to ask about who they were and where they belong. [63] The picture that emerges from Erikson's own analysis of adolescent pathology in its social context in *Childhood and Society* has some affinities with Riesman's image of the individual in the lonely crowd, though there are also telling differences in their socioeconomic explanations. Neither account, however, seemed to explain the identity problem as Erikson himself described it in the chapter on "Reflections on the American Identity" in *Childhood and Society*.

Riesman's "other-directed" self is famously dependent on other people to tell it how to live, while the inner-directed self has an "inner gyroscope" that keeps it on an independent path. The shift from "inner-directed" to "other-directed," according to Riesman, tracked the transformation of capitalism from a production-based to a consumption-driven economy. The other-directed self thus represented a Western, middle-class urban world of growing economic abundance in which the (Puritan) ethic of work, success, and acquisition had lost its importance, replaced by the pursuit of leisure and consumption directed by peer groups and the mass media. Riesman's dichotomy was not supposed to be synonymous with the opposition of autonomy and conformity—both inner-directed and outer-directed selves were "social characters" whose goals were formulated by society—but as he acknowledged, his terminology and examples tended to equate the pairs. Other-directed people "lose their social freedom and their individual autonomy in seeking to become like each other,"[64] presumably, according to this explanation, leaving the more sensitive among them to search for their own identities.

Erikson's ideal-typical adolescent grew up with a vaguely defined set of goals that had "something to do with action and motion," an individualistic core without clear direction or the possibility of true individuality.[65] This came of being raised by the American "Mom," heiress and nurturer of a frontier ethic of independence in a society that no longer had a frontier to give it purpose. To foster her son's independence she remained somewhat cold and distant, in an effort not to infantilize him with protective maternalism. But this kind of child rearing created its own problems because a mother's sensitive care of her baby's individual needs is indispensable to forming "the basis in the child for a sense of identity." In modern times this shakily independent adolescent has to enter the "machine age," run by autocratic "bosses." The young American male "finds himself confronted with superior machines, complicated, incomprehensible, and impersonally dictatorial in their power to standardize his pursuits and tastes. These machines do their best to convert him into a consumer idiot, a fun egotist, and an efficiency slave—and this by offering him what he seems to demand."[66] "The question of our time," Erikson concluded in a tone much like Riesman's, "is How can our sons preserve their freedom and share it with those whom . . . they must consider equals."[67]

If it was unclear just who or what the new tyrant was—autocratic bosses? dictatorial machines?—the nature of the tyranny was clear enough: mindless consumerism. But it was also not clear for whom "the question of our time" was a question. While Erikson claimed to draw his picture of the American family and the dilemma of its youth from what he learned from his patients, his question was drawn not from a live patient but from a literary creation. Rather than give a clinical example, he cited Biff, son of the salesman in Arthur Miller's play *Death of a Salesman*, lamenting to his mother "I just can't take hold, Mom, I can't take hold of a life."[68] But the character of Biff is embedded in a strongly tendentious thesis play dramatizing the self-destructive attitudes of Erich Fromm's "marketing personality," the conformist who tries to gain a self by selling himself to others. Fromm was Riesman's acknowledged template for the other-directed self. For all its perspicuity, cultural criticism is not historical analysis; neither Riesman's nor Erikson's analysis explains the appeal of identity to 1950s youth.

Erikson was more informative about the contemporary social context in which identity was received when he stayed closer to the evidence offered by his patients. Commenting on the change in the "presenting problems" of contemporary psychoanalytic patients, he wrote, "To condense it into a formula: the patient of today suffers most under the problem of what he should believe in and who he should—or, indeed, might—be or become; while the patient of early psychoanalysis suffered most under inhibitions which prevented him from being what and who he thought he knew he was."[69] Other psychoanalysts made parallel observations about changing psychopathology throughout the decade. Alan Wheelis pointed out that contemporary patterns of neurosis had changed since Freud's day from "symptom neurosis," such as classical hysteria, to "character disorders" marked by a generalized unhappiness pervading the entire personality.[70] Such young people were not mindless consumers.

Social historians of the 1950s have suggested that consumerism, conformity, and conservatism were only half the story of the decade. It is true that contemporary social scientists, politicians, and members of the middle class in their everyday behavior propagated a strongly cohesive set of values emphasizing domesticity—early marriage, strong families with breadwinner fathers and homemaker mothers, sexual abstinence before marriage (though mutual sexual satisfaction within it), and the virtues of work and economic success. After the anxieties of the Great Depression and World War II, amid those of the Cold War and the threat of nuclear annihilation, there was a desire amounting to an obsession in the United States with security, economic, psychological, and political. Postwar middle-class prosperity and high levels of employment seemed to make it possible; what one historian has labeled the "domestic containment" of potentially disruptive social forces like independence and sexuality seemed to promise emotional fulfillment with security.[71] But prosperity and security, along with the cultivation of the degree of independence in the young necessary for economic success, bred developments that undercut the very goals they were supposed to serve.

The 1950s were also the first decade of a truly independent and large-scale youth culture. Because of their parents' affluence, augmented by their own after-school work, more and more adolescents could participate in the expanding consumer culture with their own tastes and trends, many of which alarmed the older generation precisely because they challenged the values of domesticity. The availability of cars opened up a world of fast-food hangouts and drive-in movies, rolling laboratories of sexual experimentation. Adolescent purchasing power created a huge new market for records of the music that appealed to them, most threateningly to the adult generation rock 'n' roll with its "primitive" beat and sexualized dancing. Two popular films of the 1950s, *Rebel Without a Cause* and *The Blackboard Jungle*, featuring rebellious or out-of-control teenagers, epitomized adult fears despite their "happy endings" with the forces of good in control.[72] No doubt the psychoanalyst Robert Lindner was greatly exaggerating with his claim that *"the brute fact of today is that our youth is no longer in rebellion, but in a condition of downright active and hostile mutiny"*—Lindner had a thesis to grind about the destructive effects of conformity and wanted to encourage youthful "mutiny" against it.[73] But the social and psychological reality of the 1950s was far more brittle and conflicted than the retrospective picture of consumerism and consensus described.

Alan Wheelis astutely caught some of the double-sidedness of consumer culture in its psychological impact on identity. While the country as a whole was marked by a striking uniformity in styles of housing, dress, and entertainment, the culture that affected any individual, he claimed, had become more diverse. The very changes that had brought about an overall sameness to American life had, through the revolutions in communication, transport, and mass production, increased the variety of influences that played on any one individual because they overwhelmed the provincialism of local communities, opening them up to broader ideas and possibilities. If anything, Wheelis suggested, the tendency to conform had likely decreased rather than increased, because "experience now is pluralistic, and choice is presented in areas that formerly permitted of only one course of action."[74] Once exposed to heterogeneous manners, customs, and morals, young people could no longer ignore the relativity of those by which they had been raised, and were faced with the problem of choice in all spheres. In psychoanalytic terms, the undermining of beliefs previously taken for granted was indicated by the diminished authority of the superego, the psychic agency defined by absolute prohibitions and ego ideals.[75] If this lessened the degree to which people were motivated by the unconscious, however, it made for less centered and confident action in the world.

What neither contemporary nor recent commentators have noted, however, is that the very security the middle class achieved in the 1950s undermined parental imperatives precisely because youth were no longer driven by the anxieties and insecurities of their elders. The very successes of the Depression generation ironically made their imperatives seem outmoded and irrelevant to the needs of the newer one. The guidance such imperatives offered to identity did not answer to their situation, even as their love of and identification with their parents made those imperatives weigh heavily on them, while the possibility of making unguided choices created its own psychological difficulties. For at least a certain segment of the young population, the situation was ripe for identification with Erikson's idea of the quest for identity and identity diffusion. Among many intellectually minded college students of the 1950s, existentialism was even more in vogue than Erikson. Probably the most widely discussed work among those so disposed was Albert Camus's *Myth of Sisyphus*. Camus's description of the absurd, both in its "realist" version of the boringly repetitive daily round of work and its mythic emblem of Sisyphus's endless and pointless task reverberated in them with familiarity— though less as the metaphysical truth Camus intended it than as an echo of their march toward adulthood and career for the sake of security rather than for any intrinsic fulfillment it might offer. Identity offered them a term that could both sum up their dilemma and point a direction out of it.

* * *

Erikson's reception in Europe in the 1950s was quite different. There is hardly any evidence of Erikson's presence in France during the decade except as a name included among the ego psychologists whom Jacques Lacan excoriated. In Germany it was largely limited to interest within the psychoanalytic community, though there, in contrast with the United States, Erikson was taken very seriously. This resulted particularly from the efforts of the psychiatrist Alexander Mitscherlich, who had met Erikson on his first trip to the United States after the war, and who led the effort to reestablish Freudian psychoanalysis in Germany after its wartime destruction by the Nazis. A number of Erikson's works were translated into German, and repeated references to his idea of "ego identity" appear in articles in *Psyche*, the psychoanalytic journal Mitscherlich founded with a number of others in 1947. In 1956 Mitscherlich invited Erikson to lecture at the event honoring the hundredth anniversary of Freud's birth, thus designating him as one of the world's most important psychoanalysts. By the 1960s, however, even popular newsmagazines like *Der Spiegel* were occasionally taking notice of his work.[76] Mitscherlich's own books in the 1960s, concerned with the failures of German society to deal psychologically with the Hitler era, invoked Erikson's work as necessary to understand such failure.[77] As in the United States, his popularity spread during the decade in which his idea of individual identity was coming under increasing attack from the politics of identity.

History Again

The core of Erikson's concept of identity did not change in response to the pressures and appeals of the 1960s and 1970s, though his emphases did. In the end, however, his accommodations to the spirit of the times were not sufficient to stave off criticisms of sexism, conservatism, and more damningly, irrelevance. His most vociferous critics were feminists. Erikson's identification of the feminine with "inner space," an idea going back to observations of children at play first broached in *Childhood and Society* but republished in articles in the 1960s and 1970s, raised particular ire and scorn.[78] His interest in the identity crises of great men, epitomized in his "psychobiographies" of Luther and Gandhi, was not in keeping with the egalitarian temper of the times, and his claim for them as ethical and spiritual revolutionaries was scorned by activists for whom the only revolution worthy of the name was political.

But if Erikson's individualist version of identity was rejected by political activists in the 1960s, the term itself was not. It was a tribute both to the continuing meaningfulness of the psychosocial concerns at the heart of the concept and to the wide currency it had gained through Erikson's work that leaders of black and feminist movements appropriated it to define their constituencies and their causes, sometimes as explicit modifications of his ideas, more often not associating it with Erikson at all. By the 1970s, the word "identity" had become not only an almost exclusively collective but also a largely political concept in the American public sphere.

It could never be either of these for Erikson, even if he had always insisted on the collective dimension of personal identity and even if, as the theorist of the adolescent identity crisis, he was inevitably attuned to the impact of political protest and counterculture on contemporary adolescence. He praised contemporary youth for their idealism in embracing the civil rights movement and the Peace Corps and for being more foresighted than their parent generation, "brainwashed by McCarthyism," in opposing the war in Vietnam. Influenced by the concept of "Protean Man," a term coined by the psychiatrist Robert Jay Lifton, his friend and former student, Erikson also came to agree that in the face of the endless dynamism of modern society, identity not only had to be but could be more flexible, less clearly defined, than before, ready always to change and adapt in order to manage inner contradictions. But he did not equate Proteanism with nonidentity. Among the young, he wrote somewhat testily in his 1973 tribute to Thomas Jefferson's part in creating the American identity,

> there are those who mistrust the whole identity concept as another
> trick of the older generation, designed to impose traditional restraints
> on what one might become if one refused to make anything of oneself
> and merely continued to improvise, to drift. These young people seem

> to be permissive toward themselves and disdainful primarily toward those who believe so strenuously that they know who they are. But this does not mean that they are not seeking what they are denying. For even where new forms of consciousness and new social patterns arise in bewildering alternations, the fundamental need for a familiar identity . . . changes ever so slowly. And so, the search of a revolutionary identity often leads to stances belonging to other eras.[79]

There was no escaping identity; ironically, the effort of 1960s radicals to do so, he claimed, had resulted only in the anachronistic re-creation of old identities. The alternatives to identity were painful psychic amorphousness, unconscious self-deception, or conscious but psychologically hollow role-playing. Even in the original myth, Erikson pointed out, there was a "real and lasting Proteus in the original Protean personality, a tragic core-identity in the multiplicity of elusive roles."[80]

As for collective identities, while some groups, or their spokespersons, were starting to assert their separateness and distinctiveness in the name of identity, Erikson was moving in the opposite direction. His early insistence on individual autonomy as a sine qua non of healthy identity had been a reaction to the psychic constriction and destructive exclusiveness of totalitarian ideology. Now, in the sixties, in the climate created by battles against racism, colonialism, and nuclear armaments he took a further step away from group identity. Both ethics and human survival demanded the fostering of a universal human identity, and the rejection of what he termed "pseudospeciation," the division of humanity into sharply differentiated collectivities treating themselves and others as if they were fixed, mutually hostile biological species. Gandhi, on whose biography he spent the better part of the sixties, was for him the prophet of an ethic of active, nonviolent conflict resolution based on the premise of the common humanity of all the protagonists. In the context of the rise of cultural identity consciousness there was a particular irony in Erikson's treatment of the Indian society in which Gandhi grew up. Intent on defending the universal validity of his eight-stage life cycle, with its core value of autonomous individuality, he tried to squeeze what he himself acknowledged as the quite different Indian schematization of developmental stages into its framework. At the very historical moment when group difference was beginning to be celebrated, Erikson was championing sameness. Not long afterward, social theorists of Indian background would be the foremost expositors of a uniquely postcolonial "hybrid" identity of which Gandhi was an obvious forerunner.

Robert Jay Lifton and the Protean Self

One of the more ironic pieces of evidence for the impact of the 1960s counter-culture on the concept of identity came from within the Eriksonian camp. In an article published in 1968, the psychiatrist Robert Jay Lifton, well-known for his work on the so-called "brainwashing" of prisoners in the Korean war, broached the idea of the "Protean personality" to which, as we saw, Erikson reacted ambivalently. Although Lifton wrote that he first became aware of the possibility of Proteanism in his 1950s work with Chinese and Japanese men whose lives had undergone many radical changes of identity, his idea only crystallized during the upheavals of the 1960s, as many of the examples of Proteanism he cited clearly show.

Lifton tried to cast his idea as a continuation of Erikson's effort to under-mine the older notion of fixed character with his more plastic concept of identity, but his break with Erikson was more obvious. "Even the image of personal identity," he wrote, "in so far as it suggests inner stability and same-ness, is derived from a vision of a traditional culture in which man's relation-ship to his institutions and symbols are still relatively intact—which is hardly the case today."[81] Instead of identity, a "new style of self-process is emerging everywhere," one in which individuals, like the mythical Proteus, refuse to commit themselves to a single form but engage in an interminable series of experiments and explorations,[82] each one tentative and none final. The Pro-tean self is characterized by a sense of the absurd that finds expression in a tone of mockery toward traditional social ceremonials and rites of passage and which one finds in Sartre's ironic characterization of his existential philosophy as born of a man who lacked a superego.

There was, however, a serious confusion in Lifton's description of Protean-ism. The examples he gave were not of people who consciously cultivated it as a lifestyle but who were driven to constant change in their identities by the frequent and radical alteration in their life circumstances produced by twentieth-century war and ideological conflict. Furthermore, he characterized the Protean self as suffering from a constant sense of dislocation, overwhelmed by a flood of superficial social messages and undigested cultural elements, as feeling like an actor with many roles but no core, and hungering for an ideol-ogy that would give it meaning. On this description, the Protean self's experi-ence of identity as fragmentary seemed much more like Erikson's identity diffusion, as Lifton himself acknowledged, than a chosen way of life. Many years later, in his autobiography, Lifton recounted that when David Riesman pointed out the contradiction between Lifton's own very settled identity as scholar and family man and his idea of Protean man, he responded that his

Proteanism lay in his unconventional imagination, not his concrete lifestyle. He also conceded that for many creative people, the exercise of the most far-ranging imagination required stability within the self, an "anchored" life.[83] The idea of imagination exploring beyond the bounds of the real and conventional was a rather old-fashioned form of "Proteanism," however; the artist understood this way was a recognized identity established in the West at least since the Romantics. Years later, when he expanded his original ideas into a book, and compared Proteanism to the contingency, multiplicity, and "playful, self-ironizing patterns" of postmodernism, he insisted that this did not mean the disappearance of the self with a complete absence of coherence among its various elements. Instead, Proteanism involves "a quest for authenticity and meaning, a form-seeking assertion of self. . . . The Protean self seeks to be both fluid and grounded, however tenuous that combination."[84] "Fluid and grounded"—this was a characteristic Eriksonian note and a hallmark of the modern definition as well as dilemma of modern identity.

R. D. Laing and "Ontological Insecurity": Existentialism as Psychology

It is paradoxically necessary to conclude this chapter on the birth of psychological identity not with Erik Erikson, who gave it its name and its currency, but with another figure who for a brief moment was almost as well-known. R. D. Laing was a phenomenon of the 1960s and early 1970s, a charismatic countercultural figure whose early books and approaches to treating schizophrenia made him famous, but whose influence receded almost as quickly as it had grown when he seemed to abandon his core ideas for mysticism, bizarre techniques of psychotherapy, and self-aggrandizement.[85] Laing first came to public attention in 1960 with his book *The Divided Self*, which described symptoms of "schizoid" (near-psychotic) and schizophrenic patients in subjective terms that resonated strongly with the "normal" and neurotic because many could recognize milder versions of such feelings in themselves. But his phenomenological descriptions of symptoms in patients' terms were embedded in a concept of psychological identity derived wholly from Sartrean existentialism rather than from Erikson. It is possible that the word "identity" is as prominent as it is in Laing's book because Erikson's work had by then established it firmly in psychological thinking about the self, but Laing does not so much as mention him. Though he had trained as a medical psychiatrist and psychoanalyst of the British school of object relations, he was for someone of that background unusually invested in Continental philosophy because he believed its concepts were more helpful in understanding the state of mind of the severely disturbed. In effect, Laing translated existential ontology into pure psychology by showing how Sartre's phenomenological descriptions of supposedly universal mental operations made many apparently bizarre and meaningless manifestations of schizoid and schizophrenic patients quite intelligible. In doing so he made it transparently clear that existentialism was, with psychoanalysis, a root of modern identity thinking. It is striking evidence of the psychological convergence of the existential and psychoanalytic approaches to identity that Laing's clinical descriptions seemed to many readers more emotionally immediate, "experience-near" versions of identity pathology than almost anything to be found in the work of the psychoanalyst who first named it.

This was true despite the fact that Laing did not shy away from Heidegger and Sartre's technical philosophical terminology. What he did, however, was to psychologize it by rendering impersonal philosophical categories as subjective feelings. Existential anxiety in Heidegger and Sartre, as we saw, was not necessarily, and for the most part was not empirically, experienced as such; it was posited as a fundamental ontological truth of human existence, functioning theoretically as a causal explanation for inauthenticity and bad faith. Laing's term was "primary ontological insecurity," which he described as a complex of fully conscious and terrifying feelings. The individual suffering from ontological insecurity feels

> more unreal than real . . . more dead than alive . . . precariously differentiated from the rest of the world so that his identity and autonomy are always in question. He may lack the experience of his own temporal continuity. He may not possess an over-riding sense of personal consistency or cohesiveness. He may feel more insubstantial than substantial. . . . *The ontologically insecure person is preoccupied with preserving rather than gratifying himself.*[86]

Laing defined ontological insecurity in relation to ontological security, which was in important part a normative definition of the psychologically healthy self. That did not mean, however, that he imported it from outside the patient's experience; it was what people actually strove for and what, as his readers well understood, most people achieved only to a greater or lesser degree. A basically "*ontologically* secure person," Laing wrote, "will encounter all the hazards of life, social, ethical, spiritual, biological, from a centrally firm sense of his own and other people's reality and identity."[87] In a crucial footnote Laing explained that he was not using the word "ontological" in the philosophical sense of Heidegger and Sartre but because it is "the best adverbial or adjectival derivative of 'being.'" By ontological security, then, he meant a feeling of being at home in the world that came from having a sense of oneself as solid and permanent—the very kind of identity Sartre had condemned as bad faith. As Laing put it in his next book, "A person's identity is first of all that whereby he is the same being in this place at this time as he was at that time in the past, and as he will be at that place in the future."[88] What Sartre had declared philosophically impossible Laing, like Erikson, claimed was psychologically indispensable.

Beyond listing the general features of ontological insecurity, Laing's most evocative contribution was to name and describe the omnipresent fears that haunt the ontologically insecure self and the psychological defenses it employed against them. In the terror of *engulfment*, the self fears being overwhelmed by other people because it lacks the "firm sense of one's own autonomous identity" that is "required in order that one may be related as one human being to another. Otherwise, any and every relationship threatens the individual with loss of identity." To love or be loved is to be in danger of being wholly absorbed into the beloved, robbed of one's independence. Even just to be understood, which the self may in fact dearly want, is to feel "enclosed, swallowed up, drowned, eaten up, smothered, stifled" by the other's comprehension. The main "maneuver" used "to preserve identity" by a self threatened with engulfment is *isolation*, cutting oneself completely off from others and withdrawing into oneself. In the fear of *implosion*, the self feels that it is an empty shell. Though the person longs for the emptiness to be filled, the "nothingness" he feels is nonetheless also who he "is." "Any 'contact' with reality," Laing wrote, "is then itself experienced as a dreadful threat because reality, as experienced from this position, is necessarily *implosive . . . in itself* a threat to what identity the individual is able to suppose himself to have." As with engulfment, the self defends itself by warding off the emotional contact with the world. *Petrifaction* is the fear of being turned by another into "a stone, a robot, an automaton, without personal autonomy of action." The defense against it is to get there first by *depersonalizing* the other in order to negate his power over the self. Laing acknowledged that he was here rendering Part 3 of Sartre's *Being and Nothingness*—"the look" and being with others—in psychological terms. The risk of not dehumanizing the other, Laing summarized, is that "if one experiences the other as a free agent, one is open to the possibility of experiencing oneself as an object of his experience and thereby of feeling one's subjectivity drained away. . . . In terms of such anxiety, the very act of experiencing the other as a person is felt as virtually suicidal." And these are not, Laing insisted, just the bizarre fears of the very disturbed few: "In fact we are all only two or three degrees Fahrenheit from experiences of this order." [89]

All the defenses Laing enumerated are self-defeating. They protect the self only at the expense of depriving it of the very things it craves: connection with others, fruitful interaction with the world, feeling real and alive, *being* someone. The ontologically insecure self ultimately creates a kind of master defense that brings it back into superficial contact with others while still preserving the inner self as inviolate. It creates a "false self" of social congeniality and conformity that interacts with others on their terms, becoming what it thinks they want it to be, but without feeling and internal commitment. The "real" self is kept intact and away, preserved in the mind as completely free and rich in possibilities. Such possibilities, however, can never be revealed to others or acted on lest they be exposed as impossible, be rejected by others, or fail of realization; they must be kept hidden protectively inside, perfect and unspoiled. The tragic paradox of the false-self system is that the supposedly "real" self, the self of desire, feeling, and commitment, is only a fantasy, utterly impotent, while the embodied self that does act and interact in the world is felt to be totally unreal. As Laing put it, "if a man is not two-dimensional, having a two dimensional identity established by a conjunction of identity-for-others, and identity-for-oneself, if he does not exist objectively as well as subjectively, but has only a subjective identity, an identity-for-himself, he cannot be *real*."[90]

The inner relationship between the "real" and the false self is deeply ambivalent and complex. The false self usually identifies first with what a parent wanted the child to be, against the child's own spontaneous desires; such total identification may have been felt to be the only way to preserve the parent's love. As a result, however, the inner, secret self hates the false self. It also fears it, because "the assumption of an alien identity is always experienced as a threat to one's own."[91] "Self-destructive behavior" in the false-self system is not "self-destructive" in the common sense of the word because it is aimed psychologically at the other, the object of identification that creates the false self. Conversely the inner self may feel devouring envy of those who seem to embody the life and vitality it would like to have but is unable to express; in attacking them it is overtly or covertly attacking itself because of rage at its own impotence. Laing illustrated these apparently convoluted analyses by vivid clinical vignettes that brought them to disturbing life.

In *The Divided Self*, Laing said virtually nothing about the causes of ontological insecurity. His approach was almost purely phenomenological and individual: describing as closely as he could, often using the language of patients themselves, what "not being" felt like to them. His Sartrean point of reference was exclusively *Being and Nothingness*. But Sartre himself had already gone beyond that work. In a turn to Marxism after World War II, he had begun to see and to argue that at least some instances of the anxiety of being were the result of economic and social inequality. The omnipotent Other was not just the projection of a universal, ahistorical desire for identity but a real power in the material world; it was that real power that made the Other into a plausible candidate for idealization and projection by the weak and powerless. Laing's next works followed Sartre. In *The Self and Others*, and more concretely in *Sanity, Madness and the Family* published three years later, he elaborated a theory of family dynamics which showed how parents fostered false selves in their children by insisting on the sole reality of their definition of the world while denying the worth and even reality of the children's experience and desires. In the same year, he summarized Sartre's theoretical journey, and his own, in *Reason and Violence: A Decade of Sartre's Philosophy, 1950–1960*, coauthored with his more politically radical colleague David Cooper. It is that journey we will have to follow to begin to understand how politics turned an initial focus on individual identity both in Europe and the United States into a concern with social and collective identity. But first we should take stock of the overall meaning of individual psychological identity and the issues it raised.

*   *   *

The main difference between Laing and Erikson on identity, apart from the origins of the language in which they conceptualized it, was their starting point and hence ultimate focus. While Erikson's interest in identity was first aroused by its psychopathological breakdown, his lifelong theoretical focus was on normal development, above all of adolescence, when mature identity takes form. The "crisis" of identity crisis was normative, not pathological. Laing's conception of identity came directly out of his work with severely disturbed adult patients and consisted largely of analyses of their extreme responses to the almost total absence of an inner sense of secure being. It was Erikson's work that made identity famous and gave it solid standing in contemporary theories of psychological development, but Laing's smaller body of work supplied the conceptual center Erikson's ideas only hinted at.

This was the idea of "ontological security," an intriguing though not unproblematic effort to translate philosophical "being" into psychological identity without the latter's negative philosophical implications. It was in fact the less systematic Erikson who, parsing the psychopathology of totalitarian ideologies, made the philosophical distinction between the absolute security denied to humans in virtue of our finitude and the relative security that psychological identity affords from the "surplus anxiety" created by the failure of others to recognize our humanity and worth. But it was Laing's concept of ontological security that implicitly underlay Erikson's definition of identity as a sense of selfsameness and continuity. Both agreed that a subjective sense of well-being and oneness with one's body, the ability to care about and for others, and to function in the world while mastering the ordinary anxieties of everyday life depended on having an identity in this sense. Whether it could be had, however, without turning self-definition into the thing-like inertia of inauthenticity or bad faith was a question neither addressed.

The problem was reflected in the tension between identity and autonomy that haunted Erikson's concept from the beginning. On the one hand identity promised stability based on socially valued work and the objective standards of an ideology. On the other, the process of identity formation demanded individual choices of both work and ideology at the crisis stage, and constant openness to modification in later life as the individual faced new social and historical realities. How could the reality of choice and change comport with the desire for stability and objectivity?

A further dimension of this conflict was inherent in the idea that a positive and stable individual identity required social recognition. Laing was initially concerned with it only in the context of the nuclear family and parental recognition. Its wider presence could be taken for granted in a homogeneous society governed by social consensus, but the idea of identity itself had only emerged, as Erikson himself argued, precisely when and because such consensus had broken down. Erikson interpreted the breakdown in keeping with historians and social theorists of the 1950s as the result of the rise of individualism as manifested in the free market of nascent capitalism and the free conscience of Protestantism. Individualism ruptured the automaticity of social recognition. This was potentially a problem for the individual, though not an inherently insoluble one, as his tales of identity crisis from Luther to George Bernard Shaw demonstrated. A powerful personality like Luther could take advantage of currents of social change to create changes in the social conditions of recognition, if at the price of revolution and war. What Erikson's original standpoint did not encompass was that there were whole groups of individuals within modern society for whom recognition had always been a collective problem because the social consensus denigrated or excluded them on the basis of their group identity. It took the protest movements of the 1960s to bring this home to him. But existentialist thinkers had begun to address this fact twenty years earlier in the wake of World War II.

Chapter 4

Social Identity and the Birth of Identity Politics, 1945–1970

For decades after the 1960s, "identity politics" was taken to be a largely if not exclusively American phenomenon, driven by a newfound collective identity consciousness among politicized blacks, women, and gays in the liberation movements that began during that decade. Even more than forty years later, a French historian specializing in the history of national identities could write, "The applications of the term identity to groups . . . are of recent origin. Their political existence began with the self-affirmation movements of 'minorities' in the 1960s and 70s."[1] The conventional assumption, however, is right only in a narrow sense. The actual phrase "identity politics" apparently originated in the 1977 manifesto of the Combahee River Collective, a "collective" of American black lesbian feminists, which proclaimed that focusing on their own "'specific oppression'. . . . is embodied in the concept of identity politics."[2] The Black Power movement had advocated and practiced a politics of identity without the label—though it did talk explicitly about "black identity"—a decade before that. But a concept of group identity had become a theoretical staple of American sociology and social psychology by the mid-1950s in a quite different historical context. And the idea of politicized collective identity emerged in Europe even earlier, in the responses of Jean-Paul Sartre and Simone de Beauvoir to the Holocaust and to the racial and sexual oppression in the contemporary world to which it had awakened their attention: European colonialism, the treatment of American blacks, and the situation of the nonliberated women in post-Liberation France. Nor were the earlier French and 1960s American identity thinking unconnected. There was a direct bridge between existential social theory and the Black Power movement in the thought of Frantz Fanon, the Martiniquais psychiatrist and anticolonial intellectual who applied Sartre's ideas to the mentality of colonized blacks and the requirements of Algerian liberation. Simone de Beauvoir was in effect her own bridge; virtually all feminists from the later 1960s on acknowledged her, whether wholly in agreement with her or not, as the founder of modern feminist theory.

Existentialism and the Collective "Other"

Jean-Paul Sartre

The postwar existential concept of group identity came out of a radical shift of focus in Sartre's work from abstract ontology to history and sociology, though he interpreted both within his original philosophical framework. Sartre had first dealt with the question of collective identity in *Being and Nothingness*, where he acknowledged its factual reality while subordinating it theoretically to the ontological primacy of individual consciousness. There could not be, he claimed, such a thing as a primary collective consciousness; the sense of "we" was a derivative from the ontological needs of individual consciousness. Contradictorily, however, he introduced a concrete social factor to explain how collective identity came about. That social factor would provide his theoretical jumping-off point when he turned in the postwar years to the politics of identity groups.

Since Sartre's account of interpersonal relations took the form of an internal dialectic that showed how the passive romantic-masochistic response evolved by its internal contradictions into the active, sexual-sadistic (but no less contradictory) response, he had no need to explain why an individual might habitually choose one modality over the other. Yet empirically it was a puzzle: why, in the struggle for identity, would one consciousness *habitually* strive to be an active subject making another into its object, while a second consciousness chose to alienate its freedom and become an object for the other? Feminist criticism of the stereotypically gendered language of Sartre's descriptions of these active-passive modalities didn't solve the problem; the ontological level of analysis specifically excluded materiality, the role of body or social institutions, as the "cause" of an absolutely free choice of subjecthood or objecthood. Active and passive were simply the two possible attitudes *any* consciousness could assume to the reality of its being for others.

But the problem of why a *group* of individuals should succumb to the objectifying look of a third seemed an even greater puzzle, which Sartre did try to deal with. There are, he acknowledged—somewhat grudgingly, since it was to admit the causal influence of externalities on consciousness—"certain situations" that are "more likely than others to arouse the experience of the Us."[3] He had in mind the Marxist analysis of capitalist labor. In capitalist production, the laborers' collective activity creates the condition for group objectification in the eyes of the capitalist owners, because they are in a position to appropriate the products of the workers' labor and rob them of their agency, both material and psychological. Individuals who labor in factories are thereby objectified as "the workers" in the consciousness of both capitalists and laborers themselves. This however then creates the possibility of subjective class-consciousness on the part of the workers, who can turn in their own minds from an "us-object" as seen by the bosses into a "we-subject" who can take action against them. Or, as Sartre put it more abstractly, "Class consciousness is evidently the assuming of a particular "Us" on the occasion of a collective situation more plainly structured than usual."[4]

The obfuscating phrase "more plainly structured" at once acknowledged and downplayed the importance of the fact that by Sartre's own account the real economic power of the capitalist to control the product of the workers' labor was a necessary condition of the capitalists' power to define the workers' identity as (mere) "workers." The linkage to economics made sense even ontologically: why else would I acknowledge the absoluteness of the other's freedom over my own, and hence accept his definition of me, unless he actually wielded more effective power than I in the world? But so intent was Sartre on maintaining the absolute freedom of consciousness to create meaning, and so little concerned with its empirical context, that his attempt to keep the factual and the ontological apart was awkward and confusing. "The 'master,' the 'feudal lord,' the 'bourgeois,' the 'capitalist,'" he wrote, "all appear not only as powerful people who command but in addition and above all as *Thirds*; that is, as those who are outside the oppressed community and for whom this community exists."[5] But—as Sartre would himself soon come to see—the power of the "Thirds" to look at and define the oppressed (and to make the oppressed internalize their definition) was not simply an "addition" to their factual economic, political, and social power; it was contingent on them.

At the same time Sartre's insistence on the power to define identity as involving a motive and a conceptual register logically distinct from economic interest would make it possible for him to differentiate more clearly between material and nonmaterial sources of power and oppression, and to discriminate, describe, and locate the nonmaterial with greater precision. His attention to these nonmaterial sources was intensified by events and encounters during and after the war that made it impossible for him to continue to treat freedom and unfreedom as pure (and arbitrary) acts of consciousness: the wartime fate of French Jews, his postwar acquaintance with a group of Caribbean and African black émigrés in Paris struggling since the 1930s to define an independent black identity against French colonialism, and his friendship with the American expatriate writer Richard Wright, which made the situation of American blacks a matter of direct personal interest to him. (He did pay cursory attention to the oppression of women, in his play about the American South, *The Respectful Prostitute*, but it was his intellectual partner Simone de Beauvoir who would make women the subject of the most important and extended treatment of collective identity in the "social existentialism" of the 1940s.) Sartre was now much more concerned with the role of the concrete historical "Other" in the self-imposed subordination of the oppressed in the contemporary world. But because he did not abandon his original ontological framework, he was also better able to see it as more than a reflex of economic power.

*   *   *

The superficial surprise of *Anti-Semite and Jew*, Sartre's first and most influential exploration of collective identity,[6] begun while the war was still raging, was that its initial focus was not on the ultimate victim group but on the "victimhood" of their oppressor. This however was precisely Sartre's point. Anti-Semites were, in a real sense, victims of the economic power structure in contemporary France who responded to their inferior situation by identifying with those at the top of the hierarchy at the expense of Jews. Most anti-Semites, Sartre claimed, belonged to the lower middle class of the towns, functionaries, office workers, and small businessmen without the large-scale property that in France conferred not only economic and social power but a sense of entitlement and superiority. Sartre had earlier evoked the mentality of the wealthy French bourgeois in *Nausea* with his sardonic descriptions of the portraits of leading citizens of "Bouville"; the smug self-regard he saw in them was not just repulsive social affectation but a claim to absolute legitimacy, to the transcendent right to rule—the kind of metaphysical claim that underwrote the false ontology of identity.

Lower-class anti-Semites, deprived of the kind of property that supported such a claim, had to find property elsewhere, and they did so by asserting that they alone were the legitimate owners of France. "It is in opposing themselves to the Jew that they suddenly become conscious of being proprietors. . . . Since the Jew wishes to take France from them, it follows that France must belong to them. Thus they have chosen anti-Semitism as a means of establishing their status as possessors."[7] At some level of consciousness, however, the anti-Semite knew how precarious that status was. "If by some miracle all the Jews were exterminated as he wishes, he would find himself nothing but a concierge or a shopkeeper in a strongly hierarchical society in which the quality of 'true Frenchman' would be at a low valuation, because everyone would possess it.

He would lose his sense of rights over the country because no one would any longer contest them, and that profound equality which would bring him close to the nobleman and the man of wealth would disappear all of a sudden, for it is primarily negative."[8] The phenomenology of identity in the anti-Semite was thus necessarily quite different from that of the entitled upper classes. Though similarly based on a claim of sanctified ownership, the lower-class anti-Semite's sense of identity was accompanied by gnawing insecurity prompted by its illusoriness and by a destructive rage against the Jews that served to cover both their anxiety and their illusion. Anti-Semitism was not the calmly confident belief in their superiority that the upper classes enjoyed but a state of angry passion that eschewed rationality in order to escape examination. Only unreflecting rage could confer the feeling of hardness otherwise missing in those who lacked the real hardness of material possession, of "real" estate: "I hate, therefore I am," in place of "I own, therefore I am."

Sartre's attempt to extend the materialist explanation of group power in *Being and Nothingness* to encompass the objectification of the religious or racial other, while yielding brilliant intuitions about the different psychological registers of identity, nonetheless created conceptual dilemmas. Most obviously, his prewar novella *Childhood of a Leader* had based its protagonist's solution to his quest for identity on the anti-Semitism of a segment of the urban *upper* class, in blatant contradiction to the property analysis of *Anti-Semite and Jew*. More problematically, his analysis presumed what it set out to explain. "The Jew" must already have been singled out as other if he could be cast as the thief who would steal France from its legitimate owners. At best a Marxist approach could explain the status anxiety of the petty bourgeoisie, not the direction of its compensatory anti-Semitism. Sartre slid over the problem by acknowledging the original religious basis of anti-Semitism but relegating it to the past. Once, Jews were hated as the killers of Christ; in the modern (i.e., secular) age, they could be completely assimilated if not for their usefulness in the class wars. "Thus it is no exaggeration to say that it is the Christians who have *created* the Jew in putting an abrupt stop to his assimilation and in providing him, in spite of himself, with a function in which he has since prospered."[9] The unavoidable implication of his own argument was that modern anti-Semitism built on the originally religious pariah status of the Jew. Religious faith was an independent motive to objectify, and majority status gave it the power to do so.

For many Jewish readers at the time and after, the support proffered by Sartre's merciless anatomy of the anti-Semite's bad faith was offset by his claim that their Judaism had no internal content, that Jews did not compose an original "we-self." "The Jew," he wrote in his most controversial epigram "is one whom other men consider a Jew. . . . Jews have neither community of interests nor community of beliefs; they have no history. The sole tie that binds them is the hostility and disdain of the societies which surround them."[10] However wrong as a generalization even about Westernized Jewry, Sartre's phenomenology of the "authentic" and "inauthentic" Jew offered painfully apt descriptions of the identity struggles even of many whose Judaism was more than nominal or social. As general identity types, furthermore, they could be applicable mutatis mutandis to any group denigrated and excluded by the majority or the powerful.

The "inauthentic" Jew tries to escape his Jewishness in two ways. He may accept, with deep shame, the truth of the anti-Semite's negative stereotypes of Jews as uncouth or money-hungry but try to evade them by working consciously not to live down to them; at the extreme he may become himself anti-Semitic. The "universalist" Jew, by contrast, rejects the validity of all categorization of people by race, nationality, or ethnicity, insisting on the sameness of humanity and universal standards of reason. Discrimination according to intuition, tradition, "thinking with the blood" all serve to separate and exclude people without objective foundation.

What is inauthentic about rationalist universalism is that it denies the empirical social reality of group identities along with their spurious ontological justification. Our being-for-others is a fact in the world with which we must operate if we are to change reality. The authentic Jew recognizes that he is forced to make his choices within the framework of the society that defines him. "Jewish authenticity," Sartre wrote, anticipating by two decades the tenets of what later came to be called identity politics, "consists in choosing oneself *as Jew*—that is, in realizing one's Jewish condition. The authentic Jew abandons the myth of the universal man; he knows himself and wills himself into history as a historical and damned creature; he ceases to run away from himself and to be ashamed of his own kind. He understands that society is bad; for the naïve monism of the inauthentic Jew he substitutes a social pluralism."[11] Jewish identity may no longer be a matter of common religious belief but it is a matter of common fate; paradoxically, it is only by accepting the identity decreed by that fate that Jews become capable of making their own destiny.

* * *

Just two years later, his involvement with the self-conscious identity concerns of another victim of French racism took Sartre a big step beyond the analysis of *Anti-Semite and Jew*. The occasion was his essay "Black Orpheus," written as a preface to an anthology of poetry by a group of African and West Indian poets, French colonial subjects living in Paris. A main purpose of the anthology was to present and represent the idea of "negritude," a term coined previously by one of its contributors, the West Indian poet Aimé Césaire and later defined by the volume's editor, Léopold Sédar Senghor, as "the ensemble of values of black civilization."[12] The grammatical form of the word negritude alone was a discomfiting challenge to Sartre's existentialism. As an abstract noun, it connoted a state of being, a human essence, just the kind of thing whose legitimacy *Being and Nothingness* was intended to destroy. In the contemporary situation of colonial racism, however, this "anti-racist racism,"[13] as Sartre called it, was a prerequisite for the abolition of all racial difference. The African or Caribbean black had to be able to embrace in pride what he had been forced to endure in shame before his blackness could become irrelevant to his common humanity with the white man.

This was just a blunter version of Sartre's insistence that the "authentic" (French) Jew had to embrace his Jewish identity if only to insist on his right to "assimilate," by which Sartre meant to become as French as anyone else. But "Black Orpheus" went farther. It proclaimed the theoretical inadequacy of the Marxist explanation of the racial, and by extension the religious, objectification of others. The proletariat, he pointed out, is created by the objective economic circumstances of production. Exploitation is a structural fact; proletarian liberation does not require the proletarian's subjective self-examination but the objective analysis of his economic situation and the appropriate action to change it. The black, by contrast, is a victim first of definitional dehumanization by color. His blackness, which unlike proletarian status is ineradicable, has been defined as less than, or worse, as *other* than human by whites, who take whiteness to be synonymous with the universally human, and he has internalized that definition wherever they have ruled him. Racial subjugation is not reducible to class exploitation, though it may serve to rationalize it. Like religion, "race" has been an autonomous foundation of significant identity for humans, and identity is as much a basic human concern as producing the means of subsistence. Thus before the black can liberate himself materially and politically, he must liberate himself psychologically. He can do this only by reversing the white man's devaluation of his color into a positive identity. The quest for negritude is a quest for a valorized "Essence of blackness."[14]

What, or better where, is this "essence"? Sartre's language deliberately waffled on whether negritude was something discovered in the secret heart of black people or something created by black poets. From the purely existential point of view it could only be a poetic construction, but Sartre wanted, indeed needed, to preserve a certain ambiguity. A "created essence" not only defied the very purport of the term, which as he said denoted something preexisting and permanent, but it undermined the crucial psychological task negritude had to perform: how could a mere conscious fiction of identity transform the black psyche hungering for dignity? Sartre tried to sustain that ambiguity by interpreting negritude through his theory of the emotions, which had argued that feelings are not simply passively endured, though they are experienced that way, but ways of establishing connections with the world through choices of oneself. It was choosing to live, for example, that caused the self to interpret certain situations as dangerous; the emotion of fear inevitably followed. Negritude, he wrote, was "the Negro's being-in-the-world,"[15] structuring the meaning of all his experiences. This interpretation allowed him to cite with approbation the emotive language the poets used to celebrate negritude even when that very language seemed to imply something quite different from deliberate choice—the psychological experience of a predetermined, fated, state of being.

Toward the end of the essay, however, Sartre finally faced the ambiguity directly by asking: "Does the poet who would be the Prophet for his colored brothers invite them to *become* more Negro, or does he disclose to them what they *are*? . . . Is negritude necessity or liberty? . . . Is it a fact or a value?" Despite the stark "either/or" choice these polarities seemed to demand, Sartre initially tried to have it both ways, overtly refusing to choose between alternatives. "One will undoubtedly answer this question [of the choices between fact and value, etc.,] by saying it is all of these at once. . . . And I agree: like all anthropological notions, negritude is a shimmer of being and needing-to-be; it makes you and you make it."[16] Yet in the end Sartre insisted on the constructed nature of negritude. In part it was because he wanted to attribute philosophical correctness to his poets, but more importantly he wanted to legitimize his own vision of the brotherhood of all men by attributing it to them. The poets of negritude accordingly were "preparing the synthesis or realization of the human being in a raceless society." "Thus," he claimed in their name, "negritude is *for* destroying itself; it is a 'crossing to' and not an 'arrival at,' a means and not an end."[17] Negritude was socially real and psychologically "true" but ontologically, ethically, and so ultimately historically false.

The convolutions of Sartre's argument reflect the consequences of inescapably contradictory agendas. Once existential ontology descended into the concrete and messy arena of politics and psychology, it faced the necessity of finding a way to accommodate the "bad faith" identity needs of real people. In *Anti-Semite and Jew*, Sartre tried to remain philosophically consistent by distinguishing between "metaphysical anxiety" and "sociological anxiety," each of which could motivate bad faith. "Metaphysics," the concern with the human condition that can lead to an escape from freedom through identity, is real enough, but it "is the special privilege of the Aryan governing classes."[18] The pure anguish of existence is available only to those assured of their social rights and firmly rooted in the world, those free from the concrete anxiety of want and fear. Jews and other oppressed groups could not afford that luxury. Jewish anxiety is the result of social oppression and it demands of Jews, if they are to liberate themselves, that they first acknowledge their Jewish identity. Though this means acknowledging that they "are" Jews, however, it does not involve embracing a positive, permanent Jewish identity; it means acknowledging the Jewish "situation," one created for Jews from the outside. This pale substitute for identity would disappear in the classless society of the future, which would make anti-Semitism—hence also Jews—disappear. In "Black Orpheus," negritude has a strong content in a way that Jewish identity in *Anti-Semite and Jew* doesn't, one, furthermore, which Sartre explicitly valorized. In fact he was sharply criticized for accepting the traditional white "primitivist" stereotypes of blacks while trying to reverse their valence from negative to positive by simple fiat. Yet at the same time he undermined the ontological solidity and temporal permanence of negritude by positing a future society in which group identity as such will no longer be possible, let alone necessary. The somewhat schizoid outcome was an exhortation to blacks to believe fully in their negritude until they didn't need to.

Simone de Beauvoir

In sharp contrast, Simone de Beauvoir was not caught in the parallel dilemma of wanting to both valorize and repudiate feminine identity in her epochal call for women's liberation in *The Second Sex*. This might seem all the more surprising in light of her statement a decade after its publication: "One day I wanted to explain myself to myself. . . . And it struck me with a sort of surprise that the first thing I had to say was 'I am a woman.' "[19] But this revelation, in the context of *The Second Sex*, was not, even preliminarily, the positive embrace of a feminine identity; it was the unhappy acknowledgment of the female *situation*, one that from time immemorial had been the foundation of false identities—an existential redundancy—for both women and men. Her attitude to feminine identity was more like Sartre's toward Jewish identity than toward negritude, but much harsher. Even if Jewish identity was subjectively empty and socially negative, Sartre had insisted that to be authentic, Jews needed to affirm the fact of their Jewishness without shame to counteract the self-demeaning internalizations of anti-Semitic stereotypes. For Beauvoir, femininity certainly had to be understood—and she described it at much greater length than Sartre had either Jewishness or negritude—but it had to be unequivocally repudiated for its self-denigrating bad faith without an intermediate stage of feminine pride to ease the transition to freedom.

The reasons for her negativity become obvious through her descriptions of the female situation and the traditional feminine identity it created. Both repelled her. On its face, her revulsion was philosophical, but it was hardly dispassionate; her language exudes visceral disgust. By their biological constitutions women are subjugated to the human species, as men are not. They are fated to carry, bear, and nurse children, and they are physically weaker than men. At the dawn of human history, when life was precarious and procuring the means of subsistence difficult and dangerous, these differences doomed women to an inferior position to which they acquiesced because they also derived advantage from it. And in fact the advantages that both sexes derived from their original power relationship resulted in its perpetuation down to the present, even though external conditions had changed drastically. In practical terms women's continued social subordination made a certain sense.

What challenged and provoked Beauvoir was why women acquiesced not just to their subordinate social position but also to the inferiority of their *identity* as "feminine." Males as such had no identity, she claimed, at least not one separate from what it meant to be universally human. "It would never occur to a man to write a book on the singular situation of males in humanity," she wrote, long before studies of masculinity were thinkable, let alone commonplace. "Humanity is male, and man defines woman, not in herself, but in relation to himself" (5). Biological differences, however, were only the necessary, not the sufficient condition both for that definition and for women's collusion with it. The more fundamental cause was that biological difference was refracted through even more basic existential concerns. While in humankind's primitive beginnings virtually all of men's actions were, like women's, also bent to the service of the species—procuring the means of subsistence and defending the group—such service was at least *action*. For Beauvoir, as for Sartre, action meant freedom, "transcendence"—rising above the inert passivity of the brute given, the predetermined constraints of the human condition. Action alone conferred meaning and dignity to humans in their own eyes. "In serving the species, the human male shapes the face of the earth, creates new instruments, invents and forges the future," Beauvoir claimed. Childbearing, on the other hand, does not create, it merely re-creates: it is "nothing but a repetition of the same Life in different forms. By transcending Life through Existence, man . . . creates values that deny any value to pure repetition" (74). Childbearing is the epitome of passivity and inertness, of deterministic subordination to natural processes. It is only from this perspective that one can understand the profound alienation from the female body evident throughout the book epitomized in Beauvoir's claim that "From puberty to menopause [woman] is the principal site of a story that takes place in her and does not concern her personally" (40). Woman's reproductive biology is the alienation of her essential humanity.

And it is just because she *is* human, an "existent," in Beauvoir's philosophical terminology, who like the male values freedom and transcendence, just because "her project is not repetition but surpassing herself toward another future" that woman is complicit with men in their self-valuation and her own self-denigration. Bereft of opportunities for transformative action, she participates with men in celebrating their sovereignty, their successes and victories, able to fulfill her human destiny only through passive identification with them. "To give birth and to breast-feed are not *activities* but natural functions; they do not involve a project. . . . [Woman's] misfortune," Beauvoir lamented, "is to have been biologically destined to repeat Life, while in her own eyes Life in itself does not provide her reasons for being, and these reasons are more important than life itself" (73–74).

This extraordinarily dour evaluation of women's situation left two questions: what definition of the feminine followed from their fateful collusion with male supremacy? And, most puzzling, since technology and social mores had long since advanced to the point where not only could women control their reproduction but physical strength no longer mattered for the most prestigious work in a modern society, why did women remain submissive, in their own eyes as in the eyes of men defined as the "second" sex? The answers to these questions were integrally connected because as Beauvoir described it, the dynamic of feminine identity explained its own perpetuation.

Feminine identity, Beauvoir pointed out, could not be understood without its masculine contribution. In contradiction to her initial assertion, she claimed that there is in fact a distinctive masculine identity and that furthermore it depends crucially on men's construction of the feminine. It is true that men are in a position to attain existential authenticity by renouncing static "being" and assuming responsibility for their acts and choices, but because of the difficulties and dangers that freedom poses, authenticity demands constant effort not to surrender to the comforting temptations of bad faith. To be a man early in the evolution of the human species was to constantly court mortal danger; today it still means constantly having to prove oneself and face the eternal challenge of recalcitrant reality. As is only human, men tire of unrelenting difficulty and fear great danger, and so they have contradictory aspirations: they desire active life *and* passivity, existence *and* being. Man "dreams of restfulness in restlessness, and of an opaque plenitude that his consciousness would nevertheless still inhabit. This embodied dream is, precisely, woman" (160). Men desire to *be* without effort that which in reality they have to work at unceasingly to achieve. Because of woman's inert procreative function, she can be conceived of as "being" Nature; she is without any effort on her part the "All," the fullness man desires for himself. Loving man, woman enfolds him, making her transcendent infinitude vicariously his. She can grant him this, however, only because man also sees her as a free consciousness, though one who is, contradictorily, naturally submissive, whose freedom exists only in order to affirm his own infinite transcendence. Man has thus placed what Beauvoir called, with literal precision, a "marvelous hope" in woman: "he hopes to accomplish himself as being through carnally possessing a being while making himself confirmed in his freedom by a docile freedom."[20] Realizing that contradiction would indeed be a miracle. No wonder that, as she cuttingly put it, "No man would consent to being a woman, but all want there to be women." Men don't want to be inert and passive, as women are, but without women, men would have to be "on" all the time, having to prove their transcendence over and over with every new life challenge. Deified by woman, man can believe in his own transcendence as if it were a simple given, something to be taken for granted as existing independent of his action, or nonaction. Woman makes man that impossible possibility, a "free, omnipotent thing."

In return, of course, man deifies woman, but in a contradictory and ultimately demeaning way. He puts her up on a pedestal to worship her divine plenitude, which also enables him to sideline her from the important business of life. At the same time she is expected to take care of the necessary if uncreative business of domesticity, her métier, after all, qua natural being. Of course being a goddess has certain obvious advantages for women even if the price of empyrean divinity is mundane servitude. It means being protected physically and being taken care of materially. Above all it means being valued by the intrinsically valuable, man, being "justified" without having to face the challenges of action in the world.

Women's justification, however, does not come through man's faith alone; it demands works. Since what men desire of women is carnal possession, women must work to make themselves carnally desirable. This project is the essence of femininity, and like masculinity it is a contradictory one. Men are ostensibly the initiators, the hunters, women their prey, but to lure the hunters, they must make themselves attractive: they are not just passive but "spontaneously offered" prey. Hence the preoccupations of feminine identity: figure, clothes, deportment, sexiness, youthfulness—anything and everything that will enhance their attraction as objects. To double the contradiction, women not only work to lure men, they "capture" them, binding their freedom; they become in turn, though without full lucidity, the hunters, implicitly denying their male prey the very transcendence they seek through him. Femininity is an effortless state of being; it is also hard work. It is natural to woman yet not all women have it. Despite this fraught contradiction, women have historically found femininity rewarding enough to refuse to abandon its familiar haven for unbounded freedom. Even modern women, Beauvoir noted, who have begun to essay transcendence through meaningful work have insisted on remaining feminine, a double burden men don't bear: "She wants to live both like a man and like a woman; her workload and her fatigue are multiplied as a result" (725). More than that, her pursuit of femininity as attractiveness denies the claim to transcendence she makes through her new productivity. For Beauvoir the only existentially true and consistent response to the female situation is to reject feminine identity completely, motherhood above all, at least so long as it prevented women from being fully men's equal in freedom through creative work.

That women all over the world, at the time and later, felt themselves discovered in *The Second Sex* says much about the general relevance of her analytic portrait of feminine identity. The book's American impact is perhaps unsurprising; Beauvoir's ideas about its form and content owed much to her observations of the situation of American women during her trip to the United States in 1947.[21] But her descriptions of the life of the little girl, female adolescent, and young woman were drawn from intimate familiarity with the milieu of the early twentieth-century French upper classes into which she was born, as readers of her autobiographical *Memoirs of a Dutiful Daughter* could later easily determine. The present French political moment was also a goad: if Beauvoir believed that young American women were more willing to sacrifice independence of thought and action for domesticity than their French counterparts, she also knew that French women, who had just got the vote in 1944, were decades behind American women in political liberation. Recently, partly because we have learned more of the details of Beauvoir's life but also because we have become more attuned to the intimate subtexts of purportedly universal insights, we can see how deeply personal the book was, how much a venture in individual identity exploration. At the confusing intersection of her long-standing egalitarian intellectual partnership with Sartre and her newfound passionately sexual relationship with Nelson Algren, the " 'essay on women,' " Beauvoir's biographer writes, "offered her . . . a forum in which to analyze herself while creating a work suitable for publication. By extension, it would be suitable for a reading audience which would not know that she herself was the subject under discussion."[22] But the wider historical moment was also ripe for her venture. *The Second Sex* came out of the confluence of the existential philosophy of freedom, the post-Holocaust attention to the condition of oppressed groups in France's empire and at home, and the biographical facts of a woman's life caught by the circumstances of her background between equality with men and what she herself depicted, in the thinly veiled fictional account of her affair with Algren, *The Mandarins*, as romantic submission.[23]

* * *

Common to the work of both Sartre and Beauvoir, and their lasting contribution to the theory of collective identity, was the concept of "the Other." It would become the foundation of virtually all theorizing in the English-speaking world on negative or excluded group identities after the 1970s. Recent research by feminist scholars has worked to reverse the conventional narrative of Sartre the originator and Beauvoir the faithful epigone by claiming her priority in the discovery of the concept.[24] The issue of priority, however, is of less significance for the history of identity than the largely unnoticed fact that the two thinkers actually used the term "other" in opposite, though not incompatible, ways, and that it was Beauvoir's that became normative.

For Sartre, the Other was the absolute subject, the unbounded free consciousness with the power to make someone who encounters its look experience himself as an object. The object of the look becomes de-centered (or more accurately, allows himself to become de-centered) from his own subjectivity; he no longer sees the world from his own point of view but from that of the Other who looks at him. For Beauvoir, who introduced the concept in her novel *She Came to Stay*,[25] published before *Being and Nothingness*, the Other was not the subject but the *object* of the look, the victim, the one who feels herself turned by it into a thing-like being, other than, and less than, the one who looks. The existential interpersonal dynamic in both works was exactly the same, but the focus of the two writers was on the opposite sides of the interaction.

Use and repetition have somewhat blunted the full exclusionary force of the idea of otherness. To be Other in Beauvoir's object sense is not just to differ in some shared human characteristic; it is to be a fundamentally different kind of being. The subjects who decree the otherness of another take themselves to embody the norm of humanity, with all that entails in terms of claims to capacities, rights, and empathy; the Other, by definition, is less than human, more accurately, other than human. Phenomenologically, nonetheless, the act of rendering "other" involves a paradoxical move: the Other must give every appearance of being fully human. Humanity can only be denied someone in the face of "superficial" evidence that she or he is human; otherwise denial would not be necessary.

Frantz Fanon

That is precisely what the Martiniquais psychiatrist, philosopher, and revolutionary activist Frantz Fanon wanted to convey when he described, in *Black Skin, White Masks*, the experience of walking into a roomful of whites: "I feel, I see in those white faces that it is not a new man who has come in, but a new kind of man, a new genus. Why, it's a Negro!"[26] Years later, reviewing the 1963 English translation of Fanon's last book, *The Wretched of the Earth*, Eldridge Cleaver, a leader of the African American Black Panther group, wrote that it was "already recognized around the world as a classic study of the psychology of oppressed people [and] is now known among the militants of the black liberation movement in America as the 'Bible.' "[27] In fact the earlier *Black Skin, White Masks* was more explicitly concerned with psychology of colonized blacks than the later book, but since it was not translated until 1967 and had no political program, it did not have the same impact on restive American blacks looking for a radical alternative to the civil rights movement. Nevertheless, as a study in what Fanon explicitly called "the meaning of black identity," it was the theoretical foundation on which *The Wretched of the Earth* rested.[28]

Though he incorporated many ideas from the psychoanalysis of the day, most prominently Alfred Adler's "inferiority complex," Fanon's concept of identity came more or less directly from Sartre, particularly *Anti-Semite and Jew*.[29] But unlike the latter work, or "Black Orpheus," *Black Skin, White Masks* represented first-person testimony of the bearer of minority identity. Combining abstract theorizing with the immediacy of personal experience, Fanon was able to convey what a concept like "black identity" actually felt like.

At the level of philosophy Fanon could say that "Ontology . . . does not permit us to understand the being of the black man. . . . The black man has no ontological resistance in the eyes of the white man."[30] He meant that "blackness" was not a basic category of human existence; it was brought into being only by the white man, the Other who endowed "blackness" with negative meanings which blacks internalized. This, Fanon pointed out, was a clear parallel to what Sartre had said about "Jewishness," except that Jewishness is not visible on the surface of the body and could be hidden, while blackness could never be escaped. On the level of experience the "being of the black man" means constant feelings of "Shame. Shame and self-contempt."[31] Black feelings of inferiority vis-à-vis whites are so automatic on encounter that they should properly be described as "epidermalized" rather than internalized,[32] experienced physically on the skin as the black feels white eyes on him.

These feelings further invade the black's total experience of his—and her—body: "Consciousness of the body [for the Negro] is solely a negative experience."[33] Above all the sexual body; it is why mulatto women are physically repulsed by darker-skinned men and why black men feel driven to sexually possess white women. But such feelings also invade the mind of the most reflective, rational, and analytical person, the black philosophers and psychiatrists who try to understand such feelings. In a brilliant riff, Fanon recounted the serial attempts of someone "like" him to counter black inferiority with universal reason, then embrace the irrationality attributed to blacks by whites as a superior life-force of which whites are bereft, only to face the white rejoinder that such a stance is an outdated primitivism that has no place in the modern world. Even the foremost white champion of negritude, Sartre, repudiated it as at best a temporary stage of black consciousness to be surpassed on the way to total liberation. For a black man in quest of positive black identity Fanon lamented, "Every hand was a losing hand."[34]

In that case the only answer was to give up the identity game altogether and adopt Sartre's universalism. By reacting to the white man's definition of him, by adopting "blackness" in the first place, the black man has lost before he begins. As Fanon put it, "As I begin to recognize that the Negro is the symbol of sin, I catch myself hating the Negro. But then I recognize that I am a Negro. . . . I then try to find value for what is bad—since I have unthinkingly conceded that the black man is the color of evil. . . . I have only one solution [to this bind]: to rise above this absurd drama that others have staged round me, to reject the two terms that are equally unacceptable, and, through one human being, to reach out for the universal."[35] This meant eschewing any affirmation of black identity.

> In no way should I dedicate myself to the revival of an unjustly unrecognized Negro civilization. . . . There is no Negro mission; there is no white burden. . . . I do not have the duty to be this or that. . . . If the white man challenges my humanity, I will impose my whole weight as a man on his life. As a man, that is, as a human being like himself. That is the only "identity" that counts, which in the later reckoning of identity is no identity at all. The Negro is not. Any more than the white man.[36]

Fanon allowed one exception to the remedy of internal consciousness-raising and moral confrontation. "For the Negro who works on a sugar plantation," he asserted, "there is only one solution: to fight."[37] When oppression is external, a matter of political and physical coercion and not just negative self-definition, personal identity transformation is irrelevant: the oppressor must be defeated. While this was not the situation of black, nominally equal citizens of France—or of the United States—it was precisely the one Fanon found himself in when he took up a psychiatric position in Algeria. That the Arab majority were not equal citizens but a colonized people offered an opportunity to fight white domination directly. Soon afterward he joined the FLN, the Algerian national liberation movement. A majority people deprived of equal rights by a foreign imperial power, he argued in the work he wrote to promote its cause, could only become free by violent revolution.

Not surprisingly it was Fanon's advocacy of violence that caught the shocked and titillated attention of most contemporary readers. What many missed—though not black American activists—was that Fanon saw violence as an instrument for the creation of collective identity. In *The Wretched of the Earth* he abandoned the individualist-universalist perspectives of *Black Skin, White Masks*. He did not change his mind about the uselessness of resurrecting the glories of a culture's past, but his reason was now quite different. To focus on a group's past was to vainly attempt to raise the dead and to forfeit the chance to create a living identity in the present and future. "A national culture," he wrote, is "the whole body of effort made by a people in the sphere of thought to describe, justify and praise the action through which that people has created itself and keeps itself in existence. A national culture in underdeveloped countries should therefore take its place at the very heart of the struggle for freedom which these countries are carrying on."[38] At the level of individuals, Fanon notoriously wrote, violence is a cleansing force that frees the native from his inferiority complex, restores his self-respect and makes him fearless. But even more important, the native's violence unifies the people and makes them equal as well as free.[39] Freedom for the individual black or Arab can only come through collective struggle, which in circular fashion depends on the birth of collective identity, then continues to shape it as the fight goes on. The trajectory of Fanon's work from 1950 to 1960 was from anti-identity universality to collective identity.[40]

Sociological Identity: Collective Identity in American Thought Before Identity Politics

As Linda Nicholson argued in *Identity Before Identity Politics*, there were precursors in the early years of the century to the explicit political discourse of collective identity in the United States in the 1960s. Like the interwar European precursors of individual identity, they explored what would later be called identity issues without using the term. There were even some parallels in the underlying causes of the concern with self-definition in both cases: conflict and doubt about the status of existing identities. W. E. B. Du Bois's notion of the "double consciousness" of American blacks, forced to partly view themselves through white eyes, prefigured the 1960s quest for an authentic black cultural identity, as Marcus Garvey's black nationalism prefigured later separatist black political identity. But there were also decisive differences. In the case of American blacks and women, the idea of what would later be called group identity was taken for granted, not made an object of critical inquiry. What was problematic for them was the disjunction between the group's sense of itself and the way it was viewed by whites or males. More importantly, the ultimate aim of early black advocates and first wave feminists was not self-assertion through racial, cultural, or gender identity but equal rights and assimilation, or where that was deemed impossible because of implacable white racism, equal rights through separation.

It was not, then, out of the debates about "the souls of black folk," the "New Negro," or the feminism of the 1920s that explicit theoretical self-consciousness about group identity as such developed.[41] It first emerged as a term in the United States in the academic disciplines of sociology and social psychology during the 1950s, in reaction to what social scientists perceived as the failure of individualist paradigms of social theory. The sociological theory of group identity did have its own distinct historical and social context, even a social agenda. Couched in ahistorical abstractions, however, founded on relatively complacent notions of social integration and consensus, and without much emotional resonance, sociological identity theory did not lend itself readily to either popularization or politicization. When identity politics did emerge as a self-conscious movement, however, the sociological theory of identity contributed one of its central concepts: the idea of the social construction of reality.

*   *   *

Two currents in American social thought converged to produce sociological identity theory in the 1950s. Driving both was a reaction against the radical individualism that sociologists believed had marked prevailing trends of social and legal thinking in the later nineteenth century: William Graham Sumner's so-called "Social Darwinism" and post-Civil War corporate legal theory. Both seemed to rest on a premise of self-sufficient individuals whose competitive self-interest was the foundation of all social institutions.[42] Initially rooted in the metaphysics of social contract theory, with presocial individuals in a hypothesized state of nature, individualism had been scientifically naturalized by the application of the Darwinian struggle for survival to economic behavior. Entrepreneurial capitalism was thus rooted in man's biological constitution. Theoretical individualism was further strengthened when, with the emergence of large-scale corporations after the Civil War, legal theory extended the idea of the sovereign self to corporate entities, which were to be treated in law as "persons."[43] Socially created group entities could now also be seen as competing individuals.

In the first half of the twentieth century, however, American social thinking, often with reformist intent, sought to destroy the presumption of atomistic individualism and substitute for it a theory of the person as the developmental product of the individual's interaction with society. So strong was this reaction that it sometimes tended to the opposite extreme of reducing the individual to a function of social forces. Social identity theory was an uneasy, not wholly successful attempt to strike a balance.

One of its two basic elements was sociological role theory. Put somewhat tendentiously—though it was at times defended in just these terms—role theory claimed that the self was (nothing but) the sum of the multiple social roles it played.[44] It was an anthropologist, Ralph Linton, who in the 1930s introduced the idea that the smooth functioning of any society depends on the presence of set "patterns" of reciprocal behavior between individuals or groups, patterns that constitute their actors' respective roles. A pattern involves two or more units (individuals or groups) who occupy defined "statuses" in relation to one another, like teacher and student; when someone acts on the rights and duties that constitute his status he is performing his status role. Roles are, as the metaphor suggests, scripts of a sort, repetitive rule-governed behaviors. "Every individual," Linton claimed, "has a series of roles deriving from the various patterns in which he participates and at the same time a role, general, which represents the sum total of these roles and determines what he does for his society and what he can expect from it."[45]

Whether or not Linton himself thought that the role was the man, the increasing cachet of role theory among social scientists led some to worry that that was indeed the theory's implication. Partly to counteract it, the sociologist Nelson Foote in 1951 introduced the idea of identity as a motive force to explain why an individual subjectively identified with his social roles. His article "Identification as the Basis for a Theory of Motivation" was the first in any American journal of sociology to use the word identity as a significant theoretical term. Foote acknowledged Freud's concept of identification as his inspiration, but insisted that he intended something quite different. Freudian identification was unconscious and motivated by the desire to hold on to libidinal objects by internalizing them. Foote defined identification as the "appropriation of and commitment to a particular identity or identities. As a process, it proceeds by *naming*; its products are ever-evolving self-conceptions—with the emphasis on the *con-*, that is, upon ratification by significant others."[46] Foote made no mention of Erikson in his article, but in commenting on it the sociologist Reinhard Bendix noted some similarity between Foote's identity and the "Neo-Freudian" Erikson's concept of ego-identity.[47] One's "identity" then was one's conscious—explicitly named—conception of oneself, of who, or what, one was. Foote was not quite precise in calling identification a theory of *motivation*. It was the need for identity, for self-conception, that was the motive; identification was the process by which one created it. And it was the need for identity that according to Foote causes someone to identify with certain social roles and not with others. In the process of socialization a person learns many more social roles than he overtly uses. "The reason [a person] limits his real or realistic behavior to a selected few of all the roles he has learned," Foote claimed, "is that he knows and defines only these certain ones as *his* own. And he can only ascertain which role is his in each situation by knowing *who* he is."[48] Though the content of identity is social roles, individuals would seem to have a psychological need to know who they are by defining certain social roles as them. Erikson's influence is patent.

Nevertheless, individual motivation played a distinctly subordinate role in Foote's approach to identity. Society's needs, not the individual's, explained the existence of roles and hence of concrete identities. While he acknowledged that a person's identities "give common meaning, stability and predictability to his own behavior"—adding the proviso "as long as he clings to them," which suggested the partial freedom and lability of identities—the importance of rule-governed, predictable roles was that they "make possible a more or less orderly social life." "Every man," Foote asserted, "must categorize his fellows in order to interact with them."[49] Without the assumptions and expectations of regularity and predictability, social life would be unimaginable, each encounter demanding the reinvention of sociality.

The significance Foote attributed to the naming of roles points to the other important strand of contemporary sociology that shaped his concept of identity, the school of thought initiated by the work of Charles Horton Cooley and George Herbert Mead in the early twentieth century later called "symbolic interaction." For both men, the "self" is necessarily a product of social interaction. From early in our development we internalize the way we see others seeing us; each of us is, at least initially, what Cooley called a "looking-glass" self and what Mead referred to as "the self of reflected appraisal." These interactions take place through and are necessarily mediated by language. We are, to ourselves and to others, what we are named by others[50]—the formal social categories to which we are assigned, with all that goes into them: orientations to beliefs, values, and purposes that pattern our actions and our expectations of others. As Foote colorfully put it, "A rose by any other name may smell as sweet, but a person by another name will act according to that other name."[51]

Names are social products and in turn they socialize us; through naming, our individual identities make us integrally members of collective identities. *"One has no identity apart from society,"* Foote claimed flatly.[52] That is not to say that we are fully determined by our *initial* social identities, however, though it may feel that way at first because of the apparent absence of alternatives when we are young or if we grow up in a homogeneous environment. But this usually changes with further development. Observation and self-reflection open up the possibility of changing our identities by conscious choice.[53] Mead's developmental theory allowed for this possibility because he distinguished between the "me" that is the locus of imposed social definitions and the observing "I" who can maneuver and choose among them.

Though Foote's conception of the range of possible choices was limited to the set of collective identities furnished by an individual's society, that set might be quite large. In fact, despite the apparent stickiness of early identity, Foote and the sociologists who followed him tended to think of personal identities as equivalent to the plethora of social roles available to an individual in virtue of the richly complex division of labor in a modern society. His examples ranged from religious and political identities to those that baseball made available in the varieties of field position, membership in a particular team or even fandom. One might be a Catholic or a Protestant, but also a right fielder, a Toledo Mud Hen, or a St. Louis Cardinal fan. Understood in these terms individual identities are in principle many, evanescent, and shifting. As Foote put it, "in action it is the unique concatenation of relevant statuses at this one time and place—in this *situation*—which constitutes identity."[54] Identity is nothing more than the position of the individual in a momentary social transaction defined by its roles and rules.

The historian Philip Gleason succinctly summarized the key difference between Erikson's psychosocial identity and the sociological version, at the same time implicitly suggesting one reason why it was Erikson's that seized the historical moment and the popular imagination in the 1950s and early 1960s. For Erikson, identity was something deep within the individual that persisted through change (such that instability or uncertainty of identity could precipitate serious psychological crisis), while role theorists and symbolic interactionists thought of the self as a "flickering succession of identities adopted and shed according to the requirements of different social situations."[55] Nevertheless, in some of the most influential applications of sociological identity to contemporary social issues in the 1950s, identities were treated as significant self-identifications more limited in number, more basic in scope, and more stable within the individual than the theory suggested. These studies, which deal with the sorts of identity categories only implied in Foote's thesis about the weight of early identities, point to the concrete historical issues behind the rise of sociological identity theory in the first place: above all the role of religion and immigration in American society.

In 1954, sociologists Manford Kuhn and Thomas McPartland published a report of results from a simple but ingenious test they had devised to discover how a group of undergraduates at the State University of Iowa defined themselves.[56] The "Twenty Statements Test" was subsequently widely used both in the United States and in quite different societies abroad.[57] It consisted of a single sheet of paper with twenty numbered blank spaces. Participants were asked to fill the blanks with answers to the question, "Who am I?" without reflecting on or censoring their responses. The question, the authors wrote, "is one which might logically be expected to elicit statements about one's identity; *that is, his social statuses.*" Their definition derived directly from the symbolic interactionist thesis that "the self is an interiorization of one's positions in social systems."[58] Contrasting the sociological with the "Freudian" approach, they acknowledged that "the social scientist assumes that most human behavior is organized and directed by internalized but consciously held role recipes."[59]

Within these "recipes" the authors divided test responses between "consensual" and "subconsensual" references. The former were statements which answered the question "who am I" with reference to groups and classes whose conditions of membership were "matters of common knowledge"— "student," "girl," "Baptist." Subconsensual references were those that mentioned attributes requiring further interpretation by the subjects in order to locate them relative to others—"happy," "pretty good student," "too heavy"—answers that the authors considered "subjective" but were in fact references to observable traits or social norms rather than groups. A main conclusion of the study was that the respondents tended to exhaust all of the consensual references they would make before they made any subconsensual ones, suggesting that people's identities as members of socially well-defined groups ranked first in their self-definitions.

But a more historically specific conclusion came out of the authors' effort to correlate the frequency of references to one kind of group in particular, membership in religious denominations, with the religious affiliation of the test subjects. Analysis revealed that religious identity answers were significantly more salient among the self-attitudes of minority religious groups, Catholics and Jews, than among members of majority Protestant denominations. The authors' focus on this issue was more informative than the unsurprising results. While they did not explain why they singled out religious identity, the social integration of ethnic/religious minorities—which in the 1950s meant primarily the southern and eastern European immigrants of the late nineteenth and early twentieth centuries and their descendants—was a central concern of social science in the years after the Second World War, which had purportedly done so much to unify American society.

It was also of interest to a more general public, to judge by the wide notice of Will Herberg's book of a year later, *Protestant, Catholic, Jew.*[60] Herberg, a social theorist and Jewish theologian, argued that the two main contemporary conceptions of the immigrant experience in America were wrong. America was not the "melting pot" in which the ethnic identities of immigrant groups wholly dissolved into one homogeneous American identity, but neither was it a pluralist pastiche. Immigrants had indeed accepted and tried to assimilate to a set of idealized Anglo-American norms. Their ethnicity, however, rather than completely disappearing, had evolved into religious identification as a way of retaining something of their immigrant origins while at the same time becoming wholly American, since "all religions"—meaning, at the time, those of the so-called "Judeo-Christian tradition"—could be seen as the foundation of the central American values of respect for individuality, equality, and democracy.

"Social identity" was the central organizing category of Herberg's book. People have to self-identify by answering the question "What am I," and their answer, Herberg wrote, is couched in terms of their "social location," that is, the social group to which they belong and its relation to other groups. "Unless [someone] can locate himself," Herberg wrote, "he cannot tell himself, and others will not be able to know, who and what he is."[61] Identity in this view is a matter of social geography, which raised the question of what the significant locations were on a given social map. In the evolution of immigrant identity from the great wave of 1880 to 1920, Herberg, following the preeminent American historian of immigration Oscar Handlin, traced changes in the social maps of immigrant self-identification from neighborhoods of people from the same European town to wider groupings in terms of common language and culture, and eventually to common nationality, the trajectory making up what Handlin understood as ethnicity. For Herberg, however, it was one specific set of categories that provided the "new framework of social identities" in America by the 1950s. To be an American meant, indeed required, belonging to one of the major American religious communities. Whatever the truth of this analysis, it was itself a testimony of identity: a leading intellectual in the American Jewish community was proclaiming that Jews in the United States were not just a cluster of separate ethnicities representing their European national origins but a unified religious community as American as white Anglo-Saxon Protestants.

By the end of the 1950s, the idea of group identity in terms of social role and religion was well defined in American sociology. By then too, however, the impact of Erik Erikson's concept of psychological identity on the social-scientific as well as on the general culture was so great that sociologists were taking explicit note of it, if only to differentiate their idea of identity from his, though thereby tacitly acknowledging its influence. The symbolic interactionist Anselm Strauss, for example, while pointing out that he had made a conscious decision not to deal with identity in terms of individual personality but to limit his focus to the social process from which it emerges, titled his book of 1959 *Mirrors and Masks: The Search for Identity*.[62] This was the first sociological work to use the word identity in its title, though its hint at the centrality of an individual quest to his theme was not misleading. In discussing the subjective sense of personal continuity people often feel—or feel the lack of— across their disparate social statuses and developmental changes, he suggested that continuity of identity depended on the ability of people to create narratives that could weave them together into a coherent whole.[63] His observation foreshadowed the emergence some thirty years later of the genre of "narrative and identity" studies. Another example of Erikson's increasing influence among sociologists was the appearance in 1963 of Erving Goffman's *Stigma: Notes on the Management of Spoiled Identity*.[64] The title itself represented a significant shift in Goffman's vocabulary. Until then he had spoken not of identity but of the self and its modes of self-presentation. In *Stigma* he analyzed the feelings and coping strategies of individuals unable, because of physical or behavioral "stigmata" defined according to prevailing social norms, to conform to "normal" social identities.

Nevertheless, the point of view of both these books was unequivocally sociological. As Strauss bluntly put it, sociologists' "attention is given to persons as members of social groups and organizations. *Persons become role-players rather than individuals. Two persons in interaction are never merely* [sic] *persons but group representatives*."[65] His chapter on "Transformations of Identity" analyzed the way in which individuals in a given society moved through a regular sequence of identities prescribed by rule-governed developmental models of its available roles: thus a young woman sequentially occupies the identities of engaged woman, bride, wife, pregnant mother, and child-raiser.

Of course, Strauss pointed out, these transformations of identity are not always frictionless. Social identities are subject to historical change that may cause time lags and generational conflicts. Ordinary human emotions—jealousies, rivalries, the reluctance of elders to accept a young person newly elevated to higher status as a full equal—may act as grit in the smooth functioning of the social machinery. On the other hand, individual emotions and motives are themselves ultimately conditioned by the socially structured sequence of identities. "When positional mobility follows known sequences," Strauss noted, "different motivations frequently become appropriate at each status. . . . Indeed, the stability of a given social structure rests largely upon a proper [motivational] preparation for these sequential steps."[66] Individual motives are molded by the role development expectations of society, and these personal motivations become in turn the necessary condition of the individual fulfillment of social expectations. Social identity theory in the 1950s had a normative agenda: it interpreted the ultimate purpose of individual identity teleologically as guaranteeing social stability.

Though Strauss insisted on the necessity of conceiving social identities as changing historical constructs, and argued that individuals fashioned important parts of their personal identities out of other larger categories furnished by "public" history, such as ethnicity and nationality,[67] neither he nor Goffman was much interested in historical change. A static functionalist assumption about the purpose of social groups underlay the sociological approach to identity. Rule-governed roles and statuses were the necessary condition of any society's stability and smooth operation. Thus both Strauss and Goffman could take the prevailing structure of social identities as the fixed starting point for their theories of individual identity-formation. By contrast, the most famous American analysis of collective identity in the 1950s, Muzafer Sherif's account of his Robbers Cave experiment, was concerned with group identity precisely in the process of its making, and unmaking.[68]

Sherif actually used the word "identity" in his book only once, in reference not to the group's collective self-representation but to the self-conceptions that individual members derived from their status and role within the group; these self-conceptions he termed, with a nod to Erikson, "ego-attitudes."[69] But the significant aspect of the experiment for identity was what it revealed, in contradiction of the experimenters' own interpretation, about the formation and phenomenology of collective identities and their interaction.

Sherif assembled two groups of twelve-year-old boys, similar in economic, social, and religious background, in an isolated campsite in an Oklahoma state park. The two groups were first kept apart, but even in isolation each began to create a distinctive collective identity. There was no concrete "Other" present to constitute them as an "object group" or to react against in turn as a subjective "we-consciousness." Instead, one of the groups defined itself spontaneously as a collective entity with a name—the Rattlers—distinctive songs and rituals, and a set of group norms, including sanctions for deviate behavior. The experimenter/"counselors" had their own explanation for this. The boys' behavior seemed to bear out their initial hypothesis that "When individuals having no established relationships are brought together to interact in group activities with common goals, they produce a group structure with hierarchical statuses and roles."[70] Implicit in this hypothesis was the assumption that this was rational behavior on the part of the boys for the achievement of shared individual ends; group statuses and roles, sorted according to individual abilities, were the necessary means for realizing those ends. The assumption did not account for the boys' creation of a wholly new collective identity which each spontaneously adopted and to which each subordinated his individuality.

When the two groups were ultimately brought together for athletic and other competitions, the experimenters took the ensuing events to confirm Sherif's second hypothesis, according to which "If two ingroups are brought together under conditions of competition and group frustration, attitudes and appropriate hostile actions in relation to the outgroup and its members will arise." What actually happened was quite different. The Rattlers and the second group, who had not yet named themselves, were given hints of each other's presence before they knew they would meet. The immediate response of both to the very idea of the others' existence was hostility and rejection. The Rattlers proposed running the other boys off, and claimed possession of the various locations in the park that they were using as "ours." When the second group heard (but did not see) the Rattlers playing baseball one of them referred to those "nigger campers," and in anticipation of the possibility of playing against them decided they needed a common name to cement their unity, settling on Eagles. The racist epithet showed clearly that group formation in the park experiment was not taking place in a social vacuum; in-groups and out-groups were long since a conditioned part of the boys' social schemata. But its a priori use in a new situation without visual evidence of the identity of those to whom they were applying it also suggested the boys' spontaneous propensity to "other" the stranger. The instigated competition between Rattlers and Eagles certainly sharpened the hostility between them, to the point of physical violence, and deepened their respective identities through opposition and contrast. Since the Rattlers subscribed to manly cursing, the Eagles claimed the purity of clean speech. But the crucial fact is that distinctive collective identities preceded the actual encounter of the groups, in the case of the Rattlers even before they knew of another's existence.

If Sherif failed to attribute significance to this fact, it was out of both theoretical presupposition and ideological concern. His purpose was to see whether group solidarity and intergroup enmity could be broken down as well as created. In its final stage, Sherif's team faced the Rattlers and Eagles with a series of tasks that would have compelling appeal for both but that could only be accomplished by their cooperation. After a relatively short time, not only the hostility between the two groups but the strong intragroup identity of each broke down. The boys formed friendships across groups and by the time they left for home, Rattlers and Eagles had disappeared as separate identities. This was as the experimenters had hypothesized, and hoped. Behind the overall design of Robbers Cave lay a number of sociopolitical theses and commitments on the part of Sherif and his collaborators. Born in Turkey in 1906, Sherif had as a youth witnessed at first hand the murderous ethnic cleansing that destroyed the Greek community in Asia Minor after the First World War. Coming to the United States, where he did his graduate training, and where he perceived ethnic groups living together in mutual tolerance, he was persuaded by the prevailing sociological theories that he believed could account for American social harmony and decided to develop and test them empirically. This enterprise was all the more compelling after the carnage of World War II. If groups formed on the basis of common individual "interests," and if group antagonism was consequently the result of adventitious conflicts of interest between them, the way out of conflict was to establish what Sherif called "superordinate goals" appealing to the individual members of all groups beyond their narrower group affiliations.[71]

The ease with which Rattler and Eagle identities were conjured away, however, obscured the fact that they were only dissolved into a prior common identity. The boys had been selected precisely so that religious, racial, and economic differences would not divide them from the beginning, but this was implicitly to acknowledge their basic homogeneity. The main reason it was relatively easy to break down the Rattler and Eagle identities was that they were artificial and shallow in relation to the boys' deeper commonality. On a bus trip to a celebratory outing made possible by their cooperation, one of the boys began whistling a song that he knew would unite both groups, "The Star Spangled Banner." And as a later commentator on the experiment asked rhetorically, what might have happened if the Eagles, "these white boys with their racial slurs at the ready," had in fact come across a group of black boys.[72] In effect, Sherif had experimentally discovered an apparently deep and spontaneous urge to group identity and differentiation that, however superficial and evanescent in the particular case of Rattlers and Eagles, was not reducible to his rationalist categories. Not being noticed, however, it could not (yet) be theorized.

* * *

The work of Strauss and Goffman firmly established the concept of identity within sociological role theory by the early 1960s. Just a few years later, however, it took a radical turn that was to have a decisive impact on American social criticism. For the most part role theory and symbolic interaction were built out of native American materials.[73] The core ideas expressed both in the title of Peter Berger and Thomas Luckmann's book *The Social Construction of Reality* and in the book's central explanatory concept originated in the critical European traditions of Hegelian Marxism, the sociology of knowledge, and existentialism. "Social construction" quickly became the watchword, and eventually the cliché, of much radical social theory in the second half of the twentieth century. Its critical edge derived from its claim that the fact of "construction" was most often obscured by the mental process of reification, by which we interpret human creations as preexisting, nonhuman entities. Much American sociology and cultural anthropology, Berger and Luckmann argued, which emphasized the causal force of static, objectively given social institutions on behavior, exemplified such reification. At the same time, however, the authors "Americanized" social construction by psychologizing it. Society was only an abstraction, composed of concrete individuals. To understand the minds of those who actually do the constructing the authors incorporated both George Herbert Mead's theory of personality development and the notion of identity—without, however, mentioning Erikson.

Society in the authors' conception is both an objective and a subjective reality, in "dialectical" interaction with one another. It is at base the product of human intentions and purposes, which in turn create social institutions that both foster and constrain human possibilities. But despite their causal efficacy in molding behavior, institutions remain human phenomena, not inert things, and therefore subject to human control. "Reification," the authors explained, "is the apprehension of the products of human activity *as if* they were something else than human products—such as facts of nature, results of cosmic laws, or manifestations of the divine will. Reification implies that man is capable of forgetting his own authorship of the human world."[74]

Reification, furthermore, may distort the individual's view of himself just as it does his view of society. On the one hand, individual identity is constructed from the roles society makes available. Objective society becomes a subjective reality through the individual's internalizing of its norms and proce-dures. In this process social roles are also "identity types." "To be given an identity," the authors defined, "involves being assigned a specific place in the world. As this identity is subjectively appropriated by the child . . . so is the world to which this identity points."[75] But the assigned places of identity types are not the whole of personal identity. There are elements of subjective reality that do not originate in socialization, such as the awareness of one's own body prior to and apart from any socially learned attitude toward it. "Subjective biography is not fully social," Berger and Luckmann argued. "The individual apprehends himself as being both inside *and* outside society."[76] Individuals can react on the given social structure; mostly they tend to maintain it but they are also capable of modifying or even reshaping it.

Such a possibility is lost when identity is reified. One's role is seen as an inevitable fate, the "paradigmatic formula for which is the statement 'I have no choice in the matter, I have to act this way because of my position.'" Not only an individual role but "identity itself (the total self, if one prefers) may be reified, such that there is total identification of the individual with his socially assigned typifications. He is apprehended as nothing but that type."[77] These were Sartrian conclusions couched in Hegelian-Marxist language.

Though theirs was a significant contribution to the theory of collective identity, Berger and Luckmann actually repudiated the concept. It was "mis-leading" because it was historically associated with "undialectical" theories that hypostatized "society" as an objective entity.[78] In a word, they took the idea of "collective identity" to be reified by definition, something outside of and imposed on individuals. At its worst, they believed, such a conception had produced the determinist sociology of the conservative, later Nazi social theo-rist Othmar Spann, who based his authoritarian corporatist politics on it, but it could also be found in Durkheim's less noxious and widely influential con-ception of society as a thing external to the individual. The dialectical theory of social constructionism was intended precisely to combat the one-sided determinism of prevailing academic sociology. Its fulcrum was its conception of identity, the point at which the subjective dimension of society could exert its power, the point where the work of "social construction" actually took place. In its beginnings, the concept of social construction was defined in terms of and depended for its very possibility on the idea of identity.

From Individual Identity to the Psychology of Collective Identity

Given the rationalist and functionalist foundations of American sociological identity theory, the increasing attention historians and social scientists began paying to collective identity in the 1960s was less the result of its impact than it was the extension of Erikson's psychosocial perspective to the upheavals of colonial warfare, decolonization, and the overall collapse of European empire in Africa and Asia that had begun in the 1950s. Collective identity had always been in principle fundamental to Erikson's understanding of individual identity, even if, because of his orientation to strong individuality and creativity, he conceived his major studies of identity as biographies of world-historical individuals who in achieving their own identities amid historical turmoil had created new possibilities for others. It was no great stretch to extend the idea of the quest for identity first to small groups of creative individuals, then to nations and finally whole continents which, personified, could be described as trying to create a new collective identity in the anticolonial struggles of the era. One striking example will do for many. In 1966, the political scientist Victor Ferkiss, in his book *Africa's Search for Identity*, brought together in somewhat uneasy conjunction the developmental perspective of Erikson and the existential categories of Sartre and Beauvoir to interpret contemporary African striving:

> The search for identity is the basic dynamic of African politics. . . . Just as the adolescent comes of age and must define himself in relation to a given social environment, so Africa is seeking to come of age in the new world of the twentieth century. But the simile of adolescence is a deceptive one. . . . Africa is not a child but a captive released from bondage. It seeks now to play a role which is self-determined rather than determined by others, and in order to do this strives to know its own nature. . . . Africa is one . . . because outsiders have thought of it as one, and still do. . . . A purely Caucasian Muslim in Algeria was as much an "other," a racial and cultural inferior, as a Negro in the Ivory Coast.[79]

At about the same time, in his biography of the Senegalese poet and politician Léopold Senghor, the political scientist Irving Markovitz wrote of "negritude" as having originated in the 1930s in the quest of young black intellectuals for their "*personal identities*," while in its second phase African political leaders dealt with the central problems of establishing "*national identities.*"[80] Such interpretations, though distinguishing between individual and group identity, brought them together for a new understanding of the collective in relation to the individual. The integration of Eriksonian psychological identity into ideas of "race" (blackness), ethnicity, and nation went far beyond the concept of social role identity in defining the significance of the collective for individual identity. National and pan-African identity were taken to provide for Senegalese or Africans the personal security, psychological integration, sense of purpose, and overall ideology that Erikson had attributed to the unique identity emerging from a long, tumultuous personal quest. From the other end, the cohesion, persistence, and power of nationalism were seen to rest on the fact that it offered psychological identity to large numbers of individuals, who were thus strongly motivated to sustain it. As a result, in such studies of group identity it was the group's common denominator, not its unique individual variants, which was taken as psychologically salient for the individual. Intended or not, one result of the shift in attention from individual to collective identity was the simplification and homogenization of psychological identity. Uniqueness became an attribute of the group rather than the individual, and increasingly the identity distinctions that mattered were those between groups.

The Rise of Identity Politics in the 1960s

The shift from personal to collective identity in the academic social sciences was the symptom of changes in the larger society. Unlike the versions of collective identity thinking discussed so far, the idea of "identity politics" was broached not by intellectuals or academics but by grass roots participants in social movements in the United States in the 1960s and 1970s. Practicing identity politics, however, was initially more important to activists than theorizing it. The Combahee River Collective manifesto of 1977 was likely the first to use the term but it was also apparently the only political document that did during those years. Certainly the manifesto's drafters were picking up on the by then common use of identity in its extended Eriksonian sense of collective subjectivity, that is, individuals' identification with a group as their primary psychological identity. Black nationalists and Black Power advocates had talked about "black identity" a decade earlier, as had leaders of the feminist movement about women's identity. But it was only in subsequent reflection on the meaning of these movements that the terms "identity politics" or "politics of identity" gained currency among political theorists and historians as well activist-theorists in the 1980s and 1990s. Howard Brick's comprehensive analysis of American thought and culture in the 1960s has only a handful of references to identity politics, none of them citing contemporary use of the phrase.[81] But the reality of the new politics soon demanded a new term.

That doesn't mean that it is easy to pin down its exact nature. There was after all nothing novel in the idea of affinity groups organizing politically; it had always been the stuff of American politics. What *was* new was the basis on which some began to do so and the way they conceived their causes. Up through the 1940s, political activists and theorists had mostly framed their demands, and their general understanding of the goals of political action, within two main paradigms, the liberal-democratic principles of equal individual rights and political participation, and the Marxist analytic assumptions of class conflict, economic exploitation, and workers' needs. The battles for women's suffrage and racial integration had been fought in the name of the first, many of labor's struggles, whether for a radical new social order or for union recognition and collective bargaining within capitalism, in the name of the second. (The main exceptions were black separatist movements, which believing that neither paradigm could bring equality for blacks within American society, felt their only recourse was to opt out of it and create their own.[82]) The Marxist paradigm, however, which had never had broad purchase in the United States, was further marginalized in the 1950s by the Cold War and by the appearance of shared postwar prosperity. Social theorists across the ideological spectrum argued that the United States had achieved a "post-scarcity" society,"[83] though they differed sharply as to what economic affluence might augur for social stability and social change. Mainstream liberal and academic political theorizing celebrated consensus politics and the end of ideology. Radical and dissenting theorists agreed such notions existed but branded them as ideological because they veiled the unhappiness of an increasingly regimented corporate and bureaucratized society. Yet even radicals in those years were focused less on economic class and on alleviating the material problems of exploitation and economic inequality than on the psychological and quality-of-life issues created for a newly extended middle class by private affluence and the increasing dominance of large-scale organizations: conformity, lack of authenticity, alienation, and the cultural starvation of the public realm.

The civil rights movement in the early 1960s, and the anti-Vietnam War and counterculture movements of the mid-1960s with their indictments of capitalist imperialism and corporate-fostered consumerism, gave new impetus to the traditional reformist and radical paradigms of change. But the general diminution of class and economic modes of analysis became increasingly central to the self-awareness of black, women, and gay activists through the 1960s. They began paying specific attention to the political and psychological implications of the fact that they had always been excluded or demeaned on the basis of differences that were neither entailed in nor accommodatable by the categories of liberal individualism and socioeconomic class. Identity and the role of "otherness" seemed more open, capacious, and flexible concepts for defining their situation. In the psychological climate fostered since the

1950s by Erikson's work on identity their strategic move was to make differences of color, gender, and sexual orientation conscious objects of new forms of political thought and action by working to reverse their inner psychological and outer social valence from negative to positive.[84]

*   *   *

In the black community the emblematic initiative was not so much the demand for "black power" as such as it was the associated call for black consciousness and black pride. "Power" could in theory be assimilated into the normal understanding of American interest group and ethnic politics. If groups were particular, "interest" was universal; so long as a group was conceived as existing to pursue its members' economic and political interests, it was simply another of the factions envisioned in Madison's original constitutional theory and in contemporary American political thought about pressure-group politics. Pride, however, was a psychological category explicitly aimed at unique group characteristics. The activists who founded the Black Power movement did not in fact make basic distinctions between identity needs and demands for political and economic power; both were subsumed under the same rubric. In calling for black power they claimed to be acting like all other ethnic groups before them who had been able to participate as equals in American society and politics only by first organizing their own community institutions to represent their interests within the larger society.[85] But at the same time they were explicit about the need for blacks to make their black particularity an end in itself, to take pride in their blackness—and they well understood the provocation of a slogan that ambiguously but deliberately associated "racial" pride with power. "We aim to define and encourage a new consciousness among black people," Stokely Carmichael and Charles Hamilton wrote in their Black Power manifesto of 1967; "This consciousness . . . might be called a sense of peoplehood: pride, rather than shame, in blackness, and an attitude of brotherly, communal responsibility among all black people for one another. . . . We must first redefine ourselves. *Our basic need is to reclaim our history and our identity* from what must be called cultural terrorism."[86] To name the enemy white "cultural terrorism" was to say what such self-redefinition involved: beyond the apparently straightforward revaluation of skin color, epitomized in the contemporary battle cry "black is beautiful," it meant validating and publicly displaying a unique black culture.

The manifesto both implied new ideas about the nature of collective identity and challenged conventional ideas of politics. It proposed a series of initiatives that politicized the previously nonpolitical and questioned the relevance and validity of supposedly universal political ideals. "Negroes," for example, must change the name by which they had been up to then socially identified because, having been imposed on them by whites, it carried the stigmata of racial inferiority and was a vehicle of exclusion. But blacks must also reject political coalitions with white civil rights groups, not just because they needed to control their own organizations but above all because integration meant that "black people must give up their identity, deny their heritage."[87] Carmichael and Hamilton had relatively little to say about the specific content of that heritage, or in general of the unique culture at the heart of black identity. Though they invoked culture as the foundation of collective identity, they did not care to be precise about what they meant by it. Aside from the invocation of black "peoplehood" and history, the idea of a separate black culture amounted for them to rhetorical, psychological, and tactical separation from the white community. But that did not mean that Black Power's idea of cultural identity was merely nominal, let alone that it was easy for white liberals and radicals to assimilate it to their own political understanding of the common cause of equality.

In part this was because the current notion of black cultural identity had been inherited from the incendiary mix of Malcolm X's Nation of Islam platform, which called for a separatist black nationalism in frequently antiwhite and revolutionary rhetoric hinting at violence. In his 1964 Statement of Basic Aims, Malcolm called for recapturing black identity through the launching of "a cultural revolution to unbrainwash an entire people."[88] To the extent it had positive content, cultural revolution for the Nation of Islam meant American blacks' reclamation of their African roots through the adoption of Swahili names and Islamic religion, but to focus on these specifics would be to miss the centrality of the reactive, even adversarial dimension of Malcolm's idea of black cultural identity. To be black was to be what white was not—and not to be what white was, since revaluing blackness meant also devaluing whiteness as false universalism.

Oppositional self-definition would not be unique to the Black Power movement; it was inherent in the move to identity politics by any group protesting against the definitions imposed on it by more powerful "Others." Nor did oppositional identity of itself exclude positive content; on the contrary, it generally entailed it. Maulana Ron Karenga's Us organization, for example, laid out a comprehensive cultural program that included distinctive dress and hairstyles, a set of values, written in Swahili, which adapted purportedly traditional African virtues to the situation of the American black community, and the holiday of Kwanzaa, celebrating black unity and liberation and billed as an alternative to the "economic entrapment and alienated gift-giving" of the white community's Christmas.[89] Karenga's initiative, called *Kawaida*, offered a more traditional understanding of the politics of "identity politics" in its view of the relationship between the two terms: the cultural effort to create a new black identity was not for him in itself political but rather the prerequisite for the struggle for political power in the conventional democratic sense. Without a sense of distinctive common identity blacks could not be mobilized to fight effectively for their common interests through the democratic political mechanisms of voting, representation, and legislation.

Karenga's cultural nationalism was a natural draw for writers, poets, and dramatists like LeRoi Jones, whose vocation offered them a central role in the creation of black identity as Us defined it. Given the African name Imamu Amiri Baraka by Karenga, he became an ardent, and through the success of his off-Broadway play *Dutchman*, widely known proselytizer for Kawaida. Race, for Baraka, was "defined by a feeling—an identity—which culture preserved and art expressed."[90] His definition melded the two main prevailing definitions of culture, an older elite notion of a high culture of art and the modern anthropological notion of the organic way of life of a people. In the spirit of Us, Baraka intended the cultural fostering of black identity as a first step toward taking institutional political power. He thus became a spokesman for organizations promoting black electoral participation to gain political control of cities with majority or large black populations, like Newark and East St. Louis. But political control itself did not mean merely black voting majorities, political parties, and office holding; politics was not just process but a conception of the good. As Baraka envisaged it, black control was to be about creating a new kind of polity, an "'ecstatic vision of the soulful'" achieved by such means as "life-affirming, parklike living areas with neo-African designed homes and shops."[91] The black-run city would be a wholly different world from the white urban jungle, vibrant with a communal spirit the antithesis of white competitive egoism and exploitation.

This was real, if also utopian, politics, but Baraka's evocation of "the soulful" pointed to another, less political version of "identity politics," rather more influential at the time, in which black cultural identity was not a means to political power but a substitute for it. The aspect of urban black popular culture most easily propagated through the media and most immediately visible to the white community—the idea of "soul" as style, talk, dress, food, and music—offered a form of black self-assertion that did not require, and might even profess contempt for, traditional "white" means of social advancement and political power. Urban soul style was, as historian William Van Deburg put it, a "no-holds-barred swaggering conceptualization" that deliberately defied clear definition—you knew it if you had it, and you could have it only if you were black—but it provided the illusion of control and confidence "however powerless one might be in relation to the larger society,"[92] in other words, the illusion of politics. Yet paradoxically, to the extent that elements of the white community felt threatened by the visibility and spread of black urban culture, the idea of a "culture war" (which also embraced opposition to the concurrent sexual revolution) created a new arena of politics, or a new definition of the political, by self-fulfilling prophecy. The cultural *became* political when an upstart cultural ethos was experienced as contesting the prevailing culture for domination of the public sphere, and was opposed for that reason. One major result of the push for black cultural identity was to challenge the narrow definition of politics as electoral politics by effacing the line between the political and the cultural, and ultimately the social domain more broadly. Jazz and rock and roll had been integrated into white culture before the 1960s through the blurring of its origins as *black* music; rap and later hip-hop were promoted both as specifically black and as beneficially transformative for the entire culture.

*   *   *

The book that by common consensus inaugurated "second wave" feminism, Betty Friedan's *The Feminine Mystique*, ironically represented both the cultural triumph of Erikson's concept of psychological identity among the educated middle class in the early 1960s and its swan song. Chapter 3 is entitled "The Crisis in Woman's Identity"; the crisis was that women had no discernible identity, and no chance in the present to achieve one. Friedan took Erikson's ideas of the life cycle and identity crisis—the adolescent task of identity construction—as developmental givens, but criticized their unwitting gender bias. "It is my thesis," Friedan wrote, "that the core of the problem for women today is not sexual but a problem of identity—a stunting or evasion of growth that is perpetuated by the feminine mystique. . . . Our culture does not permit women to accept or gratify their basic need to grow and fulfill their potentialities as human beings."[93] Unlike young men, contemporary young women couldn't choose who they wanted to become as unique individuals because it had already been decided for them. Conventional femininity was not an identity, in Erikson's sense of self-fashioning, but a collective imposition on the self. So it had been for Beauvoir, though her theoretical perspective ultimately precluded Erikson's idea of a freely created identity for either sex. Like Beauvoir, however, and in contrast to advocates of black identity, Friedan was not calling for a new identity for women as a group; the deadening homogeneity of the collective norm of "femininity" was the antithesis of what identity meant to her.

The difference is instructive. It is partly a measure of class differences between the Black Power movement and early second wave feminism, partly a measure of the greater stringency, both objective and experienced, of racial oppression. For all the inhibiting mystique of femininity enforced by family, social mores, commercial advertising, and de facto discrimination, the women Friedan was writing for and about were members of the relatively comfortable white middle class who had been educated in elite colleges and universities. The point of her critique was that they were not being allowed, but also not allowing themselves, to take advantage of the opportunities they already had to fashion themselves as their male counterparts did. It was socially as well as psychologically plausible to hold up to them an ideal of individual identity, supported by a political program calling for the full realization of liberal equality through equal career opportunities and equal pay. The National Organization for Women that Friedan cofounded in 1965 did not call for women to unite in the name of identity but in the name of equality. Though it could be said that the mere fact of organizing as women was a form of identity politics, women's solidarity as conceived by NOW was a traditional political pressure-group tactic.

Only a few years later that began to change for a radical vanguard of younger feminists. Small groups of radical women began organizing in New York and elsewhere in the late 1960s; the year 1970 saw the publication of four books, very different in tone and demand from *The Feminine Mystique*, that became landmarks of a new feminist militancy: Kate Millett's *Sexual Politics*, Shulamith Firestone's *The Dialectic of Sex*, Robin Morgan's *Sisterhood Is Powerful*, and Germaine Greer's *The Female Eunuch*. They also represented a new departure in identity politics, though not yet the celebration of female difference that emerged in American and French feminist theorizing in the 1970s and 1980s.

According to Millett the politics of identity had in fact long existed, but from the point of view of women it was wholly negative. The sexual politics of patriarchy, the rule of men over women, had characterized society from prehistory to the present. Patriarchy demanded a fundamental rethinking of the category of the political. Politics should not be limited to the "relatively narrow and exclusive world of meetings, chairmen, and parties," that is, to the formal legal and institutional governance of the polis. "The term 'politics,'" she declared, "shall refer to power-structure relationships, arrangements whereby one group of persons is controlled by another."[94] Max Weber had put the state at the center of politics because it was the institution with the monopoly of legitimate violence; formal governance, law, and their enforcement mechanisms became the heart of subsequent academic political science and theory. But patriarchy reigned everywhere in society, Millett argued, and though violence was indeed its accepted, if tacit, ultima ratio, patriarchal power could be and most often was exercised in ways other than legal exclusion and physical coercion. That was why the formal grant of legal equality and voting rights to women in modern democracies had not changed the effective domination of men. Socialization into inferiority in childhood, coupled with the de facto exclusion of adult women from the commanding heights of economy and polity, continued to enforce patriarchy even when its older legal and political trappings had been abolished.

The main psychological and social instrument of patriarchal power was its power of definition, specifically the power to define "gender identity" and indoctrinate the young with it. Millett took the term from the pioneering work of the psychoanalyst Robert Stoller, who in a series of articles in the mid-1960s made the momentous distinction between sex and gender that was to be the foundation of virtually all subsequent feminist theorizing on women's identity and has since become standard American usage everywhere.[95] There are, Stoller argued, two developmental levels of "gender identity," a term he originated: "core gender identity" through which the child learns that he or she is (sexually) a boy or a girl, and gender identity (referred to later by other psychoanalytic theorists of child development as "gender role identity"),[96] through which the child learns the prevailing social behaviors that define masculinity and femininity. Core gender identity is determined by biological factors: genital organs, chromosomes, and an avowedly mysterious "biological force" that Stoller insisted on to cover clinical cases in which a person later claimed a core gender identity different from the one assigned at birth on the basis of physical structure. Gender role identity, by contrast, is cultural and psychological; what is "proper" to a boy's or girl's behavior, deportment, and future social role is learned and internalized throughout the child's social development. Crucially, there is no one-to-one correlation between core gender identity and gender role identity, which can vary considerably in content from culture to culture. In simplified terms, Stoller identified core gender identity with biological sex and gender identity with variable social roles: "*Gender* is a term that has psychological or cultural rather than biological connotations. If the proper terms for sex are 'male' and 'female,' the corresponding terms for gender are 'masculine' and 'feminine'; these latter may be quite independent of (biological) sex."[97]

What importantly did not vary in women's gender role identity, from Millett's point of view, was the subordinate position women occupied in all cultures from time immemorial in virtue of the universally decreed inferiority of feminine gender identity whatever its cultural specifics. Her "identity politics" was not a call to women to organize to overturn patriarchy but the politics *men* practiced in exercising power over women through norms of gender identity, starting with the family, "the chief institution of patriarchy."[98] Familial life was political because it was no less a sphere of power relations than the state, in many ways the more important one. The family was the first transmitter of tradition, conventional "knowledge" about the sexes, social mores, and morality and was thus patriarchy's most powerful social and psychological buttress. The politics of antipatriarchy, while calling for women's solidarity— indeed, in contrast to the reformist political goals of NOW, revolutionary solidarity, since it aimed at overthrowing an entire system of male power, formal and informal—was not identity politics in its later sense. It did not celebrate female uniqueness or difference from men; to the contrary, it rejected the idea of distinctive identities as the patriarchal ideology that had to be destroyed to realize women's equality.

In this first stage of radical feminist politics, to take difference seriously was to court despair and consequently to look to desperate remedies unlikely to have broad appeal to most women. Like Millett, Shulamith Firestone wanted to expand the category of the political, though on even more radical grounds. Taking her theoretical direction from Marx, she argued that the source of all power, and hence all power differentials, was material reality. But Marx was wrong, she claimed, to make production its most important venue; reproduction was even more fundamental to human survival. Sex, not social class, was the ultimate determinant of power in society, the foundation of all other forms. This fact, however, worked to the detriment of the sex that embodied but did not own the means of reproduction.[99] The source of woman's powerlessness was her biological role in carrying, bearing, and nursing children, which put her in need of male provisioning and protection, hence subject to male domination. The only way to equalize her status was to abolish that role through the development of artificial means of reproduction. Firestone's diagnosis and prescription shared Beauvoir's biological pessimism without the saving grace of the latter's existential activism. Whatever pro forma attention she paid to the goals of socialist cooperation and women's economic independence, her basic agenda was to free women from "the tyranny of their reproductive biology."[100] Though she did not use the term identity, her negative view of femaleness as such was so overwhelmingly determinist that paradoxically there could be no way out other than its complete extirpation. This was female identity with a vengeance.

Whether seen in terms of an inferior gender identity imposed by patriarchy or the social disadvantage imposed by biology, woman's difference was purely negative for Millett and Firestone. Neither called for the reclamation or creation of a positive cultural identity for women parallel to that demanded by Black Power. Aside from the fact that both held to the same ideal of nongendered individuality inherent in Friedan's version of Erikson's identity, it was not evident to either that "woman" as a category could have a distinct *cultural* identity in which to take pride. Women did not represent a culture in the way in which blacks, with a heritage of distinctive African custom, language, and religion might plausibly claim to. It was only in the next two decades, as arguments for something like a distinctive female way of being or for positive female difference took hold, that an explicitly feminist identity politics could emerge.

*   *   *

Looking back at the turn of the millennium on the significance of the "Stonewall Rebellion" of June 1969, when gay patrons of the bar in Greenwich Village rioted against their harassment by police, Craig Rimmerman writes, "Stonewall and its aftermath created a lesbian and gay counterculture, which helped to establish lesbian and gay identity, thus providing a foundation for the identity-politics strain in the movements today."[101] His analysis helps to locate the appearance and diffusion of the language of gay identity and identity politics. Neither existed at the time of Stonewall; thirty years later both could be taken for granted as common descriptions of the radical gay liberation movements and programs that appeared in its immediate wake. That same assessment, however, ironically contradicts the author's title, and suggests confusion about what homosexuality meant before gay become the standard term for it. In describing a trajectory from identity *to* politics, the book interpreted the insistence of the homosexual rights organizations of the 1950s that their sexual orientation was biologically determined and unchangeable, as thinking in terms of identity rather than politics. But the Mattachine Society and the Daughters of Bilitis, the main pre-1960s organizations of gays and lesbians respectively, were highly political. Their belief in the biological origin and nature of homosexuality was precisely the reason for their demands for equal rights and participation within the liberal democratic political system. Sexual orientation, they argued, was neither a moral nor a cultural category, and therefore was irrelevant to the issue of citizenship rights. In contrast, the Gay Liberation Front and the Gay Activists Alliance established in 1969 in the immediate aftermath of Stonewall insisted that to be gay was to have a unique cultural identity. Hence they rejected the historically pathologizing implications of the term "homosexual" and insisted, like Black Power advocates, on gays' right to name themselves and to take pride in who they were. "Coming out," the public acknowledgment that one was gay advocated by the GLF and the GAA, was de facto the act of claiming, and proclaiming, an identity through the creation of a gay culture, with all the things proper to it: identifying marks, folkways, idioms, and public celebrations.

The significance of coming out is effectively highlighted by contrasting the idea behind it with the use Sartre made of homosexuality to illustrate the idea of bad faith. To deny that one "was" a homosexual because one had engaged in a homosexual act, Sartre wrote, was in bad faith, but not because the claim of "not being" was false. It was because the claim was used to deny responsibility for the concrete act, to pretend that one's "real" self hadn't performed it, that it was a temporary aberration. In the metaphysical sense, however, it was true no one "was" a homosexual, because there was no "real self," homosexual or any other. To come out, however, was to announce the exact opposite. It was to proclaim that one was indeed *a homosexual*, more, that one's sexual orientation determined what one was, that it was identical with one's being. By definition, furthermore, this was a collective identity; to come out was to declare one's a priori belonging to a collective that defined its identity by sexual orientation. At least one writer later saw the commitment in explicitly ontological terms, though with an Eriksonian developmental twist: coming out "designates more than the narrow meaning usually attributed to it as a single act whereby an individual declares his or her identity. . . . [It] is a lifelong process of *becoming* lesbian or gay. . . . *[It] refers to an ontological recognition of the self by the self.* It involves recognition of one's sexuality. . . . [It] is a condition for the existence of community."[102] This does not yet say just what the substance of a "gay identity" is. I will examine that in some detail in the next chapter.

*   *   *

Within just a few years, the language of radical identity politics crossed the ocean to Germany, undergoing a sea change on the way. It was adopted not by protesting minority groups—the most significant of whom, Turkish "guest workers," had no rights of citizenship and were politically quiescent—but by middle-class German would-be revolutionaries. Following the failure of the student movements of 1968–1969 in France and Germany to achieve their

aims or to mobilize workers in a wider social movement, small groups advocating violence and resorting to terror sprang up in a number of European
countries. In 1971, Ulrike Meinhof, one of the leaders of the German terrorist
Red Army Faction known more familiarly as the Baader-Meinhof gang, talked
of "political identity" as the "permanent integration of individual character
and political motivation" and the prerequisite for revolutionary praxis; purportedly, the slogan of the gang came to be "Filthiness [*Schweinerei*] or Identity."[103] For them identity politics did not mean the politics of an identity
group in the American sense, but the identity of being political—the total
identification of the self with revolutionary political action. This usage did not
survive the gang, which was soon killed or imprisoned. In the later '70s and
'80s, however, the concept of identity was largely taken over by the conservative and radical right and increasingly associated with traditional ethnic German nationalism. What was not foreseeable, or at least not foreseen, in the
rise of identity politics in the 1960s was that it was not inherently a "progressive" cause. It could be adopted by any collective that felt beleaguered and
resentful at being, or believing itself to be, oppressed and marginalized. It
was in Europe that this first became clearly evident. Historically, nevertheless,
identity politics began even there as left-wing radical protest movement.[104]

*   *   *

The politicized idea of group identity gave the individual member of groups
excluded, subordinated, or despised by the dominant culture a valued *personal*
identity within the revised valuation of his or her group. The new politics of
identity combined the psychological dimension of identity in Eriksonian terms
with the primacy of social identity as sociology had theorized it. But rather
than a theory of social equilibrium, politicized social identity was a symptom
of social disruption and conflict. Fueled by psychological deprivation and
anger as well as by material and political disadvantage, identity politics was a
more powerful incubator and promoter of the new identity consciousness
than individual identity crises, in important part because it could become a
conduit for and major expression of personal identity crises. In fact under the
impact of identity politics, collective identity tended to become the largest
component, or determinant, of personal identity, if not in many instances
fully coterminous with it.

By the end of the 1960s, in any case, both public and intellectual attention
had shifted decisively from individual to collective identity. The events of the
second half of the decade turned out to be the beginning of a broad movement
in the next three decades to identify politically relevant collective identities by

both committed activists and by scholars attempting to define the meaning and scope of collective identity. One crucial feature of the first politicized identities, however, unremarked at the time, foretold a chronic dilemma of collective identity with practical as well as theoretical implications. Blacks and gays demanded equal recognition by converting biologically founded stigmata into positive cultural identities. While not working to valorize a specifically female culture, young feminists of the 1960s contributed to the "culturalization" of difference with the distinction between sex and gender, which turned the traits denigrating women from biological sentences into (modifiable) social constructions. Yet in all these cases, the social group identifier remained a physical-biological feature. Black culture was, after all, black; Amiri Baraka, for one, had no problem using the word "race" in referring to it. And what was "gay culture" if not the culture of those with same-sex physical desire? How was one to identify the "women" striving for equality and liberation if not by their biological sex? From the very beginnings of collective identity consciousness, equivocation between the roles of the (biological) body and the (constructed) culture in defining identity was a vexing problem.

Chapter 5

Collective Identities and Their Agendas,
1970–2000

In the decade after the first stirrings of what had not yet been labeled "identity politics," activists and theorists within the three main "liberation movements" of the late 1960s focused on defining their collective identities and articulating the aims of a politics guided by them. By the 1970s, however, this was no longer a uniquely American concern. Nor did the idea of collective identity remain bound to the major social protest movements of the 1960s. The following decades saw the extension of the language of identity to collectivities other than race, gender, and sexual orientation. Furthermore, there was no automatic overlap between interest in collective identities and radical politics. In part this was because academic anthropology, psychology, sociology, and other social science disciplines took up the study of identity for scientific and explanatory purposes. On the political side, some left-wing activists saw danger to the prospects of radical political and social change in identity thinking, even if avowedly radical in intent, and vociferously rejected it for deflecting political attention from economic issues. The extension of identity thinking into debates over the nature of nationalism and multiculturalism also involved more complex and subtle ideas about relationships between collective identity and politics than group activism allowed. Though sometimes motivated by ideological concerns, overtly or covertly, studies of ethnicity, nationalism, and culture focused analytically on the role of identity in each of these areas, challenging traditional interpretations and fundamentally altering contemporary understanding of them.

Another intellectual development beginning in the 1960s and 1970s was to intersect with and greatly affect conceptions of collective identity: the emergence of French poststructuralist thought and the idea of postmodernism. Their impact touched every sphere of identity thinking, and was so significant that it is necessary to examine how identity groups and their politics were talked about before the encounter with poststructuralism and postmodernism changed the discussion.

Sex and Gender

Of those who took up the idea of collective identity in the 1970s and 1980s, none did more than feminists to make it an increasingly familiar concept of academic discourse, political debate, and media attention. After the first wave of feminist writings that demanded full equality for women on the basis of their common humanity—in other words, their fundamental sameness—with men, some feminists in the 1970s began to think in positive and militant ways about women's difference. This was in part a somewhat belated reaction to the denigration of women inherent in sexual discrimination. Proponents of black identity, unlike middle-class white women, never had the luxury of being able to believe that they could begin from an assumption of equality; fostering pride in blackness was an inherent element in the idea of black identity from the outset. But the shift in feminist strategy was also connected in another way to the sociology of feminism. With the large and rapid expansion of American universities in the 1960s, more young women, many inspired by the feminist movement, began entering on academic careers, especially in the humanities and social sciences.[1] The difficulties they encountered in the masculine academic world, and the gender biases they found in their disciplines' research programs turned them to issues of female identity. A number of them, feminist in their politics but traditional in their scholarly approach, began to study psychological, social, and ethical differences between males and females from early childhood on.

Linda Nicholson has written that the new orientation of "difference feminism" was the "logical extension of the growing recognition by many feminists of gender as an organizing principle of individual identity and social organization."[2] This meant more than just incorporating their femaleness into their own individual identities, or acknowledging the social importance of gender differences, which was nothing new; it meant radically modifying the prevailing identity paradigms. The conceptual frameworks of the two most systematic and significant American writers on female difference in the 1970s and early 1980s, Nancy Chodorow and Carol Gilligan, were pointed revisions of Erik Erikson's and Robert Stoller's theories of psychological and sexual identity. The wide sale of their books, their adoption in many college and university courses, particularly in the new Women's Studies programs established in many universities, and the noisy controversies they generated both inside and outside academia did much to introduce the idea of a distinctive, positive female identity into the American collective consciousness.

Maternal Identity and the Primacy of Attachment

In *The Reproduction of Mothering*, Nancy Chodorow took up the gender role identity that, she argued, has been women's most basic one through time and across cultures. Though a sociologist by training, her approach in the book was largely psychoanalytic, concerned with the internal, or "intrapsychic," formation of personality. The key social fact she relied on is that women, almost universally, were responsible for early childcare. This has, she argued, a radically different impact on male and female development. Stoller's work had shown that a child's "core gender identity," that is, its sexual identity as male or female, is established for both sexes by the time the child is around three years old. Applying the developmental theory of the object-relations school of psychoanalysis, Chodorow argued that the child's gender *role* identity, as distinguished from its sexual identity, nonetheless develops hand in hand with the latter through a process of identification, or disidentification, with its mother. Mothers generally experience their daughters as more like and continuous with them. Correspondingly girls experience themselves as being like their mothers, fusing their sexual femaleness with the experiences of their own early attachment and their mother's caring role in the process of identity role formation. In contrast, mothers experience their sons as a male opposite, so boys, in defining themselves as masculine, internally separate their mothers from themselves, rejecting attachment and maternal caring as unmasculine. As a result, Chodorow concluded, "Girls emerge from early childhood with a basis for 'empathy' built into their primary definition of self in a way that boys do not. Girls emerge with a stronger basis for experiencing another's needs or feelings as their own."[3] Their identities are not threatened by attachment, as boys' are. In this way the capacity and desire for motherhood reproduces itself in girls from generation to generation.

Nothing in the book suggested any criticism of this process or of the different sex roles it produces. Only in a political "Afterword" did Chodorow claim that women's exclusive responsibility for the care of the young was the historical result of inequality in the sexual division of labor; women's sole ownership of mothering was the other side of their exclusion from the more prestigious identities in society. The reproduction of mothering was thus also the reproduction of inequality; full equality for women demanded that men take equal responsibility with them for child rearing,[4] with the implication that this would fundamentally alter the processes of identification and thus the gender identity outcomes she had described. But in a preface written twenty years later for a new edition, Chodorow, by then a full-time practicing psychoanalyst, acknowledged that she had not been aware when she wrote the book of the "tension" between the psychological descriptions of women's subjectivity in the text and the political prescription of the Afterword. More concerned now with the internal life of the individual than with social ideology, she wrote that her previous "universalizing advocacy of change cannot be taken . . . to stand for the experience and desires of many mothers." The demand for equal parenting, in other words, "ignored many women's identities." A feminism truer to women's deep subjectivity would allow for any kind of arrangement that "fostered and aided mothers to mother their children and to have a full life."[5] Though Chodorow purported simply to be honoring the subjective desires of women as she encountered them in clinical work, the priority her wording placed on motherhood seemed to be a retrospective endorsement of the notion of a primary desire for a maternal identity in many, if not most, women.

Carol Gilligan's book *In a Different Voice: Psychological Theory and Women's Development*, published in 1982 but begun in the early 1970s, can be seen as the most important theoretical bridge from an individual to a collective conception of Erikson's psychological identity. Gilligan had studied and worked with Erikson, adopted his life cycle theory of development as her psychological framework and used its own categories to critique its deficiencies from a female point of view. As she put it, "Against the background of the psychological descriptions of identity and moral development which I had read and taught for a number of years, the women's voices sounded distinct."[6] In Erikson's original eight-stage life-cycle scheme, the forging of personal identity chronologically preceded what he labeled as the stage of intimacy, the achievement of close emotional relationships through marriage and family. This sequence equated mature identity with personal autonomy, achieved by separation from childhood and adolescent ties of dependency. Gilligan's interviews with females from childhood to old age, however, revealed that at every age they put a premium not on separation but on attachment to and connection with others in every sphere of life, from moral reasoning to ambitions for the future to the most fundamental definitions of self. Girls and women tend to think of their desires for autonomy in relation to their sense of responsibility to and for others, subordinating self if they believe it necessary in the interests of relationship and the other. In female development, the creation of identity includes, indeed puts a priority on, intimacy rather than preceding it. Only if male development is taken as the norm do females look less psychologically developed; in fact what is involved in these differences between men and women are "divergent constructions of identity." Interpreting the matter this way both exposed the gender bias of Erikson's identity concept and signified a clear, if not quite explicitly avowed, normative shift. "From the different dynamics of separation and attachment in their gender identity formation," Gilligan wrote, "through the divergence of identity and intimacy that marks their experience in the adolescent years, male and female voices typically speak of the importance of different truths, the former of the role of separation as it defines and empowers the self, the latter of the ongoing process of attachment that creates and sustains the human community."[7]

Gilligan deliberately refused to take a position on the origins of the gender differences she described, attributing it vaguely to a convergence of social status and power with reproductive biology.[8] As a psychologist she took her own society as given, offering snapshots of its gendered psychologies. If it was impossible to miss the implied argument that for the health of society, the (male) ideal of autonomy as separation had to be combined with the (female) ideal of attachment, Gilligan left open the questions of whether these attributes could be combined within each sex, and what if any social changes might be needed to bring this about. The ahistorical disciplinary bias of psychology, however, along with the reference to the "different truths" expressed by male and female voices, left the strong impression that she was describing what she took to be basic attributes of a timeless, and wholly positive, female identity.

If Chodorow and Gilligan wrote primarily as social scientists, other contemporary academic feminists approached the idea of women's maternal identity with a less formal commitment to neutrality and a more overt belief that it entailed a uniquely feminine politics. In her early article "Maternal Thinking," Sara Ruddick claimed to identify a distinctive maternal kind of thinking with unique ways of "conceptualizing, ordering and valuing experience" which had developed out of long-standing traditions and practices of mothering.[9] Because mothers are attuned to children's needs that their lives be preserved, their growth fostered, and their personalities shaped to be acceptable to the next generation, "We *think* differently about what it *means* and what it takes to be 'wonderful,' to be a person, to be real."[10] Her stated position on the origins of maternal thinking was equivocal; while she neither affirmed nor denied a biological basis for maternal thinking, and insisted that it was a social category theoretically neutral between the sexes, she nonetheless asserted that maternal thought exists "for all women in a radically different way than for men."[11] She also stated unequivocally that it was her basic purpose to present maternal thought as a "contribution to an ongoing, shared feminist project: the construction of an image of maternal power which is benign, accurate, sturdy and sane."[12]

In a later book Ruddick developed the political implications of her concept. The title summed them up in a catchphrase: *Maternal Thinking: Toward a Politics of Peace.* Ruddick's claims about the reality of maternal identity remained somewhat coy and confusing; "I . . . repeatedly and provocatively hint," she wrote, "at a 'maternal identity' and in the end explicitly invoke and expand that identity for the sake of peace politics. To claim a maternal identity is not to make an empirical generalization but to engage in a political act."[13] The concept of a maternal identity inherently opposed to violence was thus made to seem something like a strategic fiction. In fact Ruddick not only acknowledged that actual mothers could be as patriotic and militaristic as men but that "the very demands of maternal practice"—loyalty to the group which defends her and her children—"often inspire a militarist politics." Nevertheless, she claimed, "The promise of maternal peacefulness lies in the work and love to which mothers are committed."[14] If not a universal truth, maternal thinking was not simply an ideological norm without empirical foundation but a potential within the real-world practice of mothering. The blurring of description and prescription, whether intentional or not, left the impression that Ruddick was arguing for an "essential" maternal identity that could derive norm from nature.

So strong was the appeal of maternal identity among certain feminists that even some of the most ambivalent ended by affirming a version of it. The poet Adrienne Rich's partly autobiographical *Of Woman Born: Motherhood as Experience and Institution* is impassioned and tormented precisely because she had herself borne her children under the "unexamined assumptions" that "a 'natural' mother is a person without further identity." "I was haunted," she saw in retrospect, analyzing the emotions she recorded in her journals as a young mother, "by the stereotype of the mother whose love is 'unconditional'; and by the visual and literary images of motherhood as a single-minded identity. If I knew parts of myself existed that would never cohere to those images, weren't those parts then abnormal, monstrous?"[15] But while she came to the apparently Beauvoirian conclusion that for a woman to be a complete human being, free and creative, "the institution of motherhood must be destroyed," she quickly qualified it with the claim that "To destroy the institution is not to abolish motherhood." It was only the identity of "mother" as patriarchy defined it that had to be put to an end because it claimed the whole woman, imprisoning her within a prescribed and narrow range of duties and responses. If, as this explanation seemed to imply, such imprisonment was what any identity entailed, Rich's attack on motherhood was also an attack on identity itself. But her qualification suggested not the elimination but the redefinition of both, and so indirectly also a reaffirmation of the centrality of woman's maternal identity. To destroy motherhood as defined by patriarchy, she wrote, "is to release the creation and sustenance of

life into the same realm of decision, struggle, surprise, imagination and conscious intelligence, as any other difficult, but freely chosen work."[16] Freely
chosen identity as self-creation within the givens of human "facticity"—
history, place, body—was no more, but no less, a paradox for Rich than it
was for Erikson. In the end her book was a call to reform society so that
individual women could apply to their identity as "mother" the creativity
that she lived by as a poet and that Erikson had so admiringly described in
Luther's and Gandhi's refashioning of their individual religious and political
identities within preexisting collective identities.

The claims of these four writers about the existence of a primary maternal
identity—or more broadly, of an underlying female desire for attachment and
connection—were in one way a reaction against the militant repudiation of
middle-class domesticity by the first wave of young radical feminists. It represented the efforts of a group of married professional white middle-class
women with children or anticipating children to insist that being a mother
was not only fully compatible with personal creativity and feminist activism,
but a prime motivating force for feminism itself. It was precisely professionals
who were also mothers who were positioned to know what laws and institutions, from maternity leave to day care to equal parenting, were necessary for
full female equality. Not coincidentally, all four were from a middle-class Jewish background. So too was Shulamith Firestone—in fact she came from the
most observant family of the five—but the very ferocity of her repudiation
and the extremeness of her solution paradoxically testified to the hold of a
strong cultural traditionalism in which family and children were women's central purpose. As important as the insistence on the psychological reality of
maternal identity, however, was the equivocation of the four writers on its
ontological status. Women had good reason to reject basing role identity in
biology, which had historically been the tool of their subjugation. But beyond
that, their equivocation was part of the pattern of thinking about identity
from the very beginning. To the extent that any identity was totalistic and
prescriptive, it was limiting of freedom. The problem endemic to identity of
paying the body, the psyche, and the culture their due while preserving individuality and choice was most dramatically evident with maternal identity.

The Female Standpoint

Not every feminist validation of women's difference explicitly referred to a
collective female identity, let alone motherhood. This was the case with perhaps the most provocative academic strand of difference feminism, feminist
standpoint theory. Standpoint theorists did talk of identity but associated it
with individual psychology, while they purportedly began from a Marxist view

of the causal relationship between knowledge and social class, women substituting for the proletariat as the primary and oppressed producer class.[17] But both the arguments and the militancy of standpoint theorists gave philosophical support to the idea of a distinctive female identity.

This was not necessarily their intent. The standpoint they argued for was *feminist*, not *female*. The distinction was meant to underline that standpoint was a consciously worked out theory with an expressly liberationist intent, derived from the situation of women who for the most part were not consciously aware of their oppression.[18] In any case, a Marxist historical sociology militated against the idea of a timeless female standpoint; what was historically and socially created could be socially changed. Despite this, standpoint theorists tended to move back and forth between the language of "feminist" and "female." Such slippage was almost inevitable. In elaborating her conception of the division of labor between men and women that according to the theory determined their distinctive world views, the philosopher Nancy Hartsock eschewed the term "gender" for the harder "sexual division of labor," because the division was partially rooted in biology and could not be reduced to purely social dimensions. Hence she felt justified in setting aside cultural and social differences among women across race and class boundaries for the purposes of theorizing. Because they were oppressed by men, because their physiology made them uniquely sensitive to the bodily processes which were the sources of their oppression, women as a sex were positioned to see the truth about "the real relations of humans with each other and with the natural world [that] are not visible" to men.[19] The "female construction of self," in contradistinction to the male adolescent's "construction of identity," leads toward "opposition to dualisms of any sort, valuation of concrete, everyday life, sense of a variety of connectedness and continuities both with other persons and the natural world."[20]

Though it characterized female selfhood in language similar to that of Chodorow, Ruddick, and Gilligan, standpoint theory was neither an empirical theory of the emotions nor of moral behavior but an epistemology, a philosophical theory about how humans come to know the world. One formulation even linked it to an ontology, defined as a general theory of human nature and social life.[21] Because it purported to be foundational rather than merely empirical, the implications of standpoint theory for female identity were more radical than those of the "maternalist" school. There are, so its argument went, two fundamentally different "ways of knowing,"[22] men's and women's, and women's way is superior because it more accurately reflects the realities of human nature and society. Furthermore, those who experienced oppression were best situated to see and analyze its dynamics because it was not in the interests of oppressors to be able to recognize its existence. The more analytically careful formulations did acknowledge that the social "reality" to which women were better attuned involved the universal normative vision of a more humanely organized society.[23]

An even more sweeping version of standpoint theory included the natural world in its scope. Ostensibly "objective" nature can never be studied as it is "out there," in itself, but only as "already socially constituted" by the contemporary cultural meanings natural objects have for everyone.[24] The cultural construction of the objects of scientific investigation reflects the interests of patriarchy. Masquerading as value-free and impartial research, modern science in fact construes nature as an object of (masculine) exploitation, conquest, and domination. This claim had significant implications for the future of scientific research. Contemporary science limits the scope of objective methodological rigor to what philosophers of science call "the context of justification"—the verification of hypotheses. It considers the "context of discovery," where problems are identified as appropriate for scientific investigation and hypotheses are formulated, to be outside the scope of objectivity, hence "irrational" or subjective. But it is precisely in the context of discovery that the hidden values of patriarchy govern science most directly, and where failure to examine them undermines scientific objectivity rather than strengthening it. Since values are an inevitable element of the context of discovery, the question is which ones promote the most comprehensive set of questions and hence the most objective research. "Democracy-advancing values," Sandra Harding argued, values that include the needs and interests of groups hitherto marginalized or excluded "have systematically generated less partial and distorted beliefs than others."[25] The "causes" of disease can only be truly known, for example, when their incidence, course and treatment are studied, as they have not been before, in those groups. Such inclusive values, according to Harding, could only exist to the extent that women's standpoint prevails in science.

"Gay": The Transformative Power of Identity

References to "homosexual identity" in both academic and popular publications appeared suddenly around 1971, and then with increasing frequency; bibliographies of writings by and about gays and lesbians published just before that date had no entries for the phrase.[26] It emerged in gay discourse when the coming-out campaign along with the proliferation of self-avowed gay communal organizations in San Francisco and New York began to make it possible for gays to think of themselves as having, like black militants a few years before, a distinctive cultural identity.[27] More than the initiative to define a distinctive female identity, which was from the outset vigorously, even bitterly contested within feminism, the notion of a "gay identity" proved transformative for many gays individually and for the gay movement as a whole socially and politically.[28]

That didn't mean that there was clear agreement on what gay "identity" actually meant. In her survey of the appearance of the term over its first decade, Vivienne Cass was struck by how imprecisely it was used in all its variants—homosexual, gay, and lesbian. None of the hundreds of articles she looked at attempted to define gay identity. She found at least five different implicit meanings, which she summarized as "(1) defining oneself as gay, (2) a sense of self as gay, (3) the image of self as homosexual, (4) the way a homosexual *is*, and (5) consistent behavior in relation to homosexual-related activity."[29] All five, obviously overlapping, were drawn from colloquial ways people talked about themselves; there was no attempt even in the academic psychological and sociological literature, Cass complained, to relate the idea to "established theory and data on the general concept of identity." Her paper proposed to fill the gap by sketching the outlines of a theory of gay identity that would combine psychological and sociological perspectives while respecting the language people actually used to talk about themselves. There was, she argued, an inescapable historical reason for undertaking such a project. Whatever its ultimate philosophical standing, "for homosexuals at this specific point in history, *the concept of an identity is built into their cultural milieu.*"[30]

A gay *identity*, she wrote, is defined by the assertion "I am a homosexual." It is to be differentiated from a gay *self-image*, which takes the linguistic form "I am a person who relates sexually to others of the same sex." The distinction for Cass was both developmental, that is, psychological, and linguistic, or social; she did not reflect on the implied ontological difference between "being" and "doing" in the two definitions. Gay identity, she argued, evolves out of the clustering of the child's early self-images derived from feelings, impulses and behaviors, initially linked together by his "idiosyncratic" understanding of what characterizes someone as "homosexual." These fragmentary personalized self-images coalesce into a fully integrated *identity*, however, only through more direct communication with others who represent to the individual the prevailing social role definition of "the homosexual." Both subjective self-images and formal social role definition are indispensable to understanding a homosexual sense of identity. For that reason "there is no such thing as a single homosexual identity."[31]

In the past, she pointed out, social definition was relatively easy to ascertain and wholly negative. The nineteenth century medical model of sexuality, in conjunction with sociological labeling theory, stigmatized the homosexual as a sexual pervert or deviant. Contemporary society has increasingly abandoned such categories.[32] The change is dramatized by the replacement of the name "homosexual" with the name "gay." Homosexuality now describes one's sexual *orientation*, but a *gay identity* implies an affiliation with the gay community in a cultural and sociable sense.[33] Cass's analysis (which despite her emphasis on the importance of the linguistic innovation confusingly referred to both "homosexual identity" and "gay identity,") rested on Berger and Luckmann's distinction between identity and identity types: "Identity is a phenomenon that emerges from the dialectic between individual and society. Identity *types*, on the other hand, are social products . . . relatively stable elements of objective social reality (the degree of stability being, of course, socially determined in its turn)."[34] "Gay" was a wholly new identity *type*, which made possible a new range of positive individual gay identities.

The qualification "relatively stable" was much to the point of the contemporary gay situation, which had changed so dramatically in the late 1960s. What Berger and Luckmann's social determination had omitted, however, was the role politics might play in destabilizing society and its identity types. Cass noted that defining oneself as gay brings about certain political consequences, but this one-directional causality does not adequately describe the relationship between gay identity and gay politics. To claim gay identity was itself a political act; gay identity was political by birth. Once established, it continued to shape the politics homosexuals would engage in.

But in just what way was assuming a gay identity political? Part of the answer was in Mary McIntosh's claim, made even before Stonewall, and before Michel Foucault's work made the idea famous, that the conception of homosexuality as a medical or psychiatric "condition" was meant as an instrument of social control, which worked by providing a clear public threshold between permissible and impermissible behavior and by segregating deviants from others in order to contain them.[35] From this point of view, coming out as "a homosexual," and changing homosexual to "gay" (analogous to the change from "Negro" to "black") was a legitimation strategy, meant to challenge the social control of the health professions through negative definition by redefining oneself as a member of a minority group having a certain quasi-"ethnic" status.[36] If being gay meant belonging to a group with its own distinct culture, it could by analogy with other ethnic groups in the United States claim a legitimate place in the American mosaic. The political need for legitimation also explains why being gay came to be embraced by many as a primary or even whole identity. Erving Goffman had pointed out that the need for the stigmatized to manage their stigma in social situations—to tell or not to tell, to confront or excuse or even to conceal—causes the stigma-identity to assume substantial proportions within the overall identity.[37] The move to transform stigma into legitimacy meant an active and positive rather than reactive embrace of gayness as the core, or totality of one's identity, akin to the call for black embrace of blackness.[38] "Totalization," soon to be the butt of the postmodern critique of identity, was the very point of gay identity.

The remaining unanswered question was the actual content of gay culture through which homosexuality legitimized itself as an identity. Applying some of the ideas of "New Social Movement" theory,[39] which argued that cultural identity movements were a new form of politics, Elizabeth Armstrong identi- fied 1971–1973 as the years that saw "The Crystallization of a Gay Identity Movement" in San Francisco, and the later part of the decade as the period in which it achieved political success. In the early years of gay liberation, she argued, there were two basic tendencies, a demand for gay *rights*, premised on a traditionally political "interest group logic," and expressions of gay *pride*, premised on a cultural "identity logic." Advocates of the struggle for rights had often been disdainful of displays of gay pride as a diversion from politics. It was in the decisive years of the early 1970s that "identity logic provided the cultural resources needed to defuse the threat [to gay unity] posed by [these] conflicting visions of the goals and strategies of gay organizing." The gay iden- tity movement was able to play successfully with both meanings of the word "identity," sameness and individuality, to provide a "generative ambiguity" that successfully united the different factions among gay activists. Gay self- assertion by the early 1970s produced a large number of openly gay self-help and community organizations, but the main expressive institution of identity logic was the lesbian/gay freedom day parade. Its central goal was the public display of gay identity, and its very structure, which united all the different groups and factions within the gay community under the banner of gay pride conveyed the message of unity through diversity. "Affirming gay cultural iden- tity," Armstrong concluded, "provided gay rights with the identity needed to claim a place on the American political scene. . . . Interest group politics was not the glue holding the project together. . . . The movement became an 'identity movement.' "[40] Identity for the gay community was not just the bor- rowing of a popular word but an internally transformative tool. And beyond that, as Armstrong argued, gay identity was a unique cultural-institutional movement that helped change the rules for producing legitimate sexual identi- ties in California and the broader American society, with indirect though ultimately hugely significant implications for American law and social institutions.

Naming Identity Politics

Given the centrality of feminism in popularizing the ideas of collective identity and identity activism, it might seem ironic that the first explicit naming of "identity politics" was the direct result of a split *within* feminism, except that the causal connection is not fortuitous. It was a consequence of the separatist logic, both psychological and political, of the emergence of group identity consciousness in the first place. "Black identity" was after all born of the long experience of exclusion by difference in the new historical context that made open black political protest on a national scale viable for the first time. The women of the Combahee River Collective, a group of radical black lesbians organized in 1974, felt multiply excluded or marginalized: as women in a patriarchal society; as blacks in a racist society; as lesbians in a heterosexual culture; finally, as former members of New Left and black radical organizations, which had treated them like handmaidens. Most of all they felt ignored as black lesbians in a feminist movement whose dominant white, heterosexual, middle-class membership, they came to feel, did not represent their situation or problems. It was marginalization within the organization they had counted on to overcome it that brought home to them their difference even from other feminists, and the significance of their unique experience for their politics. The term "identity politics" emerged, from a heightened sense of difference, as the pained but self-consciously militant program of a minority within a minority. "No other ostensibly progressive movement has ever considered our specific oppression a priority or worked seriously for the ending of that oppression," they declared; "We realize that the only people who care enough about us to work consistently for our liberation is us. . . . This focusing upon our own oppression is the concept of identity politics. We believe that the most profound and potentially the most radical politics come directly out of our own identity, as opposed to working to end somebody else's oppression."[41]

Much of the meaning and spirit of identity politics as it came to be understood by advocates and opponents alike is in these words: the splintering of identity groups into their smaller components; the turning inward of the group onto its own experiences and grievances; the cherishing and fostering of its own particularity; the felt need to take care of itself before any concern with others in reaction to others' neglect. But in this first manifestation, identity politics still retained the universalism of the New Left and the radical progressive tradition out of which it had developed. If the group was concerned with its own liberation above all, it understood liberation as an ideal for all. The objection of the black lesbians in the Combahee River Collective to the New Left and the mainstream feminist movements was that they had proved to be not truly universal. The inner tension between particularity and cosmopolitanism that had marked Erikson's notion of individual identity was no less a part of the idea of collective identity at the root of identity politics.

That tension was at the center of a book published a few years later that both dramatically illustrated and further promoted the splintering characteristic of identity politics, *This Bridge Called My Back*, edited by the Chicana writers Cherrie Moraga and Gloria Anzaldua.[42] A miscellany of poems, journal entries, essays, intimate letters, and theoretical statements, the collection by a group of "Third World women and/or women of color"—Hispanic, Asian American, Native American, African American, gay, and straight—represented a combative rejection of the claim of white middle-class heterosexual feminists to represent all women, but in its consistency also emphasized the contributors' difference from one another. On one level the project amounted to the rejection of gender by itself as an adequate category of identity because, unqualified, gender ignored the identities of race, ethnicity, class, sexual orientation, and disability, which were not incidental but central to the individual identities of women.[43] Yet all the contributors were women who felt the affinity of oppression, and who wanted to create a political coalition of the oppressed. To further complicate their situation, many saw the differences between identity groups as sometimes-contradictory fragments of their own personal identities. "We are the colored in a white feminist movement," one of the editors wrote; "We are the feminists among the people of our culture. We are often the lesbians among the straight." Uniting the different groups politically meant making a coherent whole out of their own contradictory identities: "We do this bridging by naming ourselves and by telling our stories in our own words."[44] "I am what I am and I am U.S. American," declared Rosario Morales, whose point was that she could name and claim that identity only after making a place within it for her identities as a Puerto Rican Catholic from a South Bronx working-class home, college educated and married to a Jewish man, a lover of Spanish and Yiddish who could still recite her Hail Marys in an Irish brogue, a fan of Afro-Cuban music, Dickens, and gefilte fish, and "a bit of a snob" with an English accent acquired by listening to the BBC.[45]

This accounting had a number of different, even conflicting implications. On the one hand it was a realistic insistence on the multiplicity of any one person's working identities, psychological and social. A black woman might feel solidarity with black men in the struggle against racism that necessarily crosscut her alliance with white women in the battle against sexism. As a foundation for politics, however, the inward turn to ever-narrower identities seemed to some radicals and liberals to undermine the possibility of consensus and effective political action. From a left perspective the emphasis on identity issues defined primarily in cultural and ethnic terms ignored the economic causes of poverty and social conflict and in any case made unified action to confront them impossible.[46] (As we will see, conservative critics had other kinds of objections.) A radical would find it telling that Morales's autobiographical statement omitted the fact that she had also been a pacifist and a Communist, presumably because those categories did not fit into the framework of identity as *Bridge* defined it. While identity politics might have a political intent, the markers or categories of identity were not traditionally political in a socioeconomic sense but gender, sexual orientation, ethnicity, religion, and ultimately personal idiosyncrasy. From a liberal point of view identity politics undermined the liberal democratic consensus on universal rights by setting identity groups against one another with ever more particular demands.[47]

An even more radical extension of *Bridge* identity politics insisted that only members of an identity group have the right to speak for it, and even that one's identity determines what one is able to know. Personal experience is the only legitimate access to knowledge. Those who don't share a group's identity can't legitimately speak about matters concerning the group because they can never understand what it is like to be a member. Thus Dr. Benjamin Spock (pediatrician and contemporary reigning expert on the development and care of babies) had no right to tell women how to mother a child because he was not a mother.[48] If a woman of color said that she had experienced racism, she was the authority on that experience and could not be challenged. This was standpoint theory taken to its extreme conclusion though without its philosophical underpinning. The possibility of consensually verifiable fact, let alone consensual norm, political or other, disappeared; one was right or wrong, complained Daphne Patai, a white feminist scholar who became the object of charges of racism, because of who one was. Though untenable logically and dangerous politically, this radically "experientialist" position, she suggested, could nonetheless be understood sociologically in the context of women's and ethnic studies programs in the university, as a weapon to justify positions for minorities, especially in the scarce job market and poor economy of the early 1990s.[49] If the identity claims were so extreme, it was not in this case because the stakes were so low. But it was a crucial new development that claims to positions were couched in terms of the epistemology of identity rather than of fairness, equality, or objective standards of scholarship.

At the same time identity politics did produce a full-bore version of political theory in a more traditional vein, concerned with the ideal of justice and the processes of electoral and legislative politics in a liberal democracy. In "Polity and Group Difference" and at greater length in *Justice and the Politics of Difference*, Iris Marion Young presented a set of institutional proposals based on identity group representation within the national political system.[50] While acknowledging that the paradigms of participatory democracy and liberal individualism were valid models of political freedom up to a point, she found both fatally flawed. They ignored the reality of group differences in society and their implications for full equality for all its members. The idea of participatory democracy was based on the classical republican ideal of civic virtue, in which citizens rose above their private interests to pursue the common good arrived at in rational public discussion. While republicanism's modern democratic version, unlike its classical original, presupposed the participation of all members of society, the idea of an objective common good was still premised on the false assumption of the social homogeneity of all citizens. Liberal individualism, on the other hand, acknowledged group difference but primarily as an obstacle to equality; by granting rights to all as individuals, it supposedly eliminated the invidious distinctions that had excluded members of many kinds of groups from political and social access.

But differentiated groups are an ineluctable fact of society, Young claimed. She believed that group differentiation was inevitable even in a just society, but in any case contemporary society was not just. Certain groups were historically privileged and others historically disadvantaged, even if their members were formally endowed as individuals with equal political and civic rights. They were often economically exploited, socially marginalized, kept politically powerless, stereotyped by cultural imperialism, or subject to random harassment by the dominant groups. In the United States the groups which were oppressed in one or more of these ways included "women, blacks, Native Americans, Chicanos, Puerto Ricans and other Spanish-speaking Americans, Asian Americans, gay men, lesbians, working-class people, poor people, old people, and mentally and physically disabled people."[51] And even apart from oppression there are "group-based differences between men and women, whites and blacks, able-bodied and disabled people that make application of a strict principle of equal treatment . . . unfair. . . . To the degree that there are group differences that disadvantage, fairness seems to call for acknowledging rather than being blind to them."[52]

The political remedy was to provide structural mechanisms for the effective representation of these groups by publicly subsidizing their self-organization, formally soliciting their opinions on how social policy proposals affect them as well as soliciting their own policy proposals, and giving their organizations veto power regarding specific policies that affect the group

directly, for example on reproductive rights for women. Furthermore "democ-
ratized workplaces" and government decision-making bodies should include
the specific representation of those oppressed groups.[53] In response to the
possible objection that any collectivity might constitute itself as a group for
representational purposes, Young insisted, "Only those groups that describe
the major identities . . . and which are oppressed or disadvantaged, deserve
specific representation,"[54] implying that these "major" identities were a matter
of objective knowledge and universal agreement. Her general principles,
according to Young, also justified policies already existing or currently proposed such as affirmative action, assessing the comparable worth of jobs on a
gendered basis, and bilingual and bicultural education and service.[55]

Though the practical, let alone political, problems in the way of instituting
her proposals seemed insurmountable—which group would old black women
be part of?—Young's list of the oppressed and disadvantaged is a reasonably
comprehensive if partly ideological accounting of the identity political groups
of the time. The inclusion of the working class, however, a nod to traditional
Marxism, underlined her allegiance to the radical origins of identity politics.
Hence, though written near the end of the Reagan era in American politics, it
missed what anti-identity left-wing critics pointed out: identity politics need
not be limited to the traditionally oppressed. In fact even they, like the blue-
collar "Reagan Democrats" of the 1980s, might line up with conservatives.
"The Republican tilt of white men is the most potent form of identity politics
in our time," Todd Gitlin claimed just a few years later: "a huddling of men
who resent (and exaggerate) their relative decline not only in parts of the labor
market but at home, in the bedroom and the kitchen, and in the culture."[56]
From a left-wing point of view, identity politics could well be the last refuge
of ressentiment.

Ethnic Identity

In contrast to the populist and political origins of "identity politics," two
scholarly initiatives, quite different in origin, purpose, and spirit, tried to pin
down the idea of ethnic identity in the late 1960s and 1970s. The term had
been used previously, though very rarely, and then essentially as a biological
marker more or less synonymous with race.[57] The first of the two projects,
European in origin and narrowly focused on social anthropology as an academic study, revolutionized the discipline with a new theory of ethnic groups.
The second, a wide-ranging set of essays by mostly American sociologists and
political scientists collected under the rubric of "ethnicity," was broader and
more diffuse in scope, but centrally concerned with the political implications

of what they saw as a revitalized ethnic consciousness in the contemporary world. What connected both enterprises was that identity as a simultaneously subjective and objective concept was at the core of each.

*   *   *

In his introduction to *Ethnic Groups and Boundaries*,[58] a collection of essays resulting from a colloquium of Scandinavian social anthropologists, Fredrik Barth declared their program to be a direct challenge to the conventional way of thinking in anthropology. Until then, an ethnic group had been understood to designate a population that was largely biologically self-perpetuating, shared fundamental cultural values, engaged in internal communication and inter-action, and identified itself as a category distinguishable from others of simi-lar type. Because ethnic groups were typically viewed as self-enclosed, however, the predominant view downplayed the importance of self- and other-identification. Ethnic groups could therefore be distinguished descrip-tively from one another by objectively observable differences in their overt behavior. Classifying them according to those characteristics was held to be the central task of social anthropology. Such an approach, according to Barth, ignored fundamental facts about ethnic groups.

The first was that there is no one-to-one relationship between physical ethnic units and their culture understood as behavior describable from the outside. Within an ethnic unit, the features that matter to its members are not simply the sum of its observable behaviors, but "only those which the actors *regard as significant.*" Belonging to an ethnic category implies *"being a certain kind of person, having that basic identity. . . .* It also implies a claim to be judged, and to judge oneself, by those standards that are *relevant to that iden-tity.*" The relevant standards—easily observable signs like dress and language, but also basic moral values and standards of excellence, "do not necessarily follow from a descriptive list of cultural features; *one cannot predict from first principles* which features will be emphasized and made organizationally rele-vant by the actors."[59] Ethnic groups define themselves, and identity is always and necessarily meaningfulness to a self, even if the meanings available to be subjectively affirmed within the ethnic group are given in advance and con-strict the range of individual choice.

The point about subjective relevance was sharpened by Barth's second major criticism of conventional thinking. Ethnic groups, he argued, are always in contact with others, even if just notionally, and the cultural contents that define each to itself are relevant precisely because they are intended to main-tain boundaries between groups.[60] Difference is indeed at the heart of ethnic identity, but the differences that matter to it are those that maintain exclusivity. Cultural behavior within the same ethnic group might be different under different geographical and economic conditions, and to that extent may test the subjective sense of unified ethnic identity but without necessarily undermining it; only subjective affirmation or negation could tell. While even the central cultural features that define an ethnic group to itself can change over time, what does *not* change is the "continuing dichotomization between members and outsiders [that] allows us to specify the nature of continuity." Identity is defined not only by subjectively affirmed cultural criteria but also, and centrally, by a "will to otherness."[61]

The first criterion, self-definition, would be universally agreed on by those attempting to define identity. The second, the will to otherness, would be contested, but debate on the question would be unavoidable for any theory of collective identity. Whatever the conclusions on the issue, however, after Barth's work ascertaining how a culture defined itself and not just how it looked from the outside would be central to the anthropologist's task.

*   *   *

"Ethnicity" was a new term in the mid-twentieth century. The editors of the first collection of essays on the subject, Nathan Glazer and Daniel Moynihan, noted that it first appeared in dictionaries in the early 1960s; the earliest example cited there is its use by David Riesman in 1953 to refer in passing to a form of social parochialism.[62] What the editors didn't remark is that the term appeared at about the same time as identity, and that it was the convergence of the two that shaped debates about the meaning of ethnicity itself.

The new word, they claimed, both reflected and codified a new reality. It signified the emergence of a new social category "as significant for the understanding of the present-day world as that of social class. . . . [It represents] a pronounced and sudden increase in tendencies by people of many countries and in many circumstances to insist on the significance of their group distinctiveness and identity and on new rights that derive from this group character."[63] Earlier in their careers the editors had famously argued the salience of ethnicity in the American context. Against the long-familiar cliché of the "melting pot," in which immigrant strains supposedly dissolved in a homogeneous American brew (and in implicit critique of Will Herberg's view that religion was the only surviving remnant of immigrant identities), Glazer and Moynihan asserted that "The ethnic group in American society became not a survival from the age of mass immigration but a new social form." However modified by their encounter with America, immigrant cultures remained distinct; even third-generation descendants continued to think of themselves as members of their ancestors' original group with its original name, and were so thought of by others.[64]

Less than a decade later, ethnic consciousness had impressed itself on them as a worldwide phenomenon, more purposeful and militant than the organic development they had described in America. They enlarged their previous idea of the scope of ethnicity, extending it from minority subgroups within a larger society to the majority population itself. They also sharpened their understanding of the distinctiveness of ethnicity as a social—and political—category by contrasting it with previous liberal and radical social theory. Liberals had expected that in modern societies, emphasis on individual achievement would diminish the force of identities acquired by ethnic ascription. Radicals had expected that class circumstances would become the main line of division between groups of people. Instead, ethnic identity persisted as a unifying factor of groups. But the force of the older ways of thinking about social motivation—individualism and class—for the authors themselves was obvious in the difficulty they had explaining the hold of ethnicity. As the state became the crucial arbiter of economic well-being and political status, they argued, ethnicity gained strategic efficacy in making legitimate claims on its resources in order to rectify inequality among groups. Ethnicity, in other words, was a means of advancing material interests. Yet at the same time they realized that ethnicity could only be effective precisely because it involves *more* than interest, though they seemed genuinely puzzled by what this "more" was. "Why on earth," they asked, "would one wish to be a Pole when one could be a worker?" and answered somewhat helplessly, "Well, for some reason, or set of reasons, there is a desire to be Polish."[65] At best they could only refer by way of explanation to Daniel Bell's suggestion that an "affective tie" bound an ethnic group together, without suggesting a source for such a tie.[66]

That is what other writers in the volume and in much subsequent work on ethnicity tried to do. The overall project of establishing ethnicity as a legitimate and useful category had three major aims: to offer a definition and phenomenology of ethnic identity, to ground its apparent power in some more basic explanatory theory, and to account for its contemporary emergence as force and idea.

Defining Ethnic Identity

It seemed comparatively unproblematic to arrive at a generally agreed on definition of ethnicity. An ethnic group, in one influential formulation, habitually exhibits six main features, though in different degrees in each case: a common proper *name* that identifies the essence of the community; a myth of *common ancestry*, that gives the group a sense of kinship; *shared memories of a common past*, including its important events and heroes and their commemoration; elements of *a common culture*, which normally include language, customs, or religion; *a link with a homeland*, though not necessarily its physical occupation, as in the case of diaspora peoples or immigrants; *a sense of solidarity* among the members of the group.[67] A different formulation added *commensality*, the propriety of eating together, indicating both equality within the group and physical intimacy (and hinting at the displacement of sexual intimacy), but reduced the basic elements to three: kinship, commensality, and common cult, underlining the importance of the blood tie in ethnic consciousness.[68] These were not major differences. What proved much more controversial was the effort to explain the power of ethnic identity.

Explaining Ethnicity

One major problem in explaining ethnicity was its overlap and confusion with race. Though the ancient Greek *ethnos* (a people, generally a nonmajority one) had a modern French cognate in *ethnie*, neither it nor any other derivative was much used in the late nineteenth and twentieth centuries, with the exception of Max Weber, who introduced the term "ethnic groups" into sociology without much contemporary resonance. For the most part ethnic groups and nationalities were referred to at that time as "races." The reasons for naturalizing or biologizing the *ethnie* seemed obvious to contemporaries in the heyday of Darwinism, but the temptation lingered into the postwar world, long after the biological concept of "race" had been scientifically discredited for much of the intelligentsia.[69] Sociologist Pierre van den Berghe, pointing to the persistent social significance of physical features, defined "social race" as "a group that is socially defined but on the basis of physical criteria" in contrast to ethnicity which is "socially defined but on the basis of cultural criteria."[70] But he acknowledged that both racial and ethnic groups are also socially defined by real or putative common biological descent. Many discussions of ethnicity, while nominally differentiating "racial and ethnic identity," specifically included blacks and other groups usually identified by physical features as ethnicities, because they either also had a distinctive culture, or aspired to one.[71] Ethnicity thus hovered uneasily between biology and culture.

The modern temptation to naturalize ethnicity arose in part out of the inevitable biological beginnings of an individual's ethnic identity, condensed in the word "ascription." "Ascription," as Donald Horowitz pointed out, is the "key characteristic that distinguishes ethnicity from voluntary association. *Ethnic identity is generally acquired at birth*."[72] Harold Isaacs elaborated the apparently deterministic implications:

Basic group identity [i.e., ethnicity] consists of the ready-made set of endowments and identifications which every individual shares with others from the moment of birth by the chance of the family into which he is born. . . . There is first the new baby's body itself, all the shared physical characteristics of the group acquired through the long process of selection . . . the "biological remembrance of things past". . . . The baby acquires . . . a group name. He acquires the *history and origins* of the group into which he is born. The group's culture-past automatically endows him . . . with his *nationality* or other conditions of national, regional or tribal affiliation, his *language, religion* and *value system*—the inherited clusters of mores, ethics, aesthetics and attributes that come out of the *geography* or *topography* of his birthplace itself.[73]

It is in part because ethnicity begins this way that for the members of an ethnic group, the sociologist Talcott Parsons wrote, ethnic identity characterizes "what the individual *is* rather than what he *does*."[74] His use of the copula verb implied that for many members of the group a preexisting ethnic "essence" determines their behavior.

But birth only creates presumptive ethnicity. Unlike race, ethnicity contains a significant element of voluntary association, as Parsons himself insisted. One amusing example he offered was the case of women from Irish and Polish backgrounds who, having married into Italian families, insisted on their Italian identity by virtue of their Italian cooking and eating habits.[75] Group as well as individual identity can change by collective action, so even group self-ascription is putative rather than fixed, though ethnic groups frequently maintain myths of its absoluteness.[76] Furthermore, despite the insistence of many ethnicities on membership exclusivity, individuals can and do claim more than one ethnic identity, particularly where the several identities are at different levels of generality, emphasizing now one now another depending on its relevance to or usefulness in particular circumstances. All these observations implied that there was constant tension between the social and historical realities of ethnicity and the subjective experience of ethnic identity, to the extent at least that identity wants to fix ultimate and exclusive boundaries.

That tension was embedded even more deeply and made fully explicit in the conflicting theories that attempted to explain the social power of ethnicity. Though their respective advocates took hardly any notice of it, the debate was effectively framed by the affirmation on one side and the disregard on the other of the category of identity. Applying a term from Edward Shils's typology of social attachments, the anthropologist Clifford Geertz argued that ethnic ties are "primordial." They are emotional bonds that stem from the apparently objective features of social existence, mainly kin connection and immediate physical contiguity but also the sense of "givenness" from being born into a particular religious community, speaking a particular language, and following particular social practices. These congruities of blood, speech, and custom are seen by the members of an ethnic group to have

> *an ineffable, and at times overpowering, coerciveness* in and of themselves. One is bound to one's kinsman, one's neighbor, one's fellow believer, *ipso facto*; as the result not merely of personal affection, practical necessity, common interest, or incurred obligation, but at least in great part *by virtue of some unaccountable absolute import attributed to the very tie itself.* . . . [F]or virtually every person, in every society, at almost all times, some attachments seem to flow more from a sense of natural—some would say spiritual—affinity than from social interaction.[77]

Other theorists, however, vehemently rejected the notion of an "ineffable" primordiality as an antirational mystification that ignored clear historical facts: new "ethnicities" often appeared quite suddenly, artificially created for example under colonial rule, while older ethnic ties were frequently renewed, modified, and remade by self-conscious group action in each generation. Ethnicity could only properly be understood as a "'socially constructed variable definition of self or other, whose existence and meaning is continuously negotiated, revised and revitalized.'"[78] As to its point, social constructionists claimed that ethnic attachment served wholly instrumental purposes, bureaucratic, political, or economic. "Ethnicity is essentially a political phenomenon," anthropologist Abner Cohen asserted; "traditional customs are used only as idioms, and as mechanisms for political alignment. . . . If men actually quarrel seriously on the grounds of cultural difference it is only because these cultural differences are associated with serious political cleavages. On the other hand men stick together under the contemporary situation only because of mutual interest."[79] Rational choice theory went even farther: as sociologist Michael Hechter bluntly put it, "the members of any ethnic group will engage in collective action only when they estimate that by doing so they will receive a net *individual* benefit."[80]

The occasionally sharp-elbowed arguments between social constructionists and functionalists on one side and primordialists on the other seem at points not unlike the disagreements among the blind men about the elephant, "railing on in ignorance of what each other means." Primordialists approached ethnicity from "inside," from within the subjectivity of an ethnic group's members; social constructionists looked from the outside at objectively describable events of ethnic formation and maintenance. The difference of perspective was crucial.

The ethnic groups that were forming new nation-states in the "Third World" in the early 1960s, Geertz wrote, were "searching for identity"; they wanted to be "somebody in the world," and to have who they were recognized, publicly acknowledged as having worth and importance. Identity was bound up for them in "the gross actualities of blood, race, language, locality, religion or tradition."[81] In referring to these as "natural" constituents of identity, Geertz was expressly attributing to the members of an ethnic group a belief in their absoluteness. As another primordialist argued, to talk about ethnic identity merely in terms of "emotional ties"—the most that social constructionists were willing to acknowledge on the subjective side of ethnicity—missed a philosophically crucial fact: emotions are not simply internal states but cognitions. Emotions are aroused by beliefs about their object. The fact of kinship rouses feeling because it is deeply believed to be objectively valuable and wholly binding. To insist on the cognitive dimension of the primordial is not to say that the beliefs that comprise them are true, or even that the things they refer to actually exist. "Primordiality," Steven Grosby pointed out, "only asserts that human beings classify themselves and others in accordance with primordial criteria."[82]

Instrumentalism did purport to offer an explanation of ethnicity from the inside, a theory of motivation that rested on the staple of modern social theory, "interest." But it can be questioned whether interest is a genuinely internalist theory. Applied a priori as a complete explanation of group behavior it obviated any need to look at the factors emphasized by the primordialists, or even to regard ethnic subjectivity as a field for further investigation. Instrumentalists had no difficulty giving examples of opportunistic behavior by ethnic groups, but such explanations begged the question of why interest groups were aligned along ethnic criteria in the first place. Ethnicity was a form of collectivity whose very existence seemed to many theorists to demand a concept of subjective identity as an explanatory condition. Arguments between "internalists" and "externalists" were to be found throughout the literature not only of ethnic identity but also, as we will see, of the related categories of national, cultural, and religious identity. The dispute was endemic to all of them because it involved one of the core issues of identity as such: was identity, and collective identity in particular, a fundamental or epiphenomenal category of human motivation?

What was left unexplained by primordialists was why the specific elements that made up ethnic identity were, in fact, primordial. Geertz succinctly, and provocatively, evoked what primordiality *felt* like to members of an ethnic group who experienced it (or at least what they said it felt like). But why were "ineffability," the feeling of overpowering coerciveness, or the sense of being obviously binding and absolute attached to the specific components of ethnicity, such as time, place, and connection? About this primordialism itself had little to say. It was a significant omission, about which I will offer a suggestion in a later chapter on explanations of collective identity.[83]

The Rise of Modern Ethnicity

Writers offered different reasons for the rise of militant ethnicity in the second half of the twentieth century. Their varying interpretations were shaded both by national context and by the methodological approach adopted in each case, whether empirical case study or theoretical analysis. Yet despite serious disagreements among the explanations, identity was again the pivotal issue.

Examining the rise of ethnic awareness in the United States in the late 1960s, the political scientist Martin Kilson claimed that "Negro Americans initiated the current flurry of neo-ethnicity in American political life."[84] They did so both directly with actions affirming black ethnicity and indirectly by inspiring the angry counter-assertion of white ethnic identities. Hence the term "*neo*-ethnicity," since before the rise of black self-assertion, he argued, both black and white ethnic consciousness had been on the wane.

For Kilson, the not-so-hidden issue was reclaiming honorific ethnicity from defamatory "race." The new militancy of blacks was a conscious move to assert their value against the historic refusal of white America to grant them "a quality of ethnic characterization comparable to that accorded white ethnic groups." For whites, blacks were "merely" a biological race whose inferiority was manifested precisely in the absence of an authentic black culture. Since many blacks had internalized that judgment, black militancy was aimed even more at them than at the white community; in supporting "the movement of ethnocentric revitalization," blacks were seeking "thoroughgoing identity reformation, catharsis and therapeutic benefits."[85] To be thought of, to be able to think of oneself, as having an "ethnic identity" in America was to be endowed with "positive societal and cultural attributes . . . *historical attributes that attract celebration in time, ancestry, and heritage.*"[86]

There was historical precedent in the United States for the idea of a category transition from biological race to cultural ethnicity. White immigrant groups from southern and eastern Europe, initially viewed as racially different from the original Anglo-Saxon stock, achieved acceptance by being reclassified as minority ethnic groups, leaving the stigma of racial otherness to blacks and Asians.[87] This suggests that the *claim* to ethnic identity in America was more significant than any content it might have. In support of his argument that American blacks were making such a claim, Kilson cited a 1969 survey in which a majority expressed the belief that "Negroes have a special spirit or soul that most white people have not experienced."[88] But his argument appeared to contradict itself when he wrote that the "power-mustering dimension of ethnicity," its ability to mobilize and use political power for concrete ends—rather than its identity function—"appears to endow it with legitimacy in American life."[89] Black power, it would seem, not black culture, was what impressed white Americans.

Cultural ethnicity proved even less important in his analysis of the so-called white "ethnic" reaction to black assertiveness. He characterized it as a conservative response to the relative political success of black neoethnicity, concentrated in "marginal-income, working-class and lower-middle and even some middle-class city whites, who retain some vestiges of ethnic lifestyles, values, and perceptions."[90] These cultural "vestiges" however, apparently did not figure importantly in their reaction, which he described in racial terms as a white "anti-Negro orientation" motivated by economic resentment. The only ethnic group Kilson mentioned by name was Jews, who he saw as reaffirming a specifically Jewish identity from the late 1960s in reaction to black neoethnicity. The particular example he had in mind was the bitter battle over community control of education in one district in New York City that had pitted Jews against blacks in the 1960s. But Jews fit neither Kilson's social profile nor his political analysis of "white ethnics"; they were not, as he claimed, part of the neoethnic conservative coalition that elected Richard Nixon in 1968, remaining staunchly Democratic. In fact his own arguments seem to show that the core distinguishing features of cultural ethnicity were relatively unimportant in the politics of American life in the 1970s compared to perceived racial identity. Writing just a few years later, Herbert Gans suggested that ethnicity in the United States was essentially symbolic rather than practical. By the third generation, the descendants of immigrant ethnic groups expressed their identities through a nostalgic allegiance to their ancestors' traditions or homeland that did not have to be incorporated into everyday behavior, or through the observance of certain customs or holidays that did not require belonging to functioning groups and did not disrupt the secular routines of life. "Symbolic ethnicity," he argued, "does not need a practiced culture, even if the symbols are borrowed from it."[91] Nor was he certain that even symbolic ethnicity would persist in America into the fifth and sixth generations.

This was emphatically not the case for ethnic conflict elsewhere in the world. The essays in the Glazer-Moynihan collection documented serious, deeply rooted ethnic tensions in countries across the world, old and new, First, Second, and Third World—conflicts between Walloons and Flemings in Belgium, Québécois and English-speaking Canadians, restive nationalities in the Soviet Union, Chinese and Malayans in Malaya and Singapore, tribes in Uganda, and ethnic groups in the Indian subcontinent, among others. In the following two decades many more instances were documented and analyzed.[92] The analysis of ethnicity also became increasingly sophisticated. Essays in the earlier work did not always make strict distinctions among ethnic, national, tribal, and cultural identities and conflicts, sometimes moving back and forth between different terms even in the same essay. Later work made finer-grained distinctions. Bassam Tibi, for example, in his analysis of the ruling Alawites in Syria pointed out that they represented a single *ethnie* composed of four distinct tribes, united by language, belief, and custom but differentiated by kinship ties and geographical location.[93] In the decades after 1975 work on ethnicity went into more depth analyzing the significance of its different components such as language and religion, its varying relationships with the categories of race and nationality, and the theoretical disputes about its fundamental nature.

There was, however, a real difference between empirical studies and theoretical analyses in their approach to the question of why ethnicity had emerged as a salient identity in the modern world. "All the examples of the world-wide revival of ethnicity," Canadian sociologist John Porter wrote, introducing his discussion of the French-English conflict in Canada, "can best be understood within their own local and historical contexts." That was to imply that there could be no general account. But he also pointed out that through modern communications and intellectual leadership, ethnic struggles everywhere were mutually supportive. "Fanon becomes widely read in Quebec," he noted, "and Wounded Knee takes on symbolic significance for beyond South Dakota." Among the most influential instances of ethnic self-assertion he pointed to the colonial struggles for independence against European imperialism, especially in Algeria, and the Vietnam War, seen by many protesting Westerners and many more Third World peoples as an American effort to take over the role of Western imperialist domination from the faltering Europeans.[94]

In more broad-gauged theoretical analyses of the emergence of ethnicity, however, identity once again had a central place. In "Ethnicity and Social Change," Daniel Bell attempted a global analysis of the structural sources of ethnic revival that he believed were the result of common underlying trends in many different societies. As he saw it, the most notable feature of the various contemporary ethnic movements was their expressly political form. The question then was what social structural changes had made "*ethnic* (rather than some other form of group) *identification*" the most effective form of political action, instrumentally and emotionally, in the modern world.[95]

The world, he argued in response, was becoming one of ever larger and more centralized political units, in earlier centuries through the evolution of the nation-state in the West and more recently through the anti-imperialist rebellions of European colonies, which fused smaller local units into larger states. These developments had created a worldwide tendency toward more inclusive identities. But the new identity of state citizenship was for many people purely legal and abstract. A sense of uprootedness spread throughout entire societies. Additionally government was overtaking market forces in organizing and regulating the economy. In the more advanced industrial economies this meant that class organization, and thus class identity, was becoming less significant in people's lives, while accelerating demands for equality weakened the status and power of old elites.

Consequently, Bell argued, the largest and most important category of group membership, particularly in its ability to rouse emotional feelings and therefore to act effectively, was that "broad set which we call 'communal,'—individuals who feel some consciousness of kind which is not contractual, and which involves some common links through primordial or cultural ties."[96] Of the four "kinds" he enumerated—race, color, language, and ethnicity—ethnicity, whatever its overlap with the others, was the most inclusive (and with the discrediting of race the least controversial) way of designating the currently politically salient communal groups. Following the destruction of imperialist rule in former colonies and the erosion of older authority structures in the industrial West, competition between ethnicities for political power had become the norm.[97]

Bell referred to the individual's relationship to such groups as his *identity* or *belonging*. As a political sociologist he preferred to use the sociological term "group membership," rather than the psychological term "identity," since groups were the relevant political actors, but he also insisted that "Identity is essential for individual motivation."[98] No group action, in other words, without an individual identity motivation; for many contemporary individuals, their ethnicity was increasingly who they were. In essence, then, his argument was that political and social structural change both made ethnic identity salient and politicized it, thus changing its very nature. *Modern* ethnic identity was, whatever else it might be, a political identity.

Inevitably, however, Bell's model teetered uneasily between its two poles. On the one hand for historical reasons, ethnicity furnished the most viable collective basis for personal identity in the modern world. On the other, ethnic bonding was instrumental in purpose; ethnic politics was the primary means for claiming material advantage in the modern pluralistic state. In this model, ethnicity was essentially a domestic phenomenon, and the political agenda of all ethnic communities were basically the same. Ultimately, the model subordinated identity to economics; what motivated ethnic group behavior in the public sphere was interest.

Anthony Smith, however, believed that such an explanation of ethnic revival at best fit just one outlier case, "neo-ethnicity" in the United States. He agreed with Gans that (with the exception of American blacks, Native Americans, and Puerto Ricans) ethnic consciousness in the United States was comparatively shallow, since most ethnic groups were fully integrated into American political and cultural life.[99] In much of the rest of the world, by contrast, ethnic groups live in culturally deeply divided polyethnic states or states dominated by one *ethnie*. Many ethnic groups are either "autonomist," demanding independent control of their cultural or political life within an existing state, or separatist, seeking to secede outright and form their own state. Both autonomism and separatism pointed to the motivating force of ethnic identity as an end in itself. Ethnicity is based on the reality or myth of unique cultural ties, which, Smith argued, serve to demarcate a population from neighbors and rulers. Autonomism and separatism are above all means of protecting the cultural identity formed by those ties.[100] Economic arguments that seek to explain the separatist drives of ethnic groups by their relative material deprivation or their "internal colonization" by the dominant *ethnie* are fraught with exceptions which prove that cultural ethnicity can operate quite independently of economic disadvantage.[101] Smith's basic argument was that modern ethnic movements couldn't be understood without granting both the autonomy and the primacy of identity needs. In terms of a history of identity, the claim meant that it is only the availability of the concept of identity as the basic need for self-definition that made possible an adequate understanding of ethnicity and its politics.

The full meaning of modern ethnicity can be grasped, therefore, only if the ethnic revival is seen in a much longer time perspective than just the postwar era. The "current" revival of ethnicity had in fact been going on for two centuries; postwar events represented only its most recent metamorphosis. What lay behind the longer-term movement was the birth and diffusion of nationalism, the "single most potent influence on the ethnic revival."[102] *Ethnies* themselves are as old as human society. Smith was a primordialist who believed that the core features of ethnicity are fundamental to all human identity. The prominence of ethnicity since the French Revolution represents "the transformation of passive, often isolated and politically excluded communities into potential or actual 'nations,' active participant and self-conscious in their historic identities."[103] Like Bell, Smith characterized modern ethnic identity as inherently political, but for a totally different reason; the prime manifestation of ethnicity today is the identity politics of nationalism.

In Europe, nationalism in the nineteenth century had been identified with the strivings of dominant ethnicities, more accurately their intellectual and economic elites, for territorial self-rule. It came to include a demand for national unification, where an ethnic group was fragmented into separate polities, or national liberation, where one ethnic group was under the political authority of another. The fact that virtually all of Europe's successful nation-states contained ethnic minorities at the end of the nineteenth century, a reality more or less ignored by the dominant ethnicities during the era of nation-building, provided the tinder for later flare-ups of autonomism and separatism. The paradox, if such it was, of the ethnic revival in the postwar world was that it cut *against* the nation; more precisely it cut against the ethnic *non*homogeneity of the so-called "nation-state."

The situation was in some ways clearer and more dramatic in the newly liberated countries of Africa and Asia. Imperial rulers had imposed political and administrative grids on their colonies that cut across precolonial ethnic units. These then became the territorial states of the postcolonial world, supported by the native elites created under colonial rule who feared chaos and disintegration if the established boundaries were challenged. As Smith nicely put it, they saw their task as creating culturally unified nation-states out of bureaucratic "state-nations."[104] But their very commitment to political integration in a plural setting and fragile framework fostered ethnic protest and revolt.[105]

In Europe, an additional set of events set off the latent discontent of ethnic minorities within established nation-states. The loss of economic resources and prestige accompanying the loss of their colonies created the political conditions in former imperial powers in which ethnic movements could attract support. Increasing central government direction of the economy exacerbated the felt " 'incongruence' between state boundaries and ethnic composition."[106] Existing class-based parties had no place for minority ethnic demands and aspirations. Finally, the example of Third World struggles of "national liberation" contributed ideological rhetoric and renewed impetus to the festering discontents of the long list of minority ethnic movements Smith catalogued in 1970s Europe: Scottish, Welsh, Breton, Corsican, Basque, Catalan, Flemish, Ulster, Tyrolese, Croat, Slovak, Greek Cypriot, and Maltese. Smith acknowledged that most of these movements were autonomist rather than separatist, but even at the time, some of the most militant were demanding their own states, and the surge of "ethnonationalist" sentiment and state-creation after the collapse of communism in Eastern Europe and the Soviet Union seem in retrospect to bear out his argument about the political thrust of postwar ethnic revival.

For Smith this meant that much, or most, modern ethnic identity was equivalent to national identity. While his was only one interpretation of the rise of ethnicity, his insistence on the controlling role of identity was widely shared. Identity did not simply influence the rise of ethnicity studies; it made them. From Geertz to Barth to Smith, ethnicity was the fundamental way in which humans defined themselves in relation to time, place, and other people in groups larger than the family. Even "interest" sociologists like Bell acknowledged the modern individual need for and motivating force of ethnic identity. Only the most consistent of rational choice theorists denied it any significance, their insistence on individual interest bearing all the signs of reactive zeal. Accepted or rejected, identity was the frame of reference within which contemporary ethnicity was studied and debated.

National Identity

> Nationalism provides perhaps the most compelling identity
> myth in the modern world.
> —Anthony D. Smith, *National Identity*[107]

1983 was the annus mirabilis of a resurgent interest in theories of nationalism that had begun some two decades before. That year saw the publication of three interpretations whose powerful theses attracted attention well beyond their disciplinary boundaries while generating heated debate within them: Benedict Anderson's *Imagined Communities: Reflections on the Origin and Spread of Nationalism*, Ernest Gellner's *Nations and Nationalism*, and the essay collection provocatively titled *The Invention of Tradition* edited by Eric Hobsbawm and Terence Ranger. The following year Anthony Smith published his seminal article "National Identity and Myths of Ethnic Descent," a forerunner of his larger theoretical statements a few years later, *The Ethnic Origins of Nations* (1986) and *National Identity* (1991). The reasons for this spate of books were not obvious on the surface, since much of the work seemed focused on Europe, where nationalist sentiment had presumably receded after the horrors of World War II. Indeed, the immediately preceding wave of historiography on nationalism had been concerned with the origins of the virulent strain of nationalism at the core of Fascism and Nazism, in an effort to understand the destructive fervor its authors hoped had been laid to rest once and for all. But with one exception Europe was less the focus of the new literature for itself than a pole of comparison in the effort to understand the rise of the new nationalisms of postcolonial Africa and Asia. Tellingly, all four writers were British by birth or by education and residence; all except Anderson held positions in British universities. (Two of the four, Hobsbawm and Gellner, had come to Britain as youthful Jewish refugees from Hitler's Europe.)

The most explicit, and poignant, explanation of the renewed attention to nationalism was offered by the political scientist Benedict Anderson. A Marxist scholar who despite his appreciation of the role of nationalism in the politics of Southeast Asia had believed in the premise and promise of socialist univer-salism, he was shaken by the outbreak of war between Vietnam, Cambodia, and China in 1978–1979. These wars were "of world-historical importance," he wrote, "because they are the first to occur between regimes whose indepen-dence and revolutionary credentials are undeniable" and could neither be explained nor justified from a Marxist theoretical perspective.[108] They also cast new light on the fact, whose full significance he had not previously appreci-ated, that since World War II every successful communist revolution had defined itself in national terms. The unhappy conclusion for Marxists was unavoidable: "The 'end of the era of nationalism,' so long prophesied, is not remotely in sight. Indeed, nation-ness is the most universally legitimate value in the political life of our time." His book was an effort to explain why that was and how it came about.

The testimony of the other major theorists—Hobsbawm was the one exception—tied their work no less directly to Third World ferment. Gellner traced the impulse that led him from philosophy to anthropology and the study of nationalism to his feelings about the creation of Israel in 1948. He anticipated at the time, he said, that "The solution of the Jewish national predicament by the establishment of the state of Israel would lead to a dra-matic, tragic, perhaps insoluble confrontation with the Muslim world. The least one could do was try to understand that world."[109] That aim led him to the Atlas mountains to study the local tribes (and where he could also mountain climb, a cherished hobby); while he was there violent conflict broke out between France and Morocco over independence, and he saw the families among whom he was living split between Moroccan nationalism and support of the French. His first writing on nationalism dates from the same years as his anthropological publications on the Atlas and adumbrated the theory he would develop more fully twenty years later.[110] Anthony Smith had been a student of Gellner's around that time. He had been "groping for a method of studying phenomena that had already from some time absorbed me and that were, after the wave of decolonisation in Africa and Asia, very much in the air." Gellner's work caught his imagination and he wrote the thesis that became his first book, on nationalism, in 1971 under Gellner's direction.[111] From the beginning, his work on ethnicity was part of his quest to understand modern nationalism. Acknowledging how much he had learned from his teacher, however, did not preclude differing radically with him.

Hobsbawm's work seemed to run against the grain. *The Invention of Tradition* was not specifically focused on nationalism, even if, as he pointed out, its thesis was highly relevant to it.[112] Four of its six case studies dealt with Europe; Hobsbawm's own contribution was a study in the mass production of "traditions" in the European nation-states between 1870 and 1914. Elsewhere Hobsbawm even argued that as a "vector of historical change" nationalism had actually declined in Europe compared to its role from the 1830s to the end of World War II; the burst of new-state formation following the break-ups of the Soviet Union and Yugoslavia was more the unfinished business of the post-World War I dissolution of the old multinational empires than anything new.[113] But, as he also observed, national liberation movements and state-making were driving forces in the postcolonial world, and the notion of inventing tradition was as productive for understanding the present Third World as it was for the European past.

Three fundamental disagreements, according to Smith, divided contemporary theorists of nationalism: between primordialists and instrumentalists, on the essential nature of nationalism; between modernists and "perennialists," on the question of the modernity or antiquity of nations; and between social constructionists and "ethnosymbolists" on the origins and meaning of modern nationalism, the latter arguing that even modern "civic" nations founded on equal citizenship and individual rights were built on long-preexisting ethnicities.[114] Smith stood on one side on all these issues, Gellner and Hobsbawm on the other, while Anderson occupied an odd but highly significant place in between. The second and third issues were really subordinate to the first: those who believed nations had existed in the past and that even modern nations had premodern ethnic foundations were arguing for a version of the primordialist idea that the ties that bind a collectivity and connect it to a territory are experienced as ultimate, binding, and ineffable. As with ethnicity, the fundamental differences over nationalism ultimately hinged on the place accorded by each theorist to identity. Significantly Smith, a primordialist who coined the term ethnosymbolism, was the only one of the theorists to write a book on national identity and make it central to his interpretation. "We cannot begin to understand the power and appeal of nationalism as a political force," he claimed, "without grounding our analysis in a wider perspective whose focus is national identity, treated as a collective cultural phenomenon."[115]

It is illuminating, nevertheless, to start again with Anderson, who ingeniously combined a species of primordialism with the argument that nations
were a modern creation, thereby offering a theory about the source of primordialism's power. The answer he gave to his own question about the abiding grip of nationalism was that the modern nation had inherited the mantle
of eternity from religion. The great strength of the major historical religions
was that they provided solutions to the existential questions generated by
the contingency of human life—our subjection to suffering, disease, aging,
and death. Correspondingly, the great weakness of the modern secular ideologies of progress, liberalism, and Marxism was that they ignored our concern with death and immortality, responding to our existential questions
with "impatient silence" in their exclusive focus on earthly freedom and
happiness. The waning of religion in modern times demanded the transformation of the religious answers to the fatality of life and the question of
life's purpose into a secular form of continuity and meaningfulness. "Few
things," Anderson claimed, "were better suited to this end than an idea of
nation."[116] Nation-states might be new; in their mythology, however, the
nations to which they gave concrete expression went back to time immemorial and would last to eternity, guaranteeing the immortality of its members
through the nation's identity.

Anderson's book was primarily concerned with the socioeconomic and
technological explanation for the nation-state's supplanting of religion, its
most often discussed thesis. But the role of the eternal retained central place
even within his economic interpretation. Print technology, promoted by
capitalist publishing, enabled vernaculars to replace Latin in Europe, and
laid the linguistic bases for national consciousness. The vernaculars, however, inherited the sacred function of the Latin language, if on a radically
different philosophical foundation. The sacredness of language in the
world's great religions, Anderson wrote (citing Walter Benjamin), entailed
the belief that "ontological reality is apprehensible only through a single,
privileged system of re-presentation";[117] a language was sacred because its
texts named a timeless truth that was true even "before" it happened and
could only be rendered in that language.[118] Modern secular languages, by
contrast, are disenchanted; they exist in linear time, and document unre-
peatable mundane events. But they are shared by a large number of people
who, physically dispersed but joined in a linguistically constituted imaginary
community, can talk simultaneously about events they have not directly
experienced or people they have never met, and yet know them as "theirs."
The common language enables them to create the sense of an eternal community "moving steadily down (or up) history."[119]

Both Hobsbawm and Gellner, in contrast, were strong "externalists" who looked exclusively to economic and social forces to explain the rise of nationalism and the nation-state, which they insisted were wholly modern creations. In turn they rejected self-conscious national identity as mere "deception and self-deception."[120] The idea of "nation," Gellner argued, represents the radical transformation of the traditional culture of agrarian societies. It involves the imposition of a "high," or literate, culture, on a previously oral/low literacy society. This requires universal education and "the generalized diffusion of a school-mediated, academy-supervised idiom," a language standardized "for the requirements of reasonably precise bureaucratic and technological communication." Underlying this cultural shift is the transformation of a locally centered traditional society to one that is anonymous and impersonal, composed of mutually substitutable atomized individuals held together by a shared belief in the values of individualism, rationality, and mobility. This kind of society can only be and indeed *must* be created by modern commerce and industry, with its needs for technology, education, and social fluidity, and a strong, centralized, impersonally bureaucratic state to protect them. Nationalism is the structurally necessary outcome of economic and social modernization.

But this, Gellner said, is the opposite of what nationalists claim. Nationalism conquers in the name of a "putative folk culture," based on preindustrial, agrarian idealization of peasantry and land, which it revives from the past or, if necessary, invents from the whole cloth. The truth of the modern nation is the culture of abstract individualism; its lie is that of an organic, particularist culture. Why do nations deceive themselves so? It is because modernization is an uneven process. Rural areas, entrenched in the old agrarian economy while the urban center modernized and grew wealthier, could express their resentments and grievances through whatever cultural/linguistic differences disadvantaged them from participating in the new economy; eventually this could lead to separation and the creation of a new nation-state. While Gellner protested that it travestied his position to say that he reduced national sentiment to calculations of social promotion, it is hard to see his explanation, which ultimately related everything to modernization chances, as anything else.

Hobsbawm's conclusion about the sham status of nationalism was similar, though derived from quite different premises. Traditions supporting nationalism were invented not in the interests of an economically or socially disadvantaged group but by the dominant economic and political classes attempting to safeguard the existing society and political establishment against those who would destroy it: against socialists, for example, in the case of Wilhelmine Germany, against both socialists and monarchists in the case of Third Republic

France. The idea of the unified nation with a long history represented in the symbols and observances of the present state appeared on the one hand to include everyone while on the other it branded those who dissented as unpatriotic or treasonous.

In Smith's view, neither Gellner's theory nor Hobsbawm's conception of nationalism could account for its motivating force among the mass of a nation's citizens. "A sense of national identity," he claimed, "provides a powerful means of defining and locating individual selves in the world, through the prism of the collective personality and its distinctive culture. . . . *This process of self-definition is in many ways the key to national identity.*"[121] It is impossible to understand "the power and appeal of nationalism as political force without grounding our analysis in a wider perspective whose focus is national identity treated as a collective cultural phenomenon."[122] The sense of belonging to a nation with a distinct and unique culture was for Smith the most important component of the social dimension of modern personal identity.

Smith's definition of "nation" was thus intimately related to his understanding of ethnicity. In essence, a nation was a politicized ethnicity, adding sovereignty over a territorial homeland with unified legal and economic institutions to the ethnic sense of common name, origins, myths, history, and culture. It was in these terms that Smith claimed the possibility of *nations* existing even in antiquity, though in fact he believed that only the Jews in the time of the late Second Temple approximated his definition.[123] *Nationalism* as an idea, however, was indeed something new in history. It was the ideological movement aiming to attain, or maintain, political autonomy, unity, and identity for an ethnic group that deemed itself to constitute a nation.[124] It emerged, could only have emerged, with the rise of the modern form of the *nation-state*.

Smith's distinction between ancient nation and modern nationalism followed from his position in the primordial-instrumental debate over ethnicity. Ethnic cultures, he argued, were neither the rigidly fixed patterns of ethnic self-mythologizing nor the infinitely malleable forms resulting from the instrumental manipulations of political leaders. Collective cultural identity, as something historical, subjective, and symbolic, could metamorphose over time with changing historical circumstances while still preserving the subjective sense of sameness and continuity with the past.[125] Yet again we see how modern identity theorists tried to accommodate and balance permanence and change in their understanding of identity.

The rise of modern nationalism represented for Smith the most recent metamorphosis of ethnic identity. Unified states in Europe before the end of the eighteenth century were at most "ethnic states" (if dominated by a single ethnic aristocracy) but not nation-states. Even if belief in and expressions of national character could be found earlier (for example in Shakespeare), national consciousness lacked the elements of mass cultural and political mobilization, led by an intellectual elite that formulated and inculcated an ideology purporting to speak for the whole. The creation of such an ideology depended on democratizing the idea of the nation. The modern nation was the whole people; national sovereignty was thus *popular* sovereignty, based in principle on the equal standing of all. The paradox of modern nationalism was that it combined the political unity and sovereignty of the old collective, the *ethnie*, with the new idea of the sovereignty of the individual, manifested in the idea of citizenship, which gave each individual equal rights. Depending on historical conditions one or another of these elements was foremost in the consciousness of a particular national movement, but in theory modern nationalism was at once ethnic, rooted in the claims of a dominant *ethnie* to rule its territory (however polyethnic the territory in reality) and "civic," based on the universalist idea of the rights of the individual citizen. From the point of view of identity, modern nationalism made it possible for someone to entertain two identities that were ultimately, though usually unconsciously, in tension with one another: one was at once an individual defined by his universal humanity and the rights with which it endowed the self, and a member of a particular community, bounded by its language, customs, and loyalties.

Far from denying the role of political, economic, and technological factors in the creation of the modern centralized nation-state, Smith relied on them to help explain why premodern ethnic identity evolved into modern national identity. But since for Smith it was precisely *identity* that evolved, the change could not be explained without also understanding why the older ethnic identity-consciousness was no longer adequate to the new political and economic conditions arising in Europe. The transformation of ethnic into national consciousness was not just incidental to the rise of the modern nation-state but one of its necessary conditions. Whether the nation-state was originally unified through monarchical and bureaucratic centralization, which made possible the subsequent diffusion of a unified national culture, or whether the demand for a nation-state arose from below, from the aspirations of a subject people (or its intelligentsia) for national unification and liberation, the nation-state from the nineteenth century on was both held together and motivated by the investment of its populace in their ethnonational identity.

Smith's interpretation of the reasons for the change from ethnic to national identity and the role it played in individual identity converged with Anderson's. The institutions of the modern state were grounded in rationalist and scientific thought and methods. Their power, as proved by the political, economic, and military success of the modern state, posed fundamental challenges to the traditional religious cosmic images, symbols, and theodicies which underpinned premodern ethnic identity, creating a demand for new secular forms of identity legitimation.[126] Smith's story, then, was also about the decline of religion and the replacement of transcendent images of power with secular ones. The aspiration of identity to permanence was drawn to the historical entity, the state, whose power and ubiquity seemed to promise it. Without using the term, Smith like Anderson injected ontological considerations into his interpretation of the reasons for the rise and hold of national identity. "Perhaps the most important of [the] functions [of national identity] is to provide a satisfying answer to the problem of personal oblivion. Identification with the 'nation' in a secular era is the surest way to surmount the finality of death and ensure a measure of personal immortality."[127]

The scholarly debates about national identity had obviously important implications for the political theory of nationalism. But their impact turned out to be more than theoretical. In a number of European countries national identity became, if intermittently, a consuming issue of practical politics from the 1980s into the first decade of the twenty-first century. It proved to be a galvanizing category for dealing with ethnic, religious, and political fissures within France and Germany as well as with deep anxieties about the international standing of each country. As a result the academic study of national identity itself became embroiled in debates about the issue that were taken up at the highest levels of national electoral politics. The same, as we will see, happened in connection with the problem of cultural identity. I will look at both in the following chapter.

Cultural Identity

> The international community considers it its duty to ensure
> that the cultural identity of each people is preserved and
> protected.
>
> —UNESCO, Mexico City Declaration
> on Cultural Policies, 1982

Despite the heat generated by debates over national identity in Germany and France to be described in the next chapter, it was the idea of "cultural identity" that had by the 1990s become the most prominent version of collective identity in European and North American identity discourse. It was also the one most taken for granted and the least well defined. The same reasons explain both circumstances. Cultural identity was fed from a number of different sources, each with its own context and purposes.

Cultural identity had been an integral aspect of identity politics from its beginnings in the 1960s. Black Power leaders talked of building black identity in terms of creating, or retrieving, a distinctive black culture. Proponents and theorists of gay identity based the distinction between homosexual and gay on the difference between sexual orientation and cultural institutions. Similarly, distinctive socially shared beliefs, customs, and observances were invoked to distinguish ethnicity from race. Many activists were not particularly interested in precise or comprehensive definitions of culture; they didn't need them for their purposes, which was to distinguish the social from the biological, the humanly created, and therefore honorific, from the biologically determined and merely accidental. A colloquial or popular understanding of culture would do. Others, however, were at pains to define explicitly and in detail what they intended by culture and why it was important to their groups. But both implicit and explicit definitions entailed commitments to basic assumptions about cultural identity that were not always spelled out.

In the case of black identity, for example, one such commitment was to the equal significance of the anthropological and the elitist meanings of culture—"culture" as the ensemble of a people's practices, beliefs, and folkways, and "high culture" as their most advanced artistic expressions. Maulana Karenga, founder of the Black nationalist movement Us, asserted in its statement of principles that "culture is the fundamental source of a people's identity," and named as its "core areas" history, spirituality and ethics, social organization, political organization, economic organization, and creative production in such areas as art, music, literature, and dance.[128] While culture in the anthropological sense was all-encompassing, high culture, especially for a collective identity in the (re)making, was its necessary self-conscious articulation. The spontaneity characteristic of an existing and flourishing culture could not be taken for granted in a cultural identity that had to be created anew. Art could not simply express or shape the materials of what existed; it had to take a leadership role in fashioning them.

An apparently surprising omission in Karenga's list of cultural spheres was language. This was, however, because language for him was more than just another department of culture. As the vehicle of group communication and shared behaviors and beliefs, language is its necessary form. Nor is language simply a culture's potentially interchangeable vehicle but rather its embodiment; language both expresses and creates a culture with its unique resonances. Necessarily then language was both a central focus and a serious problem for Us. A culture's history is purportedly an unbroken chain, and the origins of black culture were African. Its American phase was therefore in a crucial way deeply inauthentic. Blacks had been brought to America against their will, to an alien culture that was simultaneously barred to and forced upon them. Hence the foundation of an authentic black cultural identity had to be African both in content and language. Karenga chose a Swahili name for its basic philosophy and defined *Kawaida* as "an ongoing synthesis of the best of African thought and practice"; he gave the seven basic principles that governed its core areas Swahili names. Of necessity, however, the terms had to be translated into and promoted in the native English of American blacks. Karenga was not alone in facing the dilemma of maintaining, reviving, or recreating the culture of a group that no longer spoke its "authentic" language. That problem came to define the intrinsic yet ambiguous relationship between language and cultural identity for many minority cultures within a larger cultural community as well as, in the case of Israel, for the majority culture of an ethnic revival state.

There was another significant exclusion from Karenga's idea of cultural identity. He made no reference to the biological framework of kinship as the transmission belt for culture. Since birth into a cultural community was the most usual way culture was acquired, this was a notable omission. But this was exactly the point of a distinction between culture and ethnicity or race. Even though a common history might plausibly be assumed to rest on biological descent, even though the common history in question was that of dark-skinned people of African origin, the idea of a common culture was intentionally silent about how its patterns of behavior and belief came to be shared and transmitted by a community. Culture was just that set of shared institutions that made the community distinctly what it was, and it was transmitted by the shared will to continue it. Culture was expressly *non*-natural, indeed the opposite of nature, a structure of imaginative human creation.

A last feature of cultural identity as Karenga understood it divorced culture from the idea of a more basic grounding in a metaphysical belief system like religion. Culture was the superordinate identity category that subsumed all communal spheres of life under its head—historical commemoration, dress and custom, the arts, political organization, and what he referred to as "spirituality and ethics." This had the effect of equalizing, homogenizing, and relativizing these spheres as "elements" of culture, and thus of secularizing the idea of culture itself. Karenga was not a theist; Kwanzaa was intended as a purely secular celebration of African heritage. But while his own secular humanism may not have been incidental to his conception of the holiday, the elevation of culture to the overarching form of identity could embrace even a transcendental religion as the form of a culture's "spirituality." From the structural-functional point of view, every culture had a set of "higher" values that served to legitimize it. In this sense, all forms of spirituality, traditionally religious or not, could be considered equivalent as a functionally necessary dimension of cultural identity. Karenga's was in this sense a very "modern" version of culture and cultural identity.

* * *

A different set of concerns stemming from a different source led to a similar result with regard to the preeminence of cultural identity by the 1990s. The academic discipline of "cultural studies," which grew rapidly in the United States and Britain through the 1970s and 1980s, enrolled the main forms of "difference" in which it was invested—gender, race, ethnicity, and class—into its domain, thus in effect making them all equivalent subcategories of culture. Among other things, this disciplinary imperialism also had the effect of secularizing cultural identity by again making religion, like ethnicity, gender, and class just another sphere of cultural identity. A paradoxical if logical consequence of this move was to make it possible to claim a traditionally religious identity without being a believer. In one striking example, the Indian-born philosopher Akeel Bilgrami, of Muslim descent but a self-acknowledged "aggressive" secularist who found Islamic theological doctrine "wholly noncredible," found himself answering a Hindu hotelier's question about his religion with the words "I am a Muslim"—without, as he put it, "strain or artificiality." The essay in which Bilgrami recounts this incident is titled, significantly, "What Is a Muslim? Fundamental Commitment and Cultural Identity."[129] Other contributors to the volume in which the essay appeared, however, questioned whether it was possible to understand the real nature of a culture's "fundamental commitments," or for that matter the absolutization of culture itself, from a purely secular vantage point. Since these debates took place within the framework of a discipline transformed by poststructuralism and postmodernism, however, they will be considered in more detail elsewhere.

* * *

The most significant and broad-reaching initiative to establish the preeminence of cultural identity came neither from the liberation struggles of minority groups in the United States and elsewhere, nor from theories of cultural identity politics within the academy, but from official government action. The policy of multiculturalism initiated by the Canadian government with a series of investigation committees, declarations, and Acts of Parliament starting in the 1960s gave cultural identity its most common political name and program, and set a pattern which would soon be followed, with greater or lesser enthusiasm and success, by other countries. Its different fate in those other countries not only highlighted crucial differences in the balance between civic and ethnic nationalism that affected their receptivity to multiculturalism, but exposed serious ambiguities in the idea of cultural identity itself. I will explore them in the next chapter on the practical politics of national and cultural identity.

Religious Identity

The pro forma treatment, subordination, or total ignoring of religion in much of the original debate over cultural identity hardly meant that religious identity was not a source of bitter conflict in the last third of the twentieth century. One need only think of Northern Ireland, India-Pakistan, the Arab-Israeli conflict—despite the ethnonational label basically ethnoreligious in nature— the war between Iraq and Iran, as much intrareligious as international, and the rising political assertiveness of evangelical Christianity in the United States. As I will argue, the debates over multiculturalism in Germany and national identity in France were either open, barely veiled, or displaced religious conflicts. But for a number of reasons religious identity as such played nothing like the roles of gender, sexual orientation, race, ethnicity, and culture in the theoretical literature of identity politics. Formally and even substantively, the issue of religious identity in the West had supposedly long been solved by constitutional or de facto separation of church and state and by the secularism that increasingly marked the institutional and social public spheres. Religion, as we have seen, was taken to be one aspect of culture broadly conceived. Theorizing identity politics, with some exceptions that will be examined in the chapter on liberal democracy and identity, was still mostly impelled in the 1970s and 1980s by the social and political movements of the 1960s.

What upset this superficial consensus and introduced the most explicit discussion of religion into identity politics up to that point was the challenge of Islam to the West as perceived largely though not only by conservative observers. It had become a domestic issue in Western Europe by the 1980s, but was rarely publicly debated at first in openly religious, as opposed to cultural and political terms—the controversy over the Islamic veil in French schools was ostensibly about the lay character of the French Republic and did not single out Islamic religious garb for exclusion.[130] The work that almost singlehandedly changed this situation was an essay in international relations

by the American political theorist Samuel Huntington, "The Clash of Civilizations?" published in the influential journal *Foreign Affairs* in 1993. Three years
later he followed it with a book-length treatment of the same subject, now
with the question mark of the original title removed. Few if any articles in
specialized periodicals (at least since George Kennan's famous "Mr. X" article
outlining the policy of Communist containment) have excited more passionate commentary, for and against, than the original essay. Huntington popularized a phrase—the historian Bernard Lewis had introduced it before
him—which became a reigning idiom, not to say cliché, of identity politics.

Its impact was promoted by the blunt declarative style in which Huntington argued his thesis. The clash of civilizations as driver of international conflict represented for him both the current historical moment and an eternal
verity that could be eclipsed only temporarily. On the one hand, it was taking
center stage with the end of the conflict of ideologies that had characterized
world history since the end of World War II. On the other, it represented a
return to something far more fundamental than sociopolitical ideologies: the
question of identity. "In the post-Cold War world, the most important distinctions among peoples are not ideological, political or economic. . . . Peoples
and nations are attempting to answer the most basic question humans can
face: Who are we?"[131]

In Huntington's lexicon, a civilization was "the highest cultural grouping
of people and the broadest level of cultural identity people have short of that
which distinguishes humans from other species." It encompasses many
smaller units including families, regions, and even nations, the latter of which,
while still politically the most important actors on the world scene, are not the
most important sources of collective identity and hence of international conflict. Civilizations are the biggest "we" within which people feel culturally at
home. Many features define a civilization—language, ethnicity, history,
tradition—but by far the most important is religion. The major civilizations
in human history had been closely identified with the world's great religions.[132]

Nowhere did Huntington discuss why he thought religion was so fundamental to identity. He was primarily concerned to make the point that it had
been the cause of world conflict in the past and to venture predictions about
how and where it would be again in the future, based on what could already
be seen in the postideological revival of religion and religious tensions. What
he did note was the comprehensiveness of religious belief: "The people of
different civilizations have different views on the relations between God and
man, the individual and the group, the citizen and the state, parents and children, husband and wife, as well as differing views of the relative importance
of rights and responsibilities, liberty and authority, equality and hierarchy.

These differences are the product of centuries. They will not soon disappear. They are far more fundamental than differences among political ideologies and political regimes."[133] While an enumeration of the main issues of social and political organization on which religions differed, it did not probe religion's role and appeal as transcendental legitimation.

Nor did Huntington say why religions must inevitably clash. Indeed he sometimes asserted the opposite: "Differences do not necessarily mean conflict, and conflict does not necessarily mean violence." But that is not what he finally believed. "Civilizational identity" could not be compromised because it was what most fundamentally defined the self. As he put it, "In class and ideological conflict, the key question was 'Which side are you on?' and people could and did choose sides and change sides. In conflicts between civilizations, the question is 'What are you?' That is a given that cannot be changed. And as we know, from Bosnia to the Caucasus to the Sudan, the wrong answer to that question can mean a bullet to the head."[134] In the book version he wrote more sweepingly "it is human to hate. For self-definition and motivation people need enemies."[135] And in his later work on American national identity, Huntington cited the evidence from social identity theory to argue that ingroups will always sacrifice absolute gains for themselves so long as they come out better than their rivals.[136]

The extraordinary attention Huntington's argument drew came partly from the shock value of naming names and positing enmities, or what he more cautiously called "fault lines," between them. There were, he claimed, seven major civilizations in the modern world: Sinic, Japanese, Hindu, Islamic, Orthodox, Western, Latin American, to which African might possibly be added. While only three had overtly religious names, "Western" was the modern version of what was once explicitly "Western Christendom," Latin America was classified separately from the West for the predominance of Catholicism over Protestantism, the distinguishing religion of the Anglo-American world, and in his original article, Huntington had labeled Chinese civilization as Confucian. But from the point of view of the history of identity, the most original and provocative idea was that identity had the immediate practical value of making possible meaningful predictions about future world conflict along the fault lines he delineated as well as concrete suggestions for political action that should be taken in the light of them. If Huntington was correct, religious identity was the all-important key to practical solutions for global problems threatening the whole of humanity.

Some twenty years later, many of Huntington's predictions seemed to have been falsified, though perhaps, as Mao Zedong famously did not say when asked about the outcome of the French Revolution, "It's too soon to judge," since other of his predictions have been vindicated.[137] Even at the time, however, Huntington's "clash of civilizations" was attacked for its factual and conceptual errors as well as for its political dangers. A characteristic response by the German political scientist Thomas Meyer summarized his criticism in his title, *Identity Mania: Fundamentalism and the Politicization of Cultural Differences*, while expressing his open anger in the heading of one section, "An Indignant Look at a New Experience." The thesis of the clash of civilizations, if accepted, could become a self-fulfilling prophecy, Meyer argued, "even if its factual core is absolutely untrue."[138] Survey evidence shows that there are both significant commonalities between civilizations on basic values, and deep conflicts on other matters within each supposedly unified civilization.[139] Not religion per se but religious fundamentalists exaggerate and politicize religious differences for the purposes of seizing power, and Huntington's thesis in effect supports their claims that they are the only solution to the world's ills by declaring that the divergent civilizations of the world are "by their very nature nothing but fundamentalist action programmes."[140] But fundamentalism, Meyer argued, is only one possible *style* of religion, not its essence, and it develops only in particular historical circumstances. Contemporary fundamentalism is a form of "cultural countermodernism," directed against the principle of openness that constitutes the core of modern civilization.[141] It grows especially strong when sociocultural groups are threatened at one and the same time by humiliation in comparison with other civilizations and by the experience or threat of downward mobility and economic insecurity.[142]

Amartya Sen's dissent was aimed more directly at Huntington's basic conception of identity. The Nobel economist was far from dismissing the importance of identity; to the contrary, as an economic theorist he championed those economists who argued for incorporating it into the explanation of economic preference and behavior.[143] But Huntington's clash of civilizations was based on the opposite error of fetishizing one identity on the mistaken belief that it alone mattered to people. People have multiple, frequently competing identities, and are thus necessarily compelled to use reason to choose among them when they do conflict, not only to decide which is more important to them at any given time but to gauge the consequences for their other identities in favoring one of them. Reducing people's identity to membership in a civilization creates a one-dimensional conception of human existence. It is not only false, moreover, it is inflammatory; it has licensed bigotry and tyranny on the part of the civilizations that regard themselves as superior, and reactive, equally chauvinistic identities on the part of the tyrannized. The latter identities not only mirror the bigotry of the oppressors but also perpetuate their psychological domination, because obsessive preoccupation with the oppressor stunts the inner freedom of the tyrannized to independently develop their own possibilities.

Ironically, however, Sen's own analysis seemed to provide support for Huntington's thesis. Civilizational identities might not be the "central, inexorable, and entirely independent determinant of societal predicament,"[144] as Sen insisted, but the array of instances of cultural oppression and cultural reaction that he himself described in Africa, Arabia, and India suggested how large a part they historically played and continue to play in international strife and violence. Part of the problem in deciding the issue lay in the ambiguity of Huntington's thesis: was he making a theoretical argument for the foundational necessity of religion-based civilizations or an empirical generalization about their historical impact? But even to the extent it was the former, and thus vulnerable to Sen's objections, Sen's acknowledgement that "culture" could and did have a major impact on our identities begged the question Huntington at least tried, if unsatisfactorily, to answer: why has religion loomed so large in the history of political strife? What are its special features as a mainstay of human identity? While Benedict Anderson and Anthony Smith had ventured an answer in their explanation of the power of modern national identity as heir of religion's promise of eternity, it was more a hint at than an exploration of the hold of religious identity.

*   *   *

The argument over Huntington's thesis returns us to the most sharply debated question emerging from both advocacy and analysis of the collective identities that mobilized during the last thirty-five years of the twentieth century: primordiality or adventitious historical construction? Primordialism was explicitly espoused mainly by anthropologists and ethnographers, but it was an idea shared by difference feminists and theorists of culture who did not use the term. It held that certain kinds of groups were anchored in the fundamental nature of human beings. Yet at the same time gay advocates who took the biological basis of sexual orientation for granted could call for the construction of a wholly new gay culture. The paradox of primordiality is that it was the unique historical and political circumstances of the second half of the twentieth century that gave rise to claims about the eternal pull of collective identity, ethnic or sexual. Clifford Geertz, staunchest of primordialists, was also the theorist who insisted on the connection between the coercive power of ethnicity to command a sense of absolute belonging and the contemporary quest of the hitherto colonized and oppressed for identity and recognition.

Clearly, even if ethnicity, or primary sexual identity, or sexual orientation were primordial, a collective's sense of identity could also change over time: it could be exalted, humiliated, threatened, reconstituted, indeed be called into consciousness for the first time *as* a self-definition out of a prior state of unselfconsciousness—what Heidegger might have called "lostness" in the they-self of whatever label the group took for granted as a given. What united all proponents of identity was the claim that identity as collective self-definition was logically necessary to understand all group phenomena. What made a collective an entity persisting through time was shared self-definition; without it, there was nothing but a collection of atomistic individuals whose inner cohesion necessarily remained inexplicable. The idea of identity bridged the gap between primordiality and historicity, that is, between assertions about the permanent nature of collectives as such and the fact that such assertions in fact emerged from the historical struggles of particular groups.

By the 1960s, for a number of historical reasons, the radical contradiction between the way liberal ideology held that all should be regarded and treated, and the way certain groups were in fact regarded and treated both in the West and the colonized world, came to a political climax. Liberalism and Marxism supplied their own languages of protest and rebellion—equality, individual rights, dignity, national liberation, anti-imperialism—but not terms that could enable groups to fight back for having been denigrated and excluded because of certain shared traits, physical or cultural, that their oppressors had made socially and politically important. Identity—self-definition in terms of what made a group both unique and valuable to itself and should do so to others—supplied just such a language.

Chapter 6

The Practical Politics of National
and Multicultural Identity:
Germany, France, Canada, and
the United States, 1970–2010

Academic theorists and identity activists advanced their own ideas about what government should do or be in order to incorporate previously marginalized groups into public life; governments generally responded (if at all) with narrowly conceived measures to advance the individual rights of identity group members. But on the issues of national and cultural identity governments were not merely reactive; in a number of significant instances, their definition and promotion of both became official, and pressing, government business. Nothing is more revealing about the public impact of the idea of identity than the fact that resolutely untheoretical politicians were forced to think about its meaning for higher purposes of state and even make it part of their most opportunistic political calculations.

The Politics of National Identity

L'identité de la France
> —Title of Fernand Braudel's history of France

"Il n'y a pas d'identité française."
> —Jean-François Bayart[1]

Undoubtedly both the high and the low point of politicized "identity nationalism" in Western Europe during these years was the launching of a town-hall and online debate on national identity in November 2009 by Eric Besson, French minister of immigration and national identity. Three months later it was brought to an abrupt and ignominious halt, according to the government because it had reached a natural consensus but in fact because of the racism of many online comments. The short-lived event and the vituperation it generated made clear how much of the concern with national identity in Western Europe by the end of the twentieth century was occasioned by the increasing Muslim presence. But there had also been a vigorous public debate about national identity in Germany some three decades earlier on an issue having nothing to do with Islam: what being German could and should mean after World War II.

Before the 1980s, there were relatively few references to the idea of national identity in Germany in either academic books and articles or those intended for a more general readership. Probably the earliest essay directly concerned with the question of national self-definition, by historian M. R. Lepsius, appeared in the Catholic journal *Hochland* in 1967 with the title "The Undetermined Identity of the German Federal Republic," notable in part because it was almost alone in taking up the issue in those years.[2] Between 1980 and 1986, however, an outpouring of publications sought to bring the issue of German self-definition to public and government attention with urgency and even vehemence. The term identity appeared in many of the book titles: *The German Neurosis: On the Damaged Identity of the Germans* (1980); *German Identity* (1982); *German Identity Today* (1983); *The Identity of the Germans* (1983); *Homeland and Nation: Toward the History and Identity of the Germans* (1984); *German Identity—Forty Years After Zero* (published in English, 1985).[3] Some of these were collections of articles each of which had identity in its title. A good number of the collections were paperback editions intended for a general audience. Many more articles on identity appeared in professional and general readership periodicals.

By far the majority of these works were by right-wing or moderate conservative nationalists, upset that the prospect of German reunification appeared to be receding in the wake of *Ostpolitik*, the policy of mutual recognition of West and East Germany inaugurated some years earlier by the Socialist chancellor Willy Brandt. The return of a conservative Christian Democratic government taking an openly nationalist line after 1982 encouraged them to become more vociferous in their demands to "rethink" West German policy on reunification in the run-up to the forty-year anniversary of German defeat and division. Identity as unified national self-definition gave them the tool for conceptualizing the broken German past and justifying a way forward to the future they desired. It presupposed national identity as something necessary, permanent, and political, its concrete realization the unified national state that Germany had achieved very late in comparison with Britain and France and soon after lost again. "Whoever takes the . . . self-discovery of human beings seriously cannot in the long run overlook national identity as a value to be protected," proclaimed one writer; "Egalitarian humanism is a humanism which levels and thus shuts out identity. . . . We on the other hand speak of the identity of peoples and fatherlands . . . the freedom of peoples to be themselves."[4] Another was even more explicit about the essentially collective nature of identity. There was no such thing as purely individual identity; such a notion represented a false, modernized version of what was originally a political and national concept. The quest for identity could only be a battle for the self-conscious political determination of all Germans as *German*.[5] Nor, insisted eminent historian Ernst Nolte, could German national identity be preserved after the war by taking the easy path of denying Germany's recent history and simply identifying Germany negatively with anti-Fascism, or as fundamentally European or "Atlantic." This was to ignore the element of continuity through change that is the very essence of identity. It was no exculpation of Hitler's crimes to recognize that Nazism perverted otherwise perfectly legitimate aspects of German history, like nationalism and anti-Communism, which after all also characterized other European countries.[6] From an identity point of view, the sweep and turmoil of German history—from the Holy Roman Empire's failure to consolidate itself as a functional political entity to the fragmentation of the German states in the centuries thereafter, the perversions of the Nazi era, and the current temptation in West Germany to legitimize itself as part of Western civilization—could be understood as the continuous quest for a national political identity that had repeatedly failed or gone astray. By the same token, the political division of Germany into two states after the war could be dismissed as a false identity, artificial and temporary, imposed on Germans by the victors of World War II. Germany's permanent, real identity was as the united national state it had been between 1871 and 1949.[7] Authentic identity demanded *self*-identification.

A more temperate conservatism, which accepted the current reality of two German states with opposing political cultures, grounded its arguments for the reconsideration of German identity in a general theoretical analysis of the intensified need for collective identity in the modern world. Germans, argued Werner Weidenfeld, political theorist and adviser to German chancellor Helmut Kohl, had always had a hard time conceiving their identity. The postwar division of Germany into two separate states had greatly exacerbated the difficulty.[8] But modernity made things even worse and the need for identity even greater than in the past.

Identity, Weidenfeld argued, citing Erikson, is the sum total of the socially acquired frameworks of knowledge that orient individuals in the world—basic descriptions of the natural and social environments, fundamental expectations about the future, values, and criteria for choosing among available options. Modern mass society puts especially pressing demands on our ability to achieve such frameworks. With the dissolution of traditional ways of understanding the world and the resulting value pluralism, we face the multiple possibilities for identification without guidelines. Modern man, Weidenfeld wrote, "suffered and suffers from an ever deepening condition of homelessness [*Heimatlosigkeit*]."[9] More recently the sense of loss (*Heimatsverlust*) had been dramatically intensified by rapid technological changes that speeded up the pace of life, increased specialization, distanced people from the earth, and threatened humanity with nuclear annihilation. *Heimat* was one of the most fraught words in the German political lexicon, with its overtones of ruralism and rootedness that had been exploited in the past to justify populist, antimodernist, and reactionary politics. It remained an abiding theme of German identity even in the parliamentary republic.

Modern mass societies have a particular need for collective identity because the comprehensive transcendental interpretive systems of previous epochs (i.e., religion) have lost their binding power, and the anonymity of modern social relations, the multiplicity of existing "life worlds" and the complex needs of advanced technological production can only be mastered and directed by a society, a state, or a nation that experiences itself as a unified whole. Yet loss of faith had undermined the basis on which such a sense of collective unity was previously founded. "Collectives in the modern age do not possess the prescribed identities of a universal belief system; rather, they need to formulate their identity out of symbolically constructed life worlds. Modern societies accomplish this process through the building of community by means of legitimation, representation, institutionalization, conflict regulation and the creation of consensus." Translated into more concrete terms this meant that the creation of a modern collective identity was one of the essential tasks of the political system,[10] which could be "operationalized" using the consensus-building tools of modern communications theory.[11] The characteristic institutions of late modernity—mass communication and mass culture—should be mobilized by the state, governed by a nationalist-minded party, to foster national in place of religious identity.

The unwillingness of contemporary Germans to listen to one another, however, posed insuperable difficulties to the creation of a unified national identity. A people's "orientation frameworks," Weidenfeld claimed, have three temporal components: its memories of the past, its present social and political structure, and its goals for the future. All three constitute their identity, and in Germany all three were problematic. What was most characteristic of the

German past was its extraordinary lack of continuity. It harbored a host of contradictory tendencies: rival cultural and political definitions of the nation, opposition between romantic conservative and liberal democratic ideals, and conflict between a Western European liberal and a German *Sonderweg*, or unique path, to modernity. Nor was the contemporary political situation conducive to the creation of a collective identity. The nature of the Federal Republic was ambiguous; was it a state like others or only a partial political organization of a crippled nation? It was not just provisional—"*Provisorum*" was the term pro-unification conservatives commonly used to refer to it—but if not that, what was it? Finally, the radical difference between the fundamental ideologies of East and West Germany seemed to make reaching any kind of sociopolitical consensus impossible. A common national identity demanded both a set of common institutions and a will to identity. Under the present circumstances, it was not possible to imagine the creation of either a unified German cultural nation or a unified German nation-state. Weidenfeld quoted the writer Martin Walser to the effect that as long as both the BDR and the DDR continued to exist, a "German identity" was impossible. Somewhat more optimistically he himself concluded that while in the future Germans would have to live with a "layered identity," while both West and East Germans would likely develop an independent "state consciousness"—a political though not a national identity—Germans would nonetheless continue to will a common political community and sustain the drive for "the self-determination of all Germans."[12] The latter phrase, taken from the Basic Law that established the Federal Republic, was code for a united capitalist democratic Germany bound to the West and opposed to Communism.

Liberals discussing German identity agreed with conservatives on two things: identity was the indispensable way of talking about contemporary Germany, and German identity was highly problematic. Their reasons, however, were quite different. Some of these were set out in presentations delivered at a 1985 seminar held by the Friedrich Naumann Foundation for Freedom, a liberal German think tank associated with the market-oriented Free Democratic party with offices outside as well as within Germany. The seminar topic was "German Identity—Forty Years After Zero," the "zero hour" of Germany's new beginning in 1945; and it was attended by academics, journalists, and political figures, including the German ambassador to the United States and the chair of the Free Democratic party. Tellingly, the seminar was held in Washington, D.C., and the proceedings were published in English. Within Germany, national identity politics was dominated by conservatives.

What emerged from the various talks was the sense that Germany did not have an identity, seriously needed one, yet was unlikely to develop one soon.

Opinion surveys showed that while most West Germans, especially the younger generation, identified "Germany" with the Federal Republic and were largely uninterested in what went on in East Germany, over three-quarters of the population were in favor of reunification of the two German states.[13] When it came to defining what it meant to be *German*, however, most Germans either were not able to do so or didn't want to think about it. From the early 1950s, wrote Berlin senator Cornelia Schmalz-Jacobsen, idealistic West Germans preferred to identify themselves as Europeans. The horrors perpetrated during the Nazi era made German identity virtually a taboo subject, banned from both public discussion and personal conversation. Politicians attempted to deflect the subject by focusing public attention on Germany's economic achievements. As a popular saying of the day had it, "*Hast du was, bist du was*"—if you have something, you are something. Up to now, German identity has been at best its economic prosperity and efficiency, an identity of avoidance. Only recently, she said, perhaps after the German broadcast of the American television miniseries "Holocaust" in 1979—it was watched by some twenty million West Germans, half the population—had Germans begun to come to terms with their recent history, though it was not yet clear what this might produce by way of identity. Meanwhile it was not surprising that recent public opinion polls showed that only 21 percent of Germans expressed pride in their country, compared with 80 percent of Americans, and only 35 percent declared themselves ready to fight for it.[14]

Ralf Dahrendorf, chairman of the Foundation's board of directors and one of Germany's preeminent social theorists was even more pessimistic. "There is no German nation," he asserted. The Federal Republic is "Not a nation, not a culture, hardly a society but an entity, a country which has been successful economically and one in which economic success has been closely linked to the success of political institutions."[15] This was unfortunate because a number of currently pressing issues were forcing Germany to think about identity. One was German history, disagreement about which was a constant source of German disunity and conflict. Another involved the things that had been recently done in the name of Germany, which, in part because others would not forget, wouldn't go away and so were forcing Germans to face the question of what Germany was about.[16] Furthermore, it appeared that America was increasingly withdrawing into itself, leaving Germany to finally define a position of its own on the world scene. Not least, Germany's lack of a national identity was in principle seriously problematic for a liberal because the "Rights of Man" is an empty expression without a self-aware nation-state to legislate and enforce the "Rights of the Citizen." Unfortunately, in Dahrendorf's view, West Germany was concerned not with creating a national identity on these or any other lines but only with pragmatic solutions to such immediate problems as forging viable relations with East Germany that would not threaten the rest of the world. "There is not," he concluded, "the slightest sign of any major project of finding a well-defined identity in Germany."[17]

Barely five years later, with the collapse of the Berlin Wall and the reunification of Germany under the Basic Law, many of these considerations became moot. Reunification, though, did not put an end to the question of German identity. To the contrary, it produced a new outpouring of books and symposia on the subject.[18] Just the prospect of unification in the brief period after the Wall fell when other outcomes seemed possible had produced fierce arguments about German identity. Those who feared or actively opposed it based their hostility on their assessment of the dangers of a united Germany.[19] Nor did the argument cease even when reunification was a fait accompli. In retrospect this isn't surprising. In a sense, by getting the postwar political division of Germany forced on it from the outside out of the way, reunification prepared the scene for a deeper reckoning by Germans about who they were or might be. It was not for another seventeen years that the popular news magazine *Der Spiegel* thought it timely to take stock of the outcome with a special historical issue on "The Invention of the Germans: How We Were, What We Are."[20]

For some historians and political scientists the issues at stake in the post-unity identity debates challenged the idea of national identity itself so fundamentally that they demanded renewed inquiry into the concept. While conservative nationalists wanted to "master the past" by getting over it and recovering national pride, others believed that Germans needed to retain a sense of national guilt in order to prevent a return to the past. Their reaction to the "hypernationalism" of the Nazi era inspired among them desire for a "postnational" identity, for example the historian Karl Dietrich Bracher's suggestion of a "postnational democracy," or the "constitutional patriotism" first proposed by Dolf Sternberger and popularized by Jürgen Habermas, both of which rejected the one-sided ethnic particularism of traditional national identity.[21] Thus historian Konrad Jarausch preceded his discussion of German identity after unification with theoretical remarks on the necessity of a "postmodern" approach to German national identity in order to accommodate its enormous variability and deep conflicts,[22] while political scientist Wolfgang Bergem devoted most of his book to developing an elaborate theory about the role of cultural identity in political theory generally before broaching the subject of postunification German identity.[23] Since some of these were also contributions to the uses of poststructuralism and the ways identity transformed the social sciences, I will take them up in later chapters.

*   *   *

If anything, the theory and political practice of national identity were even more closely conjoined in France. France was the only country in the years covered in this study to formally establish a ministry of national identity. This was in fulfillment of a promise by Nicolas Sarkozy during the presidential campaign of 2007 to appeal to a constituency he feared was increasingly attracted to the ultranationalist anti-immigrant National Front of Jean-Marie Le Pen. Gérard Noiriel, France's preeminent historian of immigration, wrote afterward that a majority of observers believed that the irruption of the theme of national identity into the campaign marked the turning point of the election, allowing Sarkozy to take a decisive lead over his opponents in public opinion polls.[24] The creation of the ministry, and the public debate on national identity it initiated soon after, were in fact the culmination of three decades of increasing agitation in the country over the impact on France of large-scale Muslim immigration: the original full name of the ministry was "Ministry of Immigration, Integration, National Identity and Codevelopment." In Germany, Turkish immigration was one of a number of challenges to the formulation of a national identity, coming to the fore primarily in debates on multiculturalism, as we will see. In France, Algerian immigration essentially created the issue of national identity. But there was a symbiotic relationship between the two. It was in the language of identity that the "problem" of Algerian immigration came to be constructed and understood as a problem; the concept shaped the issues and the solutions proposed to deal with them.

One can follow the rising French concern with national identity by tracking the frequency of the term's appearance in Le Monde, one of France's three newspapers of record, its most prestigious and best-known internationally. From a mere 13 mentions in the 1950s it rose to 70 in the 1960s, 246 in the 1970s, and 476 in the 1980s. Very few early instances even referred to France—6 of 83 in the first two decades—while at least twice that number referred to British concerns about possible loss of national identity in the European community. Even as the frequency of mention rose sharply in the 1970s, French national identity remained a minor concern.

By the 1980s, however, the French context predominated. The increasing resonance of the idea of national identity was directly connected to the rising fears on the political right of the impact of France's large and growing Algerian population and to the right's success in persuading large segments of the population of the justice of their fears. A detailed study by linguist Simone Bonnafous of the language used in discussing immigrants in ten of the most influential newspapers in France across the political spectrum between 1974 and 1984 showed a striking shift over the decade. In the beginning newspaper articles focused sympathetically on the immigrants' conditions of work and life; by the end all the papers were writing anxiously about the problems of integrating the "foreigners" into France. The extreme right had succeeded in imposing its negative assessment of the immigrant problem on public opinion generally. At the extremes of both political right and left, newspaper rhetoric described the problem of integrating "foreigners" in identity terms of "self" and "other."[25]

Bonnafous did not explicitly investigate the use of the term "national identity," but it was precisely the "othering" of the Algerian immigrants that the language of national identity was used to express and codify. As Noiriel noted, the 1980s saw the triumph of a discourse of national identity that constantly pitted the French "we" against the Islamic "they."[26] The conservative newspaper *Figaro* played a major role in legitimating the extreme right discourse of national identity not only in its articles but in the public opinion polls it conducted throughout the decade, posing the question, "Do you agree with this idea: if nothing is done to limit the number of foreigners, France risks losing its national identity?" Unsurprisingly, given the wording, the yes vote oscillated between 60 and 74 percent. In the early 1980s the National Front began attracting national attention with just such a claim in its program and publicity. Mainstream conservative political parties competed by organizing colloquia in the run-up to the National Assembly elections of 1986 on the "identity of France." Some of their members joined with more extreme elements of the right wing to form the "General Alliance Against Racism and for Respect for French Identity" and a journal of political and cultural analysis called "Identity." Former president of the Republic Valéry Giscard d'Estaing threw his prestige into the anti-immigrant campaign with an article in the right-wing press insisting that immigration constituted a danger to French identity.[27]

The right suited its political proposals to its inflammatory words. Two books published in 1984–1985, one by a National Assembly deputy from the center right Union for a Democratic France, the other by a member of the far right Club de l'Horloge, proposed to radically revise French citizenship laws in the name of France's national identity by abolishing the *ius soli*, France's long-recognized right of citizenship by birth on its soil.[28] The immediate issue was the legal situation of children born in France of resident Algerians who were French citizens by virtue of their birth in preindependence Algeria. Such children were automatically French citizens, though they often felt no loyalty to their country of residence and opted to perform military service in the now independent Algeria, as by the terms of the French-Algerian treaty they were allowed to do.[29] The proposal to end their automatic citizenship was carefully defended on good republican grounds: citizenship ought to be a matter of free choice and voluntary adhesion. But the fundamental issue was the supposed incompatibility of Islam with "French identity." "Do we envisage constructing a multicultural society on the model of the late Lebanon?" asked Alain Griot-teray rhetorically, citing the recent example of a state torn apart by interreligious strife. "Or do we prefer to defend our national identity as forged by the forty kings who made France and two centuries of the Jacobin republic?" [30] His tendentious appeal deftly fused monarchical—and Catholic—France, with republican—and anticlerical—France, deadly enemies as late as the 1930s, into a unitary identity. Muslim immigrants were said to be inassimilable because there was a basic incompatibility between the political and legal culture of Islam, which recognized no separation between religion and politics, and what the republican right held to be a Christian and Republican tradition of the Rights of Man.[31] So strong was the popular response to the proposal to revise citizenship law that the mainstream conservative parties, the UDF and the Gaullist RPR, made it part of their common platform for the National Assembly elections; after their electoral success Prime Minister Jacques Chirac tried to implement it. That he failed had to do with the complexities of the law rather than lack of will.[32]

Despite the failure to amend the law, the government affirmed the key ideas behind its desire to do so in an important public document, the report of its Commission on Nationality, published under the title *Being French Today and Tomorrow* in 1988.[33] It explicitly tied nationality law to a conception of French national identity as the country whose attraction (to immigrants) "was due to its place in the history of liberty and rights, and to the permanent incarnation there of a political project of universal scope and ambition." In keeping with this universalist self-conception, the report emphasized that the nation is a community to which people choose to belong—contrasting the French conception with the "determinist" and "organic" ethnocultural German conception of nationality—and dissociated French national identity from blood, race, cultural restrictiveness, or unquestioned convention.[34] One commentator interpreted this as a concession to the new status of North Africans in postcolonial France.[35] More plausibly, the criticism of cultural restrictiveness was a hint at their distance from French identity.

It was not only politicians and propagandists who expressed fear of losing their national identity. A French Swiss writer traveling throughout France to interview newcomers and native-born about their experiences with and reactions to immigration found anxious self-questioning behind the frank and thoughtful answers that many native Frenchmen offered, which he summarized and paraphrased:

Who am I? What is becoming of my country? Who am I if the "other,"
the foreigner, maintains himself in his otherness? Doesn't he take away
from the unity of France a little of its ontological purity, its specific
mass? And as for me, from my own identity? I am going to have to
define myself, redefine myself. So disengage myself from the dailyness
of the present, disentangle myself from a *today* that is vague and
gloomy. Start examining my future. But precisely, I have doubts about
the future. I find it indefinite, disquieting. Maybe France doesn't have
a future any more.[36]

For such people the French past was better than its present because they were
sure they could find there "glorious" reasons to confirm their French identity,
"an IDENTITY OF FRANCE" once so strong it plunged the whole world into
stupefied admiration.

In cries of "France for the French" at National Front rallies the author
heard the racism once directed at Jews now directed at Muslims. Many of his
interlocutors were explicit that it was not immigrants as such but Muslims
that they feared. As one put it, "I consider Italians, Spaniards, Portuguese
[who composed a considerable fraction of past and—particularly the
Portuguese—present immigration] to be like the French. In their countries
the bronze clocks of Christianity resound." Another, an author with a long
historical memory, declared that the demands of North African immigrants to
be allowed to open mosques represented the "revenge of Poitiers"—the landmark battle of 732 in which a French army under Charles Martel defeated an
invading Muslim army and prevented the further advance of Islam into Western Europe. He added that Islam was animated by a genuine religious spirit
while the French were distancing themselves from religion.[37] His remarks
reveal the confused complexity of the key issue inspiring the rise of the
national identity issue. The French Republic was resolutely secular, yet the
identity of even staunch anticlericals included its Catholic heritage. Muslim
immigrants were not Portuguese immigrants; they had inherited the role of
religious "other" from the Jews.

The distinction between previous and present migrations into France was
precisely the focus of Gérard Noiriel's path-breaking work on the role of
immigration in modern French history. His analysis was part of a larger debate
among French historians about the validity of the idea of French national
identity. Noiriel argued that, contrary to the general opinion, modern France
had been a country of immigration since at least the mid-nineteenth
century—in fact with the United States one of the largest—that there was
nothing new about the French initially regarding immigrants as inassimilable,

and that nevertheless immigrants had fully integrated into the nation, less as the result of government action than because immigrant acceptance of existing national norms supported their own day to day interests.[38] Thus, he argued, "the role of the history of immigration in the formation of the present-day 'French identity' suggests that the framework of the nation proved less rigid than is often assumed."[39]

The most notable figure he took to task on this issue was one of France's, indeed the world's, most eminent historians, Noiriel's own former mentor, and the writer who more than anyone had recently made the idea of French identity intellectually respectable. Fernand Braudel's massive three volumes on *The Identity of France*, published in 1986, came as a shock to those who knew his reputation as the originator of the theory and practice of long-term regional history focusing on stable geographical and environmental factors, and as the opponent of short-term political narratives or "event history."[40] In fact *The Identity of France* took a similar approach, looking at France in terms of what Braudel famously called the *longue durée*, the factors that had shaped its history over the centuries. Nonetheless, and though he insisted on the necessary objectivity of the historian, the work was a self-declared labor of love for his *patrie*.

Braudel chose his title after much deliberation. The word identity, he wrote, had long both seduced and tormented him,[41] so he began with some reflections on what he meant by it:

> So what should we understand by the identity of France? If not some kind of superlative, if not a central problematic, if not France taking itself in hand, if not the living result of what the endless past has patiently deposited in successive layers, as the imperceptible deposit of ocean sediments has created by its lasting effects the powerful strata of the earth's crust? In sum, a residue, an amalgam, additions, mixtures? A process, a battle against itself, destined to be continued in perpetuity. If it is interrupted, everything collapses. A nation cannot *be* except at the cost of endlessly searching for itself, of transforming itself in the direction of its logical evolution, of opposing itself to the other without weakness, of identifying with its better, its essential, nature, consequently of recognizing itself in brand images, in passwords known by the initiates. . . . Recognizing itself in a thousand tests, beliefs, discourses, alibis, a vast unconscious without borders, obscure confluences, ideologies, myths, phantasms. . . . In addition, every national identity implies, necessarily, a certain national unity, it is like its reflection, its transposition, its condition.[42]

The somewhat florid rhetoric, a recognized hallmark of Braudel's style in general, seems here in particular evidence of two aspects of his—and perhaps all—sophisticated celebration of national identity. Its almost incantatory quality was the expression of a deep emotional identification. But it also served to obscure, though not to deny, basic contradictions. On the one hand national identity is not fixed and unchanging; it is a process, the object of perpetual contestation which if ended would mean the end of the nation. Yet the nation also has a certain essential unity, an essential nature; a nation inevitably transforms itself, but it must, if it is truly a nation, do so in the direction of its "logical evolution." In the autobiographical remarks that followed the passage, Braudel wrote of the permanent impact on him of the debacle of France's defeat in 1940. We the conquered, he wrote, on the way to unjust captivity—Braudel spent the five years until war's end as a prisoner in Germany—were the lost France, ephemeral as blown dust. But the true France, the France in reserve, remained behind us; it was surviving, it survived.[43] It is impossible that Braudel could use the term "*la France profonde*" without full awareness that it had served in the past as a right-wing slogan against the "superficial France" represented by the merely temporary liberal political institutions of the Third Republic, though he certainly did not mean it in that way. But the formative trauma of the threatened destruction of France apparently left him with the need for an indestructible one.

Noiriel pointed to other troubling implications of Braudel's concept. In his commitment to France's physical environment and the long span of history, Braudel's emphasized the idea of the "living past," especially the physical traces of the past in the rural landscape of the present. *The Identity of France*, Noiriel claimed, was profoundly marked by a philosophy of rootedness.[44] It devoted very little space to the postrevolutionary era; the France in whose creation Braudel was interested was formed before the revolution through the unification of its regions and peoples. Such a conception of the nation put him in the same camp as the conservatives. In his chapter on immigration Braudel repeated both the idea that previous immigrants had been easily absorbed and that current immigration posed a wholly new kind of problem.[45] The implication, according to Noiriel, was that for Braudel the permanent core of French identity necessarily included its Romanesque and Gothic churches—that is, Christianity in aesthetic disguise if no longer as a living belief system.

Obsessive concern with French national identity seemed to go into abeyance in the 1990s, but it came back noisily in the first decade of the new millennium, stoked by the results of the presidential election of 2002, when to France's shocked surprise Jean-Marie Le Pen defeated Socialist candidate Lionel Jospin in the first round and entered the second round run-off against

Jacques Chirac. Though Le Pen was easily defeated, it seemed clear to all that his presidential candidacy next time around had to be taken very seriously. Nicolas Sarkozy, the candidate of the right in 2007, made the theme of national identity the centerpiece of his campaign in order to siphon off potential National Front voters. His electoral rhetoric was replete with traditional conservative tropes going back to Maurice Barrès, the "father" of modern right-wing nationalism: France as spiritual principle yet "carnal soil" to which the people are attached by a mysterious bond that can't be cut without their losing part of themselves, working at the irrational level of the collective unconscious. At the same time France was the Republic, its values of dignity, liberty, and justice, the country of the rights of man, of a lay "secular morality which incorporated 2000 years of Christian values."[46] His campaign speeches reprised the efforts of the 1980s to create a definition of national identity that would reconcile right and left but exclude all those who did not adhere either to secular republican or to Christian values, the so-called "communitarians" who sacrificed individual rights to the domination of communal beliefs. The euphemism was not meant to fool anyone. Polls showed that a very large percentage of National Front adherents and voters supported the creation of a Ministry of Immigration and National Identity, understanding that the point of the second half of the ministry's mandate was the reduction or termination of the first. When the ministry was created, eight of twelve historians on the board of the newly established national museum of history and immigration, including Noiriel, resigned in protest against the political misuse of the idea of national unity. Their reason amounted to a wholesale condemnation of the conceptual validity of national identity: "There exists no definition of national identity which would be accepted by all researchers and experts. The absence of consensus stems from the fact that the expression is not a scientific concept but belongs to the language of politics."[47]

The return of national identity as a political issue in 2007 provoked a number of researchers to ask why it had emerged in the first place. In his earlier work, Noiriel had attributed the xenophobic reactions to immigration at peaks of immigration in the 1880s, the 1930s, and the 1980s to social dislocations caused by economic factors, above all the need to import foreign workers to support French industrialization from the late nineteenth century on. Unlike the situation in other industrializing countries, French peasants, owning their own land, were not attracted by the prospect of higher wages to factory employment in the city. In the process of industrialization, however, agriculture, rural life, and the peasantry suffered economic losses as well as loss of status and prestige. The oil shock of the 1970s, the huge increase in gas prices and rising industrial unemployment affected laborers in the cities as

well. Social crises, Noiriel had argued, "are moments of rupture and redefinition of social rules for the host society in general. Xenophobia is often a way
of expressing the identity crisis that overcomes social groups in such circumstances."[48] But this comparative analysis applied the idea of identity crisis as
an explanation from the outside; it did not account for the appearance of
identity language among the subjects of the analysis themselves.

Simone Bonnafous argued in response that socioeconomic conditions
alone could not explain the rise of the new discourse. The emergence of
"national identity" signified rather a fundamental transformation of the terms
in which sociopolitical issues were represented in France, made possible
because the Socialist party had abandoned the Marxist language of social class
after the election of Socialist president François Mitterand in 1981. This created an identity vacuum for many by destroying the previous terms of their
collective self-representation and leaving them bereft of a sense of group
belonging.[49] Bonnafous's point is crucial for the historical study of the idea of
national identity. It was not simply a fashionable term but an interpretive
structure that provided meaning and justification to inchoate feelings of fear
and anxiety. In his later work Noiriel essentially adopted her view. Le Pen was
able to co-opt the legacy of past socialist leaders like Jean Jaurès and Léon
Blum, praising them for their universalist values, precisely because the Socialist
party no longer spoke of class conflict, while the Communist party was no
longer influential enough to defend the idea in the public sphere.[50]

The historian Pierre Nora offered a rather different perspective on national
identity. His explicit purpose was to explain the rise of memory studies in
France, of which he was the chief author, and while he included the factors
adduced by Bonnafous and Noiriel to explain the rise of national identity, his
conclusion on that issue was dramatically opposite to theirs. In Nora's view
the 1970s saw the most important transformation of the French national
model since the revolutionary decade of 1789. From the end of World War II,
French political and ideological life had been defined by the Gaullist-
Communist opposition. That conflict did not rupture France's basic unity,
however; its "epic" historical myth of national greatness from Gallic warrior
past to heroic present could include both ideological opponents because of
their leading roles in the French Resistance. In the 1970s, however, a series of
events fundamentally undermined the national myth. The oil shock put a halt
to economic growth and destroyed the millennial stability of France's peasant
base, the foundation of the country's sense of rootedness. The election of
Valéry Giscard d'Estaing to the presidency spelled the end of Gaullist preoccupation with national grandeur and a turn to technocratic modernization. His

appointment of a free market economics minister acknowledged the international constraints on France's independence that limited its sovereignty. Finally, the political left abandoned Marxist utopianism in the wake of Alexander Solzhenitsyn's revelations about the Soviet gulags and reconciled to the Gaullist political system. When socialist president François Mitterand, elected in 1981, failed in his efforts to implement the traditional socialist policy of nationalization, socialism abandoned its discourse of class. With grandeur and national self-confidence gone, with the competing utopian vision of a classless society in ruins, France shifted politically from thinking in terms of a unified national identity to thinking in terms of multiple competing social identities.[51]

National identity, Nora argued, thus disappeared as a force animating political life and turned into nostalgic mourning for a lost past. But this claim is easily reconcilable with the creation of a new national identity consciousness in the 1980s in the form of anxiety about national identity. From Nora's perspective it could be seen as the defensive response to yet another event that appeared to be undermining French cohesion and greatness, large-scale Muslim immigration, intensified by the loss of the countervailing myth of socialist utopia.

It is significant in this connection that even some leftist critics of the idea of French national identity affirmed some version of it. Before Sarkozy's political exploitation of national identity had completely soured him on it, Noiriel had acknowledged its usefulness in explaining why, though France and the United States were both countries of immigration, the fact was a proud part of the American identity while it was denied in France. "The main difference between France and the United States," he noted, "is that French social formation paradoxically combines a full-fledged nation (rooted in history, with a homogeneous population and a rigid political framework) with a history of self-induced massive immigration that fundamentally transformed the initial makeup of its population." He then went on to claim many of the same factors that the right celebrated as making up eternal France: political centralization, underway since the Middle Ages; the official use of the French language since the reign of Francis I; the early modern conquest of peripheral regions, which with the center made up the famous "hexagon" describing France's geographical shape. Whatever the truth of constant change, there were, he was suggesting, good historical reasons for the myth of a constant core of French identity.

Anne-Marie Thiesse, foremost French historian of the European concept of national identity,[52] was also skeptical about the idea of a constant core, though somewhat more positive about the benefits of the myth and thus able to understand, while still deploring, its exclusionary tendencies. "National identity," she wrote "is not a permanent substance but an ensemble of evolving representations, and the current situation is often the result of changes more recent than we believe."[53] The contemporary international situation was particularly challenging for national identity: modern states don't control economic and financial forces, which act globally.[54] Nevertheless, this has not resulted in the reconstitution of real political power at the international level. When it expanded to the whole continent, the European Union might have been an experiment in effective transnational political power, but it had not become so; nationalist separatism had prevailed. One can understand, she continued, the attachment people maintain to their nation. Only the nation-state can realize solidarity among and social protection for its members. Education and socialization in the nation produce deep sentiments of attachment and offer people a place within a stable collective. In the absence of other perspectives, even the relative impotence of nation-states vis-à-vis globalization does not diminish the expectations people have of them. On the contrary, anxiety about the future produces fantasies of a return to the past and the illusion that the elimination of one part of the population—the most recent and fragile—would restore the protective structures to their former vigor.[55]

There were strong dissenting voices. In an interview with *Le Monde* in the wake of the online debate on national identity, the political scientist Jean-François Bayart, research director at the French National Center for Scientific Research (CNRS) declared bluntly, "There is no French identity." But this was not aimed at France in particular, since "Identities don't exist." In the case of nations, "there are contradictory processes of identification that define the changing geography of national belonging and citizenship."[56] The substitution of a process of identification for identity was an innovation of postmodernism to combat the philosophically illegitimate idea of a permanent (national) essence. In a later chapter we will examine how well it did the job. But the political vicissitudes of national identity in France exposed once again the tension between a popular ontology of permanent identity, which could be animated when its partisans felt threatened, and a more nuanced intellectual attempt to leaven it with the truths of contingency and historical change. That national identity was a "political concept" did not lessen the hold of its essentialist version on large segments of the population; the concept of identity in fact enabled many to articulate who they were for the first time.

The Politics of Multiculturalism

On October 16, 2010, in a subsequently widely publicized speech to a meeting of young leaders of her Christian Democratic party, Chancellor Angela Merkel proclaimed that the policy of "*multikulti,*" as Germans referred to multiculturalism, had utterly failed.[57] A few months later she was echoed by French president Nicolas Sarkozy and British prime minister David Cameron. Yet that same year, in a report commissioned by the Canadian federal government on "The Current State of Multiculturalism in Canada," the political scientist Will Kymlicka concluded that "recent studies . . . provide strong evidence that multiculturalism in Canada promotes integration and citizenship, both through its effects on attitudes, self-understanding and identity at the individual level and through its effects on institutions at the social level."[58] Canada was hailed throughout the world not only as the progenitor of multiculturalism but as its great success story. The difference between Western Europe and Canada reveals how significantly historical context determined the fate of multiculturalism, but also how much national self-definition in turn shaped historical context.

∗   ∗   ∗

Canadian multiculturalism was meant to solve once and for all the problem of diversity that went back to Canada's origins, though under premises supposedly far different from previous approaches, which in any case were held to have failed utterly. A half century after the British conquest of French Canada in 1759, Canada's population consisted of indigenous peoples, Indian and Inuit, a large French-speaking Catholic minority, an English-speaking and mostly Protestant majority, and the Métis, descendants of European and indigenous liaisons. Later in the nineteenth century there was an influx of immigrants from northern and central Europe invited by the government to populate the Western prairies. From the British conquest on, however, the problem of Canadian unity was seen only in terms of the French-English divide; indigenous peoples and Métis, and even Eastern Europeans, were inferior "races" to be assimilated if possible and kept subjugated if not. The Confederation of 1867 that established modern Canada was based on the myth of the equality of the two "founding races" and the reality of national domination by an English-speaking elite that tried to make Canada unequivocally British in culture and politics through rigidly exclusionary immigration policies.[59]

After World War II, however, neither the idea of "founding races" nor of the exclusively British character of Canada was tenable. World War II had made official reference to race unacceptable, and for economic reasons postwar Canada wanted immigrants wherever it could get them. In the 1960s climate of demands for equal rights and national liberation, the treatment of the

French in Canada came to be seen as increasingly unjust, especially as Quebec became restive under its own modernizing "Quiet Revolution," which ended the cultural-political domination of the Catholic Church. The first formal sign of change was the appointment in 1963 of a Royal Commission on Bilingualism and Biculturalism, charged with recommending "what steps should be taken to develop the Canadian Confederation on the basis of an equal partnership between the two founding races, taking into account the contribution made by the other ethnic groups to the cultural enrichment of Canada and the measures that should be taken to safeguard that contribution."[60]

The old language, however, proved embarrassing. In its final report, delivered seven years later, the commission took pains to reject designation by race as an unacceptable biological category. It also, however, rejected the language of ethnicity, both for its emphasis on biological descent, which could not accommodate those of mixed parentage, and because it implied that only non-majority groups were "ethnics," hence "others" and not "us." Culture was the preferred term because it was neither biological nor exclusionary.[61]

In substantive terms, the commission defined culture as "a way of being, thinking and feeling . . . a driving force animating a significant group of individuals *united by a common tongue*, sharing the same customs, habits, and experiences."[62] Crucially, a unified culture was determined in the first place by a common language. This was hardly surprising given the Canadian historical context, but in the event even it too proved problematic. For one thing the commission acknowledged that customs and habits also mattered, and that one could learn to speak the language of a culture yet not be part of it. Nevertheless it concluded, "At the practical level, an attempt to make every possible provision for cultural equality is primarily an attempt to make every possible provision for linguistic equality."[63]

There was another reason to equate culture with language: the need to deemphasize religion. "The culture of a group," it said, "must not be confused with a particular *system of thought*, even though there may be correspondence at a given moment between a culture and an *ideology*; one ideology can be replaced by another, whereas the culture continues to live."[64] "Systems of thought" and "ideology" were evasions: it was not that Francophiles were Aristotelians or communists and Anglophiles Platonists or capitalists. But French Quebec *was* largely Catholic and English Canada historically Protestant. By "system of thought" the Commission meant religion above all, though not saying so explicitly was significant. The locution doubly downgraded the importance of religion, subsuming it under the blander category of culture and declaring further that it did not define a culture's identity.

The commission did this both because it had to and because it could. It could not be seen as establishing religion, and making belief central to culture when it was arguing for officially sanctioned biculturalism would have done so de facto if not de jure. But this was now easier to avoid because religion had become less important in both French and English Canada than it had been. During the Quiet Revolution the Catholic Church lost its position of preeminence in Quebec's social and political life as the old religious, conservative, and rural authorities were replaced by a young, urban, commercial, and intellectual cadre largely secular in temperament. At the same time militant Protestantism, symbolized by the Orange Order that even in the late 1940s was still boisterously celebrating William of Orange's conquest of Ireland in 1690 with annual parades in Toronto, had pretty much faded away. Through historical circumstance confirmed by formal definition, the idea of culture in Canada was secular and devoid of substantive belief content.

One further development, however, complicated the concept of culture in a fundamental way by the time the commission report was presented to Parliament in 1971. During the commission's first year of hearings, a senator of Ukrainian origin objected to the commission's original mandate on the grounds that Canada was not a bicultural but "a multicultural nation."[65] He was credited with coining the term, and his language was incorporated in Prime Minister Pierre Elliott Trudeau's formal acceptance of the report, recorded in the official proceedings as "Announcement of Policy of *Multiculturalism* within Bilingual Framework."[66] As Trudeau now claimed, "although there are two official languages, there is no official culture, nor does any ethnic group take precedence over any other." The literal "cash value" of this claim was a pledge of budgetary assistance to all Canadian cultural groups to support institutions perpetuating their cultural heritage. A decade later multiculturalism as identity was constitutionally formalized in the Charter of Rights and Freedoms. "Multiculturalism," the Charter declared, "is a fundamental characteristic of the Canadian heritage and identity."[67] This was an astonishing declaration in a number of ways. No other country had ever formally declared an explicit national identity as such, let alone that its national identity was multicultural.

But the terms in which Trudeau announced multiculturalism created new issues: weren't national identity and multiculturalism incompatible, even contradictory? On this matter Trudeau saw no problem. "The sense of identity developed by each citizen as a unique individual," he asserted, "is distinct from his national allegiance. There is no reason to suppose that a citizen who identifies himself with pride as a Chinese-Canadian, who is deeply involved in the cultural activities of the Chinese community in Canada, will be less loyal or concerned with Canadian matters than a citizen of Scottish origin who takes part in a bagpipe band or highland dance group. Cultural identity is not the same thing as allegiance to a country. . . . Canadian identity will not be undermined by multiculturalism." So cultural identity was personal identity, distinct from national Canadian identity. What then was distinctively *Canadian* identity? Trudeau's definition was arguably circular. "Indeed," he went on to say, "we believe that cultural pluralism is the very essence of Canadian identity." Canadian identity, it would seem, was the nonidentity of universal multiculturalism.

In fact such a claim was neither necessarily contradictory nor empty. Multiculturalism in Trudeau's terms could be understood as an extension of Anthony Smith's concept of modern "civic nationalism," the idea of equal citizenship based on universal individual rights. Trudeau had explicitly framed cultural identity in individualist terms, as part of the "sense of identity developed by each citizen as a unique individual"; supporting cultural rights was logically defensible, indeed in this view necessary, as a defense of individual rights. But Smith had also argued that modern national identity had a particularist ethnic as well as a civic component; what then was the *ethnic* or particular dimension of Canadian nationalism? Trudeau seemed to be suggesting that Canadian identity didn't really have one: as a concept, multiculturalism was ethnically neutral. However by the *Commission*'s definition of culture this was not true; *culture was language*, and as bilingual, Canada did indeed have an official culture, or rather two. To avoid such a conclusion, which would relegate non-English or non-French speakers to cultural inequality, Trudeau uncoupled culture even from language. In broadening biculturalism to multiculturalism, he had no other choice: if culture was language, Canada could not be both officially bilingual *and* multicultural. Uncoupling however would seem to further empty out the concept of culture; identified by neither religion nor language, what was left to the cultures of multiculturalism?

In implicit answer to this question Trudeau, unlike the authors of the Commission report, returned to the language of ethnicity, equating it with culture. All the groups that made up Canada represented ethnic cultures. Thus, he insisted democratically, the majority French and English were no less ethnic groups than immigrant minorities. Multicultural meant multiethnic, though with ethnicity now shorn of religion and language, there seemed nothing left to culture or ethnicity other than customs, costumes, cooking, and the memory of origins. But in fact Trudeau's verbal uncoupling of language from culture was illusory. It was above all language that defined the French and English as separate groups. In Trudeau's own terms, then, maintaining English and French as Canada's only official languages amounted to making Canada officially a dual ethnonational state. It was true, of course, that the biological kinship element of ethnic cultural transmission was diluted by the linguistic emphasis: immigrants could *become* English Canadian or French Canadian by learning the language. But this meant that they were expected to do so, to assimilate to Canada's two national cultures and transmit them to their own children. The multicultural situation was thus confused. If culture was language, Canada was not truly multicultural because it demanded linguistic assimilation. If culture was ethnicity, did Canada have a national culture, or was it a mere congeries of ethnicities, and if it did what (besides language) should be included in the expectations of immigrant assimilation to an Anglo-French Canada? What, simply put, was distinctive about being "Canadian"? The problem remains real and perplexing for many citizens of Canada. But the other side of the dilemma was that widely diverse communities of foreign immigrants were able to feel welcome in their difference, particularly in Canada's larger cities.

*　*　*

Similar ambiguities about cultural identity gave the career of multiculturalism a very different path in Germany. The term "multicultural society" appeared for the first time in the German Federal Republic in 1980. It was introduced by the Catholic and Protestant churches in a statement issued for an annual event they had inaugurated called "*Tag des ausländischen Mitbürgers*"—day of the foreign fellow citizen.[68] The oxymoron pointed to the anomalous legal and social situation of the labor migrants whose public standing the churches wanted to ameliorate. Starting in the 1950s Germany had invited in a large number of foreign, predominantly Turkish, workers as so-called *Gastarbeiter*, "guest workers," to deal with labor shortages in the then-booming economy. The euphemism was less than a fig leaf; Turkish workers were expected to leave after their permits expired. Increasingly they did not, but neither were they forcibly repatriated, and even when labor importation ended in 1973, Turkish migration continued because migrant workers were allowed to bring in families and new spouses. By law, however, resident Turks could not become citizens. German citizenship was still governed by a 1913 act that conferred citizenship only on those born of German parents, according to the criterion of *ius sanguinis*, or right of blood, in contrast to the other international ground of citizenship, the *ius soli*, or right of soil, which conferred citizenship by virtue of birth within a country.

As different as it worked in practice, the 1913 law had been adopted for much the same reason as English Canadians strove to make Canada British. Germans had been dealing with problems of fragmentation and diversity since the late eighteenth century. During that period intellectuals elaborated the idea of a distinct and superior German culture to substitute for the lack of a unified national state like the French monarchy. Culture became increasingly important for the self-definition of middle-class Germans during the nineteenth century in their frustrated striving for political unification. But its achievement in 1871 made cultural nationalism even more prominent; stressing German cultural unity and superiority was one of the chief methods the new German Empire used to cope with political and cultural differences between the states, confessional conflicts between Protestants and Catholics, and the existence of large ethnic minorities of Danes, Alsatians, and especially Jews and Poles. Under these pressures there developed what a historian called the concept of the "inner homogeneity of the nation" as a guiding idea for German citizenship policy. The 1913 law was designed as a defensive measure to prevent the naturalization of foreigners deemed inassimilable because culturally inferior.[69] What Canada, as a state contiguous only with the United States and protected by oceans, could manage by immigration policy, Germany had to manage by citizenship policy. The goal in both cases was the same: cultural homogeneity through ethnic domination. The difference for citizenship was that the relatively few non-British European immigrants who were admitted to Canada could become citizens, indeed were expected to, so as to speed their assimilation. The difference for cultural identity was that the *ius sanguinis* criterion for citizenship cemented the connection between culture and biology in Germany.

Though the Federal Republic's Basic Law of 1949 established the principle of respect for human dignity and inalienable human rights as the highest constitutional value, it still kept the *ius sanguinis* as the criterion for citizenship. West Germany had immediate political reasons for renewed insistence on the ethnic unity of the German people: it wanted to retain a theoretical foundation for the reunification of the country, and it wanted to be able to grant automatic citizenship to the twelve million German refugees and expellees from Eastern Europe who flooded into Germany from 1945, and whom it integrated quite successfully despite real differences in customs and habits (and even language—some ethnic Germans from the east hardly spoke German). But the bioethnic understanding of German culture had been long deeply rooted in the public consciousness and in public policy. The presence of a large, ethnically "alien" Turkish population only caused West Germany to reaffirm its ethnonational character. In 1977, the West German government issued a set of naturalization guidelines that began with the blunt declaration, "The Federal

Republic of Germany is not a land of immigration. It does not aspire to increase the number of its citizens through naturalization."[70] It was to this declaration that the churches responded with their counterclaim that Germany had indeed become a multicultural society through immigration, and that the basis of German citizenship therefore had to be rethought.

The sharply negative reaction that followed made multiculturalism a fighting word in Germany through the next decade. Right-wing conservatives strongly reaffirmed the ethnonational foundation of German culture and peoplehood. One argument tried, ingeniously if disingenuously, to reverse the political thrust of multiculturalism by agreeing that ethnopluralism was both a reality and a positive good, but for that very reason could only be fully realized if each ethnic culture remained undiluted within its own national state. The mainstream position was that while Germany might indeed be in some sense a pluralist society, foreign residents could maintain their cultural heritage and identity on the private level so long as they did not conflict with what a parliamentary member responsible for policies regarding foreigners in the ministry of the interior called the "ethical-moral, juridical and cultural values of the German Federal Republic."[71] But the implication of continuing to deny the resident Turks citizenship was that Turkish identity was *inherently* in conflict with German values.

The reason for such a belief is in one way straightforward yet in another not. What *seems* obvious is that the continuing refusal to create a legal path to citizenship for the Turkish community was based simply on religion. It could be argued in this regard that in the postwar world Islam had replaced Judaism as the religious "other" of German ethnicity, of which Christianity had always been a defining characteristic, acknowledged or not. But matters are more complex. For one thing, the war had apparently changed more than the attitude to Jews. Neither race nor religion could henceforward be overt grounds for discrimination or exclusion. Of course such issues could simply have gone underground, and for many likely did. But the more striking fact is that by the 1980s West Germany, like many other European countries, had become a much more secular society than it had been. Church attendance plummeted, the number of self-declared people of "no religion" rose, and while a majority maintained their denominational affiliation, it was largely nominal. Paradoxically part of the deep feeling that the Turks were "other" and not "us" was because they were perceived to be pious.

Secularization revealed that the contemporary relationship of cultural identity and religion was more tortuous than simple concealment. The complex nature of the relationship was articulated a decade later, when German citizenship law was changed. After German unification in 1990, an outburst of xenophobia resulted in a number of murderous attacks against immigrants. It was evident to many that the old citizenship regime could not continue. In 1999, a recently elected socialist coalition passed a law that introduced the *ius soli* right of anyone born in Germany to become a citizen provided that one parent had been lawfully resident there for five years. Immigrant parents themselves could become citizens with a longer residence and upon proof of language competence. In a concession to the opposition, dual citizenship was ruled out; would-be citizens had to renounce their former allegiance.

It was precisely when, and because, the law came into effect that a document produced by the opposition Christian Democrats exposed the true nature of the relationship between culture and religion for many Germans. It put forward the notion of a *Leitkultur*, a guiding or defining culture that should be the basis for integrating immigrants. This included learning the German language, professing loyalty to the German nation, and accepting its legal and political institutions. But beyond these, the *Leitkultur* was to define the "national and cultural identity" to which immigrants were expected to conform: "We Germans," it declared, "have developed our national identity and culture on the foundations of European civilization [as it has developed] in the course of history." That civilization rests on "the value-order of our Christian-Occidental culture, which has been formed by Christianity, Judaism, ancient philosophy, humanism, Roman law, and the Enlightenment."[72]

The apparently startling invocation of a "Christian-Occidental" culture shaped by both Judaism and the Enlightenment was neither hypocritical nor contradictory. It pointed to the real evolution of postwar German identity. The CDU had long advocated European solidarity as a way of restoring Germany to the comity of Europe and assuaging its fears of a revived German nationalism. Being European had become part of at least "official" German identity. Nor was the inclusion of Judaism mere ritual penitence for the Holocaust, even if it had something of that flavor. By comparison with Islam, Christian Europe's external enemy for over a millennium, Jews could be considered integral to European civilization—even, as the parent religion, to Christianity itself, in a way that Islam could not. Finally, the reference to the Enlightenment, however ill it might seem to comport with the idea of traditional Christian culture was a tribute to Germany's commitment to individual rights, equality, and democracy. In fact that reference is a clue to the real meaning of the idea of a "Christian-Occidental" culture. It was a secularized Western Christianity, a retention of Christianity's perceived universalist values—the dignity of the individual, the equality of souls, the absoluteness of the ethical— with a nostalgic, emotional attachment to their religious origin, but without commitment to the dogmas religion used to entail and with outright repudiation of its past entwinement with hierarchical and authoritarian political regimes. Islam could not be trusted to have these values because it was outside the geographical-historical evolution that had produced them, hence emotionally as well as culturally alien.

Canada's dual ethnonationalism involved the same secular transformation-retention of Christianity as Germany's, without the explicit acknowledgment. As Will Kymlicka pointed out, multiculturalism could gain acceptance because Canada was lucky in timing and geography. While Canada was acclimating to the idea of multiculturalism, Muslims were a small percentage of its overall population and a tiny fraction of its nonwhite immigration. The more prominent non-European immigrant groups, Chinese, Hindu Indians, Caribbean blacks—many from former British colonies or Commonwealth countries—had frequently been characterized disparagingly in terms of old racist stereotypes, but crucially had not been seen as having a religious or cultural commitment to offensive and illiberal practices. In a word, Muslims represented what Kymlicka called a "hard case" for Canadian multiculturalism because they are not perceived as part of "Judeo-Christian/Western civilization."[73] Put another way, Kymlicka was implying that multiculturalism might not have fared much better in Canada than in Germany had Muslims comprised early on the largest and most prominent group of immigrants.

*   *   *

Though there was no comparable debate about multicultural identity at the level of government policy in the United States (the fierce political opposition to Hispanic immigration was always couched as opposition to illegal immigration) it is instructive to consider some American attitudes to multiculturalism expressed by prestigious academic opinion makers who at one time during their careers had served as government advisers. Their positions were paradoxically closer to those of Germans than of Canadians, despite the fact that the United States had long prided itself on being a land of immigration, and that the two North American countries had been, however imperfectly, liberal democracies from their beginnings. The historical reasons are not hard to find. The motto on the Great Seal of the United States *e pluribus unum*—out of many, one—expressed a deep-seated desire for a unity that had had to battle against strong centrifugal forces of state and sectional loyalty. Both the desire and the sense of struggle were later adapted beyond its original reference to respond to the great waves of ethnic immigration in the late nineteenth and early twentieth centuries. However initially resented and disdained by the Anglo-Protestant establishment, immigrant groups of different ethnic, national, and even religious origins could ultimately be accepted as long as they assimilated into the American cultural-political core ideology: the hegemony of English, political democracy, economic individualism, and American patriotism. In this sense the "melting pot" was not a myth but a reality.

It was precisely this core national identity that observers like the historian and centrist Democratic party activist Arthur Schlesinger, Jr., and the conservative political theorist Samuel Huntington (a one-time Democrat turned Republican) saw threatened by multiculturalism in the United States after the 1960s. Schlesinger's influential polemic, *The Disuniting of America: Reflections on a Multicultural Society*, was prompted by a matter close to home for him as a historian, the study of American history in primary and secondary schools. A task force charged with examining curricular materials used by the New York State Department of Education claimed that the existing curriculum was prejudiced against African Americans, Asian Americans, Latinos, and Native Americans because of its "systematic bias favoring European culture" and its omission, distortion, or marginalization of the contributions of non-European cultures. It recommended curricular changes whose purpose was to raise the "self-esteem and self-respect" of these groups while mitigating the "arrogance" of children from European cultures who feel they are part of the "group that has 'done it all.' "[74] Schlesinger regarded the report as the concrete symptom of a broader cultural danger: the insidious transformation of multiculturalism into its own kind of ethnocentrism valorizing only non-Western, nonwhite cultures. Multiculturalism's obsession with difference threatened the idea of an overarching American nationality that put the ethnic group before the whole and above the individual.[75] Schlesinger was particularly exercised by the radical leaders of the Afrocentric movement, who he saw as deliberately trying to stoke black rage and antagonism with the ultimate purpose of fostering self-ghettoization. "When a vocal and visible minority pledges primary allegiance to their groups, whether ethnic, sexual, religious, or . . . political . . . it presents a threat to the brittle bonds of national identity that hold this diverse and fractious society together."[76]

Without explicitly remarking it, Schlesinger put his finger on a problem of national identity implicit in Anthony Smith's analysis. Where a country had no discernible ethnic identity, what could take its place as the national unifier? Schlesinger's claim was that "what has held the American people together in the absence of a common ethnic origin has been precisely a common adherence to the ideals of democracy and human rights," however transgressed in practice. America is "an experiment . . . in creating a common identity for people of diverse races, religions, languages and cultures."[77] But he argued further that the American identity was not constituted by abstract universal ideals alone. Those ideals had a concrete historical-geographic origin which was therefore central to American identity. It could not be denied that "Europe was the birthplace of the United States of America, that European ideas and culture formed the republic, that the United States is an extension of European civilization."[78] American identity was more than its narrowly political ideals; it had a distinctive cultural content that was to be celebrated and transmitted.

In his relatively brief polemic, Schlesinger did not spell out what that cultural content might be beyond the general notion of European heritage. Samuel Huntington, in his longer book a decade later made an explicit distinction between what Gunnar Myrdal had famously called the "American Creed," America's liberal-democratic political belief system, and America's foundational culture, which Huntington labeled "Anglo-Protestant." Of the two, Anglo-Protestantism was primary. "Almost all the central ideas of the Creed have their origins in dissenting Protestantism," he wrote; "The American creed, in short, is Protestantism without God, the secular credo of the 'nation with the soul of a church'."[79] Though he did not put it in these terms, Huntington essentially defined America as the self-conscious exemplar of Benedict Anderson's nation as new sacred ideal, the modern repository of transcendence. Multiculturalism, which, like Schlesinger, he characterized as in essence "anti-European civilization,"[80] was an even more dangerous threat to American identity than Schlesinger said because it attacks American values at their deepest cultural root, religion. The multicultural threat he had foremost in mind, however, was from Hispanic immigration, supposedly alien to the American founding culture in both language and, more importantly, its Catholic religion. While the book was specifically about American identity, Huntington's analysis was implicitly a claim both for the primacy of cultural identity even over political and for the primacy of religious identity within culture—the same claim he had made a decade before in the wider context of world civilizations and international relations, but which he now brought home in defense of his own national identity.

* * *

National identity created certain insuperable difficulties for the ideal of multiculturalism. Even Canada officially demanded linguistic assimilation at the minimum while unofficially assuming assimilation to Canada's broader British or French cultural heritage. (On the British side, for example, this entailed at the least demonstrations of respect, if not deeper feelings, for the symbols of British monarchy, whose incumbent was after all Queen of Canada. This demand has continued to rankle French Canadians.) It was only when cultural identity was considered on the international level by UNESCO, the agency of the United Nations concerned with international policies on education, science, and culture, that fostering cultural diversity could seem to make absolute claims. Such claims were however only possible because the Universal Declaration of Cultural Diversity, adopted by UNESCO in 2002, necessarily had the existing state system as its framework and ultimately took "cultures" to be congruent with nations. It did not say so explicitly, speaking instead of the cultures of "social groups" and "societies," and it took care to assert that the defense of cultural diversity implied a commitment in particular to the rights of persons belonging to minorities and to those of indigenous people.[81] But the Declaration glossed over the possibility of conflict between the cultural identities of majority and minority within a nation-state. Its underlying intention is best gauged by the statement in the preamble that affirmed that "respect for the diversity of cultures, tolerance, dialogue and cooperation, in a climate of mutual trust and understanding are among the best guarantees of international peace and security." And as the Declaration's appended "Action Plan" made clear, the minority and indigenous cultures it was most concerned for were represented by former colonial states and developing countries with premodern traditions, who were disadvantaged in the international competition of cultural identities by lack of access to modern tools of communication and dissemination. It was the moral task of the international state system to help them obtain the means to defend and assert their national-cultural identities.

*   *   *

The international vicissitudes of multiculturalism exposed the definitional treacherousness of cultural identity with regard to ethnicity, language, and religion. In different places at different times some, all, or none of them were held to be essential to it. As perplexing as this seems, however, it should not surprise. The politicians who proposed—or who fought—multiculturalism were concerned with immediate practical problems of domestic diversity in the context of their unique national histories; their approach to defining cultural identity was pragmatic, and their theories were crude. Precisely because they were all concerned with the political problem of national unity, however, multiculturalism had ultimately to be subordinated to national identity, even where, as in Canada, it had real success in making immigrants feel accepted and the sense of what constituted distinctive national identity was particularly weak. But it was not so weak that religion did not function as a test case even in Canada. Western national identities turned out to have an obvious, if sometimes highly attenuated religious content in addition to their liberal democratic creeds; more exactly, the two were inextricably fused in the public and political mind.

Addressing culture in terms of identity not only revealed how thoroughly that concept had permeated practical political discourse but how much it had changed politics. Of necessity politicians did have identity theories, since they had to have terms in which to frame, explain, and justify their cultural and immigration policies. Trudeau advanced just such a theory when he argued that the sense of identity developed by each citizen as a unique individual derived from his or her culture, in other words, that one's cultural identity was central to, if in fact it did not wholly constitute, one's individual identity. Offered almost casually as self-evident, this single sentence made fundamental assumptions about the self that, far from taking for granted, a number of philosophers and political theorists felt had to be established against the deeply rooted and respected contrary ideas of contemporary liberalism. The two decades after Canada's constitutional adoption of multiculturalism saw a profound philosophical critique, in the name of identity, of the rival individualist idea of self its critics believed was entailed by liberal theories of ethics, justice, and democracy.

Chapter 7

The Problem of Collective Identity
in Liberal Democracy

From the moment that groups, or rather their putative spokespersons, began talking of themselves as having a collective identity, the question arose of what claims if any such identities could justly make on the liberal democratic state. This was a quite different question from claims they might rightly make for their members as individuals. To the extent that blacks, gays, and women had been discriminated against in voting, education, and public accommodation, they were only asking for equality of individual rights within the accepted framework of liberal democracy; the denial of those rights, in fact and in law, was in contradiction of its own explicit norms. Rectifying the injustices created by such contradictions posed few problems in political theory, however much struggle it took in practice. Extending equal rights to sexual orientation was more problematic because of the gap between philosophical arguments for individual rights and legal arguments about what rights the written or customary constitution of various countries recognized, but this was still an argument within the framework of individual rights, not one about group rights. The claim that a group deserved special rights precisely in virtue of its differences from the majority could not on the face of it be accommodated within the individualist and egalitarian premises of liberal democracy.

*   *   *

The problem of minority group rights within the modern national state existed long before the language of identity. It had bedeviled Central European politics in the late nineteenth century and would have continued to be an issue in the twentieth without identity talk. But identity talk, especially in terms of cultural identity, transformed political discussion of such issues in North America and Europe by the 1980s. It offered an entirely new rationale for the claim that minority cultures should be legally and politically recognized by according them differential rights within the liberal state. If individuals were significantly constituted as selves by their cultural identity, protection of their individuality demanded the preservation of their culture.

This was the claim made by Canadian prime minister Trudeau in defense of multiculturalism when he introduced it to Parliament in 1971, but he had asserted it without any serious attempt at justification. While the Royal Commission whose recommendations he was implementing had input from academics in a number of fields,[1] none of them had addressed identity as a theoretical issue. If the political argument for multiculturalism was shaped from the beginning by the Zeitgeist that had made identity a catchphrase by the end of the 1960s, politics in turn led theory to a searching analysis of cultural identity and its compatibility with liberal democracy by the middle of the 1980s. But the debate in political theory was preceded and accompanied by a more profound philosophical attack on the concept of self that critics saw as the conventional but untenable foundation of liberal individualism. In each case, the attack was carried out in the name of a rigorously argued concept of identity.

The Empty Self of Liberal Individualism

The crux of the criticism was that the self as individualism conceptualized it in politics, ethics, and ontology was an incoherent idea, incapable of performing the tasks assigned to it. Liberal theories of justice such as those of John Rawls and Ronald Dworkin, social contract theories and the Kantian ethics from which some were derived, and in a quite different yet converging way existentialist ontology—all conceived of the individual as an unencumbered freedom choosing at will among its various possibilities. As Michael Sandel put it, in both Kant and Rawls, "what is most essential to our personhood is not the ends we choose but our capacity to choose them. . . . [T]he subject, however heavily conditioned by his surroundings, is always, irreducibly, prior to his values and ends,"[2] a pure or empty will with no object or content. Charles Taylor dubbed this "the punctual self," a self with no dimensions, like the point in mathematics, abstracted from all concrete desires, tastes, and habits and identified only with the potentiality to change those it might adventitiously have.[3] To be a moral agent, Alasdair MacIntyre claimed, "Is, on this view, precisely to be able to stand back from any and every situation in which one is involved, from any and every characteristic that one may possess." This, he pointed out, is exactly Sartre's definition of the self as "'nothing' . . . a set of perpetual open possibilities."[4]

The problem for such an empty self is that it is unable to carry out the very mission for which it was conceived, freedom of choice. It is incapable of choice because it has no grounds for choosing. As pure potentiality, it has no motive or reason to choose between one alternative and another. Even conceived within the rationalist strain of moral theory, according to which action is to be judged from a purely universal and abstract point of view detached from passion and social particularity, the self still has no workable criterion. The modern foundational philosophical attempt to establish one, Kant's categorical imperative, in fact offers no substantive guidance, because many trivial nonmoral as well as blatantly immoral maxims can be vindicated by the test of their universalizability as convincingly as the moral maxims Kant sought to uphold. " 'Let everyone except me be treated as a means' may be immoral, but it is not inconsistent," MacIntyre argued, "and there is not even any inconsistency in willing a universe of egotists all of whom live by this maxim."[5]

Similarly, Sandel criticized the internal consistency of Rawls's Kantian theory of justice because the self as Rawls conceived it had no logical reason for adopting one of its two indispensable general principles. Rawls's "difference principle" holds that only those social and economic inequalities that work to the benefit of the least advantaged members of society are to be considered just. It represented Rawls's attempt to mediate between the first principle of justice, equal rights for all to basic liberties, and his realistic acceptance of the inequality of natural endowments. If allowed to operate unchecked, such inequalities would eventually but inevitably create de facto inequality of access and opportunity. The way out of this dilemma, Rawls believed, was to posit an agreement among individuals to regard the distribution of natural talents as a common asset; the difference principle thus guarantees that all would share in the benefits that natural talent produces by placing a limit on its rewards to the individual endowed with it. But, Sandel argued, such an agreement is inconsistent with the nature of the self as Rawls conceived it behind the "veil of ignorance," the hypothetical presocial condition in which individuals, in ignorance of their ultimate endowments and place in society, decide the principles of justice. Behind the veil the self is an autonomous entity, endowed only with a minimal set of supposedly universal desires, deciding with other such selves a set of principles that each could regard as fair whatever their actual embodiment, endowments and ultimate social fate turn out to be. Such a self would not rationally agree to any principle of justice that would make it, in Kantian terms, a means to the ends of others. But allowing others a basic claim on one's natural endowments, as the difference principle entailed, would seem to do just that.

The only way to avoid this consequence was to argue that people are *not* self-contained atoms, complete in themselves, as Rawls pictured them before they chose principles of justice, but that they become fully human only in social union. A major consequence is that they do have a sense of the common possession of individual assets, which develop and are effective only because they are fostered and nurtured by society. To accept this, however, was to see the self as an essentially intersubjective being, a formulation Rawls had explicitly rejected.[6] Furthermore, if becoming a self did in fact depend on the community this could not be something that fully autonomous individuals behind the veil of ignorance could freely "decide"; it was rather something true about themselves that they had to learn. Since this was in fact the case, Sandel argued, in order to make sense of Rawls's difference principle it also has to be true that "What goes on in the original position is not a contract after all, but the coming to self-awareness of an intersubjective being. . . . Community describes not just what they *have* as fellow citizens but also what they *are*, not a relationship they choose (as in a voluntary association) but an attachment they discover, not merely as an attribute but as a constituent of their identity."[7] If Rawls's theory of justice were to be consistent, it had to *begin* with the idea of the self's essential social identity.

Sandel himself had earlier used the word identity very loosely to refer to the description of Rawls's minimal self behind the veil of ignorance, stripped of all attributes except basic human desires. And even these it only "possessed," as if its qualities were external to it; the self's desires did not constitute it because the self could abstract itself from any of them: "I" am separate from, not defined by, any of my concrete desires or attributes. But Sandel's argument for the socially conditioned self excluded the idea that Rawls's minimal self could be spoken of in terms of identity at all, insofar as that word suggested having some substance. Humans considered as empty subjectivities prior to and independent of their concrete values and ends don't have identities. The term identity came to denote for Sandel the substantive intersubjective content that selves inevitably *are*, that which constituted the self's essence. To put it the other way around, "thick" social identity was definitional of selfhood.

*   *   *

Sandel's argument for the intersubjective identity of the self turns out to be a particular application to social theory of the concept of identity argued in greater philosophical depth by MacIntyre and Taylor. Their analyses made explicit the broader proposition implied by Sandel: identity was the necessary alternative to the empty self of individualist theory.

Human beings, according to Taylor's "strong thesis," can't live without an identity, which is defined by "the commitments and identifications which provide the frame, or horizon within which I can try to determine from case to case what is good, or valuable, or what ought to be done, or what I endorse or oppose." These are not simply values one holds, they are who one *is*, in the ontological sense of an essential constitution of human existence. "To know who you are," Taylor wrote, "is to be oriented in moral space." We do not invent our need for frameworks, for orienting beliefs and categories, even if in modern times their contents are often to some extent self-consciously chosen, hence historical and relative. Frameworks as templates provide answers to humanly unavoidable questions that preexist for us, independent of our answer or inability to answer: "[*Identity*] *belongs to the class of the inescapable*, i.e., it belongs to human agency to exist in a space of questions about strongly valued goods, *prior to all choice or adventitious cultural change*." Because of our inescapable need for frameworks, Taylor was ready to assert, despite his concession to historical relativism, the more controversial proposition that "We are all framed by what we see as universally valid commitments." There is an ambiguity in the phrase "what we see," which could be understood as implying that our belief in the universality of our values is intrinsically questionable. It is more likely, however, in the context of Taylor's whole work, that there was a slippage, not unintentional, between the claim for the necessity of a framework, and the claim that we need also to believe in the universality of its contents (though that claim might be wrong about some particular content). To the extent he held the latter, identity has an even more substantive ontological dimension than an absolute need for some orientation; it wants *absolute* orientation.

Taylor's thesis was expressly philosophical, but he readily deployed empirical psychological categories in arguing for it, giving them in turn a philosophical grounding. "What we call an 'identity crisis,'" Taylor wrote—taking Erikson's concept as by then so culturally established that it did not require attribution— "is an acute form of disorientation which people often express in terms of not knowing who they are, but which can also be seen as a radical uncertainty of where they stand. They lack a frame or horizon within which things can take on a stable significance." By the same token, since the questions that constitute the framework find their "original sense" through the interchange of speakers in the social space of language, such a person would be largely unintelligible to others, and "We would see this as pathological."[8] Identity originates in a social context and must be continuously confirmed by it.

*   *   *

While eschewing talk of ontology, MacIntyre similarly claimed that identity, understood as a definition of the whole self, is constitutive of human action. It is a fact of contingent, if not metaphysical, necessity, the way we factually are even if we might be otherwise. Too much of modern philosophy goes wrong because it ignores this truth. Human behavior can't be adequately understood, for example, the way contemporary Anglo-American philosophy of action approaches it, as a series of discrete acts with local intentions that can be parsed for their logical structure. When the background assumptions of even our most mundane actions are teased out, we can see they are fully intelligible to us only as elements of a much bigger narrative, one that ultimately takes in our whole life, past, present, and future. Our supposedly discrete actions are actually moments in a unified story with overall purpose and direction. Our lives have the unity of characters in fiction because we live them as future-oriented narratives with ends or goals. "Man is," as MacIntyre put it, "in his actions and practice, as well as in his fictions, essentially a story-telling animal."[9] Indeed it is *because* humans live their lives as stories that they write fictions, which serve to raise the structure of narrative to self-conscious examination and imaginative experimentation. Stories are lived before they are told.[10] The notion of narrative unity does not preclude disruption, conflict, or times of lack of direction in a life. On the contrary, since we live our lives forward, and not in circumstances wholly of our own choosing, our narratives are inevitably fraught with unpredictability, chance, and frustration, which may require us to redirect them. When we complain that our lives have become meaningless, as we can and do, we mean that our narratives have become unintelligible to us because they lack movement to an end that we see as ours. The unhappy results of the breakdown of narrative are the proof of its indispensability to life.

The bearing of MacIntyre's thesis for understanding the self becomes clearest in his critique of Derek Parfit's theory of personal identity. Parfit argued that identity in the strict sense was not what mattered to us either for our desire to survive or for ethical responsibility.[11] None of the successor selves in his science fiction thought experiments splitting the self could be said to be numerically the same as the original, but in each case there would be sufficient continuity of personality, of previous traits and aims, such that someone could be satisfied that "he" still lived on even if, for example, his original body was gone.

MacIntyre rejected Parfit's approach to the problem of self-continuity as based on a false view of how we actually relate to ourselves. "What is crucial to human beings as characters in enacted narratives," he insisted, "is that, possessing only the resources of psychological continuity, we have to be able to respond to the imputation of strict identity." That is, though we may change physically or emotionally over time, so that we feel at best only *more or less* the person we once were, we also cannot escape the fact that we *are* wholly identical with our histories. This was not a psychological proposition about experience. "I am forever whatever I have been at any time for others," Mac-Intyre claimed, "and I may at any time be called upon to answer for it—no matter how changed I may be now. . . . I am the subject of a history that is my own and no one else's."[12] Were I to be magically replicated, my past would be part of the history of each of the successor selves, who might then go on to have unique histories, and thus identities, but always on the basis of a common past neither could escape—including not least the event of replication.

The objective content of my history, my accountability for the past that comes with it, and the intelligibility of my actions that my story provides me with, all "presuppose the applicability of the concept of personal identity." Those three elements are in fact what a correct understanding of personal identity entails; they define one another. The force of MacIntyre's calling his narrative account of the self's continuity "personal identity" is that the self so understood is not simply a stream of discrete and ever-changing doings connected only by I-consciousness and memory, as Locke (and Parfit) would have it; the self always comes with a unified theme which constitutes it. That theme includes, furthermore, not just the past but the whole narrative we construct that connects our past to our present and future by a goal that must make sense out of what we did "then" and what we are doing "now" in relation to what we will be in the future. In this way we are "whole" at every moment of our lives, even before our death, before the whole temporal life can be written.[13] Such wholeness, the unity of past, present, and future in the narrative flow, is our personal identity. Change may add new content to our narratives; at every moment, however, life has the closure of narrative form.

Even granting this, why must any of our stories define who we are essentially? Why can we not be seen as constantly, or at least potentially, rewriting our stories de novo? May not the "unavoidable" past take on entirely new meaning in the light of new goals? Sartre had also argued that truth demands we acknowledge what we did in the past as our own doing, while insisting at the same time that we cannot use the weight of that past to explain or justify what we do in the future. In fact, MacIntyre's claim that identity has a necessary objective content was only completed by his further argument that our individual narratives are located within the larger narratives of a tradition (or traditions) that always impose their goals on us however we subsequently relate to them. We don't live in a social vacuum in which we create our individual narratives ex nihilo. "The story of my life," he insisted, "is always embedded in the story of those communities from which I derive my identity. I am born with a past; and to try to cut myself off from that past, in the individualist mode, is to deform my present relationships. The possession of an historical identity and the possession of a social identity coincide." The moralistic overtones of "deforming" ourselves is one of many giveaways to the book's normative intent, but there seems no way out of the logical conundrum he deduced from the fact of our embeddedness in tradition: "Rebellion against my identity is always one possible mode of expressing it."[14] There is no escape from identity. A Jew who converts to Christianity may no longer be a Jew in practice or belief, but he will always and necessarily *be* a convert from Judaism. And that fact will make him something other than a Christian by birth and upbringing, objectively but also subjectively and interpersonally, though there may be many ways to interpret the difference.

*   *   *

MacIntyre, Taylor, and Sandel were not doing political theory in their books, and only Sandel could be said to have written a work of political philosophy. But the work of all three had a direct bearing on the politics of identity. Furthermore, despite sharp differences in the implication of their arguments for politics, all three shared a common philosophical point of origin and a similar ideological animus. All began from an Aristotelian position on the necessary primacy of a concept of "the good" in ethical and political deliberation; for two of them this ultimately entailed a religious, specifically Catholic conception of the highest good. All were socialist critics of modern liberal capitalism. The two older men, MacIntyre and Taylor, represented strands, if quite different ones, of the Old Left; Sandel, just barely too young to have participated in the university New Left of the 1960s, embodied its critical spirit.[15] The convergent appearance of their work in the 1980s might have been coincidental but it spoke to the times. It represented a multigenerational critical reckoning with liberalism, which, though in gestation long before the New Left revolt of the 1960s in the cases of MacIntyre and Taylor, had been opened afresh by the social upheavals of the period. This time, however, the reckoning took place under the sign of identity, which gave it a quite different direction politically.

Unsurprisingly, MacIntyre drew no concrete implications for politics from his story of the historical decline and fall of the Aristotelian-Catholic moral traditions, which he claimed had furnished Western identities for over two thousand years. In early modern times, however, ethics governed by a socially rooted but transcendent conception of the good, a belief in the virtues objectively necessary to achieve it, and the narrative unity its pursuit gave to communal and individual life had all been replaced by the ethics of abstract rules. These could yield no concrete content and had in the end no foundation other than arbitrary desire and will. Furthermore this was not only an event in intellectual history; the state of modern ethical theory mirrored the state of modern society out of which it developed: a society of isolated individuals with at best fragmented traditions, driven by individual self-interest and competitiveness while simultaneously submitting to an impersonal coercive bureaucracy necessary to keep the peace among them. MacIntyre's apocalyptic conclusion pronounced not only the dead end of modern ethical theory but also the exhaustion of all modern political traditions, liberal, socialist, or conservative, none of which were able to devise a plausible set of political and economic institutions to replace the structures of advanced capitalism. By the same token, we had apparently also arrived at a state of almost total loss of identity. Those who kept alive and found their being in the old traditions might still individually retain some individual sense of identity, but unsupported by a society whose institutions and spirit opposed its foundations, they could neither thrive nor last.

MacIntyre notoriously compared the present to the Dark Ages.[16] This despairing comparison nonetheless implied, or so he claimed, a politics of hope. The Dark Ages came between doomed efforts to shore up the dying institutions and traditions of the Roman empire and the creation of a new kind of moral community based on the Christian institutions of medieval Europe. So long as the classical-medieval heritage could be kept intellectually alive, society might one day create the practices and institutions that would make it once again the foundation of new identities. But MacIntyre himself made no effort to suggest what they might be, nor could he have. Since the virtues of the classical and Christian traditions were by his own account embedded in the social and institutional practices of the ancient and medieval worlds in which they arose—as was true, he argued, for all systems of thought—it was impossible to imagine them outside those institutions, except at the highest level of philosophical abstraction. It was not mere nostalgia that led MacIntyre to articulate his hope for the future as the wait for another St. Benedict, the codifier of monasticism; he could only imagine the creation of new identities as re-creation of the old.

But there was another inconsistency in MacIntyre's analysis that had more interesting consequences for thinking about the prospects for identity in the modern world. If it was the case that humanity lived only by telling itself the stories that constitute its identity, moderns must also have their own stories.

And if there were, as he claimed, no escape from identity, those stories would have to reckon in some way with the old narratives. MacIntyre's own narrative of decline, despair, and hopeful waiting was one such story; Beckett's unrequited waiting for Godot, which MacIntyre invoked only to sidestep, was another. But (a possibility MacIntyre himself mentioned) the moderns' story might also be a story of liberation from the external authority of religion and tradition itself, coupled with the exhilarating if anxious possibility of—and inescapable need for—self-creation. This was in fact the plot of the story that the sociologist Anthony Giddens described in *Modernity and Self-Identity*.[17] Giddens's ultimate and overt purpose was to devise concrete policy recommendations for the British Labour Party to refresh its appeal in the 1990s after more than a decade of Conservative rule by dealing with some social consequences of the same loss of traditional identities that left MacIntyre hopeless about contemporary politics. The presuppositions of Giddens's enterprise included the notion that liberal individualism is itself an identity-conferring tradition, with its own ultimate values, practices, institutions, and evolving history, which is able, within its own narrative, to recognize and solve problems it helped to create. Moderns could no longer count on the certainties that had anchored religion and local tradition; a degree of Sartrian existential anxiety and Laingian ontological insecurity was their inescapable lot. On the other hand, the modern sense of freedom also gives them the capacity to create and sustain their own narratives. To be successful, such narratives must indeed discover and integrate answers to the moral and existential questions of meaning that modernity has repressed, but this is a task that "life politics" and the liberal-democratic political system can address by taking up causes like ecology, which aims to restore the human relationship with nature that modern exploitation of resources has destroyed.[18]

Sandel's version of the ethical and political priority of the good, the argument that rights depend for their justification on the moral importance of the ends they serve, was not, like MacIntyre's, wedded to so historically specific a set of traditional practices and institutions that it could not furnish some guidelines for contemporary politics. Quite the contrary: though his book did not much concern itself with practical consequences, he did offer a concrete example to illustrate how his identity alternative to liberal individualism could reshape the terms of contemporary political debate on social issues: the controversy over affirmative action that was roiling American universities and the judiciary in the aftermath of its institution in the late 1960s and 1970s.

Liberals defended affirmative action particularly with regard to professional schools on two grounds. Given the priority of equal individual rights in American law and culture, they first had to argue that admission policies that took such factors as race and gender into account did not violate the rights of the rejected white or male students to be judged on the basis of merit. While merit as determined by grades and test scores was certainly a relevant criterion of admission, it had never been the only one. Professional schools had always taken into account other qualities that it deemed relevant to the social purposes that the profession served. Furthermore, no one was legally entitled to claim that schools should undertake to reward any particular kind of qualification. While it could legitimately be deemed a violation of equal rights to exclude certain groups on the basis of characteristics not relevant to a profession, it was not illegitimate to discriminate in favor of some groups on the basis of such relevant characteristics as intelligence, character, or, under certain circumstances, their ability to serve an underserved community better than others.[19]

Sandel pointed out that the arguments about rights and entitlement, while sufficient to establish the nonillegitimacy of certain kinds of discrimination, were not positive arguments in favor of affirmative action. In an effort to make them, liberal advocates of affirmative action tended to shift to a utilitarian argument for its social usefulness. Crucially, however, they failed to address the stark inconsistency of appealing to social utility with their otherwise total rejection of utilitarianism because it could be used to justify violations of individual rights.

The only way for liberals to justify affirmative action consistent with individualism was to invoke the broadened sense of the self that Sandel argued for. "Since others made me," he ventriloquized such a self, "and in various ways continue to make me, the person I am, it seems appropriate to regard them . . . as participants in 'my' achievements and common beneficiaries of the rewards they bring." Instead of feeling unfairly penalized that social benefits for some limit my opportunities or tax my resources, Sandel continued, "we may come to regard ourselves . . . less as individuated subjects with certain things in common, and more as members of a wider (but still determinate) subjectivity, less as 'others' and more as participants in a common identity." More baldly, Sandel thought we *should* so regard ourselves; it is not merely an optional but the right way to think. In any case, when I do think of myself in terms of my social identity, I am less likely to experience calls on me to contribute to communal endeavors as my being used for the ends of others, and more as ways of participating in the purposes of a community I regard as my own.[20] Its purposes are mine, more precisely, in identity terms, they are me.

This way of thinking of the self would appear to have potentially very far-reaching consequences not just for the rhetoric and tone of political debate but for substantive political and social change. Sandel, however, did not develop his notion of intersubjective identity into a theory of governance or a program of reform. He gave a string of examples of communities I might regard as part of my identity—family, community, class, people, nation—without following up on the quite different consequences each of these identities might have for the structure or legislative goals of a political system. Only Charles Taylor extended his critique of the liberal "punctual self" on behalf of the self's irreducible ethical and social identity into an explicit theoretical defense of multiculturalism as political policy. In doing so he became one of the most significant contributors to the consequential debate in the political theory of the 1980s and 1990s about the relationship of cultural identity to liberal democracy.

The Political Theory of Multiculturalism

Accommodating Illiberal Identities

Everyone participating in that debate began from the same basic premise about the self: it is fatefully embedded in a more or less dense cultural matrix that gives it a "thick" identity. The political theorist John Gray provided one of its most extreme formulations: "Today, as throughout history, human identities are primarily ascriptive, not elective. For nearly everyone, belonging to a community is a matter of fate, not choice. . . . Any political ideal that neglects these realities can only be pernicious in its consequences."[21] Even if one accepted this claim, however, there were two fundamentally different ways to think about it. For those for whom individual autonomy and choice remained the supreme value, cultural identity was a fact about individuals that had to be taken into account as part of respecting and protecting their individuality. For others, some of whom, Gray among them, called themselves "value pluralists," "individualism" was only one among many possible cultural values; to assume its universality was nothing but Western parochialism. Defending identity meant defending the culture that conferred it, whatever the culture's values.[22]

The polemical thrust of value pluralism, however, was not primarily *for* polities with collectivist, authoritarian, or religious cultures, which hardly needed or wanted such a defense, but *against* the presumption of liberals to judge and restrict what it regarded as antiliberal minority cultures in their midst. This for value pluralists was just another form of Western "ethnocentrism" or cultural imperialism, attempting to force one identity on everyone. The liberal value of individual autonomy was neither universal nor an absolute good. As Chandran Kukathas pointed out, many cultures "don't place such value on the *individual*'s freedom to choose his ends. Often the individual and his interest are subordinated to the community."[23] "Asian values" for example (or in particular), such as social harmony, respect for authority, orderly society, a united and extended family and a sense of filial piety represented, according to Bhikhu Parekh, different but no less valid ways of living.[24] Genuine respect for people did not mean insisting that they conform to the narrow liberal value of autonomy. To do justice to alternative ways of life and thought, Parekh insisted, liberals had to "stop absolutizing the liberal way of life . . . to accept the full force of moral and cultural pluralism and acknowledge that the good life can be lived in several different ways."[25]

Surveying the multicultural debates some years later, Kwame Anthony Appiah offered a sharp distinction between what he called "hard" or "millet" multiculturalism (a term originally introduced by the political philosopher Michael Walzer) and "soft" or liberal multiculturalism. Millet referred to the Ottoman system of governance in which Jews and Christians were left alone to practice their religion and govern their communities internally, provided they paid taxes, kept order, and did not challenge Muslim political and cultural dominance of the state. Presumably the "hards" like Gray, Kukathas, and Parekh, wanted a modern version of such a system, at least to the extent that state power receded as far as possible from control of cultural minorities, and internal communal autocracy was indulged. But hard multiculturalists mostly stopped short of outright coercion; members of a community, they agreed, must have a right of exit from their communities, a right that should be legally protected by the state.[26] In fact even a brief look at the way in which the supposed "hards" proposed to deal with a number of contentious contemporary issues of cultural difference made them look much more like the liberals they opposed than their own rhetoric might have led one to believe.

Examining such issues as female circumcision, *sati*—the Hindu practice of a widow's immolating herself on her husband's funeral pyre—and polygamy, Parekh in every case ultimately came down on the conventional liberal side against traditional tribal or religious practices, judging that they should all be banned in the name of individual dignity and flourishing. His argumentation was elaborate, taking into careful account cultural reasons for the various practices and criticizing their out-of-hand rejection by liberals. His procedure was in fact a one-person exemplar of the dialogical process he recommended for a multicultural society.

> The good society does not commit itself to a particular political doctrine or vision of the good life. . . . It is dialogically constituted. . . .
> The dialogue requires certain institutional preconditions such as

freedom of expression, agreed procedures and ethical norms, participatory public spaces, equal rights, a responsive and popularly constituted structure of authority, and empowerment of citizens. And it
also calls for such essential political virtues as mutual respect and
concern, tolerance, self-restraint, willingness to enter into unfamiliar
worlds of thought, love of diversity, a mind open to new ideas and a
heart open to others' needs, and the ability to persuade and live with
unresolved differences.[27]

There was nothing here that a good procedural liberal could not accept, especially as the ethical norms he made a precondition of the "good society" coincided with the liberal norms of individual dignity and equality. Parekh in effect
conceded the fundamental liberalism of his position with the claim that "The
dialogically constituted multicultural society both retains the truth of liberalism and goes beyond it." Even the "beyond" could be understood without a
great stretch in traditional liberal terms, which in their Humboldtian and
Millian strain valued individuality and diversity alongside, if not as higher
than, a narrower individualism of rights. Chandran Kukathas, who argued
that a liberal culture ought to leave nonliberal cultures to flourish—or
not—on their own, explicitly identified himself as a liberal individualist.

The real issue here was not conceptual—"hard" versus "liberal"
multiculturalism—but historical: the ethnoreligious challenge to Eurocentric,
historically white Christian liberalism posed by large-scale Asian, African, and
Caribbean immigration to Europe in the second half of the twentieth century.
The challenge did not on the whole affect matters of political substance, since
liberal society was not being asked to change its fundamental principles in
accommodating immigrants so much as its social attitudes. It is no surprise
that a significant proportion of the most influential cultural critics of European liberalism, like Kukathas and Parekh, were of Asian birth, educated and
living in Britain or Australia as academics, often with political involvement as
consultants on immigrant community matters. As ex-colonials or their
descendants they were well schooled in their former imperial masters' contempt for the "inferior" peoples they had ruled.

But Parekh was right in referring to multicultural attitudes like "willingness to enter into unfamiliar worlds of thought" as *political* virtues, though of
a distinctly new kind. Changes in how one felt about those one previously
considered inferiors would mean changes in how one treated them, and with
them. Emotions, however, entail beliefs, and changing feelings demanded
changed beliefs. Traditional liberalism, founded on ideas of universal humanity and reason, had justified its judgment of the inferiority of non-European

peoples on the "irrationality" of their beliefs. The concept of identity enabled theorists to sidestep the vexed issue of rationality, faith in the exclusive posses-sion of which had long since waned in the West in any case, by placing beliefs and practices in the context of structures of thought and practice that gave meaning to a life. To understand others' differences as their *identities* put them on the same psychological and existential footing as oneself.

*   *   *

Perhaps the best example of the difficulty in making a useful distinction between liberal and hard multiculturalism is the position of the legal and polit-ical philosophers Avishai Margalit and Moshe Halbertal. It is even better evi-dence of how concrete historical situations conditioned attempts at broad generalizations about the politics of cultural identity in the last decades of the twentieth century, qualifying them to the point where it is questionable whether the generalization applied to more than the cases from which it was derived.

If any multicultural position could be said to be "hard" short of the radical relativism that reduced liberalism to a parochial Western prejudice, it was that of Margalit and Halbertal. Their claim rested its case expressly on the needs of personal identity as distinct from, indeed as often opposed to, those of individ-ual freedom. "Human beings," they declared, "have a right to culture—not just any culture, but their own."[28] The right inheres solely in the individual, though since culture can only be the attribute of a group, it entails the preser-vation of the individual's culture. Its justification lies in the even more funda-mental right to secure one's personal identity. Since "all persons are supremely interested in their personal identity," the right to culture is "basic and pri-mary."[29] It is not founded on a prior right of individual freedom, as liberals purportedly argued. The members of a culture consider it to be important because its content gives their lives meaning on a variety of levels; freedom for them may well mean the right to live their culture. Though the authors did not define just what they meant by "meaning to a life," they insisted that a culture worthy of preservation must be "comprehensive," or "encompassing," embracing all the important aspects of life, from work to family to cooking, the arts, customs, dress, and ceremonies. A culture told its members what to do or what to value in all these realms, and such imperatives became vital components of their personal identity. No other version of multiculturalism was as consequent or clear in making identity the foundational principle of political theorizing.

Given the primacy of a right to one's own culture, it could make absolutely no difference that one's culture might be illiberal. While this claim is consistent, however, what the authors failed to point out was that it mattered only for a liberal society; illiberal societies didn't need it, and not recognizing individual rights, to identity or anything else, in any case couldn't make it. The right to culture is on the other hand very important for a liberal society because it justifies serious claims on the majority to support even cultures that flout the rights of the individual.[30] Support means more than a vague "respect." It means furnishing the minority culture with all the legal protections and financial resources necessary to guarantee its present flourishing and future survival, even if that involves measures that are themselves illiberal. So a liberal government might prevent nonmembers of a minority culture from living in an area where its members constitute a majority, lest the outsiders undermine the region's cultural homogeneity. "The state is obligated to abjure its neutrality" with regard to minority cultures, "not for the sake of the good of the majority, but in order to make it possible for members of minority groups to retain their identity."[31]

The groups the authors used to illustrate their principles, Israeli Arabs and Ultra-Orthodox Jews in Israel, were particularly provocative examples for the liberal state and hence presumably ideal test cases. Both groups deny the legitimacy of the very state from which they demand support. Neither joins in singing the national anthem or serves in what is otherwise a conscript citizen army. Ultra-Orthodox culture furthermore is illiberal at its core. It controls every aspect of its members' lives, private and public, and resorts to compulsion, including physical coercion, to enforce its rulings. It makes illiberal demands even on nonmembers, such as insisting that non-Orthodox women wear modest clothing when walking through Orthodox neighborhoods or forbidding cars from driving through them on the Sabbath. Nonetheless, the authors argued, in the name of preserving their identity, the Israeli government is obligated to financially support the schools in both the Arab and Ultra-Orthodox communities, though they teach against the civic religion of the Israeli state as a secular but Jewish democracy. It is similarly obligated to enforce public observance of the Sabbath in Ultra-Orthodox areas and recognize Arabic as an official language alongside Hebrew.

These two cases, however, were not chosen simply to illustrate the authors' thesis about the requirement to support illiberal cultural identities in a liberal state. They were presented in the specific context of a crisis of Israeli national unity. The underlying problem was what to do about the fact that the two groups threatened the cohesion of the national polity because they rejected the consensual premises of its Jewish yet also secular identity. The giveaway is an inconsistency in the apparent importance the authors attributed to numbers in determining which cultures deserve governmental support. If an individual's right to culture is to obligate the state, they claimed plausibly, the minority culture he belongs to must be "viable." An additional condition of state support for a culture, then, is the existence of a sufficient number of people demanding the right to the same culture: "A group must pass some numerical threshold of rights-bearers."[32] Nowhere, however, did they suggest a way of determining what that threshold might be. Instead, they cited the fact that the Arabs at 18 percent and the Ultra-Orthodox at 7–10 percent together constituted over one-quarter of Israel's population. But there were other communities in Israel, some large, like Russian immigrants, others smaller but numerically viable, which by the identity criterion could be said to deserve the same type and level of state support as Arabs and Ultra-Orthodox Jews. Why just the latter? The reason to single them out was the combination of their numerical weight and the threat it posed to the unity of the state. Because other groups were either integrated into the country's civic culture or too small to be dangerous they did not have to be placated with financial and legal support for their subnational cultural identities. Since the two groups in question could not be integrated, it appeared the only way to avoid the breakdown of social unity, if not outright civil strife, was for the state to support their identities so that they oppose it only passively, rather than actively.

As a purely pragmatic solution to the problem of social peace in a divided society this might be workable, but one of the authors himself had given potent reasons elsewhere for believing it could never solve a problem like that posed by Israel's lack of civic consensus, and might not be practicable even in the short run. In an earlier essay addressing the question of the right to national self-determination, Margalit, with Joseph Raz, had argued that any such right derives from the value of the individual's membership in "encompassing groups." Such groups, they wrote, have certain key features: they have pervasive cultures, and their members' identities are importantly determined by it.[33] They have high "social profiles"; membership in the group is one of the primary facts by which people are identified by others as well as themselves, and the group's visibility and distinctive character form expectations as to what its members are like. Membership in encompassing groups is a matter of belonging, not of accomplishment; it is experienced as a given, a fact about oneself which affords unthreatened security.[34] The value of membership in encompassing groups, then, is the value of identity.

It followed that the cohesion and success of states founded by nationalist movements depended on their having a common identity. "To form a new political unit," the authors wrote, "*or to remain part of an existing one, all component parts should agree. . . .* [T]he more important human groupings need to be based on shared history, and on criteria of nonvoluntaristic (or at least not wholly contractarian) membership to have the value they have [for their members]."[35] Any sizable group within the state that does not identify with it must either remain forever alien and hostile or eventually become self-determining. On the other side, if unified cultural identity is the sine qua non of political cohesion, it is unclear how long or to what degree a state can tolerate the existence of large irreconcilable identities. The political crisis created twenty-five years later by the Supreme Court's ruling unconstitutional the military exemption of Ultra-Orthodox men dramatically illustrated both how right the authors were about the centrality of the issue for national unity and how ultimately unviable was their insistence that the majority tolerate it forever. The problem was precisely that of numbers, which now told against their argument. So long as the number of potential Ultra-Orthodox draftees remained small the issue could be ignored by the majority as perhaps irritating but materially insignificant; as the numbers increased, however, the exemption was perceived as both a threat to the integrity of the army and a grievous injustice to those who had to serve. At the most crucial points the equal obligations of universal citizenship in a modern liberal state had to trump the rights of minority identities.[36]

But Margalit and Halbertal had in any case already acknowledged this, in two ways: by putting some limits on minority demands that affected the rights of the majority, and by insisting that members of a minority culture must have the right of exit from it. Minority demands that affected others could claim only a prima facie, not an absolute, right to be honored. Allowing the Ultra-Orthodox control over entry to their neighborhoods in matters of dress or driving on the Sabbath had to be balanced against the danger of inflicting undue restrictions on others. If closing the community's streets to traffic on the Sabbath would block major arteries vital for people who did not abide by the ban on Sabbath driving, at least one such road had to be kept open for traffic. No culture, they argued, should be protected to the extent of enabling it to force itself on other individuals in order to preserve itself.[37] But that is exactly what they were allowing the wider society to do in putting such limitations on minority rights. This was even more obviously the case with their insistence on the right of exit for members of the minority culture, a right implicitly premised on the liberal right of consent to authority, which for the Ultra-Orthodox contravened the essence of their belief. Whether a right of exit could be more than a formal gesture, however, when education and family law was left wholly in the hands of the minority community was a potentially serious objection,[38] one that the authors themselves did not discuss or even raise. The omissions and inconsistencies in their argument resulted from the unrecognized tension between the overt purpose of advocating for majority support of illiberal cultures in a liberal polity and the implicit attempt to strike a balance between the two. "Really" hard multiculturalism was ultimately an impossible position for liberals, even those whose liberalism was founded on a basic individual right to one's own cultural identity.

Liberal Multiculturalism

Just what the balance ought to be was the explicit concern of theorists who either explicitly labeled themselves, or clearly thought of themselves, as *liberal* multiculturalists. And just as it made historical sense that a disproportionately large number of the critics of Western liberal ethnocentricity were of Asian origin, it was not by chance that the two most influential theorists of liberal multiculturalism were Canadian. Even their most abstract categories bore marks of the Canadian political experience.

To ground Canadian multicultural practice, the political theorist Will Kymlicka defined his position against what he regarded as two opposing theoretical extremes: on one hand the "communitarianism" he associated with MacIntyre, Sandel, and Taylor, which he saw rejecting liberalism altogether (true in fact only of MacIntyre), and on the other a narrowly individualistic liberalism that he believed, with the communitarians, ignored cultural identity. Multiculturalism was in Kymlicka's analysis the true liberalism because it took into account the whole individual, not just those motives of self-interest traditionally associated with the concept of individual rights. People have a "sense of identity" that is "dependent on a particular culture," hence "cultural membership gives rise to legitimate claims" that are not only "consistent with principles of liberal equality . . . but . . . indeed required by them."[39] To protect a person's culture *is* to protect his individual rights. Culture, furthermore, is not, as the communitarians argued, a rigidly deterministic straightjacket, which limits or abrogates individual freedom but a "context of choice."[40] Members of a culture are free to modify its character, as French Canadians did to dramatic effect in the 1960s with the Quiet Revolution. This example, however, rested on a distinction, more contentious than Kymlicka allowed, between what was essential to the continuity of a culture—shared language and history—and what was not: beliefs of the "moment." The argument was exactly that made by the Royal Commission on Bilingualism and Biculturalism.

Significantly, the kinds of choices Kymlicka allowed for were not of the individual's personal identity but of changes within the cultural identity that constituted him. Despite his efforts to separate himself from the communitarians, Kymlicka's view of identity was not radically different, nor could it be, since it was on the basis of an intrinsic connection between culture and identity that he argued for multicultural accommodation. His language was psychological and colloquial where MacIntyre's was philosophical and abstract but his conclusion was much the same. "Someone's upbringing," as he put it, "isn't something that can just be erased; it is, and will remain, a constitutive part of who that person is."[41] Identity is a matter of the shaping influence of language, which is not merely a neutral symbolic system for objective content but "itself a content," not merely referential but interpretive. It is crucially also a source of the emotional security, personal strength, and sense of agency provided by the sense of automatic belonging to a particular community and history. The inherent support of one's culture is the source of one's self-respect and the guarantor of the worth of one's ends.[42] These were some of the same psychological factors that Erikson had identified as necessary to individual psychic health, though with the focus on the purportedly homogeneous culture that provided them rather than on the conflicting identifications individual development inevitably brought with it, and the psychological work of integration they demanded.

But psychological arguments for cultural identity did not answer the crucial political questions of what it meant concretely to respect a culture in a liberal society, or of whether all cultures should be respected equally or in the same way. For a liberal there were two major issues. Some cultures were distinctly illiberal: should the state protect them in any way? A perhaps even thornier issue was determining which was an individual's "identitarian" culture. People generally belonged to a number of groups with a shared ethos and values, from religion to ethnicity to nationality to work. Which of these was most central to personal identity, which needed legal protection, and of what kind?

Kymlicka's answer to the first question was straightforward, if unspecific: liberals should "reject" those restrictions internal to a cultural community that limit the right of group members to question and revise traditional authorities and practices.[43] He thus rejected the belief he imputed to Sandel that, because at least some of our ends are constitutive of our personal identities, we cannot stand apart from them and judge them; they *are* our standards of judgment. In such a view, it is neither ethically important nor existentially possible for us to be free to revise them. But while doing so may not be easy or enjoyable, Kymlicka insisted, it is both possible and at times a "regrettable necessity" to revise our beliefs in the name of individual freedom.

His answer to the second set of questions, however, was determined more by the peculiarities of the Canadian polity than by the demands of liberalism. He argued that culture that mattered for identity was a "societal" culture, one which "provides its members with meaningful ways of life across the full range of human activities, including social, educational, recreational, and economic life, encompassing both public and private spheres. These cultures tend to be territorially concentrated, and based on a shared language."[44] A societal culture was marked by a high level of solidarity, dependent on "a strong sense of common identity" whose foundation was a common language and history. Kymlicka's definition seemed to be congruent with, or at least overlap, Smith's notion of ethnically based national identity, and in a way it was: Kymlicka also spoke of societal cultures as "nations." But nations were not equivalent to the political entities called states, and certainly not to the modern concept of the "nation-state," which implied a nationally homogeneous state. There was nothing inherently contradictory for Kymlicka about the idea of a multinational state.

Since, however, citizens of states, in Kymlicka's view, needed to view themselves, at least "for some purposes," as a single people,[45] how could it be determined which entities within states were "nations," and what rights separate nationalities should have in relation to the centralized state? Nations, he argued, were those entities that had at one time been territorially independent and linguistically homogeneous but that by conquest or in some other way had become incorporated into larger states—like the province of Quebec, or the indigenous peoples of what in Canada had come to be called the First Nations. To preserve their members' identities, such nations must have the legal right to preserve their original languages as the official language of the territories where they make up a majority and perhaps even as an official language of the whole country. The shaping force of the Canadian experience on Kymlicka's concepts of "societal culture," multinational state, and identity was obvious. Whatever else a societal culture might include, and whatever changes its other elements—religion, education, mores, the arts—might undergo over time, the one constant was language. A multinational state that would preserve its societal cultures and their identities was necessarily a constitutionally multilingual state.

But in many modern states there were communities of people who speak, or at one time spoke, other than the national language. Historically these were the ethnic groups who had emigrated from their home nation and state. Such immigrant groups, Kymlicka declared, "are not 'nations.'"[46] By voluntarily immigrating to a new land they had given up the right to have their original languages recognized officially, though they certainly had the right to try to perpetuate them on their own, while of necessity participating in the public sphere in the language(s) of their adopted country. They no longer made up a "societal culture." It was here that the contradictions within Kymlicka's concept of identity became evident. Though the language that was ostensibly the linchpin of their identity could not be legally recognized, other aspects of immigrant ethnic cultures should be respected by the majority society through legal protections of various kinds. Whether, by Kymlicka's own definition this amounted to full respect for the identity of ethnic groups is doubtful. Logic gave way to history.

The legal protections he would afford "non-societal" ethnic identities in a multinational and polyethnic state were nonetheless hardly negligible. At the same time they also and unavoidably represented a vital if unacknowledged shift in his criteria for the essential constituent of identity.

His specific recommendations derived from his central argument against the shibboleth of the "neutral," purely procedural, liberal state. In theory, the liberal democratic state was the guardian of universal individual rights and the guarantor of egalitarian processes of decision-making but was otherwise completely neutral toward competing ideologies and visions of the good life. Decisions about these were supposedly left to the private wills of individuals and groups. In practice, however, crucial features of public life in all liberal states enshrined aspects of the dominant societal culture's conception of the good life. This was inevitable. "There is no way," Kymlicka argued, "to have a complete 'separation of state and ethnicity.'"[47] In Western countries the traditional day of rest and many of the official holidays reflected its Christian heritage. While it was not practicable to change this, nor for the state to officially recognize every religious calendar, a truly neutral public policy would both make allowances for the needs of other religions and exempt them from certain otherwise general requirements, so long as these were not integral to liberal principles. Businesses should be mandated to permit their Muslim and Jewish employees to take days off on their respective Sabbaths, Sikh members of the Royal Canadian Mounted Police should be permitted to wear their ritual turbans instead of regulation hats, and Amish and Doukhobors should be exempted from the requirements of public schooling. When it came to matters such as these, true equality of rights requires group-differentiated rights of citizenship.

Significantly, virtually all the examples Kymlicka offered as examples of such rights concerned religion. What seemed to be most important to the identities of recent immigrants or long-established minority groups, in any case what existing law and regulation most impinged on, were their religious practices. In effect, while government could, even should be relatively intolerant in enforcing uniformity of official language, it should be very tolerant about comprehensive belief systems. This reversal of pre-modern political practice reflected the evolution of liberalism and identity in the West more generally. For a modern secular liberal, language as instrument of communication had replaced any concrete content it might express as the official marker of identity. As we saw in the previous chapter, however, language as common culture was never the full story in Canada or anywhere else; language turned out to be a surrogate for what in a liberal society could no longer be legislated. The test case of Muslim immigration, as Kymlicka himself later pointed out, made it clear that in Canada (as in Germany), "language" was partly a proxy for a secularized Judeo-Christian ethnocultural identity that Muslims, in the eyes of many Canadians in the first decades of Muslim immigration, could not satisfy simply by speaking English or French.[48]

That language was proxy for a deeper cultural identity was explicit in the liberal multiculturalism of Charles Taylor. Taylor did not see his attack on the inadequacy of the individualist concept of self as at all inconsistent with liberalism in politics. But he also argued that it entailed a different sort of liberalism, one that admitted the legitimacy of legislation on behalf of collective social goals to sustain a community's identity alongside the individualism of rights-based liberalism.

Taylor's most influential, and debated, contribution to the political theory of collective identity was the idea of recognition. In a seminal essay he drew on both the Continental philosophical tradition and American social psychology to argue that "our identity is partly shaped by recognition or its absence, often by the *mis*recognition of others, and so a person or group of people can suffer real damage, real distortion, if the people or society around them mirror back to them a confining or demeaning or contemptible picture of themselves."[49] The modern era had seen the emergence of an ideal of "individualized identity," a concept that placed value on the distinctiveness of each self. But—paradoxical as it seemed—though this ideal involves an inward sense of truly being only what feels "authentic" to oneself, the individual cannot generate such a feeling of authenticity by himself. Human life is "fundamentally *dialogical*. . . . We become capable of understanding ourselves, and hence of defining our identity . . . through . . . modes of expression . . . learn[ed] through exchanges with others . . . who matter to us."[50] This claim condensed and combined two theories of different historical and conceptual origin into a novel formulation of identity.[51] The philosophical thesis, derived from Hegel, was that humans could know themselves as autonomously acting individuals only if and when they "recognize" one another as such, that is, actively confirm one another's independence through their attitudes and actions. The psychological thesis was George Herbert Mead's theory that "significant others" are crucial to the development of our sense in early childhood of both the "me" and the "I," the objective self of internalized social values that I am to others as well as to myself, and the agent self, the "I," which can reflect on and modify the "me." Taylor insisted that the human developmental process did not culminate with the production of a fully autonomous identity impervious to the influence of others, as modern liberal theory assumed. "The making and sustaining of our identity," Taylor asserted, "remains dialogical throughout our lives." For a positive sense of identity, for a sense of ourselves as effective agents, we must be consistently affirmed as such by the society around us; failure of affirmation blights this potential.[52] In the past, general recognition was built into socially derived identities because it was based on social categories that everyone took for granted, so the need for recognition was not conscious. In modernity, this is no longer the case: recognition is not granted automatically and attempts at it can fail. That is why the need for recognition has become a matter of explicit concern in modern society.

Nonrecognition and "misrecognition" were also built into the hierarchical identities of the past. Everyone "knew" which categories of people were not fully human, incapable of being truly autonomous agents. Today, while recognition was no longer automatic by status, all might hope to achieve it. It was made thinkable for the first time in history by the "politics of universalism," the moral and social imperative to recognize the common humanity of all and its formal institutionalization through the legal equality of rights. But universalism was historically based on the philosophical homogenization of identity: everyone was worthy of dignity and respect because all were the same. Given the modern salience of individualized identity, however, the social and political challenge to recognition within liberal societies was to affirm "the unique identity of this individual or group, their distinctness from everyone else," to combine a new "politics of difference" with the older liberal "politics of universalism."[53]

The specific context in which Taylor posed this issue as a potential clash of values was the insufficiency of the idea of equal individual rights to protect the French identity of the province of Quebec within Canada. In the 1980s Quebec passed a number of laws concerning schooling and public use of language that placed restrictions on the liberty of individual Quebeckers. Taylor's defense of these laws was a crucial specification of what recognition involved beyond purely ethical norms and social attitudes of respect. Under certain circumstances it could entail legal measures backed by the coercion of the state. French-speakers and new immigrants were not legally permitted to send their children to English-speaking schools. Commercial language in any language other than French was outlawed. These laws, discriminatory on their face, defied the Canadian Charter of Rights passed in 1982 but were justified in Taylor's view because Quebeckers had the collective right to try to ensure both the flourishing of French culture in the present and its survival into the future through continuous creation of new members of the French community. This right, he argued, went beyond a purely procedural liberalism because it implied that a society could be organized around a definition of the good life without this being seen as a depreciation of those who didn't personally share that definition.[54] Quebec's laws, though restrictive, did not denigrate the identity of English speakers; it was a defensive measure to protect French Canada in a majority English culture.

However, since liberalism too was part of the definition of the good life Quebec was purportedly defending, it was not simply a neutral value on which peoples of all beliefs could agree. Because liberalism rested on the separation of politics and religion, it was, Taylor argued, incompatible with the political theology of Islam. This had recently been dramatically demonstrated by the international repercussions of Salman Rushdie's novel *The Satanic Verses*, whose supposed blasphemy against Islam evoked a *fatwa* by a Muslim cleric calling for the author's death. Liberalism, Taylor declared bluntly, is a fighting creed.[55] No liberal society could accommodate the requirement that freedom of expression be suppressed in the name of religious belief, let alone be punished by death. For that matter even the ideal of equal respect for other cultures could at most only grant an initial presumption that they have equal intrinsic *value*. While such a presumption is undoubtedly rational in the case of cultures that have provided the "horizon of meaning" for large numbers of people over a long period of time, it is not a final verdict. Cultural value has its own standards. All cultures must ultimately be brought before the bar of judgment, though Taylor was careful not to specify what the standards of "high" culture might be.

*   *   *

Taylor's "new" liberalism was not in fact different from Kymlicka's, though Kymlicka didn't think of it as another kind but as implicit in any fully self-aware and consistent liberal practice. As Jürgen Habermas pointed out, Quebeckers wanted nothing more than what would be accorded them as a matter of course if they declared themselves to be an independent nation. Even their desire to be a linguistically distinct "state within a state" could be accommodated within the broad spectrum of existing types of democratic federalism. But what was true for a state, independent or federated, was not necessarily true for subnational groups within a state. On one level, Habermas deepened Kymlicka's notion of the irretrievably particular cultural identity of the national state. At the same time he seemed to circumscribe more narrowly than Kymlicka the claims for recognition with regard to immigrant minorities or political refugees within a state. His position reflected the unique challenges to liberal multiculturalism posed on the one hand by the German history of ethnic and racist nationalism and on the other by the mass Turkish immigration starting in the 1960s and the more recent arrival of large numbers of asylum seekers. In political theory it also represented a transition toward a version of multiculturalism in some ways more skeptical about claims of identity than self-identified liberal multiculturalism, a skepticism to be most forcefully expressed in American political theory.

Kymlicka had claimed there could never be a complete separation of state and ethnicity. Habermas put the case in more philosophical terms. What he called the "ethical" dimension is an inevitable aspect of the modern state, as it is of any political entity. In Habermas's Hegelian conception, the ethical is the aspired-to unity of the particular and the universal. Every historical form of society has tried to realize the ethical by elevating its unique ways of life to the level of universally valid norms. Until modern times that meant interpreting the particular or ethnic identity of the state *as* the universal. Ethics, however, only came to fully adequate self-realization in the modern ideals of universal freedom and equality embodied in liberal democratic theory and institutions. The ethical problem for the modern state is that its social composition is the product of particular historical circumstances that preceded the principles of modern constitutionalism and individual rights. The process of actualizing universal ideals has to take place in the historical context of an already existing ethnic community. The particularity of the community—its language, territory, history, folkways, religion, in a word, its identity—constitutes an inevitable, and wholly legitimate, dimension of the ethical in a modern liberal state. The (ideal) modern state represents the fusion of a historical community in all its unique individuality with the universal—in Habermas's version of the latter, with the requirements of "discourse ethics," the participatory discussion including all members of a society that alone constitutes genuine democratic procedure. There were good historical reasons for his formulating the general problem of identity in a democracy in terms that made the particular identity of the nation essential to it. No thinker better understood the threat that particularism could pose to universalist values than the German philosopher, who had been struggling for decades to persuade his countrymen to transform their traditionally closed ethnicity-based nationalism into "constitutional patriotism," loyalty to the universal-rights based liberal republic. To fail to recognize and validate *German* identity in all its historical uniqueness would doom the effort.[56]

But Habermas's interpretation of the conversations among citizens that had to go on in the modern democratic state was also informed by his understanding of individual identity within the state. There are always differentiated identity groups within the larger national community. Discourse ethics requires ongoing discussion among such groups in order to arrive at a shared conception of the good and a desired form of life that is consensually acknowledged to be authentic.[57] "A correctly understood theory of rights," he wrote, "requires a politics of recognition that protects the integrity of the individual *in the life contexts in which his or her identity is formed*." But "This does not require an alternative model that would correct the individualistic design of the system of rights."[58] It would be wrong, even fatally wrong, for liberal political theory to separate individual rights from identity by pitting collective rights against individual rights. Collective identities could only be conceived as a necessary part of individual identity.

What are these identity-shaping "life-contexts" that the modern state has to recognize? In one sense, it is impossible to list them, since for Habermas they only emerge historically through unpredictable social change. He did, however, list some of the most relevant contexts in which contemporary identities were being fashioned in the 1990s, and which as he saw it required changes in social consciousness, law, and international relations, both in Germany and elsewhere. Among these were feminism, which demanded taking into account "gender-specific differences in life circumstances and experiences" between men and women,"[59] and multiculturalism, the domestic struggle of oppressed ethnic and cultural minorities for recognition, which in the case of Germany required a radical revision of its national identity as a nonimmigrant country.

Habermas thus fused liberal universalism and identity particularism in a unique synthesis. The modern democratic state necessarily legitimizes a particular identity in its very commitment to universal ethics. The state qua German or French, with its particular interests, is a legitimate ethical actor in the world. Its identity is codified in its official decisions about the history curriculum in public schools, the choice of an official language, and the establishment of legal holidays, among many other things. But within this national identity framework the self-consciously ethical state demands loyalty to a political culture of democratic decision making through discourse ethics. In this context Habermas argued that the state must remain neutral with regard to conflicts of basic values among social groups. Modern society is simply too complex to expect or demand consensus on other than the procedures for the legitimate enactment of laws and the legitimate exercise of power. The main emphasis of his theorizing was not on what might be owed groups in virtue of their collective identities but rather on how they ought to interact so as to arrive at consensually valid decisions. For the same reason, the state need not, indeed it must not try to guarantee a minority ethnic or religious culture's survival by, for example, subsidizing it or legally enforcing its language or hegemony over its members; that would rob the members of the freedom to say yes or no that is necessary if they are to appropriate and preserve their cultural heritage. By the same token, the modern state does not have the right to demand of immigrants that they become acculturated beyond acceptance of its ethical-political culture. This, however, from Habermas's point of view, was not necessarily a minor exception to the criterion. It meant excluding fundamentalist cultures, which by definition rejected the liberal ethical culture of the modern democratic state.

Identity Skeptics and American Individualism

It is not surprising that the theorists most wary of the claims of collective identity in a liberal democracy were American by birth or residence. It tells much about the public impact of the modern concept of identity that they felt compelled to take such claims into account at all, and the concessions they made were not insignificant. Nonetheless from an ideological vantage point that maintained individual rights as the highest political if not also ethical value these did indeed feel like concessions, both substantively and in tone.

Perhaps the most striking instance, because it involved a notable modification of his earlier position, is John Rawls's theory of political liberalism. It was a work of autorevisionism prompted by a new awareness of the importance of identity for morality and politics—the dimension of identity invested in worldviews that Erikson had called "ideological" and which Rawls largely took to be religious. His approach, however, made it clear that identity had become significant to him primarily as an obstacle to his original theory of justice. That theory had been predicated on the concept of a bare self stripped of all attributes except the desire for certain primary goods. Such selves, by definition in conditions of sameness and equality behind the pre-social veil of ignorance, decide on principles of justice that would guarantee fairness to all. But as Rawls now acknowledged, in all actually existing societies, people may and often do have "affections, devotions, and loyalties they would not, indeed could and should not, stand apart from and evaluate objectively. *They may regard it as simply unthinkable to view themselves apart from certain religious, philosophical, and moral convictions.*"[60] Rawls labeled these convictions people's "moral identity," in the strict sense that their attachments and beliefs constituted, for them, who they unchangeably were. Whatever its ontological validity, Rawls was stipulating that for the purposes of political theory belief in the permanence and indivisibility of moral self-identity must be taken as a psychological given.

The belief systems that constitute moral identity are "comprehensive doctrines" because they purport to offer answers to the most basic questions human beings could ask about their origins, meaning, and purpose, and to ground their answers in a conception of ultimate reality. Comprehensive doctrines, however, vary greatly in their basic norms and ultimate justifications. They need not in theory endorse, and most often do not in fact endorse, the stripped image of the self that Rawls had posited behind the veil of ignorance nor, consequently, the principles of justice it arrived at. In effect Rawls surrendered the enterprise of discovering a universally valid theory of justice, at least as a foundation for politics.

His solution was to lower his sights to the more limited project of trying to define a consensually just *political* system in the light of the potentially unbridgeable differences in people's comprehensive doctrines. To this end he divided moral identity into two separate parts, political and personal, and made them independent of one another. The enterprise was in one obvious sense circular: he defined in advance the particular political identity he was concerned with as that of the "citizen." His project was basically to tease out the political logic of the collective identity of "citizenship" in a religiously pluralistic liberal democratic state.

Citizens, he claimed, have both political and nonpolitical commitments. As citizens, they affirm the values of political justice in the public sphere while in their private lives they express the beliefs and values of their comprehensive doctrines. To be a citizen, committed to political justice, is to be committed to an ideal of reasonableness, which includes but is not the same as the idea of rationality. Rationality involves reasoning logically from a set of basic premises, whatever they may be and however they are derived. Reasonableness by contrast entails a specific set of normative premises. Persons are reasonable by definition when they propose principles and standards as fair terms of cooperation with others who they treat as equals, standards they themselves are willing to abide by provided that the others will also. Reasonableness necessarily takes into account the consequences of actions on the well-being of others; it is incompatible with egoism.[61] Comprehensive doctrines can be rational without being reasonable, deducing their consequences with impeccable logic from premises that originate in mystery, miracle, or authority; rational comprehensive doctrines may well sanction inequality. But many comprehensive doctrines, though disagreeing with one another in their basic beliefs, are both reasonable and rational. Reasonable belief systems are (among other things) exercises of theoretical reason that express an "intelligible view of the world,"[62] that is, one that even nonbelievers could credit as understandable. From the political point of view their most essential common feature is that because the holders of one doctrine can judge that other beliefs may also be reasonable (if untrue), they eschew the use of state coercion to enforce their own even should they have the power to do so. Reasonable comprehensive systems thus endorse some form of liberty of conscience and freedom of thought. Furthermore, they commit themselves to shareable standards of public reason in order to decide basic constitutional questions, standards their believers can appeal to with the confidence that they also bind believers in other doctrines.

For political liberalism to be practically possible, then, two things are necessary. The first is that, given the empirical fact of doctrinal pluralism in society, a political conception of justice must be one that can be endorsed by widely different and opposing, though reasonable, comprehensive doctrines.[63] The second is that "the wider realm of values" of a comprehensive system must be understandable by its adherents as congruent with, supportive of, or at least not in conflict with the values appropriate to the special domain of the political as specified by a political conception of justice. The history of religion and philosophy in the West shows that this has in fact come to be the case. As a result, it is reasonable to believe that there can be an "overlapping consensus" of otherwise radically disagreeing comprehensive doctrines on the norms and practices of a liberal political society.[64] Overlapping consensus was the social identity condition of Rawls's political liberalism.

The most consequential political implication of his reconciliation of private and public moral identity is that all debate on basic public issues should take place only within the framework of public reason, defined as the reason of equal citizens who as a collective body exercise final political and coercive power over one another in enacting laws and amending their constitution. That did not mean, as some of Rawls's critics thought, that people either should or could separate themselves from their deepest identities in proposing public policy.[65] But whatever might personally motivate them to take the stand they do, the norms of public reason impose two kinds of limitations on the role of doctrinal beliefs in public life. The first is substantive: only public reason, not comprehensive doctrine, can be allowed to define the "constitutional essentials" of the democratic polity. These included for Rawls such issues as who has the right to vote, what religions are to be tolerated, who is to be assured fair equality of opportunity or to hold property.[66] The second limitation is discursive. When citizens advocate for policy in the public forum, they should make their arguments not on the basis of their comprehensive beliefs but in the only terms that could appeal to their fellow citizens of other comprehensive beliefs, the standards of public reason. Here too Rawls was sometimes misunderstood. He was not saying that people should be forbidden to publicly argue their case in religious terms; such restrictions on speech would in any case be precluded by the very standards of public reason. He was in effect making recommendations to believers to argue policy in the only terms that had any hopes of persuading people of radically different beliefs, the shared norms that alone made a democratic polity workable.

In fundamental ways, the upshot of Rawls's political liberalism was a reaffirmation of American constitutionalism and its particular concern with religion, though with a decidedly limited accommodation of religious identity in the public sphere. Rawls's theoretical liberalism worked in effect to firmly ground both sides of the First Amendment: the separation of church and state in the public sphere and the free exercise of religion in the private. In doing so, he even rigidified the distinction between public and private spheres that the U.S. Supreme Court itself often blurred (with good reason, Kwame Anthony Appiah argued, because it was often difficult to sustain both logically and practically[67]). As for sources of difference other than comprehensive doctrines, Rawls's liberalism simply ignored identities, whether linguistic, ethnic, or cultural, that did not derive from them. The implication was that other differences were superficial in comparison to those expressing what the Protestant theologian Paul Tillich had called man's "ultimate concerns," and need not be taken into account politically. Rawls, then, accommodated identity only to the extent he thought he had to in order to make a secularly based individualistic liberalism workable in a religiously observant but pluralist society. In the end, the supposed limitation that liberalism had to be endorsed by religion was a demand on religion, not on liberalism. Liberalism only had to be acceptable to "reasonable" doctrines, a circular claim, since reasonableness was defined as either endorsing or not opposing liberalism. "Unreasonable" doctrines—any which placed appeal to an authority above public reason in all matters—did not have to be taken into political account. They should certainly be tolerated, but their refusal to endorse liberalism could be of no consequence in principle. Where they were dominant de facto, political liberalism was in any case impossible.

*   *   *

A similar point of view, but more concrete in approach and polemical in tone, informs Amy Gutmann's analysis of the place of collective identity in liberal politics. Its title, *Identity in Democracy*, was an even more direct acknowledgment of the salience the topic had assumed by the end of the millennium in American political theorizing; the two decades of identity politics since Rawls's book had done their work.

By the same token, however, Gutmann's judgment of the public role of identity was even more grudging theoretically and more skeptical politically. Democratic theory, she conceded, had long neglected the fundamental nature of mutual identification to human existence, employing the language of interest rather than identity. But while claiming that organizing politically on the basis of group identity was in itself neither bad nor good, she clearly believed the bad outweighed the good from a liberal point of view. "When identity groups put the group above opposition to injustice or the pursuit of justice," she asserted, "they are morally suspect. Identity groups do better when they offer mutual support and help combat injustice for disadvantaged people."[68] Identity was, politically speaking, mostly an instrumental good, useful as a weapon in defense of those who had been deprived of their individual rights by a society which had stigmatized them as a group. Too often, however, it became a noxious end in itself, subordinating justice and individual liberty to the collective's illiberal interests.

Gutmann was ambiguous about how fundamental collective identity was to the individual and consequently how important for democratic politics. On one hand she insisted that one's sense of identification with a group is independent of self-interest, since identity is bound up with "a sense of who people are"—a by-now standard identity formulation—rather than "what people want." Consequently, *"Democratic politics is bound up with both how people identify themselves and what they therefore want"*;[69] in other words, identity is itself an interest. She regarded this conclusion as a significant theoretical break with mainstream American political theorizing, which continued to rest largely on a material interest theory of individual motivation and an interest group theory of sociology. At the same time she thought collective identity only one possible form of individual identity, perhaps not even the most important one. "Group identification," she asserted, "is socially significant but not comprehensive of individual identity."[70] This was a far more latitudinarian view of identity than that held by most other multicultural theorists. Not everyone, she insisted, feels the need to identify strongly with groups, and when they do it is often to further individual aims. If group identification is valuable it is because "identity groups can significantly influence individual identities consistently with individual freedom." As an "inevitable byproduct of according individuals freedom of association" group identity is itself the creation of individualism.[71] And ultimately group identity is politically significant because "numbers count in democratic politics . . . and individuals are most influential in groups."[72]

Gutmann was rather less ambiguous about the compatibility of group identity with democracy than she was about its role in the economy of personal identity. "Identity groups are not the ultimate source of value in any democracy committed to equal regard for individuals," she asserted unequivocally. That is because "Equal regard for individuals—not identity groups—is fundamental to democratic justice. . . . If identity groups were the ultimate source of value, then they could subordinate the civic equality and equal freedom of persons (inside or outside the group) to their cause."[73] That concern was the lens through which she viewed the political bearing of the different kinds of group identity.

Her stance on accommodating illiberal cultural practices was unequivocally negative. It was the right, even the duty, of all citizens to oppose a minority culture's practices that violate the basic rights of its own members.[74] This meant that the liberal state should not only refuse financial support to institutions of a minority culture, like schools and religious courts, that treat women unequally but should outlaw practices like infibulation and cliteridectomy that violate their rights to bodily integrity and full sexual enjoyment, even if the women themselves acquiesce in such practices. Sensitivity to alien cultural practices does require paying respectful attention to them, and if ways can be found to honor them without compromising liberal principles, liberals should be flexible enough to accept them. When, for example, a group of doctors reached an agreement with Somali immigrant parents and their adolescent daughter to substitute a symbolic incision for full cliteridectomy, liberals were wrong to oppose it. On the other hand, it was equally wrong for the Supreme Court to uphold the right of the Pueblo to deny women who marry out of the tribe the same rights of inheritance as it grants to men who do so. The ruling, meant to protect Pueblo cultural identity, was in contravention of federal law, but more important it was a violation of the basic principle of equality.

The issue of women's rights had a pivotal role in Gutmann's stance toward cultural identity generally, as her uncharacteristic equivocation on the controversy over Muslim girls wearing headscarves in French schools suggested. Some liberals, she noted, protested the sexist symbolism of the scarf while others argued for allowing it on the grounds that the willingness of Muslim girls and their parents to be educated in public schools was a sign of cultural change. She did not come down on either side, but tellingly she did not even mention the liberal argument for allowing the headscarves on grounds of freedom of religious expression, the point most commonly made by liberal critics of the law. The omissions were connected: what mattered to her about the case was women's equality, not freedom of religion, and she apparently felt unable to judge whether allowing or forbidding the headscarf would better promote it. "Cultural survival in and of itself," she concluded, "is . . . not a human right, since the ultimate beneficiaries and claimants of human rights must be persons, and the price of enabling some cultures to survive may be violating human rights."[75] Though Gutmann cast her theoretical net more widely, her animus with regard to multiculturalism was inflected by the same concern Susan Moller Okin had more openly proclaimed in her influential article of a few years before, "Is Multiculturalism Bad for Women?"[76] The question was rhetorical. Many cultures, Okin argued, subordinated women, and even the more formally liberal ones were often patriarchal in their attitudes toward women in the private sphere. For liberal feminists like Gutmann and Okin multiculturalism was guilty unless proven innocent.

Gutmann did devote a whole chapter to religious identity, with the ambiguous title "Is Religious Identity Special?" Her answer was appropriately yes and no. Religious identity had historically played a central role in American life and politics, and religion is undoubtedly the most prominent manifestation of people's universal need for Rawlsian "moral identity." It should not, however, be more politically privileged than any other source of morality in a liberal society. Values need not be anchored in religious belief, and since the truth of their putative sources is unknowable, democracies can't be in the business of choosing amongst them. It is not respect for religion but respect for individual *conscience* that democracy presupposes in its commitment to the ideal of mutual respect entailed in the values of equality, liberty, and opportunity. Respect for conscience means "respect for the ethical identity of persons";[77] religion is only one of its forms. It therefore merits no more legal recognition than secular morality. If people are to be exempted from military service in case of a draft, claims of conscience should be treated no differently from refusal to serve on religious grounds: professing a recognized creed can't legitimately be a condition of conscientious objection. Beyond that and a few other examples, such as permitting exemptions from drug and alcohol laws for substance use in religious observances, government ought to intervene in matters of conscience as little as possible. Certainly it ought not support "faith based initiatives" by granting financial support to religious groups, even for general welfare purposes, which leads only to invidious distinctions and battles over legitimacy.[78] Because it tries to frame laws fair to all, democratic justice pushes a democracy away from routinely deferring to conscience, and it should only do so when respecting conscience is compatible with upholding a law's legitimate public purpose.[79] Then its exemptions should try to secure nondiscriminatory treatment for all—not, for example, making exceptions to substance use laws on behalf of religion only for mainstream religions, as often happened in the past.

If Gutmann was more sympathetic to ascriptive identity groups in politics than to religious identities, it was because historically those identified by traits they could not change, like race and sex, had been stigmatized by more powerful groups and denied equality. Identity groups organized around such traits are likely to be "justice friendly," fighting for the universal individual rights of the members, not special rights for the group. Even then, their political existence is justifiable primarily because they do work on behalf of rights that would not otherwise be done; their very existence is evidence of injustice in society.[80] The most appropriate way to fight for justice is for identity groups to make coalitions with justice-friendly majority associations, since the battle for equal rights is not theirs alone. Emphasizing their particular identity not only perpetuates social division but also undermines the very cause of universal rights for which they are fighting. In Gutmann's view the best way to fight for justice on behalf of difference was to fight against legitimizing difference.

*   *   *

Liberals, however, could have reasons other than the primacy of justice to oppose a significant role for collective identity in politics. If Kwame Anthony Appiah was, like Gutmann, deeply ambivalent about the political claims of collective identity, it was on behalf not of rights-based individualism but of a conception of individuality derived from John Stuart Mill, the fashioning and flourishing of a unique self, which for Appiah supported a strong version of individual identity. Appiah's primary philosophical concern was ethical rather than political, but his "ethics of identity" had direct implications for politics in its critique of the overweening claims of collective identity on the individual. Thus he rejected Charles Taylor's defense of enforcing French language instruction in Quebec schools for the purposes of preserving the province's cultural identity. "The right issue in deciding the primary language of instruction in state schools," he insisted, "is not the maintenance of a francophone ethnic identity—not *survivance*—but equality of citizenship in a francophone state." The choice of language of instruction inevitably promotes a particular culture, and mandatory French is perfectly reasonable as the democratic choice of a French-speaking majority, but the main consideration should be that it be done "within the framework of equal citizenship and a concern for the personal autonomy of citizens, not by notions of compulsory identities."[81] From this perspective, Appiah saw French instruction as necessary to offer all

Quebec residents the possibility of flourishing in a French-speaking environment and full participation in public life, not to coerce them to be French. If
Appiah's principle made no practical difference with regard to school language, its force is more obvious with respect to other aspects of Quebec's
language laws. Its original signage requirements, which mandated that commercial signs be exclusively in French, could only be explained as cultural
defense measures, and as such were unacceptable by Appiah's criterion. Government protection of group identities was permissible only if and to the
extent that it expanded the range of choices available to individuals for their
personal development.

*   *   *

Perhaps the most striking feature of the liberal debate about identity is not
that there were deep differences of opinion about the degree to which liberal
democracy should accommodate collective identities but that there was virtually unanimous agreement it should. Some versions, like Margalit's and Halbertal's, were very expansive, others, notably Gutmann's, were so restrictive as
to be almost—though never quite—prohibitive. Not surprisingly, the strongest defense of recognizing collective identity politically and legally came from
representatives of or spokespersons for substantial ethnic, cultural, or religious
minorities within other-majority states, minorities with well-defined ethnic or
religious identities. Margalit and Halbertal, though not representatives of the
minority religious cultures in Israel for whom they argued, only serve to bear
out the point. Their ultimate concern turned out to be defense of the survival
of a larger minority world cultural nation, the Jewish (but also liberal democratic) state.

The other notable feature of liberal accommodationism, however, even the
most expansive, was that it defended cultural identity in the name of individual identity. It was because collective identity was such an important dimension of individual identity that it had to be an integral part of liberalism.
Chandran Kukathas ingeniously defended the primacy of cultural identity on
the ground that the human need for collective identity offered a more secure
foundation for mutual recognition and universal rights than the idea of rationality, which had historically been identified exclusively with the West. The
real disagreements within liberalism were about just how important collective
identity was to individual identity, and this again tended to correlate with
ethnic and minority status everywhere but in the United States. American
political theorists of varying cultural backgrounds tended (with notable exceptions like Iris Marion Young) to be least impressed with the importance of

cultural identity for individual identity and more concerned about its dangers. For Amy Gutmann its importance was weak indeed, in part because of her feminism, which feared traditional cultural and religious claims that deprived women of rights, but also because as a classical American rights-based liberal she was unsympathetic to the idea of identity more generally. For Kwame Anthony Appiah, more receptive to the concept of identity because of his own background,[82] collective identity was suspect for the opposite reason: it jeopardized true individual identity. The debates of 1980–2000 did not resolve the question of the proper balance between collective identity and individual rights; nevertheless they did establish the issue as one of the central and ongoing problems for both political theory and political practice.

Chapter 8

The Contradictions of Postmodern Identity

> The purpose of history, guided by genealogy, is not to discover
> the roots of our identity but to commit itself to its dissipation.
> —Michel Foucault

> If the *modern* "problem of identity" was how to construct an
> identity and keep it solid and stable, the *postmodern* "problem
> of identity" is primarily how to avoid fixation and keep the
> options open.
> —Zygmunt Bauman

Despite deep differences in their amenability to identity politics, advocates
and skeptics of liberal multiculturalism were agreed on the reality of identity,
individual and collective. It was because they took it as a psychological and
social fact that it became a political issue. Some multicultural theorists, like
Charles Taylor, also intended their arguments on behalf of identity politics to
establish the philosophical necessity of identity. But in all cases the question
was what to do about it politically, not whether it existed.

That was the very premise challenged by a number of French thinkers
whose work began appearing in the mid-1960s. Grouped together under the
rubrics of poststructuralism and postmodernism, they were enthusiastically
taken up in the English-speaking world, first by eminent (and mostly male)
literary critics in prestigious American university departments of English
and comparative literature, then by increasing numbers of younger feminist
scholars in philosophy, literature, film, and women's studies in Britain and
Australia as well as the United States. In these sectors of the university
postmodernism[1] completely transformed the terms in which identity was
framed and contested. By the 1990s it had seriously discredited identity among
many of these scholars, a development with some resonance even beyond the

university. But their demolition work left them in a quandary, both theoretical and practical: as simultaneously political and social advocates, how other than as group identities could they describe and rally those for whom they fought? On behalf of whom, for example, were self-declared feminists advocating if not "women"? Postmodernists found it necessary to affirm—somehow—the very thing they wanted to deny.

French Theory and the "Dissipation" of Identity

Whatever the inaccuracies of a common label for the three, however different their intellectual formation, the theoretical projects of Jacques Lacan, Jacques Derrida, and Michel Foucault are legitimately linked together with regard to identity: all three centrally aimed to deny the concept philosophical legitimacy. On this issue, the history of twentieth-century Continental thought was repeating itself; with regard to identity, poststructuralism was existentialism redux. But while acknowledging their debts to Heidegger (less so to Sartre), the poststructuralists rightly claimed their originality and their radicalism vis-à-vis their predecessors. Where the existentialists had denied thing-like, permanent "being" to the self's identifications on the ground of the human subject's temporality and capacity for self-consciousness, the poststructuralists rejected the very possibility of a unified or "centered" self. It was not merely that a self could not have fixed identities; it was rather that there was no such thing as "the self."

This totalistic rejection, as it turned out, was never quite what it seemed. Poststructuralism and postmodernism emerged in the 1960s and 1970s in part as critiques of the reigning though bitterly contested and sclerotic "master narratives" of postwar France's political and intellectual life, bourgeois liberalism and orthodox Marxism, both of which embedded the subject in an objective scheme of historically predetermined "progress," a transcendental paradigm inherited from Christian eschatology.[2] In practice as well as in theory the socially conservative French liberalism of the Fourth and Fifth Republics and the rigid authoritarianism of the French Communist party were seen by many as the opposite of the freedom they claimed to stand for. Of the three figures, Foucault was the most directly concerned with the particular content of the liberal belief system he attacked, knowing himself an outcast and monster according to its norms, but the central philosophical target of all three was the objectivity, absoluteness, and totality as which all closed systems of thought represented themselves. Their political quietism during the early years—it would change in the wake of the upheavals of May 1968[3]—was a reflection of their belief that these systems were so dominant that they could not be overthrown. But beyond the false self theorized by these ideologies, poststructuralism did put forward the possibility of an authentic subjectivity, which it defined as the antithesis of identity.

The weapon poststructuralism wielded against identity was language. Lacan and Derrida adopted the structural linguistics of Ferdinand de Saussure,[4] driving it, each in his own way, to what they believed were its ultimately subversive conclusions for identity. Foucault, after a flirtation with Saussure, developed his own concept of "discourses," linguistic structures inextricably implicated in social and political power.

The theoretical ground of this "linguistic turn" in French thought was the contention that we only have our world in and through language; language is, to use a nonpoststructuralist formulation, the condition of the possibility of meaningfulness. Data of perception, desire, and experience are available to us only as interpreted through concepts, whose vehicle is a system of signs or symbols, whether phonetic, abstract, or pictographic. Symbolic structure, or language, furthermore, is governed by its own internal law. Upon analysis, that law can be seen to rule out the legitimacy of one particular use of language which, nonetheless, humankind has relied on historically to ground its norms—the use of language to name eternal truths, the unchanging essences of things, and above all, ultimate authorities.

Lacan had laid out the basics of his concept of identity before encountering Saussurian linguistics, in his famous article "The Mirror Stage as Formative of the Function of the I as Revealed by Psychoanalytic Experience." In its original version, he wrote of the child's desire to become one with its mother, and later with the image of its own wholeness and self-containment reflected in the mirror, as, in Hegelian terms "la nostalgie du tout," the longing for the whole, "the metaphysical mirage of universal harmony."[5]

The essay became widely known, however, only after Lacan had reinterpreted Hegelian identity in linguistic terms. "It is by way of this gift [of speech] that reality has come to man," he claimed; "The moment in which desire becomes human [as opposed to animal instinct] is also that in which the child is born into language."[6] Furthermore, the law of language, as Lacan put it with provocation aforethought, "has formed [man] in its image." What man can truly know and say is only what the law of language allows. Accordingly he reconceptualized Freudian phases of child development such as primary narcissism, as well as his own "mirror stage," as structures of language. More exactly they were possible but misleading deformations of the proper relationships between the elements of language. In developing this idea he took a radical step beyond Saussure.

The heart of Saussure's linguistic theory, as the poststructuralists interpreted it, is the arbitrariness of the relationship between the two parts of the linguistic sign through which we construct the world of meaning: the signifier, the sign's material element—sound, written mark, or image—and the signified, what the signifier refers to, its meaning. Crucially, signifiers have no intrinsic connection to what they signify; they get it by convention. Furthermore they get it only as part of a system of differences from other signifiers, which thus map a structure of meaning onto the world. A signifier like "red" has meaning only insofar as it signifies a color in relation to other terms that signify colors that are "not-red." The word itself is arbitrary—a rose by any other name—and the system of color signifiers could carve up the color range with ever finer-grained differences: red may exfoliate into rose, magenta, scarlet, and so on to as many shades as a group of language users care to distinguish. Meaning depends on difference, and difference by definition maps the chaotic boundlessness of experience into finite, though not permanently fixed, meanings.

But, in Lacan's interpretation of the stages of identity development, the child does not take the relationship between signifier and signified to be arbitrary, conventional, or delimited. In the mirror stage, where the self takes itself to be identical with the (false) self-image of totality and perfection it sees in the mirror, it does so via one particular sign, the phallus. The child wishes to be the object of the mother's desire, the living "mirror" that could reflect his perfection, since she is herself the absolute. But mother desires the father. The phallus, as the "most tangible element in the real of sexual copulation,"[7] is ideally suited to be the symbol of the mother's desire for him as the Other; it doesn't seem to be a purely arbitrary signifier. Thus for the child the signifier phallus *is* the signified, mother's desire incarnate; signifier and signified are one. So "If the desire of the mother *is* the phallus, the child wishes to be the phallus in order to satisfy that desire."[8] More accurately, this is not simply a wish for what is not; because his fantasy is of desire fulfilled, the child, in the mirror stage, takes itself as also being (one with) the (upright, powerful) phallus. Appropriately enough, Lacan named this level of language the imaginary stage. It is imaginary on two levels. First, the signifier is (falsely) identified with the signified, it *is* what it refers to; the phallus *is* the desire of the mother, thus to the child the very image of wholeness. And the "I" of the child, its ego or self, is one with the phallus, and therefore itself complete and perfect. As a violation of the truth of linguistic structure and the way language maps the world, through arbitrary signifiers and the finite meanings created by their difference, the imaginary of phallic identity can only be the language of fantasy and dreams.

The imaginary identity of self and the desire of the mother through the signifier of the phallus cannot, however, survive the intrusion of the father. In Lacan's interpretation of the Oedipus complex, the father, as the "real" possessor of the mother, comes to represent to the child the law, or rather the Law, objective and absolute, which forever separates him from mother and the fantasy of wholeness. The Law tells him what he must do, or not do, and what he must be in the world. The incest taboo is only its most immediately subjective aspect, the way the child first experiences it. Seen in terms of its objective function, however, "The primordial Law is . . . that which in regulating marriage ties superimposes the kingdom of culture on that of a nature abandoned to the law of mating." The law of kinship is both a microcosm of all cultural regulation and its foundation. It superimposes its absolute order through language; more exactly, Law is "identical with an order of language. For without kinship nominations no power is capable of instituting the order of preference and taboos"[9] that constitute lineage through the generations. Kinship "nominations" are not just kinship names but kinship "appointments," in another meaning of the French word, norms decreeing permissible, and impermissible, sexual and marital unions.

Lacan called this level of language the symbolic order. In it, signifier and signified are separated, but only partially. Its key signifier is "the name of the father . . . [,] the support of the symbolic function which, from the dawn of history, has identified his person with the figure of the law."[10] Signifier and signified are separated insofar as the name of the father is consciously understood as "standing for" the law, separated too insofar as the child is not one with the name of the father but is commanded by it. But separation is only partial in that *only* father stands for the law and that the law his name stands for is unchanging and absolute, wholly determining what the child is and yet must also become. In a strict sense, the name of the father is the child's identity. "Symbols in fact envelop the life of man in a network so total that they join together, before he comes into the world, those who are going to engender him 'by flesh and blood'; so total that they bring to his birth . . . the shape of his destiny; so total that they give the words that will make him faithful or renegade, the law of the acts that will follow him . . . even beyond his death."

"Unless," Lacan concluded, "he attain the subjective bringing to realization of being-for-death."[11] The "unless" points to the way out of this envelopment, and to the fact that for Lacan the symbolic order, no less than the imaginary, creates a false, alienated identity. The child may no longer "be" the phallus, as he fantasizes in the imaginary order, but in the symbolic order he does believe that there is an absolute set of "somethings" that he both is and

yet must strive to become. Only the (Heideggerian) awareness that his inevitable death is the personal destiny he cannot avoid embracing can free him from
the false objectivity of the symbolic order. He is then aware of himself as
having to create his own meanings. In linguistic terms, breaking the falsely
univocal link between the signifier (the name of the father) and the signified
(cultural norms and identities) he becomes, like Humpty Dumpty, the "master of the signifier." He can make signifiers mean what he wants them to, even
if initially he wasn't the master of the signified in which "his being took on its
original form."[12] For Lacan, as for Heidegger (at first), such liberation was not
social or political but personal and internal.[13] The purpose of psychoanalysis
was to reveal to the analysand his entrapment in the unconscious fantasies
of his imaginary union with his own phallus-mother and the unconscious
constraints of his thralldom to the norms dictated by the name of his own
father. Both created false identities, an oxymoron in fact, since from the point
of view of the structure of language, all fixed identities are false. The ends of
Lacanian psychoanalysis intend the end of identity.

*   *   *

That identity made the transition from technical psychological term to ordinary language is not hard to understand; it was already part of common speech
in a related usage. It is, however, a nice irony of twentieth-century thought
that one of its most deliberately recondite terms became popular in journalism
and social commentary. By the end of the century, writers were "deconstructing" everything from political speeches to television advertisements. In retrospect the popularity of the word may seem less remarkable because of its
linguistic connection to a much more familiar one: texts could be "deconstructed" presumably because, like any other human artifact, they had been
"constructed." And while far from the arcana of Jacques Derrida's enterprise,
popular usage was based on a valid intuition about his purpose: to deconstruct
a text meant to show its incoherencies, biases, or special pleading, to undo, or
destroy its argument.[14]

What Derrida wanted to deconstruct, however, was not just any misleading
or deceptive utterance. His target was the Word, in the sense of the evangelist
John's Logos, the word of God, which created and named—brought into being
by naming—the things of the world. What existed had thus been ordained by
God, existing by necessity. Logos, however, need not be of divine origin. In the
modern age it has been replaced by other, secularized "god-terms"—Nature,
Reason, Humanity—which purport to be the source of eternal, necessary
truths. Each of these words is a signifier intending what Derrida called the

"transcendental signified," absolute meaning, beyond local time and space. Whatever its name, the "transcendental signified" is never just understood as a descriptive term; it is taken as "the voice of the other . . . as commandment."[15] It fuses the description of what is with the norm of what ought to be, as for example in the double meaning of the word "natural": "natural" refers both to what is supposedly eternal and objective because it is not man-made, and to the supposedly objective standard it therefore decrees, to which right behavior must conform, as in the command "be natural." Derrida labeled this mode of language, which harbors an entire metaphysics, "logocentrism." Logocentrism is the "metaphysics of presence," the claim that a signifier's meaning is self-evidently and wholly contained within it, because univocal and absolute meanings are guaranteed by the transcendental signified, the Logos that decreed them.[16] When Adam, in the image of God, named the flora and fauna of the Garden of Eden, he also by that act fixed their distinct, separate, and unchanging natures.

The central argument of deconstruction is that all linguistic efforts to name the source or repository of such absolute truth must fail. Furthermore, they demonstrate their failure through the very language with which they attempt to declare it. Such failure is inevitable because of the structure of language.

On the most obvious level, failure is the consequence of Saussure's thesis that the system of differences that constitute language is conventional. That means that the way language maps reality is only one of many possible ways. That claim all by itself relativizes the signified, because conventions can change over time. "If words and concepts receive meaning only in sequences of differences," Derrida concluded, "one can justify one's language and one's choice of terms only within an historical strategy. The justification can never be absolute and definitive."[17] But the possibility of historical change in the way language carves up reality through difference was just the beginning of the argument; Derrida's deconstruction of the metaphysics of presence went deeper, into the implications of difference itself.

Difference (or *différance*, the neologism Derrida coined to mark it as an active principle) is the condition of meaningfulness; it is the breaking up of the undifferentiated, ungraspable "all," the cosmos of Genesis "without form and void," into finite units of meaning, demarcated by names that indicate "this and not that." *Différance* is the "formation of form" itself,[18] the unavoidable principle of the articulation of "everythingness" into distinct things. Because any one signifier is only an element in a structure of difference, its full meaning can't be given by what it ostensibly refers to, but only in reference to the whole chain of signs of which it is a part. Defining anything entails an implicit contrast with other meanings which locate and delimit its range of reference. It is not enough, then, to point to something and name it in order to define it, since its very meaning is dependent on those things which it is defined as not being. Any signifier necessarily also refers to all the other signifiers from which it is differentiated. Hence the full meaning of any signified is not and cannot be "present" in its signifier alone. The meaning is "dispersed," across a whole chain of signifiers. To put the paradox in terms of identity, the meaning of a sign (word) is never fully identical with itself.

To complicate matters, a signifier can be part of more than one chain of signification. It can give rise to a host of associated meanings that are not even part of the original signifying chain, even by something so crude as its similarity in sound to a word that is conventionally part of a wholly different chain of meanings. The rebus, which uses unrelated images to represent words or parts of words whose names sound like them, operates on just such a principle. From the point of view of personal identity the most striking example Derrida offered was the deconstruction of the proper name. Presumably, proper names "mean," that is, refer to, only one thing, their bearer; the full signified is thus present in—wholly contained within—the signifier. The name unmistakably and only identifies the person (leaving aside the complication that some people bear the same name). But proper names may signify other things—animals (Wolf), physical features (Linda), occupations (Taylor), locations (Frankfurter, which opens yet another chain of meanings)—that may lead it to a host of associations about the person to whom it "properly" belongs, so that he cannot claim its identity with him. "The stratification of a signifier," Derrida argued, "may thus become very complex and go beyond the empirical consciousness linked to their immediate use. . . . [T]he structure of the signifier may continue to operate not only on the fringes of the potential consciousness but according to the causality of the unconscious. Thus the name . . . is always caught in a chain or system of differences. . . . The literal meaning does not exist, its 'appearance' is a . . . function . . . in the system of differences and metaphors."[19] The associations a name can give rise to are of two kinds: the objective potentialities in the name's various signifying chains that the bearer himself does not intend and may never even think of, and connections which are in the bearer's mind but which he might not be consciously aware of. Either way, he is not in full possession of his own name, nor his name of him; it makes him subject both to the associations of others, and thus how they might see him, and to his own unconscious associations. "There is not a single signified," Derrida concluded, "that escapes . . . the play of signifying references that constitute language. . . . The signified concept is never present in and of itself in a sufficient presence that would refer only to itself."[20]

An even more sweeping consequence of this fact for personal identity is that the self or "I" can have no central core designation, even to itself, because it too is indefinitely dispersed across a range of possible meanings. Any signifier that ostensibly identifies a person to himself and others also leads to a possibly endless chain of meanings, including the meanings it wants to exclude. The Jew, defined in part as a non-Christian, necessarily has Christianity as part of his self-definition. The self becomes "de-centered" just like any other signifier, subject to the eternal play of signifying references beyond the self's control.

But while the deconstructive argument to this point shows that the full meaning of any signifier is not present in it, it doesn't yet show that to name the transcendental signified in particular was to make a false or impossible claim. The "point" of the *transcendental* signified is that it is more than the element of a finite totality (like a color set) but supposedly the very name of infinite totality, like "Nature," which could define the absolute nature of everything. There is one more crucial step in the argument.

Signifiers that attempt to name a transcendental signified, Derrida argued, always appear in binary opposition to another signifier which they purport to exclude as lesser or inferior: God versus the Devil, good versus evil, light versus darkness, the natural versus the unnatural. "An opposition of metaphysical concepts," Derrida argued, "is never [merely] the face to face of two terms but a hierarchy and an order of subordination."[21] The crucial argument of deconstruction is that the effort to demarcate the higher term by its exclusion of the lower undermines the higher by inevitably including the lesser as part of its definition. A much-simplified example would be the effort to define the "human" by contrasting it with its debased and derogatory opposite, the "inhuman." Since, however, "inhuman" behavior is necessarily the behavior of those also described as human—the term would have no normative weight otherwise—the binary opposition undoes itself by making the inhuman itself all too human. Derrida's own deconstructions were far more complex, aimed at what he took to be the most important "god-terms" of classical philosophy and modernity. In modern times our ultimate authority had become "nature," which according to the founding father of modern interiority, Rousseau, speaks to us in the authentic impulses of the heart. But Rousseau's effort to prove that (heterosexual) copulation was the only "natural" (hence normative) form of sexuality, because it created the experience of human wholeness in the timeless fusion of self and other in sexual climax, foundered on his admission that actual coitus had never provided him with the sense of perfection and fulfillment he had achieved in fantasy while masturbating. Unhappily, but inevitably, he found himself falling back on masturbatory fantasy even during sex with a real other. The supposed sublimity of physical union was thus deconstructed by the ineradicable intrusion of masturbatory fantasy, where alone perfection and wholeness proved possible.

Deconstruction was not intended, however, except by way of example, as an attack against any specific idols of the tribe, but on idolatry as such. Or better, to use the political metaphor Derrida chose, on monarchy, more exactly, absolute monarchy. "It is the determination of Being as presence, or as beingness," he wrote, "that is interrogated by the thought of *différance*. . . . *Différance* instigates the subversion of every kingdom . . . which makes it obviously and infallibly dreaded by everything within us that desires a kingdom, the past or future presence of a kingdom."[22] The metaphor is as close as Derrida got to politics in his early work, but it clearly signaled the liberatory intent of deconstruction. Without the comfort of absolute rulers, by which Derrida meant not actual human authorities but the "transcendental signifieds that they appeal to in order to legitimate their rule" (as in "the *divine right* of kings"), we have to rule ourselves, that is, take full responsibility for the way our signifiers define and normativize our reality—a democratic as well as a Sartrean conclusion.

*   *   *

"The purpose of history, guided by genealogy, is not to discover the roots of our identity," Michel Foucault wrote of his early methodological procedure, "but to commit itself to its dissipation."[23] To "dissipate" identity was indeed his life's work. His first major book, *The History of Madness*, argued that conceptualizations of "the mentally ill" had changed over the centuries as they were "deployed," in the military metaphor he favored, to support changing regimes of social and political power. Saussure's structural linguistics furnished the theoretical skeleton for his next book, *The Order of Things*, which traced changes in the "epistemes" or underlying structures of knowledge in a number of disciplines from the Renaissance to the present in terms of changing relationships between signifier and signified. It was only in his work of the mid-1970s, *Discipline and Punish* and *The History of Sexuality*, volume 1, that Foucault fully developed his unique conceptions of "discourse" and "power/ knowledge," which attacked identity on two fronts: by causally explaining particular identity categories as the tools social power fabricates and employs to establish its domination, and simultaneously extending that explanation to the emergence in modernity of the identity category of "the individual."

A "discourse" is, on the descriptive level, a linguistic scheme that stipulates the boundaries of some subject area or domain of experience. It involves a set of rules and categories, not explicitly spelled out, which define the appropriate ways to talk about that domain and the kinds of knowledge relevant to it. In his most explicitly theorized example, Foucault related how the "discourse of sexuality" had changed over time in Europe, from a religiously based "symbolics of blood" concerned with rules of legitimate marriage and purity of blood lines, to the Victorian "science of sexuality" concerned with distinguishing "healthy" from "unhealthy" sexual practices in the interests of procreative productivity.[24]

These discourses are not just repositories of knowledge or research agenda for discovering it. They produce and use knowledge to establish and institutionalize social and political power. The categories they employ and the questions they instigate serve the needs of historically dominant groups in society, though they are not merely "ideologies" in the crude sense of mere masks for self-interest. They are the most effective because the least obvious tools of power. The science of sexuality in the nineteenth century explored and tried to heal psychologically and physiologically real problems of sexual "dysfunction." But the medical obsession with masturbation and female hysteria, among other sexual difficulties, showed that the definition of dysfunction was "motivated by one basic concern: to ensure population, to reproduce labor capacity, to perpetuate the form of social relations: in short, to constitute a sexuality that is economically useful and politically conservative."[25] The science of sexuality, concerned to promote vigorous bodies and successful procreative sex, was thus an agency of the productionist worldview of the modern commercial and industrial bourgeoisie, couched in impersonal and objective terms, and aimed, in the first instance, at the bourgeoisie itself.

Within the broad abstractions of discourse and power/knowledge, the specific discourses at the heart of Foucault's interest were those of the "human" or "clinical" sciences, such as penology, criminology, psychology, psychiatry, and medicine, all resting on norms of personal and social behavior or biological functioning. But it was Foucault's insight into the *way* these discourses normalized some behaviors, classified others as deviant and attempted to correct them, that both depended on and implicated identity. In order to effectively apply their disciplinary "technology" to the criminal offender, penology and criminology had to learn who the offender "was," how he worked. To do so they constructed, through penal theory and practice, the social type, or identity, of "the delinquent," conceptualized as one manifestation of "an overall phenomenon of criminality . . . found in *quasi-natural classes*, each endowed with its own characteristics and requiring a specific treatment." The delinquent is not, or not just, someone who has committed a discrete delinquent act; he is "linked to it by a whole bundle of complex threads (instincts, drives, tendencies, character)."[26] In other words, he *is* "a delinquent," in the Sartrean sense of the copula verb; his dereliction arises from his identity. But criminology does not understand such an assignment of identity metaphysically; it naturalizes delinquency by locating it in the criminal's biological constitution. The delinquent can thus be studied, analyzed, manipulated, and altered like any other object of science. More accurately, Foucault pointed out, deviancy is only *quasi*-natural; the qualification points to the way the discourse of deviancy preserves the bourgeoisie's characteristic moralistic insistence on free will and culpability while at the same time making deviancy a deterministic causal force. The discourses of deviancy, in other terms, reify behavior into fixed syndromes or patterns that impose themselves on the subject in a unique version of bad faith—the delinquent is wholly determined yet completely responsible.

But in Foucault's overall scheme the falseness of identity is not limited to specific deviant behaviors. The modern idea of "the individual" is itself a false identity, the theoretical foundation on which all modern subcategories depend. "Individualization," the literal creation of the individual through a discourse of "individualism," is the basic operating procedure of what he called the "disciplinary society," a double entendre covering both the authoritarianism of modern society and the social disciplines through which its coercive power is exercised. The concept of the individual was invented during the eighteenth century by the need of society to find effective methods of inculcating and enforcing its productionist imperative. Thus for the prison to accomplish its goal of punishing criminal deviancy penology required "an individualization of sentences, in accordance with the particular characteristics of each criminal. . . . Individualization appears as the ultimate aim of a precisely adapted code."[27] Criminal behaviors had to be differentiated and understood causally in their specificity so that the right kind of punitive correction could be applied to the individual criminal. Disciplinary training, however, extended beyond the penal system to the institutions that formed and policed character from the beginning—the family, the school, the workplace—each governed by its own body of disciplinary knowledge, all intending the same normative outcome. Historically, training of this sort represented the very essence of the Enlightenment, the ideological origin of modernity. "The two great 'discoveries' of the eighteenth century," Foucault claimed, "—the progress of societies and the geneses of individuals—were perhaps correlative with the new techniques of power."[28]

In nakedly hierarchical and militaristic societies, there are relatively few "individuals," people with a (positively) marked individual character, which is identified with elevated lineage or heroic deeds. In the disciplinary society, where power is exercised on all anonymously through the disciplines, everyone is individualized, though those that still need to be fashioned or once more brought into line, like the child or deviant, more overtly so than those who have already been normalized. The individual, Foucault concluded, is not simply, as Marxists would have it, an ideological fiction but "a reality fabricated by this specific technology of power that I have called 'discipline.'"[29]

At this stage, Foucault failed to notice, or in any case to remark, an incoherency in his analysis that he would only later rectify. Individualization, as he described it in *Discipline and Punish*, was the creation of an individualized *type*, not of unique individuals. Diagnoses and punishments were not adapted, as he misleadingly wrote, to "the individual" as such, but to the category an individual belonged to. "Individualization" was in fact the opposite of the "creation of individuals." Looking back at his entire project in his activist mode some years later, he made a crucial distinction between the "government of individualization" and "everything that makes individuals truly individual."[30] Regimes of power objectify human beings and transform them into "subjects," who are ostensibly the agents of their own actions but in reality are subjected to the scripts of disciplinary formation, externally imposed though also internalized. Power creates individuals with collective identities. Those who resist authority and struggle against it assert "the right to be different": that is what makes them truly individual. In this formulation, the true individual, however, like Sartre's good faith consciousness, can only be defined negatively, as the absence of identity.[31]

Deconstructing Concrete Identities

Postmodernism and Female Identity

"FRENCH FEMINISM"

Undoubtedly the greatest impact of postmodernism on specific categories of collective identity was in its application to women. Lacan and Derrida themselves wrote separate works on the "problem" of woman's identity. A group of French women thinkers including most prominently Julia Kristeva, Luce Irigaray, and Hélène Çixous, the first two of whom began as Lacanian psychoanalysts, developed their own theories of female identity applying and extrapolating from Derrida's and Lacan's concepts, subverting them where they thought necessary.[32] Their work, introduced to the English-speaking academic world in 1980 under the rubric "French Feminism,"[33] strongly influenced a cadre of feminist scholars in departments of women's studies, literature, philosophy, and film not only in the English-speaking world but in Italy, Germany, and elsewhere.

The rubric itself became the object of controversy. As other writers acerbically pointed out, the three ostensibly foremost proponents of "French Feminism" were not only not part of mainstream political feminism in France but two of them had expressly disavowed being feminists.[34] These critics suggested, some more and some less charitably, that Anglo-American enthusiasm for the esoteric language of poststructuralism served as a "discourse of personal legitimation" for scholars in women's studies, who were thus able to enter into dialogue with the currently academically prestigious, and male, Continental philosophers.[35] The real focus of the controversy, however, was something that also engaged feminists who were not partisans of French theory, the question, as it became infamously termed in feminist debates in the 1980s, of "essentialism": was there or was there not a female "essence," a permanent core female identity?[36] If the debate became agitated, even quite testy, at times, it was because looming over its often abstract terms was the fraught issue of political activism. The opponents of essentialism argued either that the effort to discover and promote a timeless female identity bred political quietism, because it turned attention away from the social constraints on women effected by the patriarchal construction of woman's identity, or that any essentialist definition of "woman" inevitably privileged some women and excluded others.

It was inevitable that Lacan and Derrida should take up the issue of female identity, the psychoanalyst for obvious reasons, Derrida because of the place of the feminine in the Western transcendental imagination. For both, the answer to the question of whether there was a female identity was an obvious "no," but with a final contradictory twist.

In Lacan's general account of development the child is not sexed. And in principle, given the ontological bearing of Lacan's basic categories, there is no reason that the little girl could not identify herself in the imaginary stage with the phallus and later with the name of the father. Adult women, as Lacan said with typical double entendre, "are free to situate themselves" at the "pole where man is situated. Everyone knows there are phallic women"—just as men can situate themselves on the side of women.[37] But these are the exceptions, because from the beginning, the ontological meaning of the phallus has been falsely identified by parent and child alike with its concrete signifier, the male sexual organ.

In practice then, it is only male children who go on to identify with the name of the father, its social roles and obligations. Only males likewise identify with the father's prerogatives and powers, as agents, as subjects rather than objects of society. Men may not "be" the phallus, as they fantasized in the imaginary stage, but by virtue of having a penis they alone exercise the "phallic function" in the symbolic stage; they embody (so they fantasize) the active principle, totality *in ovo*. In a significant shift from earlier work, Lacan now claimed that it was the symbolic sphere rather than the imaginary that is the conceptual basis of what humans made into God.[38] Law, as that which commands man, conceptually transcends him, whereas desiring mother's desire is only the desire of another finite being. Man's identification with the phallic function was Lacan's version of the biblical notion that man was made in the image of God.

But this idea of himself proves to be the male's downfall in sex and love. Reaching God, according to Lacan, is in actuality what love intends. "I situate God," Lacan wrote somewhat grandly, "as the third party in this business of human love,"[39] because what lovers strive for is totality through oneness. The physical union of two finite humans, however, does not add up to infinity; there must be "something more" if the *jouissance* of sex[40] is to achieve it. Unfortunately for the male, he is not equipped to realize this "more"; the female is.

Exercising the phallic function, man, in his prerogative and power, approaches woman. But the identification of the phallus with the penis makes fulfillment doubly impossible for him. First, by literalizing the phallic function as the physical role of the penis, the male has undermined his identity as potency incarnate because he has made himself vulnerable to the threat of its loss. Castration (symbolized by detumescence) is the inevitable signifier of nonbeing when the power to achieve wholeness is identified with an intrinsically vulnerable physical organ. "There is no chance for a man to have *jouissance* of a woman's body," Lacan wrote, "otherwise stated, for him to make love, without castration, in other words, without something that says no to the phallic function." [41] And second, because in the phallic function he nonetheless takes himself to be more than the woman, he can desire a woman only as "a" woman. He desires her, that is, as what Lacan called the "object a," *an* other (*autrui*)—different from himself, to be sure, but in lower case, finite and limited. Union with such a being can't raise sex to a level beyond the physical enjoyment of another body.

To the extent that a woman thinks of herself as a man thinks of her, she has conceptualized herself as being "not-whole" in relation to his completeness. That is what, to both men and women, "woman" generally signifies. "When any speaking being whatsoever situates itself under the banner 'women' it is on the basis of the following—that it grounds itself as being not-whole in situating itself in the phallic function."[42] But it is precisely woman's not-wholeness that paradoxically allows her the possibility of real *jouissance*, of sublimity in sexual union. Her desire, unlike the man's, is not aimed simply at *an* other but at *the* Other with a capital O, the "object A" (*Autrui*), that is,

the male Other as absolute. "It is in the opaque place of *jouissance* of the Other
. . . that the Supreme Being is situated," he wrote, referring to Aristotle's
conception of the divine. "It is insofar as her *jouissance* is radically Other that
woman has more of a relationship to God" than anything Aristotle conceived
a man to be capable of in his pursuit of the supreme Good.[43]

Lacan would seem here to be describing woman's mythology about men.
At the same time, however, he spoke as if the fiction of woman's essential
nonbeing was not just the subjective belief of the phallicly mystified (men
and women) but the God's-eye view of the truth of women. "There's no
such thing as Woman," he declared, "Woman with a capital W indicating
the universal. There's no such thing as Woman because, in her essence—I've
already risked using that term, so why should I think twice about using it
again?—she is not-whole." Lacan clearly reveled in the contradiction of
denying woman a universal identity while simultaneously proclaiming it.
But whose contradiction was it? Woman's "essence" couldn't exist from the
demystified standpoint of the psychoanalyst; as Lacan himself amusingly put
it, "There are men who are just as good as women" in situating themselves
on the side of the not-whole.[44]

Clinging to an essentialist definition of woman seemed to betray Lacan's
lingering yearning for the possibility of wholeness, even if it was not available
to men. Women alone, though of course only by deifying men, could experience the bliss of union with God in sexuality. Despite his God-talk, he mocked
those who ascribed to him conventional religious belief but nonetheless
insisted that "God" was a valid signifier, if one whose meaning was not as yet
specifiable. "I believe," he declared, "in the *jouissance* of woman insofar as it
is extra (*en plus*), so long as you put a screen in front of this 'extra' until I
have been able to properly explain it."[45] As God was a signifier for the mystic
source of wholeness, woman was simultaneously the signifier of non-
wholeness—but also, because of her possibility of sexual fulfillment with the
male, of the longed-for promise of the experience of wholeness. Lacan could
not, or at any rate did not, wholly escape the metaphysical dream of absolute
identity.

*   *   *

The lure of woman in the Western male imagination, as Derrida took her up
for deconstructive analysis, is similarly the lure of the absolute. But he
approached the sexual couple from a point of view the reverse of Lacan's,
whom he charged with "phallogocentrism," elevating the phallus into a transcendental signified. More often it is man's fusion with the idealized woman—

woman as absolute—that is cast in Western literature and philosophy as the experience of human wholeness.[46] Goethe's "eternal feminine," which Derrida explicitly cited[47]—the lure that draws "us" ever upward—is perhaps the most famous modern image of the female as "transcendental signified." Derrida's discussion of female identity focused on Nietzsche's many contradictory statements about woman's relationship to "truth," but it was in the run-up to them that he made his most direct statement. Woman, he wrote, alluding to the call of the Sirens in *The Odyssey*, seduces from a distance. Distance is in fact the very element of her power, because were man to actually possess her, he would be disabused. He would discover that she is not the absolute after all but "non-identity, a non-figure, a simulacrum"—in deconstruction's central concept, "distance itself," the very emblem of finitude and nonpresence.[48] Woman is this emblem precisely in virtue of the promise of presence or totality that she seems to hold out, which when disappointed makes her the figure of its opposite.

In order to preserve her promise, then, the man must maintain "a distance from distance."[49] He must not let himself become aware of the true meaning of woman's seductive distance, of what it would tell him if he let it: that she—the promise she holds—is only a mirage of presence. He must blind himself to the truth of her metaphysical distance while yet holding on to woman's physical or emotional distance as a finite challenge to be overcome, a challenge that indeed has to be there for her to appear worthy of the quest. It is the promise of woman and its inevitable disappointment that, according to Derrida, underlies Nietzsche's contradictory depictions of woman as truth and lie, active and passive, giving herself wholly and taking total possession. It is not possible to decide on which side his texts finally come down because they don't; the contradiction stands, irresolvable.

This is true, however, only of Nietzsche's texts. From deconstruction's point of view, the contradiction would seem fully resolvable—by rejecting its premises. "Woman," Derrida declared "is not a determinable identity. . . . There is no such thing as the essence of woman." It cannot be said that the truth or lie of woman is "undecidable" if in fact "There is no such thing as a woman, as a truth in itself of woman in itself."[50] "Identity," "essence," and "truth" here don't refer to just any definition one might try to pin on women, like "compassionate" or "flighty" or "maternal." Derrida's framework is always the human desire for the absolute. For the Romantic, to be one with "woman" is tantamount to achieving the kingdom of heaven. Man's contradictory experience of woman comes about because he ascribes to her a totality that she—no more than anyone or anything else—cannot be. Once "she" is deconstructed, there is no more promise, and therefore no more lie.

The contradiction of *Derrida*'s essay, however is that he, like Lacan, did ascribe an identity to woman, in fact the same one. Woman, he had written, *is* nonidentity. In denominating her so, in his own voice, he ignored the strictures of *différance* and, like Lacan, remained within the undeconstructed male imagination of the female. While there is nothing in Derrida comparable to Lacan's outright statement of belief in—hope for—the "*jouissance* of woman," woman can be the *essence* of nonidentity only to the disappointed believer who nonetheless still holds on to the eternal feminine.

*   *   *

Despite its "regressive" contradictions, the intended thrust of the poststructuralist argument was clearly against the possibility of an essential female identity. It would seem likely that anyone adopting its methods would be led to the same conclusion. But the ambiguities of poststructuralism produced a more complicated legacy. If it seems ironic that a Lacanian psychoanalyst made the strongest and most notorious case of any feminist writer for an essential woman's identity,[51] it is an irony that could only have come out of a Lacanian reading of language.

Luce Irigaray took at face value the idea of women's exclusion from the symbolic order of language, and its identification with male dominance of social categories and resources. But for her that identification cut two ways. The symbolic order is not just male-dominated; it is more fundamentally, male-inflected. Its social categories are not, as Lacan had at least seemed to be saying, the universal laws of social organization, its ways of rendering the experience of time and space not objective; all are specifically male conceptualizations created and enforced by a patriarchal society. Above all its ways of articulating sexuality, the body, and male and female identities, are a masculine construct on the template of male sexual experience. The symbolic order was actually a "phallocratic" order.[52] The dilemma for women is that, while the symbolic order does not represent their experience, they have no other language in which to render it. They are trapped in the symbolic order's domination of meaning.

It is totalitarian domination because it controls language at every possible level, not least, for the philosopher, the highest-level philosophical abstractions. In calling the symbolic a phallocratic order Irigaray meant, literally, to root it in the male sexual body as its causal origin. Historically, Western philosophical concepts—which amounted to the "discourse on discourse" because it set the law for discourses in all other spheres—made up what she called the discourse of "the Same." Its import is to "*reduce all others to the economy of the Same.*"[53] While not entirely clear, except in its consequences for sexuality, the "economy of the Same" has a number of implications for language and logic. Utterances and signifiers can have only one meaning; ambiguity and irony are ruled out.[54] The "discursive logic" of Sameness—the logical laws of identity and noncontradiction—demands that there be clear opposition between terms such as the empirical and the transcendental, percept and concept, matter and thought.[55] Sameness also has consequences for social relations. "Proper" meanings entail the idea of propriety of meanings, hence property in meanings, that is, ideas of ownership or possession.[56] All these terms are hierarchical, since men own meaning, and reduce women to inferiority or exclude them altogether. They do so ultimately because the "male syntax" they embody excludes the possibility of articulating feminine experience, based as it is on male phallic sexuality.

In one sense there is nothing startlingly new philosophically in the way Irigaray thought of the body and its relationship to meaning. It combines Heidegger's notion of Dasein as being-in-the-world, the idea that the world becomes meaningful only in relation to Dasein's intentional directedness toward it, with Maurice Merleau-Ponty's specification that our bodies are an animating source of that directedness, constituting, for example, our sense of orientation in space, or our notions of relative size and speed.[57] But her emphasis on the role of sexuality is new, even if it had real kinship with the anatomical determinism of Freud that she scathingly rejected because of its male bias and biological drive motivation. What she was arguing is that the sexual body is a crucial source of human orientation to self, other, and world, and its modes of relating also have great impact on spheres other than sexuality. More fundamentally than the partisans of feminine difference who focused on the significance of maternity, Irigaray, though she included maternity too, made the sexed body in its entirety central to human identity.

To put it with a (masculine?) simplicity alien to Irigaray's more allusive language, men's literal-mindedness stems from the single-minded goal orientation of male sexual desire: possession, penetration, climax. That is what sex "means" in the symbolic order that dictates what "is" and ought to be. Men see women only within that framework as objects of desire with no sexual subjectivity of their own. Women's sexual modalities, however, are different because their bodies are different, and permit—or dictate—other kinds of sensual experiences and relationships. Irigaray's notorious origination of those modalities from the vaginal lips was meant literally, not as a literary trope, but it intended much more than organ pleasure. Because the lips meet, woman is always caressing herself; unlike men, whose desire is aroused by sight, her primary pleasure is in touch. But touch is more than physical; it is a way of being even with the immaterial, as evidenced in idiomatic expressions concerning emotions and thought that employ it, such as "being in touch" with feelings. Furthermore, her vaginal lips allow woman to experience herself as two as well as one, more accurately, "She *is neither one nor two*. Rigorously speaking, she cannot be identified either as one person or as two."[58] Consequently she can entertain multiple, even contradictory thoughts and ideas. "'She' is indefinitely other in herself. . . . Hers are contradictory words, somewhat mad from the standpoint of reason. . . . [I]f 'she' says something, it is not, it is already no longer, identical with what she means. What she says is never identical with anything, moreover; rather it is contiguous. *It touches (upon).*"[59] Women can hold to one meaning while playing and experimenting with other possibilities, see different sides of things simultaneously. Their mental processes are not constrained by logic. It is not surprising, Irigaray wrote, that men, thinking only in the "linear" terms of logic and cause and effect, judge women as whimsical, capricious, flitting incoherently from thought to unrelated thought, as finally incomprehensible.

That the vaginal lips touch without penetrating or incorporating one another also conditions women's orientation to personal relationships. Women are inclined to a side-by-side nearness that fosters nonpossessive relations with others, yet is so intimate that it also blurs the line between selves. "Ownership and property are doubtless quite foreign to the feminine," she claimed. "At least sexually. But not *nearness*. Nearness so pronounced that it makes all discrimination of identity, and thus all forms of property, impossible."[60] In the feminine modality, the sexual couple is both one and two, hence neither one nor two.

This is a picture of woman's identity that, like that of Lacan or Derrida, at the same time denies identity. But Irigaray's contradictoriness isn't of the same order. The characteristics that make up woman's nonidentity, her nonidentification with any one idea, role, or designation, her ability to blur self-boundaries without compromising her integrity, are solidly anchored in her body, her physical being-in-the-world. Her nonidentity is the immaterial expression of her material identity. Irigaray did try to have things both ways. Since women are one as well as two, they are as capable as men of linear thinking. On the other side, however, it is also possible to separate the processes Irigaray attributed to women from their bodily integument and find them operating in men too; that is precisely what Julia Kristeva did. Critics, women not least, found Irigaray's descriptive as well as causal claims fanciful, implausible, or unprovable at best, dead wrong or a sellout to patriarchal ways of thinking at worst. Some of her language suggests she harbored doubts about the organ specificity she credited for woman's identity. What she did not doubt was that the sexual difference of bodies mattered to identity; until women found language to describe their unique experiences, they would literally not know what they were feeling or who they were. Male language only occludes woman's agency and obscures or distorts her experience. In both form and content, Irigaray's "disconnected," fluid, dithyrambic utterances in "When Our Lips Speak Together" were her own attempt at *"parler femme,"* speaking as a woman in order to discover and project a distinctive female self.

*   *   *

Julia Kristeva, herself a Lacanian analyst, would have none of it. The nonlogical, diffuse associative styles and the bodily rhythms that Irigaray attributed to feminine anatomy are also central to Kristeva's theory of modern poetic language, but they are not exclusively the resource of women. The maternal function, it is true, has a special role in their genesis. They derive from the prelinguistic stage of life, when the child's mental processes—whatever they might look like in the absence of language—are driven by instincts and the desire to unite with the maternal body. We can know this from psychoanalytic theory, Kristeva said, but we also have evidence of it from the way these processes, which she named the "semiotic," returned in "difficult" modernist poetry like that of the French Symbolists, Georges Bataille, and Antonin Artaud. There can be no poetry without the symbolic order's deployment of conventionally univocal signifiers and linear syntax, but these appear in modern poetry in wholly unconventional connections and rhythms, introducing "wandering" and "fuzziness" into language. "Language as symbolic function," that is, in its normative constriction of meaning, Kristeva claimed, "constitutes itself at the cost of repressing instinctual drive and continuous relation to the mother"; the strangeness of modern poetic language and syntax, along with the recurrent if veiled motif of union with a maternal woman is the return of the repressed, the "equivalent of incest" and a disruption of social harmony, from that point of view inevitably linked with evil.[61] Because up to now men alone have had access to the prerogatives of the symbolic order of language, it is they who have been almost exclusively the creators of modern poetry.

That does not mean, however, that women should react in turn by claiming special status with regard to poetic language. The return of "the semiotic" in modernist poetry is an expression of the universal human longing for the free play of the instincts in the security of union with the mother, the first, unforgettable, embodiment of totality. But the semiotic is always aspiration, never fulfillment; the testimony of its inevitable, and necessary, failure is also integral to the truest poetry. Kristeva identified the illusion of fulfillment with religion, the "phantasmatic necessity," as she put it, "to procure a *representation* (which could be animal, feminine, masculine or parental, among others) that replaces the element that makes us what we are—our capacity to form symbols." Our symbolic capacity is humanity's creative glory and its despair, since it means our separation from any possibility of immediate contact with Being. By "representation" Kristeva meant our desire to name an objective source of meaning that would, through our identification with it, free us from the individual work of symbolization. Seen in this light, feminism is ersatz religion. "Feminism today seems to constitute exactly this sort of *representation*, one that complements the frustration that women feel when faced with the Christian tradition and its variation—secular humanism."[62] By feminism she meant Irigaray and Çixous as representatives of the second generation of feminists who were primarily interested in "the specificity of feminine psychology . . . [and who] seek a language for their corporeal and intersubjective experiences,"[63] which traditional Christianity and modern Enlightenment humanism both excluded. But anchoring that language in a female identity is an abnegation of individuality.

Kristeva herself wanted to support, or found, a third generation of feminists who refuse to participate in the illusion of feminine identity with privileged access to truth. "What does 'identity' and even 'sexual identity' mean," she challenged, "in a theoretical and scientific space in which the notion of identity itself is challenged?"[64] Identity is a philosophical error, which furthermore, has dangerous moral consequences in the world because it licenses violence and terrorism in the name of its exclusive truth. Getting rid of identity is an ethical, not just a truth-functional imperative. Not that undermining identity will end conflict altogether—conflict is an ineradicable feature of social life—but it will downgrade individual and group claims into particular rather than absolute demands, make compromise possible, and put an end to the fanaticism of identity wars.

THE ANGLO-AMERICAN ADAPTATION

"French Feminism" largely displaced figures like Gilligan and Chodorow in the discourse of difference and identity for many feminists in the United States, Britain, and Australia by the mid-1980s. "Psychoanalysis" came to mean Lacan rather than Freud, almost completely discredited among feminists for the biologism and patriarchalism of his view of female sexuality. The reception of the French, however, especially Irigaray, was stormy. She was avidly embraced for her analysis of the exclusionary force of conventional—phallocentric—sexual language and for making the body central to language and identity. But she was repudiated for the same reason. As the feminist literary theorist Toril Moi wrote, "Any attempt to formulate a general theory of femininity will be metaphysical. This is precisely Irigaray's dilemma: having shown that so far femininity has been produced exclusively in relation to the logic of the Same, she falls for the temptation to produce her own positive theory of femininity. But . . . to define 'woman' is necessarily to essentialize her."[65]

"Essentialism" was the buzzword, and for many the bugaboo, of the debate about identity during the decade; it designated the philosophical assumptions that the concept ostensibly entailed. Few writers bothered to define it, as they occasionally acknowledged.[66] Diana Fuss traced its use in feminist literature to the traditional Aristotelian understanding of essence as that which is irreducible and unchanging about a person or thing and constitutive of it, what makes the thing what it is. Sexual essentialism purportedly took male and female to be presocial, natural, categories to which different social characteristics could then be superadded. Typically, essentialism was opposed to "social construction," the term originating in the sociology of knowledge but now interpreted through Foucault's concept of discourse. The claim was that sexual difference was "discursively produced," elaborated as an effect of social practices rather than determined by biology.[67] Behind the philosophical debate, however, there were burning sociopolitical issues. Those most vehemently opposed to essentialism were writers representing groups who felt that their particular experiences were either excluded by or at the least not included in the purportedly universal definitions of women offered by "essentialists," above all black and Hispanic women and lesbians.

*　*　*

In a much-discussed essay of the mid-1980s, Donna Haraway introduced the cyborg, a hybrid of machine and organism that had become a staple of contemporary science fiction, as a metaphor for a postmodern feminism. It was a provocatively "perverse" suggestion, its grotesquerie intended to shake readers out of conventional ways of thinking about identity. Effacing the borders between previously rigidly differentiated categories of human and machine, the cyborg represents a radically different idea of identity that retains the word but empties it of its previous meaning. The cyborg is not only a matter of fiction but of "lived experience that changes what counts as women's experience in the late twentieth century."[68] There can be no one criterion that defines "woman" in our time; any suggestion of a universal female identity inevitably turns out to be a coercive "totalizing" that either leaves some women out—invariably "women of color"—or homogenizes them. At most "woman" can represent "fractured identities,"[69] identities that are only partial, provisional, contradictory, and permanently unclosed.[70] The term "woman" depends for its only legitimate deployment on the momentary needs of political strategy and coalitions among various groups, and for different purposes at other times might include quite a different set. "The cyborg," Haraway wrote, "is a kind of disassembled and reassembled, postmodern collective and personal self."[71] Because she knows herself to be a temporary artificial construct for shifting political purposes, "woman" as cyborg can refer to herself, whether collectively or individually, only with self-irony and "without innocence."[72] A woman "is," but knows she is not, a representative woman; a group of women "are," but know they are not, *all* women.

*   *   *

Norma Alarcon, looking back at the impact of *This Bridge Called My Back*, the collection of work by lesbian, Chicana, Hispanic, and Third World writers, went further in repudiating identity and connecting it more explicitly with white domination of minority women. Even feminists who affirm a female identity made up of disparate racial, class, cultural, and linguistic groups often end up erroneously affirming a unified female subjectivity or shared consciousness across gender. Nor does it make sense to support the idea of oppressed minority women "reclaiming" their identity from their oppressors. "In this culture," she wrote, "to grasp or reclaim an identity means always already to have become a subject of consciousness. The theory of the subject of consciousness as a unitary and synthesizing agent of knowledge is always already a posture of domination."[73] Her argument combined Foucault's thesis with Derrida's language. "Subjects" in Western discourse are really "objects" of domination, who in asserting their "own" identities are only reaffirming the categories projected on them by their oppressors, even if they reverse their valence from positive to negative. This observation put a critical spin on the ostensibly neutral sociological category of ascribed identity. It is those who wish to stigmatize and exclude who fasten onto visible physical features in order to give subjugated groups an identity. Under these circumstances liberation can only mean jettisoning identity altogether, not reclaiming it.

*   *   *

The most powerful and influential American postmodernist—or as Judith Butler insisted, poststructuralist—attack on the possibility of a general theory of femininity decisively shifted the target from essentialism to identity. The shift was a testimony to the success of identity in housing itself both in the vernacular and in academic discourse by the end of the 1980s. While Butler's work was densely theoretical, she wanted there to be no mistake about the enemy: not a philosophical abstraction like "essentialism" but what society at large took to be its most important category of differentiation. It was Butler's novel and forcefully argued theses that gave her, as she noted in the preface to the second edition, a wide audience outside academia, but her foregrounding sexual *identity* was a main reason they received so much attention.

Gender Trouble proclaimed itself at the outset as a "radical critique of the categories of identity."[74] What made it so radical was Butler's rejection of the gender/sex distinction, which even many antiessentialist feminists were willing to concede. While gender—the traits and behaviors associated with and expected of "femininity"—is culturally constructed, sex, they acknowledged, has a certain "biological intractability." In Butler's view, however, "sex itself is a gendered category. . . . [G]ender is . . . the discursive/cultural means by which 'sexed nature' or 'a natural sex' is produced and established as 'prediscursive,' prior to culture."[75] The idea of a "natural" biological sexuality is itself a social construction.

Prevailing categories of sexuality, male and female, she argued, are definitionally inseparable from the norm of heterosexuality. To be female (or male) in our society is just to "be" heterosexual; desiring the opposite sex is intrinsic to our definitions of sexual identity. But heterosexuality is a norm, and it is established and enforced through the concept of identity. Having an identity is socially understood as the coherence and continuity of the person. But, Butler argued, coherence and continuity are not in fact accurate descriptive attributes of persons—as descriptions they are often empirically false. Nor are they "logically or analytically necessary features of personhood": the concept of "person" can be defined without them (though Butler did not attempt such a definition). Identities are instead "socially instituted and maintained norms of intelligibility,"[76] that is, both knowability *and* acceptability. To have an identity is to be socially recognized and affirmed as a certain *kind* of person, one who behaves in certain regular ways and as such is knowable and predictable to others.

Identity, then, is a fiction with a purpose. In the case of sex, society creates the sexual identities of "male" and "female" in order to "heterosexualize" desire.[77] Instituting heterosexuality "requires and institutes the production of discrete and asymmetrical oppositions between 'feminine' and 'masculine,' where these are understood as expressive attributes of 'male' and 'female.'"[78] In a word, society creates males and females, who are defined by their sexual difference and sexual complementarity—along with a host of other norms of deportment, dress, and desire that exist exclusively in binary relation to one another as public manifestations of sexual identity: men are aggressive, women passive. By definition, then, gays aren't "male" and lesbians aren't "female"; fitting into neither recognized sexual category, they have no recognizable sexual identities. Socially it makes no sense to say, "That woman is a lesbian" (though the point was usually put the other way around: lesbians are not "really" women). "Woman," Butler argued, is a heterosexually exclusionary term.

Exclusion points to the political meaning of sexual identity in Foucault's sense; sexual identity enforces a regime of power. The discourse of conventional sexual identity institutionalizes the social domination of heterosexuality through the linguistic excision of nonheterosexuals; they are literally unintelligible since they do not fit into recognized classifications. Understood in the Foucauldian terms of power/knowledge, sexual identities are "discursive formations" that have no inner substance behind their social enactment. Sexual identity is purely "performative"—its performance creates the identity it is supposed to manifest. Gender is only as gender does. "There is no gender identity behind the expressions of gender; that identity is performatively constituted by the very 'expressions' that are said to be its results."[79] This was a more or less pure form of behaviorism: the person or self has no interior. Butler later tried briefly to backtrack from the theatrical implications of performance—acting as role-playing or pretense—by claiming that her notion was rooted in J. L. Austin's concept of performative language,[80] in which an utterance, like the words of the officiant at a wedding ceremony, creates what it announces, but she ultimately acknowledged that her language did in fact convey theatricality.[81] She then embraced both meanings, but in fact the distinction makes little difference. Performances, whether linguistic or theatrical, depend on prior social scripts and roles, which must be learned before they can be performed, and that was her point: sexual identities are nothing but such socially constructed scripts for performance.

But her argument entailed an even more radical conclusion. The idea that the categories of a discourse produce the "heterosexualization of desire" is ambiguous. It could be understood as society's effort to make heterosexuality the norm *for* desire, which allows that desire could be independent of social norms. However it could also be understood causally, as society's ability to make desire *itself* heterosexual through discourse. The first reading is consistent with a notion of performativity; the second demands a psychological approach to explain how social demands become personal desires. Butler meant the second, and it got her into theoretical trouble.

To explain how society creates desire, she turned to psychoanalytic theory. Her key concept was identification, but she radically altered Freud's account of it. For Freud, sexual desire exists as instinct from the beginning, but the child's final sexual identity is consolidated through the identifications that resolve the Oedipus complex. The full Oedipus complex as presented in *The Ego and the Id* involves the child's innately bisexual desires: the boy desires his father as well as his mother, and only gives up his homosexual object by identifying with him through the formation of his superego. The process follows the model Freud had first elaborated in "Mourning and Melancholia." In mourning the death of a loved object, the person gives him up by identifying with him, adopting as his own some of the object's traits; in this attenuated way one still has the lost object even as he grieves for him. The melancholic differs in that he does not grieve his loss but remains locked in a love-hate struggle with his internalized lost object. Freud's explanation of superego formation combined aspects of both mourning and melancholia. In the outcome of the Oedipal conflict, the boy identifies with his father, represses his homosexual desire for him and internalizes him as ego ideal and superego prohibition, but he does not grieve because he remains wholly unconscious of his object loss.

Butler made two radical changes to this account. First, she argued that the internalization of the lost same-sex love object creates sexual identity because it is effected through a taboo on homosexuality as well as on incest. The incest taboo is not just a prohibition; it is also a heterosexual mandate. Secondly, contrary to Freud's view that heterosexual and homosexual impulses exist prior to the Oedipal stage, the heterosexual ego ideal "produces," that is, creates, the heterosexual and antihomosexual "dispositions" that it mandates.[82]

These dispositions do not exist "inside" the psyche, however, since there is no inside. Freud's idea of identification as internalization was based on a fiction of the psyche as thing-like apparatus, built on the metaphor of three-dimensional spatial object. Nonetheless the physical implications of *incorporating* heterosexual mandate and homosexual taboo are in another way very real. They are expressed not inside the psyche but "on" the body, in its capacity for sexual pleasure in those organs, and only in those organs, sanctioned by the "gender-differentiating law." "Pleasures," Butler wrote, "are said to reside in the penis, the vagina, and the breasts . . . but such descriptions correspond to a body which has already been constructed or naturalized as gender-specific. . . . Pleasures are . . . determined by the melancholic structure of gender whereby some organs are deadened to pleasure, and others brought to life."[83] As in Freud's explanation of hysteria, the body speaks; the somaticization of the repressed conceals its origins in social law. Butler's analysis was the polar opposite of Irigaray's anchoring sexual modalities in the presocial body.

Butler's claim, however, is highly problematic. The notion of "deadening" certain organs to pleasure is easy enough to grasp within her Freudian framework; it was Freud's idea of hysterical anesthesia turned against Freud himself. What he regarded as the objective process by which "mature female sexuality" extinguishes clitoral excitation in favor of vaginal penetration is, in Butler's analysis, the paralyzing effect of a social norm. But it is much harder to imagine what the social "enlivening" of a physical organ that is not innately excitable might mean. It is equally hard to believe, as Butler's analysis would seem to imply, that women, heterosexual or homosexual, did not experience clitoral excitement until the middle of the twentieth century, or that males until recently knew nothing of anal stimulation, since anal sex was socially proscribed. Butler seemed to reject that idea that the body might have a mind of its own. A more serious problem for her own explanation, however, as she herself came to see, was that despite her behaviorist denial of an "inside" to the psyche, she had drawn upon just such a metaphor in putting forward the idea of gender melancholy, which relied on psychoanalytic concepts of unconscious fantasy, repression, and somaticization. As a result, there was an inconsistency between her idea of "gender melancholy" as an internal psychic structure, and gender performativity as (nothing but) sustained outward acts. "Certain features of the world, including people we know and lose," she acknowledged, "do became 'internal' features of the self . . . and that inner world . . . is constituted precisely as a consequence of the interiorizations that a psyche performs. . . . This suggests that there may well be a psychic theory of performativity at work that calls for greater exploration."[84] The concession would seem to demand serious qualification of her rejection of identity. A psychic theory of performativity implies at the minimum a stable disposition to act in gender-specific ways, giving them the empirical coherence and continuity that she wanted to deny to identity traits. And once the possibility of such a psychic theory is granted, the question arises of what a deeper exploration might reveal, beyond one's stable dispositions, about the beliefs such dispositions provoke about who or what the self "is" that supports them[85]—in other words, its identity.

The "Invention" of Homosexuality

Butler's psychoanalytic theory of the origin of sexual identities denied the possibility of a socially recognized sexual identity for homosexuals, though she acknowledged the proliferation of gay sexual identities *within* the homosexual community through its appropriation and redefinition of socially negative terms like "queer." But for many gay theorists, the issue of gay identity was about much more than the language of sex.

Foucault's concept of power/knowledge, which provided Butler with her basic argument for dismantling the idea of sexual identity, was also the theoretical foundation for the idea of a distinctive homosexual identity. Like other categories of deviancy, "the homosexual," according to Foucault, was a creation of the nineteenth-century discourses of bourgeois normalization: "the nineteenth-century homosexual became a personage, a past, a case history, and a childhood, in addition to being a type of life, a life form, and a morphology, with an indiscreet anatomy and possibly a mysterious physiology. . . . [T]he homosexual was now a species."[86]

Bluntly put, there was no such thing as "a homosexual" before the nineteenth century. As Jeffrey Weeks, the historian of homosexuality in Britain, put it, there is a distinction between "homosexual behavior which is universal, and a homosexual identity which is historically specific."[87] Of course Foucault's analysis was meant to dissolve the solidity of homosexual identity by exposing it as a historical artifact, but his argument for the normalization of heterosexuality depended precisely on the sociohistorical solidity of the identity of "the homosexual" in establishing the boundaries of the normal. Where Butler argued the social invisibility of homosexuality, Foucault emphasized its social prominence.

In the 1980s debate over the nature of homosexuality, Foucault's approach was the basis of much social constructionist argument against the essentialist view that homosexuality had always existed. The apparent oddity of their position, however, was that many of those who espoused social construction were not bent on exposing the historical nature of homosexual identity in order to undermine the category of identity, as Foucault was. On the contrary they supported the creation of gay identities as a legitimating strategy for homosexuality. To be gay was to have a "quasi-ethnic" status like Italians, blacks, or Jews, with a unique culture that deserved the same protection against discrimination. "The 'politics of identity,' Steven Epstein wrote, "crystallized around a notion of 'gayness' as a real, and not an arbitrary, difference."[88] But this was to fuse a voluntarist conception of social construction with the essentialist idea of a permanent core to homosexuality. In effect, social construction turned into its opposite: it meant to create a legitimate social identity out of what one "really was" internally.

Deconstructing Race

If postmodernism didn't have quite the impact on racial identity that it did on female identity, it was in part because race had already been widely discredited in the academy before its arrival. That did not prevent partisans of French theory from applying poststructuralist concepts in a renewed assault on the idea of race, particularly in literary and cultural studies. As Henry Louis Gates, Jr., put it in his editor's introduction to the collection of essays *"Race," Writing and Difference*, "Race, as a meaningful criterion within the biological sciences, has long been recognized to be a fiction." Nevertheless talk of race continues to prevail in everyday discourse, where it has become, he claimed, "a trope of ultimate, irreducible difference between cultures, linguistic groups or adherents of specific belief systems" just because of its lack of precise denotation. Cultural and religious differences were "racialized," turned into quasi-biological categories. To combat such arbitrary and indiscriminate usage, contributors to the volume were collectively engaged "to deconstruct . . . the ideas of difference inscribed in the trope of race, to explicate discourse itself in order to reveal the hidden relations of power and knowledge inherent in popular and academic usages of 'race.' "[89]

The collection of essays included a piece by Derrida himself on apartheid in which he assimilated the word to the category of language usage that deconstruction was invented to undo. Apartheid, in its linguistic form, is an "abstract essence" (which Derrida rendered in English with "apartionality," though the more literal "apartness" might have served his purpose better) that corrupts the purely descriptive status of "being apart" into "quasi-ontological separation." The word, like all racial terms, thus suggests that racial segregation is the natural state of things, legislated by the "very law of the origin."[90] Such a usage is unthinkable, he argued, outside the entire European discourse on race, rooted in both pseudoscience and Judeo-Christian ideology.[91] Religion lends the aura of ontological necessity to supposedly natural categories like race by anchoring them in the Creation. More forthrightly than in his earlier philosophical work, Derrida made clear his intention of putting an end to the political power of hierarchical categories such as race by deconstructing them.

The American contributions, both intentionally and unintentionally, had a different import. In the volume's most direct application of postmodernism to racial identity, Barbara Johnson examined how the Harlem Renaissance author Zora Neale Hurston dealt with the question of color in a number of her writings. Of Hurston's autobiographical essay "How It Feels to Be Colored Me," Johnson concluded that the author intentionally never really answered her question. Instead she "deconstructs the very grounds of an answer" by showing that "questions of difference and identity" depend wholly on the changing interpersonal contexts in which they're raised—Who's asking? At what time? Where? For what purpose?—and that Hurston's answers are always matters of momentary strategy rather than "truth." So Hurston speaks of herself at one point as "being" colored and at another as suddenly "becoming" colored, and again elsewhere as having no race but just being "me,"[92] depending on her circumstances and purposes. Any notion of a "black identity" is dissolved into a shifting kaleidoscope of contextual possibilities which are variously affirmed and denied, and often contradict one another; in any case none are permanent. Yet, Johnson concluded, "black" and "white" do continue to matter to Hurston: she "suspends the certainty of reference not by erasing the differences but by foregrounding the complex dynamism of their interaction."[93] Such a procedure did not so much deconstruct racial identity, however, as underline its salience by making the issue of her color central to the subtlest nuances of Hurston's experience and consciousness.

What for Johnson was a perhaps inadvertent confirmation of the continuity and persistence of black identity within shifting contexts of experience was for Cornel West the conscious basis for a new black cultural politics. Because of his activist purpose, however, he seemed even less aware of the contradictory thrust of his approach. In his essay "The New Cultural Politics of Difference" he praised deconstruction for exposing the political power of such binary oppositions as white/black to sustain hierarchical social structures, but criticized Derrida for promoting a purely ironic consciousness at the expense of political action. Black "cultural workers," he insisted, must create "discursive and institutional networks that deconstruct earlier modern Black strategies for identity-formation," showing how they harbor class, patriarchal, and homophobic biases that exclude many blacks from "blackness." The purpose of such deconstructive work however is ultimately constructive: as West put it, it is to articulate the complexity and diversity of black practices that must be accommodated by blacks and whites alike[94]—in effect, though he did not explicitly say so, creating a more inclusive black identity. The omission was not accidental; to articulate such a purpose would have been to suggest an identity boundary, the very thing he wanted to deny because it would, in postmodern terms, "reinscribe" color as a criterion of identity. But such reinscription was inevitable in a political enterprise meant to rally blacks.

The "Non-Identity" of Postcolonial Hybridity

If postmodernism transformed existing discussion of female identity, it was the founding discourse for the academic field of postcolonial studies that became established during the 1980s, because it seemed to provide the best account of the divided subjectivity of former subjects of European imperialism—or at least of their literary representatives. Formerly colonized peoples did not appear to have the kind of identities one normally had in mind in speaking of ethnic or national identity, with their implications of homogeneity and seamless integration. The native populations of Europe's African and Asian colonies had been forced to encounter an alien culture that was presented to them as more desirable than their own but from which they were at the same time excluded because of their inferiority.

It was this conflicted situation that Homi Bhabha, the Indian-born, British-trained, and American-based literary and cultural critic, wanted to capture with his notion of cultural "hybridity."[95] Never clearly defined, it was an ambiguous term that covered at least three distinct situations: colonial subjects of European imperialism still under the rule of white settlers, former colonial subjects become independent, and nonwhite minorities resident in and citizens of white majority democratic states.

In a chapter of his best-known book *The Location of Culture* entitled "Interrogating Identity," where he discussed Frantz Fanon's *Black Skin, White Masks,* Bhabha analyzed the educated professional black native's contradictory identification with the colonial settler through which his identity was formed. That identity was a response to the "look" of the settler, which told him that he was different from his uneducated brethren, one of "us," a (white) European. In reaction the native's self-image was split. Since the settlers would not in fact grant him real social and political equality, he fantasized being the master, occupying the settler's place. At the same time he wanted to keep his identity as the "slave" with its satisfying avenging anger. Thus he couldn't accept the colonizer's invitation to identity because he was in two places at once,[96] neither of which he could wholly believe in or commit to since each negated the other, but each of which answered a deep psychological need. Hybridity thus undercut the possibility of identity.

Bhabha went on to generalize the colonial native's situation into a full-scale theory of identity. Since the demand for identification is always the demand "to be *for* another" it is "never the affirmation of a pre-given identity. . . . [I]t is always the production of an image of identity and the transformation of the subject in assuming that image." Bhabha's point was ontological. Identification is "*always* the return of an image of identity that bears the mark of splitting in the Other place from which it comes."[97] Even if there is no obvious contradiction in the way the Other sees you, as for example in the normal white middle-class child's upbringing, there is always an ontological "difference" between self and other, so that there is an unbridgeable gap between "being for oneself" and "being for another." To be what the other is or how the other sees you, you have to manipulate yourself accordingly. In this sense, it would appear that all identity is unstably hybrid. "For identification, identity is never an a priori, nor a finished product," Bhabha wrote; "it is only ever the problematic process of access to an image of totality."[98] Identification is about the desired merging of self and Other into a unity of wholeness that can overcome our ultimate separateness, something possible only as fantasy.

Beyond restating Sartre, this analysis might have served as the beginning of a trenchant critique of the ideal of integrating conflicting identifications that, since Erikson, had been the foundation of the developmental theory of identity. Bhabha, however, did not develop the idea of a "double consciousness" into a full-blown challenge to the idea of a harmoniously integrated identity. He continued to reserve the idea of hybridity for empirical situations of cultural differences in colonial, postcolonial, and multicultural societies. And in the latter two, hybridity shifted from a purely descriptive category that seemed to undermine identity to a normative category that valorized one particular identity.

The psychic situation of liberated colonial people or "colored" minorities in white democratic societies, according to Bhabha, is different from that of the still-colonized. The excolonial or minority intellectual, politically and legally equal, is free to negotiate his relationship to the two cultures in which he is immersed. He occupies, or better constitutes, a third or "liminal" space, "in-between the designations of identity. . . . This interstitial passage between fixed identifications opens up the possibility of a cultural hybridity that entertains difference without an assumed or imposed hierarchy."[99] From their vantage point on the cultural border postcolonial and minority writers are able to dissolve the illusions of the binary oppositions that typically authorize the superiority of one culture, one identity, over another. "The contingent and the liminal," he asserted, "become the times and the spaces for the historical representation of the subjects of cultural difference in a postcolonial criticism."[100] Postcolonial critics can see through the claims of cultures—their own as well as the majority culture—to purity, wholeness, and superiority and discern a culture's historical contingency, partiality, and mongrelization.

Such claims for the creative advantage of cultural detachment were not new. In a famous article decades before, Thorsten Veblen had attributed "The Intellectual Pre-Eminence of Jews in Europe" to both Jewish marginality vis-à-vis Christian Europe and the detachment of the great Jewish intellectual and scientific innovators from their own tradition.[101] Veblen had in fact referred to the Jews as a "nation of hybrids"[102]—the biological reference in the contemporary Darwinian *Zeitgeist* was unsurprising—having physically so mingled with other populations that they were constituted of, and fertilized by, many different ethnic and cultural strains. The use of a biological metaphor by a postmodernist thinker, however, was jarring, and suggested not the end of identity but a better identity. Bhabha's postimperial "cultural hybrids" were the latest in the line of Euro-American outcasts elevated to superior intellectual status because of their existence on the boundaries of committed identity delusions. Not so ironically, it thus turned out that not only is there an identity called "postcolonial," but one that is superior to all others because it alone is able to see through illusions of totality.

Deconstructing Class Identity

One of the seemingly least likely of postmodernist initiatives was the deconstruction of the Marxist concept of class by two self-declared Marxist writers. The determinist ontology of historical materialism could not be more inimical to the poststructuralist rejection of original foundations and absolute categories. But that was exactly the point of Ernesto Laclau and Chantal Mouffe's revisionist undertaking in the mid-1980s. The contemporary emergence of gender, ethnic, national, and sexual minority protests, they pointed out, could not be accounted for in classical Marxist theory. If Marxism's radical democratic vision was to be saved, its "monist aspiration to capture with its categories the essence or underlying meaning of History"[103] had to be discarded.

Discrepancies between theory and historical fact, they argued, had challenged Marxism from the first. Classical Marxism rested on the "ontological primacy of the working class," with its "preconstituted identity" as the unified agent of a revolution that would transform society into a homogeneous community having no need for politics.[104] The problem was that "the working class" was at once a concrete, plural historical entity and the theoretically idealized unified "universal class" whose "objective" interest was to realize the freedom and wholeness of humanity. This nonempirical essentialist definition of working-class identity was the fatal flaw that had turned the Marxist vision into either totalitarian practice or narrow class politics. The real working class was a heterogeneous collection of different national experiences and local economic interests. In the face of this reality Marxists had tried to save theory by arguing that any deviations from the working class's "true identity" were either just apparent or mere contingencies, irrelevant to the basic line of historical development. Such strategies may have preserved the theoretical identity of working class as embodiment of the revolutionary ideal, but in their practical consequences proved fatal to it. Where the working class was small and fragmented, as in Russia, a small cadre claimed that their superior knowledge of its "objective interests" made them the proletariat's sole legitimate representative and justified authoritarian control over party and state. Where Marxism was a mass political party dependent on working-class organizations, as in Weimar Germany, the theoretical primacy of class led the party to become the de facto political instrument of narrow trade union interests. In reaction against the reifications of working-class identity which had perverted Marx's vision, Italian theorist Antonio Gramsci had developed the concept of "hegemony," which, they argued, pointed the way past the dead end of class essentialism, but even he had not been able to make the final break. Applying poststructuralist philosophy, however, Laclau and Mouffe believed they could redefine hegemony without falling into Gramsci's error, and use it to salvage Marxism as a viable practice.

By hegemony they meant a situation in which a particular social group purports to represent an ideal totality greater than itself. Russian Social Democrats had first used the term in claiming that the working class, given the task of creating political democracy that the Russian bourgeoisie was too backward to undertake, was acting on behalf of the whole of society. Gramsci considerably weakened the links between particular class and universalist ideology by emphasizing that there are always multiple conflicts in society, and that the desire to institute freedom and equality against domination was not limited to one group. Realizing radical democratic values called for fashioning a "bloc" of the discontented and progressive with the "collective will" to revolutionize society.[105] But because Gramsci retained the orthodox belief that there must be an "objective foundation" for both the direction of liberation and the leadership of the bloc, he could not fully grasp the historical contingency inherent in his view. The Marxist working class remained for Gramsci the historically identified hegemonic group whose situation made it the natural spokesmen for and leaders of the contemporary liberation movement. Contingency, however, meant that there were no historically determined processes or social groups with preordained identities, just groups that emerged through historical change. Nor was the goal of political action a determinate future society immanent in the logic of history; ideological visions were, in the Derridean sense, "articulations," political constructs worked out in the historical give and take between groups with different origins and goals. "The logic of hegemony," Laclau and Mouffe concluded, "as a logic of articulation and contingency, has come to determine the very identity of the hegemonic subjects."

This meant that in the postmodern view "Unfixity has become the condition of every social identity."[106] Social identities are constituted by shifting "discursive fields." There are no autonomous subjects, individual or collective, with fixed characteristics or ahistorical identities, only "subject positions" within these discursive fields. Supposedly universalist identities, like the earlier humanist conception of Man, are produced within different historical discourses where they are linked to other identities that often modify, limit, and even pervert their supposed universality. In the discourse of imperialism, for example, the "Rights of Man" were taken to be an essential part of "European values,"[107] thus undermining their universality and bending them to the interests of the colonial powers. This kind of "dispersive" analysis is necessary in the case of a term like humanism to expose what makes socialists so profoundly suspicious about the concept, and so to enable them to struggle more effectively in defense of genuinely humanist values.

But precisely for that purpose, the authors argued, the deconstruction of "humanism" is only a first step. Humanism must then be reconstructed, "retotalized" to include new historical claimants to the universal status of humanity, in order for a politically effective new hegemonic agenda to be articulated. The same two-step process is necessary in the case of contemporary radical movements like feminism. Progressive theory must first dissolve the unity of "woman," to show the specific and often unrelated sources of women's oppression in different contexts. But to create an effective movement, feminism must then reconstitute the old idea of the female sex, out of all the disparate instances of its oppression, into the idea of a unified feminine gender, because only the "imaginary signification" of "woman" as a totality can produce concrete effects in diverse social practices.[108] Simply put, the politically created unitary female identity is a necessary fiction across a wide range of quite different situations. Consequently that identity can never achieve closure; it is always precarious, always open to the vicissitudes of history.

In the examples of humanism and feminism, antagonisms aroused by exclusion and oppression play a role in mobilizing political opposition to essentialist identities. The idea of antagonism was central to Laclau and Mouffe's definition of a hegemonic bloc. To produce hegemony, however, antagonism must not focus just on the oppressors in one particular arena of conflict, like sexuality, but must see oppression as arising from exclusion and subordination as such, wherever it appears. Otherwise there can't be a bloc that cuts across social divisions with a truly hegemonic ideology, one meant to prevail over the whole of society.

This condition of generality was written into the basic purpose the authors had set themselves: "to identify the discursive conditions for the emergence of a collective action, directed toward struggling against inequalities and challenging relations of subordination."[109] In the introduction to the first edition, they claimed that their political conclusions were not uniquely Marxist; they could have been "approximated from very different discursive formations, for example from certain forms of Christianity, or from libertarian discourses alien to the socialist tradition."[110] Why then Marxism? Faithful to their belief in contingency, Laclau and Mouffe could only say that Marxism was the tradition that happened to constitute their own past; it did not represent a philosophically privileged standpoint.

At the level of generality at which they summarized their task one might be tempted to agree. But the core of their work, the detailed history of the concept of hegemony within Marxism and their ultimate definition of it, raises serious doubts. In the preface to the second edition, the authors noted that they had conceived their project in the early 1980s, at a time when Marxist theorizing had reached an impasse. As they also pointed out, it was at a time when Eurocommunism—the post-1968, ostensibly nonauthoritarian version of Western European communism—was still seen as a viable political project. A fortiori, they implied, noncommunist socialists might hope that a Marxism fundamentally revised on pluralistic and democratic lines could rejuvenate a radical socialist politics. Why they thought such a politics necessary, both initially and fifteen years later, was clear from their criticisms of the ideologies that prevailed after the collapse of Marxism in 1989. Both liberal democracy and social democracy ignored the reality of fundamental social antagonisms and abandoned the adversarial model of politics for the fallacies of consensus politics, the belief that differences could be resolved by "dialogue" between interest groups. Social democrats had given up the revolutionary ideal of "transforming the present hegemonic order." They failed to reckon with the continuing inequality of power, the reality of domination in liberal democratic society and its basic cause. In a word, they no longer stood for the overthrow of capitalism. Laclau and Mouffe had given up the Marxist idea of the revolutionary working class but not the Marxist revolutionary ideal of putting an end to capitalism—for them the unsurpassable goal of a truly democratic movement.

It is unlikely then that their conclusions could have been reached within other traditions. Marxism uniquely argues that capitalism is the root cause of domination and inequality. It was not just contingently the tradition they worked within to arrive at their concept of hegemony. Even in Laclau and Mouffe's own terms, however, there was a problem about the identity status of tradition in an individual's life. Thinking of it as mere contingency glosses over the adhesive force of the discourse and institutions in which its value commitments are embedded. It is difficult to reimagine their book's conclusions, which depend wholly on the Marxist category of hegemony, within Christian or libertarian discourses. Though they thought of their enterprise as post-Marxist, and indeed found that epithet thrown at them as a reproach by more orthodox critics,[111] their work manifested their identity as part of the

Marxist tradition, in the contestatory sense Alasdair MacIntyre had claimed characterizes all traditions.

Deconstruction and National Identity

One of the more striking because unexpected postmodern initiatives was the use some historians, generally immune to abstract theorizing, made of deconstruction to analyze national identity. Less surprisingly, it was historians of Germany who found it most useful; German history was arguably its proof case. Introducing a volume on the "reconfiguring of German identities" after German reunification in 1991, Konrad Jarausch broached certain "conceptual preconsiderations" he thought necessary in approaching his topic. He began by contrasting the older conception of "national character" with the contemporary idea of national identity. National character had been understood in an essentialist way as something fixed and probably biologically, or at least environmentally, determined. In the case of Germany, however, the many "changes in the definition of German-ness during the last centuries were so rapid and fundamental as to make it difficult to distill a stable essence that could be contrasted with a more malleable content. . . . The only fixed thing about Germany seems to have been the continual dispute about what being German might mean."[112] For Jarausch, however, that didn't mean surrendering identity but redefining it. The "identity perspective" on nationalism suggested that nations constructed their idea of self out of a shared language, history, and sense of purpose, justified and held together by a store of cultural myths and symbols. What makes it hard to determine the precise contours of the resulting "collective personality" is that they are "fiercely contested among rival parties, ideologies and interests. . . . Instead of residing in a single unified definition, a nation's self-conception is therefore more likely to be found in the competing discourses about what it ought to be."[113] With regard to any one of these discourses, however, "Postmodern approaches are particularly useful, because they seek to identify the discourses that promote certain self-images. The deconstruction of texts can uncover the politics of identity claims and guard against conflating description with prescription."[114] No single version of identity can lay claim to truth or absoluteness; it will always be shown to be partial, interested, and contested, though not as such invalid.

Nonetheless Jarausch also acknowledged that the notion of a collective identity describes the real feeling of belonging to a larger community. Debating the nature of "German-ness" entails that the debaters agree that there is such a thing as German identity. Deconstructionist historians found themselves up against the same dilemma as postmodern critics in other spheres: affirming the existence of the very thing they wanted to deny.

The Dilemma of Postmodernism and the Tactics of Rescue

In all the cases I've discussed, the attempt to deconstruct identity turned on itself, in good deconstructionist fashion, reaffirming as both idea and practice the concept it claimed was untenable. Some postmodernists simply embraced the contradiction openly as philosophically warranted. "My own position," Diana Fuss announced, "will endorse the Lacanian understanding of identity as alienated and fictitious, and it will argue for the usefulness of seeing all representations of identity as simultaneously possible and impossible."[115] Though she allied herself with other Lacanian critics, they seemed more troubled by the problem the contradiction created for personal life. The dilemma was put most poignantly by Jane Gallop, who, while protesting the idea of a stable, coherent female identity, rejected the possibility of replacing identity with something more adequate or authentic. "I do not seek some sort of liberation from identity," she wrote, "That would lead only to another form of paralysis—the oceanic passivity of undifferentiation. Identity must be continually assumed and immediately called into question."[116] How one did this without inviting the paralysis of constant self-negation she did not say. The dilemma was even more pointed in Elaine Marks's formulation "there must be a sense of identity, even though it would be fictitious."[117] What might it mean to live a psychological *sense* of identity knowing it to be a fiction?

The most dramatic affirmation of the inescapability of identity, precisely because of her root and branch rejection of it, was Judith Butler's. From her Foucauldian perspective, however, there seemed to be no other choice. "The juridical structures of language and politics," she claimed, "constitute the contemporary field of power; hence, there is no position outside this field."[118] Sexual norms are firmly entrenched in language and law as absolute truths/commands. At best there could be a critical genealogy, in Foucault's sense of tracing historical origins, of the legitimating practices of existing power and the identities that they "engender, naturalize and immobilize." Immobilization is the key word; identities are frozen solid. Since "sexuality is culturally constructed within existing power relations," she concluded, "a normative sexuality that is 'before,' 'outside' or 'beyond' power . . . is a cultural impossibility and a politically impracticable dream."[119]

Openly or implicitly, postmodernists seemed to be saying, "identity—can't live with it, can't live without it." In the face of the two unacceptable outcomes postmodern analysis seemed to produce—total indeterminateness of the self or total determination by identity—they, and others more skeptical but still compelled by postmodernism's apparently inescapable objections to identity, tried to negotiate between the alternatives. Such negotiations took a number of different paths.

Subversion by Parody

Butler herself offered one of the most controversial suggestions. If identity was nothing but performance, the way to attack it was to subvert existing roles by acting against type. The notorious example she gave of such a subversive performance was drag, which she argued "fully subverts the distinction between inner and outer psychic space and effectively mocks both the expressive model of gender and the notion of a true gender identity."[120] By creating a visible disjunction between the anatomy of the performer and the conventional gender of the performance through dress and gesture, drag displays the artificiality of the supposedly natural connections between body and gender role. "In imitating gender," she claimed, "drag implicitly reveals the imitative structure of gender itself—as well as its contingency."[121] What gender "imitates," in a word, is nothing. Gender has no natural original; it is invented out of whole cloth.

An obvious problem with subversion was the issue of who is doing the subverting. Given Butler's rejection of an autonomous subject, as well her conception of power's total dominion, where could the desire to subvert one's social identity come from?[122] The greater issue for many feminists was that subversive "pastiche," as she called it in preference to parody, left existing social identities intact. Though her avowed purpose in dismantling the identity of woman was to be politically inclusive, many feminist critics pointed out that her solution was politically empty, leading at most to symbolic individual protest that did nothing to change the power structure and the social institutionalization of exclusionary identities.[123]

Strategic Essentialism

A more widely accepted approach among postmodernists was "strategic essentialism," the use of fixed identities as a political strategy *despite* their unreality. The philosopher Gayatri Chakravorty Spivak was probably the first to introduce the idea in her work on feminist and postcolonial theory. While in the strict philosophical sense the notion of an essential female or "subaltern" identity is false, it can be instrumentally useful, she argued, and even necessary for mobilizing otherwise different groups of people for some political end. "I think we have to choose . . . strategically. . . . In fact I must say I am an essentialist from time to time," she wrote in connection with her stand against cliteridectomy as an assault on "woman's desire."[124] She similarly justified the effort of the historians in the Subaltern Studies group writing on colonial India to discover in the native subjects of the British Raj a unified "subaltern consciousness" as a "*strategic* use of positivist essentialism in a scrupulously visible political interest."[125] Left unspoken was the suspicion that a political goal might not be energizing in and of itself, that it might have to be couched in terms of an identity deeply rooted in the self because it was believed to be objectively real. Spivak herself later backed away from the strategic deployment of essentialism because the eagerness with which she saw it taken up made her fear that the idea "gave essentialism an alibi."[126] Diana Fuss, on the other hand, though also expressing the fear that strategic essentialism could be a ruse for preserving identity, nonetheless concluded that it was worth the risk because it could be an indispensable weapon for the oppressed. That she thought there was risk involved was once again evidence of the temptations of fixed identity. In a more colloquial vein, Denise Riley argued that for feminist political purposes it was sometimes useful to say that "women" don't exist and at other times act politically as if they did. "So feminism," she wrote, "must be agile enough to say, 'Now we will be "women"—but now we will be persons, not these "women."' And, in practice, what sounds like a rigid opposition—between a philosophical correctness about the indeterminacy of the term, and a strategical willingness to clap one's feminist hand over one's theoretical mouth and just get on with 'women' where necessary—will loosen."[127] Pragmatic necessity trumps consistency and truth. But like the others Riley didn't explore why it might be necessary to appeal to philosophically false collective identities in the first place. Strategic essentialism was a concession to the psychological stickiness of identity. Its advocates had a bad conscience because they had no philosophically legitimate way of conceiving it.

Identity as Conscious Identification

A more apparently psychological solution to the postmodernist dilemma was the attempt to recast identity as identification. Identification with others could explain an individual's sense of collective identity, the cultural theorist Stuart Hall suggested, though a postmodernist necessarily understood the concept differently from its usual (Freudian) connotation. The "common sense view" takes identification to be the foundation of a sense of "naturally closed" collective identity affording people feelings of solidarity with and allegiance to others. The discursive approach rejects the naturalist assumption. Identifications are not simple givens; they are continuing constructions, the fluid result of "a process never completed."[128] This was not, Hall granted, identification as psychoanalysis understood it. For psychoanalysis identification is the unconscious merging with another, but merger is based on a fantasy of incorporation. Freud had pointed out that such a fantasy replaced "having" someone with "being" that someone, but the idea of "being" is precisely what postmodernism denied.

If Hall's version of identification created an "identity" it was not, he said, an essentialist but a strategic and "positional" one. It does not indicate a "stable core of the self unfolding from beginning to end through all the vicissitudes of history without change, the bit of the self which remains always-already 'the same,' identical to itself across time." Nor, when applied to collectivities, does it refer to an inner "true self" which people with a shared history and ancestry have in common. It is fictional, a conscious creation, not ex nihilo certainly, but a self-aware acceptance of the contingencies of our initial positions in history and society. Born into a particular time and place, we are "interpellated" or addressed[129] by others as "the social subjects of particular discourses" that preexist us, but also as subjects that can react to them. Identities are thus "points of temporary attachment to the subject positions which discursive practices construct for us."[130]

From a psychological point of view, the language of construction, fiction, unending process, and temporary attachment to characterize identification seemed jarring and ill fitting. In crucial ways Hall's account of identity formation repeated George Herbert Mead's developmental distinction between the "me," the internalized social self, and the "I," the self that is capable of critical reflection, but Hall's version of the "me" was insubstantial by comparison. Whatever identification may actually be as a psychic process, it happens early and automatically; it is neither the temporary attachment nor the cool strategic calculation Hall described. Strikingly, the analysis of identification that he approvingly quoted from Judith Butler, while no less deconstructive in intent, stayed closer to the phenomenology of identification. Identifications, she wrote, "are phantasmatic efforts of alignment, loyalty, ambiguous and cross-corporeal cohabitations, they unsettle the I; they are the sedimentation of the 'we' in the constitution of any I, the structuring presence of alterity in the very formulation of the I."[131] "Phantasmatic" identification may be, but Butler's description made it a much stickier psychological and social proposition.[132] It is easy to think that Hall's adoption of identification in place of identity was itself a strategic decision. Acknowledging that social construction must be supplemented by psychology to explain the subjective attachment to identity, he gestured in the direction of psychic internalization while trying to undercut any psychological force it might have in the interest of the postmodernist evisceration of the self. Yet just by invoking psychological identification Hall was conceding more about identity than suited his poststructuralist approach.

Cultivating Contingency

The political theorist William Connolly's solution to the conundrum of identity was both more philosophically nuanced and more ironically self-aware.

"Let us feign these truths to be self evident," he wrote, in a wry postmodern mock-up of a Declaration of Identity, "that each individual needs an identity; that every stable way of life invokes claims to collective identity that enter in various ways into the interior identifications and resistances of those who share it. . . . Even if a 'way of life' without identity turned out to be possible, it would still be undesirable. I would not be, do, or achieve anything. Neither would we. . . . Identity, in some modality or other, is an indispensable feature of human life."[133] "My identity," he asserted even more categorically, using the dread copula, "is what I *am* and how I am recognized rather than what I choose, want, or consent to. It is the dense self from which choosing, wanting, and consenting proceed. . . . *Our* identity, in a similar way, is what we are."[134] But if so, why "feign" these truths to be self-evident? Because in a basic sense they are *not* true, not metaphysically and not as they are often acted out socially and politically. Though he said he did not typically call himself a postmodernist, since he rejected the claim that identity was fluid and easily changeable, he also acknowledged that his position was a version of postmodernism because his interpretation of identity was based on Derrida's conception of identity/difference.[135] Connolly's difference was that he took the identity side of the binary opposition as seriously as the difference side.

Though postmodernists have erroneously tried to base their approach on difference alone,[136] there is no difference without identity; they are the two mutually implied sides of meaning. By the same token, identity is always connected to a series of differences that, as he put it "help it be what it is."[137] To define oneself is to demarcate oneself from others. Furthermore, as Derrida had argued, since *différance* can articulate the world in different ways, such a series of differences is historically relative. So an identity is "historically contingent in its formation and inherently relational in its form. . . . *[N]o identity reflects being as such, no identity is the true identity* because every identity is particular, constructed, and relational."[138]

That does not mean, however, that identity has no weight. On the contrary, the contingencies of identity can be very deeply entrenched in the self. They might well have been otherwise for any individual, Connolly insisted, given different mixes of tradition, child rearing, the shape of dramatic public events, and so on.[139] But given what they factually are for an individual, or group, the contingencies of our identity—the gender, sexual orientation, belief, ethnicity we were born into—very frequently become what he called "branded contingencies," "instinctive" to our feelings and actions and highly resistant to modification once consolidated, not easily subject even to one's own will or decision.[140] They become a second nature.

Entrenchment is all the more likely because we have a strong and continuing temptation to turn our contingent identities into necessary ones. We tend to "congeal established identities into fixed forms, thought and lived as if their structure expressed the true order of things. When these pressures prevail, the maintenance of one identity . . . involves the conversion of some differences into otherness, into evil, or one of its numerous surrogates. Identity requires difference in order to be, and it converts difference into otherness in order to secure its own self-certainty."[141]

Why does identity want self-certainty at the expense of others? The motive is existential anxiety; the ontological "nothingness" of contingency, the dread intuition that we might be otherwise, makes us want to transform our contingent identities into the fullness and certainty of absolute "being." Identities want to defeat finitude and death by offering their divine origin, their naturalness, or their historical continuity as warrant for their permanence. And, as Sartre had pointed out, this desire for totality, which is also a desire for perfection, demands that we project any imperfection or evil we fear in ourselves onto the other; as Connolly put it, a "hegemonic" identity is one that tries to protect its purity and certainty by defining those differences that pose the greatest threat to its integrity and certainty as independent sites of evil.[142]

There is, however, another sense of ontological necessity, one appealed to by Charles Taylor and in accord with Alasdair MacIntyre's critiques of Kantianism and existentialism, with which Connolly seemed in agreement. Substantive identity—individual identification with and commitment to a tradition or group and its values—is the necessary condition for the possibility of desire, choice, and action. If we were the totally unencumbered consciousness of Sartre's early existentialism or—Connolly's concern—nothing but the origin of Derrida's *différance*, which endlessly defers identity, we would have no grounds to choose anything at all. This was the foundation of Connolly's claim that we are our identities and that without them we could not do or achieve anything, though his failure to ground it more thoroughly opened him up to criticisms of either essentialism or self-contradiction.

As both a political theorist and an ethicist, Connolly was primarily concerned about the dangerous consequences of the absolutist temptation for group conflict and democracy. The temptation of any collective identity to regard itself as the only true identity and that of others as the origin of all evil is a major source of social conflict and potentially fatal to the need of a working democracy to accommodate difference. Absolutizing identity leads to the marginalization or outright repression of others wherever one group has the social and political power to effect it. The appropriate response, however, is not to oppose identity politics but "to reconsider the *way* in which individuals and collectivities experience identities."[143]

If overcoming our finitude is the main motive for transforming contingent identities into necessary ones, conscious recognition of this needy desire can contribute to empathy with other identities as we recognize the common humanity behind them all. We must actively cultivate the sense of our contingency for political and ethical reasons, but it can only begin in a personal encounter with finitude and death. Through that encounter we can learn to appreciate what is greater than identity, the bounty and "the diversity of life flowing over and through officially sanctioned identities,"[144] each of which can only express limited aspects of life. We can see such diversity even in ourselves. Our own individual identities are multiple, the results of contingent identifications that may be incompatible and can cause us to war against ourselves. The problem, however, is not the lack of internal harmony or unity that our inner diversity creates; it is our wanting to absolutize one or another strand of our identity—our nationality, our religion—that makes us want to eliminate other such identities, other nationalities or religions.

To cultivate contingency is not, then, to eliminate identity, or the conflict between identities. If it creates a measure of distance between oneself and one's own collective identity, a sense of irony toward it, it does not necessarily overcome the distance between identities; I still feel my national or religious difference from others. What the cultivation of contingency can do is convert the usual antagonism of difference into an "agonism of difference," a kind of conflict in which respect for an adversary's rights to identity eliminates strategies of conquest or conversion as political options.[145] Connolly acknowledged the difficulty of such a stance. It is a dance on a tightrope, where the danger is falling off either into identity fanaticism or empty space. But only such a dance can honor both sides of identity/difference.

Reclaiming Identity from Postmodernism

As "entrenched" as Connolly wanted to make identity, it wasn't anchored deeply enough for some identity theorists. Starting in the mid-1990s a strong reaction against postmodernism set in among those who found it not only inadequate as a theory of the self but also socially dangerous. The objections were primarily of two kinds, psychological and sociological, but behind both, as was so often the case with identity theory after the 1960s, were concerns about fashioning a more effective identity politics. Significantly none of the objecting theorists challenged the postmodernist argument against identity as the preexisting timeless "essence" of persons to be passively discovered. The battle against this version of essentialism—whether anyone had actually held it or not—had been won.

Some critics argued, however, that from a philosophical point of view the postmodernist interpretation of essence, resting on Aristotelianism, was not the only possible one, and that on another understanding it was a legitimate, indeed necessary concept. Furthermore, there were advantages for feminism in appealing to it because the claim that there can be no female essence had a long pedigree in the history of patriarchal thought since Aristotle, who defined woman as merely a defective form of the "human," the perfection of which was male. Rethinking the metaphysics of essence would make it possible to attribute a distinctive identity to woman and to give feminists a valid conception both of what all women have in common and what differentiates them from one another.

Postmodern feminists had tried to solve the problem of exclusion through definition by getting rid of the idea of essence altogether. Because language and thought can represent particulars only through general concepts or universals, however, this is logically impossible. An adequate theory of essence, Christine Battersby argued, involved three steps. It began with John Locke's concept of "nominal essence," the idea that an essence is the name given to a thing in virtue of certain empirical properties that it shares with other things. The next step invokes the Kantian idea that the mind groups perceptions together under concepts according to certain rules or "schemata." Finally, in light of contemporary poststructuralism, Kantian schemata had to be understood not as neutral eternal structures of the mind but as regulative practices, or norms, that had their origins in discursive practices. "These privileged 'norms,'" Battersby claimed, "are what determine essence."[146] Because such norms are historical and mobile, however, they are subject to revision to accommodate new facts and values, and the corresponding essences change accordingly.

The problem that universals had historically posed for women, Battersby pointed out, was that concepts like "human," "person," or "individual" have traditionally been identified with putatively male attributes or attributes supposed to reach their highest development in males. Her approach, she argued, made it possible to challenge both the empirical adequacy and the normativity of such concepts. "What happens to the notion of identity," she asked, "if we treat the embodied female as the norm for models of the self?"[147]

This would entail taking into account five features of the female body and experience that are discrepant with the dominant models of identity in the western definition of "man," which essentializes disembodied reason and interpret the body as the external container of mind. They include the female body's "natality," its ability to give birth; its capacity to nurture the dependent; its ability in pregnancy to be both self and not-self by harboring otherness within itself; its inherent "fleshiness"; and finally the female's experiential awareness of her aberrant or "monstrous" deviation as passive flesh from the male norm of disembodied active rationality.[148] Taking these into account in defining the human would render its identity as including potentiality and flow, as having otherness "within" as well as "without," as, finally, not having a body but being body.[149]

Leaving aside feminist objections that she was simply repeating the old maternal definition of woman, there were other problems with her attempted redefinition of essence. It is not clear that there was any fundamental difference between it and the postmodern concept of social construction via discursive practices. There was, further, serious confusion about her ultimate aim: was it, as she sometimes said, to rethink the identity of woman, or was it, as she said elsewhere, to redefine "the human" as such? If the latter, starting from specifically female embodiment would seem to suggest that "the human" was apportioned differently between the two sexes, a plausible position though one whose consequences would need to be spelled out. But whatever its problems, Battersby's theory was an attempt to acknowledge and accommodate something quite real: the inescapability of the general concepts which postmodernists used even as they tried to deny their validity, and which put definitional boundaries on the entities they refer to. To use the word "women" is to circumscribe a group and attribute to it an identity, however unarticulated. The question is which identity, not whether there is one.

*   *   *

For Susan Hekman, the problem of identity for postmodernism was psychological rather than philosophical, though concerns like Battersby's about universals also came into play. Referring to clinical studies of multiple personality disorder and internal psychological gender conflicts, she cited their authors' attacks on the postmodern idea of fictive identity as a "dangerous [concept], because it posits the self as a rhetorical category, not a real, feeling, experiencing being."[150] Political theorist James Glass, who interviewed a number of schizophrenics and women diagnosed with multiple personality disorder in the context of a critique of postmodern theory pointed out that their fragmented, shattered identities are evidence of deep pain, not liberation. The psychologist and psychotherapist Lynne Layton agreed: "In postmodern work that lauds indeterminacy, fragmentation is essentialized, universalized and celebrated in a way that seems not to acknowledge what it feels like to experience it."[151] Both theorists claimed that the unity of the self is a difficult achievement and a requirement for leading any version of a good and satisfying life. A stable identity is necessary because it "locates the self in the world; it defines emotional and interpersonal knowledge; it frames the self in a historical and situational context."[152] For Hekman, the key implication was that without a stable sense of identity people could not have coherent political goals, let alone act to achieve them. "There must be a ground," she claimed, "from which the individual assesses and reacts to experience."[153]

The concept of the subject that she thought best addressed the psychological issues raised by contemporary discussions of identity was the psychoanalytic theory of object relations. This represented a return to the position of Nancy Chodorow, by this time out of favor with feminists, but with a postmodern difference. D. W. Winnicott, the most influential of the object relations theorists, had advanced the idea of what Hekman labeled the "core self" that emerged out of the interaction between infant and mother as the original nurturing figure. This core should not be confused with a "true" or "essential" self; as the product of relationships it was "a socially constituted entity." If the core self was psychologically grounded in the nurturing relationship, it was ontologically an "ungrounded ground,"[154] its contents ultimately contingent on its historical circumstances. "Each of us," she summarized, "forms a core self through relational experiences in early childhood and this core self provides us with a stable, individual identity that carries us through life. . . . But this self, like the cultural experiences we negotiate is thoroughly social,"[155] though always with individual variations.

Individual identities, however, are not the only ones we have. Central to Hekman's political argument is that each of us is also "subsumed under an array of public identities: woman/man, white/nonwhite, middle/working class and so forth." These public identities are characterized by general concepts, the "essences" whose philosophical validity Battersby tried to establish. There are spheres of life where public and personal identities interact; politics is one of the most important. To act politically demands that I identify with the public identities assigned me, because, though Hekman did not quite put it this way, it is those identities—gender, ethnicity, race, class—that can impinge negatively on my interests and needs. But "I do not and cannot bring all the aspects of my personal identity into that act of political identification." While one's political identifications are rooted in one's personal identity—there would otherwise be no motivation for political action—the complexities of personal identity exceed them.[156]

It is the distinction between public and personal identities that accounts for the existence, and the problem, of multiple identities, according to Hekman. Personal identities are composed of multiple elements, but it is only from the perspective of public identity categories that those elements are ever contradictory. The problem occurs when more than one of the public identities to which we are assigned are discriminated against or marginalized. Since the politics of each of these identity groups is exclusive and demands singular allegiance, people feel divided between them. This is often the situation of black women and Chicanas who feel torn between their gender and their racial or ethnic identities. They feel unable to speak from a single, unified "subject position."

This does not mean, however, that there is no "I" uniting all the identities, as postmodernists would have it. Their error comes from ignoring the difference between public and personal identity. "Public identity categories define all of us and demean some of us. They define elements of our personal identities as contradictory. The contradiction stems from the public categories, not personal identity."[157]

This neat distinction, however, was neither correct nor necessary. To save the idea of an "I" as the continuous subject of its multiple identifications it isn't necessary to assume that any contradictions between them are only public or external. Hekman had confused the sense of "I-ness," or "mine-ness," which she expressly mentioned,[158] with the idea of a coherent "I." It is precisely because "I-ness" permeates *all* the self's identifications that, as Erikson long ago noted about parental identifications, the "I" can feel personally torn between identities. The core self that Hekman insisted on may be a badly divided self.[159] A major reason fashioning personal identity can be an arduous task is because of internally incompatible identifications. Lack of public recognition, as Hekman discussed, is at the root of socially demeaned identities, and for this the solution may well be, as she insisted, identity politics. But to the extent that demeaned or conflicting identities are internalized, the problem is one of psychological self-division, which may demand a different solution.

*   *   *

Where Hekman insisted, against postmodernism, on the psychological reality of identity, a group of scholars working together as a self-styled "collective" at Cornell University in the 1990s attacked it in the name of identity's social reality. Their approach, to which they gave the name "postpositivist realist theory of identity," was at the same time a militant program, meant to combat the "hegemony" of postmodernism in university literary and cultural studies.

This was in part a battle for academic turf between younger and more established scholars, but it also had strong ethnoracial overtones. Members of the collective, many if not the majority of whom were self-described "women of color"—Hispanic, Chicana, Asian, black—saw postmodern feminism as the theory of privileged white middle-class women who lived intellectually in the rarified air of "discourse" and who even if lesbians did not experience the same weight of social oppression they did. To add insult, they also presumed to speak on behalf of women of color.[160]

The key objection of identity realism to the postmodernist theorizing of identity was that it recognized only a choice between essentialist and postmodernist accounts of identity.[161] Identity, however, does not live only in the precincts of closed "discourses" which can be overcome by purely intellectual distancing but in the reality of social experience. "Social experience" is not a simple concept; the impact of the external world on the self is always mediated by individual interpretation, so that there is no one-to-one causal relationship between a person's social location and her identity—that is the "postpositivist" aspect of the theory—but it is always an inescapable influence. Hence some identities have more "epistemic value"—are more true—than others because they more accurately describe someone's actual social location. The relevance of this point was that a person of color might try to identify with the part of her background that ranked higher in the estimate of the white majority—for example, her Spanish name—though later experiences of discrimination might force her to come to terms with her Mexican origins. One's own interpretation of social location as a minority person is not the only or even the determining one; it is always at the mercy of the majority's. This dynamic suggests that oppositional struggle is fundamental to one's ability as a person of color to understand the world more accurately. *Pace* Laclau and Mouffe, Moya considered this a specifically Marxist theorem.[162] One can only really understand the sexist and racist interpretations of the other, let alone free oneself from them, in the political fight against them; otherwise one takes them as natural, and conforms.

For the history of ideas, the realist theory of identity was a case of "everything old is new again." The same criticisms had been leveled by Marxists at Sartre's original existentialism sixty years earlier, labeled as "idealism." Liberation wasn't just a matter of right consciousness but of removing real material obstacles to the exercise of freedom. Such "materialist" critics generally overlooked the fact that the two positions were complementary rather than mutually exclusive, that it might first be necessary to liberate oneself from the prison house of ideology, or discourse, before one could even realize that one was in a jail with metal as well as mental bars. And even then the battle against the jailers would have to include a fight against their beliefs as well as their institutions, since the latter were based on and upheld by the former. This point was implicit in Moya's declaration that "Who we are—*that is, who we perceive ourselves or are perceived by others to be*—will significantly affect our life chances: where we can live, whom we can marry (or whether we can marry), and what kinds of educational and employment opportunities will be available to us. . . . [Present] structures of inequality . . . are often highly correlated with categories of identity."[163] "Who we are," as Moya's quick qualification acknowledged, is who we, and others, believe us to be. But as she argued against postmodernism, such beliefs are not just a matter of language but of law and social institutions, which had to be overturned to effect change. That was why *Reclaiming Identity* was not concerned with what Moya called the "reification of existing identities," which in any case postmodernism had demystified, but with their real social causes and effects, which postmodernism had ignored, as a precondition for reorienting the identity debate toward concrete political change.

Paradoxically, identity realism's most significant thrust at postmodernism was not about the insubstantiality of its purely linguistic approach in a material world but its iron determinism. The two were opposite sides of the same coin. For Butler, for example, *prise de conscience* and performative rebellion were all there could be in the face of monolithic "power"; to be anything other than subversively negative would be to fall into the essentialist trap of identity. For the realists, power was not an abstraction but a system of concrete institutions, which however deeply anchored had been historically created and were historically revisable. The question was, revisable on behalf of what? What stance toward one's socially located Chicana identity, for example, ought one to take when oppression and inequality have been overcome? If these were only pejorative identities foisted on a certain group in conditions of inequality, would they cease to exist when equality was attained? Should they? Since realism had a presentist political purpose and agenda, most identity realists did not ask the question.[164]

*   *   *

Linda Martín Alcoff was one who did. She approached the question by focusing on another dimension of the material specificity of identity, the salience of physical characteristics in the "visible identities" of race and gender.[165] Feminist theory, as epitomized by postmodernism, has an aversion to naturalism because the identification of women with nature was the traditional source of their denigration. But, she argued, this aversion does not logically rule out the facts of natural difference between men and women. What society does with them is another matter, but because natural differences exist in a sphere of life that loomed large in the life of the individual and of society, they affect identity independently of the way they are socially or discursively constructed.

Alcoff argued that it is philosophically legitimate to restore the distinction between sex and gender that, after Butler, it had almost become feminist orthodoxy to erase. But postmodernists were right about the fluidity and indeterminacy of gender. To accommodate such arguments Alcoff introduced the conception of gender "positionality," which, she claimed, allows for "a determinate though fluid identity of woman that does not fall into essentialism."[166] The existing social structure objectively determines a woman's position relative to other groups with regard to roles, mobility, and power. At the same time a woman actively takes up that position, so that while it constitutes her subjective experience of being a woman, she is also at least potentially able to choose what to make of her positionality and try to alter it.

Sex however is a different matter. Alcoff argued that it is possible to give an objective rather than a totally fluid account of sex categories, and that, furthermore, sex understood this way plays a role in the determination of gender no less significant than social or discursive construction. Applying categories developed by the philosophers W. V. O. Quine and Sally Haslinger, she argued that sex is what contemporary metaphysicians call an "objective type," because it is defined by a nonrandom unifying feature of things that is independent of us. We attribute significance to the feature, but it is present in all the objects constituting the type. In the case of sex, the objective basis of sex categories is in the differential relationship to reproductive capacity between men and woman: "*Women and men are differentiated by virtue of their different relationship of possibility to biological reproduction . . . referring to conceiving, giving birth, and breast-feeding, involving one's own body.*"[167] While this fact does not mandate a norm of either reproduction or heterosexuality, Alcoff argued that it remains in place for women who are postmenopausal, have had hysterectomies, have no desire or intention to reproduce, or who are infertile. Those classified as women will have a different set of practices, expectations, and feelings in regard to reproduction, no matter how actual their relationship of possibility to it, than men. The possibility may play a role of greater or lesser importance in a culture's definition of gender identity, or in an individual woman's personal identity,[168] but it will always be there as a consideration to be taken into account.

More broadly, "sexed identity" is what she called an "embodied horizon," meaning the range of future experiences and possibilities "visible" to someone having, or rather being, a particular kind of body. "For girls," she wrote, "this horizon will generally include the future possibility of reproduction, even if this turns out never to come to pass . . . Knowing that one may become pregnant and give birth to children in the future affects how one feels and thinks about pregnancy and childbirth, sexual relations, familial relations, and various possibilities for paid work or careers. . . . The possibility of pregnancy, childbirth, nursing, and in many societies rape, are parts of females' horizons that we carry with us throughout childhood and much or all of our adult lives."[169] That statements like these needed to be made and arduously defended suggests not just the oddity of radical postmodernism but the powerful hold it had on segments of the academy. Alcoff's almost casual inclusion of rape suggests that the determinative influence of the sexed body goes beyond its relationship to biological reproduction to the whole area of sexual experience, including the modalities of sexual pleasure and pain. And there is no reason not to consider sexual orientation part of the sexed body, as at least some gay theorists insisted, which would importantly expand the range of horizons available to and constrained by it.

Unlike those of sex, Alcoff argued, the visible markers of race—skin color, eye shape—have no proven inner connection with anything deeper like character, aptitude, or intelligence. While races might be considered "objective types" in virtue of their visible features, these superficial characteristics are their only differentials. This fact, however, has not made them any the less influential socially. Differences in skin color have been the basis for naturalizing cultural differences or the projection of inner traits. Because such physical differences are experienced as unalterable, locating race in the visible produces the experience that racial identity is both deep and immutable.[170] As a result, a "visual registry" with regard to race operates in social relations that is socially constructed and variable but powerfully determinant over individual experience, both that of the observer and that of the observed. It is this registry that makes race a stubborn social reality.

*   *   *

Theorists like Alcoff who tried to rescue identity from postmodernism insisted on acknowledging openly what postmodernists conceded unwittingly or unwillingly: society creates identities that are real because people take them as real and act on them. Furthermore some of the most socially important ones are based on physical realities that objectively affect life chances, even if their meaning and value are socially assigned and in principle revisable. What realists failed to grapple with, however, was the subjective motivation of identity itself: the self's apparent need, or desire, for definition. Postmodernists had attacked identity on precisely that ground, and for the same reason Sartre did. Like him they equated the desire for self-definition with metaphysical escapism, the need to be objectively and permanently situated, transcendentally justified. What trapped them into the contradiction of conceding identity despite what they regarded as its illegitimacy was politics. The point of deconstructing identity was the eradication of invidious identities in order to support the demands of specific identity groups for social and political recognition. On one level poststructuralist concessions to identity could be taken as the equivalent of the role played by "class" in Marxist theory: a temporary historical reality that in the ideal society would no longer exist.

William Connolly, however, undermined such a potential defense of postmodernist consistency against the charge of contradiction. While metaphysically speaking identities are false, "branded contingencies" such as our gender and ethnicity, burned into us so early in life, feel natural, not socially contingent: they are, he insisted, who we "are." Whether he fully recognized it or not, this was to allow the metaphysical sense of being in by the back door of empirical psychology. Identity could never be just a discursive production of power, just a political strategy, or just a social reality based on (if not exhausted by) physical reality. Though he offered a philosophical justification of identity in Derridean terms as the positive side of the polarity identity/difference, he remained trapped within deconstruction's all-or-nothing conceptualization of identity as wholeness or absolute being. Hence his continuing anxiety about it, and his ironic, unsatisfying conclusion that identity was necessary but not real.

Chapter 9

Identity Transforms the Social Sciences

Much of the interest in identity in the humanities through the 1980s and the 1990s—particularly in American university departments of literature, cultural studies, women's studies, and political theory—was in the broad sense politically motivated, and avowedly so. In these disciplines, theorizing identity and promoting, accommodating, or, less often, attacking identity politics were largely inseparable, even when what was at stake was something as apparently politically innocuous as the interpretation of a literary text. But this was not true everywhere in the academy. The emergence of identity as an important concept in sociology had preceded its politicization in the 1960s. What did change in its aftermath was that academic interest in identity not only intensified where it already existed but extended into such disciplines as anthropology, individual and social psychology, linguistics, and economics, where it fostered new approaches and entire subdisciplines. What differentiated these initiatives from the humanities' focus on identity politics was the attempt to formulate scientifically "neutral" theories with wide explanatory power but without immediate activist intent. This didn't mean that such work proceeded apart from any social and historical context, or even that it was "value-free," though some of its practitioners made the claim. Erik Erikson had been clear from the outset that his own work was rooted in its historical moment, and the introduction of identity into sociology in the 1950s was closely connected with the question of southern and eastern European immigrant integration in the postwar United States. In any case, from the late 1960s on it was impossible to ignore the ongoing, and noisy, political and ideological debates about identity, not least the postmodernist attacks, which had contributed much to publicizing the word and which were an unavoidable part of the contemporary context by the 1980s. Ultimately the disciplinary expansion of identity created its own backlash at the hands of social scientists who felt that the concept was not an aid but a serious, even insidious obstacle to fruitful theorizing in the social sciences.

In the United States, academic initiatives to absorb identity into the social sciences tended to be independent of one another, separated by jealously guarded departmental and methodological boundaries; even cross disciplinary references, let alone ventures, were rare. In France and Germany, by contrast, the increasing resonance of the concept in the 1970s inspired interdisciplinary colloquia focused on the uses of identity that brought together researchers from a wide variety of fields. Out of these came two volumes of papers that became landmarks in establishing the scholarly respectability of the concept and displaying its versatility in approaching old problems and broaching new ones. The first volume contained the proceedings of a seminar directed by one of the most famous French intellectuals of his day, Claude Lévi-Strauss, founder of anthropological structuralism, who in organizing it lent his immense prestige to a concept not previously associated with his work. *L'identité* included among its contributors such well-known thinkers and scientists as the philosopher Jean-Marie Benoit, the molecular biologist Antoine Danchin, the psychoanalyst André Green, the ethnologist Michel Izard and the philosopher and literary critic Julia Kristeva.[1] Contributors, however, tended for the most part to talk about identity in its older philosophical sense. The German volume, titled *Identität*, was both more ambitious and more directly concerned with the new psychological and social meanings of identity. It came out of a conference its organizers called "Poetics and Hermeneutics" but whose scope went well beyond what the name might suggest to an American reader. The organizers had, as the preface announced, invited contributions in the analysis and history of the philosophical problem of identity, on the possibilities and limits of the reception of identity in history, art history, and theology, and on the place of identity in pedagogy and linguistics.[2] Even this self-description did not do justice to the range of the contributors, who in addition to such literary eminences as Hans Robert Jauss, Wolfgang Iser, and Jean Starobinski included the historians Christian Meier and Reinhart Koselleck, the latter coauthor of the landmark history of political and social concepts that founded conceptual history, the sociologists Niklas Luhmann and Thomas Luckmann, and the philosophers Dieter Henrich and Heinrich Lübbe. The volume's timing and scope, and the reputation of the contributors, made it a touchstone for much subsequent research on identity in German universities.[3]

"Social Identity" in Social Psychology and Sociology

In an earlier chapter I discussed the transformational impact of identity on anthropology. For some theorists in sociology and social psychology as well, identity provided the answer to a long-standing dilemma that, as they saw it, had stymied progress in their disciplines. Though they posed the problem in somewhat different terms, the underlying issue was everywhere the same: there had historically been a theoretical gulf in sociology between the causal force of individuals versus that of society. As Richard Jenkins put it, "Perhaps the most persistent issue in social theory is the 'structure-action' problem. . . . From Marx to Weber to Parsons to Berger and Luckmann to Giddens to Bourdieu [the same question has been raised:] How to bring together analytically the active lives and consciousnesses of individuals, the abstract impersonality of the institutional order, and the ebb and flow of historical time?"[4] For Margaret Somers and Gloria Gibson, the problem was even older and more intractable. From its beginnings in the eighteenth century social theory continued to derive its basic categories from its original project of explaining the emergence of modernity out of traditional society. As a result, its two permanent methodological starting points were the autonomous self-interested individual on the one side and an external, coercive society on the other. By reifying the historical situation of European modernization into a set of universal sociological categories it had rendered itself incapable of explaining the purposes and continuing cohesion of social institutions. If social "relationality" is embedded in institutions that are external to the individual, they asked, where do such institutions come from?[5] How are they sustained? For these theorists the way out of this impasse was through a theory of social identity.

Henri Tajfel's Theory of Social Identity

The most striking example of the international diffusion of identity, as well as of its power to transform a discipline while also being modified by it, was Henri Tajfel's hugely influential theory of social identity. Tajfel himself insisted that the historical context of his experimental work in social psychology was a determining source of its hypotheses and operational concepts, and beyond that of his basic conception of the scope of social psychology altogether. His experience as a Jewish refugee who had lost his entire family in the Holocaust led him, he said, to his pioneering work in intergroup conflict and the social psychology of minorities: "together with many people of my generation, I share memories of a raging storm which—it seemed at the time—would never stop. Among those who died then, there were millions who formed, in the most concrete sense of the term, my 'social background': the generations of European Jews who were born in the half century straddling the eighteen and nineteen hundreds. The minority who survived came in from very cold and very far. . . . A very few . . . tried to express what happened to them and to others. Sharing their experience and feelings . . . I became an academic."[6] "The course of relations between human groups of various kinds," he was led to conclude, "is one of *the* fundamental social problems of our times."[7]

For these same historical reasons Tajfel was satisfied neither by the purely individualistic assumptions of contemporary academic psychology, which assumed a "homogeneous social medium" that could be disregarded in favor of universal laws of individual psychic functioning, nor by the causal determinism of sociological explanations solely in terms of social forces external to the self. The concept of social identity mediated between the two sorts of explanations, accommodating both individual motivation and social causation: "in an infinite variety of situations throughout his life, an individual feels, thinks, and behaves in terms of his social identity created by the various groups of which he is a member and in terms of his relation to the social identity of others, as individuals or *en masse*."[8] Identity was the subjective dimension of society, what made it internal to the individual; social norms were sustained and put into action by the self's social definition of itself. Tajfel was quite modest in his claims for the importance of social identity within the totality of an individual's identity: "social identity will be understood as that *part* of an individual's self-concept which derives from his knowledge of his membership of a social group (or groups) together with the value and emotional significance attached to that membership. It will be clear that this is a limited definition of 'identity' or 'social identity.' "[9] In light of his experimental conclusions, however, this disclaimer turned out to be overmodest.

Tajfel's critique of individualistic psychology also implicated his discipline's conventional understanding of experimentation—its basic methodology and its claim to scientific validity. By assuming that experimental subjects represent universal mankind, psychology was operating in a social vacuum. "The general case is an impossible myth," he argued, "as long as human beings behave as they do because of the social expectations with which they enter an experiment—or any other social situation. . . . If these expectations are shared—as they always are by definition to some degree in any social context—I shall obtain data from my experiment which are neither 'general' nor 'individual.' "[10] It was not even necessary to do cross-cultural experimentation to discover this fact: "*all* experiments are 'cultural' . . . . [influenced by] the contextual and background conditions which determine the subject's perception of what may be the socially appropriate behavior in the quandary in which he finds himself when faced with a row of stooges who, to the best of his knowledge, are a random collection of moderately honest citizens."[11]

Finally, it was Tajfel's historically grounded conception of social psychology that made him, though based academically in England, pursue with colleagues across the European continent the creation of a distinctly European social psychology. Europe had recently been the cockpit of murderous intergroup conflict, thus a large laboratory for experiment. At the same time Europe's national and cultural diversity created possibilities for a Continental community of social psychologists to test its analyses of social life against the intellectual and social requirements of many cultures.[12]

Yet despite all his careful contextual qualifications and his modesty about the scope of social identity, the great impact of Tajfel's work resulted from its apparently universal conclusions about the powerful hold that group identification has on the self, and the large space it takes up within the whole of a person's identity. In a series of experiments carried out by Tajfel and his associates, individuals were assigned to "groups" defined by criteria that were essentially meaningless to them. In one, boys from the same high school in Bristol, England, were separately exposed to a series of images of paintings by Kandinsky and Klee, of whom they had never heard. The images were not labeled and in fact were randomly assigned to the painters by the experimenters. The boys were asked to choose which they preferred and then arbitrarily assigned to a "Kandinsky group" or a "Klee group," though never meeting the other group "members." Each boy was then presented with a series of options for allocating monetary rewards for participation in the experiment to three anonymous pairs of boys, who were variously labeled as members of their own group, the other group, or as one from each. The options allowed the boys either to equalize rewards among all the boys in both groups, to maximize the total amount members of their own group received, or to maximize the difference between the two groups at the cost of giving less than the maximum possible to their own group. In the majority of cases, the boys chose to maximize the difference between the groups even when that meant giving less to their own group in absolute terms.[13] In an even more complete reductio ad absurdum of group criteria, subjects were assigned to groups based on the ostensible outcome of a coin toss (the actual outcome of the toss was ignored). Similar experiments were repeated with groups of various ages and both sexes, and always with the same results.[14]

Most of the subjects, Tajfel summarized, consistently favored anonymous members of their own groups at the expense of the anonymous members of the other groups, however thin, even absurd, the criterion for group identity. Ruling out an explanation in terms of the influence of the experimenters— there was no reason to believe that they desired or hinted at one possible outcome over another—he concluded that "the subjects structured the situation for themselves as one involving relations between groups and that they behaved in ways similar to those habitual to them in situations of this kind."[15]

While Tajfel did not give examples of such "habitual" behavior outside the experiments, his conclusion was that in the boys' wider society "us" versus "them" was a powerful reflex. Their group identity, in a word, was inherently adversarial. Further, Tajfel argued that there was a common denominator in both his artificial laboratory experiments and in extreme real-world events like the selection for the gas ovens in the "concentration camps" of World War II. In both there was a two-step process that began with the depersonalization of the members of the out-group followed by their dehumanization. "In the experiments," Tajfel noted, "the depersonalizing anonymity was created in a *deus ex machina* fashion by the experimenters. In real life it is generated by the actors themselves, as a function of the intergroup situation within which they act; but otherwise, certain similarities in the nature of the resulting social behavior are quite striking."[16]

When it came to explaining the habitual nature of such behavior, however, Tajfel's cautions about the inescapability of historical context gave way to the kind of universal generalizations, sociological and psychological, that he had warned against. Every society, he claimed, relies on group "categorization" to orient individuals within it by supplying them with a repertoire of socially recognized identities that create and define their place. Individuals, furthermore, depend in part on their group identity for a positive self-image. To the extent it does not afford one, they will try to leave the group, change its image, or alter its social situation. Finally, since no group lives alone, a group's self-image has meaning only in relation to other groups. Social identity depends on social comparison,[17] and comparison always plays on the differences between groups, whether of status, wealth, color, or ability.[18] Without quite saying so, Tajfel was claiming that social comparisons are always invidious; they involve hierarchical judgments of better and worse.

He did, though, explicitly highlight the difference between his results and those of Muzafer Sherif, whose Robbers Cave experiment he regarded as nearest to his own work in conception and method. Though one of the boys' groups in Sherif's experiment had formed a distinctive identity before its encounter with the other, Sherif's focus was on the way that the conflict situations set up by the experimenters *created* adversarial intergroup identities. Consequently when both groups were faced by material shortages and difficulties (these too were manufactured by the experimenters), their artificial adversarial identities could be overcome and finally obliterated by their common interest. By contrast, in Tajfel's experiments, as he emphatically noted, there was no externally defined conflict; if there was competition between the groups, *it was fully and actively brought into the situation by the subjects them-selves* as soon as the notion of group was introduced by the experiment-ers. The subjects were never together as a "group"; they neither interacted nor did they know who was in their group and who in the other; there was no *explicit* social pressures on them to act in favor of their own group; and in no way was their own individual interest engaged in awarding more money to a member of their own group. On the contrary, a consistent use of the maximum joint profit strategy would have led to *all* of them receiving more money from the experimenters.[19]

The implication seemed to be that there is a universal human need to create not only identity distinctions between "us" and "them," but explicitly exclusionary ones, in-groups and out-groups. (Anthropologist Fredrik Barth had reached a similar conclusion for tribal and ethnic identities.) Conflicts of interest between groups follow on such prior distinctions or are intrinsic to them; they are not their cause. Tajfel tried to meliorate the moral shock of this bleak conclusion by speaking in more neutral terms of the individual need to find "meaning" in social identity by inventing difference where it does not exist or assigning value to such difference as does exist.[20] His own meaning, however, was clear enough: as Jacques Derrida had argued in a more abstract philosophical context, "difference" was a binary concept meant to establish superiority and inferiority. Collective identity was a matter of hierarchy of value, of invidious comparison, not merely one of distinctive group character-istics. Coupled with his previous remarks about how the in-group depersonal-izes and ultimately dehumanizes the out-group, this analysis made his ultimate conclusion about the nature and process of intergroup conflict even less benign, identical in spirit to Beauvoir's concept of the "Other" as qualitatively lesser being. Empirical experiment verified phenomenological analysis.

Social Roles and "Identity Theory"

While crediting earlier work in symbolic interactionism,[21] Peter Burke and Jan Stets were the first to apply the name "Identity Theory" to their particular version of a long-established sociological concept, role theory.[22] Though "role" was a type of social identity, to sociologists it represented a different level of social functioning from Tajfel's "group." Groups are variable social formations of undefined purpose. Roles are derived from the stable economic, political, bureaucratic, familial, and educational structures through which a society's main functions are carried out. Two things relevant to identity follow from the structural approach. Though the repertoire of roles in a society may be historically variable, all societies must be structured by stable roles in order to function; thus social role will always be central to individual identity. And in any society, a fortiori complex modern ones, an individual will have multiple roles at any one time and throughout his life.

However, Burke and Stets pointed out, traditional role theory does not claim to be about individual people but about the objective components of social "interaction systems." Because roles are often described impersonally in terms of their interactive structural features, that is, how they relate in a rule-governed way to other roles—for example how teachers are expected to relate to students and vice versa—it is not clear what they have to do with people as agents who initiate actions or as subjects who experience their impact.[23] The function of "identity" in role theory is explicitly to bring together person and role by recognizing that the bearer of a role is someone for whom the role has subjective meaningfulness.[24] A person, they stipulated, drawing on Sheldon Stryker's definition, has a personal identity for each of the different roles he or she holds in society[25]—daughter, student, husband, teacher, citizen, and so on. Identity theory "seeks to explain the specific meanings that individuals have for the multiple identities they claim; how these identities relate to one another for any one person; how their identities influence their behavior, thought, and feelings or emotions; and how their identities tie them in to society."[26] Identity for these sociologists as for Tajfel was thus a conceptual vehicle for bringing together subjective self and objective society. It allowed them to move back and forth between agents and structures in order to explain how structures are the creations of agents and how agents act within the structures they create.[27] In this way identity theory represented the systematization of Nelson Foote's original impulse for introducing the ideas of identification and identity into sociology half a century before: identity personalizes—not to say humanizes—roles.[28]

But Burke and Stets conceived the subjectivity of role identity very narrowly. The role of a district manager might formally be defined as increasing the sales of business in a particular area; the individual manager expresses her role identity in deciding how best to fulfill it.[29] Her "role identity" is limited to the personal initiatives she takes to enact the role's requirements. Nevertheless, because a person has multiple roles, personhood is more complex than their simple aggregation. The self has to rank its identities hierarchically in order to know how to act in case of conflict among them. Ranking is necessary also because of the individual's psychological need for self-esteem, which is attached to how well she performs her roles according to their relative importance to her. In sociological identity theory psychological self-esteem is dependent on "identity-verification," which is governed by the confirmation or lack of it by those with whom one interacts in a reciprocal role-structure.[30] A large part of identity theory was concerned with the hypothesis of "perception control," according to which persons manipulate their behavior or their environment so that their perception of environmental "inputs"—reactions from others to their identity performances—match the internalized identity standards that regulate their self-esteem. Experiments in identity theory were designed to test the different parts of this hypothesis.

Burke and Stets acknowledged Tajfel's social group identity and what they called "person identity" as the two other distinct components of an individual's whole identity along with role identity.[31] Their distinctions among the three, however, were confusing. Analytically, they argued, role identities were individual-level identities because one usually referred to one's roles in the first person—"I am a student"—while social group identifications usually involved we-references. But the authors conceded that in many circumstances role-holders readily constitute themselves as groups with we-identities, when for example teachers act in concert to achieve a common aim. Similarly, while "person identity" is supposedly the set of meanings that define the person as unique individual, rather than as role-holder or group member, the criteria for ranking roles, which is the process that purportedly constitutes the uniqueness of individual identity, are themselves social. Some of the difficulties the theorists had in distinguishing the separate categories of identity and explaining how they could be synthesized into a unified concept of the self arose in part from the fact that the categories were narrowly specific artifacts of academic disciplinary and departmental divisions, reflecting the professional interests and questions of sociology, social psychology, and individual psychology respectively.

Academic specialization was not the only source of difference between Tajfel's social identity and sociological identity theory, nor the most important. While identity theory does not assume frictionless interaction—individuals can and do fail to verify one another's role identities—its interpersonal tenor is quite the opposite of Tajfel's social identity theory. Role identities are in principle nonadversarial because they are reciprocal; the parties to a role interaction normally have the same set of expectations about one another's performance. Failure of mutual identity verification can occur when agreed on role expectations are not met, or when one or the other role-player is mistaken about them. A teacher may violate his role; a student may have inappropriate expectations of a teacher. Such mistakes are objective, not subjective value judgments, because roles are defined by the consensual rules of society. For Tajfel, however, failure of mutual recognition was built into the definition of social identity as it emerged from his experiments. Identity theory was designed to explain how a society works, on the premise that it does, at least for the most part. Burke and Stets deliberately chose to build on Stryker's work, in preference to that of certain other symbolic interactionists who emphasized historical change, precisely because he took a functioning society's institutions to be structurally stable. Tajfel's social identity theory, in sharp contrast, was developed to explain why societies got into destructive antagonisms and conflict. In its way identity theory was as "American" as Tajfel's social identity was "European." In its origins a theory of the seventies and eighties, identity theory harked back to the integrationist structural-functional sociology of the 1950s and implicitly revived that decade's spirit of anti-ideology and liberal-capitalist consensus; the background to Tajfel's theory was World War II.

Social Identity as the Foundation of Sociology

For Richard Jenkins, identity offered more than a contribution to a specific branch of sociology like role theory; it was necessarily the foundation of the discipline itself. In what read like a methodological manifesto, he claimed that "identity and identification are ubiquitous, generic aspects of human life that we need to understand in order to do sociology." The basic "sociological project" of understanding the relationship between individuality and collectivity could not be carried out without utilizing both those concepts.[32] Indeed, one could not understand the human individual at all without them.

Initially, Jenkins intended these terms in their older logical meaning. Identification "is the basic cognitive mechanism that humans use to sort out themselves and their fellows, individually and collectively. This is a 'base-line' sorting that is fundamental to the organization of the human world: it is how we know who's who and what's what."[33] We identify individual things according to categories that group some things as similar to one another and different from others. Necessarily we do the same for persons, not least ourselves. It was in elaborating on the relation between selfhood and identity that Jenkins shifted the meaning of the latter to its contemporary sense as *self*-definition.

Our very sense of selfhood is an identity, he argued; in fact it is the primary identity of "internal definition," what we subjectively take ourselves to be in the first instance. Being "a self" is "the individual's reflexive sense of her own particular identity, constituted *vis-à-vis* others in terms of similarity and difference, without which she would not know who she was and hence would not be able to act."[34] In other words, to have the apparently simple identity of "being a self" is to have the complex sense that I am *me*, a being who experiences and acts, just as you, likewise a self, do, but different from you. The primary internal identity of selfhood is complemented by and intertwined with the primary identity of "external definition," which Jenkins called "human-ness."[35] "Human" is what we first implicitly and then explicitly are told that we are by others as we are socialized into the world, directed to act or not to act in ways that are appropriate or inappropriate to "our kind" of being. (As one's mother might have said about one's table manners, "Behave like a human being, not like an animal!")

Though Jenkins called his book *Social Identity*, he thought his own title misleading to the extent it implied there were any other kinds. *All* human identities, from the individual to the collective, are social identities.[36] They are meanings that can only be produced in interactions between the self and others, involving conventions governing definitions and behavior communicated from the social side, and innovations negotiated with others through the self's initiatives. Primary identities are those that develop during "primary socialization"—meaning both earliest and most basic, with the implication that they are universal—and which later exhibit the greatest solidity, though they are also the most vulnerable during their early formation. Along with the identities of selfhood and humanness, Jenkins classified gender as a primary identity, since human selfhood is self-awaredly embodied from the beginning. Gender, he claimed, "is one of the most consistent identificatory themes in human history, and one of the most pervasive classificatory principles— arguably the most pervasive—with massive consequences for the life-chances and experiences of whole categories of people."[37] Gender identity is as basic as selfhood. Kinship is also a primary identity, since one is born into permanent blood relationships, and perhaps also ethnicity, though Jenkins noted that there was disagreement about it because of its voluntary dimension. It was in fact the negotiability of ethnic, as well as other, more secondary, collective identities that lay behind another of Jenkins's central contentions about identity generally: it "can only be understood as a process of 'being' or 'becoming.' One's identity . . . is never a final or settled matter."[38]

This claim explains why Jenkins always employed the two terms "identity and identification" interchangeably, moving without notice back and forth between them. Identification is the name of a process, and as the object of that process identity remains open, potentially ever changing. Here, however, there lurked the same problem many identity theorists faced without resolving. Although Jenkins generally treated identity and identification as names for the same thing, he also suggested that they represented two different, and from one point of view even opposite, aspects of identity. On the one hand identity is, as Fredrik Barth had argued, part of the ongoing organization of group interaction in everyday life. (Jenkins was a trained anthropologist as well as a sociologist and believed in the necessity of crossing disciplinary boundaries to create an integrated theory of identity.) Ethnic identity is socially constructed at and across the boundaries a group shares with others, in a dynamic, flexible process of differentiation. On the other hand, identity is the word for what makes the group in its own eyes a solid, authentic, unique, self-contained, and continuous community. Viewed from the outside, identification is what the group continuously *does*; experienced from the inside, identity is what the group continuingly *is*. Jenkins was no more able than other social scientists—or most postmodernists—to bridge the gap between external explanations by social construction, which undid essential identity, and the internal phenomenology of the subjective experience of identity as "is-ness." Whatever the inconsistency, Jenkins's final conclusion for sociology was that any social structure it studied had to be understood as being at least partly constituted by its own self-definition or identity.

Sociology as Narrative Identity

For Margaret Somers and Gloria Gibson, the way to free sociology from the reified polarity of isolated autonomous individual and external constraining society, while bringing self and society together in a theoretically valid way, was to historicize sociology through the idea of *narrative identity*. Identity politics, they claimed, had pointed the way to such a theoretical reconstruction, but its activist purposes threatened to produce its own ahistorical totalizing fictions, such as universal gender categories. A proper theory of narrative identity would preserve the gains of identity thinking while avoiding the dangers of reifying identities.

Narrative identity, they claimed, is an "ontological" category, that is, a defining feature of human life.[39] Narratives are by definition tales of becoming, not fixed identities. They are structured by emplotment, unfolding their story line over time, guided by the sense of an ending even if the story's direction can only be read backward. These were much the same points made by Alasdair MacIntyre, but the narratives they were interested in were not those of the great moral-religious traditions. The "ontological narratives" that matter for sociology are the "public narratives" attached to the cultural and institutional formations of a concrete society. They are the stories that every society tells about itself, stories about families and churches, about national cultural icons such as American social mobility, the freeborn Englishman, the frontier, the working-class hero. Such public narratives are the contexts out of which institutions and organizations are constructed and in which social action takes place; social "structures," with their static implications, the staples of traditional sociology, cannot be properly understood outside the narratives that tell how they came be what they are and what purposes they intended. Society, like the individual, does not simply *have* a narrative identity; it *is* its story, or rather its anthology of stories, smaller ones nested within more encompassing ones. In certain modern theoretical accounts, a concrete society's stories are obscured by what the authors called "metanarratives," the postmodern "master narratives" of larger forces like progress or class struggle which govern all societies. Though they look like narratives, however, metanarratives lack the genuine historical attributes of localized time and space.[40] The idea of concrete narrative identity undercuts all such metanarratives.

Narrative social identity took the opposite tack from the sociological identity theory of Burke and Stets, emphasizing fluidity over stable structure. The narrative approach "embeds the actor within relationships and stories that shift over time and space and thus precludes categorical stability in action."[41] Its concept of identity also differs from that of role/identity theory in other crucial ways. Identity narratives can have many plots and provide people with many motivations; they are not limited to the "interest" motivation of the role identities in the social division of labor. In fact, for Somers and Gibson, a "major advantage of the concept of narrative identity is in the challenge it poses to the false dichotomy too often posed between ideal versus instrumental meanings of action," as for example and most notably in Max Weber's sociology. The narrative approach shows that what sociology often describes as purely instrumental action for material goods simultaneously serves ideal ends connected with the sense of how people define themselves in terms of family, status, morality, or spiritual goals.[42]

Narrative identity purported to be a theory of form rather than of content. It prescribes how to look at society, not, as in role/identity theory, what to look at. But narrative identity has its own structure, which also entails the possibility of its breaking down: not through the challenge of one social narrative to another, which after all preserves narrative structure, but by the breakdown of emplotment in social life altogether. If history becomes so at odds with a society's prevailing narrative that the latter no longer makes sense of actual events, the identities it provided no longer make sense either. The plot of the narrative no longer has a point and its dramatis personae no longer have roles, nor is there any other plot readily available to replace it. This was for the authors the essential description of social breakdown. Understanding social crisis as the breakdown of existing narratives in turn makes the consequent chaos and conflict intelligible as a search for a new identity narrative both to restore society's equilibrium and to make possible forward momentum. Narrative identity thus purportedly bridges the conceptual gulf between static structure and dynamic, even radical, change. To be true to reality, sociology must not only become history, but specifically the narrative history of social identities.

Identity and "New Social Movement" Theory

The freedom to have which characterized . . . industrial society
has been replaced by the freedom to be.

—Alberto Melucci, *Nomads of the Present*[43]

The creation of New Social Movement theory was one of the most transparent manifestations of identity's impact on social theory, in the broad sense of a critical theory of social dynamics. The simplest but not for that reason inaccurate way to understand the "newness" of New Social Movement theory (often referred to in the literature as NSM) is as a self-conscious reaction against and alternative to Marxism. Social scientists in Europe, where, as NSM theorists made a point of noting, systematic Marxist theorizing was always more dominant than in America,[44] took the lead in trying to forge a coherent alternative to the paradigms of class and ideology which they believed could not account for the types of social movements that swept the world in the 1960s and 1970s. Feminist, gay, ethnic, ecological, religious, and disability movements did not fit Marxist categories. They cut across class lines and they were not primarily motivated by economic interest or the traditional political ideologies tied to class. The category that seemed to embrace them all most usefully was identity. Advocates and critics of New Social Movement theory were in agreement at least on this; as one of the latter put it, "identity claims are the most distinctive features of NSMs."[45]

This was true for the genesis of the movement as well. Alberto Melucci, one of the first and most prominent NSM theorists, included an account of his own development in the English translation of his major theoretical work, *Nomads of the Present*. It appropriately personalized the theme of the book's subtitle—*Social Movements and Individual Needs in Contemporary Society*—while providing a useful overview of European intellectual and social history from the late 1960s as it affected a socially committed young intellectual just coming of age.[46] It also helped to explain why Italian thinkers were especially prominent among the originators and proponents of NSM theory.

Melucci described his youthful trajectory from working-class, left-leaning Catholic activist to ultimately disillusioned sympathizer with the student movement in 1968. He came to fear the movement's desire for homogenizing unity, and his early contacts with the Italian Communist Party reinforced his disdain for traditional leftist politics because its dogmatism too closely resembled the Catholic fundamentalism he knew early on. As a graduate student in sociology he became equally dissatisfied with the then-dominant academic paradigms in Italy, Marxism and the structural-functionalism of Talcott

Parsons, reigning theorist of American sociology in the 1950s and 1960s. Marxism omitted the spiritual dimension of life, and while Melucci was critical of the role of religion in politics, he was sensitive to the power of ethical motivation. And both Marxism and functionalism as strongly determinist theories left no room for the autonomy of social action.

There was, furthermore, a strongly individualistic element in Melucci's concerns, fostered by formal training in psychology, the clinical practice of psychotherapy, and a personal psychoanalysis. Unsurprisingly, however, he was put off by the determinism of orthodox Freudianism and drawn to the phenomenological, existential, and humanistic approaches developing at the time, which were more concerned with "how people act and how they can change their lives if they so wish." As he saw it, the purpose of collective action was not only to effect social change but also to transform personal experience—that is, foster identity creation.

All these influences converged into a series of strong propositions about the state of contemporary society. From Marxism he retained the belief that the production of a society's basic resources is riddled with conflicts, but argued that the term "class" is not necessary to describe them, since class relationships were only one historical form of the relations of production. Contemporary social movements could no longer be guided by the sense that they are fulfilling a universal plan. They can have no long-term goals, and their mobilization is limited to specific times and places, concerned with immediate problems impinging on the possibilities of full-self development for different groups of people. Hence the title of his book: modern movements resemble nomads who dwell entirely in the present and have no permanent "home," that is, no ultimate goal.

His major empirical work in sociology, a research project in the city of Milan, reinforced these ideas. He spent four years with four different groups of "movement" activists—feminists, urban youth, including the so-called "punks," ecologists, and neoreligious groups operating outside the official churches. He came to the conclusion that all such movements express something more than the substantive goals which are their publicly proclaimed agenda and by which they are socially identified. They exist in order to affirm and to live their "difference" as outsiders to mainstream society, to assert their unique identities as a group and as individuals. Even their material and political demands represented the conditions required to successfully pursue the goal of self-realization, a goal so much more easily available to the respectable and well-off.

A key feature of the movements that Melucci pointed to is their independence from organized politics. While this might seem an obvious aspect of their expressive purpose, Melucci emphasized that his view was much influenced by the peculiarities of the Italian political system. The pervasiveness of the state in all sectors of public life meant that social problems could only be dealt with through the political system. Issues that the political parties did not take up were ignored by the state, and autonomous civil initiatives were minimal to nonexistent. Italians thus saw the state as omnipresent yet unresponsive and the political system as both blocked and illegitimate. The "newness" of the New Social Movements in the eyes of Italian theorists was their existence as an alternative politics, a "meta-political" phenomenon. This was less likely to strike observers in America, with its active civil society and history of grassroots organization, as anything remarkable; what was new there, however, was the challenge represented by identity-related demands that did not fit the customary American paradigm of "interest."

One introductory anthology of essays on New Social Movements attempted to define them with a catalogue of features that differentiated them from the "old." Its subtitle offered a pithy summary: "from ideology to identity." New Social Movements have a social base that transcends traditional class analysis. They do not have an ideology in the sense of a unifying and totalizing theory of society guiding their actions. Their grievances and appeals focus on cultural and symbolic issues that are linked with issues of identity rather than on economic grievances. The movements are as much forums for individual self-definition as for collective action; they are a complex mix of collective and individual confirmations of identity. They often involve personal and intimate aspects of human life, such as sexual identity. Unlike traditional working-class movements relying on party organization and press, they commonly use tactics of disruption and resistance. The proliferation and organization of new social movements are related to a credibility crisis regarding the conventional channels for participation in Western democracies, particularly the traditional political parties often seen as serving bureaucratic or oligarchic interests despite their purportedly mass base. Finally, their organization tends to be diffuse and decentralized.[47]

The list of features seems to support criticisms that the NSM paradigm was based solely on observations of left-wing movements and reflected an ideological bias.[48] At most, though, such criticisms challenged limitations in the application of the designation, not the validity of the concept. With only minor modifications the theory was easily able to accommodate right-wing European movements like violent skinheads and neofascist youth groups (and, one might add, American Christian militias)—as the authors of the list ruefully acknowledged.[49] A more serious objection was that traditional political movements of the past also had important identity functions for their participants, while the new movements also have "old-fashioned" economic and political grievances—in other words, there was nothing new about New Social Movements. The first point might well be true, but if so the objection amounted to an acknowledgement that identity was a need long before theory became conscious of it.

For a history of identity, in any case, the more pertinent question is what NSM theorists meant by it. Some conceded that their concept was not very clear, that "a more systematic approach to NSM's requires stronger conceptual development regarding identity."[50] Overall, they seem to have adopted two different strategies in using the term. One simply imported a definition of identity drawn from other branches of psychology and sociology and examined new social movements for evidence of its appearance. A second started with a thin, largely nominal conception of identity and arrived at its full meaning only from detailed phenomenological descriptions of the actions and language of the new movements themselves. While this method ran the danger of circularity it did substantially expand the meaning of the term.

Following the first approach, Johnston divided identity in new social movements into three components: individual, collective, and public. Preexisting *individual identities*—"idiosyncratic biographies"—play a role in shaping the character and direction of social movements.[51] In turn, social movements modify individual identity, weakening or obliterating old identifications and creating new ones as they define their collective identity. A movement's *collective identity* is consciously constructed through continuous discussion and debate among its members about who they are and through joint action to achieve the ends their identity entails for them. The authors' contention was that self-definition, the creation of identity, is central to the very existence and purpose of a movement; members value attachment to their collective identity quite apart from any concrete goals they may pursue. Thus a main line of NSM research should focus on understanding the processes by which the group fashions its identity. Finally, a group's *public identity* is the way it is perceived by the world outside it. The external world's definitions of the group are imposed on the group, which reacts to it in turn. Here research needs to explore the way the ongoing interaction both modifies collective identity and shapes the public identity of the group.

Theorists like Donatella della Porta and Mario Diani rejected the a priori analytic categories of individual, group, and public identity. Instead they looked at identity as what emerged from the process of new social movement creation, the internal dynamics of the movement's functioning once formed, and its interactions with the wider society. Identity, they argued, is "neither a thing one can own, nor a property of actors, but . . . the process through which individual and/or collective actors, in interaction with other social actors, attribute a specific meaning to their traits, their life occurrences, and the system of social relations in which they are embedded." While "reference to identity evokes the continuity and solidity of allegiances over time," identity is also "open to constant redefinition."[52]

Although this approach seems close to if not identical with the first, its emphasis was quite different. It meant to liquefy, or volatilize, the solidity Johnston apparently attributed to types of identity. The essence of new social movements, its authors argued, is action, and "action 'constitutes' identity."[53] "We" are created in the first instance by the determination that our condition as created by "them" is no longer acceptable, and by our mobilization to change that condition. As we pursue our goals, our identities come to embody new networks of relationships of trust among movement actors, feelings of solidarity with people to whom we are not usually linked by direct personal contacts, and common meanings to experiences of collective action by people possibly far apart in time and space. By the same token, the continuing impingement of "them" on "us"—mostly, though not always, negatively— causes us to revitalize and reformulate our identities. We create new symbols and new rituals to consolidate them and give them more character. In these formulations, identity was inconceivable apart from action—or reaction, when, as Sartre would have said, the us-object turns into the we-subject. This version gave identity an intrinsically ephemeral quality; it exists only for the duration of the struggle.

Once again, critics of NSM theory claimed that one could see the same stages and processes in the social movements of the nineteenth and early twentieth centuries. In response, Melucci offered a full-scale theory of the contemporary social developments that had, he believed, created a new kind of identity crisis, visible as such for the first time, in large sectors of society. Society in the late twentieth century had changed from a predominantly industrial to an information system. Its most advanced sectors—education, communications, entertainment—employ over 50 percent of the population in activities involving the production, processing, and circulation of information. Consequently it is information that "structures social life."[54] Control over information depends on control over social "codes"—a key though highly condensed term in Melucci's lexicon that referred to the systems of cultural "symbols" that project social values. The power to produce social codes is not equally distributed. Access to the "knowledge," that is, the values defined by codes becomes the terrain where new forms of power, discrimination, and conflict come into being.[55] In a word, social conflicts in modern society have moved from the economic to the cultural sphere.[56]

Power differentials have an impact on individual identity because the social symbols out of which individual identity is constructed (certain icons of middle-class identity, masculine-inflected ideals) are not subjectively meaningful to the powerless. While the powerless may have the technical ability to adapt their behavior to social codes even if they can't identify with them, a split develops between their purely technical mastery and their emotional ability to translate reigning social values into personal experiences. "The result," Melucci concluded, "is the search for identity, the quest for self that addresses the fundamental regions of human action: the body, the emotions, the dimensions of experience irreducible to instrumental rationality."[57] People excluded from symbolic power and alienated from its meanings need to find meanings of their own in the spheres that matter most to human life. The search for identity is "a remedy against the opacity of the system,"[58] whose meanings do not speak to those outside it.

Melucci's analysis of the procedures he observed in the Milanese women's movement gives flesh to these skeletal abstractions. Women's way of being, he claimed, is different from that of men. Granting recognition to women *as* women entails accepting a different outlook on reality, a way of relating to one's body, to others, and to the world that differs from the male norms enforced by the dominant social codes.[59] Women rely on "the female form of communication." The official codes allow only two modes of relationship: total identification with the dominant, homogenizing codes of ideal (masculine striving) behavior or social isolation, because difference means exclusion from the very possibility of communication. Women, who know through their experiences that there are real differences among them, try in their relationships to communicate difference itself. Activities within the feminist movement often consist of meetings that can appear "pointless" to men—writing for its own sake, apparently aimless exchanges, time spent in ways that seem useless and inefficient. But this "symbolic wastefulness" is the expression of what is "valueless" only by the standards of technical rationality. "The symbolic extravagance of female output," Melucci argued, "introduces the value of the useless into the system, the inalienable right of the particular to exist, the irreducible significance of the inner life . . . by virtue of which individual experience becomes the ultimate core of experience."[60]

For Melucci, these ways of being have symbolic appeal beyond the female condition. They linked up with the values represented by other movements such as ecology in representing an alternative to the life-constricting identities fostered by the official codes. "In the ecological practice of the movement's base groups," he wrote, "Nature is lived, acted, and experienced by upsetting the operational codes of destructive production."[61] In such assertions there are more than faint echoes of the Marxist anticapitalism Melucci had supposedly abandoned.

Many of the things he said about women also seem to echo difference feminism, and Melucci did in fact cite Carol Gilligan's *In a Different Voice* in support of his claims. But while some of his assertions read as essentialist propositions in their apparently universal reference to "women," given his general sociological theory he could only see the particular forms of behavior in the Milanese feminist movement as reactions conditioned by the prevailing historical norms. If the women's movement represented an alternative identity, its most important, and for Melucci its only genuinely universal feature, the one it had in common with all the other new movements, was its promotion of the right of difference to self-fulfillment. In this sense nonconformity to the restrictive norms of male-oriented capitalist productivity was both the hallmark of the new movements and a new-old normative identity of unique individuality, one meant ultimately to undercut the hold of all stereotypical social identities.

Individual Psychology

Psychologists date the appearance of "the self" as a major determinant of human thought, feeling, and behavior that could be studied with empirical research techniques back to chapter 10 of William James's *The Principles of Psychology*, "The Consciousness of Self."[62] The authors of one account identify the 1890s as the beginning of the scientific analysis of "self and identity,"[63] though James himself never used the latter word. Since psychological identity emerged only much later, and outside the precincts of academic psychology, the interesting question is why the discipline adopted it when it already had "self," and how the two terms relate to one another.

In fact psychologists, with only a few exceptions like George Herbert Mead, did not follow James's interest in the self for many years. Psychological thought in the first half of the twentieth century was dominated by behaviorism, which rejected all talk of invisible internal entities like the self, and by its opposite psychoanalysis, whose concept of the ego was much narrower than what James had meant by "self." Sociology took up the self, as it did identity, well before university departments of psychology. When academic psychology turned to study the self in the second half of the twentieth century, initially in terms of problems of self-esteem, Erikson's concept of identity was increasingly establishing itself in both academic and popular discourse. Strikingly, the earliest book on identity by an experimental psychologist contained no accounts of psychological experiments; its declared purpose was to investigate when Eriksonian identity crises began occurring in Western history, and it relied for its evidence not on the lab but on works in history, sociology, and literature.[64] Around the turn of the twenty-first century, both a retrospective on fundamental issues in the experimental study of the self in the preceding half century and the first large-scale anthology of recent academic articles on the subject appeared bearing the title "Self and Identity." But editors and contributors did not explain why they used both terms, or what the relationship between them was.[65] The introduction to the anthology included a section on the many meanings of "self" in psychology but nothing on identity. Not until the second edition a decade later did the anthology add an essay, "Self, Self-Concept and Identity," that attempted to distinguish between the concepts.[66]

The attempt was not very successful. In large part this was because for the essay's authors (as for most psychologists) the "self," diffuse and multiple as its meanings might be, remained the overarching concept under which all other aspects of personhood were ranked. If "self" was variously identified with "the total person," "the personality," "the experiencing subject," "the reflecting subject," or "the executive agent of action,"[67] identity was more or less the same as what psychologists call the *self-concept*, the "I"'s conscious definition of the "me." A self-concept is a purely cognitive structure, even if it can include emotions, attitudes, and evaluative judgments.[68] The authors of the anthology claimed that this is what Erikson meant by identity, but this ignored both the unconscious dimension of Erikson's concept and the fact that for him identity was ultimately not just an aspect of self (hence his dropping of the term ego-identity) but its central organizer and motivator. In any case, in treating self, self-concept, and identity as "nested elements,"[69] each contained within the previous one like matryoshka dolls, the authors made identity a sort of third-level self, quite inconsistent with the equality proclaimed by the anthology's title.

It is nevertheless obvious that the authors understood identity as more than a subcategory of self. Opening their essay with examples of possible choices people might face in spheres of life both trivial and profound they claimed that "People believe that they do not need to seriously weigh the pros and cons of these choices before deciding, that their identities provide a meaning-making anchor. They know who they are, and who they are directs their choices. In that sense, choices large and small feel *identity-based* and *identity-congruent*."[70] That is, people take for granted that their identity determines their behavior; what they do in all situations flows from who they are. And though the authors went on to argue that such feelings ignore the causal effect of changing contexts on their behavior, they also pointed to empirical research showing that "psychological essentialism," the belief that "deeper essences" underlie, limit, and explain the surface features of things, is a basic human cognitive organizing schema, at the core of the process of categorization.[71] People thus tend to see themselves as having stable identities even when they in fact may behave quite differently in different circumstances. Like the sociologists Somers and Gibson, the authors failed to make anything of the contradiction they noted between what people believed about themselves and the reality of their behavior. But their concept of "psychological essentialism" seems like empirical support for Sartre's claim for the ubiquity of ontological self-deception.

A more coherent and at the same time more historical approach to the psychological relationship between self and identity placed the issue in the context of modernity and postmodernity. For Dan McAdams, the self is a process— "selfing"—in which the "I" from early on understands and appropriates its experiences as its own, as belonging "to me"—rather like Heidegger's idea of *Jemeinigkeit*.[72] Selfing is a unifying, integrative process in the sense that quite disparate experiences come together as those of the same me. It is because this process is so fundamental, he claimed, that most of us find the phenomena of multiple personality disorder or schizophrenia hard to grasp. We do not know what to make of people who claim that what would appear to be their experience does not belong to them but to another that inhabits or has invaded their body. On the other hand, the normal level of synthesizing is perfectly compatible with the idea that the different things we do or are have no necessary connection with one another: my sex, occupation, aesthetic preferences, and nationality are unified only in that they are all mine. We can be and often are quite comfortable accepting that we are all these disparate things without any intrinsic connection between them.

There is, however, another kind of internal unification process in which the self strives to construct a "me," a self-conception, which is expressive of life unity and purpose. "When I wonder what gives my collection of self-attributions a sense of unity and purpose," McAdams wrote, "I am wondering about my identity."[73] Identity is a level of synthesizing beyond "selfing" in which the unification of multiple experiences in the "me" is not unity enough; multiplicity poses a challenge to the desire for the higher unity of one's life in which all the different sides of oneself somehow hang together.

McAdams was, however, inconsistent, or at least unclear, in situating this desire for higher synthesis historically. On the one hand it was something new, a preoccupation of the modern self; identity, he claimed, "is a psychosocial issue of particular salience for modern Westerners." Yet in relying on the accounts of writers like Roy Baumeister and Anthony Giddens he also adopted their interpretations of modernity as the breakdown of traditional sources of unity and purpose. If so, people did have identities, in the sense of unified meaning and purpose, before modernity, though without the conscious sense of creating it. What would seem to be different in modern times is that identity has become both a conscious cultural norm and a personal quest rather than a given. For the past two hundred years, if one followed Baumeister and Giddens, Westerners had been expressing doubts about the extent to which they experienced themselves as essentially the same person from one situation to another, while at the same time expecting of themselves to be unique and integrated, consistently different from, but also related to, other unique persons in the environment.

In dating the quest for identity back to the beginnings of modernity, however, McAdams conflated the concepts of integration and identity, thus confusing two culturally different and temporally separate developments. Wilhelm Humboldt's late eighteenth-century ideal of individuality, popularized by John Stuart Mill and ultimately taken up by much of middle-class society in Europe and America, was indeed much as McAdams defined it, the creation of a unique, integrated self. But Humboldt's concept of individuality was not only compatible with objective norms and fixed identities in the nineteenth and early twentieth centuries, it was partly defined by them: to be individual meant to be unique but also industrious, moral, and cultured—the ideal bourgeois. It was only after World War I that the objective certainty of all identities, including the "modern" one, was called into question, and even then only by an avant garde.

A more historically accurate way of putting McAdams's point, then, is that for an influential part of the educated Western middle class the long-standing cultural demand to create a unique and integrated self has since World War II had to be realized in the absence of belief in any objective foundations for its choices and in the awareness of their intrinsic fragmentation. The result is a distinctly contemporary set of psychological demands: the self is called on to undertake a conscious quest for identity as a reflexive project of self-making on which the individual must continually work, on both the public and private levels, in order to create a unified life narrative. "The challenge of identity," he concluded, "demands that the modern adult construct a narrative of self that synthesizes the synchronic and diachronic elements of the me to suggest that (1) despite its many facets the me is coherent and unified, and (2) despite the many changes that attend the passage of time, the me of the past led up to or set the stage for the me of the present, which in turn will lead up to or set the stage for the me of the future. . . . Identity is a story that the modern I constructs and tells about the me . . . a psychosocial construction [that] has its constitutive meanings within culture."[74] Defined this way, identity is not simply a subcategory of the self, its "self-concept," but the distinctively modern way of being a self. Though it might seem like a restatement of Erikson, this definition raises identity-creation to a level of self-consciousness beyond what Erikson had understood or intended with his developmental scheme. For Erikson identity was a name for the end result of a process involving the individual's synthesizing his various concrete, often conflicting, identifications, not a conscious end in itself. McAdams's version of identity made the quest, rather than its concrete elements, the self-conscious object of the individual's attention. Yet it is not wrong to see the identity of "self-conscious identity-maker" as both the implicit novelty and the historical consequence of Erikson's work.

If McAdams's theory of narrative identity was an explicit effort to build a viable concept of identity on the ruins of its postmodern deconstruction, postmodernist critics were not persuaded. In her reading of Jeffrey Eugenides's novel *Middlesex*, the story of an intersex character born with female genitalia who discovers in adolescence that she is chromosomally male, Nicole Büchel argued that Cal/Calliope failed to arrive at a final self-understanding of who "he" is through his attempt to integrate his story into the larger narratives of his ancestors. His failure was inevitable, she claimed, because identity narratives are inherently both open-ended in themselves and parts of an infinite tapestry of narratives that makes even the qualified degree of narrative closure psychologists seek impossible.[75] But her formalist deconstruction ignored the social problem of the character's intersexuality in his failure to achieve an integrated identity. Cal's failure is more plausibly explained by the prevailing either-or social construction of sexuality, whereby the only social options available for individual identity construction make personal integration for an intersex individual impossible. Were intersexuality to become a widely socially recognized identity—which as of this writing it seems well on the way to being[76]—it would in theory be possible to construct a satisfactory psychological ending, a recognized identity, for Eugenides's character as McAdams understood it. The successful resolution of a quest for identity depended, as he saw it, on both the resourcefulness of individual creativity and the support of socially sanctioned categories. But he agreed that modernity had forever relegated reflexive identities founded on automatic belief in their ontological reality to an unrecoverable past. That was in fact his point: the discovery/invention of identity as a category represented a historically new way of having an identity.

Linguistics and Identity

An Englishman's way of speaking absolutely classifies him. /
The moment he talks he makes some other Englishman despise
him.

—Professor Henry Higgins, *My Fair Lady*[77]

Language not only reflects who we are but in some sense it is
who we are.

—Carmen Llamas and Dominic Watt, *Language and Identities*[78]

Beginning with a number of striking local investigations and theoretical works
in the 1980s,[79] the concept of identity fundamentally changed the way in which
linguists thought about the nature and purpose of language. In return, these
theorists argued that identity itself had to be understood as inescapably, if not
preeminently, a linguistic phenomenon.

Until recently, linguists had identified the primary purposes of language as
representation and communication.[80] Representation, or the denotative function of language, is concerned with the relationship between words and things
in the world, that is, with the use of words to categorize things in order to
organize the world for human meaning.[81] Since human beings are fundamentally social, language also serves to connect people through the communication of shared meanings. In the first half of the twentieth century linguists
came to recognize two other language functions, noted first by anthropologists
and philosophers, both of which pertain to the context in which certain speech
utterances are made. The psychoanalytically oriented anthropologist Bronislaw Malinowski had suggested that in "primitive" language, the point of some
utterances was not their denotative content but the act of uttering them, which
had the intention of affirming social connection or recognition. As linguists
realized, this was true of certain locutions of speech in all societies, such as the
greeting "hello" or the ostensible question "how are you?" which is not generally intended to solicit a serious answer about the interlocutor's state of health
or being. In the middle of the century a number of philosophers, notably J. L.
Austin and John Searle, also developed the notion of the performative function of language. In certain cases, language such as an officiant's pronunciation
of marriage or a bettor's wager does not name anything in the world but by
its utterance makes the marriage or the bet happen. Even ostensibly representational utterances, however, might have as their purpose something other
than informing an interlocutor of some state of affairs; depending on context,
the sentence "The window is open" might have as its "illocutionary force" a
request to close the window.

Further extending this expanded notion of language function, identity theorists came to argue that the "context" of language is not limited to the pragmatic purposes of enacting sociality, or executing such apparently universal social functions as asserting, requesting, and commanding. Many of the things that language does—for example, its performances of rituals like marriage—are in fact unique to the culture or group that speaks a particular language. Cultures, and for that matter individuals within cultures, express who they are through their language. Put in the most basic theoretical terms, identity could be considered as a third, distinct major function of language in addition to denotation and social performance.[82]

One need not even separate sharply between the representational and the identity function of language, according to some linguists, because representation itself is not neutral or objective. A group or an individual's self-representation, John E. Joseph argued, is the organizing and shaping center of their representation of the world. Treating language as an impersonal system ignores the fact that people are always present in what they say and in the understanding they construct of what others say. "Their identity inheres in their *voice*, spoken, written or signed."[83] Interpretation—not objective representation—is the "primordial linguistic function."[84] This conclusion makes identity more than one "function" of language among others; it becomes language's very foundation. One consequence would be to make translation at best highly problematic; at its extreme, it would imply that translation from one language to another is impossible. In fact Joseph left the final relationship between representation and identity ambiguous, suggesting that linguistics could either widen the traditionally purely cognitive definition of representation to include identity or keep representation in its restricted sense while recognizing its limitations.[85] Identity linguists in fact did not deny the possibility of translation, whether of propositional or attitudinal and emotional content, but insisted that the centrality of a language's identity function negates easy assumptions of mutual linguistic intelligibility.

A more formal way of linking language and identity made use of the philosopher Charles Sanders Peirce's concept of indexicality. If hearing a word pronounced a particular way is experienced by the listener as connected with a particular style of dress, a particular set of social alignments, or a particular social activity, that pronunciation may evoke or even create a social identity. In Peirce's sense of the word, the pronunciation is said to "index" the identity. In more general terms, any linguistic form used by a particular person in performing an interactional activity can come to index a social identity, as when diction comes to be identified with professional identity or accent with regional identity, both of which may in turn be identified with belief, attitude, or character.[86] (Just ask an American from a northern state what a southern accent conveys.) But the looser formulations of Joseph, John Edwards,[87] and others suggested an even tighter relationship between language and identity. Language is not simply an indexical sign of identity but its very embodiment. "Identity," Joseph concluded, is "at the very heart of what language is about, how it operates, why and how it came into existence . . . how it is learned and how it is used, every day, by every user. . . . Language . . . constitutes a text, not just of what the person says, but of the *person*, from which others will read and interpret the person's identity."[88]

If this is true, it must also be the case that those collectivities that have been generally taken as composing a person's major social identities are inescapably constructed, conveyed, and expressed through language. John Edwards, building on Tajfel's social identity theory, focused on the relationship between language and the human propensity for what he called "groupness," in particular the groupings that have seemed most central to human identity throughout history: religion, gender, ethnicity, and nationality. Perhaps the most telling example, at least in the Judeo-Christian tradition, of tight linkage between language, religion, and people is in the ancient Jewish idea of the sacredness of the Hebrew language, still called by Orthodox Jews today "*lashon hakodesh*," the holy tongue. It is the ur-language, the language by which God created the world, the language of his word, the Bible, of his commandments, and above all, of his name, which is the only correct way to address him, since God and his name are one. But as Edwards pointed out, citing Milka Rubin, the assertion of Hebrew's primordial status coincided with its place as the expression of Jewish identity. Rubin noted that "national identity and language were so closely linked that 'Nation and Language'—*umma velashon*—became a hendiadys meaning 'nation.'"[89] With the rise of modern nationalism, the identity of nation and language was claimed in secularized form, though the national language often retained its claim to superior status. J. G. Fichte, for example, making a plea for German unity and specialness in the wake of the Napoleonic occupation of Berlin in 1806, claimed in his seminal "Addresses to the German Nation" that German was the philosophical language par excellence, the one best suited to articulate moral and metaphysical truth.[90] Many a nationalist spokesman afterward was to make the claim not only for the necessity of a national language for the physical and cultural survival of the nation but for its special genius. And whether or not its "genius" was held to be superior to that of any other nation, a nation's language was the only possible expression both of its own uniqueness and of knowledge of the world available through no other language. It is not coincidence that the names of a people and of its language are frequently the same, and that we believe that to truly understand another people one must begin by learning its language.

The contemporary sociolinguistic identification of language with identity is from a historical point of view the social scientific side of modern political movements for linguistic resurrection, defense, or preservation such as those in modern Israel, Quebec, and Ireland. Separatist movements are almost always also linguistic movements. When a linguistic group is not or is no longer sovereign over its own territory, preservation of its language becomes its only way to preserve its identity. Where the substantive beliefs or ritual practice of religion have been displaced by the gauzier idea of "culture" as the main component of ethnicity, as in Quebec, culture has come above all to mean language. It is no coincidence that the first book by John Edwards, one of the earliest and foremost linguistic theorists of identity, born in England but teaching in Canada, was *Attitudes to Learning French in the English-Speaking Schools of Quebec*[91] and that he has written extensively on both the Irish language and language in Canada.

Nevertheless the idea of identity as language raises a problem about identity. If language is the essence and expression of collective identity, identity becomes the ineffable, closed "groupness" of the community that speaks a language. Not merely literary translation but all interaction between groups becomes inexplicable. Of course people do learn new languages and become members of new identity communities, but how is this possible, and why should they ever want to? The idea of linguistic identity left unresolved its relationship to the other components of identity.

History

> History is not what you thought. *It is what you can remember.*
> All other history defeats itself.
> > —Walter Sellar and Robert Yeatman, *1066 and All That*[92]

> Today, France is its own memory or is nothing.
> > —Pierre Nora, *Rethinking France*[93]

No development in historiography since 1980 had greater impact on the writing of professional history than the emergence of memory as a subject of historical interest and research.[94] The founding document of memory studies is the seven-volume work edited by Pierre Nora under the title of *Les lieux de mémoire* published between 1984 and 1992.[95] Its introductory essay "Between History and Memory," famous among historians, sounded an elegiac but somewhat mysterious note concerning the origins of the project. Memory, Nora wrote, is disappearing into history. The distinction between memory and history was the heart of his enterprise. Memory is the heritage of the past that is embodied in the living institutions of societies. Memory mythifies the past in accord with the needs of the present, situating remembrance in a "sacred context" which perpetuates past values as if they were eternally present. History, in sharp contrast, demystifies the past, stripping it of the mythic and sacred and reducing it to the cold, scientifically objective record of "what really happened." Today, "Societies based on memory are no more: the institutions that once transmitted values from generation to generation—churches, schools, families, governments—have ceased to function as they once did." As a result, these original *"milieux de mémoire,"* the living "environments" of memory, have been replaced by *"lieux de mémoire,"* objective historical recoveries of the environments which once had contemporary meaningfulness. Yet these new "sites of memory" are not quite pure dead history. An archive, be it a collection of documents or a song, monument, personage, or children's book, becomes a *lieu de mémoire* "only if imagination invests it with a symbolic aura," thus recovering the sense of the meaningfulness and value it once had. [96] In other words, a site of memory is a hybrid of present and past, or, more in keeping with the disenchanted sense of loss breathing through the essay, a kind of zombie, neither fully alive nor yet dead.

The account suggests two questions. Why should a society want to produce such deformed simulacra of living memories? And what caused the institutions of living memory to cease functioning as they once did? Nora answered the first in pointing out that minorities in a society create archives, mark anniversaries, and organize celebrations as preserves of memory to safeguarded itself against assimilation into the larger community. What such devices reveal is true of all sites of memory: without them, a group would lose its identity. "These bastions *buttress our identities*, but if what they defended were not threatened, there would be no need for them."[97] "Sites of memory" are bastions of identity erected when identity is in danger.

What then threatened French identity sufficiently to inspire his venture? His initial answer was equivocal and sketchy. On the one hand his sweeping claim that "Societies based on memory are no more" generalized about modernity at large, about the world effects of industrialization, globalization, democratization, and mass culture, which were destroying all local and particular identities. But his references to concrete changes concerned only France, and had little if anything to do with these factors. Changes in French historiography over the decades were one symptom of the threat. In the shift from national history to social history that began in the 1930s, the writing of history had shed its identification with the nation and with it the pedagogical mission of transmitting its values. "The definition of the nation ceased to be at issue, and peace, prosperity, and France's diminished status in the world did the rest."[98] The full meaning of these cryptic remarks, however, only emerged some years later in his introduction to the first volume of the second English translation, *The State*. There, Nora revealed that his history of memory was a last-ditch, and in the end futilely self-defeating rescue effort, precipitated by a final crisis of French national identity. Nora's historical masterpiece turned out to be a document in the 1980s debate about French identity examined in Chapter 6.

For a long time, he wrote, France as a nation had identified itself with the state because the state had been its director and protector, unifier and educator. As a result, the French had written their history largely as the history of the state, its forms, its struggles for power and the men who held it. This view of France, and consequently this way of writing history, were no longer viable.

> A history geared to the rhythm of the fluctuations in the nation-state has lost much of its original character and legitimacy. It assumed the reality of a power in order to justify that power's ambitions of greatness. It postulated a natural unity, now denied by all we know. It offered an exemplary history, but the world rarely looks to France for guidance nowadays. It corresponded to a conquering, universalist vision of the nation, a vision rendered naïve and pathetic by France's retraction to its own borders. It masked what was unique to the nation yet offered it as a model to the world even to the point of imposing it by colonial violence. History has swept away this imperial and military model. Today, France is its own memory or is nothing. The country is not the end result or the uncertain outcome of a history of the state, but rather the summary and actualization of a series of representations that the French call *lieux de mémoire*.[99]

This was a final, dejected farewell to France as *la grande nation*. As such, however, it was also a farewell to France. France could only be the memory of what it was because it no longer is what it was. Having outlived a self-image that it had taken for so long as its reality, contemporary France, with no self-image to replace it, had no identity. Or rather, its only possible identity now was as the memory of its former identity, the reconstructed, no longer living memory of its past. The history of memory is identity as pure nostalgia.[100]

It was with awareness of the French origins of his project that Nora opened his introduction to a collection of essays on memory and national identity with the question "Is the idea of '*lieux de mémoire*' exportable?"[101] In any case, he answered, historians elsewhere had not waited for an answer before importing it, as the volume testified. Nonetheless it was a legitimate question, because the link between memory, history, and identity could only be generalized if the notion of "sites of memory"[102] was torn from its original French context and altered in meaning. For Nora, sites of memory were the replacement for a country that had lost its identity as a world power. But as Henk Wesseling described in his essay on Dutch identity in the postwar years, the Netherlands' loss of empire in the East Indies had no immediately ascertainable negative effect on Dutch national identity. Later revelations of war crimes committed by Dutch soldiers in colonial struggles for independence did occasion national guilt and recriminations, but the effect of the Netherlands' loss of colonial vocation was compensated by the Netherlands' taking on the mission and identity of helper to the developing countries.[103]

In other national or historical contexts, where the "end of identity" was not an issue, the history of memory and its methods could be put to other identity uses. Memory studies could unpack the layers of historical meaning encoded in contemporary national celebrations, symbols, and structures of identity as a way of giving them greater historical depth and thus enriching contemporary *milieux de mémoire*. In fact this is the way the articles in Nora's *Lieux de mémoire* often functioned in practice. By way of introducing the symbolic meanings of things supposedly no longer alive in French national consciousness, they also described the contemporary resonance of those same things. An article on "Franks and Gauls," for example, speaks of "the privileged status that the Gauls enjoy today" as suggested by the large number of publications about them aimed at the general public.[104] The author attributed this to current popular associations condensed in the contemporary Gallic image of "our ancestors the Gauls," valiant warriors, depicted either in triumph or on the point of death, but in either case never without helmet and sword. On the one hand, he pointed out, representations of the Gauls were no longer to be found on the French political scene, where they were once prevalent. The chapter traced in detail the previous political uses of the Gauls to assert a particular view of French national identity, especially in relation to debates about who were the "authentic" French, a burning issue in the past based on a belief in hereditary national character. Since that belief had after World War II been displaced by the idea of France as a purely cultural community, the idea of "our ancestors the Gauls" is treated in modern times with a large measure of irony. But for all that, it remains, as the author himself asserted, an image of contemporary identification.

In the case of a more significant site of memory, that of the Old Regime and the French Revolution, François Furet, then dean of Revolutionary studies, described how the events of both had functioned as talismans of French political conflict for two hundred years, but concluded with the claim that, after the presidency of François Mitterand, they "died in an indifferent and prosperous nation." Yet he began the essay with the observation that "If the French Revolution lies at the root of the political civilization in which we still live today, it is because the Revolution wanted it that way," pointing out that contemporary France essentially accepts the Revolution's own view of itself as a foundational event, a new beginning of history.[105] The history of memory, it appeared, did not have to depend on Nora's idea that living memory had turned into dead history. Debates about the meaning of the past were an aspect of the continuous process of identity formation in any living nation or group whose factions vied for the authority to define it. Indeed, one of the unintended ironies of writing the history of supposedly dead sites of memory was that it could reanimate old memories and thus enable the current generation to deepen its identification with the past and perhaps modify its current identity.

But there were contrary ways in which the history of memory could work to buttress identity. Rather than use history to recapture dead memory, historians might use history against *current* memory to deconstruct its myths and restore identities that had been suppressed or, in the stricter Freudian sense, repressed. Nora had argued that living memory was not historical truth because it involved forgetting and distortion. "Memory is life," he had argued, "subject to the dialectic of remembering and forgetting, unconscious of the distortions to which it is subject, vulnerable in various ways to appropriation and manipulation, and capable of lying dormant for long periods only to be suddenly reawakened."[106] Memory falsifies as an aid to creating and preserving current identity. A similar idea was at the core of Michael Fischer's essay about "the contemporary reinvention of ethnic identity through remembering," which threaded its uneasy way between postmodern conceptions of identity as constantly reconstructed and fragmentary and Freudian notions of a real but buried identity welling up from the depths of the unconscious to take the conscious self by surprise.[107] Disaffiliated members of minority ethnic groups, he pointed out, have caught themselves, particularly in crisis situations, affirming an ethnic identity they did not consciously know mattered to them. More directly beholden to Nora in connecting memory and identity, the genre of trauma studies, exemplified above all in the history of the Holocaust, validated the memories of survivors as testimony of an identity Nazism wanted to destroy not only physically but also in historical memory. Dominick LaCapra, for example, defending the importance of memory studies against their academic detractors, argued that such critiques "run the risk of both pathologizing a necessary concern with memory and normalizing limit-events that must continue to raise questions for collective memory and identity."[108] Remembering the Holocaust functions both to preserve the identities of its victims and to correctly identify as "perpetrators" and "bystanders" those who would "normalize" their identities by denying it. Even supposedly objective and neutral historians, in "remembering" the Holocaust historically, disclose their own identities through the transferences onto its personages and events revealed in their interpretations. The more sweeping implication is that all history writing is on a number of levels—and not the least important ones: choice of subject and interpretive emphasis—the projection of identity.

All of these uses of the history of memory had one thing in common: they fused Locke's notion of memory as constituting sameness of personal identity through remembered I-*consciousness* with memory as preserving the substance, the continuing sameness, of selfhood's content. To put it in Paul Ricoeur's terms, in the historians' idea of memory as identity, *ipse* and *idem* are one. Memory studies link up with narrative studies in looking at the way in which we both retain identities of the past and fashion them into coherent substantive identity structures in the present.[109]

Economics

The invention of identity economics—and its proponents were quite self-conscious about being innovators—shows perhaps most clearly the difference that identity could make when incorporated into the previous stock of explanatory concepts in social science. As George Akerlof and Rachel Kranton noted, economists had long since insisted that the "utility function," the mathematical expression that characterized what people cared about in making their economic decisions, should include more than monetary motivations. To be useful for explanation and prediction it needed to take account of such nonmaterial "preferences" as status, fairness, or desire for children. But economists had previously treated such nonmonetary preferences as purely arbitrary individual tastes and choices. This ignored the fact that what people care about and how much they care about it "depends in part on their [collective] identity." [110]

Identities by the authors' definition were derived from the "social categories" into which any society divided itself, and from the "norms" that governed behavior in each category, but in identity economics these concepts involved something more than what conventional sociology implied. Social categories and norms were not just empirically observable social phenomena; their effective power was derived from the fact that they were both idealized and internalized by individuals as definitions of who they were. As the authors put it, "Norms are particularly clear when people hold an *ideal* of who they should be and how they should act."[111] Norms were most reliably enforced when they were identities, self-definitions, because identity itself was a most powerful source of motivation.

As such, it had to be invoked to explain certain phenomena that were in the domain of economics but that traditional models based on material self-interest could not. Akerlof and Kranton illustrated their argument with examples for the economics of organization, education, work, and poverty. In the case of the first they noted that productivity in organizations does not necessarily depend on monetary incentives, as traditional economics would predict. Workers in organizations tend to identify themselves either as outsiders to the organization or as insiders, members of a "workgroup." Workgroups identify with the organization, take pride in their organizational identity and work according to organizational norms. Outsiders try to get by with as little effort as possible without jeopardizing their jobs. In the case of insiders, management can pay lower wages, counting on the "identity utility" of belonging to substitute for higher pay as incentive to maintain productivity norms. In the case of outsiders, paying higher wages will make little difference to productivity, since the worker's identity depends on his oppositional stance to the organization; his "identity utility" would fall if he responded positively to monetary incentives. Based on this analysis, buttressed by empirical case studies, the authors concluded that identity economics produces a testable new theorem: "if employees think of themselves as firm insiders rather than outsiders, the pay differentials needed to induce high efforts will be lower. The difficulties that arise when employees game incentive systems [by trying to win the incentives without actually working harder] are also greatly reduced."[112]

Analysis of identity issues in the inner city also produces explanations and predictions that go against received wisdom. From the standard point of view, high levels of school dropout, crime, and drug abuse in black inner cities are irrational since they destroy any chance of economic advancement. But in an "identity model," the authors conclude, under prevailing conditions dropping out of school at an early age makes identity sense. If inner-city blacks believe they will never be accepted as insiders in the white world, working there entails an identity loss; their identity utility is best maintained by defining themselves in opposition to the white world.[113]

At the end of their book the authors offered five ways that, as they put it, "Identity Changes Economics."[114] These included offering solutions to such basic problems in economic theory as the explanation of economically "irrational" behavior in general and the mitigation of "externalities"—the negative economic effects of otherwise rational economic behavior—by fostering cooperation between economic actors and those negatively affected by them through encompassing identities. Of all the social scientists who advocated for the introduction of identity into their respective fields, economists were perhaps the most evangelical and the most concrete. Theirs was not the most in-depth analysis of the identity itself; they took the need for self-definition as self-evident and the components of identity—roles, norms, and idealization—as well established by sociology. Their hortatory zeal, however, was fostered by the egregious failures of their discipline to cope with phenomena that baffled its entrenched explanatory model. The argument for identity economics is a testimony to how deeply the concept of identity had embedded itself in the academic mind by the end of the twentieth century. As the most mathematical, hence most "scientific," of the social sciences, economics was the most impervious to humanistic considerations, including the recognition that its abstract mathematical edifice rested on the foundation of an erroneous theory of motivation. Identity economics meant to conquer this last bastion of resistance.

*   *   *

The account of identity's impact on research in social science I have offered is far from exhaustive. The essays in volumes like *Identitätsarbeit heute: Klassische und aktuelle Perspektiven der Identitätsforschung* (*Identity Work Today: Classical and Current Perspectives in Identity Research*),[115] for example, were intended as exploratory efforts in and proposals for a research program in German universities to study identity in the different disciplines. If it is difficult to generalize about the ways identity affected the social sciences it is because the effects were so disparate. At one end of a spectrum, as in economics and some NSM theory, theorists simply imported elementary definitions from other disciplines because they believed identity was necessary to explain phenomena in their own discipline not otherwise intelligible or explicable by its conventional assumptions. At the other end, Tajfel's work in social psychology contributed fundamentally new hypotheses about the nature of social identity, which could then be applied to other disciplines. In some cases, identity created new sub-disciplines or research topics within established ones, as in economics, history, and linguistics, while in others, like sociology, theorists argued that the very foundations of the discipline had to be remade in terms of identity. Finally, while some theorists insisted on the sociohistorical dimension of identity, others seemed to take it as a universal category. Tajfel claimed that all psychological experimentation took place within a context of prevailing social norms, which implicitly relativized his own findings about the adversarial nature of social identities. Further out along that spectrum, McAdams argued that for historical reasons the quest for identity itself was wholly new, the modern way of being a self. At the opposite end, however, role theorists, sociolinguists, and identity economists took identity as a universally valid analytic category. The two things all agreed on, however, were that identity as self-definition, whether implicit or explicit, was indispensable to understanding at least some individual and social phenomena, and hence to the social sciences as disciplines, and that it was both an individual psychological and a social category.

The Nay-Sayers

Identities don't exist.
—Jean-François Bayart, interview with Le Monde[116]

Tendencies to fundamentalism and coercion are inherent in
the idea of collective identity.
—Lutz Niethammer, Kollektive Identität[117]

Conceding that by the 1990s identity had lodged itself firmly in the social sciences, some dissenters nonetheless argued forcefully that this was the sciences' misfortune rather than their boon. The objections were both conceptual and political, though the two were inextricably intertwined.

The nub of the critique was that identity was inherently a closed concept that despite the intentions of even its most antiessentialist advocates could not escape a false and pernicious determinism. Appropriately, many of the critics were historians whose professional sensibilities attuned them as a matter of course to the malleability of collective self-definitions over time and to the complex social processes that continuously modified them. The core argument, however, was stated in its most pointed version by the literary theorist Walter Benn Michaels, focusing on a particularly touchy issue in American literary criticism and social thought, the relationship between race and culture. Michaels argued that social and literary theorists who sought to escape the discredited idea of biologically determined racial identity by substituting the concept of a complex, mobile cultural identity to characterize groups and their literatures inevitably failed. "The modern concept of culture is not . . . a critique of racism," he charged; "it is a form of racism."[118]

Culture means nothing more than the ensemble of a group's current practices. All one can legitimately do is describe them. When, however, we speak about people "remembering" or "recovering" a culture they never practiced, or of their obligation to practice and transmit "their" culture, we are implicitly making the claim that it constitutes their identity independently of how they actually choose to live. If they don't live a culture, in what way is it "theirs"? Similarly, people can't "lose" their culture in the sense that it still remains theirs even though they no longer practice it. If they stop practicing one culture in favor of another, they haven't "lost" or "betrayed" it; they have simply changed it. The only way we can make sense of the idea that people have a cultural identity apart from what they actually do is to acknowledge that we are asserting a deterministic conception of culture akin to the biological essentialism of race. "There are no anti-essentialist accounts of identity," he concluded.[119] Identity can only be what people do, not what they are.

Lutz Niethammer's parallel critique derived from his detailed historical account of the appearance of the word "identity" in European thought after World War I in conjunction with a number of different groups or collectivities; such usages figured for him as the roots and anticipations of the more explicit postwar concept of collective identity. The implication of a common meaning in all these interwar examples was, however, illusory, he argued. Schmitt's "identitarian democracy" of ruler and ruled, Lukacs's "proletarian revolutionary consciousness," Jung's primitive collective unconscious, Freud's ethnic Jewishness, Halbwachs's traditional cultural memory and Huxley's biologically programmed group inequality had nothing in common. "Such highly complex social formulations and demands," he argued, "are neither comparable in a formal sense nor does each individually contribute anything of real substance to the concept [of collective identity]."[120] The heterogeneous collection exposed the notion of collective identity as an empty conjuror's trick with the appearance of scientific rigor but without any substantive content.[121] It is simultaneously underdetermined, in the sense that as an abstraction it loses all concrete specification, and overdetermined in that when any supposed instance of collective identity is closely examined, it is revealed as in fact nonidentical, riven with conflict and difference among those who supposedly constitute it. Connotatively, collective identity formulations function not as descriptions at all, though they masquerade as such, but as promises of future realizations of a unity that does not exist, and as imperatives to bring that unity into being.[122]

This critique was based on the fact that the word identity does not have a logical common denominator across all its uses, and for Niethammer, it was precisely that which revealed the real historical meaning of the emergence of collective identities after World War I. All identity formulations define sameness expressly in relationship to difference, or nonidentity. In the German lineage of identity thinking, originating in German Idealist philosophy, absolute identity was understood as the union of identity with nonidentity or the incorporation of the finite into totality, a quasi-theological notion that represented the secularization of the Protestant conception of God. The identity constructs of the postwar period, steeped in this tradition, took on the connotation of identity as fullness of being in contrast to the defective being of those not included in it. This meant, crucially, that definitions of identity were designed for conflicts in which some collectivity declared its supremacy over those seen as opposing it.[123] Though usually concealed in the concept's supposed neutrality, this defining feature of identity was glaringly exposed in Carl Schmitt's claim that all politics was grounded in theology and that its essence, the notion of political unity, was founded on the distinction between friend and foe. But all the examples of identity that Niethammer exhaustively analyzed represented militantly aggressive or defensive reactions on behalf of a group against its real or perceived enemies. In one sense Niethammer could be seen as restating with historical examples the argument Fredrik Barth had made in anthropology and Henri Tajfel in social psychology, but as a political reality: collective identity is a matter of "us" versus "them."

As a historian, however, he did not treat the idea as a permanent fixture of thought. Thinking explicitly in terms of (adversarial) collective identity was a historical novum, and there were reasons for its appearance after World War I. The war and the workings of mass society it brought to the fore unsettled intellectuals who identified with those who had lost or those who were threatened by the upheavals. Schmitt and Lukacs wanted to rally their defeated idealized collectives, the German nation and the Western European proletariat, to create new fighting identities; Halbwachs, fearing precisely the militant nationalism Schmitt promoted, wanted to expose the collective illusions on which it rested; Freud defended his ethnic Jewishness in a postreligious world of increasingly virulent anti-Semitism; Jung looked to a primitive collective unconscious as a respite from modern mass society, while Huxley depicted a manufactured collective consciousness as a horror show version of it.

The Nazi genocide discredited this kind of collective thinking for a time, and when the concept of identity reappeared after World War II it was at first in the context of individual psychology. Soon afterward, however, social psychologists revived the idea of collective identity, triggering the postwar boom in the concept. Its first phase, according to Niethammer, the phase of identity politics, was progressive in the sense that it promoted the inclusion of hitherto excluded groups into civil and political society. It did not take long, however, for its inherent tendencies to fundamentalism, exclusiveness, coercion, and violence to reassert themselves in the ultraright nationalist identity movements of the 1970s in Germany. And even the more benign third phase of collective identity that Niethammer identified, the quest for identity through historical memory, led to the idea of cultural identity conflict epito-mized in Samuel Huntington's "clash of civilizations."

Given the dangerous tendencies inseparable from the historical evolution of collective identity, Niethammer offered the "modest proposal" of getting rid of it. "How would it be," he asked, "if we were to simply eliminate collec-tive identity from our political vocabulary? . . . The quasi-religious loftiness of our political discourse would be somewhat lowered, and we would be forced to greater precision. . . . If we were to stop concealing our history, our inter-ests, our differences and our coerciveness in emphatic identity formulations, it might be easier for us to think more modestly and politically and to reach accommodation in our dealings with others. . . . The boom [in collective identity talk] seems to show that this discourse is not designed for accommo-dation but for the [permanent] conflict of irreducible political-cultural entities."[124]

Jean-François Bayart's equally acerbic attack on "the illusion of cultural identity"[125] pointed in much the same direction; one of his chapters was titled "Should We Stop Using the Word Culture?" In the foreword he bluntly announced that his purpose was to "undermine identity-related nonsense by outlining an anti-culturalist examination of the relationships between culture and politics."[126] Specifically he meant to reverse the going procedure in con-temporary political science of explaining politics by cultural identity and show instead that old-fashioned power-political ends explain the vicissitudes, and the uses, of cultural identity.

A specialist in African history and politics, he heaped up examples from his own area of research and virtually everywhere else around the world—Iran, Japan, India, France, the United States—to demonstrate the artificiality and incoherence of identity claims and the ways in which interest and power poli-tics created and manipulated them for their own purposes. His opening set piece satirized the account of a party in Cameroon to celebrate the nomination of a local notable to the office of chief counselor of his village by its traditional chief. The event was billed in the local press as an example of resurgent tradi-tional culture, but even a cursory examination showed that it was everything but. The notable was a businessman who was also celebrating his initiation as a member of the Compagnons du Beaujolais, the commercial organization of wine makers and exporters founded in France less than two decades before to conquer international markets for their product. The party was in fact a mar-keting event, a Western-style Beaujolais Nouveau wine tasting dressed in native garb. And this was only one strand of the dense contemporary political and economic crosscurrents packed into this supposedly long-standing tradition.[127]

Bayart's indictment of "culturalism" was social constructionist and expressly followed the line of Hobsbawm's "invention of tradition." "There is no culture that is not created," he asserted, "and . . . this creation is usually recent. . . . Culture is less a matter of conforming or identifying than of making: making something new with something old, and sometimes also making something old with something new; making Self and Other."[128] Culturalism commits "three methodological errors": it maintains that culture is a body of representations that is stable over time, that is closed in on itself, not admitting of external influences, and that determines a specific political orientation.[129] Every one of these claims is false, but the last one was the most crucial.

Strongly influenced by poststructuralism, Bayart did not have to "concede" the role of linguistic representation in mediating politics. "The cultural interpretation of politics is necessary," he argued, "because . . . political action is cultural,"[130] expressible only through socially constructed discourses. But this did not mean that the culture norms and beliefs pointed in only one political direction. If not infinitely malleable, they were highly interpretable; the language of Islam, for example, could and did historically license quite different political goals. The inertial tendencies of "discursive genres" to foster a particular form of political action "are *merely* historical. They reflect a certain sedimentation . . . whose stability is relative and can be reopened by cultural or political innovation, socioeconomic transformations and the production of new utterances or the reinterpretation of old ones."[131]

Despite his commitment to the governing role of the cultural "imaginary"—the prevailing social myths—in political life, however, Bayart's arguments sounded at points like the most unreconstructed materialist positivism. Criticizing the French defense of support for the Hutus just before the Rwanda genocide in 1994 on the grounds that as the majority ethnic group their rule represented the principle of democratic legitimacy, Bayart wrote, "The analysis is obviously specious, assuming, as it does, that ethnicity is an objective reality, whereas it is *merely* a state of consciousness."[132] Unexpected as this distinction between "objective reality" and "mere consciousness" must be coming from a postmodernist thinker, something like it was nonetheless necessary if Bayart was to maintain the primacy of politics over cultural identity. His considered position was ultimately more nuanced, but even it epitomized the problem faced by those who wanted to eliminate talk of collective or cultural identity. Criticizing the fallacy of "primordial identity" in explaining outbursts of terrible violence between groups he wrote:

> It is not a matter of denying the efficacy of identities that are *felt* to be
> primordial. Although we are convinced of the "artificial origin of the

belief in common ethnicity," so we must acknowledge that this belief works, and that "rational association" is likely to be transformed into "personal relationships" in an overarching communal consciousness. In some sense, primordial identities "exist," but as mental facts and as regimes of subjectivity, not as structures. Instead of being explanatory factors, they must themselves be explained. . . . [I]t remains to be understood under what conditions a group of individuals apprehends [its identity] in the form of a permanent, primordial core in order to follow magicians who instrumentalise this illusion to their own advantage.[133]

The confusion in the passage is as obvious as its origins. Unable to deny the effective reality of a concept he thought was both falsely essentialist and historically pernicious, Bayart tried to simultaneously accommodate and undermine it with a rather old-fashioned materialist dualism of "real" structures and "unreal" mental events. While it was perfectly legitimate, however, to ask under what economic, social, and political conditions people come to believe in a primordial identity, it was an error to imply that the belief in primordiality itself was reducible to such historical conditions.

The same problem in a somewhat different terms marked the effort of Rogers Brubaker and Frederick Cooper to analyze the theoretical defects of the concept of identity and offer alternatives.[134] Using language similar to Michaels's, they argued that the constructivist attempt to acquit identity of the charge of essentialism by stipulating that identities are constructed, fluid, and multiple left social scientists "without a rationale for talking about 'identities' at all" and unable to resist the tendency of identity attributions to harden into the kinds of exclusive and coercive unities that characterize identity politics in practice.[135]

Like Niethammer, they claimed that identity has come to mean so many different things that it means nothing in itself. It is variously understood to refer to action governed by particularistic self-understanding rather than universal self-interest; to the fundamental sameness among members of a group; to a core aspect of individual or collective selfhood that is deep, basic, abiding, or foundational; to the interactive development of collective self-understanding that makes collective action possible, as in the New Social Movement literature; and to the unstable, multiple, fluctuating, and fragmented nature of the contemporary self. "These usages are not simply heterogeneous," they claimed, "they point in sharply differing directions."[136]

Furthermore, insofar as these various meanings refer to genuine phenomena, such as that particularistic self-understandings can shape social and political action in noninstrumental ways, they can be expressed plainly in so many words without identity. This would eliminate the danger of lapsing into "hard" understandings of the word that falsely suggest that identity is an essence to be discovered or refers to sharply delimited group boundedness and homogeneity. In any case, "it is not clear why weak conceptions of 'identity' [which admit instability and constant flux] are conceptions *of identity*. . . . '[I]dentity' suggests at least some self-sameness over time. . . . What is the point in using the term 'identity' if this core meaning is expressly repudiated?"[137]

To cover the legitimate connotations of identity without its baggage Brubaker and Cooper offered a set of alternative terms. Abstract nouns formed from verbs[138] like *identification* and *categorization* avoid reification by keeping agency, process, and change at the center of consciousness, as well as keeping separate the processes of identifying oneself and being categorized by others. The gerund *self-understanding* points to the "situated subjectivity," the social locating in terms of which persons interpret what they do. Finally, *commonality*, *connectedness*, and *groupness* could replace identity to indicate the sharing of common attributes, the relational ties that link people, and the sense of belonging to a distinctive, bounded group.[139]

These suggestions present a number of problems. It was not accurate to suggest that the different meanings of identity Brubaker and Cooper enumerated point in opposite directions. Of the five, only the notion of identity as unstable and fragmented seriously contradicts the others, and that one was the essence of the postmodern *critique* of identity, not a specification of it. As for the alternatives Brubaker and Cooper recommended, they are more or less what other social scientists in fact meant by identity; while it is quite useful to have them spelled them out in detail, it does not seem problematic to employ identity as a shorthand for them. The most serious problem with their critique, however, is that only the term identity accommodates the idea of self-definition, distinctiveness, and boundedness that the authors, like Bayart, were forced to admit is part of group consciousness even as they rejected its reality. Getting rid of the word did not get rid of the difficulty. Put simply, the observation that identities change over time, and are sometimes even deliberately manipulated and created, coexists, by the critics' own admission, with people's subjective sense of the distinctiveness and definiteness of their group identity. Nor does it solve the problem to formulate "groupness" and "boundedness" as "*emergent properties* of particular structural or conjunctural settings."[140] The notion of "emergence," a theoretical initiative in biology and the philosophy of mind to resolve the antinomies between the organic and the inorganic or brain and mind without reducing one to the other, glosses over the radical break that the phenomenological characteristics of the emergent properties represent from their initial causal conditions.

Once again the analysis of identity came up against the aporia first encountered by Erikson, the contradiction between the historical fact of identity change and the empirical experience of and belief in identity continuity and stability. After half a century of work on identity, this remained one of its main conceptual problems, if not indeed its most crucial one. What made it of more than theoretical concern and the subject of quite heated polemics were the political dangers of collective identity that even social scientists like Tajfel, whose empirical work did more than anyone's to establish its deep-rootedness, warned against. But the obvious dangers of collective identity were hardly enough reason to jettison the concept. On the contrary, the historical destruction it had wrought was if anything evidence of its reality. Depending on how it was framed, the idea of collective identity might be philosophically vulnerable, but if so, the conceptual challenge was to explain it in a way that accounted both for its truth and its falsity.

Chapter 10

The Kinds of Kinds:
Explaining Collective Identity

Not every aspect of the collective dimension of someone's
identity will have the general power of sex or gender, sexuality
or nationality, ethnicity or religion.
—Kwame Anthony Appiah, *The Ethics of Identity*

Race is not simply a bad idea; it is a deeply rooted bad idea.
—Lawrence Hirschfeld, *Race in the Making*

The concept of collective identity was at the same time a theory of collective identity. Sartre's phenomenological descriptions of the nature of the collective experience, for example—the group as "us-object" and "we-subject"—was embedded in an ontological theory of how and why identity is constructed. Pre-1960s American sociological role theory provided its own quite different description and explanation of group identity. It first theorized social roles as the basic collective categories of social structure. When Nelson Foote linked the individual to his/her social roles through the concept of identification, roles could be seen as both collective and individual identities, with the latter, however, wholly subsumed by the former.

In each of these cases, the range of possible collective identities was paradoxically both infinite and constricted. In Sartre's version, the "third" whose "look" created the objectified identity of the "looked at" was an ontological placeholder; the place could in principle be filled by anyone, but the individuals caught in the look were irremediably fixed in their objectified collective identity. In sociological theory, the number of roles available as identities was delimited by the existing social division of labor. But since many role theorists understood society as historical, ever changing, and for the most part progressively more complex, social roles and identities were potentially open-ended.

Under the impact of political events these approaches to collective identity came to seem even to some of their original authors incomplete, inadequate, or both. For Sartre and Beauvoir, the Other, whether as the origin of the demeaning look or its object, could no longer be just an ontological abstraction or a fictional character caught up in a domestic love triangle.[1] There were all too obvious historically concrete Others—anti-Semites and Jews, whites and blacks, imperial masters and colonial subjects, men and women—locked in a sadomasochistic embrace of negative identity projection and submissive identification. Even before the advent of self-conscious identity politics, American sociology had been concerned with the political and social integration of the great migration wave of 1880–1920, interpreting it as the gradual accommodation of initially scorned ethnic identities within the framework of an increasingly pluralistic American national identity. Religious identity was a central focus of the psychologists who designed the Twenty Questions test, and Will Herberg made American religious pluralism central to his thesis about the successful postwar acculturation of eastern European Jews. But none of them explicitly analyzed the relationship of religious identity to role identity or provided any other systematic theory of collective identity.

Only when identity became politicized from the bottom up in the 1960s by popular movements for black, gay, women's, and ethnolinguistic rights did collective identity became a topic of broad public and sustained academic focus. Just for that reason, however, there was at first little interest in more abstract questions like the purpose of collective identity itself, the basis on which distinct collective identities got to be defined and established, or their possible range. What was immediately obvious however was that the rise of identity politics made the sociological role theory of collective identity seem both too narrow and too broad. There were larger sources of collective identity that, from the activism they inspired, were obviously much more salient to their members than the social roles they occupied in the division of labor (though the group's exclusion from high-status social roles was a factor motivating their activism). At the same time, these motivating sources were relatively few in number—sex, sexual orientation, race, ethnicity, nationality, and religion. It was not until the 1980s, after identity groups as such had become recognized and important social players, that social theorists turned to the questions of why identity groups form in the first place and whether there is a systematic way of thinking about the range of collective identities human beings inhabit.

Explaining Collective Identity

"Us" and "Them": The Other as Adversary

Any "us" presupposes a "them," since "we" are defined in relation to those who are "not we." This logical necessity says nothing in itself about either the boundaries of "us" or the relationship between "us" and "them." Nevertheless, the polarity itself carries for many people implications of conflict. For one, it is generally invested with normative meaning. "We" are defined by norms of behavior to which "they" do not adhere, which must mean that they are lesser. Even if we recognize that "they" have their own norms, we often judge them as inferior to ours. Furthermore humans often display what in infants is called "stranger anxiety," which first appears as a spontaneous response to unfamiliar faces at about nine months. Whatever its source (evolutionary biology argues its survival value), adults manifest it by registering the difference of those they encounter outside their own group, and if not fear, tentativeness. Stranger means danger.

Conflict, in any case, was built into Sartre's original interpretation of intergroup relationships, derived as it was from the ontological dialectic of self and Other. Unlike Hegel's concept of consciousness's struggle for recognition, however, which while initially aimed at the death of the other ultimately ideally ended in their mutual recognition, the existential struggle for identity remained a zero-sum game. One group was ontologically up and the other down. One had absolute identity and the power to define the other in relation to itself as deficient or negative identity. The other either colluded in its derogatory definition while simmering in resentment or fought to turn the tables and assert its own superior identity. From this perspective the only way to end conflict was to end identity.

This remained true even when Sartre anchored the power to define identity in material economic and social power. To abolish identity now required the abolition of differences of material power, but identity still remained an independent category. Thus to abolish power differences between identity groups required first a seizure of consciousness on the part of the subordinate identity by which it would confer on itself the right to act in the first place. Sartre dramatized the point in "The Respectful Prostitute," where the hunted black man is unable to shoot at his pursuers to escape a lynching because he believes he has no right to shoot at whites.[2] Before the utopian abolition of difference and identity, it was necessary if anything to first sharpen the sense of conflict by emphasizing the identity of "otherness." In this context, as I noted earlier, it was Beauvoir's identification of otherness with the object group rather than Sartre's version of the Other as absolute subject that won out. In political polemics this meant focusing on the ways in which the majority, the powerful, the subjects of society, turned the powerless, the outgroup, the objects, into ontological Others, less than fully human beings.

The role theory of collective identity did not provide politically useful categories like otherness for fighting negative identity. Role theory was based on the assumption of social harmony. Stereotyped, rule-governed, and interlocking roles were the foundation of orderly and smooth social interaction. Muzafer Sherif's ground-breaking exploration of group identity formation in the Robbers Cave experiment did not even recognize the category of collective identity as such, let alone its possibly adversarial nature, despite the clear evidence he himself gave for it. Observation was made to conform to theory. Sherif and his collaborators interpreted group organization, including the group's collective self-consciousness, in instrumental terms as creating the division of labor necessary for executing its members' purposes more effectively; it also provided individual role identities for them. The subsequent conflict between the Eagles and the Rattlers was not at bottom a clash of collective identities but a conflict over resources. When the experimenters threatened the resources of both groups, the boys were easily able to overcome their identity difference and pool their efforts for the benefit of all their members. Sherif's basic theoretical perspective remained that of individual self-interest. Group organization was the means to its ends.

Erving Goffman's concept of stigma came closer to attributing autonomous psychological power to group identity as such. He defined stigma as a discrepancy between a person's "virtual" social identity, what he socially ought to be, and his "actual" social identity—the attributes he is perceived to have—that deeply discredit that person among society's "normals."[3] Goffman's subject was the ways in which people who deviate from a society's normative categories manage what he called their "spoiled identity." Stigma originally carried the connotation of a physical sign, and while Goffman pointed out that contemporary usage referred more directly to the disgrace than to the bodily evidence of it, the examples he gave of "spoiled identities" did involve visual or behavioral "deviancies" from the norm: the "crippled," the blind and deaf, homosexuals, and blacks. These identities were "discredited" in the most shocking way even if "normal" people were unaware of the meaning of their judgments. "By definition, of course," Goffman wrote bluntly, "we believe the person with a stigma is not quite human."[4] To add psychological injury to social insult, the stigmatized tend to hold the same beliefs about identities as everyone else. Ashamed of their own and sensitive to social rejection, they correct what they can, try to conceal what they can't, and struggle to find ways to compensate for what they can neither correct nor conceal.

Stigma was evidence of the increasing spread of identity in the study of conflictual social phenomena that sociology had previously dealt with under the rubrics of social labeling, prejudice, in-groups and out-groups, and marginalization. In Goffman's own work, the introduction of identity marked his recognition of the subjective, psychological dimension of social role that he had peremptorily dismissed in *The Presentation of Self in Everyday Life*. The meaning and the dynamics of stigma, particularly from the side of the stigmatized, Goffman was suggesting, could not be fully understood without the identity notions of individual and group self-definition and the value that their subjects attached to them.

Stigmatization, however, was only a special case of adversarial collective identity as Goffman interpreted it, the exception that proved the rule since it dealt with the fate of outliers from the consensually accepted identities. The implied standpoint of stigmatization theory was again the supposed harmony of recognized identities, which even the stigmatized themselves acknowledged. It was the experimental work of Henri Tajfel that made conflict the essential principle of collective identity, demonstrating that "us and them" is always "us versus them."

The jarring conclusion of Tajfel's experiments was that group conflict wasn't "about" anything but difference itself. Any set of markers around which individuals could coalesce into identity groups, no matter how trivial by any scale of reckoning, automatically created antagonism and competition between them. As the example of the "Kandinsky-ites" and the "Klee-ites" showed, conflict over material goods followed from their respective group identifications; it did not provoke it. Where the conflict did involve material rewards, the aim of each group was not to maximize its own but to put the other group down by maximizing the difference between them. What mattered was relative superiority, not absolute gain.

To establish that people spontaneously group themselves in adversarial identities left matters hanging, some felt; the phenomenon needed to be further explained. Evolutionary-minded critics argued survival; the precariousness of human life drives us to find allies—as David Berreby put it, to "team up with others"[5]—to face the struggle for existence. Besides reducing Tajfel's result to something quite different, this was a circular claim, like many evolutionary explanations, assuming what it wanted to prove. Another sort of criticism attacked the trivial criteria of group identity in Tajfel's experiments. As Donald Horowitz argued, the identities that seem to matter most to humans, such as ethnic identity, don't compete in just one task or game but "in lifelong games." Between ethnic identities, "competition has an urgency, a centrality, that [Tajfel's] experiments do not capture."[6] This was true, but it was not a criticism of Tajfel's thesis and could in fact be taken as support for it. Tajfel himself, after all, had been inspired to study the origins of competitive group identities precisely by the deadliness of its national and racial manifestations in contemporary European history. If it were true for trivial differences, would it not hold a fortiori for more significant ones? But Tajfel also insisted that experimental results could not be taken out of their sociohistorical context. Was social identity conflict a universal fact, or true only for the society in which Tajfel's experiments took place? The latter was the core argument of the sharpest critics of the idea of collective identity, such as Niethammer and Bayart. For critics like them, the idea that collective identity was inherently adversarial served the ideological purposes of its proponents, whether nationalist or capitalist ideologues.

Collective Identities and the Power of "Knowledge"

If Tajfel's experimental initiative was rooted in the desire to understand the genocidal catastrophes of the mid-twentieth century, another approach to the question of the origin of collective identity took its cue from the politics of the contemporary moment as interpreted by poststructuralism. In his often cited essay, titled with colloquial provocation "Making Up People," Ian Hacking credited Michel Foucault as his chief inspiration.[7] Hacking was concerned there and in subsequent writings with the way government bureaucracies and modern social, medical, and biological science create new "human kinds" (a term he later rejected in favor of "kinds of people"). His first example, the split or multiple personality, strongly suggested that such human kinds were both fictitious and ephemeral. The multiple personality didn't exist until psychiatrists named it on the basis of one famous case and a series of assumptions they read into it. Following that, people who ostensibly fit the published description began showing up in clinics and psychiatric offices and quickly outbid previous patients in the number of their personalities. This was an example of what Hacking later named "the looping effect,"[8] in which people respond to the institutional invention of a new kind of person by expanding its meaning. But almost as quickly as it appeared, the multiple personality went out of psychiatric and popular fashion, he claimed, its reality challenged to the point where both the label and the assumptions about it disappeared from both scientific literature and the entertainment media.[9]

Multiple personality was just one dramatic example of his general thesis. Hacking had begun his researches by looking at nineteenth-century government statistical surveys of so-called deviant groups such as criminals, prostitutes, suicides, and homosexuals. Bureaucratic classification and counting of such groups, backed by the "normalizing" human sciences of medicine, penology, and psychiatry that defined their deviancy, raised the questions of whether "making up people [is] intimately linked to control" and whether "making up people [is] of recent origin." He was inclined at first to answer yes to both questions. "We may be observing," he wrote, "a particular medico-forensic-political language of individual and social control,"[10] the power/knowledge instrument of Foucault's middle-class disciplinary society. Most importantly, counting and labeling were not a matter of recognizing a kind of person that had always existed but had gone unrecognized; rather, a "kind of person came into being at the same time as the kind itself was being invented."[11] Hacking significantly described a new kind as a new way for a person "to be." The copula implied that such kinds, despite their recent invention and constant modification, were nonetheless thought of by the classifiers and experienced by the classified as fixed, permanent, and naturalized.

In later work Hacking changed his mind about the recent origin of made-up people, but not about the causal importance of power. It was in fact his belief that political and social control was the ultimate purpose of classifying people that enabled him to broaden his historical perspective and turn his theory from a claim about modernity into a claim about the broad spectrum of human kinds through the ages. But inconsistencies on this point threw his more general causal theory of identity group formation into question.

"There has been making up of people in all times and places," he now asserted.[12] As an example of how political power had invented ethnicities and nationalities from early on he cited the political and administrative procedures of the ancient Persian Empire. His analysis and conclusion, however, were equivocal. For the convenience of governing and taxing the polyglot peoples of his empire, the emperor Darius imposed on it a structure of satrapies corresponding more or less to previously existing geographical demarcations, political allegiances, social cohesion, and similarities of bodily structure and skin color. "*In some cases,*" Hacking claimed, the kinds of people classified by the satrapies did not exist "*as a kind of people*" until they had been so classified, organized, and taxed, while others were "cemented" as kinds of people by classification and administration.[13] His qualifications acknowledged that kinds of some sort, including well-established nationalities, had existed prior to imperial organization and recognition, rather weakening his thesis that centralized power "made up" the nations and ethnicities of the empire out of the whole cloth.

However hedged, the example did broaden Hacking's notion of making up kinds by extending it to the rigidifying and formalizing, if not actual creation, of ethnicities by imperial rulers throughout history—the same point made by Bayart and many other historians about so-called primordial tribal structures in Europe's African colonies. In another essay Hacking noted how the imperial urge to control might help explain the race theories of modern

European and American empires, which were otherwise expressly committed to egalitarianism. Modern race sciences from the seventeenth century on, Hacking argued, "were devised to discover a lot of differences that do not follow from the marks of color and structure by which we distinguish them. You do not have to treat people equally, if they are sufficiently different."[14] The racial obsession of modern egalitarian empires thus had the same cause as the urge to classification of older hierarchical ones: the "single historical source" was the imperial desire for "conquest and control." Furthermore, that liberal empires classed their subject people as inferior also showed that imperial kind making was not just about the practical exigencies of ruling: "The end is to magnify the exploits, glory, and power of the ruler."[15]

If Hacking did not explore the political creation of ethnic kinds beyond this, it was because he thought of the imperial organization of peoples as a straightforward matter of brute force. What interested him more was the indirect and subtle creation of kinds fostered by modern science, whose ostensible purpose was not power but the "neutral" accumulation of knowledge. "Kinds of People" laid out a progression of ten "scientific imperatives," basic discovery procedures in the human sciences, which together revealed that their ultimate purpose was not objectively scientific at all. These so-called "engines of discovery" started with the requirement that science imposed to count, quantify, and classify people, followed by the demand to normalize the classifications by explaining them biologically and institutionalizing them bureaucratically. The last of the imperatives was the exhortation to "reclaim our identity!" Identity creation, Hacking proposed, was the teleological bottom line of the social scientific process. "Neutral" knowledge machines are simultaneously "engines for making up people," and the kinds of people they invent—"the obese," "the autistic," "the homosexual"—are negative identities that serve to confirm socially normative ones. Sooner or later, therefore, these classifications rouse the resistance of the classified. The latter, however, do not look to repudiate their identities but to take control of them back from the experts who created them and the institutions that administer them, sometimes by creating new experts and institutions, in any case by reversing their negative valence. Hacking cited homosexuality as the paradigm case of how pathologically designated "homosexuals" took back control of their identity, creating a positive version through the idea and institutions of gay pride.

The way kinds of people are created led Hacking to the question of their "ontological," or reality status. After all some people do weigh more than is healthy, do have same-sex desires, do manifest unusual behaviors. Hacking was not denying any of this. His question was not whether obesity, homosexuality, or autism existed, but whether they are incidental attributes of people or essential to identifying who those people "are." In the case of autism, Hacking was inclined to accept the argument advanced by parental advocates for autistic children that "autism" is what their child *is*;[16] in others, like obesity, he was more skeptical, while recognizing the aim of those who make parallel claims about obesity in order to remove its stigma. But even in the case of autism he resisted the idea that it defined the "essence" of the person, preferring instead John Stuart Mill's concept that people who have many enduring characteristics in common—like those who suffer from autism—constitute a "real kind," in contrast to those who share only one superficial characteristic—like white skin—who do not.

Hacking's resistance to essentialism was motivated both by philosophical qualms and his fear of how easily it could lead to negative stereotyping. Nevertheless, it is hard to see the difference between the essentialism he repudiated and the statement that autism is who, or what, someone "is." Once again, the use of the copula suggested thing-like permanence, closed definition by one unchangeable feature. Significantly, Hacking's ultimate formulation of the meaning of kind-making did not allow for a distinction between "real" and "unreal" kinds of people. The naming of a kind, he said—whether real or unreal—presented people with a new "way to be" a person. True, this was an especially striking way of putting matters in the case of "real kinds," because in one sense they had existed before they were named. Same-sex desire was as old as the human race, but naming "the homosexual" in the nineteenth century or "gays" in the twentieth had created new sets of expectations of and judgments about people physically attracted to their own sex that fundamentally affected how they were seen and treated by others, how they thought of themselves, and how they acted privately and socially. "Being gay" was more than a matter of same-sex attraction; it was a set of principles, practices, and attitudes that governed every sphere of life, premised on but going well beyond sexual orientation. As both objectively structured and subjectively internalized ways of being a person, identities like "being gay" constituted a historically and socially defined *ontology*. Despite his qualms about the term's metaphysical baggage, Hacking wrote that some of the old philosophical connotations of ontology suited his purposes. Ontology is often defined as the study of the most general kinds that exist in the universe, and he wanted to talk about the most general kinds of things—in his case, of people—that exist in the social universe.[17]

The notion that naming a kind of person can bring into being new ways to be was a significant clarification of the concept of identity. "Naming" pointed to the elements of fixed definition and self-awareness that seem central to the sense of having an identity. Identity as a "way of being" brought together both its static and dynamic aspects, with the implication also that it encompassed every aspect of self in its relationship to the world. Along these lines it might be argued that "having an identity" is itself one of those "real kinds" that only came into being by being named. Even if it can be claimed that in a meaningful sense people had identities before identity became a word, the contemporary naming of identity as conscious self-defining (along with the looping effects it generated) created an entirely new way of being a person—as the psychologist Dan McAdams argued on historical grounds.

But the identities created by modern scientific engines of discovery compose only a small subset of kinds of persons, and focus on them puts too great an emphasis on artifice and control as the origin of collective identities. Hacking himself insisted that "ideas of race and of 'others' began long before the sciences of race, and will probably outlast them. They have a life of their own (as do ideas of sex), that is far more entrenched than any science."[18] To race and sex Clifford Geertz and Anthony Smith would add ethnicity and nationality. How is their prior existence to be explained? Are we led back by an infinite regress to some original empire which started it all off? Are power differentials and the desire to control the ultimate sources of all collective identity? In his focus on the power/knowledge procedures of modern science and the brute force of ancient empires, Hacking left such questions unanswered.

Kind-Making as Innate Cognitive Category:
The Question of Race

Taking up Hacking's notion of human kinds, the anthropologist Lawrence Hirschfeld tackled what in the contemporary West was the most fraught of all the apparently long-existing collective identities: race.[19] As a social and political liberal he found his own conclusions unsettling. On the basis of both comparative historical anthropology and psychological experiments he conducted with children, he concluded that "children are more than aware of diversity; they are driven by an endogenous curiosity to uncover it. . . . [three-year-olds] believe that race is an intrinsic, immutable, and essential aspect of a person's identity. *Moreover, they seem to come to this conclusion on their own.*"[20] If this is true for such young children it is because humans are endowed with a "special-purpose conceptual device: a domain-specific competence [analogous to Chomsky's notion of biologically programmed grammatical rules that govern the human acquisition of language] for creating knowledge of and reasoning about human kinds."[21] Just as children know far more about how to construct grammatically valid sentences than they learn from their environment, automatically generalizing the rules of grammar to new vocabulary they acquire, they also reason about the differences between people that they discover are important to the adults in their environment in terms they could not have learned just from observation (or even indoctrination).

Children's spontaneous race theories include three elements: an ontology—the notion that humans divide into kinds, analogous to their spontaneous "folk biology" assumptions about animal species; a specific pattern of explanatory causal principles, according to which the differences that define kinds are immutable through development from childhood to adulthood and heritable by a person's children; and a set of concepts about which differences among people matter in defining races and which don't. The analogy between a child's naïve biological and racial thinking, he claimed, is not causal; both are governed by a similar preexisting cognitive structure for constructing kinds in their respective domains of living things. Like any domain-specific cognitive competency, racial cognition functions to increase knowledge beyond what everyday experience warrants. It promotes inductive inference by encouraging children to make "educated," if sometimes erroneous guesses about nonobvious aspects of human difference, to generalize from observable similarities to less concrete ones.

The relevant observable similarities are not simply empirical descriptions. "Enmeshed" in the hard-wired principles of racial thinking, Hirschfeld claimed, is the "notion of a material and nonobvious essence. . . . In the folk [which is also the child's] view, a child does not simply resemble its parent in being black; the black child *is* black in virtue of having black parents. . . . The notion of essence is a conceptual attempt to capture kinds rather than properties or attributes."[22] Children may believe that tall people generally (though not always) produce tall offspring but they don't regard differences in height as fundamental distinguishing marks of groups; height is a contingent personal attribute applicable to both blacks and whites. The indicators of race, in contrast, are not seen as just a set of properties associated with a race but as signaling in each race a hidden "*distinguishing essence.*"[23] Black people are black, in other words, because of some essential "blackness," and they are also whatever else black people are thought to be by their environment in virtue of that same blackness. (It was such essentialist thinking that underlay the notorious "one-drop rule" in American racial thinking under Jim Crow segregation, according to which someone with a black ancestor no matter how far removed was black even if he was indistinguishable in skin color from the whitest white; his "essence" remained black even if his color didn't.)

Despite the focus on blackness that emerged from his experiments with young American children, however, what Hirschfeld meant by "race" was not determined primarily by physical features. Children learn which groups are different from them from their environment and then spontaneously supply an essentialist theory about what underlies the difference. There were, he pointed out, examples throughout history of distinguishing races by other than physical characteristics. Explicitly differing with Hacking, he argued that quite aside from the constructions of modern science or the centralized state, societies have always thought in terms of "primordial groups,"[24] groups of individuals that a person recognizes as being like (or unlike) himself in some fundamental and enduring way. Such groups are not unified in their members' minds simply by superficial visible similarities or activities, or even just shared sentiments and beliefs: "Rather, the cut is determined by a commonsense partitive logic or social ontology that picks out the 'natural' kinds of people that exist in the world. People of this kind are relevant to what it is like to be you *and* yours." "What it is like to be you" is a phenomenological description of the sense of individual identity; "what it is like to be yours" is the inner sense of collective identity. Racial categorization ultimately serves the purpose of fixing both. Borrowing a term from the philosopher and social theorist David Goldberg, Hirschfeld called such identity groups "ethnoraces."

People everywhere and at all times have discriminated between members of their own ethnorace and others. The defining characteristic of ethnoracial thought is that it *naturalizes* differences among groups: people identify the social differences of culture or language with natural differences, though not necessarily biological ones; biologizing difference is a feature only of *modern* ethnoracial thinking. Naturalization, however, does make differences seem unchangeable by rooting them in physical *causes*, for example the effects of environmental influence. Furthermore, naturalization is not morally neutral. Many traditional tribal names, Hirschfeld noted, originate in the native names for "people" or "real humans." A consequence of naturalization is the implication that those outside the group are less than or other than fully human.[25] But because his own purpose was to argue that humans bring innate cognitive structures to bear on the various domains of their experience, Hirschfeld did not emphasize the exclusionary or demeaning aspect of ethnoracial distinctions. To the contrary, he was arguing the primacy of kind-making cognitive structures against the more commonly accepted theory in contemporary sociology that race is created out of empirical perceptions of difference for the purposes of exploitation.

In the latter view, a society's race concept is shaped exclusively by existing social relations of domination, and can be explained only in the context of a particular society's power structure. According to Hirschfeld, however, this approach ignores the ubiquity and sameness of the "race concept" across time and societies, in contrast with the diversity of "racial thinking" produced by

the variety of ethnoraces and their unique interrelationships in different societies. Race is one of the few categories that is reliably naturalized across cultures
and that withstands changes of social and power relationships. It is true that
as naturalized, races easily lend themselves to exploitation. The causal relationship between power and race, however, is the opposite of what it is conventionally taken to be. "Race," Hirschfeld argued, "was taken up as a category of
power in part because of its unique characteristics as a *category of the mind*";[26]
difference could be exploited because it was there.

In the contemporary United States, popular racial thinking is almost exclusively a matter of black and white skin color. But in the nineteen twenties, he
pointed out, Irish and Italian Catholics were considered by many to be a different race from Northern Europeans of Protestant descent. In one of the
earliest examples of modern race doctrine, apologists for the aristocracy in
seventeenth-century France claimed superior Frankish descent against racially
inferior commoners descended from the original Gallic population. And in
perhaps the most salient example from European history, Jews were considered racially different from Christians at least as far back as the Spanish
conquest.

In light of these examples, it is rather confusing that Hirschfeld defined his
"cognitive race theory" as

> the recurrently encountered folk belief that humans can be partitioned
> into distinct types on the basis of their concrete observable constitu-
> tion. The notion of observable constitution captures the following fea-
> tures of racial thinking: racial differences are thought to be embodied,
> natural and enduring, and are thought to encompass nonobvious or
> inner qualities (including moral and mental ones) as well as outward
> physical ones.[27]

Despite his desire to downplay the importance of visible physical differences
in racial classification, his definition nonetheless began with them.

Ambiguity about the salience of physical features in race-making was again
evident in Hirschfeld's interpretation of the results of his empirical work in
France. In experiments he conducted with young French school children, he
noted that when they were asked to retell a simple story that included references to the protagonists' gender, race, size, clothing, and occupation, there
was a significant statistical difference in their mention of racial identity when
the story was narrated to them without visual aids and when the story was
told through drawings. There was a much higher frequency of mention of

race, both in absolute terms and relative to the other categories, after the narrated stories than after the visual stories. Hirschfeld concluded that in building racial categories, "obvious surface cues like skin color are not *defining* for young children. Perceptual cues are not extraneous to racial concepts; they simply (and grossly) underdetermine them. Young children's racial categories initially derive less from visual than from verbal (i.e., discursive) information. . . . Such categories contain little perceptual but a great deal of conceptual (i.e., ontological and causal) knowledge."[28] When prompted to think about what they had heard, rather than to report what they had seen, race was much more salient for them because race was more a conceptual than a visual category for them. This, Hirschfeld thought, also explained the otherwise peculiar disjunction between children's racial attitudes and their behavior. Preschoolers may display gross racial prejudice in experimental tests yet play easily with children from the supposedly despised group; racial attitudes as determined by tests are a weak predictor of playmate choice. With regard to gender, by contrast, attitudes tend to be consistent with behavior: children with negative test attitudes to the other gender will not choose to play with them.

Hirschfeld wanted to wrench the concept of race out of the narrow and as he thought conceptually illegitimate constraints imposed on it by modern racial thought. From the mid-nineteenth century on, Europeans and Americans expressly categorized the races by skin color—white, yellow, black, and red—linked them with specific moral and intellectual traits and rooted the differences in biological constitution. This way of thinking about race overvalued the observable physical component of race at the expense, Hirschfeld thought, of the essentialist beliefs crucial to the way children, and adults, inherently theorize group difference. But in all of his experiments with both American and French children, race and color fully overlapped.

There was in fact no contradiction between the ideas that racial classifications depended on physical signs and that they were essentialized cognitive categories. Hirschfeld's own examples confirmed this. As they acculturated, Southern and Eastern European immigrants to America were able to escape their racial classification as "non-white" because they were in fact "white"; blacks and Asians, no matter how long they were in the country, never could.[29] In the cases of the French aristocracy and European Jews, where there were no immediately obvious physical markers, differences were "naturalized" by rooting them in "blood," a precursor to modern biological race theory, but naturalization was accompanied by the drive to discover visible distinguishing marks that reached maniacal extremes in the twentieth century in Nazi "racial science."

Hirschfeld's attempt to minimize the importance of physical difference was not just the confused fallout of his cognitive argument but was partly motivated by the cultural demands of contemporary egalitarianism. The shock of acknowledging the deep-rootedness of "racial" thinking could be mitigated by emphasizing its fallacy as biology. What he was in fact arguing for was a human cognitive propensity to "essentialize" physical difference, which entailed seeing it also as a marker of fundamental character differences. He *also* observed that we naturalize other kinds of group distinctions as well, such as those of ethnicity and religion, by anchoring them in the body; where there is no easily visible physical difference, visible markers would be found, or invented. But, as the evolution of American immigrant groups from race to ethnicity showed, where these markers were not prominent or were largely imagined, they could "disappear" when the salience of difference on the grounds of culture and language was mitigated by acculturation. "Racialization" should thus be seen as distinct from the naturalizing of non-physical differences, even if the result of both is the conjoining of cultural-moral-intellectual and physical traits and thus the occasional blurring of the distinction. Strictly speaking, *racial* essentializing moves from visible physical difference to moral and cultural difference; the essentializing naturalization of ethnicity or religion moves from the cultural to the physical. It is the first that was most prominent and pernicious in Western racism in the last two centuries (with the exception of a deadly strand of modern anti-Semitism, which explicitly racialized religion based on the supposed close kinship of Jews). Modern "scientific" race theory in the twentieth century took the relationship between the physically visible and the moral/intellectual an ominous step farther by anchoring it in deep genetic structure. Modern antiracism in turn took the form of denying the significance of genetic differences between the so-called races. Recently it has become common in some quarters to speak of anti-Muslim prejudice as "racializing" Islam. This amounts to the persuasive displacement of terminology in an effort to mobilize liberal society's total repudiation of racial bigotry against an apparently more acceptable religious prejudice, though an element of true racialization persists in anti-Islamic sentiment in the more or less overt identification of Islam with brown, or in any case nonwhite, peoples.

The denial of any genetic foundation to racial difference has turned out to be too sweeping. As Ian Hacking pointed out, something of value is lost by completely discounting biological differences between certain human populations.[30] Since the publication of Richard Lewontin's seminal article in 1972, liberal antiracists have been claiming that the idea of biological races does not pick out significant differences among the groups traditionally classified as racially distinct by physical feature. The genetic variation between two randomly chosen members of one racial group was just as great as that between two randomly chosen members of "different" races. Deeper analysis of the statistical reasoning behind this claim, however, showed it to be fallacious.[31] Some stereotypical physical features of conventional racial classification are in fact associated both with ancestral geographical origin and with genetic markers of significance for medicine and health. Modern epidemiological practice recognizes biological differences among traditionally classified racial populations by establishing racial registries for bone marrow transplants, since such groups show different genetic factors affecting transplant success. Much contemporary scientific work on race-based medicine is carried out under essentially African American auspices because of the special susceptibility of African Americans to diseases like sickle-cell anemia. While recognizing the dangers of misusing genetic identification, Hacking wrote that he took a "rather benign view of the use of genetics to trace identities"[32] because of its positive consequences for health. He did insist, quite forcefully, that "A set of people with risk factors is a biological, not social, group." Nevertheless, he also argued, determining such a biological group has fruitful social consequences in the formation of advocacy and support groups. Such groups introduce something new into the discussion of identity—the insistence on the biological susceptibility of their members couched in the language of essence. People with genetically caused disabilities, Hacking pointed out, can hardly avoid thinking of their genetic inheritance as "part of what constitutes them, as part of who they are, as their essence."[33] In these cases it is not their disease itself that furnishes their identity (as in the case of autism or obesity) but their race, because race is the marker of higher susceptibility to the disease.

This limited rehabilitation of biological race makes it all the more import to distinguish it from Hirschfeld's broader claim that human beings, from childhood on, naturalize all sorts of difference among human beings, creating all-encompassing theories of ontological kinds—fixed and permanent—out of the differences their society valorizes. Since the modern concept of race has some (narrowly defined) biological validity, it is an error to automatically identify the idea of biological race as such with racial essentialism. The temptation to do so arises out of its historical linkage of race with cultural differences and judgments of inferiority and superiority. Furthermore, legitimate biological race classification should be distinguished from essentialism because essentialism flies in the face of modern biology itself. Essentialism implies permanence or fixity, but genetic population-based diseases can be and are diluted by interbreeding, and genetic manipulation holds out the possibility of curing them. It is not biology *tout court* but biological essentialism—rooting cultural difference in unchangeable biological constitution—that gave rise to socially pernicious racism.

Formal Criteria for Collective Identity

Taking off from Ian Hacking's insight that kinds of persons are brought into being by the creation of labels for them, Kwame Anthony Appiah advanced a set of criteria for establishing social identities. While intended as analytic rather than causal, they included necessary social and individual conditions for identity recognition.

Identities require first the *availability of terms in public discourse* that can be used to pick out the bearers of an identity and *criteria for ascribing them* to individuals. There can be no "black" or "gay" or "Jewish" identity if there are no words to designate the group to which individuals are to be assigned and specific features by which society can assign them. "Availability" in this context means that most members of a society know that the labels exist, and that there is a fairly high degree of consensus on how to identify those to whom they should be applied. The set of relevant characteristics does not have to have sharp boundaries, as long as there is enough agreement about the range of things it may include that there is no serious social dispute about them. (This has not always been the case, as obsessive racist efforts to establish precise criteria for "blackness" or "Jewishness" abundantly show. Nor are these efforts confined to racists.)

Second, at least some of those labeled by society must have *internalized the label* as part of their individual identities. A social category is not an identity unless people whom society labels in a certain way self-identify with the label in a way that actually affects their feelings, behavior, or beliefs. Hence identities often have ethical and moral weight for their bearers. On the other hand, since identity labels are generally organized around stereotypes, it isn't necessarily the case that the labeled and those labeling them have the same characteristics in mind. African Americans, Appiah noted, may well have different social conception of black identity than whites. What does matter for identity is that enough blacks and nonblacks agree that there is such a thing as a distinctive "black identity" to constitute one. Typically also, identification has a strong *narrative dimension* such that a person fits his life story into certain patterns predetermined by his identity and also into the larger story of his identity group's history.

Finally, a social identity involves *a pattern of social behavior* toward a collective that involves society's treating them as that identity. Historically these behaviors have often been negative and discriminatory; treating blacks *as* blacks and Jews *as* Jews has often meant demeaning, persecuting, and excluding them. But logically, treating someone as a particular something could involve positive recognition.

Appiah summarized his analysis this way, using "L" (for label) as the marker of an identity: "Where a classification of people as Ls is associated with a *social conception* of Ls, some people *identify as* Ls, and people are sometimes *treated as* Ls, we have a pattern of a social identity that matters for ethical and political life."[34] The problem with this definition is that it doesn't really accomplish what Appiah intended. He meant it to pick out those collective identities that have the greatest impact on people's individual identities, pointing out that "Not every aspect of the collective dimension of someone's identity will have the general power of sex or gender, sexuality or nationality, ethnicity or religion." These of course were also the forms of collective identity that had roiled the politics of the preceding forty years. But the stripped down set of formal criteria he offered applied to any kind of group identity. Even his more extended version of social identity labeling, which included additional criteria such as normative commitments and long-range historical narratives, could well apply to many if not all occupational, civic, and familial roles—doctors, chimney sweeps, bureaucrats, fathers—all of which come with their own codes of ethics and venerable histories. Purely formal criteria are not sufficient to pick out the social identity categories that had excited the identity politics of the recent past and that also, according to all the theorists discussed above, seemed to have been the most important sources of both individual identity and group conflict throughout history.

An "Existential" Approach to Collective Identity

Can any set of criteria accomplish this? Both the historical reality of modern identity struggles and Hirschfeld's suggestion about the naturalization of important difference classifications point to one possibility. There is, I want to argue, a useful way of thinking about certain collective identities that can clarify what it means to call them "primordial." It does not seem particularly controversial to suggest that there is a small set of features of human lives, including both commonalities and differences, that is determined by the universal human condition, by certain ineluctable realities—Heidegger and Sartre called them our "facticity"—about which we have no choice and which are of salient importance to us as we live our lives. (Or historically have had no choice. Whether genetic manipulation or as yet undiscovered possibilities in the future will give us the power to change elements of our facticity remains to be seen.) These furnish what human beings have historically regarded as the weightiest of the categories of collective identity.

SEX

The most physically obvious, and historically most basic of our differences, as evidenced by its subjective importance to humans and by the fact that it cuts across all other group distinctions, is our sexual identities as male and female, determined for most of our species history by our reproductive organs and secondary sexual characteristics, now also by our genetic makeup. The binary identities are so deeply rooted in us that even the contemporary recognition of individuals who apparently don't fit into the binary scheme takes place in relation to it. The supposed exceptions are far fewer in number than some nowadays like to think. They do *not* include the transgendered, for example, who accept the binary distinction between male and female but believe that they were born with the "wrong" sexual organs and wish to alter them to those of the other sex. If anything, transgender is strong evidence for the subjective importance of a primary sexual identity. Nor do gays, lesbians, and bisexuals represent a challenge to the division into male and female, although so long as male and female sexual identity was also held to include sexual orientation, they were thought to do so. Exclusive sexual orientation however, whether heterosexual or homosexual, clearly affirms male-female distinction, while bisexuality, as the word says, is defined in relation to it as inclusive rather than exclusive, and in any case bisexual people generally identify as one sex or the other.[35]

Integrating homosexuality and bisexuality into the binary sexual classification did mean hiving off sexual orientation from core sexual identity and making it into an independent sexual identity category, but it did not change the fact that being male or female matters in relation to sexual desire. Core sexual identity also expresses itself in our concern for sexual desirability, which in turn affects behavior as much as sexual orientation. Desire itself may be biologically "automatic," but the desire to be desirable requires that one consciously attend to and emphasize one's sexual identity. Perhaps intersex individuals who have the physical or genetic characteristics of both sexes constitute the only genuine, if rare, "third sex," though it too is necessarily defined in relation to the male and female polarity. And even many, though not all, intersex individuals have a decided gender identity and sexual orientation.

On the other hand, contemporary acceptance of the normality of homosexual desire in many places points to the social malleability of human attitudes toward our core sexual identities. It has not always been the case that society accepted as male men who desire other men. Primordial collective identities have to be plotted along not one but two axes, the existential and the sociohistorical. Collective identity changes over time *within* the bounds of the fundamental existential categories established by our facticity. Even more telling than the separation of sexual orientation from core sexual identity as an example of historical change within binary sexual identity—since both sexual orientation and core identity are (most likely) biologically determined—is the emergence of the category of gender. If historically it resulted from the political push for women's equality, theoretically it marked the breakthrough awareness of the distinction between the biological and the social dimensions of sexual identity. While far from complete or uncontested even in those societies where women have achieved the greatest degree of social, economic, and political equality, the idea of equality both depends on and in turn continues to foster radical change in traditional concepts of femininity and masculinity. But those same societies give clear evidence that, however confused or in flux, "feminine" and "masculine" continue to exist as primordial identities along with male and female; sexual equality does not mean gender homogeneity. Sexual difference continues to matter for identity both physically and socially; more exactly, it continues to matter socially because it matters physically.

Sexuality is the foremost expression of the embodiedness of human existence as it relates to collective identity. As the phenomenologist Maurice Merleau-Ponty was the first to argue in detail, we do not only "have" bodies, we *are* bodies. Our experience of the world, of spatial and temporal location, up and down, big and small, ecstasy and pain, and much else, is not just oriented in relation to the body but happens through and in the embodied self. Subjectivity is not pure reflection only but also body consciousness. Most of how the world is for the embodied self is the same for males and females, but not everything, and it makes a great difference for life experience, expectation, and decision making that only females menstruate and carry, bear, and nurse children and only males inseminate. One need not go to the speculative extremes of Luce Irigaray to think that the sexual experience of males and females must be different because of the differences in sexual organs and the variable modalities of initiation and reception, aggression and vulnerability both entail.[36] Though imagination and fantasy make it possible for some to feel that they can enter into the sexual experience of the other sex, and for a rarer few to write it persuasively to the other sex, though what Freud called our innate bisexuality makes it possible for all of us, male and female, to experience both active and passive, aggressive and receptive sex, the embodiment of sexuality makes the difference between the sexes in a fundamental sense unbridgeable and perhaps ultimately incommunicable. However any of that difference gets translated into social behaviors, contemporary relations between the sexes even in the most sexually equal environments suggest that it does translate socially, and likely always will.

"RACE"

Embodiment is also at the core of the criteria differentiating groups that in modern times have been called races. Though the word "race" and its cognates in European languages appeared only from the middle of the sixteenth century on,[37] salient visual differences like skin color, eye shape and color, and physiognomy generally have always mattered for group classification. It is the physical that distinguishes racial classification from ethnicity, though physiognomy is always connected to behavioral and cultural traits in the concept of race. Race has also characteristically been interpreted as constituting a hierarchy of value. Even Ivan Hannaford, who argued forcefully against the interpretation of *ethnos* and *barbaros*, the standard Greek terms for non-Greek peoples, as early instances of invidious racial thinking, acknowledged that physical appearance generally played a role in Greek classifications of human groups. Hesiod and Herodotus characterized the basic difference between the Greeks and the *ethnos* or *barbaros* in political terms, between those who lived according to reason and law and those who brutishly or unthinkingly obeyed nature and tradition, but Greeks and Romans, he acknowledged, lumped all dark-skinned peoples of sub-Saharan Africa together as "Ethiopians" (uniting the Greek words for "burn" and "face"), though presumably without antipathy.[38] Hippocrates wrote of the Scythians inhabiting the southeast coast of the Black Sea as a "gross, fleshy, yellowish, corpulent people who speak with deep voices," attributing these characteristics to the quantity of water in their lower bowels.[39]

Aristotle was the most explicit and systematic of ancient thinkers, according to Hannaford, in explaining political differences between peoples by physical causation. In the *Politics* he wrote of the "natural differences" between the people of the colder regions of Europe, the Greek people, and the peoples of Asia. Those of the northern parts of Europe were deficient in skill and intelligence but full of spirit; they were comparatively free but did not develop politically and showed no capacity for governing others. Asians, by contrast, living in warmer climates, were endowed with skill and intelligence but deficient in spirit, and for that reason continued to be subjects and slaves. Between the two extremes were the Greeks, who united spirit and intelligence and were thus both free and politically developed and capable of ruling others.

Though Hannaford claimed that Aristotle's principle of differentiation was solely political, physiology and politics went together and each signified the other in this mode of thinking. Aristotle argued that there is a direct connection between bodily and mental characteristics: "It seems to me that soul and body react on one another; when the character of the soul changes it changes also the form of the body, and conversely, when the form of the body changes, it changes also the form of the soul."[40] Furthermore the basic purpose of Aristotle's classification was unquestionably to establish a hierarchy of virtue. So while Hannaford did not regard Aristotle's analysis as based on race in the modern understanding of the term, the classical scholar Benjamin Isaac did, or at least on something that could be regarded as racial prototypes. "Early forms of racism," he declared unequivocally in his introduction, "to be called [in his book] proto-racism, were common in the Graeco-Roman world."[41]

The term "proto-racism" was a concession to the fact that Greek and Roman antiquity had no conception of biological determinism, the hallmark of the modern concept of race. But the ancient world did have a range of prejudices, phobias, and hostilities toward specific groups of foreigners, based on the belief that their inferior characteristics were produced by physical forces over which they had no control and hereditarily transmitted to their off-spring.[42] Isaac defined racism as positing a "direct and linear connection between physical and mental qualities." In essence it regards individuals as superior and inferior because they are believed to share physical, mental, and moral attributes with the group to which they are deemed to belong, and it is assumed that they cannot change these traits individually. Change is held to be impossible because the negative traits are determined by their physical makeup, shaped by uncontrollable factors like climate and geography and transmitted by heredity.[43] By these standards, race and racism in the West are at least as old as recorded history.

In modern racial thinking since at least the eighteenth century the emphasis in criteria for discriminating races shifted from climate and geography to the physical signs by which the Other was recognized. Certainly after Darwin, Isaac noted, it was believed possible to classify human beings on the basis of physiological traits, on the assumption that certain groups possess hereditary traits that are sufficiently constant to characterize them as distinct human types. By the end of the nineteenth century it was a commonplace in Europe and America that there were at least white, black, and yellow races, if not also red, brown, and others of varying hues while Jews, who were "racialized" in Christian Europe originally for religious reasons, had to be caricatured with the "typical" Semitic features of swarthy complexions and hooked noses. Color in the contemporary world, especially in America, has pretty much become the stand-in for race, though as Hirschfeld's cognitive thesis explained, the essentializing of color also led to the absurdity that "blacks" could in fact be white.

Virtually all contemporary commentators on race have noted both that the concept has been largely discredited scientifically in the version that invidiously links color and character, and that it nonetheless continues to maintain its hold on popular discourse. There is no proven relationship between visible physical characteristics and intelligence, ability, or character, yet race unquestionably remains a socially and politically significant category. Its hold is evidence not only of the legacy of past racism but also of the deep propensity identified by the existentialists to anchor ourselves in the permanent and unchanging. The body is "nature," meaning that which was there before human fashioning. In her discussion of purity and order, the anthropologist Mary Douglas tellingly quoted Sartre to explain why people might ignore reason—as in the arguments against the idea of biological race—when it threatens the felt need of many people for experience that could be hard set and fixed in form:

> How can anyone choose to reason falsely? It is simply the old yearning
> for impermeability. . . . There are people who are attracted by the
> permanence of stone. They would like to be solid and impenetrable,
> they do not want to change; for who knows what change may bring?
> . . . They have no wish to acquire ideas, they want them to be innate.
> . . . They want to adopt a mode of life in which . . . one never becomes
> anything else but what one already is.[44]

To which one can add, a mode of life that guarantees the permanent superiority of one's own kind to every other kind. Racial embodiment does this for many. It may be a bad idea, wrong factually and disastrous morally, but it is, as Hirschfeld sadly noted, a deeply rooted bad idea. And as long as color, eye shape and physiognomy create invidious distinctions, those who differ from the dominant ones in any society will have to embrace their own, whether in pride or as neutral fact, for a sense of positive identity.

"ETHNICITY"

The prominence of geographical location, kinship, and behavior in the ancient classifications of groups by physical feature suggests another existential factor as a basis for collective identity, one that before the advent of modern race thinking was perhaps even more important for classification than physical differences and that will likely continue to be so even should race ultimately yield to science and disappear as an important social category. We call it "ethnicity" after the Greek word for non-Greek peoples, though I want to give the term a rather broader sense than it usually calls up. As finite beings located in time and space, we are born into groups defined by geography, descent, and culture, including, most important, language. Contemporary liberal, especially academic thought tends to be much more impressed by the mobility and hybridity of populations than their fixity, and it is now the fashion to argue that these rather than fixed boundaries and stability have been the truth of humanity throughout history. But hybridity and mixing presuppose separateness and difference. We are the heirs of a not so distant past where kinship counted for almost everything in human connectedness to and separateness from others, and in somewhat altered form it still counts for a great deal.

Culture is the ensemble of formal rules and informal customs that regularize and ritualize the basic functions of human life, individual and collective. Birth and death, social interactions, the most basic biological functions of eating, sex, and elimination, and finally rule making itself, that is, the political function—all are governed by interpretations, meanings, norms, and customs that differ from collective to collective but, along with the language in which they are couched are the necessary structures of all societies, in fact what define a society for us. If, however, establishing a legitimate authority for rule-making is one of the fundamental practices of any society, the particular form of that authority is not. Like all other culture content, the principles and institutions of governance are locatable not on the existential but the sociohistorical axis of collective identity. Clans and tribes mutate into city-states, empires, feudal societies, monarchies, and nation-states. From this point of view, for example, modern national identity, so important to us today as a category of identity is not primordial but only the most recent form of the political dimension of ethnicity.

Kinship is a biological tie, though the significant degrees of "blood relationships" are defined by culture and augmented by rules governing legitimate reproduction. Blood, visible on the outside only through its loss, is deemed nature itself, the very essence of life. In classical "proto-racist" thinking, descent from a common ancestor, thus sharing the same blood, was if anything more important than physiognomy in defining collective identity. But kinship and culture were in the past always seen to go together, because though culture is the expression of the human symbolic capacity, it is initially transmitted by birth; one is born into a community of culture, which in the first instance defines for us who we are collectively and individually. It is only relatively recently—and imperfectly—that culture has been separated from blood and seen as an autonomous collective identity.

If we think of kinship only in the narrow familial or clan sense of consanguinity, it is easy to imagine that it no longer matters in a modern individualist society or nation-state defined only by common legal citizenship. But even traditionally kinship was always a broader category than family or clan; common culture often defined those who were of the "same" blood even if they were not directly blood relatives. In this wider sense the modern nation with its own history, myths, and heroes, its own language, holidays, and commemorative events, can be seen as a kinship group, situated above the nuclear family as the tribe also was, transmitting its culture organically to those born into it. Both citizenship by birth and citizenship by blood confirm the kinship—born into or born of—of the national idea. The American word for citizenship acquired by domicile is, tellingly, "naturalization." Because of immigration and regional differences, there can be more circumscribed ethnicities within wider ones, though their modern significance may be more notional than real for successive generations of immigrants; if so, the process of acculturation strengthens the "national ethnicity."

Part of the reason for this is the ineluctability of geographical location, the spatial element of ethnicity. One badge of our finitude is the inescapability of being "here" and not "there" at any given moment. For the modern dual or triple citizen or the cosmopolitan citizen of the world "here" may encompass sequentially more than one physical location and many more than those in imagination or empathy, but one is always somewhere, never everywhere— though part of our existential reality is often to want to understand *our* somewhere as everywhere, as the only true and absolute "where," or conversely, to deny the necessity of having to be limited by our somewhere. Human collectivities are territorial and tend to think territorially; they want to be rooted in, to belong as of right to, their own space—though perhaps also to elevate their space to universality by calling it holy, or making it correspond with spatiality as such through expansion and conquest. But even were they to entirely escape that propensity, they cannot escape their finite communality and their need to define it.

LABOR

Within culture there is one sphere that can be regarded as an independent existential category, furnishing a distinctive and necessary range of collective identities. It is so fundamental that, for example, both religious and secular scripture in the West have agreed on it. Because we are only partly instinctual creatures, humans have to produce the means of our subsistence by the sweat of our brow and the application of intelligence and imagination, that is, by labor. Labor is an existential category, as evidenced by its various ontological interpretations as the result of sin and divine decree or as man's distinctive species being, the first stressing its necessitarian and the other its free creative aspect. The cultural conditions under which we labor, however, change with social organization and technology, producing different kinds of labor, different structures of division, and different criteria for distributing its roles. Labor roles are collective identities; whether one is peasant or priest, engineer or undertaker, financier or factory worker, one is a member of a category with a distinctive identity that determines much of one's life activity and self-definition. For Karl Marx, the distinctive factor in the division of labor was whether one owned or worked the means of production, which determined one's class identity; "class" has been taken over—though without much of Marx's substance—by non-Marxists who define it hierarchically in terms of differences in levels of wealth, education, church, and occupational type. With or without its Marxist connotations, social class, along with occupation, are determinative collective identities for all human beings, even those who don't "have to" work or enjoy the pastimes of the "idle rich." In both primitive and modern societies, one is defined and defines oneself in part by what one does, though in primitive divisions of labor what one typically did might be included in one's sexual identity; men were hunters by the definition of masculinity (though not necessarily in every society). In advanced industrial and technological societies, where productivity is a value, the division of labor is complex, and many kinds of work demand high levels of skill, intelligence, and training, work has become—as Erikson's emphasis on it testifies—a more prominent category of identity.

TRANSCENDENCE

A final existential category requires separate classification, though historically it has often been fused with ethnicity and in secularizing social science is often classified as a subcategory of culture. I might have called it religion, but what I mean by it isn't restricted to recognizably theistic faiths, even if they have been its most prominent historical expressions. It is rather what Wilhelm Dilthey meant when he generalized, and relativized, religion by calling it one kind of Weltanschauung, an all-encompassing interpretation of the world. Closer to the topic at hand, it is the category of "ideology" that Erik Erikson added to the requirements of a fully developed identity, a basic belief system that grounded all the self's other identifications and norms.

Religions and their secular kin perform two existential tasks. As self-aware beings capable of reflection, we ask the most basic questions about our human existence: where did we come from? Why are we here? How ought we to live while we are here? What happens to us when we are no longer here? As finite beings, we understand those questions in relation to our ephemerality and to what might transcend it. Humanity through history has shown a strong desire to answer its basic questions with transcendent schemes of absolute beings or powers which offer grounds for our being, objective purposes for which to live, absolute codes to live by, and eternal consolations for our death. But secular or humanist answers also position themselves in relation to transcendence, if only to deny its possibility for us, though not its pull. We may live without religion but not without a Weltanschauung or an ideology, which tells us ethically what the good life is for us and morally what is right and wrong in relation to others. These may be, for a minority of modern people, individual and self-chosen belief systems, though even these are unimaginable for us today without the heritage of previous thinking on such issues; historically and still most commonly, however, they are collective belief systems based on universal principles, held to be objective, that unite—and separate—large numbers of people.

In her study of the idea of purity and pollution in primitive cultures and in the dietary laws enumerated in Leviticus, Mary Douglas made two essential arguments. The concern in primitive cultures and in ancient Judaism to preserve "purity" from dirt and pollution represents a desire for order. Dirt is "matter out of place," the "by-product of a systematic ordering and classification of matter."[45] The specifics of that order are without doubt derived from the way of life of a group. In the case of the Israelite laws of edible and nonedible animals, Douglas argued, "Cloven-hoofed, cud-chewing ungulates are the model of the proper kind of food for a pastoralist. If they must eat wild game, they can eat wild game that shares these distinctive characters and is therefore of the same general species."[46] But to think of this ordering as sacred or holy is to declare it absolute and objective, guaranteed true by the highest power, by "divinity." "Holiness," she wrote, "means keeping distinct the categories of creation,"[47] the separations that are inherent in the structure of being that God made. Holiness also means that the separate categories constitute a structure that is whole and complete.[48] In turn it demands perfection, being without blemish, of the objects of ritual and of those who perform it. (Ultimately too, though Douglas did not note this, holiness is demanded not just of priests but of the whole community of Israel, who are commanded "You shall be holy, as I the Lord your God, am holy."[49]) The separation between clean and unclean in the dietary laws was mirrored in rules of social separation within the Israelite community. Thus obeying the dietary laws, she concludes, would have "inspired meditation on the oneness, purity, and completeness of God" and the order he sanctioned.[50]

Douglas's second major point, however, was that such concepts of dirt and purity are not just primitive but part of modern ways of thinking and that they go beyond the considerations of health and hygiene by which we try to explain them. The desire for sanctioned order is universal. To extend the existential explanation Douglas herself invoked, humans are strongly tempted to endow the contingent historical order of their primordial factical characteristics with Being, timeless metaphysical necessity. If not by divinizing them, it feels plausible to do so by naturalizing them, rooting them in physical nature that has historically seemed to humans objective and eternal because it was there before and beyond human intervention. The imperative to "be natural," the concept of "natural law," the figure of "Mother Nature" all suggest a reliable authority transcending the arbitrary will of man.

*   *   *

Sex, "race," "ethnicity," labor, the aspiration to transcendence—these have been the foundations of the most impactful collective identities throughout history. They are "primordial" in the sense that they are unavoidable. I put "race" in quotation marks because I mean by it the propensity for human beings to derive significance beyond the physical from the visible physical differences that demarcate large human populations, out of the desire to anchor identity in the "natural," supposedly nonarbitrary features of the human body. It is why race mixing has been branded "unnatural" in various times and places—and seen to be threatening precisely because "interbreeding" proves that it is not so at all, and that even supposedly defining physical differences can be effaced. Race is the most problematic of the existential categories of identity because it is the most pernicious and misleading instance of the broader category of naturalization. It appears to wear the obviousness of its identity criterion on its face, while in reality what gets naturalized in racial identity is much more than skin deep: it is the moral and intellectual qualities of humanness that have no provable connection either with the physically visible or with the supposedly causal physically invisible.

I put "ethnicity" in quotes for similar reasons. I might have separated out culture and governance from ethnicity as autonomous sources of collective identity. The governed in a society may well be multi-ethnic, and their identity may also be defined by their allegiance to whatever entity exercises power through the monopoly of force that their voluntary obeisance legitimizes. But I wanted again to point to the powerful human propensity to anchor the existential facts of symbolization (culture) and rule making (governance) in the permanence and solidity of kinship: to put it in its most ominous and ugliest modern form, in "blood and soil," or less tendentiously, in ancestry, place, and time. Kinship naturalizes community, the existential fact of our

"communality," with all it entails. Like Anthony Smith I see modern nationalism as the latest political form of ethnicity. Perhaps our existential capacity
for symbol making and our modern aspiration to self-determination and the
universal ideal of citizenship will someday become wholly autonomous determinants of community, so that culture and blood, governance and Authority,
will become wholly separable—though can culture or citizenship ever be
imagined apart from local place, from tradition, from language? But however
differently one might parse my categories, some such set of permanent, existential needs and propensities underlies the collective identities that most
importantly define us to ourselves as members of groups. Call it a contingent
ontology of collective identities. What renders collective identities theoretically
suspect and dangerous in practice is the metaphysics of naturalization, which
takes the form of conflating the particular instance of an existential category—
our sex, *our* nation, *our* interpretation of transcendence—with the broader
category and absolutizing it as its highest or only true version. Shorn of pretensions to inherent superiority or exclusivity, however, our sexuality—
including gender and sexual orientation; our race—a set of linked physical
and biological features; our ethnicity—today likely foremost nationality, the
most organized though hardly the only contemporary expression of ethnicity;
the work we do; and our Weltanschauung—religious or secular—necessarily
constitute the collective identities that most saliently define us to ourselves
and others, as in different historical versions they always have, and so far as
we can see now, always will. The "only" difference from the past, which however makes all the difference, is that knowing this enables us to distinguish
between what is fixed and what is not in our identities and to exercise our
freedom to choose and to create accordingly.

Chapter 11

Identity as an Ethical Issue

For Jean-Paul Sartre, the problem of identity was intrinsically ethical, defined by the issue of personal responsibility for one's choices. Denying responsibility by pleading the necessity of "who one is," identity was nothing less than moral dereliction, wearing its transgression on its face as "bad faith." When identity first became a widespread term of discourse in the 1950s and 1960s, by contrast, it had strongly positive connotations, first as a criterion of individual psychological health, then as a collective demand for social and political recognition and justice, but no explicit argument was made for its distinctively ethical value. Postmodernism's judgment of identity was again wholly negative, but primarily from the standpoints of philosophy and politics. It was only in the 1980s that moral philosophers began to explicitly examine the bearing of identity on ethics. The popular currency of the concept brought to their attention the significant consequences it could have for many issues in the main traditions of modern ethical discourse: virtue ethics; deontology—moral theory based on universal rules and obligations; and utilitarianism. Identity's most immediate moral affinity seemed to be with the Aristotelian tradition of virtue ethics, whose central question concerns the good life for man. The quest for identity could be seen as another way of asking that same question, though not within the original framework of Aristotelian metaphysics, with its preordained teleological answer. Identity, however, might also serve an ethics that started from the premises of modern individualism, while at the same time repeating some of individualism's typical moral problems. If, for example, the idea of a unique individual identity were itself an ethical value, what might be its rights? What were its obligations to the collective identities that in part composed it? What was the relationship of identity rights to universal rights? Finally a third philosophical approach held that individual identity, while inescapable and important, was also an obstacle for a binding universal morality. Moral theory would have to work around, rather than with, identity.

*   *   *

In Chapter 7 I looked at Alasdair MacIntyre's concept of the narrative identity of the self as the only viable alternative to the empty self of liberal theory. His notion of the unity of a life constructed out of the tradition into which it is born was meant, however, as the linchpin of a more basic argument about the nature of ethics. He employed identity to rescue Aristotelian virtue ethics from its long-since discredited biological teleology and to restate it in a form both philosophically defensible and meaningful to a modern audience.

MacIntyre's starting point was his notorious claim that modern moral theory was totally bankrupt after the failure of the Enlightenment project of justifying morality in abstract terms. When Enlightenment philosophy rejected the Aristotelian idea of man as having an essential nature that dictated an objective human purpose, it replaced it with a purely formal ethics based on principles that were purportedly universal, categorical, and internally consistent, and which could therefore be recognized by any rational person regardless of his particular circumstances. But MacIntyre argued that such abstract formulations, epitomized by Kant's categorical imperative, led nowhere because they could lead anywhere. The supposedly empirical utilitarian alternative fared no better. The utilitarian ethical requirement to maximize happiness took no account of the fact that happiness was not a definable end state in itself, let alone one that could be quantified, but rather the byproduct of satisfaction and fulfillment in very different kinds of pursuits. Different pleasures are therefore incommensurable.[1] Utilitarianism leaves the fundamental question of what ends humans should pursue unresolved because "happiness" by itself is a directionless guide.

The only alternative to such failed moral theorizing, MacIntyre argued, was a revived Aristotelianism, "*philosophically* the most powerful of pre-modern modes of moral thought. If a pre-modern view of morals and politics is to be vindicated against modernity, it will be in *something like* Aristotelian terms or not at all."[2] "*Something like*" them, because Aristotelianism itself had to be rescued from an unanswerable objection to its original major premise. The merit of Aristotle's approach was that it provided objectively knowable content to ethical demands; they derived from the understanding of man's fundamental nature and purpose, and the virtues required to realize and fulfill them. But Aristotle derived his view of human purpose from an untenable metaphysical biology, according to which man's highest end, determined by his nature as rational being though realizable in fact only by a very few, was contemplation of the impersonal, unchanging divinity which had endowed him with it. The question for a viable modern Aristotelian ethics was whether it was possible to keep the idea of an objective human *telos* or end without Aristotle's objectionable metaphysics.[3]

That was achievable, in MacIntyre's view, if one took into account the fundamental historical nature of man. For Aristotle, history could not be a source of genuine knowledge because he defined the latter as the knowledge of essential natures, necessary truths logically derivable from first principles, not from contingent, ephemeral events. It was precisely man's historicity however, MacIntyre argued, with all its contingency and unpredictability, which provided the human being with his purposes and determined the virtues that were necessary to achieve them. For MacIntyre, historicity furnished objective principles that could replace those of Aristotle's metaphysics, principles that were empirically defensible not least because they allowed for the reality of change.

MacIntyre derived his first principle from the sociology of knowledge, which was the basis of his critique of modern ethical theories. Morality, he argued "is always to some degree tied to the socially local and particular. . . . [T]he aspiration of the morality of modernity to a universality freed from all particularity is an illusion."[4] What are held to be virtues in any given society are rooted in the institutional practices of that society; they are the qualities that enable their members to achieve the goods internal to those practices. But the sociological understanding of the virtues is not enough by itself to offer a guide to the ethical life, since a society generally offers a range of practices among which the individual must choose and whose goods may conflict with one another. What is required in addition is a *telos* that "transcends the limited goods of practices by constituting the good of a whole human life, the good of a human life conceived as a unity."[5] MacIntyre found this *telos*, as we saw earlier, in the modern concept of narrative identity.

Man, he argued, "is in his actions and practice, as well as in his fiction, essentially a story-telling animal."[6] Stories are narratives that link past, present, and future in the continuous behavior of characters. "Personal identity," MacIntyre wrote, "is just that identity presupposed by the unity of the character which the unity of a narrative requires. Without such unity there would not be subjects of whom stories could be told."[7] This claim can be understood as both psychological and ontological: we humans need/want our lives to be unified and purposeful, and as the historical creatures we are, our life's unity can only be that of a narrative, which binds past, present, and future together in a plot with beginning, continuous action, and dénouement. Most important, the purposeful directedness of our actions, the plot or "point" of our lives, demands that we have an overarching conception of "the good" for ourselves, so that through it we can order all the other goods we may pursue and maintain the integrity and constancy of our selves through time. It was the contemporary concept of substantive personal identity that supplied MacIntyre with the idea of the unity of a life. His crucial contribution to it was to show that identity as a unified life was an inherently ethical concept. "What I am" tells me what to become if I am not there yet, or if I fall short of it, and it tells me what virtues or qualities I must aspire to in order to achieve or sustain my identity.

To this point, MacIntyre was describing identity from a purely individual point of view. But, he argued, we are never able to seek the good only as individuals. We all approach our own circumstances as bearers of a particular social identity, or rather a number of them—familial, political, work, ethnic. The story of my life, he argued, "is always embedded in the story of those communities from which I derive my identity."[8] In a word, personal identity is necessarily collective identity. "To ask 'What is good for me?' is to ask how best I might live out [the unity of my life] and bring it to completion. To ask 'What is the good for man?' is to ask what all the answers to the former question must have in common."[9] Collective identity is no more static than individual; living in time, communities, like individuals, tell stories about themselves relating their past to their present and envisioning a future in its light. The story of its past is its tradition. In principle, there are many kinds of communities to which one belongs and which have their own traditions, but at their apex is the overarching community that defines the good not just for a particular practice or particular group but the good for man as such. Though he only mentioned religion in specific examples, it is obvious MacIntyre believed that it was ultimately only what Rawls called "comprehensive" traditions like the world religions that offered individuals an adequate framework for deciding the good for themselves.

Tradition, as its etymology indicates, is handed down from past to present, but any existing collective identity is a *living* tradition, not inert repetition but a practice subject to reinterpretation by its devotees in the face of new social and historical conditions. Because of our historicity, change and interpretation are so integral to tradition that the best way to define it is as a "historically extended, socially embodied *argument*, and an argument precisely in part about the goods which constitute that tradition."[10] Anyone participating in the debate is by definition part of the tradition.[11] MacIntyre's "argument theory" of narrative identity was his way of negotiating the dialectic of sameness and change at the heart of identity since its original formulation by Erikson. From the point of view of the history of ethics it was salutary because it offered a rational procedure for conducting disputes about ethics. Disputes were not

irresolvable clashes of absolute differences but differences over how to interpret, or whether and how to modify, a collective identity about which there
was at least a modicum of agreement.

Whether or not MacIntyre's concept of tradition in fact offered such a
rational procedure for ethics was, however, questionable. For one thing, Mac-
Intyre himself left open the possibility that a tradition can produce moral evil.
Such a judgment would seem to imply a standard of ethics outside any particular tradition, or perhaps more plausibly in his case, the valorization of one
particular tradition whose standards were implicitly being invoked as absolute.
Not all "virtues," defined abstractly as the qualities that are necessary to realize
the goals of practices, are "virtuous." It was not adventitious that MacIntyre
announced at the end of his book that we await the second coming of St.
Benedict, the founder of that supremely anti-individualist institution devoted
to Christian communal worship, the monastery.

There was also a problem of internal consistency in MacIntyre's attempt
to reconcile the poles of change and stability within a tradition. If the question
of what goods constitute a tradition is *wholly* up for grabs, there can be no
decision procedure; each side in a dispute may invoke the tradition, but there
is no arbiter to decide which of them is interpreting it correctly. The result is
precisely the ethical anarchy that a revived Aristotelianism was supposed to
obviate.[12] If, on the other hand, there is a body invested with the authority to
determine the correct interpretation, the potentiality of argument to modify
tradition is severely limited by the orthodoxy such authority proclaims. At the
extreme, dissenters may have no choice but to secede. Are they then part of
the same tradition? Christianity, after all, originally claimed—and in a sense
still claims—that it is true normative Judaism.

My point, however, is not to analyze MacIntyre's arguments in depth but
rather to suggest that their internal problems, no less than the solution they
purport to offer to the dilemma of modern ethics, derive from the problems
at the heart of the idea of substantive identity. Erikson's original concept
wanted to combine the autonomy of the self and the possibility of change with
the binding stability of sameness. Though MacIntyre associated the idea of
individual autonomy with the ethical individualism he rejected, it was nonetheless entailed by his own notion of historicism, of tradition as living and
subject to interpretation and change. Not all traditionalists take this position.
Many have conceived tradition as never changing, or as changing only in order
to return to its eternal truth from contemporary errors and distortions. Such
a view explicitly denies the role of argument and innovation to adjust tradition
to contemporary circumstances except as sources of error. MacIntyre's view

of tradition as narrative collective identity through internal debate was as distinctively modern as identity itself, arguably, in fact, part of its definition.

*   *   *

For Charles Taylor the reality of identity had similarly transforming consequences for ethics. If it is somewhat more difficult to sort them out, it is because Taylor used the word in three different ways, or at least in three different contexts. Most fundamentally, he interpreted identity ontologically, as a necessary structure of human existence. Like MacIntyre, he understood it in Aristotelian terms as the framing structure of the self that answers to our inescapable need to define the good in order to know how to orient our lives. In another context, however, he meant identity as a literal term that had only come into being at a particular moment in history, for reasons having to do with the breakdown of previous ways of understanding the origin and nature of the good. Lastly, he used the word in the phrase "the modern identity" for the particular worldview which ostensibly defines the troubled situation of contemporary ethical thought.

Taylor's concept of the good differed from MacIntyre's in that it explicitly entailed a set of universal moral demands with regard to others: respect for their lives, integrity, well-being, and flourishing. These, he thought, were so deeply embedded in us that they were quasi-instinctual, experienced as feelings or "gut reactions," but they differed from pure instinct in that they also involved, implicitly or explicitly, ontological claims about the nature and status of human beings, and thus were subject to reasoned analysis.[13] It was only the philosophical claims which backed our moral intuitions that changed through history. In modern times our moral obligations to others had come to be couched in a metaphysics of universal individual rights. The burden of his book was that the reasoning that supported these philosophical claims was inadequate to sustain them. His analysis of the historical causes of the rise of modern individualist moral philosophy, and ultimately the emergence of the concept of identity, was intended to both define and explain the contemporary ethical dilemma. His version of it strongly resembled MacIntyre's in its religious thrust, if not in its apocalyptic pessimism. On this level, "identity," or at least "modern identity," was the problem, not the solution.

As Taylor pointed out, Erik Erikson explained Luther's crisis of faith in terms of a psychological identity crisis which Luther would have been unable to recognize, or to accept if he could. Faith was a matter of divine truth and theological, not psychological, need. The reason we talk about moral orientation today in terms of the question "Who are we?" is that we no longer believe that the moral order can be defined in universal terms. The word "identity" connotes a complex of comparatively recent ideas about the self. To be faithful to these modern ideas, each of us is expected to develop a unique identity as the source of the framework of values that guides our life.[14] Our moral dilemma derives from the fact that we are still also "framed by what we see as universally valid commitments (being a Catholic or an anarchist)" as well as "by what we understand as particular identifications (being an Armenian or Québecois)."[15] While our particular identifications don't require grounding in anything more than contingencies of birth and the affinities of feeling, our putatively universal commitments do. Moderns, however, have no universal ground to stand on. We have given up the original theistic foundation of morality, while "the naturalism of disengaged reason," that is, formal reasoning about morality, divorced from substantive considerations of the good, cannot ground our intuitions about universal benevolence and justice. Morally we are left floating in the air with nothing but our feelings, sympathies, and intuitions.

These subjective sources, however, are not enough even for those who claim to be satisfied with them as the basis for their moral choices. Often there is an inner contradiction between the purely affective or expressive reasons people publicly offer for their value choices and their unarticulated, inchoate beliefs about the truth of those values. This contradiction opens up space for rational argumentation on behalf of the idea of objective goods. While such goods can't be demonstrated to someone who really is impervious to them, one *can* argue convincingly for the truth of the goods which people already respond to at some emotional level but which they may nonetheless refuse to acknowledge they believe are *objectively* good.[16] And there are good and important moral reasons for trying to make the arguments for the objective validity of such beliefs.

Intuitive or emotional causes of moral behavior are not only obscurely felt to be inadequate by those who claim to be motivated solely by them; they are also morally self-defeating. Our normal understanding of the ideals of self-realization and emotional expressivity presupposes that some things are important beyond the self, even as we explain them only in terms of the self's desires. And because such feelings are the emotional residues of older absolute belief systems, we are subject to no longer justifiable but still powerful peremptory moral demands, as well as feelings of guilt when we fail them and self-satisfaction when we fulfill them. This is an intolerable emotional and ethical situation. "There is something morally corrupting, even dangerous,"

Taylor argued, "in sustaining the [moral] demand simply on the feeling of undischarged obligation, on guilt, or its obverse, self-satisfaction."[17] Peremptory moral demands without foundations in reasoned beliefs may breed self-condemnation without moral resolve, and even resentment of morality, because such demands seem incompatible with modern ideals of enjoyment and self-realization—the very point of Nietzsche's attack on morality. Furthermore the threatened sense of unworthiness when we transgress may be so strong that it can be defended against only by projecting our sense of evil onto others, who then become the object of hatred and worse, liquidation. Thus a humanist-based morality turns into antihumanism.

What then can be the moral answer to the dilemma of "the modern identity?" Taylor's overt answer was modest and tentative but jarringly paradoxical. "We are now in an age," he acknowledged, "in which a publicly accessible cosmic order of meanings is an impossibility. The only way we can explore the order in which we are set with an aim to defining moral sources is through . . . personal resonance."[18] That is, the very subjectivity that is the source of the moral problem of modern identity is the road to solving it. Spiritual poets like Rilke can be our guides to the inward journey that will reveal, as Taylor put it, the objective claims the world makes on the self. By world, however, he meant more than all that there is; he was pointing to its Source. The attempt at a humanist foundation of ethics cannot, he intimated, sustain our deepest ethical intuitions. If our supreme value is the highest that humans can achieve we are not likely to value those who are irremediably broken and incapable of such achievement. On the other hand, the original Christian notion of *agape* is of a love that God has for humans that is connected with their unconditional goodness as creatures and in which human beings participate. "My hunch," as he put it, is that "the potential of a certain theistic perspective is incomparably greater" in its ability to support our aspirations to benevolence and justice for all. But, he also admitted, if he did not develop that hunch it was largely for lack of good arguments.[19]

In fact, however, he had already offered a strong argument, if not for theism then at the least for some form of absolute belief, in his initial definition of identity. Theism, while always lurking at the edges of his history of the self, would have taken him outside the parameters of the book's basic concepts. A more internally consistent way of putting its central thesis—and the real paradox he was exploring—was that our modern identity contravened the demands of ontological identity. Identity was for Taylor neither optional nor (only) psychological. It is the structure of commitments and identifications which constitute the necessary framework of our values and actions and which is constitutive of human agency. Without identity in this sense we could not orient ourselves in the world. Furthermore, he believed that our deepest identity commitments do in fact include, though they are not limited to, some that we hold to be universally valid. This claim was empirical, though one he obviously thought would be supported in every case by an honest exploration of the "personal resonance" of moral intuitions. Even if we intellectually reject all absolute belief systems, we feel and we act—we *must* feel and act—as if our moral judgments are "right," and this implicit appeal to an objective standard of the good entails just the kind of belief we say we reject. This part of his claim about identity *was* psychological: our feelings show us that we believe even when we don't think we do. And the consequences of a breakdown of belief in ourselves are also psychological: an identity crisis that produces acute disorientation and incapacity to function in the world. As with MacIntyre, a psychological concept of identity came to the rescue of a search for an objective foundation for morality that could no longer be confidently defended in traditional metaphysical or religious terms.

*   *   *

Toward the end of his book Taylor conceded that "the great spiritual visions of human history have also been poisoned chalices, the causes of untold misery and even savagery" and that appalling destruction had certainly been wrought in the name of faith. But, he argued, radical secularism does not avoid the problem of human evil either, while relying on secularism as a foundation of ethics means stifling some of our deepest and most powerful spiritual aspirations.[20] It was in just these aspirations, however, that William Connolly saw the greatest danger to ethics in political life. And to the extent that these aspirations were rooted in a falsely essentialist concept of identity, Connolly claimed that the "affirmation of the relational and constructed character of identity can . . . make a difference to the ethical quality of political life."[21]

Connolly's starting point was the basic poststructuralist idea that identity presupposes difference; difference defines identity in part as that which identity excludes and which therefore always inhabits it. The exclusionary relationship between identity and difference, he argued, is "the site of two problems of evil" in politics. The first problem is a version of an originally theological maneuver to handle responsibility for evil in the world, which was then replicated in secular identities. Religion saves the idea of the goodness of an omnipotent god with the doctrine of human free will, which exempts god from responsibility for evil and makes men its sole source. In secular political terms, the need to preserve the absolute goodness of secular collective identities drives a similar attempt to protect the purity and certainty of a "hegemonic identity"—say national or imperial or ethnic—by defining as "independent sites of evil" the attributes or behavior that pose the greatest threat to the collective's self-definition. The potential taint of such attributes is then projected onto an "Other," constructed for the sole purpose of making it the external repository of those taints, the ultimate source of evil which must be excluded, fought, even extirpated. ("We are clean, they are dirty; we are believers, they are infidels; we must destroy them before they destroy us.") Thus circumstances of the greatest political danger derive from a polarizing attempt to secure "the surety of self-identity" against self-doubt.[22] Connolly's diagnosis of the psychology of political Manichaeism (Sartre had used the term for the maneuvers of individual bad faith) was the same as Taylor's but his remedy was the exact opposite. Identity aspirations to absolute goodness were, to paraphrase Karl Kraus's famous slam at psychoanalysis, the disease which Taylor offered as its cure.

Great ethical danger lay in just that idea of "personal resonance" that Taylor had advanced as the best path in modern times to the disclosure of people's hidden beliefs in absolute morality. What Connolly labeled as Taylor's "doctrine of quasi-radical self-questioning" was basically a veiled restatement of St. Augustine's path to the God of Catholicism. It was based on a model of "the self as a deep self able to become more attuned to deep truths pursued through an internal process of confession and self-inquiry; the more carefully and honestly one probes the inner self, the closer one gets to one's fundamental identity and the deepest mysteries of divinity; but this truth, because it is infinite and we are finite, is never achieved 'fully or satisfactorily.'"[23] The confessional model was only "quasi-radical" because too much of its "persuasive power . . . moves below the threshold of critical reflection and . . . the faith it embodies may even discourage efforts to engage its own practices of conversion and confession. This doctrine depends for its effectiveness upon a fundamental, contestable faith" whose questionable status is concealed by the rhetoric in which it is couched.[24]

To avoid the ethical-political dangers such partial self-analysis inevitably produces, we have to revise the notion of personal identity it presumes and embed our new understanding of ourselves in our "political imaginary," the set of beliefs and myths which structures our political norms and institutions. The demand for a "true identity" in Augustine's and Taylor's sense is "rooted in an entire array of linguistic, psychological, epistemic, and political pressures built into the human condition. The drive to strong identity . . . is overdetermined as a disposition of life. What one must refuse to do . . . is to invest these dispositions with the blessing of unambiguous truth." A strong identity

is thing-like in its solidity and inertia, ostensibly guaranteed true by the structure of reality. Unspoken but inherent in Connolly's evocation of "the human
condition" was the motivating power of existential anxiety, which must be
recognized in order to be fought against. In place of "true" or "strong" identity Connolly posed a demystified version, unmatched in the postmodern literature of identity for its specificity and above all for its effort to balance the
psychological and orientational necessities of identity with its always lurking
ontological temptations and illusions. His description of the right sort of identity was in effect a manifesto, infused with ethical passion:

> Identity without capitalization: my identity is entrenched, as well as
> particular in the sense that no set of universal statements about
> humanity or reason or rights or the necessity of death can exhaust it;
> but it is neither chosen in its fullest sense nor grounded in a harmoni-
> ous direction in being. It is deep in its contingency. It is contingent in
> the sense that happenstances of genetics, family life, historically specific
> traditions, personal anxieties, demands and aspirations, surprising
> events . . . all enter into its composition and give shape to the porous
> universals that mark me as human. It is deep in the sense that some of
> these elements become impressed into me as second nature, bonded to
> my first nature and not readily detachable from it. The attempt to
> detach them might foster personal breakdown, but that does not mean
> they are necessarily true. This recognition may enable me to live more
> of the elements of my identity as contingent formations that do not
> reflect the truth of being as such. And that, in turn, to the degree it is
> accomplished, can relieve pressures to hold the other responsible for
> not living up to the hope embodied in my existence.[25]

This was an exhortation to individuals to rationally commit to the philosophically correct understanding of personal identity despite its potential psychological dangers. For Connolly such an understanding was above all the
prerequisite of an ethical politics, one that accepted the legitimacy of difference and avoided the demonization of the other that licensed group contempt,
exclusion, and finally annihilation. He called his vision "agonistic democracy,"
defined as "a practice that affirms the indispensability of identity to life, dis-
turbs the dogmatization of identity, and folds care for the protean diversity of
human life into the strife and interdependence of identity difference." [26] One
might think, and as far as its practical consequences were concerned with
some justice, this was just a high-minded expression of multiculturalism. But

in probing the existential roots and temptations of identity it offered a much deeper support for multiculturalism than the glib optimism of many of its political and even intellectual spokespersons, and a reasoned response to its equally too-easy dismissal by its political and intellectual opponents.

*   *   *

MacIntyre's concept of personal identity as derived wholly from a comprehensive tradition was explicitly directed against modern individualism. Since his argument from historicity allowed for argument and change within a tradition, he necessarily admitted a degree of individual autonomy, though without quite acknowledging it as such and certainly without allotting it independent value. Even Taylor, more hospitable to individual autonomy, argued that it could only be defended as part of a comprehensive and grounded notion of the good. But the Aristotelian pursuit of the (objective) good was not the only way ethicists conceived of the origin, content, or moral implications of identity. Quite in opposition to MacIntyre's and Taylor's Aristotelian approach, Kwame Anthony Appiah explicitly anchored identity in and allied it firmly with John Stuart Mill's ideal of individuality.

So firmly, in fact, that one might ask just what Appiah thought identity added to individuality, the more so because he referred to his own position as "ethical individualism." His answer was implicit in the example he chose to illustrate it, the character of the butler Mr. Stevens in Kazuo Ishiguro's novel *The Remains of the Day*. At first glance Stevens hardly seems a paragon of individuality, since his life's purpose is to meld his personality wholly with the role of butler; nor does he believe in self-fashioning, let alone individual uniqueness, as ideals. Yet, Appiah argued, Stevens exemplifies individuality even if he does not affirm it as a value because his life is founded on a plan that he has chosen. He plan is to live *as* a butler, as his father's son, as a loyal Englishman—the best butler, the most faithful son, the most loyal Englishman he can be. Living *as* something is precisely what it means to have an identity.[27] And it is impossible to live without living as *something*.

We are fated to the autonomy of choice as well as to the givenness of social identities. But both the (Heideggerian) idea of authenticity, which calls us to be true to our destinies, and the (Sartrian) notion of pure self-creation ex nihilo are wrong. We do create our own lives, but "To create a life is to create a life out of the materials that history has given you."[28] These materials are collective identities, which Appiah defined as historical narratives with (preexisting) "scripts" that help us shape our individual projects and tell our personal life stories. Collective identities are independent sources of value for us.

Since there are many values proposed in the world, we have no way of ordering them except in and through a collective identity that ranks the goods of the world. Insofar as I adopt that identity as my own, or better, as what I am, it structures my way through life. Structuring includes not least picking out in advance those with whom I feel a sense of solidarity. Solidarity, in Appiah's view, is a universal value for human beings, but it manifests itself in attachments to particular others who share my collective identity, and therefore entails concrete acts of solidarity with them that are particular values for me.

Appiah's narrative scripts might look at first glance like MacIntyre's narrative traditions, but they differ in important respects and finally suggest a quite different range of ethical issues. Because some of these involve questions about the kind of life it is good or bad for an individual to live while others raise questions about how one treats other people, Appiah adopted Ronald Dworkin's distinction between "ethics" as concern with the good life for the self and "morality" as our obligations to others.

Despite the Aristotelian reference to the good life, Appiah did not think of the ethical in universal terms. Unlike MacIntyre, he held prevailing collective identities to be necessary but in themselves insufficient elements of personal identity. The ethically good life is the good life *for me*. The identities promoted by ethical individualism require autonomy at their core (as in Mr. Stevens' choice and unique amalgam of existing scripts as a life-plan), and Appiah defended that idea against a variety of contemporary philosophical and sociological objections, including some like MacIntyre's. The idea of autonomy as both a necessary truth of human practice and an ethical value in itself made him more than a little skeptical of the claims of communitarians that "culture" constituted the whole of identity, and quite critical of normative recommendations to preserve it at all costs. His opposition to cultural identity was not based just on abstract theoretical grounds. As he acknowledged in his disagreement with Charles Taylor over the degree to which government should accommodate group identities, "In a rather unphilosophical nutshell, my suspicion is that Taylor is happier with the collective identities that actually inhabit our globe than I am."[29] Many identities, like sectarian fundamentalism, stifled individuality, and Appiah was quite prepared to use government coercion to counter them when they are imposed on others. "If," he stated forthrightly, "intolerance of other identities is built into an identity, or if learning the views of others except as a shameful error is one of their norms, we will be seeking, in public education, to reshape those identities so as to exclude this feature. This is liberal soul-making."[30] But his unhappiness with collective identities also came from the totalistic claims on the individual that even acceptable identities sometimes made.

A key problem with prevailing identities stemmed from the fact that society ascribes identities to people for things over which the individual has no control, such as gender, race, and sexual orientation. "Whether you identify with that identity," he wrote, "whether, for example, you think of yourself as gay and act sometimes as a gay person, is not only up to you."[31] Social attribution of negative identities poses ethical problems about their place in one's individually chosen life plan and moral problems about the obligations owed to those with whom society lumps you. In reaction to the historically negative identities imposed on Negroes and homosexuals, for example, these groups had recently been able to reverse their value and demand to be respected *as* blacks and gays. The embrace of their social identities, as Sartre had argued in the case of Jews faced with anti-Semitism, was both necessary for their self-respect and for enlarging their sphere of autonomy. But while accepting its necessity, Appiah was equivocal about it. We have to ask, he said, whether we should be happy in the longer run with identities constructed reactively: "Demanding respect for people *as blacks* and *as gays* can go along with notably rigid strictures as to how one is to be an African American or a person with same-sex desires. . . . Someone who demands that I organize my life around [my race and my sexuality] is not an ally of individuality."[32] Taken just a little further this could be a problem with any social identity, even ones adopted with full volition. All social scripts are written before actors choose them, and anyone might find himself chafing at aspects of plot or character and suggesting revisions. But being able to choose a scritp, or to modify a script that one chooses to act in is qualitatively, not just quantitatively, different from being forced by others to act only one role, in one way.

By far the most interesting moral questions for ethical individualism, however, concerned the relationship between individual ethical goods and universal moral obligations. As Appiah put it, "Ethical concerns and constraints arise from my individuality; moral ones arise from my personhood."[33] This distinction cut two ways. On the one hand, ethical concerns—the goals and chosen norms of one's individual identity—are both real values and qualitatively different from moral ones. They are particular and partial, not universal. We are right to prefer those to whom we feel closest, family, friends, members of our particular group. We love our spouses and friends not as instances of the universal value of partnership or friendship but as the unique individuals they are. Nevertheless, and precisely for this reason, our moral obligations must discipline our ethical values,[34] lest in preferring some we do serious harm to those not in our circle. We shouldn't, in my example, toast along with Commodore Decatur, "My country: may she always be in the right, but my country, right or wrong," if this implies that I will choose my country above the right when it does moral wrong to other peoples. At the same time, Appiah argued, ethical preferences bring with them real obligations to those we feel close to. Ethical "oughts," however different in kind from moral "oughts" in that they are not universal but tied to my identity, are nonetheless real. In this sense, identity is an autonomous and important source of obligations as well as rights.

There was, however, a serious equivocation in Appiah's discussion of ethical obligation. Strictly speaking, by his definition ethical obligations are determined by the kind of person we are or wish to be; at the deepest level they are only "obligations" to ourselves, that is, to the identities we have chosen. This does not mean that such obligations are not sometimes highly constraining; having chosen to be a doctor, I incur extensive and quite rigid obligations to my profession, its standards, my fellow practitioners, and above all to my patients, well beyond the basic moral obligations I have to them as fellow human beings. Nonetheless it is I who have chosen them. But accidents of birth determine particular relationships that we have not chosen, and, Appiah insisted, these too create obligations: "The fact that you did not choose to be your mother's son does not mean you have no special responsibilities [to your mother] as a result."[35] Such responsibilities compose what he called "a zone of 'ought,' of ethical obligation that is intermediate between the wholly required and the wholly supererogatory."[36] It is difficult to see, however, why in Appiah's terms filial loyalty is such an intermediate zone. It is indeed an obligation to my mother, not to mothers as such. But there is no element of choice with regard to one's parents, and choice was Appiah's basic criterion of identity values. Traditionally, of course, this kind of difficulty had been obviated by making responsibilities to one's parents, as in the Ten Commandments, universal *moral* obligations—the very position from which he wished to distinguish his own. (The Decalogue in fact commands us just to honor our parents, presumably because we may not in fact love them, though in the cases of one's neighbor and of God love is a divine command.) Neither of the two grounds Appiah claimed for values, individual identity and universal morality, in fact prescribe obligation where he wanted it, the sphere of "non-elective affinities," unchosen personal relationships. The defense of identity values is a defense of our right to love some people more than others, and it is hard to see how the notion of "an intermediate zone of ethical obligation" is consistent with the right of ethical *partiality*. Partiality toward particular persons is a matter of emotion, affinity, and desire; it is these that motivate preference above and beyond the minimal demands of moral obligation. Partiality, then, is the opposite of obligation; if one doesn't love one's mother, so much for her, except as another person to whom one has basic moral obligations—a conclusion Appiah obviously didn't want to accept. In the end what he could legitimately justify from the starting point of individual identity was not the idea of special ethical obligations to one's loved ones but our right to partiality in preferring them to all others. It is telling that in order to include obligation within our partiality for those we love, he felt it necessary to abandon the sharp distinction between ethical individuality and moral universality and invoke the Aristotelian notion of an "objective good": "The most powerful defense of partiality is the simplest," he wrote; "relationships are an important good—I would be inclined to say they were objectively valuable—and many (non-instrumental) relationships . . . require partiality."[37] Thus founded in part on the idea of an objective good, identity can include not just choice of a plan and affinity for particular persons, but ethical obligations to them. Expanded in this way, our particular identities become an even more important source of values for the kind of beings we are. We are not only allowed to favor some people more than others simply because they are ours, we also have greater obligations to them than to everyone else because they are ours.

This conclusion lay at the heart of Appiah's most sweeping ethical-moral ideal, which he called "rooted cosmopolitanism," a term with deliberately ironic echoes of the old anti-Semitic charge of Jewish "rootless cosmopolitanism." Its essence is the reconciliation of morals and ethics, which is to say the universal and the particular, which is in turn to say personhood and identity. Appiah's cosmopolitanism is militantly liberal. Its moral core is a doctrine of universal individual rights, though one based on a unique ontological rationale: not that we are all the same in some descriptive sense but that all human beings struggle to understand a single world with a similar mental apparatus. Our mental apparatus does include universal reason in the Enlightenment sense, but for Appiah its more important feature is the human grasp of narrative logic that allows us to construct individual worlds to which our imaginations respond.[38] It is our common capacity to tell and understand stories about our relationship to the world, rather than our ability to arrive at common beliefs about it, that is the ground of human sharing; our stories, unlike our rational beliefs, can and do differ radically. If there is any hope of coming to agreement about the value of autonomy—not its reality, which is a matter of objective fact—it is by telling and listening to one another's unique stories, and the mutual recognition that our individual differences are local variations of a common human struggle to make ourselves at home in the world.

Differences in our stories are unavoidable but they are ethically beneficial, because a world of cultural and social variety is a precondition for the self-creation that is at the heart of a meaningful human life.[39] Though Appiah didn't put things this way, "localism" or particularism, that is to say, identity itself, is the badge of human finitude. As finite, we are situated; our only approach to the universal is through the particulars of our situation, our concrete identities. This is the "rooted" part of rooted cosmopolitanism. It was not out of narcissism or "anecdotalism" that Appiah ended his book with autobiographical remarks about the origins of his own ideas in those of his Ghanaian father and about the latter's roots in both Asante and the liberal traditions of British colonialism, against whose domination he also fought. These and many other autobiographical vignettes sprinkled throughout the book are methodologically justified, indeed required, because they exemplify the theoretical importance Appiah assigned to personal identity as the unique path each individual and group must take to arrive at their ethical values and ultimately their universal moral obligations.

*   *   *

Appiah's distinction between ethics and morality rested, as we saw, on a further distinction between individual identity and personhood. Paul Ricoeur made the same distinction and also saw it decisive for morality. In one way, his analysis tended to the same conclusion: Ricoeur assigned morality to, or rather derived it from, "ipse-identity," or selfhood and not "idem-identity," or sameness. But his more sustained investigation of the relationship between the two showed that identity as self-sameness was more problematic for universal morality than Appiah implied.

The two kinds of identity are not morally symmetrical. Character, or sameness, entails selfhood because it is the result of processes by which the self internalizes identifications, adopts habits, and changes to adapt to new circumstances. That is why the self as a whole can only be understood as a narrative identity, which in Ricoeur's formulation is the "dialectic" of selfhood and sameness. Our character, our stable traits and goals, directs our story, but we also construct ourselves along the way as we choose among the possibilities the world offers. We thus move back and forth between stability and change, though always on the way to some end which shapes us. At the extreme, however, identity as character can collapse and disappear, as it does in Musil's novel *The Man Without Qualities*. We lose and cannot find a goal, hence we lose our character. But while sameness identity can be lost, selfhood never is. What remains when identity breaks down, to brutally summarize the last and climactic third of Ricoeur's book, is the elemental human capacity to act and to suffer. It is in light of these capacities that we can see most clearly the potentiality of the self for permanence as self-constancy. We glimpse that potential in our awareness of the impact of our actions on others, and we experience it as a demand for accountability for our actions as we recognize ourselves in others. At that point we can achieve permanence, self-constancy, by the act of committing ourselves to our responsibilities to them, including not least commitments we made in the past though we may feel we no longer are who we were when we made them. This kind of permanence is more stable, more permanent, than sameness of character. Only as a moral being does one finally attain true identity. Identity in the modern sense, identity as sameness of "character" through substantive self-definition, was an impediment to morality because it was vulnerable to dissolution. He might also have added that it was unreliable because of its relativism. Ricoeur did not have to be reminded that there are evil narrative identities; he insisted on it. Stable character-identity is in itself morally neutral, and while any complete analysis of the self had to take account of it, the quest for a reliably certain foundation of morality had to go beyond it. Founding morality in personhood, furthermore, offered the only reliable source of stable sameness.[40]

Ricoeur was the most insistent about this, but in fact all those who considered the implication of identity for moral theory were committed to a doctrine of universal morality, however they derived it. What distinguished their moral theories, even Ricoeur's, however, was the argument that identity, whether individual or collective, was a legitimate source of "right" in the broadest sense of that term. All were concerned to harmonize ethical particularity with universal morality, and none in the end were ready to subordinate the latter to personal or collective identity. But in arguing for the rights of identity, they greatly enlarged the traditional sphere of moral debate. Personal choices and affinities, and most transgressively of all from the deontological point of view, ranking some people over others and treating them preferentially were not in and of themselves immoral. To the contrary, for a moral theory that took account of the human need for and unavoidable reality of identity, such preferences were required. Without sacrificing the rights of others, we have the right, indeed the "obligation" to ourselves, to prefer our own.

Conclusion. The Necessity of Identity

I'm singing again because . . . your identity is the thing you
never stop becoming.
                    —Yusuf/Cat Stevens (explaining why he resumed
                                singing after a decades-long hiatus)

The simple definition of modern identity is that it is the response to the question "Who, or what, am I?" But even this apparently straightforward notion needs qualifying. The question is not satisfactorily answered, for example, by defining what I am as human, a concern as old as classical philosophy and perhaps the dawn of *Homo sapiens* (and not coincidentally the only way modern rights theory since the Enlightenment cares to identify me). Nor is it answered by John Locke's formulation that I am my present consciousness and my memory of its past states. Modern identity asks about my self-definition under a set of rubrics that ostensibly determine my stable beliefs, commitments, loyalties, and, in consequence, my actions. It is in this sense that identity is a new idea.

The need for a more complicated answer has to do with the fact that even this recent sense of identity has a complex history, which among other things involved efforts to resolve serious ambiguities in the question itself. To begin with, the equivocation between "who" and "what" in the question "Who, or what, am I?" implies fundamental differences about the nature of the self that asks. "Who" implies subjectivity, "what" implies thingness, and the implications of each for identity are radically different. "Am" is problematic for parallel reasons. To paraphrase a former president of the United States, who whatever his evasive purposes was on to something, it *does* depend on what the meaning of "is" is. In the identity expression "I am X," the copula verb skates over crucial differences between the ways humans can experience themselves as temporal creatures. "Is" can mean "now" or permanently. Even the "I" is a problem, since it appears to assume the existence of a self wholly independent of others. Can there be an "I" without a "we"? And beyond these difficult issues there are also the large questions of what the rubrics are under which I define myself, and where they come from.

*   *   *

When we turn to the history of identity, we see that these difficulties were there from the start. The idea of identity originated in paradox: it was born as the negation of the previously taken for granted possibility of fixed and permanent definitions of the self. Interwar writers and philosophers, reacting to the discrediting of deeply embedded Western identities by the unanticipated perversion of values, the dislocations, and the horrors of World War I, ultimately called into question the very idea of identity in this sense. The notion that a person could be something in a fixed and permanent way was, they claimed, an illusion and an act of self-deception. It denied that human beings are able to reflect on, and by doing so distance themselves from, their self-definitions, realizing they could be other than what they ostensibly "were." The illusion of identity, they further argued, is driven by a fundamental anxiety about the fact that our existence is not necessary in the ultimate scheme of things. We are merely contingent beings who want desperately to deny our contingency by endowing our existence, the categories we use to define ourselves, with necessity, permanency, and value. Inevitably, however, for all these writers skepticism about identity went hand in hand with the question of how we can live without it. Some of its critics, like Pirandello and Broch, seemed to believe we couldn't. Their works on identity ended in chaos and despair (or, as in the case of Kafka, did not end at all). Other writers, like Proust, Musil, and Woolf, fashioned their critiques of identity within attempts to reimagine it by accommodating the facts of contingency, flexibility, and change. The most reasoned yet also dramatic instance of such a two-track enterprise was Heidegger's. In the first part of *Being and Time* he launched the definitive philosophical attack on the foundations of individual identity as a prelude to trying in the second part to found the idea of collective identity on unshakeable philosophical ground.

In the wake of World War II the problem of identity was taken up and for the first time explicitly named not by a creative writer or philosopher but by a psychoanalyst. In the psychic paralysis of soldiers suffering from "battle fatigue" Erik Erikson saw a trauma of identity: what they had done or seen in war so violated their sense of who they thought they were before that they could no longer function in the world because they no longer knew who they were. For Erikson this turned out to be one particular instance of a much larger-scale undermining of previous Western self-definitions in the wake of the breakdown of traditional society, whose ramifications he had experienced in his own early life in Germany and in his forced emigration from Europe to America. Permanent, thing-like identity might be philosophically problematic, but humans needed something like it, a psychological experience of stable, objective meaningfulness, a feeling of legitimately and wholeheartedly being someone in themselves while belonging to some larger collectivity, in order to feel at home in their own bodies and function effectively in the world.

This soon became further apparent for the realm of politics. Jean-Paul Sartre's initial destruction of identity rebounded on him when he became politically active after the war on behalf of the exploited and oppressed. His own analysis had shown that Marxist economic explanations were inadequate to understand the state of mind of groups like Jews and blacks (or their persecutors). They suffered not just from material deprivation—and not necessarily even from that—but from a sense of themselves as less worthy beings, imposed on them by the powerful who justified their denigration in terms of an implicit ontology that defined the excluded as "other." Marxism had to be supplemented by the existential understanding of "otherness," which meant also the qualified validation of identity. Simone de Beauvoir and Frantz Fanon similarly analyzed the situation of women, blacks and the colonized in greater detail and even more persuasively, though only Fanon defended identity.

In the American context, Erik Erikson's psychological formulation of individual identity, which emphasized autonomy, was in keeping with the values of American liberalism he enthusiastically took to as a refugee from totalitarianism. But contemporary liberalism was also a provocation: the popularity of Erikson's conceptions of identity and identity crisis in the 1950s and early 1960s was due in good part to youthful discontent with the narrow success orientation of contemporary individualism, fostered by the economic security anxieties and consumption avidity of the parent Depression generation. Erikson's concept of identity was more spacious and inclusive; it was founded on the individual's creative self-fashioning in choice of work and Weltanschauung even as it incorporated identifications with parents, whose own ideal of individuality could be turned against the lives they actually lived.

A decade and a half after its introduction, Erikson's psychological focus on individual identity in a consensus society was overtaken by political concern with collective identity. Again American liberalism was the provocation, this time because of the contradiction between the liberal ideal of equal rights and the social reality that denied recognition and equality to blacks, women, and gays. But founded on the idea of the abstract individual, liberalism was no better able than Marxism to account for society's defining and excluding people on the basis of physical or cultural characteristics. The category of identity both offered an explanation of this and supplied the conceptual weapon that enabled those groups to fight back against it. Erikson had always taken for granted that collective identity was a necessary part of individual identity, but identity politics reversed his emphasis. The collective dimension soon almost completely swamped concern with individual identity. Nonetheless, after Erikson it was of the essence of the idea of collective identity that it was inherently psychological. Collective identity existed only in the psychological identity of a group's individual members; it was not a mysterious "collective consciousness" but the product of deep identification of individual women, blacks, or Germans with those they defined as their gender, their race, their nation. The concept of identity bridged the gap between externally describable social realities and subjective consciousness. In sociological identity theory, for example, identity was specifically meant to link objective social role with the individual's psychic need for self-definition and self-esteem, which explained why people are motivated to sustain what social norms prescribe. For social scientists identity could be a transformative category that at the least opened up new areas of research in traditional disciplines, as in economics, and at the most could transform a discipline's entire theoretical foundation, as some anthropologists and sociologists argued it should.

If social scientists were able to see collective identity as a valuable, ideologically neutral explanatory category, however, this was far from the case in political debate. The idea of collective identity was fatefully shadowed throughout the twentieth century by its initial appearance as identity politics. Defended by many as politically indispensable to achieving dignity and power for marginalized groups, collective identity was also seen by others as a false and dangerous idea. Minority activists criticized it for homogenizing real differences among those classified as the same, either in the interests of or because of the myopia of white elites. Liberals and progressives attacked the idea of distinct collective identities for denying human universality and privileging group difference at the expense of economic equality and real social reform. Worse, as recent history had devastatingly shown, it could be used to legitimize group particularity, exclusion, hatred, and genocide. The rise of identity created a bitter backlash, political and philosophical. While identity consciousness was spreading to ever increasing kinds of collectivities, making its broadest claim for the acceptance of difference in the demand for multiculturalism, postmodernism renewed, with different philosophical tools but more explicit focus, the original existentialist campaign to expose its illegitimacy. The backlash in turn inspired its own reaction: on behalf of whom, identity realists asked, was the political struggle for recognition and rights being waged if not on behalf of socially recognizable and self-defined identity groups?

Clearly identity must have some kind of legitimacy, and it should be possible to spell that out in ways that avoid erroneous metaphysical assumptions. Identity, they argued, is a social, psychological, and historical fact.

A number of influential philosophers who almost completely ignored the debates over postmodernism agreed and went even further. Identity as self-definition was constitutive of human reality, both as the necessary framework for the important choices we have to make and as that which unifies us as the characters we are in the stories we tell about ourselves as beings living in time. To the extent that identity, both individual and collective, expresses needs and desires in all the basic spheres of human life, it is an inescapable and legitimate source both of meaning and of value.

It is this course of development that this book has tried to trace historically.

*   *   *

While the vicissitudes of identity were in part responses to historical events, however, the very adaptability of the idea demanded constant reflection on its meaning and renewed efforts at its definition. Theorizing identity, I claimed in the introduction, was oriented from the beginning—implicitly, if not systematically or deliberately—along four conceptual axes: ontological, psychological, social, and historical. These determined the kinds of issues that were talked about in the different spheres of human life in which identity was considered and contested, the spheres, I have argued, that constitute the basic domains of human existence—our embodiedness, our locatedness in space and time, our being with others, and our aspirations for transcendence. Each of the axes was further specified by a set of questions whose implications, I hope, are now both clearer and richer. *Ontological*: Is identity a necessary category for the interpretation of human life or is it philosophically indefensible? Even if we come to think of identity as a human construct rather than a predetermined essence, something human beings create for themselves rather than a preexisting truth about themselves that they passively discover, to what degree are our identities determined by our facticity—our unchosen birth in a concrete time, place, and body, our need for orienting values—and to what degree by our capacity for reflection and choice? *Psychological*: Do our emotional and physical well-being, as well as our ability to act effectively in the world depend on having a felt *sense* of identity, whatever its philosophical standing? What are the elements of such a sense of identity, and where do they come from? If we say that they are fashioned from our "identifications" with different individuals and groups, how does identification actually work? What is the relationship between identification as a psychological process and identity as stable self-definition? *Social*: What is the relationship between individual identity and the collectives we are unavoidably part of? Is individual identity nothing but the ensemble of our group identities, and if not that, what else? What kinds of collective identities are there and how do we recognize them? What is the cement, the purpose of group identity and how do different collective identities relate to one another? *Historical*: How does the sense of identity stability relate to the reality of historical changes within identities or the appearance of new ones? Is identity nothing but the product of history, or does identity make history? If identity is a necessary category of human existence, why did it emerge only recently?

Despite the different and sometimes conflicting answers to all these questions, despite the efforts of serious thinkers to reject the validity of identity altogether, I believe that the best arguments support one conclusion: within certain limits, identity is a valid, useful, and ultimately indispensable category for understanding psychological, social, and historical reality. This is true not in spite of but precisely because of its recent emergence, more exactly, because of what its emergence at a particular point in time revealed about what is true and what is false about the concept of identity.

Virtually all identity theorists rejected the notion that identities are fixed essences dictated by metaphysical necessity, that people are what they are because they were so created by some Ultimate Reality. Religious thinkers like Charles Taylor came closest to such a view, but at most just hinted at it, at least in their work on identity. Rather he, like Alasdair MacIntyre and more explicitly secular thinkers like William Connolly couched their argument for the inescapability of identity expressly in terms of contingent necessity. There may be no metaphysical explanation or justification for the way we humans, or the universe, are constituted; we might indeed have been otherwise. But given how we are in fact constituted, we must deal with some inescapable realities: that we have bodies constructed in specific ways; that we are born into groups with similar physical features or speaking the same language, living at a specific point in historical time and geographical space; that we have enough freedom (or apparent freedom) to have to make choices and to decide on criteria for them. For Taylor, MacIntyre, Connolly, and others such realities were reason enough to insist that identity, which answers to and incorporates them, was indeed an ontological category of human existence. Sometimes their interpretation of contingent necessity seemed to come as close to total determinism as any metaphysics; the most obvious, and serious, case in point is Heidegger, who converted the contingent historical fatedness of birth into absolute historical destiny. But for most of them contingent necessity at most limited the scope of freedom, not the fact of it. Even Heidegger could only transform freedom into necessity through a falsely one-dimensional interpretation of historicity, a view which MacIntyre, the other main proponent of the authority of collective tradition, decisively rejected.

On the other side, many of those who rejected identity determinism in the name of "social construction" found it necessary to make concessions to the reality of identity as (closed) self-definition. Identity might be socially malleable and historically mutable, and in that sense "constructed," but was it—could it even be—experienced as such? Sartre had written poetically of negritude that it was an ambiguous "shimmer of being and needing to be." William Connolly pointed out more prosaically that the contingencies of our birth—sex, cultural location—often become our "second nature," quasi-instinctual, so deeply entrenched in our feelings and desires that they are beyond our conscious will to change, except perhaps superficially in our outward actions. One obvious problem with the metaphor of "construction" is its implication of conscious intention and rational procedure. Collectivities do not normally create or sustain their identity in that way, nor for the most part do individuals, though it can and does happen under certain circumstances, as when someone immigrates, converts, or theorizes for a living. But even in these cases the assumption of identity is rarely so calculated or coldblooded, and if it is we are hard-pressed to think of it as identity. One of the major problems in understanding what identity "means" is in knowing how it is truly felt by the self in everyday life. Is it avowed, or avowable? Does it govern one's behavior? Is it, to paraphrase Kierkegaard, something for which one lives, and might perhaps die? It is possible to intellectually hold the idea of identity as social creation in the abstract, knowing and accepting the contingencies of one's own birth and of history at large, while feeling deeply that nonetheless one "is" a woman, a gay man, a Kennedy, a Muslim, a German, with all their accompanying baggage of attachments, feelings, habits, and norms. We may call that "is" a fantasy, as existentialists and poststructuralists insisted, but we do not know exactly what identification in fantasy means or how it works. Is it, as one philosophical model of unconscious fantasy argues, an unconscious belief, powered by desire, that one is literally "one with" a certain "kind" and with the others of the same kind? Is it a preverbal, prelogical pictorial image, like a Freudian dream element, that fuses things that are unlike according to their normal categorization into a unified being? If it is an act of commitment, as many theorists wanted, it is certainly not in most cases a matter of the conscious will. Whatever it is, however, the most radical postmodernists conceded not only its power to motivate but even its indispensability for political orientation and action.

Ontological identity, as we see, quickly shades into the psychological. Erikson first introduced the idea of identity based on clinical case studies and on his observations of "normal" adolescent development. Both pathology and normality, he concluded, show that without a stable, integrated identity, without a positive secure self-definition however complex, individuals did not feel at home in their bodies, their most intimate personal relationships, their work, or their wider society. At the extreme they would be riven by inescapable aimlessness, crippling anxiety—what R. D. Laing called "ontological insecurity"—self-loathing, and bottomless rage at others. These were empirical observations, but Charles Taylor did not hesitate to use Erikson's psychological findings as evidence for his philosophical arguments about the ontological necessity of identity. Erikson had shown, Taylor argued, that the price of lack of value orientation was a seriously compromised psyche. Yet Erikson himself hedged about his notion of stable identity with qualifications intended to challenge the psychological health of identities that were based on exclusionary absolutes, best exemplified by the totalitarian ideologies of the twentieth century. Such ideologies created rigid identities that could only ward off the threat of difference by excluding or annihilating others. A healthy identity was one that was flexible, adaptable, capable of further development, and able to recognize identities that differed from theirs. At the same time tolerance and openness to change could not mean complete lack of definition. Healthy identity had to walk the tightrope between the two, though Erikson never came up with a precise formulation for it, just exemplars of it, like Luther and Gandhi. It was only by its fruits, the creative personality, that the successful balance could be known.

To speak of "an" identity, however, begs another large question. Assuming the psychological importance of identity, is it correct to speak of it in the singular? Do we not in fact have many identities—as many as we have social roles, as many as the different collectives we may belong to, as many unique ones as we may devise for ourselves? There was a wide though not unanimous agreement among identity theorists that we do in fact have multiple identities. What they disagreed about is whether we rank them in relative and contextual or in absolute terms. Even those who argued for multiple identities acknowledged that different ones become salient at decision points in our lives. Any one of them may become the decisive one at some crossroads: whether to change jobs or careers, whether to marry or divorce, whether to emigrate, to abandon one's religion or convert to another. But is it also the case that one of these identities is more important than all the others? Do we necessarily rank our identities in a hierarchy, so that we will, if circumstances force us to choose, sacrifice all others to that of family member, artist, patriot, or believer?

Or, finally, dissenting from both these alternatives, does each of us have some complex overarching identity, perhaps incorporating all our other identities in a unique amalgam, such that without it one knows with certainty that he or she would not be? The novelist Amin Maalouf, a Lebanese-born Christian and native Arab speaker who resides in France and writes in French made the case this way: "So am I half French and half Lebanese? Of course not. Identity can't be compartmentalized. You can't divide it up by halves or thirds or any other separate segments. I haven't got several identities; I've got just one, made up of many components in a mixture that is unique to me, just as other people's identities are unique to them as individuals."[1] Kwame Anthony Appiah worried that the individuality of members of embattled minorities might be completely swallowed up by the demands of the group struggle for recognition. On the issue of multiple versus individual identity, then, there is no final consensus, which arguably points to the simple reality that people can experience the balance between individual and collective identities very differently. On the other hand, those who completely efface individual identity, defining themselves wholly by a collective identity, while quite possibly psychologically healthy, content, and functioning well, deny the existential freedom they do not and cannot avoid. They are self-deluded.

But this issue does not exhaust the question about the relationship between individual and collective identity. No one, not even Maalouf, denied that social identity—identification with named groups with more or less clear identifying criteria—is an inescapable dimension of individual identity. The presocial individual had no place in identity theory. Everywhere its premise was that we become individuals and begin shaping identity only through socialization, even if individuation ultimately enables us to turn even against the groups and norms that originally furnished the sources of our identity. For those who thought in terms of ontology, social embeddedness was one of the self's ontological features. Nevertheless the idea of collective identity was vexed from the beginning because it initially emerged as a politicized category. It was, and in the political context remains, highly contentious, perhaps the most contentious of all identity issues.

Roughly speaking, those for whom collective identity was not only a necessary truth but a positive good were members of groups which had been, or felt, excluded, demeaned, oppressed, or threatened because of certain physical or cultural characteristics. The feeling was not confined to minorities, the colonized, nonwhite races, or women; Germans, Frenchmen, and white Anglo-Saxon Protestants have all at one time or another expressed it. While advocates of collective identity did not necessarily deny the importance of individual identity, their political purposes and engagements fostered a strong tendency to emphasize group identity to the point where the individual dissolved in it almost completely. This is exactly what frightened opponents of collective identity: not only might individual rights and human universality be diminished in importance, they might even be dismissed entirely in the interests of collective ideals. In some cases cultural ideals expressly opposed the idea of the autonomous individual or absolute individual rights. Furthermore, collective identities had been reified and absolutized throughout history as the highest or only legitimate ones, licensing the demeaning, persecution, and elimination of others. Those who championed the liberation of oppressed identity groups and subjugated nationalities, often of a younger generation, faced those, often though not always older, who had lived through or kept in mind the horrors wrought by recent collective identities.

What made the exclusionary, chauvinist, or totalitarian potentials of collective identity loom more threateningly for such critics was that highly influential theories like Henri Tajfel's concept of social identity and more provocatively Samuel Huntington's clash of civilizations, held that collective identities were inherently mutually antagonistic. Theory reinforced history in prompting the alarmed to attack the validity of the concept. Theirs was a conceptual and not just a political argument, but it threw the baby out with the bath water. Even opponents were forced to acknowledge that collective identities exist as social and psychological facts with real historical effects, but bent as they were on exposing both the flaws in claims of collective identity to permanence and its hidden ideological motives, they were not able to give a satisfactory explanation of its hold. Outside the arena of politics, social scientists trying to understand how groups function had no problem with the proposition that self-definition was a prerequisite for constituting groups in the first place, and that identity was an indispensable explanatory category in their fields because it alone could bridge the gulf between explanation by external social structure and explanation by subjective values and motivation.

On the other hand even the strongest proponents of collective identity acknowledged and in fact actively insisted on the proposition that collective identities were historical. They saw no contradiction between the idea that collective identities come to be in time, even if the precise moment or circumstances of their birth can only sometimes be determined, and the idea that how a group defines itself in the present is one of the decisive causal forces of history. Nor is there any in principle. When critics insisted on the (transient) historical nature of group identities, on their internal changes over time, on the provable fact that "hoary" tradition is sometimes a recent invention, they were rightly objecting to the metaphysical pretensions, and the political uses, of collective identity. These were, and are, salutary warnings, given the terrible consequences of founding identity superiority metaphysically in cosmic legitimacy, biology, or History itself. Furthermore the errors they pointed to were not just those of unthinking racists, chauvinistic nationalists, and true believers, but of the most ingenious and subtle of thinkers.

In an excess of theoretical caution, however, critics of identity failed to credit the ontological bases of historical identities. These are the inescapable existential realities that have always been the foundation of our most salient collective identities, which are in this sense rightly referred to as "primordial"—our sexuality and its implications for our lives, our "racial" and ethno-national-linguistic features, our work and the social place it gives us, and our "God," spiritual or natural (as Spinoza put it, *Deus sive natura*) but in any case transcendent. It has been easy for humans to absolutize the historical particulars of these dimensions of human existence because they are ineluctably there and central to the ways we have to live our lives. For the same reason it has been particularly easy to make visible physical differences into more than they are, to turn biological sex into the destinies of cultural gender, to read skin color or eye shape as outward signs of inward differences in intelligence, temperament, and character. The temptation to absolutize, naturalize, or magnify differences as badges of metaphysically necessary distinctions, and hence of superiority, is also a primordial human reality that, on their side, proponents of identity sometimes fail to see at the risk of theoretical error, and worse. Human beings rarely walk the fine line between metaphysical and existential necessity carefully.

It is the wakened awareness of this reality precisely as a *temptation*, as a source of error, that is the real story of the emergence of identity as self-conscious discourse in the years between and after the two World Wars. Identity as self-definition, individual and collective, has existed as long as humans, something so obvious that it didn't need to be said. Representation and self-representation are ineluctable dimensions of human facticity. Popeye the Sailor Man put the past common sense of it most pithily when he proclaimed "I yam what I yam and that's all what I yam"—though his saying it already betokened a level of self-consciousness and assertiveness that suggested doubt.[2] What the crisis of identity clearly revealed after World War I is that "what I am" is not in fact "all that I am," and because of that, it is impossible to say "what I am" with finality. Since that is the way we were used to saying it, it seemed to those who first realized it that we could not talk of identity at all. But that was not satisfactory either. First, because of our facticity, we are something, in fact a number of things. And secondly, we want to be something. The disenchantment of Identity with a capital letter did not destroy identity; it forced us to revise it. It showed us that identity exists for those who think of themselves as moderns as partly a matter of self-fashioning, of choosing among the alternatives history makes available to us within the framework of our predetermined facticity.

But—and here is the final rub—is choice and indeterminacy what, in the end, we mean by, or want out of, identity? It is with the deepest of insights about identity that the biblical narrator has God define himself to Moses in the burning bush with the words "I shall be what I shall be," and though the Hebrew is in the future tense, they are also legitimately translated as "I am what I am." God is both ongoing self-making and permanence, futurity and eternal present. The keenest theorists of identity, philosophical and psychological, saw the goal of fusing stability and change, eternity and history, as implicit in the historical quest for identity. (This is also how theorists of national identity like Anderson and Smith explained its particular salience within modern identity.) But in rejecting the goal philosophers tended to overlook its psychological necessity and in embracing it psychologists tended to ignore its metaphysical impossibility. William Connolly was perhaps the most clear-eyed and the most ironic about this situation, though not, I think, without genuine anguish. "Let us feign these truths to be self-evident, that each individual needs an identity; that every stable way of life invokes claims to collective identity that enter in various ways into the interior identifications and resistances of those who share it. . . . Identity, in some modality or other, is an indispensable feature of human life." If the last sentence is true, however, why do we have to "feign" its truth? Because, the implication seems to be, it is false as we mean it yet we cannot do without its falsity. We feel we cannot have an identity without the implicit metaphysical claim to permanence and totality.

This is the challenge of identity in the age of self-consciousness about it. Perhaps, though, Connolly is wrong. Perhaps we can have identity without the pretense of totality or metaphysical justification, or self-deception if, taking a cue from Jürgen Habermas and Kwame Anthony Appiah, we embrace the legitimacy of our nonuniversality, our particularity as embodied, localized, and temporal beings, our finitude or our "rootedness." (We in fact do something like this when we proclaim the right of each person and each nation to self-determination. The right is universal, but we also affirm the uniqueness of its outcome.) Then there would be nothing contradictory about adapting our identity to change while at the same time trying to preserve its continuous core. Both would be striving to honor aspects of our finite nature without making any claims beyond it. Nor, for the same reason, would there be anything a priori contradictory about trying to make major changes in our identities. It is when we claim transcendental justification for them—changes and identities—that we ignore the truth that the rise of the modern discourse of identity revealed. We can't do without identity; we are not nothing and nowhere. But to be true to who and what we are (and safer from one another), identity must be disenchanted; we are not everything either. Because of the danger that a particular identity may believe it is, some would like to jettison identity altogether and become only universalists. But universalists ironically run into the very same danger that haunts identity by declaring themselves in effect to be everywhere, without even the saving grace of a somewhere. Identity need not be the unhappy default of beings who would be God but know they're not. Rightly understood it can be the positive affirmation of the particular beings we partly are and have partly made ourselves to be. Unique identity, individual and collective, has its absolute rights. But by the same token, distance from who we are is also never far from us.

Notes

Introduction. The New "Discourse" of Identity

Epigraph: Wolfgang Bergem, *Identitätsformationen in Deutschland* (Wiesbaden: VS Verlag für Sozialwissenschaften, 2005) 14.

1. For a wry account, with numbers, of his adventures in quest of identity titles in library catalogs in Brazil, Germany, and the United States, see Lutz Niethammer, *Kollektive Identität: Heimliche Quellen einer unheimlichen Konjunktur* (Reinbek bei Hamburg: Rowohlt, 2000), 23–24n25. Since 2000, of course, the numbers have risen greatly. In the spring of 2009 an undergraduate research assistant printed out lists of over 300 English titles in psychology, social psychology, and sociology for the decade 1991–2000 before we ended the exercise.

2. The pioneering work on the history of identity in the United States is Philip Gleason's article "Identifying Identity: A Semantic History," *Journal of American History* 69, 4 (March 1983): 910–31.

3. So, for example, Linda Nicholson titled her book about blacks' and women's consciousness in the United States before the 1960s *Identity Before Identity Politics* (Cambridge, Mass.: Harvard University Press, 2008). Along the same lines, Kwame Anthony Appiah published his lectures on W. E. B. Du Bois under the title *Lines of Descent: W. E. B. Du Bois and the Emergence of Identity* (Cambridge, Mass.: Harvard University Press, 2014), which includes a section titled "Identity Before 'Identity.'" In his corrosive analysis of the origins of the term collective identity, Niethammer registered the concept's "boom" in the postwar marketplace of ideas with acerbic skepticism. He dismissed as "legend" the claim that identity was first introduced into social thought in the United States after World War II as an individual psychological concept (*Kollektive Identität*, 55) and only later developed into collective identity: "Everything that seemed new [about collective identity] in the postwar years had its roots in the previous period" in the thought of such figures as Carl Schmitt, Georg Lukacs, Sigmund Freud, C. G. Jung, Maurice Halbwachs, and Aldous Huxley (634). Collective identity, he claimed, preceded individual identity in Erik Erikson's own work on national identities in the context of World War II (301–7). I will discuss his argument later in the introduction, but I note his dissent here since I cite, and up to a point side with, the conventional wisdom. I fully agree with Niethammer, however, on the importance of the interwar years for the origins of Western concern with identity.

4. Although one of the *Grundbegriffe*'s coauthors, historian Reinhart Koselleck, had a few years earlier presented a paper on the role of war monuments in establishing the identity of survivors at a seminal interdisciplinary colloquium in Germany on identity, which then appeared in the published proceedings. See Reinhart Koselleck, "Kriegerdenkmale als Identitätsstiftungen der Überlebenden," in *Identität*, ed. Odo Marquard and Karlheinz Stierle (Munich: Fink, 1979), 255–76.

5. Maryanne Cline Horowitz, ed., *New Dictionary of the History of Ideas*, vol. 3 (Farmington Hills, Minn.: Thomson Gale, 2005), 1084–98.

6. The handy *Desk Reference* for the revised *DSM IV* of 2000 included a general diagnostic category, "Identity Problem," which was to be used "when the focus of clinical attention is uncertainty about multiple issues relating to identity such as long-term goals, career choice, friendship patterns, sexual orientation and behavior, moral values, and group loyalties." Michael B. First, ed., *Desk Reference to the Diagnostic Criteria from DSM-IV-TR* (Washington, D.C.: American Psychiatric Association, 2000), 313.

7. Ronald L. Jackson, II, ed., *Encyclopedia of Identity*, 2 vols. (Los Angeles: Sage, 2010).

8. For example, one among hundreds, a headline in the *Chicago Tribune* of July 2, 1888, above a story about police efforts to identify an abandoned baby, "Establishing a Baby's Identity." I would argue that the concept of "identity theft" is a contemporary extension of the older notion of civic identity. For a different view see Peter Brooks, *Enigmas of Identity* (Princeton, N.J.: Princeton University Press, 2011), 196. My research of the French newspapers *Le Temps* (published 1861–1942) and *Le Matin* (1884–1944) found the same bureaucratic usages of the term.

9. An article in the *New York Times* of August 22, 1857, with the lead "Personal Identity," noted how easy it is in court for someone to pretend to be someone else and how difficult it is to prove that one is oneself. Another *New York Times* story from January 2, 1880, headlined "The Man Who Lost His Identity," concerned an amnesiac unable to recognize anyone from his past.

10. Thus "Personal Identity Must Continue," a headline in the New York *Times*, May 5, 1895, reporting a sermon by a minister on life after death, and another from April 20, 1931, on a similar occasion, "Man a Perpetual Identity."

11. Milan Kundera, *Identity*, trans. Linda Asher (New York: HarperCollins, 1998). In 1984, he had published the most philosophically probing postwar novel on identity, *The Unbearable Lightness of Being*, without using the word. It was adapted as a popular Hollywood movie two years later, though Kundera repudiated it as having nothing to do with his original themes and characters.

12. Movie review of "Identity," April 23, 2003, www.rogerebert/identity-2003.

13. Brad Meltzer, *Identity Crisis* (New York: DC Comics, 2004, 2005).

14. Wolfgang Bergem, *Identitätsformationen in Deutschland* (Wiesbaden: VS Verlag für Sozialwissenschaften, 2005), 13.

15. Rogers Brubaker and Frederick Cooper, "Beyond 'Identity,' " *Theory and Society* 29, 1 (February 2000): 1. Niethammer sharply criticized the vagueness of and contradictions in contemporary, mostly German usages of identity in a section titled "Semantische Ver(un)sicherung" ("Semantic (Un)certainty"), *Kollektive Identität*, 28–54.

16. Cited in Niethammer, *Kollektive Identität*, 33.

17. Derek Parfit, *Reasons and Persons* (Oxford: Clarendon, 1984).

18. Jerrold Seigel, *The Idea of the Self: Thought and Experience in Western Europe Since the Seventeenth Century* (Cambridge: Cambridge University Press, 2005), 6.

19. Ibid., 14–15.

20. Raymond Martin and John Barresi, *The Rise and Fall of Soul and Self: An Intellectual History of Personal Identity* (New York: Columbia University Press, 2006).

21. Ibid., 3.

22. Ibid., 54.

23. John Locke, *Essay Concerning Human Understanding*, 2nd ed. (London, 1694), 448.

24. Ibid., 451.

25. Ibid., 460, 467.

26. Katherine Mansfield, *Journal*, ed. J. Middleton Murray (London: Constable, 1954), April 12, 1920.

27. Amélie O. Rorty, ed., *Identities of Persons* (Berkeley: University of California Press, 1976), 2.

28. See Natalie Z. Davis, *The Return of Martin Guerre* (Cambridge, Mass.: Harvard University Press, 1983) and Partha Chatterjee, *A Princely Impostor? The Strange and Universal History of the Kumar of Bhawal* (Princeton, N.J.: Princeton University Press, 2002).

29. Paul Ricoeur, *Oneself as Another*, trans. Kathleen Blaney (Chicago: University of Chicago Press, 1992), 116.

30. Ibid., 118.

31. Ibid., 149.

32. I will discuss it further in Chapter 11 on ethics and identity.

33. Mark R. Leary and June Price Tangney, eds., *Handbook of Self and Identity* (New York: Guilford, 2003). I discuss the distinction in more detail in Chapter 9.

Though I have said that the contemporary philosophical debate about identity initiated by the work of Derek Parfit remained within the Lockean tradition of personal identity, and so is not relevant to my subject, I want to address it if only very briefly because of his notorious conclusion that the question of identity is "undecidable," and that in any case "our identity is not what matters" (*Reasons and Persons*, 245). To dramatize his argument, Locke had offered the thought experiment of a prince whose memory is somehow transplanted into the body of a cobbler. Does the cobbler become the prince, who he remembers having been, or does he remain the cobbler, who other people recognize as such? In keeping with his thesis, Locke answered unequivocally that the cobbler is now the prince since that is how he remembers himself. Parfit deployed more up-to-date science fictions to argue that in such cases it is impossible to decide the question. A person's existence, he claimed, consists only in the existence of a body and brain, and the occurrence of a series of interrelated physical and mental events. Suppose I am scanned by a machine that makes an electronic blueprint of my brain and body, and teleports it to another planet, where a replicator makes an exact copy of me, molecule for molecule. In the process my original brain and body are destroyed. Am I gone, or do I survive in my replica? Am I, that is, identical with my replica? The question, in Parfit's view, can't be answered definitively. If by my survival I mean numerical survival—I am numerically singular and thus different from any replica—my replica is not me. In terms of qualitative identity, however, my replica is in every way indistinguishable from me, hence substitutable for me. There is no way, Parfit concluded from this and other examples, to define identity that does not yield such an impasse. But identity doesn't matter anyway for what is important to me. If, for example, instead of being destroyed while my replica is being created my heart is badly damaged, so that I know I will die before my replica does, I can take consolation that my existence in all the things that matter to me—my loyalties, feelings, values, and so on—will continue on after "my" death. Whether "original me" and "replica me" are to be considered the "same person" or not is irrelevant to my wish for survival. Most importantly for Parfit, the impossibility of logically sustaining the idea of identity is beneficial for ethics. Getting rid of concern about identity, he argued, mitigates the force of self-interest as a rational moral consideration. In his own case, he claimed, it had made him less concerned about his own future and death, and more concerned about others (347).

One need hardly be persuaded by Parfit's arguments about the irrelevance of identity to take consolation from the fact that what one holds dear will live on in some way after one's death. In fact the consolation Parfit offers *presumes* the continuity of identity as "character" precisely in Ricoeur's sense. Ricoeur himself argued against Parfit's definition of the self as a set of impersonal mental and body "events" separable from a sense of their "mine-ness," their belonging to an embodied subjectivity. If, miraculously, my "mental events" were reembodied in a replica, they would necessarily be part of another subjectivity experiencing, and saying, "I." Even if one's self could be replicated, then, both selves would be faced with answering anew, just because of the other's existence, "Who am I?"

34. Charles Taylor, *Sources of the Self: The Making of the Modern Identity* (Cambridge, Mass.: Harvard University Press, 1989), 28.

35. Ibid., 29.

36. Ibid., 28.

37. Ibid., 492.

38. Ibid., 516.

39. Anthony Giddens, *Modernity and Self-Identity: Self and Society in the Late Modern Age* (Stanford, Calif.: Stanford University Press, 1991), 16.

40. Ibid., 20.

41. Ibid., 32.

42. Ibid., 35.

43. Ibid., 76.

44. Niethammer, *Kollektive Identität*, 63.

45. Ibid., 73.

46. Erik H. Erikson, *Childhood and Society*, 2nd ed. (New York: Norton, 1963), 281. The phrase "inner identity" (a translation of the original German "innere Identität") is in Freud's 1926 "Address to the Society of B'nai B'rith," in *The Standard Edition of the Complete Psychological Works of Sigmund Freud*, ed. James Strachey, vol. 20 (London: Hogarth, 1959), 274 (*S.E.*).

47. Niethammer, *Kollektive Identität*, 242.

48. Sigmund Freud, *Gesammelte Schriften*, vol. 12 (Vienna: Internationaler Psychoanalytischer Verlag, 1924–34), 385; my translation.

49. Niethammer, *Kollektive Identität*, 252.

50. On this point see the discussion about the logical and social conditions of group identification in Chapter 10. As we will also see, however, proponents of so-called "primordial" identities do also talk about their "ineffability."

51. Sigmund Freud, *Group Psychology and the Analysis of the Ego*, S.E. 28: 67–143.

52. For an extended argument about the way Freud's biological metapsychology translates into the categories of psychological and ideological individualism, see Gerald N. Izenberg, *The Existentialist Critique of Freud: The Crisis of Autonomy* (Princeton, N.J.: Princeton University Press, 1976), 175–210.

53. Niethammer, *Kollektive Identität*, 178.

54. Cited by Niethammer from the German translation of Halbwachs's original French *Les Cadres sociaux de la mémoire* (1925) in *Kollektive Identität*, 354.

55. Cited in Hans Kohn, "The Crisis in European Thought and Culture," in *World War I: A Turning Point in Modern History*, ed. Jack J. Roth (New York: Knopf, 1967), 29.

56. Virginia Woolf, *Mrs. Dalloway* (San Diego: Harcourt, 1981 [1925]), 8.

Chapter 1. Identity Becomes an Issue: European Literature Between the World Wars

An earlier version of this chapter appeared with the title "Identity Becomes an Issue: European Literature in the 1920s," *Modern Intellectual History* 5, 2 (2008): 279–307.

Epigraphs: André Gide, *The Counterfeiters*, trans. Dorothy Bussy (New York: Vintage, 1973), 70–71; André Malraux, *The Temptation of the West*, trans. Robert Hollander (New York: Vintage, 1961), 121.

1. Virginia Woolf, *Orlando* (London: Penguin, 1993 [1928]), 271–72. (I give the date of the first publication of a book in square brackets after the edition cited where it is important for historical context.)

2. Well before this scene, of course, Woolf had apparently challenged the premise of identity even more dramatically by abruptly transforming Orlando from a man into a woman, without benefit of surgery. But there she claimed that the sex change "did nothing whatever to alter their [sic] identity" (124). In this instance she was using identity in the Lockean sense that equates identity with continuity of memory (though there is physical continuity as well, which hints at the bisexuality Woolf was playing with): "Their faces remained, as their portraits prove, practically the same. His memory . . . [now we must say] her memory . . . went back through all the events of her past life without encountering any obstacle."

3. Robert Musil, *The Man Without Qualities*, vol. 2, trans. Sophie Wilkins and Burton Pike (New York: Vintage, 1996 [written late 1920s]), 762.

4. Marcel Proust, *Time Regained*, trans. Andreas Mayor, Terence Kilmartin, and D. J. Enright (New York: Modern Library, 2003 [1927]), 257.

5. Ibid., 3. Italics added.

6. Ibid., 413.

7. Ibid., 23.

8. Ibid., 7.

9. Musil, *The Man Without Qualities*, vol. 1, 9.

10. The classic account is Arno J. Mayer, *The Persistence of the Old Regime* (New York: Pantheon, 1981). See also Gerald N. Izenberg, "Die 'Aristokratisierung' der bürgerlichen Kultur im 19. Jahrhundert," in *Legitimationskrisen des deutschen Adels 1200–1900*, ed. Peter U. Hohendahl and Paul Michael Lützeler (Stuttgart: Metzler, 1979), 233–44.

11. Musil, *The Man Without Qualities*, 10; italics added.

12. Hermann Hesse, *Steppenwolf*, trans. Joseph Mileck (New York: Holt, Rinehart and Winston, 1963 [1927]), 65.

13. Robert Musil, *Young Törless*, trans. Eithne Wilkins and Ernst Kaiser (New York: Pantheon, 1982 [1906]), 50, 56.

14. Ibid., 137.

15. The English translation omits the names of the characters associated with each type and turns the abstract substantives ("Romanticism") into descriptive nouns ("Pasenow the Romantic"). This undermines Broch's intention to make the characters archetypes of an era. Hermann Broch, *The Sleepwalkers*, trans. Willa Muir and Edwin Muir (New York: Vintage, 1996 [1930–32]).

16. Broch, *The Sleepwalkers*, 20–21.

17. Luigi Pirandello, "Henry IV," in *Naked Masks: Five Plays by Luigi Pirandello*, ed. Eric Bentley (New York: Dutton, 1952), 195.

18. Ibid., 204–6.

19. Pirandello, "Six Characters in Search of an Author," in *Naked Masks*, 266.

20. André Gide, *The Counterfeiters*, trans. Dorothy Bussy (New York: Vintage, 1973), 70–71.

21. Hesse, *Steppenwolf*, 192.

22. Virginia Woolf, *Mrs. Dalloway* (San Diego, Calif.: Harcourt, 1981 [1925]), 37.

23. Musil, *The Man Without Qualities*, 140.

24. Ibid., 137.

25. Franz Kafka, *The Castle*, trans. Mark Harman (New York: Schocken, 1998 [1926]), 24.

26. Ibid., 74.

27. Ibid., 170.

28. Ibid., 70.

29. Ibid., 48.

30. Musil, *The Man Without Qualities*, 157.

31. Ibid., 30.

32. Ibid.

33. Ibid., 31, 35.

34. Ibid., 285.

35. Woolf, *Mrs. Dalloway*, 9.

36. Musil, *The Man Without Qualities*, 30.

37. Ibid., 181.

38. Paul Fussell, *The Great War and Modern Memory* (New York: Oxford University Press, 2000), 35.

39. Modris Eksteins, *Rites of Spring: The Great War and the Birth of the Modern Age* (Boston: Houghton Mifflin, 1989).

40. See, for example, David S. Luft, *Robert Musil and the Crisis of European Culture, 1880–1942* (Berkeley: University of California Press, 1980) and Paul Michael Lützeler, *Hermann Broch, A Biography*, trans. Janice Furness (London: Quartet, 1987), esp. 31–35.

41. Jay Winter, *Sites of Memory, Sites of Mourning: The Great War in European Cultural History* (Cambridge: Cambridge University Press, 1995), 1–5.

42. For a book-length discussion of World War I as a major turning point in and influence on Woolf's work, see Karen L. Levenback, *Virginia Woolf and the Great War* (Syracuse, N.Y.: Syracuse University Press, 1999).

43. Woolf, *Mrs. Dalloway*, 16–17.

44. Ibid., 126.

45. Ibid., 50.

46. Fussell, *The Great War*, 157.

47. Woolf, *Mrs. Dalloway*, 86.

48. Ibid., 88–89.

49. Ibid., 184.

50. Virginia Woolf et al., *The Mrs. Dalloway Reader*, ed. Francine Prose (Orlando, Fla.: Harcourt, 2003), 11.

51. Ibid., 373.

52. Ibid., 374.

53. Hermann Broch, "Kultur," in *Philosophische Schriften*, vol. 1, *Kritik*, ed. Paul Michael Lützeler (Frankfurt: Suhrkamp, 1977), 13.

54. Ibid., 21.

55. The "Ethical Reality of Our Time" was first published in the Suhrkamp edition of Broch's collected works in 1977. Paul Michael Lützeler, its editor, points out that the origins of the three essays he has included under the general title "Towards an Understanding of Our Area," of which "Ethical Reality" is the first, go back in part to the period before the war, though most were written during the war itself. Nothing in the prewar fragments, however, let alone the published essays, anticipates either the rage and despair or the scope of the historical analysis in the three wartime essays.

56. Broch, *The Sleepwalkers*, 407; *Die Schlafwandler* (Frankfurt: Suhrkamp, 1996), 454.

57. Broch, *The Sleepwalkers*, 642.

58. Hesse, *Steppenwolf*, 78.

59. Ralph Freedman, *Hermann Hesse, Pilgrim of Crisis: A Biography* (New York: Fromm, 1997), 168.

60. Stefan Jonsson, *Subject Without Nation: Robert Musil and the History of Modern Identity* (Durham, N.C.: Duke University Press, 2001), 7.

61. Robert Musil, *Gesammelte Werke*, vol. 2, *Prosa und Stücke, Kleine Prosa, Aphorismen, Autobiographisches, Essays und Reden, Kritik* (Hamburg: Rowohlt, 1978), 1010.

62. Ibid., 993.

63. Musil, *The Man Without Qualities*, 101.

64. Ibid., 107.

65. Ibid., 359.

66. See Rita Felski, *The Gender of Modernity* (Cambridge, Mass.: Harvard University Press, 1995), especially 91ff. This is a central theme in my *Modernism and Masculinity: Mann, Wedekind, Kandinsky Through World War I* (Chicago: University of Chicago Press, 2000).

67. Musil, *The Man Without Qualities*, 103.

68. Ibid., 304.

69. Ibid., 421.

70. Ibid., 423.

71. Musil, "Die Nation als Ideal und als Wirklichkeit," in *Gesammelte Werke*, vol. 2, 1073–74.

72. Musil, *The Man Without Qualities*, 405–6.

73. Ibid., vol 2, 1126.

74. Ibid., 1116.

75. Pirandello justified his allegiance to Fascism by turning it into Pirandellism. Il Duce's doctrine of action for action's sake derived from his understanding that while life requires form, all form, subject to change and motion, is doomed to death. See Gaspare Giudice, *Pirandello: A Biography* (London: Oxford University Press, 1975), 145–46.

76. Woolf, *Mrs. Dalloway*, 9.

77. Ibid., 152–53.

78. Ibid., 122.

79. Quoted in Levenback, *Virginia Woolf*, 13.

80. Ibid., 76.

81. Hesse, *Steppenwolf*, 203.

82. Ibid., 213.

83. See Gerald N. Izenberg, *Impossible Individuality: Romanticism, Revolution and the Origins of Modern Selfhood, 1787–1802* (Princeton, N.J.: Princeton University Press, 1992), 55–60.

84. Hesse, *Steppenwolf*, 216.

85. See my discussion of Romantic incest in *Impossible Individuality*, 245–48, 285–86, 303–4.

86. Musil, *The Man Without Qualities*, 2, 982.

87. Ibid., 1116–17.

88. Ibid., 947.

89. Ibid., 1024.

90. Proust, *Time Regained*, 261.

91. Ibid., 264.

92. Ibid., 273.

93. Ibid., 306.

94. Ibid., 290.

95. Ibid., 301.

96. Ibid., 302.

Chapter 2. The Ontological Critique of Identity: Heidegger and Sartre

Epigraph: U.S. President William J. Clinton, testifying before the grand jury on his relationship with Monica Lewinsky, August 17, 1998. Full text available at www.enquirer.com/clinton/com plete_text.html.

1. I have capitalized the English word here in keeping with the practice of the Macquarrie-Robinson translation (see my note 3). Though it gives the word a portentousness it does not necessarily have in German, which capitalizes all nouns, I retain it to highlight both its centrality and ambiguity in Heidegger's argument. The translation also capitalizes many other nouns. Except for "Being" and "Dasein," however, I will use capitals only when citing the translation.

2. We have little information about Heidegger's political commitments before *Being and Time*; my claim about his politics in the 1920s rests on the interpretation of that book. There is now an extensive and impassioned literature on the question of its relationship to ideology and politics. Even those who agree that there is an important connection disagree on exactly what it was. I will argue at greater length for the position I take here later in the chapter. Tellingly, *The Cambridge Companion to Heidegger's* Being and Time, ed. Mark A. Wrathall (Cambridge: Cambridge University Press, 2013) deals with the issue by ignoring it completely. The controversy about Heidegger's recently published "Black Notebooks" from the 1930s and 1940s, which equate the German spirit with the truth of Being and reveal his radical anti-Semitism, does not tell us anything specific about the previous decade, even if the notebooks strengthen the presumption that radical nationalism infuses *Being and Time*.

3. Martin Heidegger, *Being and Time*, trans. John Macquarrie and Edward Robinson (New York: Harper and Row, 1962), 150. Citations from this edition will be given in the text in parentheses. Italics are in the original except where noted. Because Heidegger used both single and double quotation marks which the translators preserve, the citations will keep both to avoid confusion.

4. I discuss these points and their historical context at greater length in *The Existentialist Critique of Freud: The Crisis of Autonomy* (Princeton, N.J.: Princeton University Press, 1976), 90ff.

5. See Chapter 4, on the origins of sociological role theory in the United States.

6. For a detailed analysis of Heidegger's antimodernism that covers his whole career and connects its beginnings with the broader current of right-wing reactionary thought in Germany after World War I, see Michael E. Zimmerman, *Heidegger's Confrontation with Modernity: Technology, Politics, and Art* (Bloomington: Indiana University Press, 1990).

7. The translation does not quite give the sense of the common German expression "*Alles in Ordnung*," which has the sense that everything is as it should be, that the actual state of affairs matches what is objectively right.

8. The importance of religion in the evolution of Heidegger's thinking leading up to *Being and Time* is one of the main themes of Theodore Kisiel's *The Genesis of Heidegger's* Being and Time

(Berkeley: University of California Press, 1993). See also John van Buren, *The Young Heidegger: Rumors of the Hidden King* (Bloomington: Indiana University Press, 1994).

9. In preference to the Macquarrie-Robinson translation of *Nichtigkeit* as "a nullity."

10. For the classical discussion of the trope with regard to political theory see Leonard Krieger, *The German Idea of Freedom* (Chicago: University of Chicago Press, 1957).

11. There is no basis in the original for the Macquarrie-Robinson insertion of the words "some sort of" before position, with its hint of vagueness. To the contrary, Heidegger's *Standgewonnenhaben* indicates the finality of Dasein's (at last) having achieved a firm footing.

12. This is more or less the position I took in *The Existentialist Critique of Freud*. It is also the one argued by Richard Wolin in *The Politics of Being: The Political Thought of Martin Heidegger* (New York: Columbia University Press, 1990). I have been persuaded by Johannes Fritsche's analysis that it is incorrect, though I do not accept his further argument that *Being and Time* is already an argument for Nazism. See his *Historical Destiny and National Socialism in Heidegger's* Being and Time (Berkeley: University of California Press, 1999). More on this in what follows.

13. This is how Johannes Fritsche reads the phrase "of the community, of the people." Even if that is a step too far, I am in full concurrence with his broader assertion that in the five pages of section 74, "Heidegger . . . concisely summarizes the common motif uniting the parties on the revolutionary political Right in their fight against romantic right-wingers, liberals and leftists" (*Historical Destiny*, 129). Furthermore, Fritsche's detailed philological and historical arguments are persuasive in ruling out other interpretations of historicality which claim that Heidegger either left the future open to completely free choice of self, licensed utopian political possibilities, or, by advancing a radical voluntarism inconsistent with his conservative politics, left him open to a pure political opportunism which, had the Communists been successful, might have allowed Heidegger to choose Bolshevism as easily as Nazism. See *Historical Destiny*, 216–24, and throughout.

14. Charles Bambach makes an extended argument that Heidegger's turn toward politics in 1933 was part of the right-wing revolutionary consciousness whose aim was to "restore rootedness to historical Dasein," but he also locates the strong desire for rootedness or "autochthony" in Heidegger's work of the 1920s. See *Heidegger's Roots: Nietzsche, National Socialism and the Greeks* (Ithaca, N.Y.: Cornell University Press, 2003), 23 and passim.

15. Martin Heidegger, "German Students," in *German Existentialism*, trans. Dagobert D. Runes (New York: Philosophical Library, 1965), 27; originally published in *Freiburger Studentenzeitung*, November 3, 1933, 1.

16. See Chapter 7.

17. "German Students," 28.

18. For my more detailed discussion of Sartre's indictment, as expressed in *Nausea*, see *The Existentialist Critique of Freud*, 234–35.

19. Simone de Beauvoir wrote that Sartre said of his hated stepfather Joseph Mancy, a philistine factory owner whom his mother married when he was eleven and who was disdainful of Sartre's early interest in writing, "he was always the person I wrote against. All my life." Annie Cohen-Solal, *Sartre: A Life*, trans. Anna Cancogni (New York: Pantheon, 1987), 48.

20. Brilliantly skewered in the novella "Childhood of a Leader," in *The Wall and Other Stories*, trans. Lloyd Alexander (New York: New Directions, 1948), 84–144.

21. Jean-Paul Sartre, *Les Mots* (Paris: Gallimard, 1964), 210.

22. Jean-Paul Sartre, *Being and Nothingness: An Essay on Phenomenological Ontology*, trans. Hazel E. Barnes (New York: Philosophical Library, 1956), 24. References to this text appear in square brackets after the citation.

23. Jean-Paul Sartre, *Nausea*, trans. Lloyd Alexander (Norfolk, Conn.: New Directions, 1949), 176.

24. Cohen-Solal, *Sartre*, 17.

25. "Success is not important to freedom. . . . The empirical and popular concept of 'freedom' which has been produced by historical, political, and moral circumstances is equivalent to 'the ability to obtain the ends chosen.' The . . . philosophical concept of freedom, the only one which we are considering here, means only the autonomy of choice" (483).

26. The body in Sartre has only recently become the focus of sustained critical attention. See Katherine J. Morris, ed., *Sartre on the Body* (Houndmills: Palgrave Macmillan, 2010).

27. Maurice Merleau-Ponty, *Phenomenology of Perception*, trans. Colin Smith (London: Routledge, 1962); *The Structure of Behavior*, trans. Alden L. Fisher (Boston: Beacon, 1963).

28. Sartre himself soon after felt the need to qualify the supposed absoluteness of his descriptions of human relations in terms of the Other. In his *Notebooks for an Ethics*, written in the course of his own conversion to Marxism, he described them as "ontology before conversion." In that work, published only posthumously, he canvassed the possibilities of "good faith" interpersonal relationships, the supportive relations possible in love and reciprocity. While ontologically valid, however, Sartre's rectification of the partial analysis of interpersonal relationships in *Being and Nothingness* obscured their force as a critique of identity. *Notebooks for an Ethics*, trans. David Pellauer (Chicago: University of Chicago Press, 1992.)

29. My own discussion of them can be found in *The Existentialist Critique of Freud*, 239–43.

30. For an overview of twentieth-century feminist critiques (and defenses) of Sartre, including bibliographies of earlier work, see Julien S. Murphy, ed., *Feminist Interpretations of Jean-Paul Sartre* (University Park: Pennsylvania State University Press, 1999). For how inner conflicts about activity and passivity played out in Sartre's own relationships with women, see Jean-Pierre Boulé, *Sartre, Self-Formation and Masculinities* (New York: Berghahn, 2005).

Chapter 3. Identity Becomes a Word: Erik Erikson and Psychological Identity

1. Erik H. Erikson, *Childhood and Society*, 2nd ed. (New York: Norton, 1963), 282. The first edition appeared in 1950. Though I cite the second edition, all citations appear in the first unless otherwise noted. He had used the word identity earlier in more technical articles.

2. Erik H. Erikson, "Ego Development and Historical Change: Clinical Notes," in *Identity and the Life Cycle: Selected Papers*, Psychological Issues 1 (New York: International Universities Press, 1959), 42. The essay was originally published in 1946.

3. Erikson, "Growth and Crises of the Healthy Personality," in *Identity and the Life Cycle*, 90. The original version was published in 1950.

4. Erikson, "Ego Development and Historical Change," 21.

5. Ibid., 22; emphasis added.

6. Erikson, *Childhood and Society*, 35. This idea was the foundation of Erikson's concept of "psychohistory" and of his biographical studies of identity crisis in Luther and Gandhi.

7. Erikson, "Ego Development and Historical Change," 23.

8. Erikson, "The Problem of Ego Identity," in *Identity and the Life Cycle*, 102.

9. Erikson, *Childhood and Society*, 35. Italics added.

10. Erik H. Erikson, *Identity: Youth and Crisis* (New York: Norton, 1968), 227.

11. Lawrence J. Friedman, *Identity's Architect: A Biography of Erik H. Erikson* (New York: Scribner, 1999), 433. Friedman's biography is the source of most of my information about Erikson's life.

12. Friedman describes the episode in *Identity's Architect*, 429–36. It was initiated by Marshall Berman's highly critical *New York Times* review of Erikson's autobiographical essay " 'Identity Crisis' in Autobiographic Perspective," in Erikson, *Life History and the Historical Moment* (New York: Norton, 1975).

13. See Chapter 4.

14. For examples of such criticisms, see Chapter 4.

15. For Fromm's Orthodox Jewish background, his study with figures like Martin Buber and Franz Rosenzweig, and the origins of his fusion of Marxism and Jewish sensibility, see Lawrence J. Friedman, *The Lives of Erich Fromm: Love's Prophet* (New York: Columbia University Press, 2013).

16. Friedman, *Identity's Architect*, 162. Friedman states bluntly that Erikson "neglected to mention the importance of Erich Fromm in the formation of his concept of identity."

17. Erich Fromm, *Escape from Freedom* (New York: Rinehart, 1941), 156.

18. Ibid., 254.

19. For the classical formulations of this ideology, see Fritz Stern, "The Political Consequences of the Unpolitical German," in *The Failure of Illiberalism: Essays on the Political Culture of Modern Germany* (New York: Knopf, 1972) and Fritz K. Ringer, *The Decline of the Mandarins: The German Academic Community, 1890–1933* (Cambridge, Mass.: Harvard University Press, 1969).

20. Friedman, *Identity's Architect*, 52, 54. Erikson's effusions were a very junior version of but nonetheless quite similar to Thomas Mann's classical conservative statement in *Reflections of an Unpolitical Man*, which appeared in 1918.

21. For a discussion of the connection between Humboldt's ideal of *Bildung* and his liberalism, see my essay "Reconciling Individuality and Individualism in European Liberalism," *Intellectual History Newsletter* 24 (2002): 23–37.

22. Erikson, *Childhood and Society*, 138.

23. Ibid., 323.

24. Ibid., 282.

25. Ibid., 287.

26. Ibid., 322.

27. Erikson, "Problem of Ego Identity," 158.

28. Ibid., 159.

29. The term was introduced by Heinz Hartmann in one of the founding works of psychoanalytic "ego psychology," *Ego Psychology and the Problem of Adaptation*, 1939.

30. Erikson, "Eight Ages of Man," chapter 7 in *Childhood and Society*.

31. Ibid., 250.

32. Ibid., 253.

33. Ibid., 262.

34. Erik H. Erikson, "Identity and Uprootedness in Our Time," in *Insight and Responsibility* (New York: Norton, 1964), 103. It was first delivered as an address in 1959. It is hard to believe that Erikson's formulation was not influenced by Sartre as well as Fromm, though his acknowledged connection to existential thought was through his personal relationship with the theologian Paul Tillich, his colleague at Harvard University in the early 1960s .

35. With a nod to Herbert Marcuse's notion of "surplus repression" in *Eros and Civilization*.

36. As in the construction of the superego. One might also identify with them and then ostensibly turn one's anger onto oneself to punish them for abandonment, as Freud had described in "Mourning and Melancholia," *Standard Edition*, vol. 14, 237–58.

37. Erikson, "Problem of Ego Identity," 113.

38. Ibid., 114.

39. Erik H. Erikson, *Young Man Luther: A Study in Psychoanalysis and History* (New York: Norton, 1958), 217.

40. Erikson, "Problem of Ego Identity," 102.

41. Ibid., 110.

42. Ibid., 118.

43. Ibid., 140.

44. Diane McShane, "Group Told: Try Retiring for a Year," *Chicago Tribune*, October 1, 1963.

45. The computerized complete text database for the *Tribune* only begins in 1963. I was unable to check earlier years. But see below.

46. D. Barclay, "After the First Year of College," *New York Times*, May 28, 1961.

47. M. Bender, "Edie Pops Up as Newest Superstar," *New York Times*, July 26, 1965.

48. P. H. Dougherty, "Advertising: After the Game, a Bit of Glory," *New York Times*, October 13, 1966.

49. C. A. Pinderhughes, *Los Angeles Times*, November 2, 1968.

50. M. Cheshire, originally in the *Washington Post*, *Los Angeles Times*, May 1970.

51. "Clergymen Seek Ways to Ease 'Identity Crisis,'" *Los Angeles Times*, June 26, 1971.

52. J. A. Morris, "Yugoslavia Suffers New Identity Crisis," *Los Angeles Times*, February 11, 1973.

53. T. Green, "IDENTITY CRISIS: Squash: It's Just a Khan Game," *Los Angeles Times*, February 6, 1975.

54. L. Lieber, "What James Bond," *The Sun*, February 4, 1968.

55. F. P. McGehan, "The Medical Society Probes Itself," *The Sun*, December 17, 1968.

56. R. S. Browne, "Negro Separatists Say Black May Be Beautiful But Not Next to White: Despair over Integration Stimulates Identity Crisis," *The Sun*, August 4, 1968.

57. L. Berton, "After the Merger: Firms That Combine Often Find the Period of Adjustment Painful," *Wall Street Journal*, March 13, 1968.

58. Warren I. Sussman, "'Personality' and Twentieth Century Culture," in *New Directions in American Intellectual History*, ed. John Higham and Paul K. Conkin (Baltimore: Johns Hopkins University Press, 1979), 224.

59. Quoted in Friedman, *Identity's Architect*, 304, 241.

60. Anecdotal personal evidence suggests that a university student could be excited by the concept of identity in the 1950s without even having read the book.

61. F. Keene, "A Desperate Need for Identity: *The Pillar of Salt*, by Albert Memmi," *New York Times*, October 23, 1955.

62. G. Samuels, "People in Search of Identity: In the Camps of the Refugees," *New York Times*, September 23, 1956.

63. Philip Gleason, "Identifying Identity: A Semantic History," *Journal of American History* 69, 4 (March 1983): 926–28.

64. David Riesman, *The Lonely Crowd: A Study of the Changing American Character* (New Haven, Conn.: Yale University Press, 1950), 373.

65. Erikson, *Childhood and Society*, 308, 320.

66. Ibid., 323.

67. Ibid., 324.

68. Cited in ibid., 307.

69. Erikson, "Introduction to Part Four," in *Childhood and Society*, 279.

70. Alan Wheelis, *The Quest for Identity* (New York: Norton, 1958), 41.

71. Elaine Tyler May, *Homeward Bound: American Families in the Cold War Era* (New York: Basic, 1988), 14.

72. For a more detailed description, see James T. Patterson, *Grand Expectations: The United States, 1945–1974* (New York: Oxford University Press, 1996), 350–72. The now standard work on American consumer culture is Lizabeth Cohen, *A Consumer's Republic: The Politics of Mass Consumption in Postwar America* (New York: Knopf, 2003), but it has no specific comments on youth consumption.

73. Robert M. Lindner, *Must You Conform?* (New York: Rinehart, 1956), 5; italics in original.

74. Wheelis, *Quest for Identity*, 91.

75. Ibid., 127–28.

76. "Erik Erikson: *Der Junge Mann Luther*," notice and comment on the German translation of *Young Man Luther* in *Der Spiegel*, September 2, 1964.

77. Alexander Mitscherlich, *Society Without the Father: A Contribution to Social Psychology*, trans. Eric Mosbacher (New York: Harcourt, Brace and World, 1969 [1963]); Alexander Mitscherlich and Margarete Mitscherlich, *The Inability to Mourn: Principles of Collective Behavior*, trans. Beverly R. Placzek (New York: Grove Press, 1975 [1967]).

78. Famously, for example, Germaine Greer's less than politic comment that "Erik Erikson invented the lunatic concept of an *inner space* in a woman's *somatic design*, a hole in the head, as it were, which harbours the commitment to take care of children." *The Female Eunuch* (New York: McGraw-Hill, 1970), 109; italics in original.

79. Erik H. Erikson, *Dimensions of a New Identity* (New York: Norton, 1974), 104–5.

80. Ibid., 106.

81. Robert Jay Lifton, "Protean Man," *Partisan Review* 35 (Winter 1968): 13.

82. Ibid., 17.

83. Robert Jay Lifton, *Witness to an Extreme Century: A Memoir* (New York: Free Press, 2011), 369–70.

84. Robert Jay Lifton, *The Protean Self: Human Resilience in an Age of Fragmentation* (Chicago: University of Chicago Press, 1993), 8–9.

85. For a balanced view of Laing's development, see Daniel Burston, *The Wings of Madness: The Life and Work of R. D. Laing* (Cambridge, Mass.: Harvard University Press, 1996).

86. R. D. Laing, *The Divided Self: An Existential Study in Sanity and Madness* (Harmondsworth: Penguin, 1960), 42; italics added.

87. Ibid., 41.

88. R. D. Laing, *The Self and Others: Further Studies in Sanity and Madness* (London: Tavistock, 1961), 75.

89. Laing, *Divided Self*, 44–47; italics in original.

90. Ibid., 95.

91. Ibid., 103.

Chapter 4. Social Identity and the Birth of Identity Politics, 1945–1970

1. Anne-Marie Thiesse, *Faire les français: Quelle identité nationale?* (Paris: Stock, 2010); my translation.

2. Combahee River Collective, "A Black Feminist Statement," in *The Second Wave: A Reader in Feminist Theory*, ed. Linda Nicholson (New York: Routledge, 1997), 65.

3. Jean-Paul Sartre, *Being and Nothingness: An Essay on Phenomenological Ontology*, trans. Hazel E. Barnes (New York: Philosophical Library, 1956), 419.

4. Ibid., 420.

5. Ibid., 421.

6. I fully agree with Sonia Kruks's assertion that *Anti-Semite and Jew* is "a locus classicus for the emergence of identity politics." Sonia Kruks, *Retrieving Experience: Subjectivity and Recognition in Feminist Politics* (Ithaca, N.Y.: Cornell University Press, 2001), 97.

7. Jean-Paul Sartre, *Anti-Semite and Jew*, trans. George J. Becker (New York: Schocken, 1965), 25.

8. Ibid., 26.

9. Ibid., 68.

10. Ibid., 69, 91.

11. Ibid., 136.

12. Adrian Haddour, "Sartre and Fanon: On Negritude and Political Participation," in Adrian van den Hoven and Andrew Leak, *Sartre Today: A Centenary Celebration* (New York: Berghahn, 2005), 287. This formulation represented a shift in the concept of negritude from its original focus on personal identity to one of collective or national identity. See Irving Leonard Markovitz, *Léopold Sédar Senghor and the Politics of Negritude* (New York: Heinemann, 1969), 49.

13. Jean-Paul Sartre, "Black Orpheus," in Sartre, *"What Is Literature?" and Other Essays* (Cambridge, Mass.: Harvard University Press, 1988), 296.

14. Ibid., 297.

15. Ibid., 314.

16. Ibid., 326.

17. Ibid., 327.

18. Ibid., 133.

19. Simone de Beauvoir, *The Second Sex*, trans. H. M. Parshley, intro. Deirdre Bair (New York: Vintage, 1989), viii. Citations in parentheses are from this edition.

20. Simone de Beauvoir, *The Second Sex*, unabridged trans. Constance Borde and Sheila Malovany-Chevallier, intro. Judith Thurman (New York: Vintage, 2011), 161. The English translation mistakenly omits the reflexive pronoun of the original French. See Simone de Beauvoir, *Le deuxième sex*, vol. 1, *Les faits et les mythes* (Paris: Gallimard, 1949), 242. What Beauvoir so succinctly summarizes is precisely the Romantic project, and contradiction, I tried to describe in *Impossible Individuality: Romanticism, Revolution and the Origins of Modern Selfhood, 1787–1802* (Princeton, N.J.: Princeton University Press, 1992).

21. Deirdre Bair, *Simone de Beauvoir: A Biography* (New York: Simon and Schuster, 1990), 386ff.

22. Ibid., 386.

23. Simone de Beauvoir, *The Mandarins*, trans. Leonard M. Friedman (New York: Norton, 1991).

24. Edward Fulbrook and Kate Fulbrook, *Sex and Philosophy: Rethinking De Beauvoir and Sartre* (London: Zed Books, 2008); Christine Daigle and Jacob Golomb, eds., *Beauvoir and Sartre: The Riddle of Influence* (Bloomington: Indiana University Press, 2009).

25. Simone de Beauvoir, *She Came to Stay* (New York: Norton, 1990 [1943]).

26. Frantz Fanon, *Black Skin, White Masks*, trans. Charles L. Markmann (New York: Grove, 1967 [1952]), 116.

27. Eldridge Cleaver, *Post-Prison Writings and Speeches* (New York: Random House, 1969), 18.

28. Fanon, *Black Skin*, 14.

29. For an excellent discussion of the connection, see Kruks, *Retrieving Experience*, 97–104.

30. Fanon, *Black Skin*, 110.

31. Ibid., 116.

32. Ibid., 11.

33. Ibid., 110.

34. Ibid., 132.

35. Ibid., 197.

36. Ibid., 226, 228, 231.

37. Ibid., 224.

38. Frantz Fanon, *The Wretched of the Earth*, trans. Constance Farrington (New York: Grove, 1968 [1961]), 233.

39. Ibid., 94.

40. James D. Le Sueur claimed that the impact of the Algerian War on identity went well beyond Fanon. "The war," he wrote, "gave rise to an identity politics that continues to influence debates in France and Algeria as well as academic discussions around the world." In this connection he quoted from the diaries of the Algerian writer Mouloud Ferouan, who was assassinated by the French OAS during the war, "What am I, dear God? Is it possible that as long as there are labels, there is not one for me? Which is mine? Can somebody tell me what I am! Of course they want me to pretend that I am wearing a label because they pretend to believe in it. I am sorry, but this is not enough." *Uncivil War: Intellectuals and Identity Politics During the Decolonization of Algeria* (Lincoln: University of Nebraska Press, 2005), 28.

41. Though the women's suffrage movement sometimes grounded the demand for the vote on the ground of women's moral superiority to men.

42. As Jerry Muller points out, Sumner applied Darwinian language only after developing his own ideas, and was concerned with institutional, not individual selection, but the institution that he believed had proved its survival value was the competitive market. See Jerry Z. Muller, *Conservatism: An Anthology of Social and Political Thought from David Hume to the Present* (Princeton, N.J.: Princeton University Press, 1997), 233–36.

43. See Jeffrey Sklansky, *The Soul's Economy: Market Society and Selfhood in American Thought, 1820–1920* (Chapel Hill: University of North Carolina Press, 2002).

44. Most notoriously, Erving Goffman in *The Presentation of Self in Everyday Life* (Garden City, N.Y.: Doubleday, 1959).

45. Ralph Linton, *The Study of Man: An Introduction* (New York: Appleton-Century-Crofts, 1936), 113–14.

46. Nelson R. Foote, "Identification as the Basis for a Theory of Motivation," *American Sociological Review* 16, 1 (February 1951): 17; italics in original.

47. Reinhard Bendix, "Identification as the Basis for a Theory of Motivation: Discussion," *American Sociological Review* 16, 1 (February 1951): 22.

48. Foote, "Identification," 16; italics in original

49. Ibid., 17, 18.

50. Ibid., 19.

51. Ibid., 17.

52. Ibid., 19; italics added.

53. Ibid.

54. Ibid.; italics in original.

55. Philip Gleason, "Identifying Identity: A Semantic History," *Journal of American History* 69, 4 (March 1983): 917–18.

56. Manford H. Kuhn and Thomas S. McPartland, "An Empirical Investigation of Self-Attitudes," *American Sociological Review* 19, 1 (February 1954): 68–76.

57. See, for example, Michael H. Bond and Tak-Sing Cheung, "College Students' Spontaneous Self-Concept: The Effect of Culture Among Respondents in Hong Kong, Japan and the United States," *Journal of Cross-Cultural Psychology* 14, 2 (June 1983): 153–71.

58. Kuhn and McPartland, "Self-Attitudes," 72.

59. Ibid., 69.

60. Will Herberg, *Protestant, Catholic, Jew: An Essay in American Religious Sociology* (Garden City, N.Y.: Doubleday, 1960 [1955]).

61. Ibid., 12.

62. Anselm Strauss, *Mirrors and Masks: The Search for Identity* (Glencoe, Ill.: Free Press, 1959). Strauss both drew on and contrasted his approach with Erikson in a number of places, e.g., 130, 146ff.

63. Ibid., 148.

64. Erving Goffman, *Stigma: Notes on the Management of Spoiled Identity* (New York: Simon and Schuster, 1963).

65. Strauss, *Mirrors and Masks*, 72. Italics added.

66. Ibid., 104.

67. "Persons may be conceived as taking some particular stance toward the historical, suprapersonal past" (ibid., 171).

68. Muzafer Sherif et al., *The Robbers Cave Experiment: Intergroup Conflict and Cooperation* (Middletown, Conn.: Wesleyan University Press, 1988 [1961]).

69. Ibid., 10.

70. Ibid.

71. Ibid., 160–88.

72. David Berreby, *Us and Them: Understanding Your Tribal Mind* (New York: Little, Brown, 2005), 178; republished as *Us and Them: The Science of Identity* (Chicago: University of Chicago Press, 2008).

73. This is of course the roughest of generalizations, which elides the background influence of such European contributions as Durkheimian sociology.

74. Peter L. Berger and Thomas Luckmann, *The Social Construction of Reality: A Treatise in the Sociology of Knowledge* (Garden City, N.Y.: Anchor, 1967, 1966), 89.

75. Ibid., 132.

76. Ibid., 134.

77. Ibid., 91.

78. Ibid., 174.

79. Victor C. Ferkiss, *Africa's Search for Identity* (New York: George Braziller, 1966), 5–6, 10.

80. Markovitz, *Léopold Sédar Senghor and the Politics of Negritude*, 49, 75.

81. Howard Brick, *Age of Contradiction: American Thought and Culture in the 1960s* (New York: Twayne, 1998). See the index under "identity politics," 238.

82. On the traditional political dimension of Marcus Garvey's black nationalism and the innovative nature of Black Power identity politics, see L. A. Kauffman, "The Anti-Politics of Identity," in *Identity Politics in the Women's Movement*, ed. Barbara Ryan (New York: New York University Press, 2001), 25–26.

83. Brick, *Age of Contradiction*, 4.

84. In *Retrieving Experience: Subjectivity and Recognition in Feminist Politics*, Sonia Kruks lists five core "propositions" that define identity politics. The first asserts that there exist "significant differences of social status and experience (such as those of race, class, ethnicity, gender and sexuality) that have for too long been obscured by the dominance of the ideas of a hegemonic white, male, upper-class and heterosexual elite" (80). The inclusion of class in the list is a historical, or rather ahistorical, mistake. It is an attempt, in keeping with the temper of contemporary middle-class feminist radicalism, to be inclusive, phrased as if Marxism had never existed. In fact identity politics emerged in important part *against* the felt irrelevance of traditional left-wing class politics.

85. Stokely Carmichael and Charles V. Hamilton, *Black Power: The Politics of Liberation in America* (New York: Random House, 1967), 44.

86. Ibid., viii, 34–35; italics added.

87. Ibid., 55.

88. William L. Van Deburg, *New Day in Babylon: The Black Power Movement and American Culture, 1965–1975* (Chicago: University of Chicago Press, 1992), 5.

89. Ibid., 172.

90. Ibid., 177.

91. Ibid., 179.

92. Ibid., 197.

93. Betty Friedan, *The Feminine Mystique* (New York: Norton, 2001 [1963]), 133.

94. Kate Millett, *Sexual Politics* (Urbana: University of Illinois Press, 2000 [1970]), 23.

95. Robert J. Stoller, "A Contribution to the Study of Gender Identity," *International Journal of Psychoanalysis* 45 (1964): 220–26 and "A Further Contribution to the Study of Gender Identity," *International Journal of Psychoanalysis* 49 (1968): 364–68.

96. Phyllis Tyson and Robert Tyson, *Psychoanalytic Theory of Development: An Integration* (New Haven, Conn.: Yale University Press, 1990).

97. Robert J. Stoller, *Sex and Gender: On the Development of Masculinity and Femininity* (New York: Science House, 1968), 9.

98. Millett, *Sexual Politics*, 33.

99. Shulamith Firestone, *The Dialectic of Sex: The Case for Feminist Revolution* (New York: Morrow Quill, 1970), 6, 8, 10.

100. Ibid., 233.

101. Craig A. Rimmerman, *From Identity to Politics: The Lesbian and Gay Movements in the United States* (Philadelphia: Temple University Press, 2002), 27.

102. Mark Blasius, "An Ethos of Lesbian and Gay Existence," in *Sexual Identities, Queer Politics*, ed. Mark Blasius (Princeton, N.J.: Princeton University Press, 2001), 155.

103. Klaus Bitterman, "Wie die Identität unter die Deutschen kam. Die Linke als Geburtshelfer nationaler Gefühle," in *Geisterfahrer der Einheit: Kommentare zur Wiedervereinigungskrise* (Berlin: ID-Archiv, 1995), 94–120. Cited in Niethammer, *Kollektive Identität*, 20. My translation.

104. For an argument to this effect in the British context, see Grant Farred, "Endgame Identity? Mapping the New Left Roots of Identity Politics," *New Literary History* 31, 4, *Is There Life After Identity Politics?* (Autumn 2000): 627–48.

Chapter 5. Collective Identities and Their Agenda, 1970–2000

1. See for example Nancy Chodorow's autobiographical remarks in *Individualizing Gender and Sexuality: Theory and Practice* (New York: Routledge, 2012), 2–3.

2. Linda Nicholson, ed., *The Second Wave: A Reader in Feminist Theory* (New York: Routledge, 1997), 147.

3. Nancy Chodorow, *The Reproduction of Mothering: Psychoanalysis and the Sociology of Gender* (Berkeley: University of California Press, 1999 [1978]), 167.

4. Ibid., 211–19.

5. Ibid., xvi.

6. Carol Gilligan, *In a Different Voice: Psychological Theory and Women's Development* (Cambridge, Mass.: Harvard University Press, 1993 [1982]), 1.

7. Ibid., 157, 156.

8. Ibid., 2.

9. Sara Ruddick, "Maternal Thinking," *Feminist Studies* 6, 2 (Summer 1980): 346, 359.

10. Ibid., 359; italics in original.

11. Ibid., 346.

12. Ibid., 345.

13. Sara Ruddick, *Maternal Thinking: Toward a Politics of Peace* (Boston: Beacon, 1989), 56.

14. Ibid., 221.

15. Adrienne Rich, *Of Woman Born: Motherhood as Experience and Institution* (New York: Norton, 1986 [1976]) 22.

16. Ibid.

17. See Nancy Hartsock's reference to identity in "The Feminist Standpoint: Developing the Ground for a Specifically Feminist Historical Materialism," in *The Feminist Standpoint Theory Reader: Intellectual and Political Controversies*, ed. Sandra G. Harding (New York: Routledge, 2004), 44. This essay from 1983 is generally seen as the beginning of standpoint feminism.

18. Ibid., 40.

19. Ibid., 37.

20. Ibid., 45.

21. Alison Jagger, "Feminist Politics and Epistemology: The Standpoint of Women," in Harding, *Feminist Standpoint Theory Reader*, 62.

22. See for example Mary F. Belenky et al., *Women's Ways of Knowing: The Development of Self, Voice, and Mind* (New York: Basic, 1997 [1986]).

23. "A feminist standpoint can allow us to understand patriarchal institutions and ideologies as perverse inversions of more humane social relations." Hartsock, "The Feminist Standpoint," in Harding, *Feminist Standpoint Theory Reader*, 36.

24. Sandra Harding, "Rethinking Standpoint Epistemology: What Is 'Strong Objectivity'?" in Harding, *Feminist Standpoint Theory Reader*, 133.

25. Ibid., 137.

26. Vivienne C. Cass, "Homosexual Identity: A Concept in Need of a Definition," *Journal of Homosexuality* 9, 2–3 (December 1983): 105–26.

27. For the growth of gay self-help and other forms of community organizations in San Francisco after 1971 see Elizabeth A. Armstrong, "The Crystallization of a Gay Identity Movement, 1971–1973," chap. 5 in *Forging Gay Identities: Organizing Sexuality in San Francisco, 1950–1994* (Chicago: University of Chicago Press, 2002).

28. In the early 1970s, "gay" was used to refer to both male and female homosexuals. Later it was used mostly for males, with lesbian the exclusive term for females.

29. Cass, "Homosexual Identity," 108.

30. Ibid., 120; italics added.

31. Ibid., 111.

32. The American Psychiatric Association had formally removed the designation of mental illness from homosexuality in 1973.

33. Cass, "Homosexual Identity," 117.

34. Berger and Luckmann, *The Social Construction of Reality*, 160, quoted in ibid., 120.

35. Mary McIntosh, "The Homosexual Role," in *Forms of Desire: Sexual Orientation and the Social Constructionist Controversy*," ed. Edward Stein (New York: Routledge, 1992), 29.

36. Steven Epstein, "Gay Politics, Ethnic Identity: The Limits of Social Construction," in Stein, *Forms of Desire*, 243. Epstein took the notion gay "ethnicity" from Dennis Altman, *The Homosexualization of America* (Boston: Beacon, 1982). As Epstein points out, Altman's earlier work, *Homosexual: Oppression and Liberation*, published in 1971, took the opposite position of favoring the abolition of sexual and gender categorization in favor of creating a "new human" for whom all such distinctions would be irrelevant (253). The difference between the two books marks the shift over the decade from the universalism of the demand for equal rights for homosexuals to gay identity. I will discuss the legitimating function of ethnic status in a later section. It should also be pointed out that the word gay preceded the idea of a gay identity. Robert Lindner, for example, used the word quite unselfconsciously in a public lecture and essay in 1954. See Robert Lindner, "Homosexuality and the Contemporary Scene," in *Must You Conform?* (New York: Rinehart, 1956), 34.

37. Goffman, *Stigma*, 14, 88.

38. Steven Epstein, following Goffman, calls this an "ironic effect" of asserting legitimacy but it is not clear what's ironic about it; the outcome was not an unintended intensification of the stigmatized identity but a conscious move to eliminate stigma from the identity.

39. See Chapter 9.

40. Armstrong, *Forging Gay Identities*, 98.

41. Combahee River Collective, "A Black Feminist Statement," in Nicholson, *The Second Wave*, 65.

42. Cherrie Moraga and Gloria Anzaldua, eds., *This Bridge Called My Back: Writings by Radical Women of Color* (New York: Women of Color Press, 1981).

43. See Norma Alarcon, "The Theoretical Subject(s) of *This Bridge Called My Back* and Anglo-American Feminism," in Seidman, *The Postmodern Turn*, 140–52.

44. Moraga and Anzaldua, *This Bridge Called My Back*, 23.

45. Rosario Morales, "I Am What I Am," in ibid., 14–15.

46. "The politics of identity is silent on the deepest sources of social misery: the devastation of cities, the draining of resources away from the public and into the private hands of the few." Todd Gitlin, "The Fate of the Commons," in Ryan, *Identity Politics in the Women's Movement*, 37. For a more ambivalent view, see Kauffman, "The Anti-Politics of Identity," which argues that a politics of identity that was effective in the public sphere in the 1960s and early 1970s degenerated in the later 1970s into an antipolitical, purely personal "lifestyle politics," in Ryan, *Identity Politics in the Women's Movement*, 31–32.

47. See Arthur Schlesinger, Jr., *The Disuniting of America: Reflections on a Multicultural Society* (New York: Norton, 1992). The problem of identity in liberal democracy will be taken up in detail in Chapter 6.

48. June Jordan quoted in Kruks, *Retrieving Experience*, 82.

49. Daphne Patai, "The Struggle for Feminist Purity Threatens the Goals of Feminism," in Ryan, *Identity Politics in the Women's Movement*, 41–42.

50. Iris Marion Young, "Polity and Group Difference: A Critique of the Ideal of Universal Citizenship," *Ethics* 99, 2 (January 1989): 250–74; *Justice and the Politics of Difference* (Princeton, N.J.: Princeton University Press, 1990). The theoretical argument of the book, though not the article, invokes certain postmodernist premises but is not dependent on them.

51. Young, "Polity and Group Difference," 261.

52. Ibid., 268.

53. Ibid., 262, 263.

54. Ibid., 266.

55. Ibid., 270–71.

56. Gitlin, "The Fate of the Commons," 35.

57. The first mention of ethnic identity I have found in scholarly literature is in an article on "The Prehistoric Inhabitants of the Mississippi Valley," *Journal of the American Geographical Society*

of New York 5 (1874). Its next appearance is in the journal *Science* in 1896, and the one after that in 1903. The first reference to ethnic identity in the *New York Times* dates from 1917 ("Germany's Mexican Intrigue—and What It Means," *New York Times*, March 11). Only by the 1940s did the racial implications begin to fade away. See the discussion later in this chapter on the relationship between race and ethnicity.

58. Fredrik Barth, ed., *Ethnic Groups and Boundaries: The Social Organization of Culture Difference* (Long Grove, Ill.: Waveland, 1989 [1969]), 14.

59. Barth, "Introduction," *Ethnic Groups and Boundaries*, 14; italics added.

60. Ibid.

61. Ibid., 14.

62. Nathan Glazer and Daniel P. Moynihan, eds., *Ethnicity: Theory and Experience* (Cambridge, Mass.: Harvard University Press, 1975), 1. There were no cognates in French or German until the English word was imported into French. Arthur Schlesinger attributes the first use of the word to the sociologist W. Lloyd Warner in the initial book of the Yankee City series, published in 1941 (misdated as 1940). Schlesinger, *The Disuniting of America*, 42.

63. Ibid.

64. Nathan Glazer and Daniel P. Moynihan, *Beyond the Melting Pot* (Cambridge, Mass.: Harvard University Press, 1963), cited in John Hutchinson and Anthony D. Smith, eds., *Ethnicity* (Oxford: Oxford University Press, 1996), 137, 135.

65. Glazer and Moynihan, *Ethnicity*, 15.

66. Ibid., 19.

67. Hutchinson and Smith, *Ethnicity*, 6–7; italics added.

68. Manning Nash, "The Core Elements of Ethnicity," in ibid., 25.

69. Elizabeth Tonkin and colleagues pointed out that the biological aspect of race was only a part of a complex use of the word in the nineteenth century that included culture and language, but it was not simply one element among many; it was the grounding concept that explained the existence and transmission of the others. Elizabeth Tonkin, Maryon McDonald, and Malcolm Chapman, eds., *History and Ethnicity* (London: Routledge, 1989); Hutchinson and Smith, *Ethnicity*, 21.

70. Pierre L. van den Berghe, *Race and Racism: A Comparative Perspective* (New York: Wiley, 1967), 9–10.

71. For a discussion of the tortured relationship between the two terms, see Thomas H. Eriksen, "Ethnicity, Race, Class and Nation," in Hutchinson and Smith, *Ethnicity*, 28–30. While he himself didn't want to distinguish between race and ethnicity, he conceded that groups who "look different" from majorities or dominating groups find it more difficult to escape from their ethnic identities.

72. Donald L. Horowitz, "Ethnic Identity," in Glazer and Moynihan, *Ethnicity*, 113; italics added.

73. Harold R. Isaacs, "Basic Group Identity: The Idols of the Tribe," in Glazer and Moynihan, *Ethnicity*, 31–32.

74. Talcott Parsons, "Some Theoretical Considerations on the Nature and Trends of Change of Ethnicity," in Glazer and Moynihan, *Ethnicity*, 56.

75. David M. Schneider, *American Kinship: A Cultural Account* (Englewood Cliffs, N.J.: Prentice-Hall, 1968), cited in Parsons, "Some Theoretical Considerations," 64.

76. D. Horowitz, "Ethnic Identity," 114.

77. Clifford Geertz, "Primordial Ties," in Hutchinson and Smith, *Ethnicity*, 42. Italics added.

78. Jack Eller and Reed Coughlan, "The Poverty of Primordialism," in ibid., 46.

79. Abner Cohen, "Ethnicity and Politics," in ibid., 84.

80. Michael Hechter, "Ethnicity and Rational Choice Theory," in ibid., 90; italics added.

81. Geertz, "Primordial Ties," 41.

82. Steven Grosby, "The Inexpungeable Tie of Primordiality," in Hutchinson and Smith, *Ethnicity*, 51.

83. See Chapter 10.

84. Martin Kilson, "Blacks and Neo-Ethnicity in American Life," in Glazer and Moynihan, *Ethnicity*, 236.

85. Ibid., 237.

86. Ibid., 240; italics in original.

87. David R. Roediger, *Working Towards Whiteness: How America's Immigrants Became White* (New York: Basic, 2005).

88. Kilson, "Blacks and Neo-Ethnicity in American Life," 246.

89. Ibid., 240.

90. Ibid., 260.

91. Herbert J. Gans, "Symbolic Ethnicity," in Hutchinson and Smith, *Ethnicity*, 149.

92. See, for example, David Taylor and Malcolm Yapp, eds., *Political Identity in South Asia* (Dublin: Curzon, 1979), as well as the local studies excerpted in Hutchinson and Smith, *Ethnicity*.

93. Bassam Tibi, "Old Tribes and Imposed Nation-States in the Middle East," in Hutchinson and Smith, *Ethnicity*, 174–78.

94. John Porter, "Ethnic Pluralism in Canadian Perspective," in Glazer and Moynihan, *Ethnicity*, 268.

95. Daniel Bell, "Ethnicity and Social Change," in ibid., 142; italics in original.

96. Ibid., 155.

97. Ibid., 161.

98. Ibid., 153.

99. Anthony D. Smith, *The Ethnic Revival in the Modern World* (Cambridge, Mass.: Harvard University Press, 1981), 154–55.

100. Ibid., 13.

101. Ibid., 35.

102. Ibid., 18.

103. Ibid., 24.

104. Ibid., 138.

105. Ibid., 140.

106. Ibid., 167.

107. Smith, *National Identity*, viii.

108. Benedict Anderson, *Imagined Communities: Reflections on the Origin and Spread of Nationalism* (London: Verso, 1991 [1983]), 3.

109. John Davis, "An Interview with Ernest Gellner," *Current Anthropology* 32, 1 (February 1991): 63–72.

110. Ernest Gellner, *Thought and Change* (London: Weidenfeld and Nicolson, 1964).

111. Anthony D. Smith, "Nations and Their Pasts," The Warwick Debates (debate between Smith and Gellner at Warwick University, 1995), www2.lse.ac.uk/researchAndExpertise/units/gellner/WarwickDebate.

112. Eric J. Hobsbawm and Terence O. Ranger, eds., *The Invention of Tradition* (Cambridge: Cambridge University Press, 1983), 13.

113. Eric J. Hobsbawm, *Nations and Nationalism Since 1780: Programme, Myth, Reality* (Cambridge: Cambridge University Press, 1990), 165.

114. Anthony D. Smith, *The Nation in History: Historiographical Debates About Ethnicity and Nationalism* (Cambridge: Polity, 2000), 2–4. The United States was the obvious exception to the ethnosymbolist argument.

115. Smith, *National Identity*, vii.

116. Anderson, *Imagined Communities*, 10–11.

117. Ibid., 14.

118. In the Jewish tradition, the Talmud famously held (in Tractate *Pesachim*) that "there is no before and after in the Torah"; linear time was of no consequence, and a practice or commandment enunciated at some late date had in fact been "true" since the beginning of time and for all time. For observant Jews, Hebrew is "lashon hakodesh," the language of holiness, and the most pious will speak it only on the Sabbath.

119. Anderson, *Imagined Communities*, 26.

120. Ernest Gellner, *Nations and Nationalism* (Ithaca, N.Y.: Cornell University Press, 1983), 57.

121. Smith, *National Identity*, 17; italics added.

122. Ibid., vii.

123. Ibid., 50.

124. Ibid., 51.

125. Ibid., 25.

126. Ibid., 96.

127. Ibid., 160.

128. Maulana Karenga, "Us: Philosophy, Principles, and Program," http://us-organization.org/30th/ppp.html. Though dating from 1999, it repeats the original formulations of 1977.

129. Akeel Bilgrami, "What Is a Muslim? Fundamental Commitment and Cultural Identity," in *Identities*, ed. Kwame Anthony Appiah and Henry L. Gates, Jr. (Chicago: University of Chicago Press, 1995), 199.

130. This would change dramatically in Europe with the murders of anti-Muslim Dutch politician Pim Fortuyn in 2002 and Dutch filmmaker Theo Van Gogh in 2004, along with publication of Ayaan Hirsi Ali's *The Caged Virgin: An Emancipation Proclamation for Women and Islam* in 2004 and Caroline Fourest's attack on Tariq Ramadan, a Swiss Muslim intellectual calling for the modernization of Western Islam, whom she criticized as a dangerous fundamentalist in reformist clothing and as such a serious threat to Western liberal values. Caroline Fourest, *Brother Tariq: The Doublespeak of Tariq Ramadan* (New York: Encounter, 2008).

131. Samuel P. Huntington, *The Clash of Civilizations and the Remaking of World Order* (New York: Simon and Schuster, 1996), 21.

132. Ibid., 42–43.

133. Samuel P. Huntington, "The Clash of Civilizations?" *Foreign Affairs* 72, 3 (Summer 1993): 25. Huntington was clearly referring to the work of Henri Tajfel on social identity. See Chapter 9.

134. Ibid., 27.

135. Huntington, *Clash of Civilizations*, 130.

136. Samuel P. Huntington, *Who Are We? The Challenges to America's National Identity* (New York: Simon and Schuster, 2004), 25.

137. Most jarring at the moment of this writing (September 2014) is his claim that the likelihood of violent conflict between Russia and Ukraine over territory, particularly Crimea, is low ("Clash of Civilizations?" 38).

138. Thomas Meyer, *Identity Mania: Fundamentalism and the Politicization of Cultural Differences*, trans. Madhulika Reddy and Lew Hinchman (London: Zed, 2001), 3.

139. Ibid., 79 and passim.

140. Ibid., 13.

141. Ibid., 18.

142. Ibid., 94.

143. Amartya Sen, *Identity and Violence: The Illusion of Destiny* (New York: Norton, 2006), 22. See the discussion of identity economics in Chapter 9.

144. Ibid., 112.

Chapter 6. The Practical Politics of National and Multicultural Identity: Germany, France, Canada, and the United States, 1970–2010

1. Jean-François Bayart, interview, "Politique," *Le Monde*, June 11, 2009.

2. M. Rainer Lepsius, "Die unbestimmte Identität der Bundesrepublik," *Hochland* 60 (1967/68): 562–69.

3. Anton Peisl and Armin Mohler, *Die deutsche Neurose: Über der beschädigte Identität der Deutschen* (Frankfurt: Ullstein, 1980); Caspar von Schrenk-Notzing and Armin Mohler, eds., *Deutsche Identität* (Krefeld: Sinus Verlag, 1982); Peter Berglar, ed., *Deutsche Identität heute* (Mainz: Hase and

Koehler, 1983); Werner Weidenfeld, *Die Identität der Deutschen* (Munich: Bundeszentrale für politische Bildung, 1983); Konrad-Adenauer-Stiftung, ed., *Heimat und Nation: Zur Geschichte und Identität der Deutschen* (Mainz: Hase and Koehler, 1984); Friedrich-Naumann-Stiftung, Wolfgang Pollak, and Derek Rutter, *German Identity—Forty Years After Zero* (Sankt Augustin: Liberal Verlag, 1985).

4. P. Dehout, "Nationale Selbstfindung," *Nation Europa* 31, 4 (April 1981): 3–4. All translations from the German are mine unless otherwise noted.

5. Bernard Willms, "Die Zukunft der deutschen Identität," in Berglar, *Deutsche Identität heute*, 80–95.

6. Ernst Nolte, "Die Faschismus in seiner Epoche and seine weltpolitischen Konsequenzen bis zur Gegenwart," in ibid., 25–47.

7. Robert Pflüger, "Identität als Oktroi," in Von Schrenk-Notzing and Moller, *Deutsche Identität*, 50–58.

8. Weidenfeld, *Die Identität der Deutschen*, 9.

9. Ibid., 19.

10. Ibid., 21.

11. Ibid., 40.

12. Ibid., 42–43.

13. Wolfgang Gibowski, "A Democracy at Last: An Empirical Perspective of Germany's Political Culture," in Friedrich-Naumann-Stiftung, *German Identity—Forty Years After Zero*, 83–84.

14. Cornelia Schmalz-Jacobsen, "What Do We Mean by the German Fatherland," in Friedrich-Naumann-Stiftung, *German Identity—Forty Years After Zero*, 103–13.

15. Ralf Dahrendorf, "The Search For German Identity: An Illusory Endeavor?" in Friedrich-Nauman-Stiftung, *German Identity-Forty Years After Zero*, 134, 137.

16. Ibid., 133.

17. Ibid., 142.

18. For just a small sampling from the six years after reunification, see the footnotes on pages 4–5 of Konrad H. Jarausch, ed., *After Unity: Reconfiguring German Identities* (Providence, R.I.: Berghahn, 1997).

19. The famous *Historikerstreit*, the quarrel of historians in the late 1980s over the attempts of some conservative writers to offer revisionist accounts of Nazism, "master" the past and justify pride in a renewed nationalism, served as an overture to the reunification debate. As the title of Charles Maier's account indicates, it too was a battle over German national identity. See Charles Maier, *The Unmasterable Past: History, Holocaust and German National Identity* (Cambridge, Mass.: Harvard University Press, 1988).

20. "Die Erfindung der Deutschen: Wie wir wurden, was wir sind," *Der Spiegel*, Geschichte 1, 2007.

21. Konrad H. Jarausch, "A Struggle for Unity: Redefining National Identities," in *Shattered Past: Reconstructing German Histories*, ed. Konrad H. Jarausch and Michael Geyer (Princeton, N.J.: Princeton University Press, 2003), 240.

22. Jarausch, *After Unity*, 4–8.

23. Wolfgang Bergem, *Identitätsformationen in Deutschland* (Wiesbaden: VS Verlag für Sozialwissenschaften, 2005).

24. Gérard Noiriel, *À quoi sert "l'identité nationale"* (Marseille: Agone, 2007), 9.

25. Simone Bonnafous, *L'immigration prise aux mots: Les immigrés dans la presse au tournant des années 80* (Paris: Kimé, 1991), 272.

26. Noiriel, *À quoi sert*, 61.

27. Ibid., 72.

28. Alain Griotteray, *Les immigrés: Le choc* (Paris: Plon, 1984); Jacques-Yves le Gallou et le Club de l'Horloge, *La préférence nationale: Réponse à l'immigration* (Paris: A. Michel, 1985).

29. For a detailed discussion of the law and the issue see Rogers Brubaker, "'Être France, c'est se mérite,'" chap. 7 in *Citizenship and Nationhood in France and Germany* (Cambridge, Mass.: Harvard University Press, 1992).

30. Griotteray, *Les immigrés*, 175.

31. Brubaker, *Citizenship and Nationhood*, 149.

32. Ibid., 151ff.

33. Marceau Long, *Être français aujourd'hui et demain* (Paris: Union Générale d'Éditions, 1988).

34. *Ibid.*, 89–90.

35. Adrian Favell, *Philosophies of Integration: Immigration and the Idea of Citizenship in France and Britain* (New York: St. Martin's, 1998), 64.

36. Jean-Pierre Moulin, "Identité française," in *Enquête sur la France multiraciale* (Paris: Calman-Lévy, 1985), 237; capitals in original.

37. Ibid.

38. Gérard Noiriel, *The French Melting Pot: Immigration, Citizenship, and National Identity*, trans. Geoffroy de Laforcade (Minneapolis: University of Minnesota Press, 1996), 5–6, 189–90, 277.

39. Ibid., 250.

40. Fernand Braudel, *La Méditerranée et le monde méditerranéen à l'époque de Philippe II* (Paris: Colin, 1949).

41. Fernand Braudel, *L'identité de la France*, vol. 3, *Espace et histoire* (Paris: Flammarion, 1990 [1986]), 18.

42. Ibid.; my translation.

43. Ibid., 19.

44. Noiriel, *The French Melting Pot*, 40.

45. Ibid., 30.

46. Nikolas Sarkozy campaign speech of March 9, 2007, in ibid., 87.

47. Ibid., 142.

48. Ibid., 210.

49. Bonnafous, *L'immigration prise aux mots*, 273.

50. Noiriel, *À quoi sert*, 103.

51. Pierre Nora, *Présent, nation, mémoire* (Paris: Gallimard, 2011), 13, 20.

52. Anne-Marie Thiesse, *La création des identités nationales: Europe XVIIIe–XXe siècle* (Paris: Seuil, 1999).

53. Anne-Marie Thiesse, *Faire les français: Quelle identité nationale?* (Paris: Stock, 2010), 12.

54. This was one of the reasons offered by the political philosopher Pierre Manent in his conversation with the author for his concern with the threat to France's national identity.

55. Thiesse, *Faire les français*, 191–92.

56. Jean-François Bayart, "Il n'y a pas d'identité française," *Le Monde*, June 11, 2009.

57. "Merkel Says German Multicultural Society Has Failed," *BBC News*, Europe, October 17, 2010.

58. Minister of Public Works and Government Services, Canada, 2010.

59. Another early concern in defining Canadian identity was its relation to the United States. Probably the earliest use of the word identity in the Canadian context was in the title of a book written by a Canadian academic for an American audience intended to differentiate Canada from the United States. See W. L. Morton, *The Canadian Identity* (Madison: University of Wisconsin Press, 1961).

60. Canada, Royal Commission on Bilingualism and Biculturalism, *Report of the Royal Commission on Bilingualism and Biculturalism*, Privy Council Office, 1967–1970, xxi, www. lac-bac.gr.ca.

61. Ibid., xxii–xxiv.

62. Ibid., xxxi. Italics added.

63. Ibid., xxxviii.

64. Ibid., xxxi.

65. For more detail on this, see Michael Temelini, "Multicultural Rights, Multicultural Virtues: A History of Multiculturalism in Canada," in *Multiculturalism and the Canadian Constitution*, ed. Stephen Tierney (Vancouver: UBC Press, 2007), 48–49.

66. Trudeau, Pierre Elliott, "Multiculturalism," speech delivered to the House of Commons accepting the Report of the Royal Commission on Bilingualism and Biculturalism, October 8, 1971, http://www.canadahistory.com/sections/documents/.

67. Canada, Constitution Act, 1982, Part 1, Canadian Charter of Rights and Freedoms, www. laws-lois.justice.gc.ca/eng/const/page-15.html.

68. Sabine Dierke, "Multikulti: The German Debate on Multiculturalism," *German Studies Review* 17, 3 (October 1994): 516.

69. Douglas B. Klusmeyer and Demetrios G. Papademetriou, *Immigration Policy in the Federal Republic of Germany: Negotiating Membership and Remaking the Nation* (New York: Berghahn, 2009), 45.

70. Brett Klopp, *German Multiculturalism: Immigrant Integration and the Transformation of Citizenship* (Westport, Conn.: Praeger, 2002), 7.

71. Dierke, "Multikulti," 522.

72. Klusmeyer and Papademetriou, *Immigration Policy*, 231–32.

73. Will Kymlicka, "The Canadian Model of Diversity in a Comparative Perspective," in Tierney, *Multiculturalism and the Canadian Constitution*, 74.

74. New York State Special Task Force on Equity and Excellence in Education, *A Curriculum of Inclusion: Report of the Commissioner's Task Force on Minorities: Equity and Excellence* (July 1969), http://eric.ed.gov/?id = ED338535.

75. Arthur Schlesinger, Jr., *The Disuniting of America: Reflections on a Multicultural Society* (New York: Norton, 1991), 74.

76. Ibid., 113.

77. Ibid., 118.

78. Ibid., 122.

79. Samuel P. Huntington, *Who Are We? The Challenges to America's National Identity* (New York: Simon and Schuster, 2004), 68–69.

80. Ibid., 171.

81. UNESCO, Universal Declaration on Cultural Diversity, November 2, 2001, Article 4.

Chapter 7. The Problem of Collective Identity in Liberal Democracy

1. Christopher R. Adamson, Peter C. Findlay, Michael K. Oliver, and Janet Solberg, "The Unpublished Research of the Royal Commission on Bilingualism and Biculturalism," *Canadian Journal of Political Science* 7, 4 (December 1974): 709–20.

2. Michael J. Sandel, *Liberalism and the Limits of Justice*, 2nd ed. (Cambridge, Mass.: Harvard University Press, 1998 [1982]), 19, 22.

3. Charles Taylor, *Sources of the Self: The Making of the Modern Identity* (Cambridge, Mass.: Harvard University Press, 1989), 171–72.

4. Alasdair MacIntyre, *After Virtue: A Study in Moral Theory* (Notre Dame, Ind.: University of Notre Dame Press, 1981), 30–31.

5. Ibid., 44–45. His critique of Kierkegaardian decisionism argued that Kierkegaard cannot with consistency base the authority of ethical principle on a choice between the aesthetic and the ethical that by Kierkegaard's own insistence is purely arbitrary.

6. Sandel, *Liberalism*, 80.

7. Ibid., 132, 150. Italics in original.

8. Taylor, *Sources of the Self*, 27–31; italics added.

9. MacIntyre, *After Virtue*, 201.

10. Ibid., 197.

11. See Introduction, note 33.

12. MacIntyre, *After Virtue*, 202.

13. This is more than a parallel with, it is the same analysis in different words as Heidegger's explication of temporality.

14. MacIntyre, *After Virtue*, 205.

Notes to Pages 270–284

15. MacIntyre was a one-time Trotskyite, Taylor is a long-time socialist in the Canadian social-democratic tradition. In his valedictory speech on his graduation from Brandeis University in 1975, Sandel lamented the loss of the activist spirit of the 1960s, with its notion of citizenship wedded to social engagement and reform.

16. MacIntyre, *After Virtue*, 244.

17. Anthony Giddens, *Modernity and Self-Identity: Self and Society in the Late Modern Age* (Stanford, Calif.: Stanford University Press, 1991).

18. Ibid., 54, 221–23.

19. Sandel, *Liberalism*, 136–37.

20. Ibid., 143; italics added.

21. John Gray, *Two Faces of Liberalism* (New York: New Press, 2000), 121.

22. Gray, for example, argued that liberalism must eschew any claim to base itself on the superiority of individualist values and define itself as a politics of toleration aiming solely at social peace between differing conceptions of the good. See also William A. Galston, *Liberal Pluralism: The Implications of Value Pluralism for Political Theory and Practice* (Cambridge: Cambridge University Press, 2002).

23. Chandran Kukathas, "Are There Any Cultural Rights?" *Political Theory* 20, 1 (February 1992): 120.

24. Bhikhu Parekh, *Rethinking Multiculturalism: Cultural Diversity and Political Theory* (Cambridge, Mass.: Harvard University Press, 2000), 139.

25. Ibid., 110.

26. Kwame Anthony Appiah, *The Ethics of Identity* (Princeton, N.J.: Princeton University Press, 2005), 73–79.

27. Parekh, *Rethinking Multiculturalism*, 340.

28. Avishai Margalit and Moshe Halbertal, "Liberalism and the Right to Culture," *Social Research* 61, 3 (Fall 1994): 491.

29. Ibid., 502, 506.

30. Ibid., 491.

31. Ibid., 492.

32. Ibid., 500.

33. Avishai Margalit and Joseph Raz, "National Self-Determination," *Journal of Philosophy* 87, 9 (September 1990): 444.

34. Ibid., 446–47.

35. Ibid., 456; italics added.

36. At the moment of this writing (August 2015), with ultra-Orthodox parties back in the governing coalition, the ultimate fate of the ruling is in question. Perhaps an even more intractable example of the problem is the inevitable alienation of the Israeli Arab population from the national anthem Hatikvah, which speaks of the eternal hope of the Jewish people to be free in its own homeland.

37. Margalit and Halbertal, "Liberalism and the Right to Culture," 508.

38. See on this Amy Gutmann, *Identity in Democracy* (Princeton, N.J.: Princeton University Press, 2003), 61, and Appiah, *Ethics of Identity*.

39. Will Kymlicka, *Liberalism, Community and Culture* (Oxford: Clarendon, 1989), 3–4.

40. Ibid., 166.

41. Ibid., 175.

42. Ibid., 192.

43. Will Kymlicka, *Multicultural Citizenship: A Liberal Theory of Minority Rights* (Oxford: Clarendon, 1995), 37. In fact his position on particular issues was less clear-cut. While he acknowledged the restrictions on individual liberties inherent in the collective ownership of tribal lands by indigenous people, he emphasized the importance of such ownership for the preservation of indigenous culture and identity.

44. Ibid., 76.

45. Ibid., 13.

46. Ibid., 14.

47. Ibid., 115.

48. Until 2005 the province of Ontario permitted Orthodox Jews to settle civil matters such as divorce in rabbinic courts if all parties consented. When Muslims requested the same privilege for sharia courts, the government banned all religious arbitration.

49. Charles Taylor, "The Politics of Recognition," in Charles Taylor, *Multiculturalism: Examining the Politics of Recognition*, ed. Amy Gutmann (Princeton, N.J.: Princeton University Press, 1994), 25. Italics in original.

50. Ibid., 28.

51. For a much more extended account of the relationship between the two, see Axel Honneth, *The Struggle for Recognition: The Moral Grammar of Social Conflicts*, trans. Joel Anderson (Cambridge, Mass.: MIT Press, 1995).

52. Taylor's language often suggests a psychological perspective absent not only in Hegel but also in Mead. It evokes the idea of narcissistic needs for self-esteem and the need for empathy to foster it that are at the center of Heinz Kohut's self-psychology.

53. C. Taylor, "The Politics of Recognition," 38.

54. Ibid., 59.

55. Ibid., 62.

56. For an extensive theoretical discussion of the importance of the political community as a collective identity see Jürgen Habermas, *Between Facts and Norms: Contributions to a Discourse Theory of Law and Democracy*, trans. William Rehg (Cambridge, Mass.: MIT Press, 1998), 281–83 and *passim*.

57. Jürgen Habermas, "Struggles for Recognition" in Taylor, *Multiculturalism*, 119, 125.

58. Ibid., 113. Italics added.

59. Ibid., 117.

60. John Rawls, *Political Liberalism* (New York: Columbia University Press, 2005 [1993]), 30–31; italics added.

61. Ibid., 49.

62. Ibid., 61.

63. Ibid., 38.

64. Ibid., 140.

65. See on this issue Michael Kenny's discussion in his *The Politics of Identity: Liberal Political Theory and the Dilemmas of Difference* (Cambridge: Polity, 2004), chap. 3.

66. Rawls, *Political Liberalism*, 214.

67. Appiah, *Ethics of Identity*, 83–99.

68. Gutmann, *Identity in Democracy*, 2–3.

69. Ibid., 15; italics in original.

70. Ibid., 10.

71. Ibid., 4.

72. Ibid., 8.

73. Ibid., 7–8.

74. Ibid., 70.

75. Ibid., 77.

76. Susan Moller Okin, *Is Multiculturalism Bad for Women?* ed. Joshua Cohen, Matthew Howard, and Martha C. Nussbaum (Princeton, N.J.: Princeton University Press, 1999).

77. Ibid., 171.

78. The cited phrase refers to a policy under the first administration of President George W. Bush, 2000–2004.

79. Ibid., 177.

80. Ibid., 132.

81. Appiah, *Ethics of Identity*, 103–4.

82. See Chapter 11.

Chapter 8. The Contradictions of Postmodern Identity

Epigraphs: Michel Foucault, "Nietzsche, Genealogy, History," in *Language, Counter-Nemory, Practice*, ed. Donald F. Bouchard, trans. Bouchard and Sherry Simon (Ithaca, N.Y.: Cornell University Press, 1977), 162; Zygmunt Bauman, "From Pilgrim to Tourist—or a Short History of Identity," in *Questions of Cultural Identity*, ed. Stuart Hall and Paul du Gay (Los Angeles: Sage, 1996), 18.

1. The definitions of, and the relationship between, poststructuralism and postmodernism are highly problematic. Poststructuralism is the narrower term, denoting primarily the work of Lacan, Derrida, and Foucault, a grouping that has itself been challenged by intellectual historians because of important differences among the three. Postmodernism may have specific reference to the ideas of Jean-François Lyotard and Jean Baudrillard, but it also has a broader and more diffuse sense connoting a critique of closed systems of thought purportedly explaining all of reality, or fixed aesthetic norms and forms purporting to define or embody objective Beauty. These are held to be untenable, to be replaced by local and partial truths, fragments, eclectic mixes, and irony. Postmodernism is thus often taken as the more general and inclusive term. I use postmodernism to refer to the Weltanschauung that includes poststructuralism. The relevant literature is vast. For an informative and amusing discussion of some of these terminological issues, see Kevin Hart, *Postmodernism: A Beginner's Guide* (Oxford: Oneworld, 2004), chap. 1.

2. The other part of the background is the rich context of philosophical debate on the meaning and legacy of Husserl's phenomenology and Heidegger's existentialism in postwar France, through which the issues of ideology were mediated, in the case of Derrida and Foucault. For how philosophy and ideology critique intersected in Derrida's early work, see Peter E. Gordon, "Hammer Without a Master: French Phenomenology and the Origins of Deconstruction (Or, How Derrida Read Heidegger)," in *Histories of Postmodernism*, ed. Mark Bevir, Jill Hargis, and Sara Rushing (New York: Routledge, 2007), 103–30; and Edward Baring, *The Young Derrida and French Philosophy, 1945–1968* (Cambridge: Cambridge University Press, 2011).

3. For an overview and fine analysis of these developments, see Richard Wolin, "From the 'Death of Man' to Human Rights: The Paradigm Change in French Intellectual Life," in Bevir, Hargis, and Rushing, *Histories of Postmodernism*, 171–92.

4. It was largely through the work of the French anthropologist Claude Lévi-Strauss, the "father" of structuralism in France, that they became familiar with it and it was his version that they attacked, though much influenced by it; hence *post*structuralism. See François Dosse, *History of Structuralism*, vol. 1, *The Rising Sign, 1945–66*, trans. Deborah Glassman (Minneapolis: University of Minnesota Press, 1997), chap. 2. Dosse's two-volume history is an indispensable introduction to both structuralism and poststructuralism.

5. Jacques Lacan, *Écrits: A Selection*, trans. Alan Sheridan (New York: Norton, 1977 [1966]), 1–7; Jacques Lacan, "Le complexe, facteur concret de la psychologie familiale," in *Encyclopédie française*, vol. 8, *La vie mentale*, ed. Henri Wallon (Paris: Société Nouvelle de l'Encyclopédie Française, 1938), 40.

6. Lacan, "The Function and Field of Speech and Language in Psychoanalysis," in *Écrits*, 103, 106.

7. Lacan, "The Signification of the Phallus," in ibid., 287.

8. Ibid., 289; italics in original.

9. Lacan, "The Function and Field of Speech," 66.

10. Ibid., 67.

11. Ibid., 68

12. Ibid., 81.

13. This is not quite accurate, since for Heidegger the "authentic resolve" enabled Dasein to become the active master, with others of its generation, of its collective destiny. For Lacan mastery meant breaking the prison house of conventional significations, on the model of the Surrealists.

14. Valid also as an intuition about Derrida's choice of name for his method; he said that he invented it in homage to the Heideggerian terms *Destruktion* and *Abbau*, "unbuild." Cited in Gordon, "Hammer Without a Master," 115.

15. Jacques Derrida, *Of Grammatology*, trans. Gayatri Chakravorty Spivak (Baltimore: Johns Hopkins University Press, 1997 [1967]), 17.

16. Ibid., 20.

17. Ibid., 70.

18. Ibid., 63.

19. Ibid., 89.

20. Ibid., 7.

21. Ibid.

22. Ibid., 150.

23. Foucault, "Nietzsche, Genealogy, History," 162.

24. Michel Foucault, *The History of Sexuality*, vol. 1, *An Introduction*, trans. Robert Hurley (New York: Vintage, 1990 [1976]).

25. Michel Foucault, *Discipline and Punish: The Birth of the Prison*, trans. Alan Sheridan (New York: Vintage, 1979 [1975]), 36–37.

26. Ibid., 253; italics added.

27. Ibid., 99.

28. Ibid., 160.

29. Ibid., 194.

30. Michel Foucault, "The Subject and Power," in *The Essential Works of Michel Foucault, 1954–1984*, ed. Paul Rabinow, vol. 3, *Power*, ed. James D. Faubion (New York: New Press, 2000), 330.

31. Although in the realm of sexuality Foucault posited a specific way of being that was authentic and free, if not exactly "individualistic." Sadomasochism is not a normalizing discipline with external rules that strictly regulate proper sexual behavior but a play of "bodies and pleasures" in which each participant can experiment freely with all the possible variants of domination and submission. Foucault's attempted justification of sadomasochism is a most ingenious effort to incorporate these opposites of freedom and equality into the tradition of autonomy.

32. Julia Kristeva was born in Bulgaria and only moved to France as a young adult, but her cultural formation was French and she writes in French.

33. The first English translations appeared in Elaine Marks and Isabelle de Courtivron, eds., *New French Feminisms* (Amherst: University of Massachusetts Press, 1980).

34. See Christine Delphy, "The Invention of French Feminism: An Essential Move," in *Another Look, Another Woman: Retranslations of French Feminism*, Yale French Studies 87 (New Haven, Conn.: Yale University Press, 1995), 190–221; Claire G. Moses, "Made in America: 'French Feminism' in Academia," in *Disciplining Feminism? The Future of Women's Studies*, special issue, *Feminist Studies* 24, 2 (Summer 1998): 241–74.

35. Nancy Fraser, "Introduction" to *Revaluing French Feminism: Critical Essays on Difference, Agency, and Culture*, ed. Nancy Fraser and Sandra. L. Bartky (Bloomington: Indiana University Press, 1992), 2.

36. Elizabeth V. Spelman does not mention the French writers in her influential attack on essentialism, *Inessential Woman: Problems of Exclusion in Feminist Thought* (Boston: Beacon, 1988). The essentialist error she attacks is most prominently represented by nonpostmodernists like Nancy Chodorow and Carol Gilligan.

37. Jacques Lacan, "God and Women's *jouissance*," in *On Feminine Sexuality: The Limits of Love and Knowledge*, Book 20, *Encore 1972–1973*, trans. Bruce Fink, Seminar of Jacques Lacan (New York: Norton, 1999 [1975]), 71, 76.

38. Lacan, "A Love Letter," in ibid., 83.

39. Lacan, "God," in ibid., 70.

40. The French word slides from sexual enjoyment to sexual climax to, in Lacan's case, transcendent sexual ecstasy.

41. Lacan, "God," 72.

42. Ibid.

43. Lacan, "A Love Letter," 83.

44. Lacan, "God," 76.

45. Ibid., 77.

46. Though with Neo-Platonic and Christian antecedents this is above all the heart of the Romantic trope of woman. See my *Impossible Individuality: Romanticism, Revolution, and the Origins of Modern Selfhood, 1787–1802* (Princeton, N.J.: Princeton University Press, 1992).

47. Jacques Derrida, *Spurs: Nietzsche's Styles*, trans. Barbara Harlow (Chicago: University of Chicago Press, 1979), 67.

48. Ibid., 49.

49. Ibid., 109.

50. Ibid., 51, 101.

51. This interpretation is hardly universally accepted by Irigaray's commentators. It was the subject of heated contestation during the essentialism debate. On the "essentialist" side, Elizabeth Gross claimed that "Irigaray's concern throughout all her works is the articulation of a femininity, an identity or subjectivity which is women's." Elizabeth Gross, "Philosophy, Subjectivity and the Body: Kristeva and Irigaray," in *Feminist Challenges: Social and Political Theory*, ed. Carol Pateman and Elizabeth Gross (Boston: Northeastern University Press, 1987), 134. The opposite view is epitomized in the title of the essay by Naomi Schor, "This Essentialism Which Is Not One: Coming to Grips with Irigaray," in *The Essential Difference*, ed. Naomi Schor and Elizabeth Weed (Bloomington: Indiana University Press, 1994), 40–62. For a more detailed, if not quite comprehensive review of the controversy, see Diana Fuss, "Luce Irigaray's Language of Essence," in her *Essentially Speaking: Feminism, Nature and Difference* (New York: Routledge, 1989), 55–72. I find the antiessentialist view, including Fuss's more nuanced interpretation of Irigaray's essentialism as metonymical and strategic, unpersuasive in view of the indelible centrality of the body to Irigaray's concept of language, and hence identity.

52. Luce Irigaray, *This Sex Which Is Not One*, trans. Catherine Porter (Ithaca, N.Y.: Cornell University Press, 1985 [1977]), 68.

53. Irigaray, "The Power of Discourse," in ibid., 74; italics in original.

54. Irigaray, "Questions," in ibid., 134.

55. Ibid., 161.

56. Ibid., 134.

57. Maurice Merleau-Ponty, *Phenomenology of Perception*, trans. Colin Smith (London: Routledge, 1962); Merleau-Ponty, *The Structure of Behavior*, trans. Alden L. Fisher (Boston: Beacon, 1963).

58. Irigaray, *This Sex Which Is Not One*, 26; italics in original.

59. Ibid., 29; italics in original.

60. Ibid., 31.

61. Julia Kristeva, "From One Identity to an Other," in *French Feminism Reader*, ed. Kelly Oliver (New York: Rowman and Littlefield, 2000), 161, 162.

62. Kristeva, "Woman's Time," in ibid., 197.

63. Ibid., 187.

64. Ibid., 197.

65. Toril Moi, *Sexual/Textual Politics: Feminist Literary Theory* (London: Methuen, 1985), 139.

66. Elizabeth Grosz, "Sexual Difference and the Problem of Essentialism," in Schor and Weed, *The Essential Difference*, 84.

67. Fuss, *Essentially Speaking*, 2–3. The essentialist-social construction debate was not limited to feminism. See for example Edward Stein, ed., *Forms of Desire: Sexual Orientation and the Social Constructionist Controversy* (New York: Routledge, 1992).

68. Donna Haraway, "A Manifesto for Cyborgs," in *The Postmodern Turn: New Perspectives on Social Theory*, ed. Steven Seidman (Cambridge: Cambridge University Press, 1994), 83.

69. Ibid., 91.

70. Ibid., 94.

71. Ibid., 102.

72. Ibid., 84.

73. Norma Alarcon, "The Theoretical Subject(s) of *This Bridge Called My Back* and Anglo-American Feminism," in Seidman, *The Postmodern Turn*, 150.

74. Judith Butler, "Preface 1990," in *Gender Trouble: Feminism and the Subversion of Identity* (New York: Routledge, 1999), xxix.

75. Ibid., 11.

76. Ibid., 23.

77. The wording in context is "the heterosexualization of desire."

78. Ibid.

79. Ibid., 33.

80. Judith Butler, "For a Careful Reading," in *Feminist Contentions: A Philosophical Exchange*, ed. Linda Nicholson (New York: Routledge, 1995), 134.

81. Butler, *Gender Trouble*, xiv–xv.

82. Ibid., 86.

83. Ibid., 90.

84. Ibid., xv.

85. Butler's attempt to offer "a psychoanalytic criticism of Foucault" in *The Psychic Life of Power* (Stanford, Calif.: Stanford University Press, 1997) added little to the psychoanalytic account she had already given in *Gender Trouble*; even after its publication she wrote, "I continue to think that it is a significant theoretical mistake to take the 'internality' of the psychic world for granted" (*Gender Trouble*, xv). It is a striking feature of virtually all postmodernist discussion of behavior that it ignored Anglo-American philosophy of action, with its analyses of the role of intention, desire, and belief in describing and explaining human action as distinct from physically caused behavior. Of particular relevance to Butler's discussion is Richard Wollheim's argument that the psychoanalytic idea of unconsciously motivated behavior can be understood—indeed, if empirical sense is to be made of it must be understood—on the desire-belief model of action. See Richard Wollheim, *Freud* (Cambridge: Cambridge University Press, 1981).

86. Foucault, *History of Sexuality*, vol. 1, 42.

87. Jeffrey Weeks, *Coming Out: Homosexual Politics in Britain from the Nineteenth Century to the Present* (London: Quartet, 1977), 3.

88. Steven Epstein, "Gay Politics, Ethnic Identity: The Limits of Social Construction," in Stein, *Forms of Desire*, 243.

89. Henry Louis Gates, Jr., ed., *"Race," Writing, and Difference* (Chicago: University of Chicago Press, 1986), 5–6.

90. Jacques Derrida, "Racism's Last Word," in ibid., 333.

91. Jacques Derrida, "But Beyond . . . ," in ibid., 364.

92. Barbara Johnson, "Thresholds of Difference: Structures of Address in Zora Neale Hurston," in ibid., 319–20.

93. Ibid., 328.

94. Cornel West, "The New Cultural Politics of Difference," in Seidman, *The Postmodern Turn*, 74.

95. Homi K. Bhabha, *The Location of Culture*, 2nd ed. (London: Routledge, 2004).

96. Ibid., 63–64.

97. Ibid.; italics added.

98. Ibid., 73.

99. Ibid., 5.

100. Ibid., 256.

101. Thorsten Veblen, "The Intellectual Pre-Eminence of Jews in Europe," *Political Science Quarterly* 34, 1 (March 1919): 33–42.

102. Ibid., 35.

103. Ernesto Laclau and Chantal Mouffe, *Hegemony and Socialist Strategy: Towards a Radical Democratic Politics*, 2nd ed. (London: Verso, 2001 [1985]), 4.

104. Ibid., 2.

105. Ibid., 67.

106. Ibid., 85.

107. Ibid., 116.

108. Ibid., 118.

109. Ibid., 153.

110. Ibid., 3.

111. In *The Politics of Identity*, Stanley Aronowitz seconded Laclau and Mouffe's poststructura-list critique of existing Marxist theory, but claimed that it offered at best a democratic rather than truly socialist program. The latter must rely on the "broad social vision" of radical unions in the new social movements in countries like Brazil and South Africa, in other words, the traditional identity of the working class as the bearers of the socialist vision. *The Politics of Identity: Class, Culture, Social Movements* (New York: Psychology Press, 1992), 268–70.

112. Konrad H. Jarausch, ed., *After Unity: Reconfiguring German Identities* (Providence, R.I.: Berghahn, 1997), 6.

113. Ibid., 5.

114. Ibid., 7.

115. Fuss, *Essentially Speaking*, 102.

116. Jane Gallop, *The Daughter's Seduction: Feminism and Psychoanalysis* (Ithaca, N.Y.: Cornell University Press, 1982), xii.

117. Elaine Marks, "Feminism's Wake," in *On Feminine Writing: A Boundary 2 Symposium*, special issue, *Boundary 2*, 12, 2 (Winter 1984): 110.

118. Marks, "Feminism's Wake," 8.

119. Ibid., 40.

120. Butler, *Gender Trouble*, 174. Ironically, the psychological explanation she gave in *The Psychic Life of Power* for why people cling to identities that are injurious to them only heightened the mystery of rebellion. They do so out of narcissism, the need to cling to the identity that constitutes them, however negative.

121. Ibid., 175.

122. This was the crux of a sharp confrontation between Butler and the critical theorist Seyla Benhabib. See their respective essays in Seyla Benhabib et al., *Feminist Contentions: A Philosophical Exchange* (New York: Routledge, 1995).

123. See the notorious attack on Butler by Martha C. Nussbaum, "The Professor of Parody," *New Republic*, February 22, 1999.

124. Gayatri Chakravorty Spivak, "Criticism, Feminism and the Institution, Interview with Elizabeth Grosz," in Gayatri Chakravorty Spivak, *The Post-Colonial Critic: Interviews, Strategies, Dialogues*, ed. Sarah Harasym (New York: Routledge, 1990), 11.

125. Gayatri Chakravorty Spivak, *In Other Worlds: Essays in Cultural Politics* (New York: Methuen, 1987), 205. Italics in original.

126. Gayatri Chakravorty Spivak, "In a Word. Interview, with Elizabeth Rooney," *Differences* 1, 2 (Summer 1989):124–54.

127. Denise Riley, *"Am I That Name?" Feminism and the Category of "Women" in History* (Minneapolis: University of Minnesota Press, 1988), 113.

128. Stuart Hall, "Introduction: Who Needs Identity?" in *Questions of Cultural Identity*, ed. Stuart Hall and Paul du Gay (London: Sage, 1996), 2.

129. The reference is to the Marxist theorist Louis Althusser's concept of "interpellation" according to which we are come into social existence by being "hailed" or addressed as instances of specific social categories.

130. Hall, *Questions of Cultural Identity*, 6.

131. Cited in ibid., 16.

132. This was even truer of Joan Wallach Scott's quasi-psychoanalytic theory of the idea of unified female identity in feminist movements as fantasy. Arguing that collective identities are fictions invented for political mobilization, she insisted nevertheless that they take on psychic reality.

Because fantasy as a "setting for desire. . . . reproduces and masks conflict . . . [and] operates as a (tightly condensed) narrative" it is a "formal mechanism" for the articulation of scenarios of female power that are specific in detail yet transcend historical specificity. *The Fantasy of Feminist History* (Durham, N.C.: Duke University Press, 2011), 45–67.

133. William E. Connolly, *Identity/Difference: Democratic Negotiations of Political Paradox* (Minneapolis: University of Minnesota Press, 1991), 158.

134. Ibid., 76. My italics for "am."

135. Ibid., xix, 47.

136. Ibid., 158.

137. Ibid., xix.

138. Ibid., 46; italics added.

139. Ibid., xxii.

140. Ibid., 176.

141. Ibid., 64.

142. Ibid., ix.

143. Ibid., 160; italics in original.

144. Ibid., 170.

145. Ibid., 179.

146. Christine Battersby, *The Phenomenal Woman: Feminist Metaphysics and the Patterns of Identity* (New York: Routledge, 1998), 31.

147. Ibid., 38.

148. Ibid., 8–9, 38–39.

149. Ibid., 57.

150. Susan J. Hekman, *Private Selves, Public Identities: Reconsidering Identity Politics* (University Park: Pennsylvania State University Press, 2005), 17.

151. Lynne Layton, *Who's That Boy? Who's That Girl: Clinical Practice Meets Postmodern Gender Theory* (Hilldale, N.J.: Analytic Press, 2004), 124.

152. James M. Glass, *Shattered Selves: Multiple Personality in a Postmodern World* (Ithaca, N.Y.: Cornell University Press, 1993).

153. Hekman, *Private Selves*, 30.

154. Ibid., 22, 26.

155. Ibid., 29.

156. Ibid., 7.

157. Ibid., 87.

158. Ibid., 106.

159. On this issue see the important essays in *The Multiple Self*, ed. Jon Elster (Cambridge: Cambridge University Press, 1986), which deal with issues of self-division such as self-deception and internal conflicts of interest.

160. For all these points, see Paula M. L. Moya, "Postmodernism, 'Realism,' and the Politics of Identity," in *Reclaiming Identity: Realist Theory and the Predicament of Postmodernism*, ed. Paula M. L. Moya and Michael R. Hames-Garcia (Berkeley: University of California Press, 2000), 67–101.

161. Ibid., 79.

162. Ibid., 86.

163. Ibid., 8; italics added.

164. An example of this kind of thinking from a less theoretically self-conscious source is Beverly Daniel Tatum's book *"Why Are All the Black Kids Sitting Together in the Cafeteria?" and Other Conversations About Race* (New York: Basic, 2003 [1997]). As she demonstrates, for black students, their racial identity as reflected back to them in the attention paid to it by the majority white society is a basic fact of their everyday lives.

165. Linda Martín Alcoff, *Visible Identities: Race, Gender, and the Self* (Oxford: Oxford University Press, 2006).

166. Ibid., 149.

167. Ibid., 172; italics in original.

168. Ibid., 174.

169. Ibid., 176.

170. Ibid., 192.

Chapter 9. Identity Transforms the Social Sciences

1. Claude Lévi-Strauss, *L'identité: Séminaire interdisciplinaire dirigé par Claude Lévi-Strauss au Collège de France, 1974–1975* (Paris: Presses Universitaires de France, 1977).

2. Odo Marquard and Karlheinz Stierle, eds., *Identität*, Poetik und Hermeneutik 8 (Munich: Wilhelm Fink, 1979). The conference took place in 1976.

3. Personal communication from Andreas Wirsching, director of the Institute for Contemporary History in Munich.

4. Richard Jenkins, *Social Identity*, 3rd ed. (London: Routledge, 2008 [1996]), 46.

5. Margaret R. Somers and Gloria D. Gibson, "Reclaiming the Epistemological 'Other': Narrative and the Social Constitution of Identity," in *Social Theory and the Politics of Identity*, ed. Craig Calhoun (Oxford: Blackwell, 1994), 45–52.

6. Henri Tajfel, *Human Groups and Social Categories: Studies in Social Psychology* (Cambridge: Cambridge University Press, 1981), 1.

7. Ibid., 31; italics in original.

8. Ibid.

9. Ibid., 255.

10. Ibid., 21.

11. Ibid., 22.

12. Ibid., 6.

13. For a more detailed description, see the account Tajfel published in "Experiments in Intergroup Discrimination," *Scientific American* 233, 5 (1970): 96–102.

14. Tajfel, *Human Groups*, 234.

15. Ibid., 236.

16. Ibid., 241.

17. Ibid., 255–56. His sociological claims referred to the work of Berger and Luckmann and his account of the strategies an individual might use with regard to dissatisfaction with his group relied on Albert O. Hirschman's *Exit, Voice and Loyalty: Response to Decline in Firms, Organizations and States*, 2nd ed. (Cambridge, Mass: Harvard University Press, 1972).

18. Tajfel, *Human Groups*, 258.

19. Ibid., 273.

20. Ibid., 276.

21. Above all the work of George J. McCall and J. L. Simmons, *Identities and Interactions: An Examination of Human Associations in Everyday Life* (New York: Free Press, 1966) and Sheldon Stryker, *Symbolic Interactionism: A Social Structural Version* (Caldwell, N.J.: Blackburn, 2002 [1980]).

22. Peter J. Burke and Jan E. Stets, *Identity Theory* (Oxford: Oxford University Press, 2009).

23. Ibid., 7.

24. George J. McCall and J. L. Simmons first introduced the term "role/identity." McCall and Simmons, *Identities and Interactions*, 13, and passim.

25. Burke and Stets, *Identity Theory*, 25. See Stryker, *Symbolic Interactionism*, 60ff.

26. Burke and Stets, *Identity Theory*, 3.

27. Ibid., 13.

28. See Chapter 4.

29. Burke and Stets, *Identity Theory*, 13.

30. Ibid., 79ff.

31. Ibid., chap. 6, "Bases of Identities: Role, Group and Person."

32. Jenkins, *Social Identity*, 200.

33. Ibid., 13.

34. Ibid., 73.

35. Ibid., 75.

36. Ibid., 17. This of course marks the difference in usage with Tajfel.

37. Ibid., 83.

38. Ibid., 17.

39. Somers and Gibson, "Reclaiming the Epistemological Other," 61.

40. Ibid., 62–63.

41. Ibid., 65.

42. Ibid., 71–72.

43. Alberto Melucci, *Nomads of the Present: Social Movements and Individual Needs in Contemporary Society* (London: Hutchinson Radius, 1989), an expanded translation of the Italian original published in 1982, 177.

44. Hank Johnston, Enrique Laraña, and Joseph R. Gusfield, "Identities, Grievances and New Social Movements," in *New Social Movements: From Ideology to Identity*, ed. Enrique Laraña, Hank Johnston, and Joseph R. Gusfield (Philadelphia: Temple University Press, 1994), 7, 26.

45. Nelson A. Pichardo, "New Social Movements: A Critical Review," *Annual Review of Sociology* 23 (1997): 414.

46. Melucci, *Nomads of the Present*, 180–233,The biographical information is in an interview with Melucci conducted in 1988 by John Keene and Paul Mier.

47. Johnston, Laraña, and Gusfield, "Identities, Grievances, and New Social Movements," 6–8.

48. Pichardo, "New Social Movements," 413.

49. Johnston, Laraña, and Gusfield, "Identities, Grievances, and New Social Movements," 30.

50. Ibid., 28.

51. Ibid., 12.

52. Donatella della Porta and Mario Diani, *Social Movements: An Introduction*, 2nd ed. (Oxford: Blackwell, 2006 [1998]), 92.

53. Ibid., 93.

54. Alberto Melucci, "A Strange Kind of Newness: What's 'New' in New Social Movements?" in Laraña, Johnston, and Gusfield, *New Social Movements*, 111.

55. Ibid., 112.

56. Ibid., 109.

57. Ibid., 112.

58. Ibid., 114.

59. Ibid., 119.

60. Ibid., 121.

61. Ibid., 122.

62. Richard D. Ashmore and Lee Jussim, eds., *Self and Identity: Fundamental Issues* (New York: Oxford University Press, 1997), 3; Mark R. Leary and June Price Tangney, eds., *Handbook of Self and Identity* (New York: Guilford, 2003), 4. For a broader historical perspective on the development of Western interest in and concepts of the self since classical times by a psychologist see Roy F. Baumeister, "How the Self Became a Problem: A Psychological Review of Historical Research," *Journal of Personality and Social Psychology* 52, 1 (1987): 165–76. For an interdisciplinary approach to contemporary issues in defining the self see Shaun Gallagher and Jonathan Shear, *Models of the Self* (Thorverton: Imprint Academic, 1999).

63. Leary and Tangney, *Handbook of Self and Identity*, 4.

64. Roy F. Baumeister, *Identity: Cultural Change and the Struggle for the Self* (Oxford: Oxford University Press, 1986), vii–viii.

65. This is also true of Baumeister's review article on the history of the idea of self, where he identified one of the four problems defining the self as "how identity is actively or creatively defined by the person" ("How the Self Became a Problem," 163). In a later overview he distinguished more

sharply between "self" as knowledge structure, interpersonal being and agent, and "identity" as "being the same person across time—different from others." See Roy F. Baumeister, "Self and Identity: a Brief Overview of What They Are, What They Do, and How They Work," in *Perspectives on the Self: Conversations on Identity and Consciousness*, Annals of the New York Academy of Sciences 1234 (Boston: Blackwell, 2011), 48–49.

66. Daphne Oyserman, Kristen Elmore, and George C. Smith, "Self, Self-Concept and Identity," in Leary and Tangney, *Handbook of Self and Identity*, 2nd ed., 69–104.

67. Leary and Tangney, *Handbook of Self and Identity*, 6–7.

68. Ibid., 2nd ed., 72.

69. Ibid., 74.

70. Ibid., 69; italics in original.

71. Ibid., 79.

72. Dan P. McAdams, "The Case for Unity in the (Post)Modern Self: A Modest Proposal," in Ashmore and Jussim, *Self and Identity*, 57.

73. Ibid., 61.

74. Ibid., 63. For longer discussions of the psychological concept of narrative identity see Dan P. McAdams, Ruthellen Josselson, and Amia Lieblich, eds., *Identity and Story: Creating Self in Narrative* (Washington, D.C.: American Psychological Association, 2006); also Wolfgang Kraus, *Das erzählte Selbst: Konstruktion von Identität in der Spätmoderne* (Pfaffenweiler: Centaurus, 1996).

75. N. F. Büchel, "Narrative Identity in Jeffrey Eugenides's *Middlesex*," in *Rethinking Narrative Identity: Persona and Perspective*, ed. Claudia Holler and Martin Klepper (Amsterdam: Benjamins, 2013), 129–46.

76. There is a significant anthropological literature on so-called "two-spirit" or mixed-gender individuals in some Native American cultures, and a growing therapeutic literature on dealing with the identity problems of the transgendered. See for example Sue-Ellen Jacobs, Wesley Thomas, and Sabine Lang, eds., *Two-Spirit People: Native American Gender Identity, Sexuality and Spirituality* (Urbana: University of Illinois Press, 1997) and Dallas Denny, ed., *Current Concepts in Transgender Identity* (New York: Routledge, 1997).

77. http://www.metrolyrics.com/why-cant-the-english-lyrics-my-fair-lady.html.

78. Carmen Llamas and Dominic Watt, "Introduction," in *Languages and Identities*, ed. Carmen Llamas and Dominic Watt (Edinburgh: Edinburgh University Press, 2010), 1.

79. For a brief account of the beginnings of the linguistic interest in identity see John E. Joseph, "Identity," in *Language and Identities*, ed. Llamas and Watt, 12–13. The most influential works in each category were Robert Brock le Page and Andrée Tabouret-Keller, *Acts of Identity: Creole-Based Approaches to Language and Identity* (Cambridge: Cambridge University Press, 1985) and John Edwards, *Language, Society and Identity* (Oxford: Blackwell, 1985).

80. John E. Joseph, *Language and Identity: National, Ethnic, Religious* (Houndmills: Palgrave Macmillan, 2004).

81. Barbara Johnstone, "Locating Language in Identity," in Llamas and Watt, *Language and Identities*, 29.

82. Joseph, *Language and Identity*, 20.

83. Ibid., 21.

84. Ibid., 39.

85. Ibid., 40.

86. Johnstone, "Locating Language," in *Language and Identities*, 31–32.

87. John Edwards, *Language and Identity: An Introduction* (Cambridge: Cambridge University Press, 2009).

88. Joseph, *Language and Identity*, 224–25.

89. Milka Rubin, "The Language of Creation or the Primordial Language: A Case of Cultural Polemics in Antiquity," *Journal of Jewish Studies* 49 (1998): 306–33, cited in Edwards, *Language and Identity*, 104.

90. J. G. Fichte, *Addresses to the German Nation*, ed. and intro. George Armstrong Kelly (New York: Harper and Row, 1968), xxiii. Kelly referred to the *Addresses* as "an essay in identity" (xxviii), though he did not particularly stress identity's linguistic dimension.

91. Province of Quebec Official Publisher, 1973.

92. Walter Carruthers Sellar and Robert Julian Yeatman, *1066 and All That* (London: 1993 [1930]), Compulsory Preface.

93. Pierre Nora, "General Introduction," in Pierre Nora, ed., *Rethinking France*. Vol. 1, *The State*, trans. Mary Trouille (Chicago: University of Chicago Press, 2001), xxxvii.

94. For an interesting overview of this development, which takes a different approach than mine to the meaning of what its author calls the "memory industry," see Kerwin Lee Klein, "On the Emergence of Memory in Historical Discourse," *Representations* 69 (Winter 2000): 127–50. The poststructuralist-inspired "linguistic turn" was methodologically very influential through the 1980s, though at the time of this writing it has largely run its course, while memory studies are still going strong.

95. Pierre Nora, ed., *Les lieux de mémoire*, 7 vols. (Paris: Gallimard, 1984–92). There are two partial English translations with nonoverlapping selections from the French essays totaling somewhat more than half the original number: *Realms of Memory: The Construction of the French Past*, ed. Lawrence D. Kritzman, 3 vols. (New York: Columbia University Press, 1996–98), and *Rethinking France*, ed. David P. Jordan, 4 vols. (Chicago: University of Chicago Press, 2001–2010).

96. Pierre Nora, "General Introduction: Between Memory and History," in *Realms of Memory*, vol. 1, 3–6. The essay is a translation of the original French introduction "Entre mémoire et histoire: La problématique des lieux," in *Les lieux de mémoire*, vol. 1, *La République*; italics added.

97. Ibid., 7.

98. Ibid., 6.

99. Pierre Nora, "Volume Introduction," in *Rethinking France*, vol. 1, *The State* (Chicago: University of Chicago Press, 2001), xxxvii.

100. Ironically, this is precisely the idea behind the spoof of British history *1066 and All That*, written in 1930 before the advent of identity, from which the epigraph at the head of this section is taken. The history of England had come to an end, the authors claimed, because England was no longer "top Nation." All that was left was to memorialize the few dates, events, and kings most people remembered from the time when England mattered.

101. Pierre Nora, introduction to *Lieux de mémoire et identités nationales*, ed. Pim den Boer and Willem Frijhoff (Amsterdam: Amsterdam University Press, 1993), 3.

102. I will use this term to translate *lieux de mémoire* rather than the one Nora preferred for the English translation, "realms of memory," because of its connotation of specific entities, whether material or conceptual.

103. Henk L. Wesseling, "Fin des empires, fin des nations?" in Den Boer and Frijhoff, *Lieux de mémoire et identités nationales*," 283.

104. Krzyzstof Pomian, "Franks and Gauls," in Nora, *Realms of Memory*, vol. 1, 28.

105. François Furet, "The Ancien Régime and the Revolution," in Nora, *Realms of Memory*, vol. 1, 106, 79.

106. Nora, "Between Memory and History," 3.

107. Michael M. J. Fischer, "Ethnicity and the Post-Modern Arts of Memory," in *Writing Culture: The Poetics and Politics of Ethnography*, ed. James Clifford and George E. Marcus (Berkeley: University of California Press, 1986).

108. Dominick LaCapra, *History and Memory After Auschwitz* (Ithaca, N.Y.: Cornell University Press, 1998), 12–13.

109. Ricoeur brought the two together in his three-volume study *Time and Narrative*, trans. Kathleen McLaughlin and David Pellauer (Chicago: University of Chicago Press, 1984–88). See especially part 2 of vol. 1, "History and Narrative." See also Jürgen Straub, "Telling Stories, Making History: Toward a Narrative Psychology of the Historical Construction of Meaning," in *Narration, Identity, and Historical Consciousness*, ed. Jürgen Straub (New York: Berghahn, 2005).

110. George A. Akerlof and Rachel E. Kranton, *Identity Economics: How Our Identities Shape Our Work, Wages, and Well-Being* (Princeton, N.J.: Princeton University Press, 2010), 10.

111. Ibid., 11.

112. Ibid., 59.

113. Ibid., 104.

114. Ibid., 121.

115. Edited by Heiner Keupp and Renate Höfer (Frankfurt a.M: Suhrkamp, 1997).

116. Interview with Jean-François Bayart, *Le Monde*, Politique, November 6, 2009.

117. Lutz Niethammer, *Kollektive Identität: Heimliche Quellen einer unheimlichen Konjunktur* (Reinbek bei Hamburg: Rowohlt, 2000), 625.

118. Walter Benn Michaels, "Race into Culture," in *Identities*, ed. Kwame Anthony Appiah and Henry L. Gates, Jr. (Chicago: University of Chicago Press, 1995), 60. See also Michaels, *Our America: Nativism, Modernism and Pluralism* (Durham, N.C.: Duke University Press, 1995) and *The Trouble with Diversity: How We Learned to Love Identity and Ignore Inequality* (New York: Metropolitan, 2006).

119. Michaels, "Race into Culture," 61.

120. Niethammer, *Kollektive Identität*, 415.

121. Ibid., 33ff.

122. Ibid., 39.

123. Ibid., 625.

124. Ibid., 627, 631.

125. Jean-François Bayart, *The Illusion of Cultural Identity*, trans. Steven Rendall, Janet Roitman, Cynthia Schoch, and Jonathan Derrick (Chicago: University of Chicago Press, 2005). The French original, published in 1996, is titled more sweepingly *L'illusion identitaire*.

126. Bayart, *Illusion of Cultural Identity*, xii.

127. "The Beaujolais Nouveau Is Here!" part 1 in ibid., 1–6.

128. Ibid., 59, 96.

129. Ibid., 65.

130. Ibid., 117.

131. Ibid., 120; italics added.

132. Ibid., 22; italics added.

133. Ibid., 95; italics in original. The words in quotation marks are citations from Max Weber, *Economy and Society*.

134. Rogers Brubaker and Frederick Cooper, "Beyond 'Identity,'" *Theory and Society* 29, 1 (February 2000): 1–47.

135. Ibid., 1.

136. Ibid., 7–8.

137. Ibid., 11; italics in original.

138. Grammatically, "deverbal nouns."

139. Brubaker and Cooper, "Beyond 'Identity,'" 14, 17, 19.

140. Ibid., 28.

Chapter 10. The Kinds of Kinds: Explaining Collective Identity

Epigraphs: Kwame Anthony Appiah, *The Ethics of Identity* (Princeton, N.J.: Princeton University Press, 2005), 65; Lawrence A. Hirschfeld, *Race in the Making: Cognition, Culture, and the Child's Construction of Human Kinds* (Cambridge, Mass.: MIT Press, 1996), xi.

1. Simone de Beauvoir, *She Came to Stay* (New York: Norton, 1990 [1943]).

2. Jean-Paul Sartre, "The Respectful Prostitute," in *No Exit and Three Other Plays* (New York: Vintage, 1989), 271.

3. Erving Goffman, *Stigma: Notes on the Management of Spoiled Identity* (New York: Simon and Schuster, 1963), 2–3.

4. Ibid., 5.

5. David Berreby, *Us and Them: Understanding Your Tribal Mind* (New York: Little, Brown, 2005), 210. Also published as *Us and Them: The Science of Identity* (Chicago: University of Chicago Press, 2008).

6. Donald L. Horowitz, *Ethnic Groups in Conflict* (Berkeley: University of California Press, 1985), 147.

7. Ian Hacking, "Making Up People," in *Historical Ontology* (Cambridge, Mass.: Harvard University Press, 2002). The paper was given originally in 1983.

8. Ian Hacking, "The Looping Effects of Human Kinds," in *Causal Cognition: A Multidisciplinary Approach*, ed. Dan Sperber, David Premack, and Ann James Premack (Oxford: Oxford University Press, 1995), 351–83.

9. This is not quite true of psychiatry and psychotherapy and certainly not true of popular culture. The clinical diagnosis of Multiple Personality Disorder (MPD) has been formally replaced by the term Dissociative Identity Disorder, but some mental health professionals think of them as more or less equivalent, the formal term just more technically accurate.

10. Hacking, "Making Up People," 104.

11. Ibid., 106.

12. Ian Hacking, "Kinds of People: Moving Targets," *Proceedings of the British Academy* 151 (2007): 305.

13. Ibid., 288. First set of italics mine.

14. Ian Hacking, "Why Race Still Matters," "On Race," special issue, *Daedalus* 134, 1 (Winter 2005): 104.

15. Ibid., 113.

16. Hacking, "Kinds of People," 313.

17. Hacking, *Historical Ontology*, 2.

18. Hacking, "Kinds of People," 290.

19. Lawrence A. Hirschfeld, *Race in the Making: Cognition, Culture, and the Child's Construction of Human Kinds* (Cambridge, Mass.: MIT Press, 1996).

20. Ibid., xi; italics added.

21. Ibid., 12.

22. Ibid., 84–89.

23. Ibid., 54; italics in original.

24. See the discussion of Geertz and others in Chapter 5.

25. Hirschfeld, *Race in the Making*, 21.

26. Ibid., 188; italics in original.

27. Ibid., 42.

28. Ibid., 155.

29. David R. Roediger, *Working Towards Whiteness: How America's Immigrants Became White* (New York: Basic, 2005).

30. Ian Hacking, "Genetics, Biosocial Groups and the Future of Identity," "On Identity," special issue, *Daedalus* 135, 4 (Fall 2006): 81–95.

31. Ibid., 85.

32. Ibid., 87.

33. Ibid., 92.

34. Kwame Anthony Appiah, *The Ethics of Identity* (Princeton, N.J.: Princeton University Press, 2005), 66–69.

35. I maintain this despite Thomas Laqueur's brilliant demonstration that prior to the seventeenth century Europeans held to a "one-sex model" of males and females in which it was a "commonplace" that women had the same genitals as men except that men's were on the outside and women's on the inside. Thomas Laqueur, *Making Sex: Body and Gender from the Greeks to Freud* (Cambridge, Mass.: Harvard University Press, 1990), 8, 4. His conclusion, however, that "Sex before the seventeenth century . . . was still a sociological and not an ontological category" does not follow. God, Genesis says, created humans male and female. For believing Jews and Christians this was (and is) an ontological claim.

36. Which is not the same as saying, for example, that males alone are "active" because they penetrate the passive or receptive female. "Penetration" may feel, to both to male and female, like active female enfolding and male receptive being enfolded—let alone like fantasies of swallowing up and being castrated.

37. Ivan Hannaford, *Race: The History of an Idea in the West* (Baltimore: Johns Hopkins University Press, 1996), 5.

38. Hannaford, *Race*, 19.

39. Ibid., 29.

40. Cited in Benjamin Isaac, *The Invention of Racism in Classical Antiquity* (Princeton, N.J.: Princeton University Press, 2004), 71.

41. Ibid., 1.

42. Ibid., 37–39.

43. Ibid., 23.

44. Mary Douglas, *Purity and Danger* (London: Routledge, 2002 [1966]), 200.

45. Ibid., 44.

46. Ibid., 68.

47. Ibid., 67.

48. Ibid., 63.

49. Leviticus 19:2.

50. Douglas, *Purity and Danger*, 71.

Chapter 11. Identity as an Ethical Issue

1. Alasdair MacIntyre, *After Virtue: A Study in Moral Theory* (Notre Dame, Ind.: University of Notre Dame Press, 1981), 62.

2. Ibid., 111; italics in original.

3. Ibid., 148–52.

4. Ibid., 119.

5. Ibid., 189.

6. Ibid., 201.

7. Ibid., 203.

8. Ibid., 205.

9. Ibid., 203.

10. Ibid., 207; italics added.

11. MacIntyre made this point explicitly in conversation with the author about the obsessive question within the Jewish community of "Who is Jew?"

12. MacIntyre addressed this issue in the context of whether it can be rational to leave one tradition for another in his later work *Whose Justice? Which Rationality?* For a critical analysis of his argument, see the review of both this book and *After Virtue* by R. Jay Wallace in *History and Theory* 28, 3 (October 1989): 326–48.

13. Charles Taylor, *Sources of the Self: The Making of the Modern Identity* (Cambridge, Mass.: Harvard University Press, 1989), 4–5.

14. Ibid., 28, 495.

15. Ibid., 29.

16. Ibid., 505.

17. Ibid., 516.

18. Ibid., 512.

19. Ibid., 516, 517. He did try to develop it in his later book *A Secular Age* (Cambridge, Mass.: Harvard University Press, 2007).

20. C. Taylor, *Sources of the Self*, 519–20.

21. William E. Connolly, *Identity/Difference: Democratic Negotiations of Political Paradox* (Minneapolis: University of Minnesota Press, 2002 [1991]), ix.

22. Ibid., x.

23. Ibid., 110.

24. Ibid., 111.

25. Ibid., 119.

26. Ibid., x.

27. Kwame Anthony Appiah, *The Ethics of Identity* (Princeton, N.J.: Princeton University Press, 2005), 16.

28. Ibid., 19.

29. Ibid., 108.

30. Ibid., 211.

31. Ibid., 70.

32. Ibid., 110.

33. Ibid., 232.

34. Ibid., 235.

35. Ibid., 234.

36. Ibid., 235.

37. Ibid., 236.

38. Ibid., 257.

39. Ibid., 268.

40. The moral philosopher Ernst Tugendhat reaches a strikingly similar conclusion about what he called moral identity with somewhat different arguments. Moral identity, he claimed, is our primary intersubjective identity, foundational for all our other intersubjective identities and therefore for our self-understanding as persons. Ernst Tugendhat, "Die Rolle der Identität in der Konstitution der Moral," trans. Barbara Reiter and Alexander Staudacher from the original English lecture "The Role of Identity in the Constitution of Morality," in *Moral und Person*, ed. Wolfgang Edelstein, Gertrud Nunner-Winkler, and Gil Noam (Frankfurt a.M: Suhrkamp, 1993), 41.

Conclusion. The Necessity of Identity

Epigraph: Yusuf/Cat Stevens, quoted in "Nine Lives," by Tad Friend, *New Yorker*, April 21, 2014.

1. Amin Maalouf, *In the Name of Identity*, trans. Barbara Bray (New York: Penguin, 2000 [1996]), 2.

2. The line appeared in the Paramount Studios cartoon short, "I Yam What I Yam," 1933.

Bibliography

Library Catalogues, Newspapers, Magazines, Periodicals
(Online Data Bases)

American Journal of Psychology (1887–
American Journal of Sociology (1895–
American Periodicals
American Sociological Journal (1936–
American Sociological Review (1936–
Atlanta Constitution (1868–1945)
Baltimore Sun (1837–1988)
Bibliothek des Instituts für Zeitgeschichte (Munich)
British Periodicals
Chicago Daily Tribune (1949–1990)
Deutsche National Bibliothek
Gallica
Los Angeles Times (1881–
Le Matin (1884–1944)
Le Monde (1944–
New York Times (1851–2010)
Psyche: Zeitschrift für Psychoanalyse und ihre Anwendungen
Der Spiegel (1947–
St. Louis Post-Dispatch (1878–1922)
Le Temps (1861–1942)
Wall Street Journal (1889–1996)

Books and Articles

Abelove, Henry, Michèle Aina Barale, and David M. Halperin, eds. *The Lesbian and Gay Studies Reader*. New York: Routledge, 1993.

Adamson, Christopher R., Peter C. Findlay, Michael K. Oliver, and Janet Solberg. "The Unpublished Research of the Royal Commission on Bilingualism and Biculturalism." *Canadian Journal of Political Science* 7, 4 (December 1974): 709–20.

Akerlof, George A., and Rachel E. Kranton. *Identity Economics: How Our Identities Shape Our Work, Wages, and Well-Being*. Princeton, N.J.: Princeton University Press, 2010.

Alarcon, Norma. "The Theoretical Subject(s) of *This Bridge Called My Back* and Anglo-American Feminism." In *The Postmodern Turn*, ed. Seidman, 140–52.

Alcoff, Linda Martín. *Visible Identities: Race, Gender, and the Self*. Oxford: Oxford University Press, 2006.

Alcoff, Linda Martín, Michael Hames-Garcia, Satya P. Mohanty, and Paula M. L. Moya, eds. *Identity Politics Reconsidered*. New York: Palgrave Macmillan, 2006.

Ali, Ayaan Hirsi. *The Caged Virgin: An Emancipation Proclamation for Women and Islam*. New York: Atria, 2008.

Altman, Dennis. *The Homosexualization of America*. Boston: Beacon, 1982.

Anderson, Benedict. *Imagined Communities: Reflections on the Origin and Spread of Nationalism*. London: Verso, 1991.

Appiah, Kwame Anthony. *The Ethics of Identity*. Princeton, N.J.: Princeton University Press, 2005.

———. *Lines of Descent: W. E. B. Du Bois and the Emergence of Identity*. Cambridge, Mass.: Harvard University Press, 2014.

Appiah, Kwame Anthony, and Henry L. Gates, Jr., eds. *Identities*. Chicago: University of Chicago Press, 1995.

Armstrong, Elizabeth A. *Forging Gay Identities: Organizing Sexuality in San Francisco, 1950–1994*. Chicago: University of Chicago Press, 2002.

Aronowitz, Stanley. *The Politics of Identity: Class, Culture, Social Movements*. New York: Psychology Press, 1992.

Arthur, Paige. *Unfinished Projects: Decolonization and the Philosophy of Jean-Paul Sartre*. London: Verso, 2010.

Ashmore, Richard D., and Lee Jussim, eds. *Self and Identity: Fundamental Issues*. New York: Oxford University Press, 1997.

Assmann, Aleida, and Heidrun Friese, eds. *Identitäten*. Erinnerung, Geschichte, Identität 3. Frankfurt: Suhrkamp, 1999.

Badinter, Elisabeth. *On Masculine Identity*. Trans. Lydia Davis. New York: Columbia University Press, 1995.

Bair, Deirdre. "Introduction to the Vintage Edition." In Beauvoir. *The Second Sex*, xix–xxxvi. New York: Vintage, 1989.

———. *Simone de Beauvoir: A Biography*. New York: Simon and Schuster, 1990.

Bambach, Charles. *Heidegger's Roots: Nietzsche, National Socialism and the Greeks*. Ithaca, N.Y.: Cornell University Press, 2003.

Baring, Edward. *The Young Derrida and French Philosophy, 1945–1968*. Cambridge: Cambridge University Press, 2011.

Barth, Fredrik, ed. *Ethnic Groups and Boundaries: The Social Organization of Culture Difference*. Long Grove, Ill.: Waveland, 1989.

Battersby, Christine. *The Phenomenal Woman: Feminist Metaphysics and the Patterns of Identity*. New York: Routledge, 1998.

Bauman, Zygmunt. *Identity: Conversations with Benedetto Vecchi*. Cambridge: Polity, 2004.

Baumeister, Roy F. "How the Self Became a Problem: A Psychological Review of Historical Research." *Journal of Personality and Social Psychology* 52, 1 (1987): 165–76.

———. *Identity: Cultural Change and the Struggle for the Self*. Oxford: Oxford University Press, 1986.

———. "Self and Identity: A Brief Overview of What They Are, What They Do, and How They Work." In *Perspectives on the Self: Conversations on Identity and Consciousness*. Annals of the New York Academy of Sciences 1234. Boston: Blackwell, 2011. 48–55.

Bayart, Jean-François. *The Illusion of Cultural Identity*. Trans. Steven Rendall, Janet Roitman, Cynthia Schoch, and Jonathan Derrick. Chicago: University of Chicago Press, 2005.

Beauvoir, Simone de. *Le deuxième sex*. Vol. 1, *Les faits et les mythes*. Paris: Gallimard, 1949.

———. *The Mandarins*. Trans. Leonard M. Friedman. New York: Norton, 1991.

———. *The Second Sex*. Unabridged trans. Constance Borde and Sheila Malovany-Chevallier. Intro. Judith Thurman. New York: Vintage, 2011.

———. *The Second Sex*. Trans. H. M. Parshley. Intro. Deirdre Bair. New York: Vintage, 1989.

———. *She Came to Stay*. New York: Norton, 1990.

Beck, Ulrich. "Jenseits von Stand und Klasse? Soziale Ungleichheiten, gesellschaftliche Individualisierungsprozesse, und die Entstehung neuer sozialer Formationen und Identitäten. In *Soziale Ungleichheiten*, ed. Kreckel, 35–74.

Belenky, Mary F. et al. *Women's Ways of Knowing: The Development of Self, Voice, and Mind*. New York: Basic, 1997.

Bell, Daniel. "Ethnicity and Social Change." In *Ethnicity*, ed. Glazer and Moynihan, 141–76.

Benhabib, Seyla, Judith Butler, Drusilla Cornell, and Nancy Fraser. *Feminist Contentions: A Philosophical Exchange.* New York: Routledge, 1995.

Bendix, Reinhard. "Identification as the Basis for a Theory of Motivation: Discussion," *American Sociological Review* 16, 1 (February 1951): 22.

Benhabib, Seyla, Ian Shapiro, and Danilo Petranovic, eds. *Identities, Affiliations and Allegiances.* Cambridge: Cambridge University Press, 2007.

Benoist, Alain de. "On Identity." Trans. Kathy Ackerman and Julia Kostova. *Telos* 128 (Summer 2004): 9–64.

Bergem, Wolfgang. *Identitätsformationen in Deutschland.* Wiesbaden: Verlag für Sozialwissenschaften, 2005.

Berger, Peter L., and Thomas Luckmann. *The Social Construction of Reality: A Treatise in the Sociology of Knowledge.* Garden City, N.Y.: Anchor, 1967.

Berglar, Peter, ed. *Deutsche Identität heute.* Mainz: Hase and Koehler, 1983.

Berreby, David. *Us and Them: Understanding Your Tribal Mind.* New York: Little, Brown, 2005.

Bevir, Mark, Jill Hargis, and Sara Rushing, eds. *Histories of Postmodernism.* New York: Routledge, 2007.

Bhabha, Homi K. *The Location of Culture.* 2nd ed. London: Routledge, 2004.

Bickford, Susan. "Anti-Anti-Identity Politics: Feminism, Democracy and the Complexities of Citizenship." In "Citizenship in Feminism: Identity, Action and Locale." Special issue, *Hypatia* 12, 4 (Autumn 1997): 111–31.

Bilgrami, Akeel. "What Is a Muslim? Fundamental Commitment and Cultural Identity." In *Identities,* ed. Appiah and Gates, 198–219.

Billig, Michael. "Rethinking the Particular Background of Social Identity Theory." In *Social Groups and Identities: Developing the Legacy of Henri Tajfel.* Ed. W. Peter Robinson, 337–58. Oxford: Butterworth Heinemann, 1996.

Billig, Michael, and Henri Tajfel. "Social Categorization and Similarity in Intergroup Behavior." *European Journal of Social Psychology* 3, 1 (March 1973): 27–52.

Bitterman, Klaus. "Wie die Identität unter die Deutschen kam. Die Linke als Geburtshelfer nationaler Gefühle." In *Geisterfahrer der Einheit. Kommentare zur Wiedervereinigungskrise,* ed. Bitterman, 94–120. Berlin: ID-Archiv, 1995.

Blasius, Mark. "An Ethos of Lesbian and Gay Existence. In *Sexual Identities, Queer Politics,* ed. Blasius, 143–77.

———, ed. *Sexual Identities, Queer Politics.* Princeton, N.J.: Princeton University Press, 2001.

Bloom, William. *Personal Identity, National Identity and International Relations.* Cambridge: Cambridge University Press, 1990.

Bond, Michael H., and Tak-Sing Cheung. "College Students' Spontaneous Self-Concept: The Effect of Culture Among Respondents in Hong Kong, Japan and the United States." *Journal of Cross-Cultural Psychology* 14, 2 (June 1983): 153–71.

Bonnafous, Simone. *L'immigration prise aux mots: Les immigrés dans la presse au tournant des années 80.* Paris: Kimé, 1991.

Borst, A. "Barbarossas Erwachen—zur Geschichte der deutschen Identität." In *Identität,* ed. Marquard and Stierle, 17–60.

Boulé, Jean-Pierre. *Sartre, Self-Formation and Masculinities.* New York: Berghahn, 2005.

Bourdieu, Pierre. "L'identité et la représentation." *Actes de la Recherche en Sciences Sociales* 35 (November 1980): 63–72.

Bowen, John R. *Blaming Islam.* Cambridge, Mass.: MIT Press, 2012.

Braudel, Fernand. *La Méditerranée et le monde méditerranéen à l'époque de Philippe II.* Paris: Colin, 1949.

———. *L'identité de la France.* Vols. 1 and 2, *Les hommes et les choses.* Vol. 3, *Espace et histoire.* Paris: Flammarion, 1990.

———. *The Identity of France.* Vol. 1, *History and Environment.* Vol. 2, *People and Production.* Trans. Sian Reynolds. London: HarperCollins, 1988, 1990.

Breakwell, Glynis M., ed. *Threatened Identities*. New York: Wiley, 1983.

Breuilly, John. "German National Identity." In *The Cambridge Companion to Modern German Culture*, ed. Eva Kolinsky and Wilfried van der Will, 44–66. Cambridge: Cambridge University Press, 1998.

Brick, Howard. *Age of Contradiction: American Thought and Culture in the 1960s*. New York: Twayne, 1998.

Broch, Hermann. *Philosophische Schriften*. Bd. 1, *Kritik*. Ed. Paul Michael Lützeler. Frankfurt: Suhrkamp, 1977.

———. *Die Schlafwandler*. Frankfurt: Suhrkamp, 1996.

———. *The Sleepwalkers*. Trans. Willa Muir and Edwin Muir. New York: Vintage, 1996.

Brooks, Peter. *Enigmas of Identity*. Princeton, N.J.: Princeton University Press, 2011.

Brubaker, Rogers. *Citizenship and Nationhood in France and Germany*. Cambridge, Mass.: Harvard University Press, 1992.

Brubaker, Rogers, and Frederick Cooper. "Beyond 'Identity.'" *Theory and Society* 29, 1 (February 2000): 1–47.

Brunner, Otto, Werner Conze, and Reinhart Koselleck, eds. *Geschichtliche Grundbegriffe: historisches Lexikon zur politisch-sozialen Sprache in Deutschland*, vol. 3. Stuttgart: Klett, 1982.

Büchel, Nicole Frey. "Narrative Identity in Jeffrey Eugenides's *Middlesex*." In *Rethinking Narrative Identity*, ed. Holler and Klepper, 129–46.

Bucholtz, Mary, A. C. Liang and Laurel A. Sutton, eds. *Reinventing Identities: The Gendered Self in Discourse*. Oxford: Oxford University Press, 1999.

Burke, Peter J., and Jan E. Stets. *Identity Theory*. Oxford: Oxford University Press, 2009.

Burston, Daniel. *The Legacy of Erich Fromm*. Cambridge, Mass.: Harvard University Press, 1991.

———. *The Wings of Madness: The Life and Work of R. D. Laing*. Cambridge, Mass.: Harvard University Press, 1996.

Butler, Judith. *Gender Trouble: Feminism and the Subversion of Identity*. New York: Routledge, 1999.

———. *The Psychic Life of Power*. Stanford, Calif.: Stanford University Press, 1997.

Calhoun, Craig, ed. *Social Theory and the Politics of Identity*. Oxford: Blackwell, 1994.

Camilleri, Carmel et al. *Stratégies identitaires*. Paris: Presses Universitaires de France, 1990.

Canada Royal Commission on Bilingualism and Biculturalism. *Report of the Royal Commission on Bilingualism and Biculturalism*. Privy Council Office, 1967–1970. www.lac-bac.gr.ca.

Carmichael, Stokely, and Charles V. Hamilton. *Black Power: The Politics of Liberation in America*. New York: Random House, 1967.

Cass, Vivienne C. "Homosexual Identity: A Concept in Need of a Definition." *Journal of Homosexuality* 9, 2–3 (December 1983): 105–26.

Castells, Manuel. *The Power of Identity*. Oxford: Blackwell, 1997.

Chatterjee, Partha. *A Princely Impostor? The Strange and Universal History of the Kumar of Bhawal*. Princeton, N.J.: Princeton University Press, 2002.

Chodorow, Nancy. *Individualizing Gender and Sexuality: Theory and Practice*. New York: Routledge, 2012.

———. *The Reproduction of Mothering: Psychoanalysis and the Sociology of Gender*. Berkeley: University of California Press, 1999.

Cleaver, Eldridge. *Post-Prison Writings and Speeches*. New York: Random House, 1969.

Clifford, James, and George E. Marcus, eds. *Writing Culture: The Poetics and Politics of Ethnography*. Berkeley: University of California Press, 1986.

Cohen, Abner. "Ethnicity and Politics." In *Ethnicity*, ed. Hutchinson and Smith, 83–85.

Cohen, Lizabeth. *A Consumer's Republic: The Politics of Mass Consumption in Postwar America*. New York: Knopf, 2003.

Cohen-Solal, Annie. *Sartre: A Life*. Trans. Anna Cancogni. New York: Pantheon, 1987.

Combahee River Collective. A Black Feminist Statement. In *The Second Wave*, ed. Nicholson, 63–70.

Connolly, William E. *Identity/Difference: Democratic Negotiations of Political Paradox*. Minneapolis: University of Minnesota Press, 1991.

Dahrendorf, Ralf. "The Search for German Identity: An Illusory Endeavor?" In *German Identity*, ed. Friedrich-Naumann-Stiftung, 131–56.

Daigle, Christine, and Jacob Golomb, eds. *Beauvoir and Sartre: The Riddle of Influence*. Bloomington: Indiana University Press, 2009.

Davis, John. "An Interview with Ernest Gellner." *Current Anthropology* 32, 1 (February 1991): 63–72.

Davis, Natalie Z. *The Return of Martin Guerre*. Cambridge, Mass.: Harvard University Press, 1983.

Day, Richard J. F. *Multiculturalism and the History of Canadian Diversity*. Toronto: University of Toronto Press, 2002.

Dehout, P. "Nationale Selbstfindung." *Nation Europa* 31, 4 (April 1981): 3–8.

Deissler, Gerhard. *Die deutsche Identität: Gedanken zur Identitätsfrage Deutschlands*. Norderstedt: GRIN, 2010.

Della Porta, Donatella, and Mario Diani. *Social Movements: An Introduction*. 2nd ed. Oxford: Blackwell, 2006.

Delphy, Christine. "The Invention of French Feminism: An Essential Move." In *Another Look, Another Woman: Retranslations of French Feminism*, ed. Lynne Huffer, 190–221. Yale French Studies 87. New Haven, Conn.: Yale University Press, 1995.

D'Emilio, John. *Sexual Politics, Sexual Communities. The Makings of a Homosexual Minority in the United States, 1940–1970*. 2nd ed. Chicago: University of Chicago Press, 1988.

Den Boer, Pim, and Willem Frijhoff, eds. *Lieux de mémoire et identités nationales*. Amsterdam: Amsterdam University Press, 1993.

Denny, Dallas, ed. *Current Concepts in Transgender Identity*. New York: Routledge, 1997.

Derrida, Jacques. "But Beyond. . . ." In *"Race," Writing, and Difference*, ed. Gates, 354–69.

———. *Of Grammatology*. Trans. Gayatri Chakravorty Spivak. Baltimore: Johns Hopkins University Press, 1997.

———. "Racism's Last Word." In *"Race," Writing, and Difference*, ed. Gates, 329–38.

———. *Spurs: Nietzsche's Styles*. Trans. Barbara Harlow. Chicago: University of Chicago Press, 1979.

Dierke, Sabine. "Multikulti: The German Debate on Multiculturalism." *German Studies Review* 17, 3 (October 1994): 513–36.

Dosse, François. *History of Structuralism*. Vol. 1, *The Rising Sign, 1945–66*. Trans. Deborah Glassman. Minneapolis: University of Minnesota Press, 1997.

Douglas, Mary. *Purity and Danger*. London: Routledge, 2002.

Eakin, Paul John. *Living Autobiography: How We Create Identity in Narrative*. Ithaca, N.Y.: Cornell University Press, 2008.

Edelstein, Wolfgang, Gertrud Nunner-Winkler, and Gil Noam, eds. *Moral und Person*. Frankfurt a.M: Suhrkamp, 1993.

Edwards, John. *Language, Society and Identity*. Oxford: Blackwell, 1985.

———. *Language and Identity: An Introduction*. Cambridge: Cambridge University Press, 2009.

Eisenstein, Hester, and Alice Jardine, eds. *The Future of Difference*. New Brunswick, N.J.: Rutgers University Press, 1994.

Eksteins, Modris. *Rites of Spring: The Great War and the Birth of the Modern Age*. Boston: Houghton Mifflin, 1989.

Eller, Jack, and Reed Coughlan. "The Poverty of Primordialism." In *Ethnicity*, ed. Hutchinson and Smith, 45–51.

Elster, Jon, ed. *The Multiple Self*. Cambridge: Cambridge University Press, 1986.

Epstein, Steven. "Gay Politics, Ethnic Identity: The Limits of Social Construction." In *Forms of Desire*, ed. Stein, 239–94.

Eriksen, Thomas H. "Ethnicity, Race, Class and Nation." In *Ethnicity*, ed. Hutchinson and Smith, 28–34.

Erikson, Erik H. *Childhood and Society*. 2nd ed. New York: Norton, 1963.

———. *Dimensions of a New Identity*. New York: Norton, 1974.

———. "Ego Development and Historical Change: Clinical Notes." In Erikson. *Identity and the Life Cycle*, 18–49.

————. *Gandhi's Truth: On the Origins of Militant Nonviolence.* New York: Norton, 1969.

————. "Growth and Crises of the Healthy Personality." In Erikson. *Identity and the Life Cycle,* 50–100.

————. *Identity and the Life Cycle: Selected Papers.* Psychological Issues 1. New York: International Universities Press, 1959.

————. *Identity: Youth and Crisis.* New York: Norton, 1968.

————. *Insight and Responsibility.* New York: Norton, 1964.

————. *Life History and the Historical Moment.* New York: Norton, 1975.

————. "The Problem of Ego Identity." In *Identity and the Life Cycle,* Erikson, 101–64.

————. *A Way of Looking at Things: Selected Papers from 1930 to 1980.* Ed. Stephen Schlein. New York: Norton, 1987.

————. *Young Man Luther: A Study in Psychoanalysis and History.* New York: Norton, 1958.

Fanon, Frantz. *Black Skin, White Masks.* Trans. Charles L. Markmann. New York: Grove, 1967.

————. *The Wretched of the Earth.* Trans. Constance Farrington. New York: Grove, 1968.

Farred, Grant. "Endgame Identity? Mapping the New Left Roots of Identity Politics." In "Is There Life After Identity Politics?" Special Issue, *New Literary History* 31, 4 (Autumn 2000): 627–48.

Favell, Adrian. *Philosophies of Integration: Immigration and the Idea of Citizenship in France and Britain.* New York: St. Martin's, 1998.

Felski, Rita. *The Gender of Modernity.* Cambridge, Mass.: Harvard University Press, 1995.

Ferkiss, Victor C. *Africa's Search for Identity.* New York: George Braziller, 1966.

Fichte, J. G. *Addresses to the German Nation.* Ed. and intro. George Armstrong Kelly. New York: Harper and Row, 1968.

Firestone, Shulamith. *The Dialectic of Sex: The Case for Feminist Revolution.* New York: Morrow Quill, 1970.

First, Michael B., ed. *Desk Reference to the Diagnostic Criteria from DSM-IV-TR.* Washington, D.C.: American Psychiatric Association, 2000.

Fischer, Michael M. J. "Ethnicity and the Post-Modern Arts of Memory." In *Writing Culture* ed. Clifford and Marcus, 194–233. Berkeley: University of California Press, 1986.

Foote, Nelson R. "Identification as the Basis for a Theory of Motivation." *American Sociological Review* 16, 1 (February 1951): 14–21.

Foucault, Michel. *Discipline and Punish: The Birth of the Prison.* Trans. Alan Sheridan. New York: Vintage, 1979.

————. *The Essential Works of Michel Foucault, 1954–1984.* Ed. Paul Rabinow. Vol. 3, *Power.* Ed. James D. Faubion. New York: New Press, 2000.

————. *The History of Sexuality.* Vol. 1, *An Introduction.* Trans. Robert Hurley. New York: Vintage, 1990.

————. *Language, Counter-Memory, Practice: Selected Essays and Interviews.* Trans. Donald F. Bouchard and Sherry Simon. Ithaca, N.Y.: Cornell University Press, 1977.

Fourest, Caroline. *Brother Tariq: The Doublespeak of Tariq Ramadan.* New York: Encounter, 2008.

Fraser, Nancy, and Sandra L. Bartky, eds. *Revaluing French Feminism: Critical Essays on Difference, Agency and Culture.* Bloomington: Indiana University Press, 1992.

Freedman, Ralph. *Hermann Hesse, Pilgrim of Crisis: A Biography.* New York: Fromm, 1997.

Freud, Sigmund. "Address to the Society of B'nai B'rith." In *The Standard Edition,* vol. 20. 1959.

————. "Ansprache an die Mitglieder des Vereins B'nai B'rith." In *Gesammelte Werke,* vol. 17. Frankfurt: S. Fischer Verlag, 1983.

————. *Group Psychology and the Analysis of the Ego.* Vol. 18 of *The Standard Edition.* 1955.

————. *The Standard Edition of the Complete Psychological Works of Sigmund Freud.* Ed. James Strachey. London: Hogarth, 1953–74.

————. *Totem und Tabu.* Vol. 12 of *Gesammelte Schriften.* Vienna: Internationaler Psychoanalytischer Verlag, 1924–34.

Friedan, Betty. *The Feminine Mystique.* New York: Norton, 2001.

Friedman, Lawrence J. *Identity's Architect: A Biography of Erik H. Erikson.* New York: Scribner, 1999.

———. *The Lives of Erich Fromm: Love's Prophet.* New York: Columbia University Press, 2013.

Friedrich-Naumann-Stiftung, Wolfgang Pollak, and Derek Rutter. *German Identity: Forty Years After Zero.* Sankt Augustin: Liberal Verlag, 1985.

Friese, Heidrun, ed. *Identities: Time, Difference and Boundaries.* New York: Berghahn, 2002.

Fritsche, Johannes. *Historical Destiny and National Socialism in Heidegger's* Being and Time. Berkeley: University of California Press, 1999.

Fromm, Erich. *Escape from Freedom.* New York: Rinehart, 1941.

Frosch, Stephen. *Identity Crisis: Modernity, Psychoanalysis and the Self.* New York: Routledge, 1981.

Fulbrook, Edward, and Kate Fulbrook. *Sex and Philosophy: Rethinking de Beauvoir and Sartre.* London: Zed Books, 2008.

Fullbrook, Mary. *German National Identity After the Holocaust.* Oxford: Oxford University Press, 1991.

Furet, François. "The Ancien Régime and the Revolution." In Nora. *Realms of Memory,* vol. 1, 79–108.

Fuss, Diana. *Essentially Speaking: Feminism, Nature and Difference.* New York: Routledge, 1989.

Fussell, Paul. *The Great War and Modern Memory.* New York: Oxford University Press, 2000.

Gallagher, Shaun, and Jonathan Shear. *Models of the Self.* Thorverton: Imprint Academic, 1999.

Gallop, Jane. *The Daughter's Seduction: Feminism and Psychoanalysis.* Ithaca, N.Y.: Cornell University Press, 1982.

Galston, William A. *Liberal Pluralism: The Implications of Value Pluralism for Political Theory and Practice.* Cambridge: Cambridge University Press, 2002.

Gans, Herbert J. "Symbolic Ethnicity." In Hutchinson and Smith. *Ethnicity,* 146–55.

Gates, Henry Louis, Jr., ed. *"Race," Writing, and Difference.* Chicago: University of Chicago Press, 1986.

Geertz, Clifford. *The Interpretation of Cultures.* New York: Basic, 1973.

———. "Primordial Ties." In Hutchinson and Smith. *Ethnicity,* 40–45.

Gellner, Ernest. *Nations and Nationalism.* Ithaca, N.Y.: Cornell University Press, 1983.

———. *Thought and Change.* London: Weidenfeld and Nicolson, 1964.

Gibowski, Wolfgang. "A Democracy at Last: An Empirical Perspective of Germany's Political Culture." In Friedrich-Naumann-Stiftung. *German Identity,* 73–102.

Giddens, Anthony. *Modernity and Self-Identity: Self and Society in the Late Modern Age.* Stanford, Calif.: Stanford University Press, 1991.

Gide, André. *The Counterfeiters.* Trans. Dorothy Bussy. New York: Vintage, 1973.

Gilligan, Carol. *In a Different Voice: Psychological Theory and Women's Development.* Cambridge, Mass.: Harvard University Press, 1993.

Gillis, John R. *Commemorations: The Politics of National Identity.* Princeton, N.J.: Princeton University Press, 1994.

Gitlin, Todd. "The Fate of the Commons." In *Identity Politics in the Women's Movement,* ed. Ryan, 35–38.

Giudice, Gaspare. *Pirandello: A Biography.* London: Oxford University Press, 1975.

Glas, Gerrit. "Idem, Ipse, and Loss of the Self." *Philosophy, Psychiatry, and Psychology* 10, 4 (December 2003): 347–52.

Glass, James M. *Shattered Selves: Multiple Personality in a Postmodern World.* Ithaca, N.Y.: Cornell University Press, 1993.

Glazer, Nathan, and Daniel P. Moynihan, eds. *Ethnicity: Theory and Experience.* Cambridge, Mass.: Harvard University Press, 1975.

Gleason, Philip. "Identifying Identity: A Semantic History." *Journal of American History* 69, 4 (March 1983): 910–31.

Goffman, Erving. *The Presentation of Self in Everyday Life.* Garden City, N.Y.: Doubleday, 1959.

———. *Stigma: Notes on the Management of Spoiled Identity.* New York: Simon and Schuster, 1963.

Gordon, Peter E. "Hammer Without a Master: French Phenomenology and the Origins of Deconstruction (Or, How Derrida Read Heidegger)." In *Histories of Postmodernism,* ed. Bevir at al., 103–30.

Gray, John. *Two Faces of Liberalism*. New York: New Press, 2000.

Greenberg, David F. *The Construction of Homosexuality*. Chicago: University of Chicago Press, 1988.

Greenhouse, Carol J., and Roshanak Kheshti, eds. *Democracy and Ethnography: Constructing Identities in Multicultural Liberal States*. Albany: State University of New York Press, 1988.

Greer, Germaine. *The Female Eunuch*. New York: McGraw-Hill, 1970.

Griotteray, Alain. *Les immigrés: Le choc*. Paris: Plon, 1984.

Grosby, Steven. "The Inexpungeable Tie of Primordiality." In *Ethnicity*, ed. Hutchinson and Smith, 51–57.

Gross, Elizabeth. "Philosophy, Subjectivity and the Body: Kristeva and Irigaray." In *Feminist Challenges*, ed. Pateman and Gross, 125–43.

Grosz, Elizabeth. "Sexual Difference and the Problem of Essentialism." In *The Essential Difference*, ed. Schor and Weed, 82–97.

Gutmann, Amy. *Identity in Democracy*. Princeton, N.J.: Princeton University Press, 2003.

Habermas, Jürgen. "Struggles for Recognition." In Taylor, *Multiculturalism*, 107–48.

———*Between Facts and Norms: Contributions to a Discourse Theory of Law and Democracy*. trans.- William Rehg. Cambridge, Mass.: MIT Press, 1998.

Hacking, Ian. "Genetics, Biosocial Groups and the Future of Identity." In "On Identity." Special issue, *Daedalus* 135, 4 (Fall 2006): 81–95.

———. *Historical Ontology*. Cambridge, Mass.: Harvard University Press, 2002.

———. "Kinds of People: Moving Targets." *Proceedings of the British Academy* 151 (2007): 285–318.

———. "The Looping Effects of Human Kinds." In *Causal Cognition: A Multidisciplinary Approach*, ed. Dan Sperber, David Premack, and Ann James Premack, 351–83. Oxford: Oxford University Press, 1995.

———. "Why Race Still Matters." In "On Race." Special issue, *Daedalus* 134, 1 (Winter 2005): 102–16.

Haddour, Adrian. "Sartre and Fanon: On Negritude and Political Participation." In *Sartre Today: A Centenary Celebration*, ed. Adrian van den Hoven and Andrew N. Leak, 286–301. New York: Berghahn, 2005.

Hall, Stuart, and Paul du Gay, eds. *Questions of Cultural Identity*. London: Sage, 1996.

Hannaford, Ivan. *Race: The History of an Idea in the West*. Baltimore: Johns Hopkins University Press, 1996.

Haraway, Donna. "A Manifesto for Cyborgs: Science, Technology, and Socialist Feminism in the 1980s." In *The Postmodern Turn*, ed. Seidman, 82–118.

Harding, Sandra G., ed. *The Feminist Standpoint Theory Reader: Intellectual and Political Controversies*. New York: Routledge, 2004.

———. "Rethinking Standpoint Epistemology: What Is 'Strong Objectivity?'" In *The Feminist Standpoint Theory Reader*, ed. Harding, 127–40.

Hart, Kevin. *Postmodernism: A Beginner's Guide*. Oxford: Oneworld, 2004.

Hartsock, Nancy. "The Feminist Standpoint: Developing the Ground for a Specifically Feminist Historical Materialism." In *Feminist Standpoint Theory Reader*, ed. Harding, 35–54.

Hayward, Clarissa R., and Ron Watson. "Against Recognition. Identity Politics and Democratic Non-Domination." Manuscript, 2009.

Hechter, Michael. "Ethnicity and Rational Choice Theory." In *Ethnicity*, ed. Hutchinson and Smith, 90–98.

Heidegger, Martin. *Being and Time*. Trans. John Macquarrie and Edward Robinson. New York: Harper and Row, 1962.

———. *Being and Time*. Trans. Joan Stambaugh. Albany: State University of New York Press, 1996.

———. *German Existentialism*. Trans. Dagobert D. Runes. New York: Philosophical Library, 1965.

Hekman, Susan J. *Private Selves, Public Identities: Reconsidering Identity Politics*. University Park: Pennsylvania State University Press, 2005.

Herberg, Will. *Protestant, Catholic, Jew: An Essay in American Religious Sociology*. Garden City, N.Y.: Doubleday, 1960.

Hesse, Hermann. *Steppenwolf.* Trans. Joseph Mileck. New York: Holt, Rinehart and Winston, 1963.

Higham, John, and Paul K. Conkin, eds. *New Directions in American Intellectual History.* Baltimore: Johns Hopkins University Press, 1979.

Hirschfeld, Lawrence A. *Race in the Making: Cognition, Culture, and the Child's Construction of Human Kinds.* Cambridge, Mass.: MIT Press, 1996.

Hirschman, Albert O. *Exit, Voice and Loyalty: Response to Decline in Firms, Organizations and States,* 2nd ed. Cambridge, Mass: Harvard University Press, 1972.

Hobsbawm, Eric J. *Nations and Nationalism Since 1780: Programme, Myth, Reality.* Cambridge: Cambridge University Press, 1990.

Hobsbawm, Eric J., and Terence O. Ranger, eds. *The Invention of Tradition.* Cambridge: Cambridge University Press, 1983.

Holler, Claudia, and Martin Klepper, eds. *Rethinking Narrative Identity: Persona and Perspective.* Amsterdam: Benjamins, 2013.

Honneth, Axel. *The Struggle for Recognition: The Moral Grammar of Social Conflicts.* Trans. Joel Anderson. Cambridge, Mass.: MIT Press, 1995.

Honneth, Axel, and Avishai Margalit. "Recognition." *Proceedings of the Aristotelian Society, Supplementary Volumes* 75 (2001): 111–39.

Horowitz, Donald L. "Ethnic Identity." In *Ethnicity,* ed. Glazer and Moynihan, 111–40.

———. *Ethnic Groups in Conflict.* Berkeley: University of California Press, 1985.

———. . "Ethnic Identity." In Glazer and Moynihan. *Ethnicity,* ed. Glazer and Moynihan, 111–40.

Horowitz, Maryanne Cline, ed. *New Dictionary of the History of Ideas.* Vol. 3. Farmington Hills, Minn.: Thomson Gale, 2005.

Howells, Christina, ed. *The Cambridge Companion to Sartre.* Cambridge: Cambridge University Press, 1992.

Huntington, Samuel. "The Clash of Civilizations?" *Foreign Affairs* 72, 3 (Summer 1993): 22–49.

———. *The Clash of Civilizations and the Remaking of World Order.* New York: Simon and Schuster, 1996.

———. *Who Are We? The Challenges to America's National Identity.* New York: Simon and Schuster, 2004.

Hutchinson, John, and Anthony D. Smith, eds. *Ethnicity.* Oxford: Oxford University Press, 1996.

Irigaray, Luce. *Speculum of the Other Woman.* Trans. Gillian C. Gill. Ithaca, N.Y.: Cornell University Press, 1985.

———. *This Sex Which Is Not One.* Trans. Catherine Porter. Ithaca, N.Y.: Cornell University Press, 1985.

Isaac, Benjamin. *The Invention of Racism in Classical Antiquity.* Princeton, N.J.: Princeton University Press, 2004.

Isaacs, Harold R. "Basic Group Identity: The Idols of the Tribe." In *Ethnicity,* ed. Glazer and Moynihan, 29–52.

Izenberg, Gerald N. "Die 'Aristokratisierung' der bürgerlichen Kultur im 19. Jahrhundert." In *Legitimationskrisen des deutschen Adels 1200–1900,* ed. Peter U. Hohendahl and Paul Michael Lützeler, 233–44. Stuttgart: Metzler, 1979.

———. *The Existentialist Critique of Freud: The Crisis of Autonomy.* Princeton, N.J.: Princeton University Press, 1976.

———. *Impossible Individuality: Romanticism, Revolution and the Origins of Modern Selfhood, 1787–1802.* Princeton, N.J.: Princeton University Press, 1992.

———. *Modernism and Masculinity: Mann, Wedekind, Kandinsky Through World War I.* Chicago: University of Chicago Press, 2000.

———. "Reconciling Individuality and Individualism in European Liberalism." *Intellectual History Newsletter* 24 (2002): 23–37.

Jackson, Ronald L., II, ed. *Encyclopedia of Identity.* 2 vols. Los Angeles: Sage, 2010.

Jacobs, Sue-Ellen, Wesley Thomas, and Sabine Lang, eds. *Two-Spirit People: Native American Gender Identity, Sexuality and Spirituality.* Urbana: University of Illinois Press, 1997.

Jagger, Alison. "Feminist Politics and Epistemology: The Standpoint of Women." In *The Feminist Standpoint Theory Reader*, ed. Harding, 55–66.

James, Harold. *A German Identity: 1770 to the Present Day*. London: Phoenix, 1989.

Jarausch, Konrad H., ed. *After Unity: Reconfiguring German Identities*. Providence, R.I.: Berghahn, 1997.

———. "A Struggle for Unity: Redefining National Identities." In *Shattered Past*, ed. Jarausch and Geyer, 221–44.

Jarausch, Konrad H. and Michael Geyer. *Shattered Past: Reconstructing German Histories*. Princeton, N.J.: Princeton University Press, 2003.

Jenkins, Richard. *Social Identity*. 3rd ed. London: Routledge, 2008.

Johnson, Barbara. "Thresholds of Difference: Structures of Address in Zora Neale Hurston." In *"Race," Writing, and Difference*, ed. Gates, 317–28.

Johnston, Hank, Enrique Laraña, Joseph R. Gusfield. "Identities, Grievances and New Social Movements." In *New Social Movements: From Ideology to Identity*, ed. Laraña et al., 3–35.

Johnstone, Barbara. "Locating language in identity." In *Language and Identities*, ed. Llamas and Watt, 29–38.

Jones, Anne Rosalind. "Writing the Body: Toward an Understanding of 'L'Écriture Feminine.'" *Feminist Studies* 7, 2 (Summer 1981): 247–63.

Jonsson, Stefan. *Subject Without Nation: Robert Musil and the History of Modern Identity*. Durham, N.C.: Duke University Press, 2000.

Joseph, John E. "Identity." In *Language and Identities*, ed. Llamas and Watt, 18–28.

———. *Language and Identity: National, Ethnic, Religious*. Houndmills: Palgrave Macmillan, 2004.

Kafka, Franz. *The Castle*. Trans. Mark Harman. New York: Schocken, 1998.

Karenga, Maulana. "Us: Philosophy, Principles, and Program." http://usorganization.org.

Kauffman, L. A. "The Anti-Politics of Identity." In Ryan. *Identity Politics in the Women's Movement*, 23–34.

Kaufmann, Jean-Claude. *L'invention de soi: Une théorie de l'identité*. Paris: Armand Colin, 2004.

Kenny, Michael. *The Politics of Identity: Liberal Political Theory and the Dilemmas of Difference*. Cambridge: Polity, 2004.

Keupp, Heiner et al. *Identitätskonstruktionen: Das Patchwork der Identitäten in der Spätmoderne*. Reinbek bei Hamburg: Rowohlt, 1999.

Keupp, Heiner, and Renate Höfer. *Identitätsarbeit heute: Klassische und aktuelle Perspektiven der Identitätsforschung*. Frankfurt a.M.: Suhrkamp, 1997.

Kilson, Martin. "Blacks and Neo-Ethnicity in American Life." In *Ethnicity*, ed. Glazer and Moynihan, 236–66.

Kisiel, Theodore. *The Genesis of Heidegger's Being and Time*. Berkeley: University of California Press, 1993.

Klapp, Orrin E. *Collective Search for Identity*. New York: Holt, Rinehart and Winston, 1969.

Klein, Kerwin Lee. "On the Emergence of Memory in Historical Discourse." *Representations* 69 (Winter 2000): 127–50.

Klopp, Brett. *German Multiculturalism: Immigrant Integration and the Transformation of Citizenship*. Westport, Conn.: Praeger, 2002.

Klusmeyer, Douglas B., and Demetrios G. Papademetriou. *Immigration Policy in the Federal Republic of Germany: Negotiating Membership and Remaking the Nation*. New York: Berghahn, 2009.

Kohn, Hans. "The Crisis in European Thought and Culture." In *World War I: A Turning Point in Modern History*, ed. Jack J. Roth. New York: Knopf, 1967, 25–46.

Konrad-Adenauer-Stiftung, ed. *Heimat und Nation: Zur Geschichte und Identität der Deutschen*. Mainz: Hase-Köhler, 1984.

Koselleck, Reinhart. "Kriegerdenkmale als Identitätsstiftungen der Überlebenden." In *Identität*, ed. Marquard and Stierle, 255–76.

Kramsch, Claire. *Language and Culture*. Oxford: Oxford University Press, 1998.

Krappman, Lothmar. *Soziologische Dimensionen der Identität*. Stuttgart: Klett-Cotta, 1971.

Kraus, Wolfgang. *Das erzählte Selbst: Konstruktion von Identität in der Spätmoderne*. Pfaffenweiler: Centaurus, 1996.

Kreckel, Reinhard, ed. *Soziale Ungleichheiten*. Soziale Welt, Sonderband 2. Göttingen: A. Schwartz, 1983.

Krieger, Leonard. *The German Idea of Freedom*. Chicago: University of Chicago Press, 1957.

Kristeva, Julia. "From One Identity to an Other." In *French Feminism Reader*, ed. Oliver, 158–65.

———. "Woman's Time." In *French Feminism Reader*, ed. Oliver, 181–200.

Kruks, Sonia. *Retrieving Experience: Subjectivity and Recognition in Feminist Politics*. Ithaca, N.Y.: Cornell University Press, 2001.

Kuhn, Manford H., and Thomas S. McPartland. "An Empirical Investigation of Self-Attitudes." *American Sociological Review* 19, 1 (February 1954): 68–76.

Kukathas, Chandran. "Are There Any Cultural Rights?" *Political Theory* 20, 1 (February 1992): 105–39.

———. "Liberalism and Multiculturalism: The Politics of Indifference." *Political Theory* 26, 5 (October 1998): 686–99.

Kundera, Milan. *Identity*. Trans. L. Asher. New York: HarperCollins, 1998.

Kymlicka, Will. "The Canadian Model of Diversity in Comparative Perspective." In *Multiculturalism and the Canadian Constitution*, ed. Tierney, 61–90.

———. *The Current State of Multiculturalism in Canada*. Government of Canada: Minister of Public Works and Government Services, 2010. Online.

———. *Liberalism, Community and Culture*. Oxford: Clarendon, 1989.

———. *Multicultural Citizenship: A Liberal Theory of Minority Rights*. Oxford: Clarendon, 1995.

Lacan, Jacques. "Le complexe, facteur concret de la psychologie familiale." In *Encyclopédie française*, vol. 8, *La vie mentale*, ed. Henri Wallon. Paris: Société Nouvelle de l'Encyclopédie Française, 1938.

———. *Écrits*. Paris: Seuil, 1966.

———. *Écrits: A Selection*. Trans. Alan Sheridan. New York: Norton, 1977.

———. *Feminine Sexuality: Jacques Lacan and the école freudienne*. Ed. Juliet Mitchell and Jacqueline Rose. New York: Palgrave Macmillan, 1982.

———. *On Feminine Sexuality: The Limits of Love and Knowledge*. Book 20, *Encore 1972–1973*, trans. Bruce Fink. Seminar of Jacques Lacan. New York: Norton, 1999.

LaCapra, Dominick. *History and Memory After Auschwitz*. Ithaca, N.Y.: Cornell University Press, 1998.

Laclau, Ernesto, and Chantal Mouffe. *Hegemony and Socialist Strategy: Towards a Radical Democratic Politics*. 2nd ed. London: Verso, 2001.

Laing, R. D. *The Divided Self: An Existential Study in Sanity and Madness*. Harmondsworth: Penguin, 1960.

———. *The Self and Others: Further Studies in Sanity and Madness*. London: Tavistock, 1961.

Lamizet, Bernard. *Politique et Identité*. Lyon: Presses Universitaires de Lyon, 2002.

Laqueur, Thomas. *Making Sex: Body and Gender from the Greeks to Freud*. Cambridge, Mass.: Harvard University Press, 1990.

Laraña, Enrique, Hank Johnston, and Joseph R. Gusfield, eds. *New Social Movements: From Ideology to Identity*. Philadelphia: Temple University Press, 1994.

Lawler, Steph. *Identity: Sociological Perspectives*. Cambridge: Polity, 2008.

Layton, Lynne. *Who's That Boy? Who's That Girl: Clinical Practice Meets Postmodern Gender Theory*. Hilldale, N.J.: Analytic Press, 2004.

Leary, Mark R., and June Price Tangney, eds. *Handbook of Self and Identity*. New York: Guilford, 2003; 2nd ed. 2010.

Lee, Hermione. *Virginia Woolf*. London: Vintage, 1999.

Le Gallou, Jacques-Yves, et le Club de l'Horloge. *La préférence nationale: Réponse à l'immigration*. Paris: A. Michel, 1985.

Le Page, Robert Brock, and Andrée Tabouret-Keller. *Acts of Identity: Creole-Based Approaches to Language and Identity*. Cambridge: Cambridge University Press, 1985.

Lepsius, M. Rainer. "Die unbestimmte Identität der Bundesrepublik." *Hochland* 60 (1967/68): 562–69.

Le Rider, Jacques. *Modernity and Crises of Identity: Culture and Society in Fin-de-Siècle Vienna*. Trans. Rosemary Morris. New York: Continuum, 1993.

Le Sueur, James D. *Uncivil War: Intellectuals and Identity Politics During the Decolonization of Algeria*. Lincoln: University of Nebraska Press, 2005.

Levenback, Karen L. *Virginia Woolf and the Great War*. Syracuse, N.Y.: Syracuse University Press, 1999.

Levin, Jerome D. *Theories of the Self*. Washington, D.C.: Hemisphere, 1992.

Lévi-Strauss, Claude. *L'identité: Séminaire interdisciplinaire dirigé par Claude Lévi-Strauss au Collège de France, 1974–1975*. Paris: Presses Universitaires de France, 1977.

Levita, David J. *The Concept of Identity*. The Hague: Gruyter, 1965.

Lifton, Robert Jay. "Protean Man." *Partisan Review* 35 (Winter 1968): 13–27.

———. *The Protean Self: Human Resilience in an Age of Fragmentation*. Chicago: University of Chicago Press, 1993.

———. *Witness to an Extreme Century: A Memoir*. New York: Free Press, 2011.

Lindner, Robert M. *Must You Conform?* New York: Rinehart, 1956.

Linton, Ralph. *The Study of Man: An Introduction*. New York: Appleton-Century-Crofts, 1936.

Llamas, Carmen, and Dominic Watt, eds. *Language and Identities*. Edinburgh: Edinburgh University Press, 2010.

Locke, John. *Essay Concerning Human Understanding*. 2nd ed. London, 1694.

Lohauss, Peter. *Moderne Identität und Gesellschaft: Theorien und Konzepte*. Opladen: Leske + Budrich, 1995.

Long, Marceau. *Être français aujourd'hui et demain*. Paris: Union Générale d'Éditions, 1988.

Lott, Eric. "After Identity Politics: The Return of Universalism." In "Is There Life After Identity Politics?" Special issue, *New Literary History* 31, 4 (Autumn 2000): 665–80.

Luft, David S. *Robert Musil and the Crisis of European Culture, 1880–1942*. Berkeley: University of California Press, 1980.

Luhmann, Niklas. "Identitäten in selbst-substitutiven Ordnungen, besonders Gesellschaften. In *Identität*, ed. Marquard and Stierle, 315–46.

———. "Suche der Identität und Identität der Suche—über teleologische und selbstreferentielle Prozesse.' In *Identität*, ed. Marquard and Stierle, 593–94.

Lützeler, Paul Michael. *Hermann Broch, A Biography*. Trans. Janice Furness. London: Quartet, 1987.

Lynd, Helen Merrell. *On Shame and the Search for Identity*. New York: Harcourt Brace, 1958.

Maalouf, Amin. *In the Name of Identity*. Trans. Barbara Bray. New York: Penguin, 2000.

MacIntyre, Alasdair. *After Virtue: A Study in Moral Theory*. Notre Dame, Ind.: University of Notre Dame Press, 1981.

Mackey, Eva. *The House of Difference: Cultural Politics and National Identity in Canada*. Toronto: University of Toronto Press, 2002.

Maier, Charles. *The Unmasterable Past: History, Holocaust and German National Identity*. Cambridge, Mass.: Harvard University Press, 1988.

Malraux, André. *The Temptation of the West*. Trans. Robert Hollander. New York: Vintage, 1961.

Mansfield, Katherine. *Journal*. Ed. J. Middleton Murray. London: Constable, 1954.

Margalit, Avishai, and Moshe Halbertal. "Liberalism and the Right to Culture." *Social Research* 61, 3 (Fall 1994): 491–510.

Margalit, Avishai, and Joseph Raz. "National Self-Determination." *Journal of Philosophy* 87, 9 (September 1990): 439–61.

Markovitz, Irving Leonard. *Léopold Sédar Senghor and the Politics of Negritude*. New York: Heinemann, 1969.

Marks, Elaine. "Feminism's Wake." In "On Feminine Writing: A *Boundary 2* Symposium." Special issue, *Boundary 2* 12, 2 (Winter 1984): 99–111.

Marks, Elaine, and Isabelle de Courtivron, eds. *New French Feminisms*. Amherst: University of Massachusetts Press, 1980.

Marquard, Odo, and Karlheinz Stierle, eds. *Identität*. Poetik und Hermeneutik 8. Munich: Wilhelm Fink, 1979.

Martin, Raymond, and John Barresi. *The Rise and Fall of Soul and Self: An Intellectual History of Personal Identity*. New York: Columbia University Press, 2006.

May, Elaine Tyler. *Homeward Bound: American Families in the Cold War Era*. New York: Basic Books, 1988.

Mayer, Arno J. *The Persistence of the Old Regime*. New York: Pantheon, 1981.

McAdams, Dan P. "The Case for Unity in the (Post)Modern Self: A Modest Proposal." In *Self and Identity*, ed. Ashmore and Jussim, 46–80.

McAdams, Dan P., Ruthellen Josselson, and Amia Lieblich, eds. *Identity and Story: Creating Self in Narrative*. Washington, D.C.: American Psychological Association, 2006.

McCall, George J., and J. L. Simmons. *Identities and Interactions: An Examination of Human Associations in Everyday Life*. New York: Free Press, 1966.

McCartney, John T. *Black Power Ideologies: An Essay in African-American Political Thought*. Philadelphia: Temple University Press, 1992.

McIntosh, Mary. "The Homosexual Role." In *Forms of Desire: Sexual Orientation and the Social Constructionist Controversy*, ed. Edward Stein, 25–42. New York: Routledge, 1992.

Meltzer, Brad. *Identity Crisis*. New York: DC Comics, 2004, 2005.

Melucci, Alberto. *Nomads of the Present: Social Movements and Individual Needs in Contemporary Society*. London: Hurchinson Radius, 1989.

———. "A Strange Kind of Newness: What's 'New' in New Social Movements?" In *New Social Movements*, ed. Laraña et al., 101–32.

Merleau-Ponty, Maurice.. *The Phenomenology of Perception*. Trans. Colin Smith. London: Routledge, 1962.

———. *The Structure of Behavior*. Trans. Alden L. Fisher. Boston: Beacon, 1963.

Meuter, Norbert. *Narrative Identität: Das Problem der personalen Identität im Anschluss an Ernst Tugendhat, Niklas Luhmann und Paul Ricoeur*. Stuttgart: Wissenschaft und Forschung, 1995.

Meyer, Thomas. *Identity Mania: Fundamentalism and the Politicization of Cultural Differences*. Trans. Madhulika Reddy and Lew Hinchman. London: Zed, 2001.

Michaels, Walter Benn. "Race into Culture." In *Identities*, ed. Appiah and Gates, 32–62.

———. *Our America: Nativism, Modernism and Pluralism*. Durham, N.C.: Duke University Press, 1995.

———. *The Trouble with Diversity: How We Learned to Love Identity and Ignore Inequality*. New York: Metropolitan, 2006.

Miller, Arthur. *Death of a Salesman*. New York: Penguin, 1976.

Millett, Kate. *Sexual Politics*. Urbana: University of Illinois Press, 2000.

Mitscherlich, Alexander. *Society Without the Father: A Contribution to Social Psychology*. Trans. Eric Mosbacher. New York: Harcourt, Brace, 1969.

Mitscherlich, Alexander, and Margarete Mitscherlich. *The Inability to Mourn: Principles of Collective Behavior*. Trans. Beverly R. Placzek. New York: Grove, 1975.

Moi, Toril, ed. *French Feminist Thought: A Reader*. Oxford: Blackwell, 1987.

———. *Sexual/Textual Politics: Feminist Literary Theory*. London: Methuen, 1985.

Moraga, Cherrie, and Gloria Anzaldua, eds. *This Bridge Called My Back: Writings by Radical Women of Color*. New York: Women of Color Press, 1981.

Morales, Rosario. "I Am What I Am." In *This Bridge Called My Back*, ed. Moraga and Anzaldua, 145–46.

Morris, Katherine J., ed. *Sartre on the Body*. Houndmills: Palgrave Macmillan, 2010.

Morton, W. L. *The Canadian Identity*. Madison and Toronto: University of Wisconsin Press and University of Toronto Press, 1961.

Moses, Claire G. "Made in America: 'French Feminism' in Academia." In "Disciplining Feminism? The Future of Women's Studies." Special issue, *Feminist Studies* 24, 2 (Summer 1998): 241–74.

Moulin, Jean-Pierre. "Identité française." In *Enquête sur la France multiraciale*. Paris: Calman–Lévy, 1985.

Moya, Paula M. L. "Postmodernism, 'Realism,' and the Politics of Identity." In *Reclaiming Identity*, ed. Moya and Hames-Garcia, 67–101.

Moya, Paula M. L., and Michael R. Hames-Garcia, eds. *Reclaiming Identity: Realist Theory and the Predicament of Postmodernism*. Berkeley: University of California Press, 2000.

Mucchielli, Alex. *L'Identité*. Paris: Presses Universitaires de France, 2009.

Muller, Jerry Z. *Conservatism: An Anthology of Social and Political Thought from David Hume to the Present*. Princeton, N.J.: Princeton University Press, 1997.

Murphy, Julien S., ed. *Feminist Interpretations of Jean-Paul Sartre*. University Park: Pennsylvania State University Press, 1999.

Musil, Robert. *Gesammelte Werke*. Vol. 2, *Prosa und Stücke, Kleine Prosa, Aphorismen, Autobiographisches, Essays und Reden, Kritik*. Hamburg: Rowohlt, 1978.

———. *The Man Without Qualities*. Vols. 1 and 2. Trans. Sophie Wilkins and Burton Pike. New York: Vintage, 1995.

———. *Young Törless*. Trans. Eithne Wilkins and Ernst Kaiser. New York: Pantheon, 1982.

Nash, Manning. "The Core Elements of Ethnicity." In *Ethnicity*, ed. Hutchinson and Smith, 24–28.

Nicholson, Linda, ed. *Feminist Contentions: A Philosophical Exchange*. New York: Routledge, 1995.

———. *Identity Before Identity Politics*. Cambridge, Mass.: Harvard University Press, 2008.

———, ed. *The Second Wave: A Reader in Feminist Theory*. New York: Routledge, 1997.

Nicholson, Linda, and Steven Seidman, eds. *Social Postmodernism: Beyond Identity Politics*. Cambridge: Cambridge University Press, 1995.

Niethammer, Lutz. *Kollektive Identität. Heimliche Quellen einer unheimlichen Konjunktur*. Reinbek bei Hamburg: Rowohlt, 2000.

Noiriel, Gérard. *À quoi sert "l'identité nationale."* Marseille: Agone, 2007.

———. *The French Melting Pot: Immigration, Citizenship, and National Identity*. Trans. Geoffroy de Laforcade. Minneapolis: University of Minnesota Press, 1996.

———. *Population, immigration et identité nationale en France, XIXe–XXe siècle*. Paris: Hachette, 1992.

Nolte, Ernst. "Die Faschismus in seiner Epoche and seine weltpolitischen Konsequenzen bis zur Gegenwart." In *Deutsche Identität heute*, ed. Berglar, 25–47.

Nora, Pierre. "General Introduction: Between Memory and History." In *Realms of Memory: The Construction of the French Past*, vol. 1, *Conflicts and Divisions*, 1–20. Ed. Lawrence D. Kritzman. Trans. Arthur Goldhammer. New York: Columbia University Press, 1996.

———, ed. *Les lieux de mémoire*. 7 vols. Paris: Gallimard, 1984–92.

———. *Présent, nation, mémoire*. Paris: Gallimard, 2011.

———. *Rethinking France*. 4 vols. Ed. David P. Jordan and Pierre Nora. Chicago: University of Chicago Press, 2001–10.

———. "Volume Introduction." In *Rethinking France*. Vol. 1, *The State*, xxxv–xl..

Nussbaum, Martha C. "The Professor of Parody." *New Republic*, February 22, 1999.

Okin, Susan Moller. *Is Multiculturalism Bad for Women?* Ed. Joshua Cohen, Matthew Howard, and Martha C. Nussbaum. Princeton, N.J.: Princeton University Press, 1999.

O'Leary, Brendan. "On the Nature of Nationalism: An Appraisal of Ernest Gellner's Writings on Nationalism." *British Journal of Political Science* 27, 2 (April 1997): 191–222.

Oliver, Kelly, ed. *French Feminism Reader*. Lanham, Md.: Rowman and Littlefield, 2000.

Ott, Hugo. *Martin Heidegger: A Political Life*. Trans. Allan Blunden. New York: Basic, 1993.

Oyserman, Daphne, Kristen Elmore and George C. Smith. "Self, Self-Concept and Identity." In *Handbook of Self and Identity*, 2nd ed., ed. Leary and Tangney, 69–104.

Parekh, Bhikhu. *Rethinking Multiculturalism: Cultural Diversity and Political Theory*. Cambridge, Mass.: Harvard University Press, 2000.

Parfit, Derek. *Reasons and Persons*. Oxford: Clarendon, 1984.

Parsons, Talcott. "Some Theoretical Considerations on the Nature and Trends of Change." In *Ethnicity*, ed. Glazer and Moynihan, 53–83.

Patai, Daphne. "The Struggle for Feminist Purity Threatens the Goals of Feminism." In *Identity Politics in the Women's Movement*, ed. Ryan, 39–42.

Pateman, Carol, and Elizabeth Gross, eds. *Feminist Challenges: Social and Political Theory*. Boston: Northeastern University Press, 1987.

Patterson, James T. *Grand Expectations: The United States, 1945–1974*. New York: Oxford University Press, 1996.

Peisl, Anton, and Armin Mohler. *Die deutsche Neurose: Über der beschädigte Identität der Deutschen*. Frankfurt: Ullstein, 1980.

Pflüger, Robert. "Identität als Oktroi." In *Deutsche Identität*, ed. Von Schrenk-Notzing and Moller, 50–58.

Pichardo, Nelson A. "New Social Movements: A Critical Review." *Annual Review of Sociology* 23 (1997): 411–30.

Pirandello, Luigi. "Henry IV." In *Naked Masks: Five Plays by Luigi Pirandello*, ed. Eric Bentley, 139–208. NewYork: Dutton, 1952.

———. "Six Characters in Search of an Author." In *Naked Masks*, ed. Bentley, 211–76.

Plummer, Kenneth, ed. *The Making of the Modern Homosexual*. London: Rl Innactive Titles, 1981.

Pomian, Krzyzstof. "Franks and Gauls." In Nora. *Realms of Memory*, vol. 1, 27–78.

Porter, John. "Ethnic Pluralism in Canadian Perspective." In *Ethnicity*, ed. Glazer and Moynihan, 267–304.

Proust, Marcel. *Time Regained*. Trans. Andreas Mayor, Terence Kilmartin, and D. J. Enright. New York: Modern Library, 2003.

Rajchman, John, ed. *The Identity in Question*. New York: Routledge, 1995.

Rawls, John. *Political Liberalism*. New York: Columbia University Press, 2005.

Raz, Joseph. *Ethics in the Public Domain: Essays in the Morality of Law and Politics*. Oxford: Oxford University Press, 1994.

Rich, Adrienne. *Of Woman Born: Motherhood as Experience and Institution*. New York: Norton, 1976.

Ricoeur, Paul. *Oneself as Another*. Trans. K. Blaney. Chicago: University of Chicago Press, 1992.

———. *Time and Narrative*. 3 vols. Trans. Kathleen McLaughlin and David Pellauer. Chicago: University of Chicago Press, 1984–88.

Riesman, David. *The Lonely Crowd: A Study of the Changing American Character*. New Haven, Conn.: Yale University Press, 1950.

Riley, Denise. *"Am I That Name?" Feminism and the Category of "Women" in History*. Minneapolis: University of Minnesota Press, 1988.

Rimmerman, Craig A. *From Identity to Politics: The Lesbian and Gay Movements in the United States*. Philadelphia: Temple University Press, 2002.

Ringer, Fritz K. *The Decline of the Mandarins: The German Academic Community, 1890–1933*. Cambridge, Mass.: Harvard University Press, 1969.

Roazen, P. *Erik H. Erikson: The Power and Limits of a Vision*. New York: Free Press, 1976.

Robinson, W. Peter, ed. *Social Groups and Identities: Developing the Legacy of Henri Tajfel*. Oxford: Butterworth-Heinemann, 1996.

Roediger, David R. *Working Towards Whiteness: How America's Immigrants Became White*. New York: Basic, 2005.

Rorty, Amélie O. "The Hidden Politics of Cultural Identification." *Political Theory* 22, 1 (February 1994): 152–66.

———, ed. *Identities of Persons*. Berkeley: University of California Press, 1976.

Rost, Dietmar. "In der Geisterbahn kollektiver Identität. Lutz Niethammers Kritik einer Begriffskonjunktur." *Forum: Qualitative Social Research* 4, 2 (May 2003).

Roth, Jack J., ed. *World War I: A Turning Point in Modern History*. New York: Knopf, 1967.

Ruddick, Sara. "Maternal Thinking." *Feminist Studies* 6, 2 (Summer 1980): 342–67.

———. *Maternal Thinking: Toward a Politics of Peace*. Boston: Beacon, 1989.

Ryan, Barbara, ed. *Identity Politics in the Women's Movement*. New York: New York University Press, 2001.

Sandel, Michael J. *Liberalism and the Limits of Justice*. 2nd ed. Cambridge, Mass.: Harvard University Press, 1998.

Sartre, Jean-Paul. *Anti-Semite and Jew.* Trans. George J. Becker. New York: Schocken, 1965.

———. *Being and Nothingness: An Essay on Phenomenological Ontology.* Trans. Hazel E. Barnes. New York: Philosophical Library, 1956.

———. "Black Orpheus." In *"What Is Literature?" and Other Essays,* Cambridge, Mass.: Harvard University Press, 1988, 289–330.

———. *Les Mots.* Paris: Gallimard, 1964.

———. *Nausea.* Trans. Lloyd Alexander. Norfolk, Conn.: New Directions, 1949.

———. *Notebooks for an Ethics.* Trans. David Pellauer. Chicago: University of Chicago Press, 1992.

———. "The Respectful Prostitute." In *No Exit and Three Other Plays,* 243–75. New York: Vintage, 1989.

Schlesinger, Arthur, Jr. *The Disuniting of America: Reflections on a Multicultural Society.* New York: Norton, 1992.

Schmalz-Jacobsen, Cornelia. "What Do We Mean by the German Fatherland." In *German Identity,* ed. Friedrich-Naumann–Stiftung, 103–13.

Schor, Naomi. "This Essentialism Which Is Not One: Coming to Grips with Irigaray." In *The Essential Difference,* ed. Schor and Weed, 40–62.

Schor, Naomi and Elizabeth Weed, eds. *The Essential Difference.* Bloomington: Indiana University Press, 1994.

Scott, Joan Wallach. *The Fantasy of Feminist History.* Durham, N.C.: Duke University Press, 2011.

Seidman, Steven, ed. *The Postmodern Turn: New Perspectives on Social Theory.* Cambridge: Cambridge University Press, 1994.

Seigel, Jerrold. *The Idea of the Self: Thought and Experience in Western Europe Since the Seventeenth Century.* Cambridge: Cambridge University Press, 2005.

Sellar, Walter Carruthers, and Robert Julian Yeatman, *1066 and All That.* London: 1993.

Sen, Amartya. *Identity and Violence: The Illusion of Destiny.* New York: Norton, 2006.

Sherif, Muzafer, O. J. Harvey, B. Jack White, William R. Hood, Caroline W. Sherif. *The Robbers Cave Experiment: Intergroup Conflict and Cooperation.* Middletown, Conn.: Wesleyan University Press, 1988.

Shimada, Shingo. "Constructions of Cultural Identity and Problems of Translation." In *Identities: Time, Difference and Boundaries,* ed. Friese, 133–52.

Simon, Bernd. *Identity in Modern Society: A Social Psychological Perspective.* Oxford: Blackwell, 2004.

Sklansky, Jeffrey. *The Soul's Economy: Market Society and Selfhood in American Thought, 1820–1920.* Chapel Hill: University of North Carolina Press, 2002.

Smith, Anthony D. *The Ethnic Revival in the Modern World.* Cambridge, Mass.: Harvard University Press, 1981.

———. *National Identity.* Reno, Las Vegas: University of Nevada Press, 1991.

———. *The Nation in History: Historiographical Debates About Ethnicity and Nationalism.* Cambridge: Polity, 2000.

———. "Nations and Their Pasts." The Warwick Debates, 1995. www2.lse.ac.uk/researchAndExpertise/units/gellner/WarwickDebate.

Somers, Margaret R., and Gloria D. Gibson. "Reclaiming the Epistemological 'Other': Narrative and the Social Constitution of Identity. In *Social Theory and the Politics of Identity,* ed. Calhoun, 37–99.

Spelman, Elizabeth V. *Inessential Woman: Problems of Exclusion in Feminist Thought.* Boston: Beacon, 1988.

Spiegel, Der. "Die Erfindung der Deutschen: Wie wir wurden, was wir sind." In "Geschichte 1." Special issue, *Der Spiegel,* 2007.

Spivak, Gayatri Chakravorty. "In a Word. Interview. With Elizabeth Rooney." *Differences* 1, 2 (Summer 1989): 124–54.

———. *In Other Worlds: Essays in Cultural Politics.* New York: Methuen, 1987.

———. *The Post-Colonial Critic: Interviews, Strategies, Dialogues.* Ed. Sarah Harasym. New York: Routledge, 1990.

Stein, Edward, ed. *Forms of Desire: Sexual Orientation and the Social Constructionist Controversy*. New York: Routledge, 1992.

Stern, Fritz. "The Political Consequences of the Unpolitical German." In *The Failure of Illiberalism: Essays on the Political Culture of Modern Germany*. New York: Knopf, 1972.

Stoller, Robert J. "A Contribution to the Study of Gender Identity." *International Journal of Psychoanalysis* 45 (1964): 220–26.

———. "A Further Contribution to the Study of Gender Identity." *International Journal of Psychoanalysis* 49 (1968): 364–68.

———. "Primary Femininity." *Journal of the American Psychoanalytic Association* 24 (1976): 59–78.

———. *Sex and Gender: On the Development of Masculinity and Femininity*. New York: Science House, 1968.

Straub, Jürgen, ed. *Narration, Identity, and Historical Consciousness*. New York: Berghahn, 2005.

Strauss, Anselm. *Mirrors and Masks: The Search for Identity*. Glencoe, Ill.: Free Press, 1959.

Stryker, Sheldon. *Symbolic Interactionism: A Social Structural Version*. Caldwell, N.J.: Blackburn, 1980.

Sussman, Warren I. " 'Personality' and Twentieth Century Culture." In *New Directions in American Intellectual History*, ed. Higham and Conklin, 212–26.

Tajfel, Henri. "Experiments in Intergroup Discrimination." *Scientific American* 233, 5 (1970): 96–102.

———. *Human Groups and Social Categories: Studies in Social Psychology*. Cambridge: Cambridge University Press, 1981.

———. ed. *Social Identity and Intergroup Relations*. Cambridge: Cambridge University Press, 1982.

Tatum, Beverly Daniel. *"Why Are All the Black Kids Sitting Together in the Cafeteria?" and Other Conversations About Race*. New York: Basic, 2003.

Taylor, Charles. *Multiculturalism: Examining the Politics of Recognition*. Ed. Amy Gutmann. Princeton, N.J.: Princeton University Press, 1994.

———. "The Politics of Recognition." In Taylor, *Multiculturalism*, 25–73.

———. *Sources of the Self: The Making of the Modern Identity*. Cambridge, Mass.: Harvard University Press, 1989.

Taylor, David, and Malcolm Yapp, eds. *Political Identity in South Asia*. Dublin: Curzon, 1979.

Temelini, Michael. "Multicultural Rights, Multicultural Virtues: A History of Multiculturalism in Canada." In *Multiculturalism and the Canadian Constitution*, ed. Tierney, 43–60.

Thiel, Udo. *The Early Modern Subject: Self-Consciousness and Personal Identity from Descartes to Hume*. Oxford: Oxford University Press, 2011.

Thiesse, Anne-Marie. *La création des identités nationales: Europe XVIIIe–XXe siècle*. Paris: Seuil, 1999.

———. *Faire les français: Quelle identité nationale?* Paris: Stock, 2010.

Tibi, Bassam. "Old Tribes and Imposed Nation-States in the Middle East." In *Ethnicity*, ed. Hutchinson and Smith, 174–78.

Tierney, Stephen, ed. *Multiculturalism and the Canadian Constitution*. Vancouver: UBC Press, 2007.

Tonkin, Elizabeth, Maryon McDonald, and Malcolm Chapman, eds. *History and Ethnicity*. London: Routledge, 1989.

Trudeau, Pierre Elliott. "Multiculturalism." Speech to House of Commons, with Government Response to Report of the Royal Commission on Bilingualism and Biculturalism, October 8, 1971. http://www.canadahistory.com/sections/documents/Primeministers/trudeau/docs-on multiculturalism.htm.

Tugendhat, Ernst. "Die Rolle der Identität in der Konstitution der Moral." Trans. Barbara Reiter and Alexander Staudacher. In *Moral und Person*, ed. Edelstein, 33–47.

Turner, J. C. "Henri Tajfel: An Introduction." In *Social Groups and Identities*, ed. Robinson, 1–24.

Tyson, Phyllis, and Robert Tyson. *Psychoanalytic Theory of Development: An Integration*. New Haven, Conn.: Yale University Press, 1990.

UNESCO. "Mexico City Declaration on Cultural Policies." World Conference on Cultural Policies. Mexico City, July 26–August 6, 1982. Online.

———. Universal Declaration on Cultural Diversity, November 2, 2001. Online.

Van Buren, John. *The Young Heidegger: Rumors of the Hidden King*. Bloomington: Indiana University Press, 1994.

Van Deburg, William L. *New Day in Babylon: The Black Power Movement and American Culture, 1965–1975*. Chicago: University of Chicago Press, 1992.

Van den Berghe, Pierre L. *Race and Racism: A Contemporary Perspective*. New York: Wiley, 1967.

Van den Hoven, Adrian, and Andrew Leak. *Sartre Today: A Centenary Celebration*. New York: Berghahn, 2005.

Veblen, Thorsten. "The Intellectual Pre-Eminence of Jews in Europe." *Political Science Quarterly* 34, 1 (March 1919): 33–42.

Von Schrenk-Notzing, Caspar, and Armin Mohler, eds. *Deutsche Identität*. Krefeld: Sinus Verlag, 1982.

Wallace, R. Jay. Review of Alasdair MacIntyre, *After Virtue* and *Whose Justice? Which Rationality?*, *History and Theory* 28, 3 (October 1989): 326–48.

Wallerstein, Robert S., and Leo Goldberger. *Ideas and Identities: The Life and Work of Erik Erikson*. Madison, Wis.: International Universities Press, 1998.

Wang, Ban. "'I' on the Run: Crisis of Identity in *Mrs. Dalloway*." *Modern Fiction Studies* 38, 1 (Spring 1992): 177–91.

Weeks, Jeffrey. *Coming Out: Homosexual Politics in Britain from the Nineteenth Century to the Present*. London: Quartet, 1977.

Weidenfeld, Werner, ed. *Die Identität der Deutschen*. Munich: Bundeszentrale für politische Bildung, 1983.

Weizsäcker, Richard von. "Die Deutschen und ihre Identität." In *"Denk Ich an Deutschland . . . :" Grundlagen eines Dialoges beider deutschen Staaten*, ed. Steffen Käser, 9–26. Hamburg: Bleicher Verlag, 1987.

Wesseling, Henk L. "Fin des empires, fin des nations?" In *Lieux de mémoire et identités nationales*," ed. Den Boer, 275–84.

West, Cornel. "The New Cultural Politics of Difference." In *The Postmodern Turn*, ed. Seidman, 65–81.

Wheelis, Alan. *The Quest for Identity*. New York: Norton, 1958.

White, Harrison C. *Identity and Control: A Structural Theory of Social Action*. Princeton, N.J.: Princeton University Press, 1992.

Willms, Bernard. "Die Zukunft der deutschen Identität." In *Deutsche Identität heute*, ed. Berglar, 80–95.

Winter, Jay. *Sites of Memory, Sites of Mourning: The Great War in European Cultural History*. Cambridge: Cambridge University Press, 1995.

Wolin, Richard. "From the 'Death of Man' to Human Rights: The Paradigm Change in French Intellectual Life." In *Histories of Postmodernism*, ed. Bevir, Hargis, and Rushing, 171–92.

———. *The Politics of Being: The Political Thought of Martin Heidegger*. New York: Columbia University Press, 1990.

Wollheim, Richard. *Freud*. Cambridge: Cambridge University Press, 1981.

Woolf, Virginia. *Mrs. Dalloway*. San Diego, Calif.: Harcourt, 1981.

———. *Orlando*. London: Penguin, 1993.

Woolf, Virginia et al. *The Mrs. Dalloway Reader*. Ed. Francine Prose. Orlando, Fla.: Harcourt, 2003.

Wrathall, Mark A., ed. *The Cambridge Companion to Heidegger's Being and Time*. Cambridge: Cambridge University Press, 2013.

Young, Iris Marion. *Justice and the Politics of Difference*. Princeton, N.J.: Princeton University Press, 1990.

———. "The Politics of the Un-Identified Woman." *Nous* 20, 1 (1986): 52.

———. "Polity and Group Difference: A Critique of the Ideal of Universal Citizenship." *Ethics* 99, 2 (January 1989): 250–74.

Zimmerman, Michael E. *Heidegger's Confrontation with Modernity: Technology, Politics, and Art*. Bloomington: Indiana University Press, 1990.

Index

absolute, lure of the, 316
absolute being, in Sartre, 90
absolute beings, 423–24. *See also* God
absolute identity, 3, 344, 391–92, 400
absolute monarchy, 310
absurd, sense of, 137
action: constituting identity, 372; desire-belief model of, 487n85; meaning and dignity conferred by, 153
Action Française, 87, 466n20
active male/passive female trope, 496n36
active strategy, Sartre's, 99, 100–101, 145
Addresses to the German Nation (Fichte), 381, 492n90
Adler, Alfred, 158
adolescence, 122–23, 179, 191
Adorno, Theodor, 115
adversarial collective identity, 392
aesthetics, 32, 47
affective ties, within ethnic groups, 206
affirmative action, 273–74
Africa's Search for Identity (Ferkiss), 173
Afrocentric movement, 260
agape, 434
"agnostic democracy," 437
Akerlof, George, 387–89
Alarcon, Norma, 324
Alawites, 213
Alcoff, Linda Martin, 351–53
Algeria: decolonization of, 160, 471n40; immigration from, to France, 241, 242, 243
Algren, Nelson, 156, 157
Ali, Ayaan Hirsi, 478n130
alienation: from self, 36, 121; and women's reproductive biology, 154–55
Althusser, Louis, 488n129
Altman, Dennis, 475n36
"American Creed," 261
American "Mom," 131
American Psychiatric Association, 2. *See also* psychoanalysis

Amish schooling, 285
amnesia, and loss of identity, 460n9
am-ness, sense of, 104
ancestry, myth of common, 207
Anderson, Benedict, 217, 218, 219, 220, 232, 261, 456
anguish, 88–90. *See also* anxiety
annihilation of being, 87
antagonism, and hegemony, 336
anthropology: and definition of ethnicity as self-definition, 204; and identity, 448
anticipatory resolve, 76, 78
anticolonial struggle, 173–74
anti-Fascism, 56
antimodernism: fundamentalism as, 231; Heidegger's, 70–71; in Wilhelmine Germany, 112
antirationalism: and the Great War, 46; nineteenth-century Romantic, 30
Anti-Semite and Jew (Sartre), 147, 151–52, 158
anti-Semitism, 412; French, 147–49
"antitotalitarian moment," 116
anti-Vietnam War movement, 1960s, 175
anxiety, 73–75, 139–41, 143, 344, 437. *See also* anguish
Anzaldua, Gloria, 200
apartheid, 330
Appiah, Kwame Anthony, 96, 276, 294, 298, 300, 398, 414–15, 438–43, 453, 456, 459n3
Arabs, Israeli, 279–82
archetypes, 15
Arendt, Hannah, 115
aristocracy-"mobocracy" conflict, in American identity, 115
Aristotle: on racial characteristics, 418–19; teleological ethics, 427, 428–29; virtue ethics, as rescued by MacIntyre, 427, 428–32
Armstrong, Elizabeth, 198
Aronowitz, Stanley, 488n111
Artaud, Antonin, 321
ascription, 207, 298, 324

"as if" beliefs, 122
assets, individual, common possession of, 266–67
assimilation, 161, 243; and the "naturalized" citizen, 422
attachment, 189–93, 190
Attitudes to Learning French in the English-Speaking Schools of Quebec (Edwards), 382
Augustine of Hippo, Saint, 436
Austin, J. L., 326, 379
Austria-Hungary, 41–42, 51
authenticity: achieving of, 75–78; of being with others, 68, 102; *eigentlich* and *eigenst*, 74; in handing down of tradition, 82; of identity, and self-identification, 236; Jewish, and being-for-others, 149; of subject vs. identity, 303; and temporality, 78; through anticipatory resoluteness, 78. *See also* inauthenticity
authentic possibility, as determinism, 72
authentic resolve, 484n13
authority, in tension with autonomy, 123
autism, as identity, 405–6
autochthony, 466n14. *See also* rootedness
autonomism, 215
autonomy, 120, 123, 131, 136, 190, 276, 431, 442
"averageness" of *das Man*, 70

Baader-Meinhof gang, 185
bad faith, 92, 97, 103, 143, 148, 151–52, 153, 427, 436
Badinter, Elizabeth, 20
Bambach, Charles, 466n14
Baraka, Amiri (LeRoi Jones), 178, 186
barbaros, 418
Barrès, Maurice, 247
Barresi, John, 6
Barth, Fredrik, 204–5, 361, 365, 392
Basic Law of 1949, German, 256
Bataille, Georges, 321
Battersby, Christine, 346–47, 348
battle fatigue, 105, 446–47
Baudrillard, Jean, 484n1
Bauman, Zigmunt, 301
Baumeister, Roy, 377, 491–92n65
Bayart, Jean-François, 234, 250, 390, 393–94, 403, 404
Beauvoir, Simone de, 18, 97, 144–45, 147, 182, 399, 400, 447, 466n19, 471n20
Beckett, Samuel, 94–95, 273
becoming, narratives as tales of, 367
behavior, reciprocal, 162
being: absolute, in Sartre, 90; annihilation of, 87; and categories of human existence, 62–63; in

Erikson, 107; in Heidegger, 62, 465n2; way of, identity as, 406–7
Being and Nothingness (Sartre), 86–87, 90–103, 140, 142, 150
Being and Time (Heidegger), 62–86, 446–47, 465n2
being-for-others: vs. being for oneself, 332; and Jewish "authenticity," 149
Being French Today and Tomorrow (Commission on Nationality), 243
being-in-the-world, 74, 319
being with others, 449; authenticity of, 68, 102; psychologizing of, in Laing, 140
Belgium, Fleming-Walloon conflict in, 213
beliefs: liberal democracies' religious protections, 285–86; revision of, and individual freedom, 283
belief systems: as comprehensive doctrines, 292–93; and identity, 29
Bell, Daniel, 206, 213–15
Bendix, Reinhard, 163
Benedict, Ruth, 113
Benedict of Nursia, Saint, 431
Benhabib, Seyla, 488n122
Benjamin, Walter, 220
Benoit, Jean-Marie, 356
Bergem, Wolfgang, 1, 240
Berger, Peter, 171, 172, 197
Bergson, Henri, 16
Berman, Marshall, 467n12
Berreby, David, 402
Besson, Eric, 234
Bhabha, Homi, 332
Bildung, 32, 50, 58, 112, 115, 468n21
Bilgrami, Akeel, 227
binary oppositions: black/white racial, 331; identity/difference, 343, 361; illusory, dissolved by liminal-space writers, 333; of the transcendental signified, 309. *See also* Derrida; dualism
bisexuality, 416
Blackboard Jungle (film), 133
black culture, 178, 212, 225–27
black identity, 110, 144, 161, 176–79, 186, 225–26, 331, 414, 440, 489n164; in Sartre, 146–47, 149–51
black inner-city youth, and identity utility, 388
black nationalists, 174
blackness, 158, 408. *See also* black identity; negritude
"Black Notebooks" (Heidegger), 465n3
"Black Orpheus" (Sartre), 149–51, 158
Black Power, 212; manifesto of 1967, 176–77; movement for, 144, 174, 225

black rights movement, 399

black separatist movements, 175

Black Skin, White Masks (Fanon), 158, 332

blood: and Jewish identity, 411; and kinship, 421–22

Blum, Léon, 248

body: "being" vs. merely "having," 417; black consciousness of, 159; centrality to language, 486n51; desire of consciousness to become, 101; female, 346–47; genetic foundations of racial difference, 412–14; group distinctions anchored in, 412; oneness with one's own, 143; relationship to meaning, 319; role of, in identity, 97–98; women's alienation from, through reproductive biology, 153–54. *See also* embodiment

bone marrow transplants, and racial identity, 413

Bonnafous, Simone, 241–42, 248

boundedness, as substitute for identity, 396

bourgeoisie, 17, 32, 70, 87

Bracher, Karl Dietrich, 240

Brandt, Willy, 235

Braudel, Fernand, 234, 245–46

Brick, Howard, 174

Broch, Hermann, 26, 33–34, 42, 45–50, 446, 463n15, 464n55

Brockhaus Concise Dictionary, 3

Brubaker, Rogers, 395–96

Buber, Martin, 467n15

Büchel, Nicole, 378

Burke, Peter, 361–64

Burns, Robert, 98

butler, Ishiguro's, and identity, 96, 438. *See also* sincere waiter

Butler, Judith, 324–28, 340, 342, 487n85, 488n122

Cameron, David, 251

Camus, Albert, 134

Canada: Charter of Rights and Freedoms, 253, 287; conflict between Québécois and English-speakers, 213; French instruction in, 287–88, 298–99; language as culture in, 261; multiculturalism in, 227–28, 251–55, 259, 261–62, 282–88

Canadian identity, 254, 480n59

capitalism: and individual anxiety, 112; productivity in, 374; and the rise of individualism, 143; as root cause of domination and inequality, 337

Carmichael, Stokely, 176

Cass, Vivienne, 196–97

The Castle (Kafka), 37–39, 111

castration, 315

categorical imperative, 266, 428

categorization, as substitute for identity, 396

certainty, desired by Dasein, 83, 89

Césaire, Aimé, 149

chains of signification, 308

character, and identity, 8–9, 461n33

Charles Martel, 244

Charter of Rights and Freedoms, Canada, 253

childbearing, 153–54. *See also* mothering

child development: and identification with the phallus, 304–5; in Mead, 164; and race theory formation, 408–9, 410–11; sexlessness of child, 314–16; stages of, as structures of language, 303

Childhood and Society (Erikson), 114–15, 116, 129–30

"Childhood of a Leader" (Sartre), 148, 466n20

child rearing practices: differences in, 343; and "sanity," 114–15

Chinese-Malayan conflict, on Malay Peninsula, 213

Chirac, Jacques, 243, 247

Chodorow, Nancy, 188, 189–90, 322, 348, 485n36

choice: to be oneself, 78; free, and destiny, 80–86; identity-based and identity-congruent, 375; and indeterminacy, 456; and midcentury American youth culture, 133; of self, 113; of work commitments, 123. *See also* free will

Chomsky, Noam, 407

Christian Democrats, Germany, 235, 250, 258

Christian militias, American, 370

church-state separation, 228

citizenship, 223, 254, 255, 256, 258, 285, 292–93, 422

civic identity, 3, 460n8

civic nationalism, 254

civil rights movement, 1960s U.S., 135, 175

Cixous, Hélène, 313, 322

"clash of civilizations," 229, 393, 454

class, 110, 146, 206, 473n84; and anti-Semitism, 147; ignored by gender identity politics, 200; and knowledge, 193–94; and work identity, 423

class conflict, 175; utility of Jews in, 148

class identity, 29, 214, 334–38

clean/unclean distinction, dietary, 424

Cleaver, Eldridge, 158

Clinton, William J., 62, 465n1

clitoridectomy, 296, 340
Club de l'Horloge, 242
CNRS (French National Center for Scientific
    Research), 250
coercion: ethnicity's power of, 209, 232; in illib-
    eral culture, 279; and Québec's Francophone
    laws, 287–88
Cohen, Abner, 209
Cohen, Lizabeth, 469n72
coherence, and personhood, 325
collapse of communism, 217
collective identity, 12, 21, 390, 397, 399, 438–39,
    447, 450, 457; absolutizing of, 22; in American
    thought before identity politics, 160–72; in
    decolonized countries, 173; and ethnicity,
    420–22; existential approach to, 415; facilitat-
    ing individuality, 63; formal criteria for,
    414–15; and gay/lesbian coming out, 184;
    held to be impossible by Sartre, 102; histori-
    cal, 454–55; Jemeinigkeit compatible with, 21;
    labor as, 422–23; in liberal politics, 294–98; as
    living tradition, 430; as loss of self, 15; mass
    societies' need for, 237; and personal identity,
    290, 371, 430, 448; race, 417–20; rendered sus-
    pect under Nazism, 86; in the "Robbers Cave"
    experiment, 169; in second-wave feminism,
    188–95; sex, 416–17; and transcendence,
    423–25; violence, and creation of, 160. See
    also group identity
collective memories, of nationalism, 16
collective Other, 145–52
collective tradition, 16
collective unconscious, Jungian, 13, 15, 391, 392
colonial warfare, 173. See also anticolonial
    struggle
the colonized, quest for identity and recognition
    by, 232, 447
color, and race, 411, 419
Combahee River Collective, 144, 199; manifesto
    of 1977, 174
coming out, as assertion of collective identity,
    184
Commission on Nationality, France, 243
commitment, denial of, in das Man, 69
commonality, 207, 266–67, 274, 396
common knowledge, 70. See also (das) Man
communal destiny of birth, 86
communism, collapse of, 217
community: imaginary, linguistically consti-
    tuted, 220; naturalized by kinship, 425; peo-
    ple's (Volksgemeinschaft), 80–81, 83
Community and Society (Tönnies), 81

companionship, in work, 126
competence, domain-specific, 407
comprehensive doctrines, 292–93
conformity, 131, 132, 133
connectedness, 83, 396; of Dasein, 79
Connery, Sean, 128
Connolly, William, 342–45, 354, 435, 450, 451,
    456
conscience, 76, 118; Christian, in Luther, 123;
    respect for, and military service exemption,
    297
consciousness, 3, 105, 126; absolute, Other as,
    96; attempts to constitute identity through
    self-definition, 95; and body, 101, 159; of
    class, 146; "double," of American blacks, 161;
    ethnic, transformed into national, 223; free-
    dom as act of, 146; and good faith, 313; self
    as, 90–91; separate from its past, 88
consensus politics, 175
conservatism, American, at midcentury, 131,
    132
constancy of self, 77–78, 84. See also self-
    continuity
constitutionalism, 289, 294
consumerism, 131, 132, 133
A Consumer's Republic (Cohen), 469n72
context of discovery, 195
contingency, 37, 335, 342–45; branded, 354;
    necessary, of identity, 90, 104, 450–51
continuity: of identity, 84, 107, 397; of memory,
    in Locke, 27; with past, Germany's lack of,
    237–38; and personhood, 325; sense of, and
    cultural identity, 222; unconscious striving
    for, 125
Conversations-Lexikon oder kurzgefasstes Handw-
    örterbuch, 3
Cooley, Charles Horton, 163
Cooper, David, 142
Cooper, Frederick, 395–96
core self, 348
corporate legal theory, 161, 162
cosmopolitanism: vs. particularity, 200; rooted,
    442. See also universalism
countercultural movements: of 1960s, 115, 116,
    175; in Wilhelmine Germany, 112
The Counterfeiters (Gide), 25, 36
countermodernism, fundamentalism as, 231. See
    also antimodernism
criminality, 311–12
crisis: of credibility, over political participatory
    channels, 370; social, and breakdown of exist-
    ing narratives, 367. See also identity crisis

"cult of the uniform," 33

cultural identity, 224–28, 391; biological stigma converted to, 186; definition problematic, 262; vs. ethnicity, 226; and government-initiated multiculturalism, 227–28; and the nation, 222; as personal identity, 254; primacy of, 299

"culturalism," 394

cultural memory, 391

cultural transmission, 207, 255

culture, 113–14; aligned with identity, 282–83; ethical-political, of liberal democracies, 291; and ethnicity, 206–7, 226, 254; fundamentalist, state exclusion of, 291; German unity of, 256; as group's common practices, 390–91; "identitarian," 283; and ideology, 252; vs. kinship, 421–22; language equated with, 252, 254, 261, 382; minority, recognition of, 265; and race/ethnicity, 226, 390; as a right, 278–79; secularized, spirituality and ethics in, 226–27; "societal," 283–84, 284; women as carrier, trope of, 54. *See also* fundamentalism

culture war, spread of black urban culture as, 179

cyborg, 323–24

Dahlendorf, Ralf, 239–40

Danchin, Antoine, 356

Darius Hystaspis, emperor of Persia, 404

Dasein, 64, 65, 319, 466n11, 485n13; connectedness of, 79, 83; dispersed in *das Man*, 83; empirical psychology of, 105; facticity of, 77; as "having to be," 66–67; historicality of, 72; negation only real power of, 76; as source of meaning, 72; in subjection to Others, 68, 71; "thrownness" and "fallenness" of, 71, 73, 74, 76, 77, 78, 79, 84, 89. See also *(das) Man*

Daughters of Bilitis, 183

death, 220; awareness of, as personal destiny, 306; as common destiny, 306; Dasein's aggregate of enacted possibilities after, 75; as "impossibility of Dasein," 76; persistence of identity after, 6, 460n10, 461n33

death instinct, 119

Death of a Salesman (Miller), 131

"The Death of the Hired Man" (Frost), 74

Decatur, Stephen, 440

decisionism, Kierkegaardian, 481n5

decolonization, 172

deconstruction: of god-terms, 309; of homosexuality, 328–29; of humanism, 335–36; linguistic, 307; and national identity, 338; of proper names, 308; of race, 329–31

delinquent, as quasi-natural class, 311–12

della Porta, Donatella, 371–72

Demian (Hesse), 51

democracy, liberal: accommodation of illiberal cultures, 275–78, 279–80, 283, 296; agnostic, 437; credibility crisis over conventional participatory channels, 370; ethical political culture, immigrant acceptance of, 291; as foundational U.S. belief, 261; politics of, and collective identity, 294–98; separation of politics and religion in, 288; state neutrality in values conflicts, 290

democratic republicanism, 85

deontology, 427

Derrida, Jacques, 302, 306–10, 316–18, 330, 361, 484nn1–2

Descartes, René, 65

descriptive phenomenology, 62

desire: clitoridectomy as assault on, 340; of consciousness to become body, 101; fantasy as setting for, 480–89n132; female, 315, 319; heterosexualizing of, 325–26; lost objects of, retained through identification, 122; to merge with the Other, 333; mother's, phallus as signifier of, 304–5; personal, social demands translated into, 326–27; protected by nonconsummation, 59; for self-definition, 353–54; "to be" something, identity as, 111; for transcendence, 449

desire-belief model of action, 487n85

destiny, 104; collective, 484n13; death as, 306; vs. fatedness, 82; and free choice, 80–86. *See also* determinism

determinism: authentic possibility as, 72; of identity, 451; and living one's heritage, 80; security of, 86; in sociology, 358

detumescence, as castration and non-being, 315

Diagnostic and Statistical Manual of Mental Disorders (DSM), 2

Dialectic of Enlightenment (Adorno and Horkheimer), 115

The Dialectic of Sex (Firestone), 180

Diani, Mario, 371–72

Dictionary of the History of Ideas, 2

dietary laws, Jewish, 424

différance, 307, 310, 318, 343, 344

difference, 385; as binary concept, 361; in children's racial theorizing, 408; "culturalization of," 186; group, and social reform, 448; and hybridity, 421; illuminated by stories, 442–43; language as conventional system of, 307; lived by new social movements, 369; multiculturalism obsessed with, 260; presupposed by

difference (*continued*)
identity, 435; women's attempt to communicate, 373. *See also* hybridity
difference feminism, 232, 374. *See also* standpoint theory
difference principle, Rawls's, 266
differentiation from the other, 170–71
diffusion of identity, 120, 126, 134
Dilthey, Wilhelm, 423
dirt, vs. purity, 424
disabilities: genetically caused, 413; ignored by gender identity politics, 200. *See also* stigma
disciplinary vs. hierarchical/militaristic societies, 312–13
Discipline and Punish (Foucault), 310, 313
discontinuity: of memory, 26–28; of temporal moments, 75–76
discourse ethics, 288
discourses, 303, 310–11; closed, 350; of deviancy, 311–12; on discourses, 318; of imperialism, 335–36; of individualism, 312; of race, in Canada, 251, 252; of sexuality, 311, 326; of "the Same," 318–19
disidentification with mother, 189. *See also* identification
"The Disintegration of Values" (Broch), 45–48
dispersal of Dasein, 83
"dissipation" of identity, in French theory, 302–13
Dissociative Identity Disorder, 495n9
"distantiality" of *das Man*, 70
The Disuniting of America (Schlesinger), 260–61
diversity, domestic, 262
The Divided Self (Laing), 138, 141–42
division of labor, sexual, 189, 194
domination, racial concepts shaped by, 409
"double consciousness" of American blacks, 161
Douglas, Mary, 420, 424–25
Doukhobor schooling, 285
drag, as performance against type, 340
drive theory, psychoanalytic, 119, 327
DSM IV—Revised Desk Reference, 459n6
dualism, in pre-Great War identity, 28–34. *See also* binary oppositions
DuBois, W. E. B., 161
il Duce (Benito Mussolini), 464n75
Durkheim, Émile, 172
Dutchman (Baraka), 178
Dworkin, Ronald, 265, 439
dystopia, homogeneous, 13

economic exploitation, 175
economics, and identity, 387–89, 448

education, minority community control of, 281, 285
Edwards, John, 381, 382
The Ego and the Id (Freud), 118, 327
ego identity, 2, 117–24, 163, 375. *See also* psychosocial identity
ego psychology, 118–19
ego synthesis, 125
egotism, 266
1888: Pasenow, or Romanticism (Broch), 33–34
Eksteins, Modris, 42
embodied horizon, 352
embodiment, 449; of sexuality, 417. *See also* body
emergence, as explanation of identity, 396
empathy, 189, 483n52
empires, European, dissolution of, 51, 173, 219
empty self, of liberal individualism, 265–75
"encompassing groups," 280
Encyclopedia of Identity, 2
Encyclopedia of the Social Sciences, 2
"engines of discovery," 405
English-speakers and Québécois, conflicts between, 213
engulfment, 140
Enlightenment rejection of Aristotelian teleology, 428
environments of memory, vs. sites, 383
epistemic value, of identities, 350
epistemology: gendered ways of knowing, 194–95; of identity, and claims to positions, 201; Lockean empiricist, 6–7
Epstein, Steven, 329, 475nn36, 38
equal opportunity, 293
equal rights: individual, 161, 175, 201, 202, 447; and citizenship, 223, 254; and common humanity, 287; for homosexuals, 198, 475n36; and humanism, 236; under liberal democracy, 264; for minorities, 262; and sameness, 188; for women, 180
Eriksen, Thomas H., 476n71
Erikson, Erik, 14, 105–7, 164, 355, 374, 397, 423, 459n3; becomes celebrity, 129; biographical influences, 108–9; on collective identity as part of individual identity, 448; and decolonized collective identities, 173; diffusion of his identity model, 127–34; ego-identity concept, 163; feminist revisions of, 188; on Gandhi, 135, 193, 452; ideological influences on, 109–16; influence of Fromm on, 468nn16, 34; life cycle model, 108, 119–20, 190; on Luther, 432–33, 452; "The Problem of Ego Identity,"

124–27; psychoanalysis-based identity concept, 1–2, 12–13, 17–18, 106, 117–24; sameness and possibility of autonomous change, 431; and 1960s counterculture, 134–36; and Tillich, 468n34; on trauma of identity, 446–47; on women's "inner space," 469n78; on work, 423; youthful Romantic conservatism of, 468n20

Eros, 119

Escape from Freedom (Fromm), 111

Essay Concerning Human Understanding (Locke), 6–7

essences, 348; created, 150; distinguishing, and race, 408; rethinking metaphysics of, 346; as what was, 89

essentialism, 18; female, 135, 314, 373, 471n41, 485n36, 486n51; Heidegger's, 76; physical difference conducive to, 412; psychological, 376–77; racial, biological race erroneously identified with, 413; sexual, 323; strategic, 340–41

the "eternal feminine," 317

"ethical individualism," Appiah, 438

ethical particularity, and universal morality, 444

"The Ethical Reality of Our Time" (Broch), 47–48, 464n55

ethics: and the good, 271; and identity, 7, 8, 10, 19, 27, 298, 427–44; Kantian, 265; vs. morality, 439, 440; motivational power of, 369; narrative and tradition in, 428–32; within secularized culture, 226; subordinated to aesthetics, 32; as unity of particular and universal, 289

"Ethiopians," Greco-Roman, 418

ethnic consciousness, and the nation-state, 223

ethnic groups: immigrant, as non-native speakers, 284; self-definition by, 204

Ethnic Groups and Boundaries (Barth) 204

ethnic identity, 203–6, 206–7, 285, 365, 366, 476n57

ethnicity, 203–6, 252, 426; coercive power of, 209, 232; and cultural identity, 262; differences in, anchored in the body, 412; equated with culture, 254; explanations of, 207–11; gay, 475n36; ignored by gender identity politics, 200; as mere state of consciousness, 394; modern, rise of, 211–17; origins of term, 205; vs. race, 207, 225, 476n71; as socially constructed, 209; symbolic, 212

"Ethnicity and Social Change" (Bell), 213–15

The Ethnic Origins of Nations (Smith), 217

ethnic states, vs. nation-states, 222–23

ethnic struggles, mutually supportive, 213

ethnolinguistic rights, 399

ethnonationalism, 216–17, 223

ethnopluralism, 257. *See also* multiculturalism

ethnoraces, 409

ethnos, 418

ethnosymbolists, 219

Eugenides, Jeffrey, 378

European Union, and transnational identity, 20

everdayness, 71; inauthenticity of, 74

"everyman" identity, 69–70

"everythingness," articulation of, into distinct things, 307

evil: God not responsible for, 435; independent sites of, 436; moral, produced by traditions, 431

existentalia, in Heidegger, 63

existential anxiety, 73–75, 139–41, 143, 344, 437

existentialism: and the collective Other, 145–52; French, 302; as psychology, in Laing, 138–42; social, of 1940s, 147; in vogue among midcentury students, 134. *See also* Beauvoir; Heidegger; Sartre

existential ontology, 265

Existenz as "identity," 48

experientialism, radical, 201

exploitation, economic, 175

externalism, and the rise of nations and nationalism, 221

facticity, 84, 85, 415, 417, 455

faith, 90, 91, 124, 432–33, 436; loss of, 237. *See also* religion

"fallenness" of Dasein, 71, 73–74, 76

false self, 141

family, as chief institution of patriarchy, 182

family law, minority-community control of, 281

Fanon, Frantz, 144, 158–60, 332, 447

fantasy, 102, 304–5, 309–10, 488–89n132

Fascism, 42, 56, 63, 217, 464n75

father, name of, as standing for the law, 305

Faust (Goethe), 29–30

fear: denial of, 72; of implosion, 140

"female," as category, 181

female circumcision, 276. *See also* clitoridectomy

female essentialism, 135, 314, 373, 471n41, 485n36, 486n51

The Female Eunuch (Greer), 180

female hysteria, 311

female identity: essentialist (*see* essentialism: female); Firestone's determinism, 182; and postmodernism, 313–28 "feminine," as category, 181

The Feminine Mystique (Friedan), 127, 179–80

feminism, 290; critique of Sartre's gendered active-passive modalities, 145; difference, 232, 374; as ersatz religion, 322; first wave, 161; French, 313–22; identity politics as split within, 199; postmodern, 301–2, 350, 351; second wave, 179–83; standpoint, 193–95, 201, 474nn17, 23

"The Feminist Standpoint" (Hartsock), 474nn17, 23

Ferkiss, Victor, 173

Ferouan, Mouloud, 471n40

Fichte, J. G., 381, 492n90

finitude, 456

Firestone, Shulamith, 180, 182–83, 193

First Nations, 284. *See also* indigenous peoples; Native American cultures

First World War. *See* Great War

Fischer, Michael, 386

Fleming-Walloon conflict, 213

flesh, reduction of identity to, 101–2. *See also* body

FLN (National Liberation Front), Algeria, 160

Foote, Nelson, 162–64, 362, 398

forensic identity, 7, 460n9

"for-itself," Hegelian, 91, 93, 96

Fortuyn, Pim, 478n130

Foucault, Michel, 197, 301, 302, 310–13, 329, 403, 484nn1–2, 485n31

Fourest, Caroline, 478n130

France: anti-Semitism in, 147–48; *la France profonde*, 246; imagined Gauls and Franks, 385, 410; impact of Algerian War, 471n40; lay character of the state, 228; national identity, 147–48, 384; school headscarf controversy, 296–97; student movement of late 1960s, 184–85; Third Republic, 221–22

Frankfurt School, 115

Frankish descent claims, aristocratic, 410

free choice, and destiny, 80–86

Free Democrats, Germany, 238

freedom, personal: and revision of beliefs, 283; as acceptance of necessity, 77; as act of consciousness, 146; and fear, 72; Hegelian, 90; modern sense of, 273; native, achieved through collective struggle, 160; negative, 40–41; vs. personal identity, 278; success not important to, 466n25; through socialism, 112

free market, 143

free will, 435

French feminism, 313–22; Anglo-American adaptation of, 322–28

French Revolution, 385–86

Freud, Anna, 118

Freud, Sigmund, 391, 392, 459n3, 468n36; on biological drives, 118–19; feminist discrediting of, 322; on identification, 341; and inner identity, 461n46; on Jewish identity, 13, 14; and the Oedipus complex, 327

Friedan, Betty, 127, 179–80

Friedman, Lawrence J., 467n12, 468n16

Friedrich Naumann Foundation for Freedom, 238

Fritsche, Johannes, 466nn12–13

Fromm, Erich, 105, 110–12, 131, 467n15, 468n16

Frost, Robert, 73–74

fulfillment, illusion of, 321–22

fundamentalism, 439; as countermodernism, 231; cultural exclusion of, 291

Furet, François, 385–86

Fuss, Diana, 323, 339, 341, 486n51

Fussell, Paul, 42, 44

future, as primary meaning of existentiality, 79

Gallop, Jane, 339

Gandhi, Mohandes K., 135, 136, 193, 452

Gans, Herbert, 212, 215

Garvey, Marcus, 161, 473n82

Gastarbeiter. See "guest workers"

Gates, Henry Louis, Jr., 330

Gauls, 385, 410

gay, as term, 474n28

Gay Activists Alliance, 183–84

gay and lesbian identity, 183–84, 186, 195–98, 196, 225, 326, 406, 414, 440, 475n36

gay culture, 186, 232

Gay Liberation Front, 183–84

gay movement, 399

gay pride, 405; displays of, 198

gaze, self-consciousness of other's, 99. *See also* look

Geertz, Clifford, 208–9, 210–11, 232, 407

Geist, modernity and, 54

Gellner, Ernest, 217, 218–19, 221

Gemeinschaft, 81, 85

Gemeinschaft und Gesellschaft (Tönnies), 81

gender, 417; biological vs. role identity, 181–82, 189; children's attitude toward other's, 411; internal psychological conflicts over, 347; as positioned, 352; vs. sex, 181, 186, 188–95, 352; "two-spirit" persons, Native American, 492n76

gender identity, 101–2, 326, 328

Gender Identity Disorder (*DSM-III*), 2
gender melancholy, 328
Gender Trouble (Butler), 325–28, 487n85
General Alliance Against Racism and for Respect for French Identity, 242
genetics, and racial difference, 412–14
"German Identity—Forty Years After Zero" (Naumann Foundation seminar), 238
German-ness, 63, 83–84, 85, 235, 338, 381
Germany: destiny of, 81–82; multiculturalism in, 255–59, 290; national identity, 235–40, 289; reunification of, 239, 240, 257, 479n19; student movement of late 1960s, 184–85; Turkish/Muslim immigration into, 184, 241, 255, 256, 286; ultraright nationalist identity movements of 1970s, 392; Weimar-era, 83, 85, 112, 334–35; Wilhelmine, 83, 112, 221. *See also* Nazism
Geschichtliche Grundbegriffe, 2
Gesellschaft, 81, 83
Gibson, Gloria, 357, 366–67
Giddens, Anthony, 11–12, 273, 377
Gide, André, 25, 26
Gilligan, Carol, 188, 190–91, 322, 374, 485n36
Giscard d'Estaing, Valéry, 242, 249
Gitlin, Todd, 203, 475n46
Glass, James, 347
Glazer, Nathan, 205–6
Gleason, Philip, 130, 164, 459n2
God: loves unreservedly and freely, 100; secularization of Protestant conception of, 392; self-definition from burning bush, 456; as ultimate object of love, 315; as valid signifier, 316
god-terms, 306; deconstruction of, 309
Goethe, Johann Wolfgang von, 29–30, 50, 317
Goffman, Erving, 167, 168, 171, 197–98; on stigma, 401–2
Goldberg, David, 409
the good, objective, 271, 442; argumentation about, 433, 435; and the black urban utopia, 178; and ethics, 273; and individual identity, 90; in politics, 273.
good faith, in interpersonal relationships, 467n28
Gramsci, Antonio, 335
Gray, John, 275, 276, 482n22
Great War, 446; antirationalism fostered by, 46; and redefinition of human contribution to identity, 22–23; and unmaking of identity, 41–42
The Great War and Modern Memory (Fussell), 42
Green, André, 356

Greer, Germaine, 180, 469n78
Griotteray, Alain, 243
Grosby, Steven, 210
Gross, Elizabeth, 486n51
group identity, 4, 15, 143, 398; claims of, 19; and differentiation from other, 170–71; hold on the self, 359; individual identity as variant of, 106, 109; vs. "person identity," 363; and revised valuation of personal identity, 185. *See also* collective identity
group inequality, biologically programmed, 391
groupness, 381, 396
groups: culture as common practices of, 390–91; deviant, 403–4; identification with, 295; language as vehicle for communication, 225–26; membership in, 123, 214; mutual support by, 295; primordial, 409. *See also* collective identity
"guest workers," in Germany, 184, 255
Gutmann, Amy, 294–98, 299, 300

Habermas, Jürgen, 240, 288–89, 456
Hacking, Ian, 403–7, 409, 412–14
hailing, and coming into social existence, 488n129
Halbertal, Moshe, 278–82, 299
Halbwachs, Maurice, 13, 16, 391, 459n3
Hall, Stuart, 341–42
Hamilton, Charles, 176
Handbook of Self and Identity, 10, 375
Handlin, Oscar, 166
Hannaford, Ivan, 418–19
Haraway, Donna, 323–24
Harding, Sandra, 195
Hartsock, Nancy, 194, 474nn17, 23
Haslinger, Sally, 352
"Hatikvah," Israeli national anthem, 482n36
headscarves, in French schools, 296–97
Hebrew, privileged status of, 381, 478n118
Hechter, Michael, 209
Hegel, Wilhelm Friedrich, 3, 89, 90–91, 286, 483n52
hegemony: in deconstruction of class, 335, 336, 337; and identity, 344; of postmodernism, 349
Heidegger, Martin, 17, 61, 105; antimodernism of, 70–71, 484n2; and authentic resolve, 485n13; *Being and Time*, 62–86, 446; "Black Notebooks," 465n2; on destiny, 450, 451; on facticity, 415; and French postmodern identity theory, 302; "lostness" in, 233; time in, 481n5; turns toward politics, 466n12
Heimatlosigkeit, 74; and *Heimatsverlust*, 237

Heinrich, Dieter, 356
Hekman, Susan, 347–49
Henry IV (Pirandello), 34–35, 37, 40, 79
Herberg, Will, 166–67, 205, 399
the hero, authority of, 86
Hesiod and Herodotus, on politics of non-
    Greeks, 418
Hesse, Hermann, 26, 29–31, 50–51, 57–59, 112
heterosexualizing of desire, 325–26
hierarchical/militaristic societies, vs. disciplinary
    societies, 312–13
hip-hop, 179
Hippocrates, on Scythian racial characteristics,
    418
Hirschfeld, Lawrence, 398, 407–12, 420
Hispanic immigration, to U.S., 259, 261
historical construction, vs. primordiality, 232,
    233
historical identity, 20, 21, 35, 450, 454–55
historicality of Dasein, 63, 72
Historikerstreit, 479n19
historiography, identity in, 382–87, 389
The History of Madness (Foucault), 310
The History of Sexuality (Foucault), 310
Hitler, Adolf, 86
Hobsbawm, Eric, 217, 218, 219, 221–22, 394
Holocaust, 144
Holy Roman Empire, failed consolidation efforts
    of, 236
Homburger. *See* Erikson
homeland, link with, 207. *See also*
    Heimatlosigkeit
homosexuality, 405–6; and binary sexual taxon-
    omy, 416; identity vs. self-image, 196; "inven-
    tion" of, 328–29; and naming, 474n28;
    politics of, 183–84; taboo on, 327; termino-
    logical changes in, 197. *See also* gay and les-
    bian identity
Horkheimer, Max, 115
Horowitz, Donald, 207, 402
humanism, 87, 236, 335–36
Humboldt, Karl Wilhelm von, 113, 116, 377,
    468n21
humiliation, 95
Huntington, Samuel, 229–32, 260, 261, 393, 454
Hurston, Zora Neale, 330
Husserl, Edmund, 62, 484n2
Huxley, Aldous, 13, 391, 392, 459n3
hybridity, 136, 331–34, 421
hysteria, 311, 328

id, 118
Idealism, German, 20, 391

idem-identity, 8, 16; and ipse-identity, 8–9, 387.
    See also sameness
identification, 332, 396, 433, 449–50; and collec-
    tive identity, 448; conscious, identity as,
    341–42; with group, 146, 295; interchangeable
    with identity, 365; mutual, 295; narrative
    dimension, 414; with the nation, as path to
    immortality, 224; with parents, 15, 189, 447,
    468n36; postmodern substitution of, for iden-
    tity, 250; religious, 166–67; and retention of
    lost objects of desire, 122; in sociology, 364–
    67, 398; submissive, 399; as theory of motiva-
    tion, 162–63. *See also* collective identity;
    group identity
"Identification as the Basis for a Theory of Moti-
    vation" (Foote), 162–63
"Identifying Identity: A Semantic History"
    (Gleason), 459n2
Identität, 2–3, 24;
Identität, anthology, 356
identité, 2–3, 24
L'identité, anthology, 356
identity, 1, 22, 38, 39, 60, 171, 343, 469n60;
    absolute, 3, 344, 391–92, 400; active and pas-
    sive strategies, 99–101; adolescent construc-
    tion of, 179; affirmed through identification,
    122; aligned with culture, 282–83; American,
    cultural content of, 261; anxiety as motive for,
    73–75; vs. authentic subjectivity, 303; as bad
    faith, 92–93, 427; of the Beloved, 100; Ber-
    gem's "culture" of, 1; Braudel's definition,
    245–46; bridging primordiality and historic-
    ity, 233; buttressed by history of memory,
    386; Canadian, 254, 480n59; as character,
    461n33; as choice and indeterminacy, 456;
    civic, 460n8; and claim to exclusive truth, 322;
    as conscious identification, 341–42; consti-
    tuted by action, 372; contingent necessity of,
    21, 437, 450–51; continuity of, 397; conver-
    gence with ethnicity, 206; creation of, 369,
    378, 405; criminality arising from, 312;
    Dasein's desire for, 83; definitional history
    and evolution summarized, 445–49; depic-
    tions of life without, 34–41; as desire "to be"
    something (Fromm), 111; deterministic, 451;
    and economics, 448; essentialism of, 52,
    114–15; and ethics, 19, 27, 289, 427–44; eth-
    nic, 14; *Existenz* as, 48; fixed, falsity of, 306;
    fractured, 323–24; French, 147–48, 241–50,
    384; gendered strategies of making, 101–2;
    gender role, 181–82; German, 235–40, 289,
    338; the Great War and the unmaking of,

41–56; and group membership, 214, 280; hegemonic, 344; in historiography, 382–87, 389; honorific, 50; idem- vs. ipse-, 8–9; and identity types, 172, 197; illiberal, accommodation of, 275–78; inauthentic, 64–65, 69–70, 71; incestuous desire as obstacle to, 60; incommensurable with social class, 110; indispensibility of, 343; "individualized," 286; inherent in voice, 380; inner, 461n46; in interwar fiction, 61; Johnston's three-way division, 371; in Laing, 138–42; legal, 7; in linguistics, 379–82, 389; markers of, 3, 150, 201; Marxism conceptually dissonant with, 110–12; maternal, 189–93; mature, and autonomy, 190; as meaningfulness to a self, 204; modern, 11, 434; moral, 497n40; multiculturalism as, 253; multiple, 345, 452; and narrative, 8, 269–71, 366–67; national, 4; necessary, social role as, 96; need for, as bad faith, 151–52; and New Social Movement theory, 368–74; no escape from, 271, 273; and normative heterosexuality, 325; as nostalgia, and history of memory, 384; and ontology, 20–21, 62–103; past, as myself-in-error, 94; "patrician," 115; and personal psychology, 374–78; phallic, imaginary, 304–5; politicization of, 18–19; postcolonial hybrid, 136, 331–34; post-Great War reinvention of, 56–61; pre-Great War dualism in, 28–34; presupposes difference, 435; primordial, alleged, 394–95, 462n50; and psychic health, 126; psychological, 167; public and personal, distinction between, 349; qualitative, 461n33; Québécois French, 287; quest for, 133, 455; ranking within, 362, 452; reappearing claimant to, 8; reclaiming of, from postmodernism, 345–54; reification of, 172; role of the body in, 97–98; and Sartre's "absolute being," 90; in 1960s counterculture, 134–36; secular forms of legitimation, 224; and self, 3, 5, 491–92n65; as self-definition, 449; self-injurious, 488n120; and selfsameness, 1, 125; sense of, 21–22, 449; sexed, 352; shifting meaning of, in everyday discourse, 2–3; shut out by humanist leveling, 236; skeptics of, and American individualism, 291–300; and social context, 268; and social roles, 172, 361–64; in sociology, 160–61, 171, 355, 448; as solution to self-alienation, 121; "spoiled," 401; subjectivity of, 107; "thick," 275; through encompassing-group membership, 280; and time, 75–76, 84; transnational, 20; use-frequency of term in English, German, and

French, 24T; vulnerable to dissolution, 444; as a "way of being," 406–7; and white domination of minority women, 324; women's lack of, 320; in Woolf, 26. *See also* authenticity; black identity; collectivity; diffusion of identity; ego identity; ethnicity; feminine identity; German-ness; group identity; historical identity; Jewish identity; language; Locke; multiple personality disorder; negative identity; personal identity; postmodern identity; psychosocial identity; religion; religious identity; self; social identity

Identity (film), 4
"Identity" (French journal), 242
Identity (Kundera), 4
"Identity" (Moore song), 4–5
"Identity and Uprootedness in Our Time" (Erikson), 468n34
Identity Before Identity Politics (Nicholson), 160
identity crisis, 2, 125–26, 142, 179, 185, 435, 447; in great man, 135; popular diffusion of term, 127–29; Taylor on, 268; xenophobia as resolution to, 248
Identity Crisis (Meltzer), 4
identity economics, 387–89
identity groups: ascriptive, 298; mutual support among, 295
Identity in Democracy (Gutmann), 295–98
Identity Mania (Meyer), 231–32
The Identity of France (Braudel), 245–46
identity politics, 174–86, 184–85, 198, 199–203, 355, 399, 448, 473n84
"Identity Problem" as psychiatric diagnosis, 459n6
identity realism, 349–51, 448–49
identity theft, 460n8
identity utility, 388
identity verification, 362–63
ideology, 423; culture aligned with, 252; Erikson's, influence on psychosocial identity concept, 109–16; healthy vs. unhealthy, 117; totalitarian, 117, 136, 452
Ideology and Utopia (Mannheim), 117
idolatry, 310
ignorance, veil of, and the minimal self, 266, 267
illiberal cultures: within liberal democracies, 275–78, 279–80, 283, 296; right of exit from, 276, 281; societies dominated by, 279
illusion of fulfillment, 321–22
imaginaries, political, 436
Imagined Communities (Anderson), 217
immigration, 249; to Canada, 251–52, 286; and choice of self, 113; experience of, as uprootedness, 121; to France, 243; Hispanic, to U.S.,

immigration (*continued*)
259, 261; integration of, in U.S., 355; and
non-native speakers, 284; and religious identification, 166–67; Turkish, to Germany, 184,
241, 255, 256, 289
immortality, 220; of the soul, 6; through identification with the nation, 224
imperialism, discourse of, 335–36
implosion, fear of, 140
inadequacy of memory, 26–28
In a Different Voice (Gilligan), 190–91, 374
inauthenticity, 143; in being with others, 68,
102; of determinism, 86; of everydayness, 71,
74; of individual identity, 63, 64–65; of Sartre's being-with, 102. *See also* authenticity
"inauthentic Jew," Sartre's, 149
incest: as Romantic trope, 59; as taboo, 305, 327
independence ethic, American, 131
indexicality, of identity markers, 380
indigenous peoples, Canadian, 251–52, 262. *See
also* First Nations
individualism, 143, 206, 221, 447; American, and
identity skeptics, 291–300; and the empty self,
265–75; ethical, and autonomy, 431; liberal,
202, 273; presumption of, in academic psychology, 358; radical, 161–62; secular, 11; and
self, in liberal democracy, 263
individuality, 113; facilitated by collective identity, 63; vs. personhood, 440
individualization, 312, 313
"individualized" identity, 286
individual sovereignty, 223
inferiority and superiority, use of difference to
establish, 361
inferiority complex, 158, 160
infibulation, 296
information, control over, 372. *See also*
knowledge
in-groups, and Tajfel's "Klee/Kandinsky" group
experiment, 359–61
inheritance: claims to, and markers of identity,
3; rights, among Pueblos, 296
"in-itself," Hegelian, 91–92, 95–96
inner-city youth, and identity utility, 388
inner-directed self, 130
inner identity, 461n46
"inner space," and female essentialism, 135
In Search of Lost Time (Proust), 27–28
instrumentalism, 210, 219
interbreeding, 413
internalization of labels, as part of individual
identities, 415

interpellation, 488n129
"Interrogating Identity" (Bhabha), 332
intersexuality, 378, 416
intersubjective identity, 266–67, 274–75
intimacy, 190
The Invention of Tradition (ed. Hobsbawm and
Ranger), 217, 219
inward turn, in identity politics, 199, 200–201
ipse-identity, 8; and idem-identity, 8–9, 387. *See
also* selfhood
Irigaray, Luce, 313, 318–21, 323, 417, 486n51
Irish Catholics, as racial category, 412
Isaac, Benjamin, 419
Isaacs, Harold, 207–8
Iser, Wolfgang, 356
Ishiguro, Kazuo, 96, 438
Islam: American black adoption of, 177; as challenge to the West, 228; European reactions to,
478n130; as German religious "other,"
257–59; Muslim presence in Europe, and
national identity concerns, 235; political theology of, 288; racialization of, 412; religiosity
of, 244
isolation, 140
Israel: accommodating the Ultra-Orthodox,
279–82; creation of, 218; linguistic "authenticity" in, 226; national anthem, 482n36
Italian Catholics, as racial category, 412
ius sanguinis, 255
ius soli, 242, 255
Izard, Michel, 356

James, William, 374
Jarausch, Konrad, 240, 338
Jaurès, Jean, 248
jazz, 179
Jefferson, Thomas, and the American identity,
135–36
Jemeinigkeit, 65, 68, 85, 376; denial of, 69, 72
Jenkins, Richard, 357, 364–66
Jewish identity, 13–15, 212, 414; "authentic" vs.
"inauthentic," 149; and conversion to Christianity, 271; as defense against anti-Semitism,
440; Erikson's, 109, 116; French, 146, 147–49;
in Freud, 391, 392; as non-Christian, 309;
privileged status of Hebrew, 381, 478n118; in
Sartre, 151–52; "universalist," 149
Jews: French, 146, 147–49; integral to European
civilization, 258; otherness of, 257, 279–82;
postwar American acculturation of, 399;
racialized, 244, 410, 419; Sabbath observance
rights, 285; supposed close kinship of, 412;
Ultra-Orthodox, in Israel, 279–82

Johnson, Barbara, 330–31
Johnson, Lyndon B., 129
Johnston, Hank, 371
Jones, LeRoi. *See* Baraka, Amiri
Jonsson, Stefan, 51
Joseph, John E., 380, 381
Jospin, Lionel, 247
jouissance, 315, 318
Jung, C. G., 13, 15, 391, 392, 459n3
justice: democratic, vs. deference to conscience, 297–98; liberal theories of, 265; political conception of, and competing comprehensive doctrines, 293
Justice and the Politics of Difference (Young), 202
justification: context of, 195; in Sartre, 89–90; women's, through male valorization, 155

Kafka, Franz, 37–39, 446
"Kandinsky/Klee Groups" experiment, Tajfel's, 359–61
Kant, Immanuel, 266, 428; ethics, 265, 266; schemata, 346
Karenga, Maulana Ron, 177–78, 225–27
kawaida, 178, 226
Kelly, George Armstrong, 492n90
Kennan, George, 229
Kierkegaard, Søren, 74, 481n5
Kilson, Martin, 211–12
"kinds of people," 403, 404, 405; and race, 407–14
kinship, 207, 365, 412, 421–22, 425
knowledge: about human kinds, 407; of the body as object, 97–98; and class, in Marxism, 193–94; disciplinary, 312; gendered ways of knowing, 194–95; and power, 310, 311, 329; sociology of, 171, 429
knowledge machines, 405
Kohl, Helmut, 236
Kohut, Heinz, 119, 483n52
Koselleck, Reinhart, 356, 459n4
Kranton, Robert, 387–89
Kristeva, Julia, 313, 320, 321–22, 356, 485n32
Kroeber, Alfred, 113
Kruks, Sonia, 473n84
Kuhn, Manford, 165–66
Kukathas, Chandran, 275–76, 277, 299
Kundera, Milan, 4, 460n11
Kwanzaa, 177–78, 226
Kymlicka, Will, 251, 259, 282–86, 284, 288, 482n43

labeling, social-identity, 414, 415. *See also* naming

labor, 120, 145–46, 422–23. *See also* work
Lacan, Jacques, 134, 302, 303–6, 314–16, 322, 484nn1, 13
LaCapra, Dominic, 386
Laclau, Ernesto, 334–38, 488n111
Laing, R. D., 138–42, 452
language: acquisition of, and becoming Canadian, 255; Arabic and Hebrew in Israel, 279; child developmental stages as structures of, 303; competence required for German citizenship, 258; as conventional system of difference, 307; and culture, 252, 254, 261, 262; identity shaped by, 283; meaning and "male syntax," 319; performative, 326, 379; as possibility of meaningfulness, 303; as proxy for secularized ethnocultural identity, 286; sacredness of, and community, 220, 381, 478n118; as text of person, 381; as vehicle for group communication, 225–26; "wandering" and "fuzziness" in, 321
Language and Identities (Llamas and Watt), 379
Laqueur, Thomas, 495n35
lashon hakodesh. See Hebrew
Latin, sacred function of, 220
Layton, Lynne, 347–48
legitimation of identity, secular forms of, 224
Leitkultur, 258
Le Pen, Jean-Marie, 241, 247
Lepsius, M. R., 235
Lerner, Alan Jay, 379
lesbian, as term, differentiated from gay, 474n28
lesbian/gay freedom day parades, 198
lesbians, 350; and identity, 326. *See also* gay and lesbian identity
Le Sueur, James D., 471n40
"leveling down" of *das Man*, 70
Lévi-Strauss, Claude, 356, 484n4
Leviticus, dietary laws in, 424
Lewinsky, Monica, 465n1
Lewis, Bernard, 229
Lewontin, Richard, 412
liberal-democratic political systems, 273. *See also* democracy, liberal
liberal individualism, 273
liberalism, 233; American, 447; founded on universal humanity and reason, 277–78; Humboldt's, 468n21; identity-centered critiques of, 271–73; "impatient silence" of, on metaphysical matters, 220; individualist, 202; political, Rawls's theory of, 291–94; and toleration, 482n22
lieux de mémoire, 383, 384–85, 493n102

"life-contexts," 290
life cycle theory of development, Erikson's, 108, 119–20, 190
Lifton, Robert Jay, 135, 137–38
liminal spaces, 333
Lindner, Robert, 133, 475n36
linguistics, and identity, 379–82, 389. *See also* language
Linton, Ralph, 162
Littré, Emil, 3
living tradition, collective identity as, 430
Llamas, Carmen, 379
localism, 442–43
The Location of Culture (Bhabha), 332
Locke, John, 5, 6–7, 27, 346, 387; on continuity of self, 1, 3, 270, 387, 445; "prince and cobbler" thought experiment, 461n33
logocentrism, 307
logos, 306
The Lonely Crowd (Riesman), 130
longue durée, 245
look: of the colonial settler, 332; objectifying, and other's power, 99, 141, 145; by "thirds," and power to define identity of the oppressed, 146, 398
"looking-glass" self, 163
love: and disconnected memory, 28; freedom of the Beloved, 100–101; God as ultimate object of, 315; identity through, 40; for mother, 441–42; as passive identity strategy, 100; and post-Great War skepticism, 43
Lübbe, Dietrich, 356
Luckmann, Thomas, 171, 172, 197, 356
Luhmann, Niklas, 20, 356
Lukacs, Georg, 13, 391, 459n3
Luther, Martin, 10, 104, 123–24, 135, 193, 432–33, 452
Lützeler, Paul Michael, 464n55
Lynd, Helen Merrell, 130
Lyotard, Jean-François, 484n1

Maalouf, Amin, 453
MacIntyre, Alasdair, 85, 338, 438, 450, 482n15, 496nn11–12; and Aristotelian virtue ethics, 428–32, 496n11; critique of Kierkegaardian decisionism, 481n5; on ethics and identity, 265, 428–32; on inadequacy of Kantian ethics, 266, 344; on narrative identity, 269–73, 366; on temporality and continuity, 481n13
madness: and changing regimes of social and political power, 310; and Pirandello's theory of identity, 34

Magic Theatre (*Steppenwolf*), 58, 59, 61
Maier, Charles, 479n19
"Making Up People" (Hacking), 403–4
Malayan-Chinese conflict, 213
Malcolm X, 177
"male," as core gender identity, 181
Malinowski, Bronislaw, 379
Malraux, André, 25
das Man, 69–70, 72, 103; and the surrender to publicness, 77, 78
Mancy, Joseph, 466n19
The Mandarins (Beauvoir), 157
Manichaeanism, political, 436
Mann, Thomas, 468n20
Mannheim, Karl, 117
Mansfield, Katherine, 7–8, 16, 19
The Man Without Qualities (Musil), 8, 16–17, 26–29, 32, 37, 39–41, 50, 56, 59–60, 443
Mao Zedong, 230
Margalit, Avishai, 278–82, 299
"marketing personality" (Fromm), 131
Markovitz, Irving, 173
Marks, Elaine, 339
Martin, Raymond, 6
Marxism, 87–88, 171, 218, 233; analysis of labor in, 145–46; analytical assumptions of class, exploitation, and workers' needs, 175; conceptually dissonant with identity, 110–12; knowledge and class in, 193–94; New Social Movement theory as alternative to, 368; omits spiritual dimension of life, 369; and otherness, 447; poststructuralist critique of, 488n111; Sartre's conversion to, 467n28; utopian, abandoned by French leftists, 249; and working-class identity, 334
"masculine," as category, 181, 189
masculine identity, 154–55
masochism, 95, 100, 111, 145. *See also* sadomasochism
masses, the, 70. *See also* proletariat
masturbation, 311; and fantasy, 309–10
maternal identity, 189–93. *See also* mothering
"Maternal Thinking" (Ruddick), 191
Maternal Thinking: Toward a Politics of Peace (Ruddick), 191
matter vs. mind, 65. *See also* thingness; things
McAdams, Dan, 376–78, 390, 407
McCarthyism, 135
McIntosh, Mary, 197
McPartland, Thomas, 165–66
Mead, George Herbert, 163, 164, 286–87, 342, 374, 483n52

Mead, Margaret, 113, 129–30
meaning, 62–63; and Dasein, 71–72
meaningfulness, language as possibility of, 303
Meier, Christian, 356
Meinhof, Ulrike, 185
Mekeel, H. Scudder, 113
"melting pot," American, 259–60
Meltzer, Brad, 4
Melucci, Alberto, 368–70, 372–74
Memmi, Albert, 130
Memoirs of a Dutiful Daughter (Beauvoir), 156
memory, 382–83; continuity of, 7, 27; disconti-
    nuity of, 26–28; fusion of ipse and idem, 387;
    history of, and identity, 384, 386; sites of, 383,
    384–85
memory studies, 248, 382, 385, 386–87, 493n94
Merkel, Angela, 250–51
Merleau-Ponty, Maurice, 92, 97, 319, 417
metanarratives, 367
Métis, Canadian, 251–52
Mexico City Declaration on Cultural Policies,
    UNESCO, 224
Meyer, Thomas, 231–32
Michaels, Walter Benn, 390–91, 395
Middlesex (Eugenides), 378
military service: conscientious objection to, 297;
    Ultra-Orthodox exemption, Israel, 281
Mill, John Stuart, 298, 377, 406
Miller, Arthur, 131
"millet" multiculturalism, 276
Millett, Kate, 180–82, 183
mind vs. matter, 65
"mine-ness" (*Jemeinigkeit*), 65
Ministry of Immigration and National Identity,
    France, 241, 247
minorities: cultures of, to be recognized, 265;
    rights of, 262
Mirrors and Masks: The Search for Identity
    (Strauss), 167–68
"The Mirror Stage as Formative of the Function
    of the I as Revealed by Psychoanalytic Experi-
    ence" (Lacan), 303
Mitchell, Martha, 128
Mitscherlich, Alexander, 134
Mitterand, François, 248, 249
mixed-gender persons, in Native American cul-
    tures, 492n76
mobility, 221
"mobocracy"-aristocracy conflict, 115
modernity, 11, 12, 49, 54, 70, 106, 273; critics of,
    115. *See also* antimodernism
Modernity and Self-Identity (Giddens), 273

modernization, 221
Moi, Toril, 323
monasticism, 431
Le Monde, frequency of references to national
    identity in, 241
money, as symbol of modernity, 49
Moore, Lecrae, 4–5
Moraga, Cherrie, 200
moral agency, 265
moral bourgeois, 17
Morales, Rosario, 200, 201
moral evil, traditions productive of, 431
moral identity, 297, 497n40
morality: universal, and ethical particularity,
    444; vs. ethics, 439, 440
"moral space," orientation in (Taylor), 10
moral theory, 427
Morgan, Robin, 180
mother, love for, 441–42
mothering, 189, 190, 191–92. *See also* pregnancy
motivation, identification as theory of, 162–63
Mouffe, Chantal, 334–38, 488n111
"Mourning and Melancholia" (Freud), 327,
    468n36
Moya, Paula, 350, 351
Moynihan, Daniel, 205–6
Mrs. Dalloway (Woolf), 17, 26, 36–37, 41, 43–
    45, 56–57
Muller, Jerry, 472n41
multiculturalism, 187, 437–38, 448; in Canada,
    227–28, 251–55, 261–62, 282–88; debates
    over, and religious conflict, 228; in Germany,
    255–59, 290; liberal, 282, 283; politics of, 250–
    51, 261–63, 275–300; in United States,
    259–61
multinational state, 284
multiple identities, 452
multiple personality disorder, 347, 376, 403–4,
    495n9. *See also* Personality Identity Disorder
Musil, Robert, 9, 19–20, 26–29, 31–32, 39–41,
    42, 50, 51–56, 59, 443, 446
Muslims: identification as, 227; immigration of,
    into Europe, 184, 235, 241, 255, 256, 286; Sab-
    bath observance rights, 285; schoolgirls' head-
    scarves, in France, 296–97. *See also* Islam
Mussolini, Benito ("il Duce"), 464n75
My Fair Lady (Lerner and Loewe), 379
Myrdal, Gunnar, 261
The Myth of Sisyphus (Camus), 134

name of the father, as absolute law, 305
naming: of ethnic community, 207; and fixed
    definition, 406; as legitimation strategy, 197;

naming (*continued*)
   right of, and identity, 184; of roles, 163–64; of
      subdivisions of homosexuality, 474n28. *See
      also* labeling
narrative: as dimension of identification, 414;
   explanatory, capacity to create, 273; public, as
      ontological narrative, 366; unity of, 269–71,
      429
"narrative and identity" studies, 167
narrative identity, 8, 366–67, 429
natality, 347
National Center for Scientific Research, France
   (CNRS), 250
National Front, France, 241, 242, 244, 247
national identity, 4, 187, 217–24, 456; Canadian,
   254, 480n59; and Dasein's historicality, 72,
      80–86; of the decolonized, 173–74; and
      deconstruction, 338; in Erikson's *Childhood
      and Society*, 116; French, 234–35, 241–50;
      German, 235–40, 479n19; multiculturalism
      subordinated to, 262–63; and Muslim pres-
      ence in Europe, 235; and self-definition, 222;
      vacuity revealed by Great War, 42, 44, 45, 53.
      See also statehood, sense of
National Identity (Smith), 217
"National Identity and Myths of Ethnic
   Descent" (Smith), 217
nationalism, 215–17, 217, 218, 219, 221; civic,
   254; and collective memories, 16; Hesse's war-
      time critique of, 51; modern, vs. ancient
      "nation" (Smith), 222; Musil's critique of,
      41–42, 55; patriotic, 17; reactionary, of Action
      Française, 87; and sense of statehood, 41;
      shifting allegiances to, 86
National Organization for Women (NOW), 180
"The Nation as Ideal and Reality" (Musil), 55
nation-ness, 218
Nation of Islam, 177
nations. *See* nation-states; states
Nations and Nationalism (Gellner), 217
nation-states: ethnonational identity of, 216,
   223; modern, nationalism predicated upon,
      222; and myths of timelessness, 220; separate
      from church, 228; vs. ethnic states, 222–23;
      vs. "nations," 284. *See also* states
Native American cultures, "two-spirit" persons
   in, 492n76. *See also* First Nations; indigenous
      peoples
"natural," double meaning of, 307
naturalization: of American citizens, 422; metaphysics of, 426; of race, 425; through kinship,
      425

natural law, 425
nature: identification of women with, 351, 425;
   in nostalgic Romanticism, 31; as socially con-
      stituted, 195
Nausea (Sartre), 87, 89, 147
Nazism, 81, 86, 217, 236, 386, 392, 411; "hypernationalism" of, 240; revisionist accounts of,
      479n19
necessity: absolute, certainty of, 89; contingent,
   of identity, 90, 104, 450–51; freedom as
      acceptance of, 77; metaphysical, and facticity,
      84. *See also* determinism
negation, as Dasein's only real power, 76
negative freedom, 40–41
negative identity, 108, 126–27, 313, 399, 400,
   405, 440
negritude, 110, 150–51, 173, 451, 470n12
neo-ethnicity, 211–12, 215
neofascist youth groups, 370
New Dictionary of the History of Ideas, 2
New Social Movement (NSM) theory, 198, 368–
   74, 389
Nicholson, Linda, 160, 188, 459n3
Niethammer, Lutz, 12–15, 16, 390, 391–93, 403,
   459n3, 460n15
Nietzsche, Friedrich, 43, 108, 317, 434
nihilism, 56, 63, 108
1918: Huguenau, or Realism (Broch), 33, 45,
   48–50
1903: Esch, or Anarchy (Broch), 33
Nixon, Richard M., 129, 212
Noiriel, Gérard, 241, 242, 244–45, 246, 247, 248,
   249
Nolte, Ernst, 236
nominal essence, 346
nonbeing, castration and detumescence identified with, 315
nonconsummation, sexual: desire protected by,
   59–60; as putting off the inevitable, 60–61
"non-societal" ethnic identities, legal protections for, 285
Nora, Pierre, 248–49, 382–85, 386, 493n102
nostalgia: for forfeited paradise, 120; identity as,
   and history of memory, 384; Romantic, for
      nature, 31
the "not-at-home," 73–74. See also
   Heimatlosigkeit
Notebooks for an Ethics (Sartre), 467n28
nothingness: and dread of the female body, 102;
   in Heidegger, 76, 88; in Sartre, 88
NSM. *See* New Social Movement (NSM) theory

obesity, as identity, 405–6
objectification: of female subject, 324; from religious motives, 148
object relations theory, 189, 348
Oedipus complex, 106, 304–6, 327
The Odyssey (Homer), song of the Sirens, 317
"O Friends, Not These Tones" (Hesse), 51
Of Woman Born: Motherhood as Experience and Institution (Rich), 192
Oglala Sioux, 114
oil shock of 1970s, 248
Okin, Susan Moller, 297
Old Regime, 385
"one-sex" model, 495n35
On Shame and the Search for Identity (Lynd), 130
ontological identity, 20–21; and contingency, 344, 449, 450–52; historical bases for, 455
ontological insecurity, 139–41
ontological narratives, 366
ontology: of "being gay," 406; children's, of racial categories, 408; existentialist, 265
the oppressed: group representation of, 203; quest for identity and reconition by, 232
Orange Order, Canada, 253
The Order of Things (Foucault), 310
orientation, vs. identity, 197
Orlando (Woolf), 25–26, 462n2
Ostpolitik, 235
other-directed self, 130
Other/otherness, 399; as absolute consciousness, 96–97; adversarial, 400; in Beauvoir, 157–58; collective, 145–52; constructed as source of evil, 436; and cultural inferiors, 173; Dasein in subjection to, 68–69, 72; depersonalizing of, 140; desired merging of self with, 333; and devalued selves, 18; of foreigners, 242, 244; harboring of, in pregnancy, 347; identity of, emphasized, 400; infinite freedom of, 99; as object of female desire, 315–16; perception of the body by, 98; of place, and splitting of identity, 332; in politics of identity, 175–76; racial, 173, 211; recognition by, 96; in relation to us as group, 102–3; religious, 257–59; sadomasochistic relations with, 95; sameness and continuity of identity recognized by, 107; in Sartre, 93, 94, 467n28; of the "stranger," 169; in wholly internal fantasy, 102; will to, 205

pan-African identity, 174
Parekh, Bhiku, 276
Parfit, Derek, 5, 269–70, 270, 460–61n33

parody, subversion of identity by, 340
Parsons, Talcott, 208, 368–69
partiality, ethical, 441
particularity, 442–43, 456; vs. cosmopolitanism, 200; ethical, and universal morality, 444; group, legitimizing of, 448; in identity politics, 199, 200; in tension with universalist values, 289
passive strategy, Sartre's, 99, 100, 145
past: and former identity as self-in-error, 94; German, lack of continuity with, 237–38; putting out of play, 88; "unavoidable," 270
Patai, Daphne, 201
patriarchy: family as chief institution of, 182; hidden values of, in science, 195; "mother" as defined by, 192–93; sexual politics of, 180
Peace Corps, 135
penetration, sexual, 496n36
peoplehood, 81, 85
perennialism, 219
perfectio, 74
performative language, 326
permanence of individual identity, 21–22, 90. *See also* continuity
Persian Empire, Achaemenid, 404
persona, Jungian, 15
personal desire, social demands translated into, 326–27
personal identity, 363, 429, 457; as collective identity, 430; continuity of, 5, 6 (*see also* self-continuity); cultural identity as, 254; in Erikson, 1–2; vs. individual freedom, 278; lack of core designation, 309; in Locke, 1, 5, 6; postmortem, 6, 460n10, 461n33; revised valuation of, by group, 185; nineteenth-century American connotations of, 3–4
Personality Identity Disorder (*DSM-IV*), 2
personhood: coherence and continuity not necessary features of, 325; corporation as, 162; forensic, 7, 460n9; and moral concerns, 440; morality founded in, 444
Peter Camenzind (Hesse), 30–31
petrifaction, as defense against ontological insecurity, 140
"phallegocentrism," 316
phallocracy, symbolic order as, 318
phallus: child's fantasy of equivalence with, 304–5, 314–15; ontological meaning of, 314–15
phenomenology, Husserl's, 62, 484n2

philosophy of life, 123; made coherent by work, 126

Pierce, Charles Sanders, 380

The Pillar of Salt (Memmi), 130

Pirandello, Luigi, 26, 34–35, 61, 63, 75, 79, 111, 446, 464n75

place, and ethnicity, 422

pleasure, deadening of organs to, 328–29. *See also* desire

Plutarch, and the Theseus ship problem, 1

"Poetics and Hermeneutics" conference, Germany, 356

poetry, modernist, and longing for totality, 321

"Political Confession of a Young Man. A Fragment" (Musil), 51

politics: and cultural identity, 393; and the good, 271; grounded in theology, 392; of identity, 355, 399; independence of new social movements from, 369–70; life, 273; lifestyle, 475n46; of multiculturalism, 250–51, 261–63; of national identity, 234–50; redefined by second-wave feminists, 180–81; separate from religion, 288; of universalism, 286. *See also* identity politics

"Politics in Austria" (Musil), 52

pollution, vs. order, 424

polygamy, 276

Popeye the Sailor Man, and identity, 455

Pörker, Uwe, 5

Porter, John, 213

positionality, 201, 352. *See also* standpoint feminism

possibilities: authentic, as determinism, 72; of change, 75; enacted, Dasein's aggregate of, after death, 75; filled with anguish, 89; of freedom, 90; ownmost (*eigenst*), 74; thrownness as, 79; of totality, 90

postcolonial hybrid identity, 136, 331–34

postcolonial states, 214, 216

postmodernism, 18–19, 138, 187, 427, 448, 484n1; discrediting of identity by, 301–2; and female identity, 313–28; hegemony of, 349; reclaiming identity from, 339–54; and substitution of identification for identity, 250

poststructuralism, 18–19, 187, 302, 324, 484nn1, 4, 488n111

potentiality, pure, self as, 265–75

power: coercive, of ethnicity, 209, 232; to define, Other's, 93; differentials in, affecting individual identity, 373; female, articulated by fantasy, 488–89n132; and knowledge, 310, 311, 329; in relationship between sexes, 153; of

"thirds" to look at and define the oppressed, 146; transcendent images of, replaced by secular ones, 224

pregnancy, and the harboring of otherness, 347

"presence-at-hand," in Heidegger, 64

The Presentation of Self in Everyday Life (Goffman), 402

primordialism, 209–10, 210–11, 219, 232, 233, 394–95, 409, 464n50

The Principles of Psychology (James), 374

"The Problem of Ego Identity" (Erikson), 124–27

"progress," 302

proletariat: revolutionary consciousness among, 391; solidarity of, 87–88

proper names, deconstruction of, 308

Protean self, 135–36, 137–38

Protestant, Catholic, Jew (Herberg), 166

Protestantism, and free conscience, 143

"proto-racism," 419

Proust, Marcel, 26, 27–28, 60

"pseudospeciation," 136

Psyche (psychoanalytic journal), 134

psychoanalysis: deconstructive of unconscious semiotic fantasies by, 306; discrediting of Freud, 322; and Erikson's psychosocial identity, 106, 117–24; identification in, 341; marginal status of, 109; object-relations school, 189, 348

psychology: individual, and identity, 374–78; individualist assumptions in, 358. *See also* psychosocial identity; social psychology

psychosocial identity, 1–2, 12–13, 17–18, 20, 21, 167; and Erikson's biography, 107–8; historical influences on, 116–17; and ideology, 109–16; initial definitions, 105–7; sense of, and identification, 449–50. *See also* personal identity

public identity, 371

public vs. private spheres, U.S. religion in, 294

"publicness," 70, 77. See also *(das) Man*

Pueblo inheritance rights dispute, 296

"punctual self," Taylor's, 265, 275

purity, as order, 424

qualitative identity, 461n33

Québécois: French-only laws, 298–99; speakers of, and English-speakers, 213

quest for identity, 133

The Quest for Identity (Wheelis), 130

Quiet Revolution, Canada, 282

Quine, W. V. O., 352

race, 426; biological aspects of, 476n69; Canadian discourse of, 251, 252; and collective identity, 417–20; and culture, 390; deconstruction of, 329–31; defamatory, vs. honorific ethnicity, 211; ignored by gender identity politics, 200; and kind-making, 407–14; modern-era Western imperial theories of, 404–5; naturalization of, 425; in Sartre, 149–51; and stigma of otherness, 211; vs. ethnicity, 225, 476n71

"Race," Writing, and Difference (Gates), 330
racism, 200, 419
Ramadan, Tariq, 478n130
Ranger, Terence, 217
ranking of identities, 452
rape, and female identity, 353
rap music, 179
rational choice theory, 209
rationality, 221, 292; applied to ethics, 428, 433; bourgeois, rebellion against, 30; disembodied, 346–47; scientific thought and methods, 223; and universalism, 149, 277. See also reason; reasonableness
Rawls, John, 265, 266, 267, 291–94, 430
Raz, Joseph, 280
readiness-to-hand, 67
Reagan Democrats, 203
reality principle, 118
reason, and liberalism, 277. See also rationality
reasonableness, citizenship as commitment to, 292–93, 294
Reason and Violence: A Decade of Sartre's Philosophy (Laing), 142
Rebel (Moore CD), 4–5
Rebel Without a Cause (film), 133
recognition, 286–87; claims to, from immigrant minority groups, 289; mutual, failure of, 349, 363–64; from the Other, 96; quest for, by the oppressed, 232; of rights, 96; social, 143, 349
Red Army Faction, Germany, 185
refugees and expellees, German, post-World War II, 256
re-identification of self, 8
reification, 171–72
religion, 143, 148, 166, 220, 261, 322, 423, 435; change of, 94; and culture, 226–27, 262, 263; decline of, 224; deemphasized in Canada, 252; as defining a civilization, 229; differences in, anchored in the body, 412; as escape from freedom and nothingness, 90; fundamentalist, 231, 291, 439; in Heidegger, 465–66n8; and illusion of fulfillment, 321–22; liberal democracies' protections for, 285–86; pluralism in,

399; and post-Great War skepticism, 43; sectarian courts and arbitration, within liberal democracy, 483n48; separate from politics, 288; timelessness and practices of, 477–78n118; toleration of, 293; in U.S. public sphere, 294. See also church-state separation; ethics; Islam; secularization
religious identity, 228–32, 297–98, 399
The Remains of the Day (Ishiguro), 96, 438
repeatability, as authenticity, 82
reproduction: capacity for, 352–53; and gender, 182
The Reproduction of Mothering (Chodorow), 189–90
The Respectful Prostitute (Sartre), 147, 400
responsibility: accepted by the self, 78; denial of, as das Man, 69
reunification of Germany, 239, 240, 257, 479n19
revolutionary consciousness, proletarian, 391
Rich, Adrienne, 192
Ricoeur, Paul, 8–9, 16–17, 387, 443–44, 461n33
Riesman, David, 130, 137, 205
rights: of citizenship, group-differentiated, 285; ethnolinguistic, 399; of exit, from illiberal community, 276, 281; gay and lesbian, 198; numerical threshold of bearers of, 280; recognition of, 96; of self-determination, 280, 456; to vote, 293. See also equal rights
"rights of man," 247; and "rights of the citizen," 239; in traditional French identity, 243. See also equal rights
Riley, Denise, 341
Rilke, Rainer Maria, 434
Rimmerman, Craig, 183
The Rise and Fall of Soul and Self (Martin and Barresi), 6
Rites of Spring (Eksteins), 42
"Robbers Cave" experiment, Sherif, 168–71, 360, 401
rock 'n' roll, 132–33, 179
role theory, 68, 162–63, 361–62, 400–401
Romanticism, 30, 31, 33–34, 59, 317, 471n20
rootedness, 456, 466n14; and cosmopolitanism, 442; French philosophy of, 246
Rorty, Amélie, 8
Rousseau, Jean-Jacques, 309–10
Royal Canadian Mounted Police (RCMP), 285
Royal Commission on Bilingualism and Biculturalism, Canada, 252–53, 254, 265, 282
Rozenzweig, Franz, 467n15
RPR (Rally for the Republic), France, 243
Rubens, Peter Paul, 128

Rubin, Milka, 381
Ruddick, Sara, 191–92
Rushdie, Salman, 288
Russell, Bertrand, 5

sadomasochism, 101, 145, 485n31; and negative
    identity, 399; and the Other, 95; and safe-
    word, 100
salvation by faith, 124
sameness, 8; discursive, 318–19; and equal
    rights, 188; sense of, and cultural identity,
    222. See also idem-identity
Sandel, Michael, 265–67, 273–75, 482n15
sanity, identity as condition for, 115
Sanity, Madness and the Family (Laing), 142
Sarkozy, Nicolas, 241, 247, 249, 251
Sartre, Jean-Paul, 139, 398, 399; on acknowledg-
    ment of past actions, 270; Being and Nothing-
    ness, 86–104; and black identity, 145–52; and
    ethics of identity, 427; on facticity, 17; on
    freedom and success, 466n25; and the Hege-
    lian "for-itself," 91, 96; on his philistine step-
    father, 466n19; on homosexuality, 184; on
    identity as bad faith, 436; on incommensura-
    bility of identity and social class, 110; Note-
    books for an Ethics, 467n28; and the Other, 18,
    447; on refusal to reason, 420; and the
    "respectful prostitute," 147, 400; self as set of
    perpetually open possibilities, 265
The Satanic Verses (Rushdie), 288
sati, 276
Saussure, Ferdinand de, 304, 310
schemata, Kantian, 346
schizophrenia, 138, 347, 376
Schlesinger, Arthur, Jr., 260–61, 476n62
Schmalz-Jacobsen, Cornelia, 239
Schmitt, Carl, 13, 391, 392, 459n3
Schor, Naomi, 486n51
Schweitzer, Charles, 90
science: and hidden values of patriarchy, 195;
    knowledge machines and identity creation,
    405; thought and methods of, and rational-
    ism, 223
Scott, Joan Wallach, 488–89n132
Searle, John, 379
"second nature" of contingencies as identity,
    451
The Second Sex (Beauvoir), 152–56, 471n20
secular humanism, 322
secularization: in black cultural identity, 226; in
    forms of identity legitimation, 224; of French
    state, 244; in Germany, 257; and individual-
    ism, 11; of Protestant conception of God, 392;
    in Western nations, 228

security: middle-class, of 1950s, 132, 133; onto-
    logical, 142–43. See also ontological insecurity
Sedgwick, Edie, 128
self: 26, 111, 137, 333, 348, 436; choice of, 113;
    collective identity as loss of, 15; as conscious-
    ness, 90–91; constancy of, 77–78, 84; deval-
    ued, through otherness, 18; empirical research
    on, 374–75; empty, of liberal individualism,
    52, 265–75; and group identity, 359; and indi-
    vidual identity, 5, 10, 52, 204, 263, 491–
    92n65; inner-directed vs. other-directed, 130;
    intersubjectivity of, 266–67, 274–75; moral,
    permanence and indivisibility of, 292; "punc-
    tual," Taylor's, 265, 275; Rawls's minimal,
    266, 267, 291; real vs. false, 141; as reflexive
    project, 12; re-identification of, 8; rejection of,
    in French postmodern identity theory, 302;
    and sameness, dialectic of, 443–44; sense of;
    sovereign, corporate entity as, 162; unity of,
    84, 348. See also self-continuity; sense of
    identity
self-alienation: self-identification as, 70; in the
    "They," 67
The Self and Others (Laing), 142
self-assertion of identity, 38
self-awareness, and naming, 406
self-concept, 10, 375
self-constancy, 443–44
self-continuity, 5–6; and narrative unity,
    269–70; vs. self-identity, 7–8. See also perma-
    nence of identity
self-control, 120
self-definition, 143, 204, 205, 233, 448, 451;
    alternatives to, 56; consciousness's attempt to
    constitute identity through, 95; desire for,
    353–54; and group formation, 454; identity
    as, 26, 29, 449; and need for enemies, 230;
    oppositional, 177; substantive, 1
"self-destructive" behavior, 141
self-determination, right of, 456; national, 280
self-esteem, 120, 362–63, 374, 448; narcissistic
    need for, 483n52
self-estrangement, 36
self-ghettoization, 260
selfhood, 8; ethical nature of, 7, 8, 10. See also
    ipse-identity
self-identification: and authentic identity, 236;
    as self-alienation, 70; of West Germans as
    Europeans, 239, 258
"selfing," 376
self-judgment, critical, 121
self-making, and revisions of identification,
    122–23

self-rule, territorial, 216

selfsameness, 1, 107–8, 125

self-understanding, 396

Sellar, Walter, 382

semiotics, 321–22. *See also* signifiers

Sen, Amartya, 231–32

Senghor, Léopold Sédar, 149, 173

sense of being, 354

sense of freedom, modern, 273

sense of identity, 21–22, 449

sense of solidarity, 207

sense of well-being, 143

separatism, 215; feminist, 199; linguistic-group based, 382. *See also* Nation of Islam

sex: active male/passive female trope, 496n36; and collective identity, 416–17; vs. gender, 181, 186, 188–95, 352; intersexuality, 378, 416; as sociologial category, 496n35; transgendered, 416, 492n76

sexual essentialism, 323. *See also* essentialism, female

sexual identity, in Butler, 325–26

sexuality, 426; bisexual, 416; embodiment of, 417; intersexual, 378, 416; orientation ignored by gender identity politics, 200; sadomasochistic, 485n31; Victorian discourse of, 311. *See also* gay and lesbian identity; gays; homosexuality; lesbians

Sexual Politics (Millett), 180–82

shaming, 120, 121

sharia courts, Canada, 483n48

She Came to Stay (Beauvoir), 157

Sherif, Muzafer, 168–71, 401

Shils, Edward, 208

sickle-cell anemia, and biological race, 413

Siegel, Jerrold, 5

"significant others," 286–87

signifiers: and chains of signification, 308; in child development, 304–6; and dispersed meaning, 308; god-terms, 306, 309; interpretive function of signs and symbols, 303; and link to signified, 304, 306; stratification of, 308

Sikhs, RCMP, 285

sincere waiter, Sartre's, 92–94, 95, 96

Singapore, Chinese-Malayan conflict in, 213

Sirens, Homeric, and female identity, 317

Sisterhood Is Powerful (Morgan), 180

sites of memory, 384–85

Sites of Memory, Sites of Mourning (Winter), 42

Six Characters in Search of an Author (Pirandello), 34, 35–36

skinheads, as right-wing identity, 370

The Sleepwalkers trilogy (Broch), 33–34, 47

Smith, Anthony, 215–17, 217, 218–19, 222–24, 232, 254, 260, 407, 425–26, 456

social constructionism, 219, 451; and ethnicity, 209

The Social Construction of Reality (Berger and Luckman), 171–72

social contract theory, 161–62, 265

social crisis, and breakdown of existing narratives, 367

Social Darwinism, 161, 472n41

social demands, transformed into personal desires, 326–27

social existentialism, 147

social experience, 350

social identity, 20, 21, 160, 356–57, 450, 453–54; as foundation of sociology, 364–66; identity theory and social roles, 361–64; indexing of, 380; in Tajfel's social psychology, 357–61, 389; virtual vs. actual, 401.

Social Identity (Jenkins), 365

sociality, 63

social psychology, 168–71, 357–61, 360, 389, 401

social recognition, 143

social roles, 95; as identity types, 172; as necessary identity, 96

"societal culture," 283–84, 284

sociology: identity in, 160–61, 171, 401–3, 448; of knowledge, 171, 429; as narrative identity, 366–67

solidarity: proletarian, 87–88; sense of, 207

solipsism, 98

Solzhenitsyn, Alexander, 249

Somali immigrants, and clitoridectomy substitute, 296

Somers, Margaret, 357, 366–67

Sonderweg, 238

soul: continued postmortem existence of, 3–4; dual, trope of, 30; and self, 6

Sources of the Self (Taylor), 10

sovereignty of the individual, 223

Spann, Othmar, 172

spatiality, 449; and ethnicity, 422

Spelman, Elizabeth V., 485n36

Spinoza, Benedict, 455

"spirituality" within secularized culture. *See* religion

Spivak, Gayatri Chakravorty, 340–41

Spock, Benjamin, 201

standpoint theory, 193–95, 201, 474nn17, 23

statehood, sense of, 41. *See also* national identity

The State (Nora), 384

states: dependent on common identity, 280–81; as legitimate ethical actors, 290; numerical threshold of rights-bearers, 280; postcolonial, 214, 216–17. *See also* nation-states

status role, 162

Steppenwolf (Hesse), 29–30, 32, 36, 50–51, 56, 57–59

Sternberger, Dolf, 240

Stets, Jan, 361–64

Stevens, Cat (Yusuf), 445

stigma, 186, 197–98, 211, 401–2, 475n38

Stigma: Notes on the Management of Spoiled Identity (Goffman), 167

Stoller, Robert, 181, 188, 189

Stonewall Rebellion of 1969, 183

stories: and differences, 442–43; and narrative identity, 449

stranger, "othering" of, 169

strategic essentialism, 340–41

stratification of signifiers, 308

Strauss, Anselm, 167–68, 171

stream of consciousness, 28

Stryker, Sheldon, 362

student movements of 1968–69, French and German, 184–85

subaltern consciousness, 340

subjectivity, 445; Cartesian, 66; entities without, 64; of identity, in Erikson, 107; Kantian, 64–65; transformation of us-object into we-subject, 372; women's, 190, 324

submission, 68–69, 72, 399

subversion: of identity by parody, 340; instigated by *différance*, 310

Sumner, William Graham, 161, 471n42

superego, 106, 117, 468n36; diminished authority of, at midcentury, 133

superiority and inferiority, established by difference, 361

Supreme Court, U.S.: and public-private boundary blur, 294; upholds Pueblo inheritance laws, 296

surplus anxiety, 143

Surrealism, 484n13

Swahili names, and African roots, 177

symbolic ethnicity, 212

symbolic interaction, 163

symbolic wastefulness, 373

Symbolist poets, French, 321

Syrian Alawites, 213

Tajfel, Henri, 357–61, 389, 392, 397, 402–3, 454

Talmud, timelessness in, 477–78n118

Tatum, Beverly, 489n164

Taylor, Charles, 450, 482n15, 483n52; on ethics and identity, 10–11, 432–35; on government accommodation of cultural identity, 286–88, 298, 439; and ontological necessity of identity, 301, 344, 452; and the punctual self, 265, 275; "strong thesis," 268

temporality: and authenticity, 78–79; and the sincere waiter problem, 94. *See also* time

The Temptation of the West (Malraux), 25

1066 and All That (Sellar and Yeatman), 382, 493n100

theater, interior identities in, 35

The Caged Virgin (Ali), 478n130

"them/us," 103

Theseus ship problem, 1

"they-self," 69. See also *das Man*

Thiesse, Anne-Marie, 249–50

thingness, 445

third consciousness, objectifying, 102–3, 146

This Bridge Called My Back (Moraga and Anzaldua), 200, 324

"thrownness" and "fallenness" of Dasein, 71, 73, 74, 76, 77, 78, 79, 84, 88, 89

Tibi, Bassam, 213

Tillich, Paul, 294, 468n34

time: discontinuity of temporal moments, 75–76; in Heidegger, 79; irrelevance of, in religious observance, 477–78n118; locatedness in, 449; and the unified self, 84. *See also* self-continuity; temporality

Time Regained (Proust), 27–28, 56

Tocqueville, Alexis de, 115

toleration, 482n22

Tonkin, Elizabeth, 476n69

Tönnies, Ferdinand, 81

totalitarianism, 117, 136, 452

totality: female, 317; as human possibility, 90. *See also* wholeness

totalization, 198

Totem and Taboo (Freud), 14

touch, women's, 319–20

"Towards an Understanding of Our Era" (Broch), 47–48, 464n55

tradition, 82, 86, 126, 343, 496n12; Aristotelian-Catholic metaphysics, 271–72, 427; and collective identities, 430, 454; embodying narratives, 270–71; fostering moral evil, 431; and individual identity, 273, 337; invented, 394

transcendence, 426; and collective identity, 423–25; desire for, 449

the transcendental signified, 306, 309, 310, 316

transgendered persons, 416, 492n76
trauma studies, 386
The Trial (Kafka), 37–38
Trudeau, Pierre Elliott, 253–54, 263, 265
truth: absolute, futility of attempts to name, 307; divine, and faith, 432–33; exclusivity claim, identity's, 322; woman's relationship to, 317
Tugendhat, Ernst, 497n40
Turkish immigration to Germany, 184, 241, 255, 256
"Twenty Statements Test," 165–66, 399
"two-spirit" persons, in Native American cultures, 492n76

UDF (Union for French Democracy), 243
Uganda, tribal conflict in, 213
ultimate concerns, 294, 299
Ultra-Orthodox Jews, in Israel, 279–82
The Unbearable Lightness of Being (Kundera), 460n11
uncanny, the (*unheimlich*), 74
unconscious: fantasies deconstructed through pychoanalysis, 306; Sartre's critique of Freud's, 95–96
"The Undetermined Identity of the German Federal Republic" (Lepsius), 235
UNESCO, policy declarations on cultural diversity, 224, 262
United States: Canadian identity self-defined relative to, 480n59; and church-state separation, 294; foundational culture of, 261; identity skeptics and individualism, 291–300; multiculturalism in, 259–61
unity of the self, 348. *See also* continuity
Universal Declaration of Cultural Diversity, UNESCO, 262
universalism/universality, 457; collective identities as denial of, 448; fused with identity particulism, 290; in morality, and ethical particularity, 444; politics of, 286; Sartre's, 159; sociological assumptions about, 358
uprootedness, 120; self-chosen, 121. *See also* alienation: from self
"us": as object, vs. we-subject, 398; and "them," 360, 400. *See also* Other/otherness
utilitarianism, 427, 428
utility of identity, 388

vaginal lips, and female identity, 319–20
Valéry, Paul, 17
values: instilled in child-rearing practices, 114–15; naturalized, 114–15; pluralism

toward, 275–76; state's neutrality in conflicts of, 290
Van Deburg, William L., 178
van den Berghe, Pierre, 207
Van Dyck, Anthony, 128
Van Gogh, Theo, 478n130
Veblen, Thorsten, 333
verification of identity, 362–63. *See also* forensic identity
vertigo, 88
violence: and creation of collective identity, 160; inherent in patriarchal sexual politics, 181
virtual social identity, vs. actual, 401
virtue ethics, 427, 428–32
voice, identity inherent in, 380
Volk, 80–81. *See also* ethnicity
Volksgemeinschaft, 80–81, 83

waiter, Sartre's, as model of identity, 92–94, 95, 96
Walser, Martin, 238
Walzer, Michael, 276
war: aesthetic sensibility, and the will to life, 47; culture, spread of black urban culture as, 179; as "preposterous masculine fiction" (Woolf), 57
Warhol, Andy, 128
Warner, W. Lloyd, 476n62
Watt, Dominic, 379
ways of knowing, gendered, 194–95
"we": defined relative to "not-we," 400; the proletariat as, 103; as subject, vs. "us" as object, 398
Weber, Max, 180–81, 207
Weeks, Jeffrey, 329
Weidenfeld, Werner, 236–38
Weimar Germany, 83, 85, 112; theoretical primacy of working class in, 334–35
well-being, sense of, 143
Weltanschauung, 423, 424, 426, 447, 484n1
Wesseling, Henk, 385
West, Cornel, 331
"What Is a Muslim?" (Bilgrami), 227
Wheelis, Alan, 130, 133
wholeness: identified with phallus, 304–5, 315–16; of individual identity, 90; longing for, 303; temporal, 270; woman as, 317
Wilhelmine Germany, 83, 112, 221
will: to life, aesthetic sensibility, and war, 47; to otherness, 205
Winnicott, D. W., 348
Winter, Jay, 42

Wittgenstein, Ludwig, 5
Wolin, Richard, 466n12
Wollheim, Richard, 487n85
"woman" as term, 324, 336
women: absolute, and wholeness, 317; bodies, features distinct from dominant models of identity, 346–47; "carrier of culture" trope, 54; and female form of communication, 373; and hysteria, 311; identified with nature, 351; as lure, in Western male imagination, 316; and motherhood, 189–93; nonidentity of, 320; as objects of male desire, 319; rights of, and identity, 399; standpoint theory, 193–95; suffrage movement, 471n41. See also female identity
Woolf, Virginia, 17, 25–26, 36–37, 41, 43–45, 57, 446, 462n2

work, 123, 125–26, 155–56, 156, 426, 447. See also labor
workers' needs, 175
workgroups, and work identity, 388
World War I, see Great War
The Wretched of the Earth (Fanon), 158–60, 160
Wright, Richard, 146–47

xenophobia, as resolution to identity crisis, 248

Yeatman, Robert, 382
Young, Iris Marion, 202–3, 299
Young Törless (Musil), 31–32
youth culture, midcentury, 132–33
Yugoslavia, breakup of, 219
Yurok, Pacific coast, and cohesive identity, 114

"zone of 'ought'" in identity ethics, 441

Acknowledgments

The mention of a name in a list of acknowledgments is paltry recompense for the assistance its bearer has given the author. Those named here should know, however, how deeply grateful I am for their interest in and contributions to this book. It has been long enough in the making that I fear I have forgotten some of those who along the way suggested books, articles and themes I should look at and think about. If so, I beg their forgiveness, and hope they will feel thanked by seeing the fruits of their suggestions in the book.

My greatest debts are to Sam Moyn, Jerry Muller, and Jerrold Seigel, who generously undertook to read the entire manuscript in its original draft version before the University of Pennsylvania Press sent it out for formal review. Thorough, discerning and sharp, they, along with a most insightful anonymous reader for the press, made invaluable suggestions for revision, most of which I have tried to incorporate. They will judge with what success, but whatever the book's shortcomings, it is certainly better for their contributions than it would otherwise have been.

My thanks to Howard Brick, John Bowen, Matthew Brown, John Edwards, Philip Gleason, Dagmar Herzog, Stephan Heblich, Michael Lützeler, Pierre Manent, Robert Milder, Linda Nicholson, Laya Seghi, Corinna Treitel, Andreas Wirsching, and Steven Zwicker for reading parts of the manuscript or for assistance with issues that came up in the course of my research and with bibliographical suggestions. My debt to Alasdair MacIntyre, from whom I learned about and with whom I discussed central issues in the book years before I glimpsed my project, goes back a very long way. Washington University students in my undergraduate courses and graduate dissertation seminar on the topic of identity contributed not only critical comments on some of the texts I discuss and some of the theses I broach here but also their candid personal responses to questions of identity in their own lives.

A Fellowship from The Center for the Humanities at Washington University in the spring of 2007 allowed me the time to research and write Chapter 1, initially published in somewhat different form in *Modern Intellectual History*. One of the Fellowship requirements was a presentation of work in progress to a colloquium including the other fellows, Center board members, and invited faculty. The lively discussion and questioning that followed was most helpful not only with that chapter but in prompting me to clarify the project as a whole. Joseph Lowenstein's invitation to give the keynote talk at the tenth anniversary colloquium of Washington University's Mellon Foundation Post-doctoral Program, Modeling Interdisciplinary Inquiry, was the occasion for writing Chapter 6; the response of the participants was most useful and grati-fying. A Mellon Foundation Emeritus Fellowship for 2010–2012 enabled me to travel to France and Germany for research and interviews and to purchase a good number of the works I wrote about. Unhappily the program, a wonder-ful source of financial and moral support for scholars wanting to continue their research and writing after retirement, has been cancelled.

I am very grateful to Damon Linker for the enthusiasm with which he greeted my project and the support he has given it from the beginning. His assistant Hannah Blake kindly took over the task of properly formatting the manuscript and whatever else was involved in preparing it for editing that baffled my limited technical resources. Thanks to my project editor Alison Anderson and copy editor Ellen Douglas, whose careful reading caught textual errors and infelicities of style and kept me on the straight and narrow path of accuracy in citations and references.

My thanks to my family for their unflagging interest in and unfailing per-sonal support for my project over its years of gestation. My brothers Samuel and Daniel Izenberg, non-academic but close and discerning readers in their own fields of psychiatry and journalism, read and critiqued a number of chap-ters, as did my wife Ziva. I hope the dedication conveys the measure of my gratitude to her.